John R. Vacca

7-13-01

WIRELESS BROADBAND NETWORKS HANDBOOK

Wireless Broadband Networks Handbook

3G, LMDS, and Wireless Internet

John R. Vacca

McGraw-Hill

New York   Chicago   San Francisco
Lisbon   London   Madrid   Mexico City
Milan   New Delhi   San Juan   Seoul
Singapore   Sydney   Toronto

McGraw-Hill

A Division of The McGraw·Hill Companies

Copyright © 2001 by The McGraw-Hill Companies, Inc. All rights reserved. Printed in the United States of America. Except as permitted under the United States Copyright Act of 1976, no part of this publication may be reproduced or distributed in any form or by any means, or stored in a data base or retrieval system, without the prior written permission of the publisher.

2 3 4 5 6 7 8 9 0   DOC/DOC   0 5 4 3 2 1

ISBN 0-07-213031-8

The executive editor for this book was Steven M. Elliot, the editing supervisor was Penny Linskey, and the production supervisor was Daina Penikas. It was set in New Century Schoolbook by V&M Graphics, Inc.

Printed and bound by R. R. Donnelley & Sons Co.

To Marvin Bernard, for his inspiration, support, interest, and friendship over the past few years; and, for giving me Bee who changed my life for the better.

CONTENTS

Contents

Contents

PREFACE

Wireless broadband technology is picking up steam. The technology will let enterprises prepare data for mobile access.

Vendors and solution providers say there will be a shift in the focus of wireless broadband development during 2002. For one, there will be less attention on the wireless broadband Web and more emphasis on information access. That will come in the form of applications that support user-initiated requests for data and software agents that alert users when some piece of information has changed.

Your cellular phone is not a browsing appliance. It's an appliance for immediate access.

Wireless broadband hooks will be built into mission-critical applications such as Customer Relationship Management (CRM), sales-force automation and supply chain and order management software. In 2002, solution providers can expect mobile development platforms to offer support for the simultaneous use of voice and text in wireless broadband applications.

Thus, wireless broadband is the next telecommunications revolution. Telcom customers have shown heightened interest in preparing data for wireless broadband applications.

With that in mind, wireless broadband is fundamentally a part of whatever system you're building. In this book, I'll examine in detail many of these wireless broadband systems, and show you how to build and maintain them.

Purpose

The purpose of this book is to show experienced (intermediate to advanced) networking professionals how to install wireless broadband networks. It also shows through extensive hands-on examples how you can gain the fundamental knowledge and skills you need to install, configure, and troubleshoot wireless broadband networks. This book also provides the essential knowledge required to deploy and use wireless broadband network applications: integration of data, voice, and video. Fundamental broadband wireless concepts are demonstrated through a series of examples where the selection and use of appropriate high-speed connectivity technologies are emphasized.

In addition, this book provides practical guidance on how to design and implement satellite and fixed wireless broadband networks. You will also learn how to troubleshoot, optimize, and manage a complex wireless broadband network using LMDS technology.

In this book, you will learn the key operational concepts behind fixed wireless broadband networks. You will also learn the key operational concepts behind the major fixed wireless broadband network services: LMDS, MMDS and WLL. You will gain extensive hands-on experience designing and building resilient wireless broadband networks, as well as the skills to troubleshoot and solve real-world wireless network communications problems. You will also develop the skills needed to plan and design large-scale wireless network communications systems.

Also, in this book, you will gain the knowledge of concepts and techniques that allow you to expand your existing wireless broadband network, extend its reach geographically and integrate global wireless network systems. This book provides the advanced knowledge that you'll need to design, configure and troubleshoot effective wireless broadband network solutions for the Internet.

Through extensive hands-on examples (field and trial experiments), you will gain the knowledge and skills required to master the implementation of advanced residential wireless broadband applications. In other words, in this book, you will gain the knowledge and skills necessary for you to take full advantage of how to deploy advanced residential wireless broadband applications.

Finally, this intensive hands-on book provides an organized method for identifying and solving a wide range of problems that arise in today's wireless broadband applications and networks. You will gain real-world troubleshooting techniques and skills specific to solving hardware and software application problems in wireless network environments.

Scope

Throughout the book, extensive hands-on examples will provide you with practical experience in installing, configuring, and troubleshooting wireless broadband applications and networks. It will also provide you with advanced extensive hands-on examples in configuring wireless broadband applications and networks. In addition to advanced wireless broadband application technology considerations in commercial organizations and governments, the book addresses, but is not limited to, the following line items as part of installing wireless broadband networks:

- Wireless Broadband technologies and deployment issues.
- Current Wireless Broadband Networks deployment information.
- Deployment profiles for major Wireless Broadband Networks high-speed operators.
- Competitive positioning of Wireless Broadband Networks high-speed technologies.
- Wireless Broadband Networks high-speed demand profiles and characteristics.
- Wireless Broadband Networks high-speed subscriber forecasts.
- Wireless Broadband Networks high-speed service and equipment revenue forecasts.
- Overview of the wireless phone industry and the conditions for higher speed data.
- Current state of high-speed data in the wired world (DSL and cable modems) and implications.
- Internet-user demographics and usage characteristics.
- Wireless-user demographics and usage characteristics.
- Migration path to 3G.
- Market potential for high-speed mobile data in top 100 BTAs.
- Market potential for fixed mobile data in top 100 markets.
- Service revenue and equipment revenue forecasts.
- How higher speed cellular and PCS data solutions fit in the spectrum of wireless access to the Internet.
- Assessment of the wireless broadband network market environment: licensing, regulation, and competition.
- Analysis of the wireless broadband network market opportunity including:
  - Profile of ideal markets.
  - Supply and demand factors.
  - Advantages of LMDS.
  - Hurdles to widespread deployment.

- The economics of build-out.
- Current LMDS, MMDS, and broadband WLL trials and deployments.
- Demand wireless broadband network forecasts including:
  - Regional and top country trends.
  - Business and residential demand.
  - Projected services revenues.
  - Equipment overview, vendor profiles, and revenue forecasts for sales of end-user equipment.
- Country profiles for over 40 top wireless broadband network markets in Asia-Pacific, Western and Eastern Europe, North America, and Latin America include:
  - Regulatory and competitive environment.
  - Fixed wireless broadband licensing, regulation, and spectrum allocation.
  - Telecommunication network profiles: wireline, cable, satellite, and Internet.
  - Current broadband activity: LMDS/fixed wireless, wireline, cable, and satellite.
  - Projection of business and residential wireless broadband demand through 2009.
- Projection of LMDS including:
  - Penetration rates.
  - Market share.
  - Service revenues.
  - End-user equipment sales through 2009.

This book will leave little doubt that a new architecture in the area of advanced wireless broadband network installation is about to be constructed. It will benefit organizations and governments, as well as their networking professionals.

Intended Audience

This book is primarily targeted toward domestic and international network managers, technicians, designers, and consultants who are involved in designing, implementing and troubleshooting wireless broadband networks. Basically, the book is targeted for all types of people and organizations around the world that are involved in planning and implementing their wireless broadband networks.

Plan Of The Book

The book is organized into seven parts as well as an extensive glossary of wireless broadband networks, 3G, LMDS and wireless Internet networking terms and acronyms at the back. It provides a step-by-step approach to everything you need to know about wireless broadband networks as well as information about many topics relevant to the planning, design, and implementation of high-speed-performance wireless broadband network systems. The book gives an in-depth overview of the latest wireless broadband technology and emerging global standards. It discusses what background work needs to be done, such as developing a wireless broadband technology plan, and shows how to develop wireless broadband plans for organizations and educational institutions. More importantly, this book shows how to install a wireless broadband system, along with the techniques used to test the system, as well as the certification of system performance. It covers many of the common pieces of wireless broadband equipment used in the maintenance of the system, as well as the ongoing maintenance issues. The book concludes with a discussion about future planning, standards development, and the wireless broadband industry.

PART 1—Overview Of Wireless Broadband Networks Technology

Part 1 presents the fundamentals of wireless broadband networks technology: platforms; services, and applications; marketing environment; and standards for next generation high-speed wireless broadband connectivity.

1. *Wireless Broadband Networks Fundamentals.* Chapter 1 lays the groundwork for the rest of the book by examining how you can gain the fundamental knowledge and skills you need to install, configure, and troubleshoot wireless broadband networks. This chapter provides the essential knowledge that is required to deploy and use wireless broadband network applications: integration of data, voice, and video. Fundamental broadband wireless concepts are presented through a series of examples where the selection and use of appropriate high-speed connectivity technologies are emphasized.

2. *Wireless Broadband Networks Platforms.* This chapter examines the following wireless broadband network platforms: enhanced copper; fiber optics and HFC; third generation cellular (3G); satellites; and, ATM and relay technologies.

3. *Services And Applications Over Wireless Broadband Networks.* This chapter describes wireless broadband network software technologies, their functional components, and intended use. In addition, this chapter provides descriptions of the application-specific technologies required for residential gateways, IP phones, and IP fax devices.

4. *Wireless Broadband Marketing Environment.* The markets for fixed and mobile broadband wireless networks have been evolving at a rapid pace. This chapter will enable you to understand where the major opportunities in these markets will arise.

5. *Standards For Next Generation High-Speed Wireless Broadband Connectivity.* The technical parameters contained in this chapter build upon the very successful CDMA harmonization activities undertaken to date between Telecommunications Industry Association (TIA), ARIB, European Telecommunications Standards Institute (ETSI), TTA and TTC. However, the proposal contained herein is strongly focused on a solution that would meet operators' needs based on available technical information on the merits of the various techniques without regard to intellectual property rights (IPR).

PART 2—Planning And Designing Wireless Broadband Networks Applications

Part 2 of the book is the next logical step in wireless broadband technology: planning and design. It shows you how to plan and design wireless broadband and satellite applications. Part 2 also examines local multipoint distribution service (LMDS) design technology; broadband fixed wireless network design; broadband wireless access design; designing millimeter wave devices; wireless broadband services; and, U.S.-specific wireless broadband design.

6. *Planning And Designing Wireless Broadband And Satellite Applications.* Data applications are key to the business cases of almost all the new technologies, systems and services discussed in this chapter. In many cases, voice and video are secondary considerations.

7. *Local Multipoint Distribution Service (LMDS) Design Technology.* This chapter presents a very detailed discussion on LMDS. With an introduction on LMDS and then a discussion on fixed wireless broadband networks, this chapter looks into different ways fixed wireless broadband communication can be achieved and then gives a detailed description on the various wireless broadbands available for communication. It also discusses technical and design issues involved with LMDS.

8. *Broadband Fixed Wireless Network Design.* This chapter discusses how millimeter wave technologies are growing; proving that fixed broadband wireless networks are the most efficient and economical bridge for the *last mile*. These systems, operating alone and in conjunction with others, are causing an explosion in the service offerings. Given the rapid developments being made in technology and the associated expansion of wireless services, *fixed broadband wireless* will remain in the forefront of the communications industry.

9. *Broadband Wireless Access Design.* This chapter defines broadband wireless access and its advantages.

10. *Designing Millimeter Wave Devices.* This chapter discusses wireless broadband technology related to the design of integrated microwave, millimeter wave devices, and submillimeter wave device (Terahertz) components. Very, very high level discussions include fundamental design analysis, modeling and measurement of millimeter wave devices and circuits that have applications ranging from commercial microwave integrated systems to radio astronomy.

11. *Wireless Broadband Services: The Designing Of The Broadband Era.* This chapter shows you how to design wireless broadband services. It shows you how to fuse together all of the different wireless broadband elements into a single sweeping strategic assessment and opportunity. Its insights and recommendations are exclusive, as are die models used to project growth into this. This chapter is essential reading for anyone involved in one of the most dynamic markets of this or any other industry-wireless broadband networks.

12. *U.S. Specific Wireless Broadband Design.* This chapter explores U.S.-specific wireless broadband design: LMDS, MMDS and Unlicensed Spectrum; and, the vast potential of wireless broadband as a competitive local access technology in the voice, video and Internet access markets. Following an extensive exploration of current trends in telecommunications demand and competitive broadband markets, the case for wireless broadband technologies is detailed and industry forecasts developed.

PART 3—Installing And Deploying Wireless Broadband Networks

This third part of the book discusses how to deploy wireless broadband satellite networks; implement terrestrial fixed wireless broadband networks; and, implement broadband wireless and satellite applications. It also examines packet-over-SONET/SDH specification (POS-PHY level 3): deploying high-speed wireless broadband networking applications; and, wireless broadband access implementation methods.

13. *Deploying Wireless Broadband Satellite Networks.* This chapter is required reading if you want to know why broadband without wires is causing so much excitement and where the most profitable opportunities will arise. In other words, this chapter will help you understand the business case for LMDS and the new satellite networks. You will also grasp how international markets for these new services differ from North American ones and which markets are ripe for penetration by wireless broadband and satellite services. Furthermore, this chapter includes a detailed ten-year forecast of broadband satellite and wireless equipment and services of both industry giants and start ups.

14. *Implementing Terrestrial Fixed Wireless Broadband Networks.* This chapter offers a brief but comprehensive look at the implementation of terrestrial fixed wireless broadband technologies. With the first LMDS auction completed, license winners now are faced with the challenge of implementing and building out their systems. What strategy is best? Should your business plan exploit the full potential of the spectrum and offer voice, data and video? Or, would a gradual ramp up of services be better? This chapter also examines the implementation of enterprise terrestrial fixed wireless broadband technology, services and equipment.

15. *Implementing Broadband Wireless And Satellite Applications.* The explosive growth of wireless broadband satellite users will exact a tremendous burden on Internet businesses. If you do business via the Web, this chapter shows you why you need to rethink your strategies with regard to implementing wireless broadband satellite applications.

16. *Packet-Over-SONET / SDH Specification (POS-PHY Level 3): Deploying High-Speed Wireless Broadband Networking Applications.* This chapter covers the building and deployment next-generation multiservice switches and routers possessing attributes like frame relay, ATM infrastructure as well as emerging traffic types such as POS and Gigabit Ethernet; and, the requirement of a protocol agnostic physical to data link layer interface such as POS-PHY Level 3 (PL3).

17. *Wireless Broadband Access Implementation Methods.* This chapter discusses the new construction of an open wireless broadband core for the implementation of mobile and access applications. As wireless broadband goes multidimensional and the Internet goes wireless, this new compact architecture will surely trigger a new revolution in wireless broadband communications.

PART 4—Configuring Wireless Broadband Networks

Part 4 shows you how to configure wireless lans; unlicensed band systems to enhance wireless broadband services in multichannel multipoint distribution services (MMDS); wireless broadband satellite networks; and, residential wireless broadband access technology.

18. *Configuring Wireless LAN: Microcells And Roaming.* This chapter introduces the benefits, uses, and basic technologies of configuring wireless LANs (WLANs). The chapter also describes the business benefits and applications of configuring WLANs and explains how WLANs differ from other wireless broadband technologies. It explains the basic components and technologies of configuring WLANs and how they work together. It explores the factors that customers must consider when evaluating and configuring WLANs for their business applications needs. Finally, it introduces the Wireless LAN Alliance (WLANA), a non-profit consortium of wireless LAN vendors that provides ongoing education about specific applications, current technologies, and future directions of wireless LANs.

19. *Configuring Unlicensed Band Systems To Enhance Wireless Broadband Services In Multichannel Multipoint Distribution Services (MMDS).* Here, in this chapter, a few examples of scenarios are given where this concept of using multiple frequency bands can be very effective, especially for second tier markets. Generally, for first tier markets consisting of large cities, a large number of mini cells using the MMDS band spectrum can address the capacity and coverage needs fairly well.

20. *Configuring Wireless Broadband Satellite Networks.* This chapter contains detailed in-depth configuration profiles of wireless broadband and satellite equipment including customer premises equipment (CPE)`, cell site equipment, other microwave radios and even the wireless broadband satellites themselves. The chapter also profiles the leading service providers including both the emerging providers of high-speed wireless alternatives (companies such as WBL, Winstar and Teligent) and wireless broadband satellite projects, such as those planned by Hughes and Alcatel.

21. *Configuring Residential Wireless Broadband Access Technology.* This chapter offers considerations for implementing security in enterprise networks where DSL-based services are applied. It does not profess to address every security issue for every enterprise IT manager. In the course of this chapter, security products are mentioned that may satisfy a security need for an IT manager, and may direct the IT manager to a review of certain products. Any such mention does not represent an endorsement of any kind by this author.

PART 5—Managing Wireless Broadband Networks

Part 5 discusses how to manage wireless broadband: LMDS, MMDS and broadband wireless local loop (WLL); test wireless broadband satellite networks; and, troubleshoot fixed wireless broadband networks.

22. *Managing Wireless Broadband: LMDS, MMDS and Broadband Wireless Local Loop (WLL).* This chapter focuses on LMDS and their operational management principles, their potential and areas of application.

23. *Testing Wireless Broadband Satellite Networks.* This chapter discusses the testing systems developed by European space industries with support from the European Space Agency.

24. *Troubleshooting Fixed Wireless Broadband Networks.* The objective of this chapter is to provide a broad overview of the system. It briefly discusses fixed wireless broadband access, then describes AT&T's experimental system, and finally highlights their observations and lessons.

PART 6—Advanced Wireless Broadband Networks And Future Directions

This sixth part of the book discusses wireless broadband network applications: the teleservice model and adaptive QoS provisions; residential high-speed internet: wireless broadband; the nest wave: wireless broadband/wireless hybrids; next generation wireless broadband networks; and, global broadband demand methodology and projections. It also presents a summary, conclusions, and recommendations.

25. *Wireless Broadband Network Applications: The Teleservice Model And Adaptive QoS Provisions.* This chapter describes a paradigm for wireless broadband multimedia applications matching the adaptive QoS approach and reports the test results of its flexibility in a high-bit-rate multitier mobile environment. The overriding concept is that the multimedia application is prone to accept a variable QoS within a given acceptability range to face a momentary lack of resources or overall degradation of a radio link. The teleservice model proposed in this chapter suggests how this adaptation can be simply and effectively performed.

26. *Residential High-Speed Internet: Wireless Broadband.* The goal of this chapter is to provide a rational and objective opinion of the wireless broadband Internet access market, as it appears today and how it will evolve over the next few years. Wireless broadband technology in this context means anything that sends multiple signals over a single line or transport carrier. This chapter focuses on those technologies that provide a bandwidth level of at least 1.5 Mbps, because this is considered a minimum for carrying simultaneous voice, video, and data. The chapter also discusses the technologies that fall below this point if they provide multiple services over a single medium and will increase to higher bandwidth levels sometime in the near future.

27. *The Nest Wave: Wireless Broadband / Wireless Hybrids.* The issues involved with untethered communications are extensive. This chapter discusses some of these from a high level with the purpose of addressing the considerations that extend across many of the detailed analyses and discussions. No single multi-access scheme is considered in detail. Instead, the discussion centers around more general themes.

28. *Next Generation Wireless Broadband Networks.* This chapter provides information beyond the typical overview of standards committees related to 3G. Based on detailed financial models and market research, this chapter analyzes the business case for mobile and fixed wireless broadband, looking at demand and financial viability.

29. *Global Broadband Demand Methodology And Projections.* This chapter discusses future-generation mobile communication systems and global wireless broadband demand methodology and projections.

30. *Summary, Conclusions, and Recommendations.* This last chapter outlines the new challenges this bring to service providers and addresses key properties that are critical to a robust wireless broadband provisioning system. Summary, conclusions, and recommendations with regard to the information presented in the book are also presented.

PART 7—Appendices

This last part provides a very extensive glossary of wireless broadband networks, 3G, LMDS and wireless Internet networking terms and acronyms.

ACKNOWLEDGEMENTS

There are many people whose efforts on this book have contributed to its successful completion. I owe each a debt of gratitude and want to take this opportunity to offer my sincere thanks.

A very special thanks to my editor Steve Elliot, whose continued interest and support made this book possible. And, acquisitions coordinator, Alex Corona, who provided staunch support and encouragement when it was most needed. Special thanks to my technical editor, Steve Shepard, who ensured the technical accuracy of the book and whose expertise in cabling and telecommunications system technology were indispensable. Thanks to my production supervisor, Daina Penikas; Editing Supervisor, Penny Linskey; all of the individuals at V&M Graphics; and, copyeditor James Madru whose fine editorial work has been invaluable. Thanks also to my marketing manager, Jason Z. Stanbrough, whose efforts on this book have been greatly appreciated. And, a special thanks to Michael Erbcshloe who wrote the Foreword for this book.

Thanks to my wife, Bee Vacca, for her love, her help, and her understanding of my long work hours.

I wish to thank the organizations and individuals who granted me permission to use the research material and information necessary for the completion of this book. Finally, thanks to all the other people at McGraw-Hill Professional Book Group whose many talents and skills are essential to a finished book.

FOREWORD

Wireless broadband is one of the technologies of the future and that future is coming at us very quickly. The wireless broadband market is expected to boom over the next five years. New Internet applications as well as new media applications that are still in the experimental stage including interactive television and custom multi-channel news feeds will help to drive this boom. There is a wide range of new manufacturing monitoring and control systems that need wireless broadband connections. There is also a huge demand for more connectivity and Internet users want more speed, more bandwidth and more functions delivered to an ever-growing array of devices. Many manufacturers are speedily bringing these new gadgets to the store shelves and starting to fight for market share.

Wireless broadband, like other emerging technologies of the past, is coming at us from many different directions. There are standards that must be understood and a cast of players that technicians must get to know. *Wireless Broadband Networks Handbook* puts this massive amount of information at the fingertips of technicians, application developers, and product planners. There are over 800 pages of essential information that would take readers months and maybe even years to go out and assemble themselves. But *Wireless Broadband Networks Handbook* is more than just a lot of information between two covers. It is well organized into easy-to-read chapters that save the reader hours and hours of time sorting through the mountains of new information just to prepare to read through it all.

Wireless Broadband Networks Handbook also tackles hundreds of new terms and provides clear and concise definitions for the reader. It is an essential guide for the seasoned technician and a great starting place for the beginner or student who needs to quickly gain a thorough understanding of wireless broadband technology.

—MICHAEL ERBSCHLOE
VICE PRESIDENT OF COMPUTER ECONOMICS
CARLSBAD, CALIFORNIA

Overview of Wireless Broadband Networks Technology

CHAPTER 1

Wireless Broadband Networks Fundamentals

The last 25 years have seen an explosion in wireless broadband communications and computer technology. The last 5 years have seen the explosion of the Internet. Standing at the center of this convergence is the wireless broadband networks industry.

Wireless broadband networks are defined as communication without wires over distance by the use of arbitrary codes and increased bandwidth. Primitive examples include waving lanterns by night or sending smoke signals. Modern examples include hand-held devices such as pagers, "smart" phones, personal digital assistants (PDAs), and personal communication services (PCS) using wireless broadband modems or satellites to enable wireless broadband data communications.

So welcome to the revolution in communications! Today, many communication companies (Hughes Spaceway, AT&T Wireless, CAI Wireless, MaxLink, NextLink, WavePhone, WinStar, Skybridge, Skystation, Teledisc, etc., to name a few) are starting to provide high-speed bandwidth-on-demand satellite communications and changing the way the world communicates. From high-speed Internet access, to corporate intranets, to virtual private networks, to multimedia broadcasting and high-speed data delivery, these companies will lead the new generation of broadband delivery systems.

NOTE   The corporate landscape will continue to evolve and change, and the big players of today will be joined by others in the future.

While the technologies, protocols, and network infrastructure supporting wireless broadband are often complex, most data applications can be simply divided into three main types: bursty, query-response, and batch files. *Bursty data* refers to quick bursts of data sent from point to point. Emerging applications in this area include remote electric power meter readings, wireless broadband burglar alarms, and other remote sensing applications. *Query-response* lies at the heart of new wireless broadband applications and devices that allow for wireless broadband e-mail and Internet access.

NOTE   Batch files are files that contain a sequence, or batch, of commands. Batch files are useful for storing sets of commands that are always executed together because you can simply enter the name of the batch file instead of entering each command individually.

Nevertheless, while the customer usually sees seamless and reliable service, behind the curtain, the wireless broadband networks industry is still working out the kinks in developing and building data transmission networks and agreeing on standards and protocols. There is more than one competing vision. In the end, many experts believe that the growing market for wireless broadband networks will support multiple networks and protocols and faster speeds.

Current revenue forecasts/projections for the wireless broadband networks market predict strong industry growth. According to the following sources, the wireless marketplace is exploding.

- *Frost & Sullivan*. The compound annual growth rate (CAGR) for wireless broadband from 2000 through 2007 is projected to be 46 percent. The market is expected to grow to 10 times its current value and reach close to $11.4 billion by the year 2006.

- *Yankee Group*. The Yankee Group projects that more than 5 million wireless broadband intelligent terminals (WBITs) will be sold in the year 2004. This total will comprise almost 8 percent of total wireless broadband terminal sales that year.

- *Gartner Group*. The opportunity for wireless broadband communication in the United States is huge. Growth will be slow and steady, with 69.7 million of the 156.5 million workforce having a mobile job requirement.

- *The Strategis Group*. Five and one-half million wireless broadband subscribers exist in 2000. The market is predicted to grow at an average annual rate of over 40 percent through 2005.

- *Ovum (U.K.)*. By the end of the year 2004, there will be over 30 million users of data over Global Systems for Mobile (GSM) communications in western Europe, rising from a current installed base of around 3 million. In the United Kingdom, there will be 9 million users of data over GSM services by 2004, rising from the current installed base of around 900,000. GSM is a TDMA-based standard used in many parts of the world and the de facto standard in Europe. GSM is used and promoted by Wireless Data Forum (WDF) member companies such as Wireless Data Services. It incorporates telephony, two-way radio, short messaging, and paging, all in a single handset.

Overall, according to Killen & Associates, current estimates of the potential of the wireless broadband networks industry range as high as $37.5 billion in revenues for the year 2002 for wireless broadband Internet applications alone. The Wireless Data Index, now under development by the WDF, will track these statistics and trends more completely/accurately in the months to come.

On the other hand, according to the latest results from The Strategis Group, the broadband wireless access (BWA) markets are on the verge of tremendous growth (see sidebar, "Broadband Wireless Access Made Simple"). Demand is high, and supply is growing.

NOTE   What is broadband access? Broadband has been defined in many ways. The Strategis Group has defined broadband as networks that provide end users with downstream data speeds of 128 kbps or higher; two-way capabilities, although upstream data speeds may be less than 128 kbps; and digital transmission.

Broadband Wireless Access Made Simple

BWA uses high-frequency microwave signals to send and receive data (voice, video, Internet, etc.) wirelessly between *hubs* located in the center of Local Multipoint Distribution Service (LMDS) cells and rooftop antennas on subscriber's buildings and homes. Once the antennas are established, the connection can be constant and move data in both directions. One hub antenna can serve hundreds or thousands of subscribers in each cell. The cells are limited in size by the fact that microwave signals lose strength as they travel through space. Figure 1-1 is a simplified visualization of three LMDS cells and a master headend interconnected by a fiber loop.[1] The hub towers transmit LMDS signals to the homes and businesses in the cells, which in turn transmit signals back to the hub tower. The master headend coordinates the signals and connects the LMDS network with the Internet and the telephone system and feeds the network with television signals received from satellites and off-air antennas (see sidebar, "Wireless Broadband Point-to-Multipoint Microwave Technology").

NOTE   BWA is not purely an LMDS-based technology phenomenon. The term is used here to describe broadband wireless in general.

Wireless Broadband Point-to-Multipoint Microwave Technology

The demand for affordable, fast data connections is increasing both in the United States and around the globe. There are several reasons why faster connections are not readily available and affordable. They are a complex mix of entrenched interests of the incumbent connection providers, the high costs of wireline upgrades and the associated slow pace, cumbersome regulations and tariffs, and the difficulty of forcing more data through already crowded data pipes.

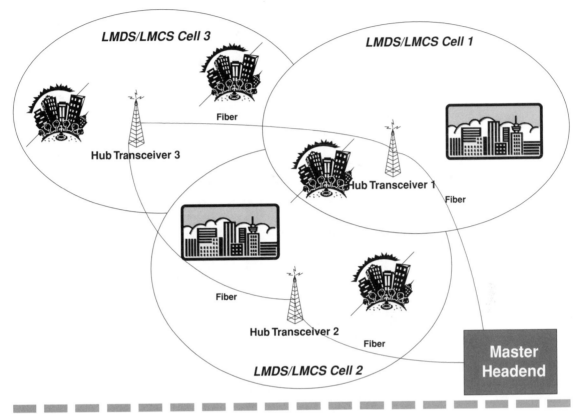

Figure 1-1
Simplified LMDS cell structure. Master headend feeds a series of hubs each in its own cell with data, voice, and video connections. The hubs use the wireless broadband Local Multipoint Distribution Service/Local Multipoint Communication Service (LMDS/LMCS) spectrum to transmit the data, voice, and video to homes and businesses that receive the signals on rooftop transceivers. These transceivers also transmit responses or requests for additional information back to the hub.

A new wireless broadband point-to-multipoint microwave technology called Local Multipoint Distribution Service (LMDS) stands ready to bypass these barriers to readily available broadband connections. In the United States, incumbent connection providers were prevented from owning or controlling the large block of LMDS microwave spectrum in their territory for a period of 36 months (from the auction). Consequently, the chances of entrenched interests limiting bandwidth availability are small. In Canada, Local Multipoint Communication Service (LMCS) applications from entrenched landline providers were not accepted. The 1-GHz of LMCS spectrum was awarded to newly established companies and consortiums.

LMDS is wireless broadband and consequently does not require landline wire upgrades, which makes it affordable when compared with landline technologies. And LMDS is lightly regulated and can be used for two-way transmission of voice, video, and data. Finally, the LMDS spectrum is immense. This large amount of radiofrequency spectrum allows operators to realize data rates above 1 billion bits per second.

The key to business and consumer acceptance of LMDS as an attractive solution is the affordability and availability of the systems. Because of its point-to-multipoint nature, one LMDS cell with a single hub transceiver can serve hundreds or thousands of simultaneous customers. The affordability of the overall LMDS solution therefore is largely dependent on the cost of the customer premises equipment.

Internationally, governments are working quickly to enable the use of high-gigahertz microwave spectrum for broadband data, voice, and video transport. In many ways, the opportunities internationally are greater than those domestically because of the poor state of the communications infrastructure internationally and the desire of the ministries of telecommunications to move rapidly to make their systems competitive with those in the United States.

On February 18, 1998, the Federal Communications Commission (FCC) commenced the auctions for 1.3 GHz of lightly regulated LMDS radiofrequency spectrum in the 28- to 31-GHz range. In March 1998, the auctions were completed successfully, raising almost $600 million. Several years of auction delays have created a pent-up demand for LMDS operators, who are very interested in earning a return on their investment by providing reliable broadband wireless services to customers in as short a time frame as possible.

Untangling the Wireless Ruling   Recently, though, the FCC issued a ruling that takes the shackles off wireless broadband transmission of data. The agency hopes the result will be more consumer choices and falling prices for wireless home networking and multimedia gear.

The problem is that in this market for low-power local wireless broadband data transmission, the players, the technologies, and the industry groups all go by a variety of names, nicknames, and acronyms.

The winners at the FCC ruling are members of the HomeRF Group, which includes Intel, Siemens, Motorola, and Compaq. Their supporters call themselves CUBE. Their technology is *frequency-hopping spread spectrum*, and its nickname is *SWAP*.

The losers in this ruling are members of an industry group called WECA, which includes Cisco, 3Com, Apple, and Lucent. These companies' technology, *direct-sequence spread spectrum*, sometimes goes by the number of its IEEE standard, 802,11B, and sometimes by the nickname *Wi-Fi*.

The FCC ruling quintupled the bandwidth available per channel for the first group, the makers of frequency-hopping equipment. This will enable frequency-hopping equipment to run six to seven times faster, allowing it to catch up with the direct-sequence competition.

Several industry analyst outlets implied that frequency-hopping equipment is cheaper than direct-sequence equipment, but no one said why. The context from the industry analysts is such that you cannot really figure out how much either kind of gear is likely to cost.[2]

Within this escalating wireless broadband market, fixed terrestrial wireless broadband systems (LMDS, MMDS, and broadband WLL) are expected to generate global service revenues approaching US$10 billion in 5 years and US$28 billion in 10 years. Cumulative end-user equipment sales are projected to approach US$4 billion by the end of 2009 [see Appendix F, "Ten-Year (2000–2009) Forecasts of World Broadband Satellite and Fixed Wireless Broadband Markets. LMDS, MMDS, and Broadband WLL").

The bottom line here is that global interest in wireless broadband networks is really taking off with potential in both developed and developing telecom markets. In developed markets, the technology holds benefits for new competitive operators seeking to enter the local access market. For developing countries, wireless broadband offers state-of-the art, cost-efficient, flexible networks that can be deployed quickly without the high cost and time involved in wireline infrastructure projects.

In 2000, early adopters such as the United States, Canada, and Argentina are rolling out commercial networks in major cities. Other large markets, including Japan and Germany, are conducting trials and issuing licenses. By 2002, it is likely that close to 60 countries will have licensed or be moving toward licensing broadband wireless networks.

NOTE   Over 2 billion people in the world will have access to these types of networks by 2002.

Recently, The Strategis Group examined the current status of wireless broadband in 39 key countries and projected the market opportunities over a 10-year time frame. As defined previously, *wireless broadband networks refer to technologies that use point-to-point or point-to-multipoint microwave, in various frequencies between 2.5 and 43 GHz, to transmit signals between hub sites and end users.* The technology can be used to provide voice, data, and video services and requires line-of-sight between the hub site and the end-user receiver. LMDS is the term used in the United States for 28 GHz.

NOTE   The Strategis Group, an edr (e-data resources) company—with offices in Washington, D.C., London, and Singapore—publishes in-depth market research reports and provides customized consulting services and continuous information solutions to the cable TV, satellite, Internet, competitive telephony, and wireless broadband communications industries. The Strategis Group's market studies, valuations, and strategic planning projects provide crucial information to communications industry leaders throughout the world.

With all the preceding information in mind, the purpose of this introductory chapter (as well as the rest of the book) is to show experienced (intermediate to advanced) networking professionals how to install wireless broadband networks. It also will lay the groundwork for the rest of the book by examining how you can gain the fundamental knowledge and skills you need to install, configure, and troubleshoot wireless broadband networks. This book (as well as this chapter) provides the essential knowledge that is required to deploy and use wireless broadband networks applications: integration of data, voice, and video. Fundamental broadband wireless concepts are presented through a series of examples where the selection and use of appropriate high-speed connectivity technologies are emphasized.

In addition, this book provides practical guidance on how to design and implement satellite and fixed wireless broadband networks. You also will learn how to troubleshoot, optimize, and manage a complex wireless broadband network using LMDS technology.

In this book you will learn the key operational concepts behind fixed wireless broadband networks. You also will learn the key operational concepts behind the major fixed wireless broadband network services: LMDS, MMDS, and WLL. You will gain extensive hands-on experience designing and building resilient wireless broadband networks, as well as the skills to troubleshoot and solve real-world wireless network communications problems. You also will develop the skills needed to plan and design large-scale wireless network communications systems.

Also, in this book you will gain the knowledge of concepts and techniques that allow you to expand your existing wireless broadband network, extend its reach geographically, and integrate global wireless network systems. This book will provide the advanced knowledge that you will need to design, configure, and troubleshoot effective wireless broadband networks solutions for the Internet.

Through extensive hands-on examples (field and trial experiments), you will gain the knowledge and skills required to master the implementation of advanced residential wireless broadband applications. In other words, you will gain the knowledge and skills necessary to take full advantage of how to deploy advanced residential wireless broadband applications.

Finally, this intensive hands-on book provides an organized method for identifying and solving a wide range of problems that arise in today's wireless broadband applications and networks. You will find real-world troubleshooting techniques and gain skills specific to solving hardware and software application problems in wireless networks environments.

What Are the Driving Forces Behind Broadband?

Wireless broadband networks services will become a $380 billion worldwide business in 5 years, assuming effective competition emerges in global telecom markets. The combined effects of the global Internet explosion and businesses' rapidly growing data communications needs are fueling broadband demand. The next few years are a critical window of opportunity for wireless broadband networks equipment manufacturers. The end-user equipment market is projected to generate $40 billion over the next 5 years.

> **NOTE**　One of the driving forces is the perception of demand on the part of businesses and private individuals. And as new broadband optimized applications such as interactive TV and application services emerge, the demand probably will go up.

In other words, the promise of the full-service network, delivering high-speed interactive voice, data, and video services into every U.S. home, has devolved rapidly into a patchwork of alternative technologies for often less ambitious networks. Wireless broadband networks for one-way video services and Internet access over enhanced copper wires are now the telephone companies' main service strategies and the driving forces behind broadband.

Furthermore, development and deployment of wireless broadband networks are driven by competition to incumbent telephone companies, and without competitive providers, broadband needs are not likely to be met. The number of businesses using wireless broadband services will more than triple over the next 5 years, and the number of households with broadband service will increase ninefold. In 2005, the average business using wireless broadband services will spend about $1000 per month for wireless broadband access, whereas the average wireless broadband household subscriber will spend $39 a month—mostly for high-speed Internet access.

Carriers have made some especially bold moves into wireless broadband services. Witness AT&T's $148.6 million buy into the DirecTV satellite service and MCI Communications Corp.'s winning $793 million bid for direct broadcast satellite (DBS) frequencies auctioned off by the U.S. government. Meanwhile, Pacific Telesis Group has purchased the rights to offer wireless broadband cable service in parts of California, and Verizon (the new name for Bell Atlantic Corp. and Nynex Corp.) has bought wireless broadband video properties.

The strides forward into wireless broadband services have been matched by sidestepping and backpedaling on wireline broadband networks. PacTel has downscaled plans to build a hybrid fiber-coax network in Los Angeles. Verizon turned on a commercial full-service network using fiber to the curb in one New Jersey town, but it has outlined no specific plans for wireline broadband beyond that one community. The company has abandoned asymmetric digital subscriber line (ADSL) trials to offer video-on-demand services over existing copper wires; instead, it is now thinking about using ADSL technology for Internet access.

NOTE   ADSL stands for *asymmetric digital subscriber line*. It is a high-speed transmission technology using existing local loops to transmit plain old telephone service (POTS) and data to and from a customer location.

How did the full-service network fizzle so fast? In mid-1994, the ILECs (formally the Bell companies) and GTE Corp. projected that some 5 million U.S. homes would have access to wireline broadband networks by the end of 1995. When 1996 rang in, however, wireline broadband passed fewer than a half million U.S. homes. U.S. telephone companies may not hit the 35 million mark until 2002—the date when their earlier projections had called for 140 million homes passed. What happened to the rosy projections made by the phone companies was fairly simple: A solid business case simply has yet to develop for the full-service network. As the millions of projected customers for video-on-demand gave a collective shrug, telephone companies beat a hasty retreat to the drawing boards.

Here are some of the basic telco economics that awaited them there: The book value, or original price, of each line installed for basic telephone service is $2000. This represents $2000 per home passed and per subscriber, because virtually 100 percent of all homes in the United States have phone service. Annual revenues are about $800 per line; operating cash flow (earnings before interest, taxes, depreciation, and amortization) is about $450 per line. The ratio between book value and cash flow is high (more than 4:1), but it is considered acceptable because of the long-term predictability of cash flow for basic phone service.

The telephone companies estimated that they could install broadband wireline networks offering interactive video and phone service for $1400 per home passed. At first glance, this looked like a bargain compared with the $2000 book value for basic phone lines. However, the telcos cannot expect anywhere near 100 percent market penetration for broadband wireless services. Cable TV operators have achieved only about 64 percent market penetration for their services, and they are not likely to give up their customers without a fight. Even if the telcos were able to get 36 percent of their residential customers to subscribe to broadband wireless services, the line cost per subscriber would soar to $2900. A market penetration of only 24 percent would push the per-subscriber cost to $5400.

NOTE   The cable TV operators are not going to give up without a fight, and there will be a fight. One of the advantages of cable operators is the installed base and the possibility of being able to leverage that with additional services and programming that a pure connectivity provider cannot provide on its own.

The arithmetic gets even more depressing. For one thing, the cost per home passed does not include some essential equipment, such as set-top video converters and video servers. And as for per-user revenues, broadband may not be much more lucrative than conventional phone service. Right now, cable operators pull in about $700 per subscriber in annual revenues, with a cash flow of about $400. Granted, services like video-on-demand should boost these numbers, but demand for such services still is uncertain. Given the major up-front costs and the enormous risks involved in wireline residential broadband, it is easy to see why the telcos have put the brakes on deployment.

Nevertheless, the United States will continue to lead the world in adopting wireless broadband services and technologies. For example, North America will have 47 percent of global wireless broadband service revenues in 2003, whereas Europe will capture over one-quarter of global wireless broadband service revenues, and the Asia-Pacific region will gain another quarter. Japan, on the other hand, would argue with these projections because it claims to be on the verge of winning the broadband wireless war.

How Are Networks and Operators Positioned to Provide Broadband Service?

The window of opportunity for delivering Local Multipoint Distribution Service (LMDS) is open wide—for operators that can position their companies networks just right. The LMDS industry, however, needs a viable business plan. We are only just seeing it occur. Like many in the LMDS industry, businesses—mainly small to medium in size—make up the most appropriate target market for wireless broadband networks.

NOTE   The competition is fierce (as indicated above). A business plan can be difficult to create in a fast moving business environment. Therefore, the LMDS industry "needs to move faster" if it is going to compete.

Some industry experts believe that the residential market should be left to other technologies for the time being. Although most players agree that the business market makes the best target, some believe that large residential buildings could offer lucrative targets.

The case for chasing the business market is strong. Fiber today reaches nearly 5 percent of the 970,000 office buildings in the United States. Even though that 5 percent actually reaches 46 percent of fiber-addressable businesses, it still leaves 54 percent of the market not served by fiber and open for LMDS players to target.

This portion of the market is looking for alternatives. The incumbents are underserving small and medium-sized businesses. In the future, this lack of attention to small to medium-sized businesses may hurt the incumbents and offer opportunity to LMDS players. The revenues of incumbent local exchange carriers (ILECs) should begin to decrease around 2008, and competitive local exchange carriers will experience 589 percent growth until that same time.

NOTE   Actually, the revenues of the ILECs are already starting to decline. The competitive local exchange carriers (CLECs) are having a significant impact in many market areas.

Although the opportunity for wireless broadband networks solutions is strong, LMDS players do not imply that they can replace existing or even future fiber connections. The industry experts believe that the infrastructure that is in place to get to the concentrated customer units should be used.

LMDS operators can choose a building already connected by fiber as a *minihub point*. After all, wireless broadband is just an access technology[3] (Figure 1-2). One can do anything with wireless broadband that one could do with fiber. On the other hand, wireless suffers from such things as interference (Rayleigh fading), limited bandwidth (certainly less than fiber), security, and frequency availability/licensing.

However, the lower cost of implementing broadband wireless networks and the speed with which operators can implement them offer LMDS players an advantage over those laying fiber. Where 80 percent of the cost of implementing wireline systems is dedicated to labor and 20 percent to capital, the opposite is true for wireless broadband networks, and the capital expense is much less.

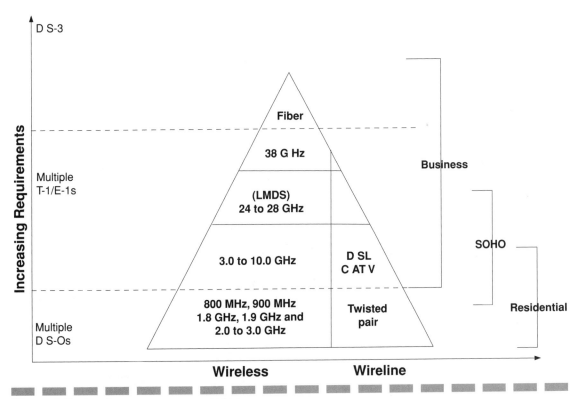

Figure 1-2 Local access user segmentation.

In addition, repair times are much shorter with broadband wireless systems than with fiber. Also, point-to-multipoint systems offer a fourfold improvement of spectrum efficiencies over point-to-point systems. Much of this efficiency stems from the LMDS hubbing capability, which eliminates the need for antennas dedicated to each link.

The scalability of LMDS systems also offers operators a cost advantage over fiber competitors. New operators do not know what penetration and churn will be like. Operators can start with one sector, placing one radio at a hub and adding equipment as traffic builds.

Can't Match

For the most part, today's technology alternatives cannot match wireline broadband's ultimate promise of giving residential customers everything from conventional phone service to interactive video and high-speed access to the Internet (see sidebar, "Weighing Wireline Options"). However, wireline broadband is increasingly viewed as a high-cost alternative with questionable payback.

CAUTION   We must keep in mind, though, that the wireline infrastructure is already in place as coax and xDSL over twisted pair, whereas wireless deployment is still somewhat spotty. Therefore, while wireless may well be the winner in the future, it still has a long way to go to oust wireline technologies.

Weighing Wireline Options

Here's a look at the wireline alternatives, along with their specific strengths and weaknesses:

ADSL   The main advantage of Asymmetric Digital Subscriber Line technology is its fairly low up-front cost. ADSL can run over the twisted-pair copper wires that telcos now use for basic phone service to most homes. ADSL offers up to 2 Mbps of downstream bandwidth to subscribers; upstream bandwidth is 64 kbps, or one uncompressed voice channel. ADSL actually can offer up to 9 Mbps downstream and 256 kbps upstream.

ADSL is still very much in the trial stage. Only about 28,000 lines have been installed in the United States to date. Improvements in the technology are on the way. ADSL's downstream capacity is expected to reach 24 Mbps soon. New digital subscriber line technologies are increasing the upstream path to 6 Mbps. And ADSL's operating range is expected to increase from the current 72,000 ft to 108,000 ft from a central office or remote terminal. This would put about 84 percent of all U.S. telco customers within ADSL's potential reach.

> **NOTE** ADSL's operating range is actually around 12,000 ft maximum without the addition of a Next Generation Digital Loop Carrier (NGDLC).

Still, ADSL does not look like a winner for video. Despite low upfront costs, overall deployment costs are now about $6000 per subscriber, putting ADSL on the expensive side. True, volume production of ADSL gear could push basic infrastructure costs down to a more attractive $900 per user, but this does not include the additional cost of the servers and digital set-top converters needed for video service. ADSL's better chance is with Internet access. Even at 6 Mbps, ADSL is far superior to competing access technologies such as basic-rate ISDN, which delivers only 128 kbps per B channel. However, ISDN is virtually universally available today, whereas ADSL is still spotty and limited by loop age and other impairments.

Hybrid Fiber/Coax (HFC) HFC is the favorite among cable operators, which already have coaxial cable running out to all 60 million of their U.S. subscribers. About 40 percent of U.S. cable TV networks now have fiber backbones. But cable operators still have plenty of work to do on the interactive front. Less than 10 percent of cable subscribers have access to two-way service. Cable companies have to pay only about $200 to $300 per home passed to upgrade their coaxial networks to HFC. This is where the technology is expected to come on strong. Telcos installing HFC have to pay about $300 to $500 per home passed for basic infrastructure. Additional costs for both telcos and cable operators include the ability to handle analog video (which costs about $200 per user to add) and voice (which costs another $300 per subscriber).

Furthermore, HFC broadband systems that operate in residential areas are usually capable of delivering 60 gigabits of bandwidth. This is billions of bits per second! Before HFC broadband, this kind of capacity was equivalent to the capacity of the entire state of Maine[4] (Figure

Figure 1-3
HFC broadband
technology.

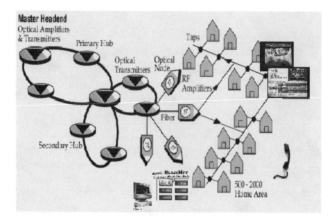

Figure 1-3
HFC broadband
technology.

1-3.) Broadband also delivers high-speed data, digital television services on demand, and standard voice services all on the same wire.

In other words, HFC broadband technology offers extremely high bandwidth at prices never before heard of in the world of data services. Even today a comparable service can cost hundreds of dollars per month with another provider.

One potential drawback with HFC is that it requires sophisticated frequency-allocation technology to offer voice because it has a bus architecture on which multiple conversations share the same path. This could present technical problems and potentially raise costs. HFC is a good choice for high-speed data services as long as the network is engineered properly.

Fiber to the Curb   At the high end of all the wireline broadband options is fiber to the curb (FTTC). FTTC runs fiber deeper into the neighborhood than HFC. Where HFC serves up to 6000 homes with a bus architecture running from a single fiber node, FTTC serves no more than a few hundred homes with direct coax or copper links from its fiber nodes. FTTC still remains a drawing-board technology: By the end of 1999, well below $250 million had been spent on FTTC deployment. The cost of running fiber averages about $700 per home passed; digital video costs another $500 per subscriber, whereas phone service costs another $600.

FTTC is ideal for high-speed data, but this service alone will not justify the cost to install. Phone and video revenues can help with payback, but they require high penetration to make up for the large up-front investment.[5]

Instead, wireline carriers are focusing on Direct Broadcast Satellite (DBS) and the two wireless broadband cable approaches: Multichannel Multipoint Distribution Service (MMDS) and Local Multipoint Distribution Service (LMDS). The big advantage of wireless broadband is its low cost. Basic infrastructure can be installed for less than $46 per home passed.

Even at market penetration as low as 14 percent, the cost per subscriber (less than $300) is more than competitive for both LMDS and MMDS. Customers often buy their own equipment, at about $300 to $500 for set-top box and receiver.

The main drawback of wireless broadband options is that they are primarily one-way only, which means no interactive video and no Internet access. However, wireless broadband offers a fast way for carriers to enter the home video market. This is not a bad tradeoff. What's more, the FCC is planning to make additional radiofrequency spectrum available, and this will improve prospects for wireless broadband video. And services like DirecTV's cousin, DirecPC, are offering two-way capabilities.

Wireless broadband networks are coming on strong. The bottom line: Telcos will deploy wireline residential broadband networks even more slowly. Ultimately, they will employ a mix of technologies. Wireless broadband is looming as an ever bigger part of that mix.

NOTE It appears that the telcos also need a business plan.

Overview of Wireless Broadband Network Activity

Since the demand for broadband access is closely related to demand and developments in the personal computer (PC) and Internet markets, as well as to events in the semiconductor, long-distance, local telephony, and cable television markets, it is apparent that the wireless broadband market is ready to arrive. Consumer and business markets are becoming dependent on data and Internet content, and the growing number of applications is driving us all further into an Internet Protocol (IP)–based world in which information is available anytime, anywhere. While wireline operators have the advantages of a head start and brand recognition, wireless broadband operators have the advantage of higher speeds and quick deployment. Fiber, on the other hand, has significantly more bandwidth than wireless technologies and enjoys a broad and growing installed base.

LMDS, for example, appears to be the most promising of all broadband technologies assessed on a cost and throughput basis. Residential satellite service users should expect from 16 kbps to 10 Mbps downstream and from 16 kbps to 500 Mbps upstream (see Chapter 26, "Residential High-Speed Internet: Wireless Broadband"). Higher rates will be available to the commercial sector. The bandwidth for MMDS recently has been transformed from a path for plain old cable television to another digital two-way high-speed conduit for data as large players in telecommunications have bought up the under-used spectrum. Even 38-GHz operators have a chance to find a profitable niche through this seemingly never-ending appetite for data. Mobile wireless broadband operators will be able to take advantage of its infrastructure with the introduction of third-generation (3G) systems and 2.5G radios, promising providers much higher data speeds on stackable voice channels and up to twice the voice capacity per radio.

NOTE   The *third generation* (3G, or IMT-2000) is the next generation of wireless technology after PCS. 3G is characterized by high-speed, high-bandwidth services that support a variety of applications, including wireline-quality voice and high-resolution video, wirelessly. 3G or IMT-2000 is an initiative of the International Telecommunication Union that seeks to integrate the various satellite, terrestrial, fixed, and mobile systems currently being deployed and developed under a single standard or family of standards to promote global service capabilities and interoperability after 2001.

NOTE   Amid the hype surrounding 3G mobile communications, general packet radio service (GPRS) often has been seen as a poor relation to 2.5G radio (between second- and third-generation wireless technology) technologies or dismissed as merely a stepping stone. However, with the bulk of operators running GPRS trials and many planning full commercial rollout within the next few years, GPRS is being reassessed. Many vendor and operator executives see GPRS, rather than 3G, as the driver of a fundamental shift in mobile communication habits. 3G remains the buzz technology, but GPRS is increasingly recognized as a bridge to it.

Wireless Broadband Technology Assessment and Services

Wireless broadband cable, also called *fixed wireless broadband*, is emerging as a legitimate local access platform for the delivery of high-quality digital data, video, and voice services. Like their cable competitors, wireless broadband operators are increasingly using their spectrum to offer high-speed Internet services.

Just like wired cable, a 6-MHz wireless broadband television channel can support 27 Mbps of downstream data throughput using wireless modems with 64 QAM (quadrature amplitude modulation) technology. Historically, a telephone-return path has been used for upstream communications, but operators are now transitioning to full two-way wireless broadband delivery.

Wireless broadband cable technology has limitations, but it also has key benefits, most notably the ability to rapidly introduce high-speed data access throughout a metropolitan area without the cost or delay of wired plant upgrades. Rather than stringing thousands of miles of fiber, coax, or twisted-pair wiring, a wireless broadband operator installs a headend and transmission tower and is open for business. The technology received a major endorsement in April 1999 when telecom giants Sprint and MCI WorldCom purchased three wireless broadband operators for more than $1 billion to build a wireless broadband local loop network.

> **NOTE** The wireless broadband operator still needs to interconnect the remote wireless offices to the wireline network, and this requires infrastructure, typically fiber. This is a significant cost item.

Wireless Broadband Cable Primer

There are several wireless broadband spectrum blocks in the 2.1- to 2.7-GHz band (Table 1-1) that can be used for cable television and Internet services, including Multipoint Distribution Service (MDS), Multichannel Multipoint Distribution Service (MMDS), and Instructional Television

TABLE 1-1

Wireless Broadband Cable Spectrum in the 2.1- to 2.7- GHz Band

Frequency Range	Service Type	Number of Channels	Channel Width
2.150–2.162 GHz	MDS	2	6 MHz
2.305–2.320 GHz	WCS	2	5 and 10 MHz
2.345–2.360 GHz	WCS	2	5 and 10 MHz
2.500–2.596 GHz	ITFS	16	6 MHz
2.596–2.644 GHz	MMDS	8	6 MHz
2.644–2.686 GHz	ITFS	4	6 MHz
2.686–2.689 GHz	MMDS	31	125 kHz

Fixed Service (ITFS).[6] Actually, ITFS was the original service from which spectrum was coopted for the creation of MMDS.

Additionally, Wireless Broadband Communications Service (WCS) spectrum allocated in 5- and 10-MHz increments, can be used for digital data or video. Ultrahigh frequency (UHF) broadcast television spectrum also can potentially be used for high-speed data access with cable modem technology, as can Local Multipoint Distribution Service (LMDS) spectrum, located in the 27.5- to 29.5-GHz frequency range.

In the United States, traditional wireless broadband cable system operators have aggregated available MDS, MMDS, and ITFS spectrum in a given market, providing up to 200 MHz of bandwidth, the equivalent of 33 analog 6-MHz television channels. Like broadcast television, MDS/MMDS/ITFS transmission is based on line-of-sight technology. Wireless broadband cable signals are transmitted from a broadcast tower, usually located on a mountain or tall building, to special antennas affixed to residences or businesses throughout a local market.

Reliable wireless broadband service delivery requires a direct line of sight between the transmitter and the receiving antenna. As is the case with broadcast TV, obstructions such as dense tree cover, hills, tall buildings, or even heavy precipitation can hinder reception. Multipath distortion (which results from signal reflections off of buildings or other structures) also can cause problems. Distance is a consideration too, since wireless broadband cable signals typically can only be received within a 30-mile radius of the transmitter. Wireless broadband cable operators believe these impediments can be overcome by dispersing a number of transmitters throughout a market in a cellular-like architecture.

Wireless Broadband Cable Modem Access Networks

Similar to delivering wired cable data services, a cable modem router and related networking gear are installed in the wireless broadband operator's headend. Digital data signals, such as Internet content requests, are then modulated onto radio frequency (rf) channels for broadcast transmission to rooftop antennas at subscriber locations. Coaxial cable is run from the antenna to a downconverter (which shifts the microwave signal frequency into the cable television band) and then into the cable modem inside the customer premise. The cable modem demodulates the incoming high-speed data signal and passes it onto an individual PC or local-area network (LAN) through a 10base-T Ethernet link. Wireless broadband operators offering Internet access typically have used a telephone-return path for upstream communications, but they are migrating to full two-way wireless broadband data delivery.

For example, one 6-MHz wireless broadband cable channel (MDS, MMDS, ITFS, or UHF) can support 650 to 1500 simultaneous active high-speed data users, providing peak downstream burst rates up to 1.5 Mbps or more to individual users. Assuming that only 20 percent of users are online at a given time, a single channel can support 5000 subscribers, whether they are home-based consumers or individuals connected to a business LAN.

Wireless Broadband Cable Modem Service Availability

A number of MDS/MMDS/ITFS operators have deployed high-speed data services commercially to date, mostly using wireless broadband cable modem technology. American Telecasting, Inc. (ATI), has launched service in Denver and Colorado Springs, Colorado, plus Portland, Oregon. CAI Wireless, Inc., has launched in Rochester, New York and in New York City. CS Wireless, Inc., has deployed high-speed Internet service in Dallas, Texas. People's Choice TV (PCTV) has launched its SpeedChoice service in Phoenix, Arizona, and Detroit, Michigan, whereas DirectNET is offering service commercially in Ft. Lauderdale, Florida.

These wireless broadband operators typically are pricing unlimited high-speed Internet access at $50 to $90 per month for consumers and $80 to $110 for small office/home office (SOHO) businesses. For larger businesses, some wireless broadband operators are charging $160 to $210 to connect one user on a business LAN plus $60 to $85 for each additional LAN user.

Two-Way Wireless Broadband Cable Modem Services

In the past, a key issue facing wireless broadband cable modem technology was the lack of two-way capabilities. Reliance on a telephone-return path limits upstream transmission speeds for end users. Furthermore, it adds costs to the wireless broadband service provider for incoming telephone lines and dialup modem pools.

In the United States, the FCC is approving use of the MDS, MMDS, and ITFS spectrum for upstream and downstream broadcasts. A number of operators are trialing two-way services, and PCTV is now offering two-way wireless broadband cable modem service commercially in Phoenix.

Upgrading wireless broadband cable systems to support two-way transmission is technically challenging because it requires operators to convert broadcast television systems into networks that more closely resemble a cellular telecommunications platform. Additionally, a transverter must be added at the customer premises to transmit data upstream.

NOTE   A *transverter* is a receive converter and a transmit converter joined by a common local oscillator. Its intentions are to convert a transceiver to a different set of frequencies or band. It will do so being totally transparent to the existing transceiver. This means that most functions of the transceiver will also be the same on the converted band. The transverter may be used in any mode that the transceiver is capable of. All filtering, signal processing, memory storage, scanning, frequency splitting, and all the other bells and whistles that your transceiver can do can be done on another band. There are a few things that are not transparent to all transceivers. Two of them are power control and frequency readout. Although there are a few transceivers on the market that allow these two functions, most transceivers will not. Power control is addressed in the transverter setup and can be adjusted in other ways. The frequency readout will become a minor, not noticeable inconvenience the more you use your system.

Cable TV–Based High-Speed Internet Services

In addition to providing high-speed Internet access to PCs with cable modems, multiple system operators (MSOs) are also working to provide fast Internet connections to TVs through digital cable set tops. Like cable modems, digital settops support 27 Mbps of downstream data throughput per 6-MHz TV channel. They also have enough processing power and memory to run basic browser software.

NOTE   *Multiple system operator* is a cable industry term that describes a company that operates more than one cable TV system.

By selling TV-based Internet services, cable operators can achieve a better return on the capital investments they make for two-way cable modem deployments by leveraging common infrastructure. Capital investments that could be shared by both TV- and PC-based Internet services include upgraded cable plant, Internet connectivity, network management systems, routers, servers, and broadband content.

Bolstered by the success of the Multimedia Cable Network System (MCNS) Partners' Data Over Cable System Interface Specification (DOCSIS) initiative, which defined North American standards for cable modem interoperability, Cable Television Laboratories, Inc., launched a similar project in August 1997 called OpenCable that is working to set standards for interactive digital cable set-top boxes.

OpenCable Project

CableLabs issued a request for information (RFI) in August 1997 and received responses from more than 20 cable equipment, consumer electronics, and technology companies in October 1997[7] (Table 1-2). The OpenCable Task Force sorted through the vendor submissions and issued initial product guidelines in November 1997.

OpenCable basically specified the same physical-layer transmission scheme used in MCNS cable modems. This included the International Telecommunications Union's (ITU) Annex B implementation of 64/256 quadrature amplitude modulation (QAM) for downstream modulation and a QPSK/16QAM-based real-time return path.

NOTE   Quadrature amplitude modulation (QAM) is a modulation technique that uses two carriers in quadrature (90 degrees between the carriers) that are amplitude modulated.

TABLE 1-2

Companies Responding to OpenCable RFI

ACTV	PowerTV
Cisco Systems	Samsung
Criterion Software	Sarnoff
IBM	Scientific-Atlanta
Intel	SCM Microsystems
Lucent Technologies	Sony
Microsoft	Sun Microsystems
Netscape	Texas Instruments
Network Computer, Inc.	Thomson Consumer Electronics
NextLevel Systems	Toshiba
Oracle	Wink Communications
Panasonic	WorldGate Communications
Pioneer	Zenith Electronics

The MPEG-2 (Moving Picture Experts Group) standard is specified for digital video transport with audio following the Dolby Audio AC-3 system. For signal security, OpenCable selected NextLevel Systems, Inc.'s, implementation of the DES encryption standard. Through a harmony agreement reached between NextLevel (which changed its name back to General Instrument) and Scientific-Atlanta, Inc., OpenCable supports multiple conditional access and control data streams over the core encryption scheme, specifically GI's DigiCipher and S-A's PowerKEY solutions.

The OpenCable standard will not specify a single vendor's microprocessor or operating system (OS). Instead, it plans to spell out basic requirements for processing power and memory that OpenCable manufacturers must meet, as well as rules of the road for OS vendors to follow. With this "OS agnostic" approach, most interactive services will be implemented with middleware using open Internet specifications, including HTML, CGI, JavaScript, and popular plug-ins.

In January 1998, CableLabs selected S-A to manage key elements of the OpenCable project. S-A will produce a network architecture reference model, help define network interfaces (including the physical layer and communication protocols), and also provide system integration services. The project was completed in the first quarter of 1998, enabling the OpenCable specification to be completed by the second quarter of 1998.

TCI's OpenCable Maneuvers

In December 1997, cable giant Tele-communications, Inc. (TCI), now part of AT&T, committed to purchase 6.5 million to 11.9 million digital set tops from General Instrument (GI) over the next 5 years. In 1998, TCI deployed GI's DCT-1000 set top, a one-way digital video receiver. The MSO deployed interactive set tops from GI that meet the emerging OpenCable specification in 1999.

As part of the deal, GI issued TCI and its affiliates a warrant convertible for 3.2 shares of GI common stock at a discounted price of $14.75 per share for every digital box purchased. Since TCI cable fulfilled the full potential of its purchase commitment, the stock-for-boxes strategy yielded a 16 percent equity stake in GI. GI also acquired TCI's Headend in the Sky digital authorization business in exchange for a 10 percent equity interest in GI.

In January 1998, TCI announced that it had agreed to license Microsoft's Windows CE operating system for at least 5 million of the OpenCable set tops it deployed. The deal also called for Microsoft to provide key elements of its WebTV technology for the TCI set tops. Separately, TCI also inked a deal with Sun to add PersonalJava to some of the boxes.

NOTE AOL-TV potentially will be a factor at this level.

Windows CE serves as the operating system for TCI's advanced set tops, whereas PersonalJava runs on top of the OS, providing an open application environment. In this way, TCI could run software that is written expressly for Windows CE as well as Java-based Internet applications.

Also in January 1998, Sony Corp. purchased a 5 percent interest in GI for $187.5 million to ensure that it got a piece of the emerging digital cable set-top market. As a part of the investment, Sony helped GI fulfill the TCI order as a second-source supplier.

Pegasus Flying First

TCI is not the only MSO with big OpenCable plans. Under a project called Pegasus, Time Warner Cable developed specifications for a two-way digital set-top box that was deployed commercially in April 1998—beating the TCI-GI team to the punch.

Time Warner selected Scientific-Atlanta as the prime contractor for the Pegasus program, with Toshiba and Pioneer tapped as secondary suppliers. In total, Time Warner bought 1 million digital set tops from the three vendors. The company also has purchased 500,000 boxes from GI.

S-A's Pegasus box, called the Explorer 2000, is now compliant with OpenCable specifications. At its initial release, Explorer included HTML and JavaScript engines within the PowerTV operating system to support TV-based Internet services. Eight other MSOs deployed S-A's Explorer 2000 digital set tops in 1998: Adelphia, Comcast, Cox, Marcus Cable, MediaOne, Rogers, Videotron, and Cogeco.

Other Internet TV Solutions: ICTV and WorldGate

In addition to the digital OpenCable approach, two other vendors championed complementary Internet TV technologies for analog cable systems: Interactive Cable Television (ICTV) and WorldGate Communications. Los Gatos, California–based ICTV has developed a high-powered *virtual PC* service that can be delivered to cable subscriber TVs over hybrid fiber-coax (HFC) networks. ICTV and Cox Communications started a market trial of the service in March 1997 in Santa Barbara, California. Cox has priced the service at $9.95 per month for equipment rental and 5 hours of use, plus $4.99 for each additional hour. Today, the ICTV services include Web access, e-mail, and multimedia games. Service is now priced at $8.95 per month for equipment rental and 8 hours of use, plus $3.99 for each additional hour.

ICTV essentially builds a client-server network in the cable headend by installing a massively parallel architecture of multimedia PCs running Windows 2000. Proprietary ICTV hardware is used to take the VGA output from each PC board and translate it into National Television Systems Committee (NTSC) or MPEG video streams for over-the-cable system to subscriber homes. The signal can be received through any cable-ready television set or set-top box. A small ICTV box and wireless broadband keyboard are installed in the home to handle upstream communications from the subscriber to the headend.

In an analog cable environment, each ICTV subscriber is allocated a full 6-MHz television channel during their session. The subscriber receives a dedicated 10-Mbps stream to the home, enabling him or her to receive the video output from the headend-based PC he or she is using in real time. In effect, the subscriber's TV set operates as a remote monitor, allowing them to view any Windows 2000 application running on the PC, whether it's surfing the Web, sending e-mail, or playing a multimedia game.

While ICTV is focused on providing a high-performance multimedia service, WorldGate Communications is working to deliver cheap, no-frills Internet access to the masses. Rather than requiring the use of a full TV channel, WorldGate's TV On-Line service operates in the vertical blanking interval (VBI). Normally an unused portion of the video spectrum, a typical cable system may have 60 or more slots. WorldGate's platform delivers 100 kbps of shared downstream data throughput in each VBI to addressable analog set-top boxes manufactured by GI and S-A.

To make it work, WorldGate needed to pull a few tricks because VBI bandwidth cannot deliver a real-time video stream, like ICTV, and analog set tops do not have enough memory to run a full-featured Web browser. At the headend, HTML coding is stripped off any Web page a customer requests. The display output is then sent down to the TV set in the home as a bitmap image.

WorldGate foresees cable operators selling the TV On-Line service, which includes Web and e-mail access, for $7.95 per month, with World-Gate receiving a 33 percent share of the revenue. Rental of a wireless broadband keyboard would cost subscribers another $5 per month. The company has deployed TV On-Line service with MSOs Charter Communications and Shaw Communications.

Cable IP Local and Long-Distance Telephony

The idea of offering competitive residential telephone services has captivated cable operators for years. Although reliable telephony equipment for hybrid fiber-coax (HFC) networks is available commercially, significant economic and operational barriers have discouraged most MSOs in North America from deploying it widely. Rather than offering telephone services, cable operators have responded to growing market demand for high-speed Internet connections by rolling out cable modems. The effort has been largely successful. Currently, North American MSOs have served more than 500,000 cable modem subscribers, outpacing telcos in the race to offer wireless broadband Internet access.

Now, with IP networks emerging as viable platforms for the delivery of voice traffic, MSOs hope to use their high-speed data networks to support packet telephone services instead of deploying standalone HFC telephony equipment. The rationale is clear. Deploying separate telephony and high-speed data architectures creates capital and operational and spectrum inefficiencies, since a cable operator must purchase two hardware platforms, allocate a pair of upstream and downstream channels for each service, integrate two operations support systems, and assign staff to manage each service offering.

Using IP, cable operators hope to create an integrated multiservice communications platform that operates on a lower cost structure than existing circuit-switched alternatives, enabling aggressive service price discounting without sacrificing margins.

Besides undercutting competitors, MSOs hope the flexibility of IP networks will allow them to deliver a host of unique value-added features, such as integrated voice mail and e-mail messaging and the real-time provisioning of additional phone lines without rewiring a home. However, to make this vision a reality, cable operators must overcome a number of hurdles. The first-generation Data Over Cable Service Interface Specification (DOCSIS) cable modem standard was not specifically designed to support IP telephony and must be enhanced. Cable packet telephony operations support systems must be developed to handle customer provisioning, management, and billing. And MSOs must develop interconnection standards for their IP backbone networks to effectively share packet telephony traffic.

In September 1997, Cable Television Laboratories, Inc., initiated a project on behalf of its North American MSO members called PacketCable to address these issues. Most leading networking and telecommunications vendors are participating in the cable IP telephony initiative.

Packet Telephony Overview

A telephone call is a highly isochronous (time-sensitive) network application. If transmission delays greater than a few hundred milliseconds occur, telephone call quality suffers. Conventional telephone networks avoid delays, also called *latency*, by establishing a dedicated circuit between two end points for the duration of a call. On digital telecommunications networks, each circuit requires up to 64 kbps. However, the latency control offered by circuit-switched networks comes at a price: wasted bandwidth. Even though there are numerous pauses or silent periods during a telephone conversation when no data are transferred, a full 64-kbps stream is still required for the entire call.

Connectionless packet data networks have the opposite characteristics. Rather than employing dedicated connections, network resources are shared and only used when data are sent or received in quick bursts. Using aggressive compression algorithms, telephone calls can be delivered at rates as low as 8 kbps in a packet format, offering even more bandwidth efficiency. The challenge is that shared data networks can be subject to delay levels that harm call quality.

Anyone who has placed a phone call over the Internet understands this issue. Since no performance guarantees are available, the sound quality is often wretched. This need not be the case over private IP networks, such as a corporate intranet or cable modem network. While traffic patterns on the Internet can be as rough and unpredictable as currents in the Atlantic Ocean, a well-engineered and well-managed IP network can be as placid as a swimming pool.

This said, even on private IP networks, strict quality-of-service (QoS) and prioritization schemes are required to ensure that voice packets reach their destination within a maximum delay window. Otherwise, jitter can occur, causing distortion or unacceptable pauses during a call.

Assuming that network quality levels can be maintained, mechanisms for call setup and management must be implemented to route IP voice traffic. A leading candidate for the job is H.323, an umbrella standard for audio and video conferencing over shared data networks adopted in 1996 by the International Telecommunications Union (ITU). H.323 specifies protocols for call signaling and control, plus several compression and decompression algorithms (codecs) ranging from 8 kbps (called G.729) to 64 kbps (called G.711). It also specifies techniques for delivering supplementary services such as call waiting, call park, and other PBX-like capabilities.

The H.323 architecture specifies several network elements, including terminals (that connect PCs, telephones, or other devices to the network), a gatekeeper (that authorizes and manages calls), and a gateway (that translates H.323 calls into other voice formats, enabling communication with conventional telephone networks). In addition to H.323, cable operators and vendors plan to support Simple Gateway Control Protocol (SGCP) and Media Gateway Control Protocol (MGCP), a more centralized packet telephony architecture that may prove to be a more scalable solution.

Driving DOCSIS

The North American cable industry developed the DOCSIS standard to create a competitive consumer market for cable modem equipment. Seeking to capitalize on the most obvious service opportunity (delivering high-speed Internet access), the DOCSIS standard was designed as a cheap consumer Web-surfing platform. While well suited for its intended application, DOCSIS does not provide all the QoS and latency controls required to offer toll-quality IP voice services.

AT&T Corp. joined major cable companies to uncover this problem in early 1997 when it assigned a team of engineers and business executives to thoroughly evaluate the potential of DOCSIS as a telephony platform. The team at AT&T Labs identified three key items that must be added to DOCSIS to support toll-quality telephone calls: upstream packet fragmentation and reassembly techniques, support for a national clock, and an advanced isochronous scheduling system.

Because DOCSIS products employ an asymmetric architecture, offering 27 Mbps of downstream capacity and typically less than 1 Mbps upstream, packet fragmentation is required to avoid upstream congestion that has an impact on call quality. Specifically, the largest Ethernet packet size is 1500 octets. Thus, sending this full-size packet upstream over a 768-kbps cable modem would take about 15 ms, straining the delay budget for a packet voice call. Using fragmentation techniques, these large data packets are broken into smaller ones to prevent unacceptable transmission delays.

The second item, a national clock, is necessary to properly synchronize transmissions between cable modems on the network. The final enhancement is adding a high-quality isochronous scheduler to headend-based DOCSIS cable modem termination system (CMTS) equipment. Because the DOCSIS standard was designed as a consumer Internet access platform, system latency can run in the 50- to 70-ms range. While this window is fine for Web surfing, it seriously affects packet telephone call quality. To support packet telephony, CMTS vendors are working to offer an isochronous scheduling solution closer to a 2-ms time scale.

Due largely to AT&T's efforts, these key enhancements should be added to the DOCSIS standard. DOCSIS products have been available since mid-1999.

PacketCable Products

In the PacketCable architecture, a number of DOCSIS-based client devices support IP telephone connections, including cable modems, digital set tops, and media terminal adapters (MTAs)—standalone devices that link telephone handsets to the cable data network. All these devices can be served in the same cable spectrum by a single DOCSIS CMTS.

Based on its initial traffic modeling, Cisco Systems believes its CMTS product, which includes an integrated router, can support between 300 and 3000 simultaneous IP telephone calls when intermixed with other data traffic. The high-end number assumes the use of a G.729 standard-bandwidth-saving codec, which is 8 kbps, whereas the smaller number assumes a full 64-kbps codec.

Vendors expect that the addition of IP telephony support will only increase the cost of a DOCSIS cable modem by 24 to 34 percent. Thus an integrated cable modem and PacketCable MTA could be priced as low as $550 at its initial release.

Of course, if a cable operator wants to offer a lifeline IP telephone service, it also will need to add a battery pack to the device to provide power during an electrical outage. Vendors estimate that a battery pack with 8 hours of standby power will add $50 to $60 to the price of a cable IP telephony device. Over time, consumer electronics companies are likely to offer cable IP telephony products in a variety of configurations, such as incorporating the technology into a cordless telephone system base station.

End-to-End Issues

Building DOCSIS headend and client products with IP telephony support will not be easy. An even greater challenge, however, according to cable operators and vendors, will be efficiently provisioning and managing the devices once they are installed on the network. Additionally, engineering disparate local cable data systems and backbone networks to offer high end-to-end IP voice quality is not trivial. This means voice packets need to be specially identified and given priority by the CMTS, routers, and switches as they traverse the network.

As a starting point, many cable operators may opt to initially deploy IP telephony merely as a local-loop bypass service. In this scenario, voice packets would be transferred directly from the CMTS to an IP telephony gateway and then onto the public switched telephone network (PSTN). This would enable cable IP telephony users to place and receive calls without using the incumbent local exchange carrier (ILEC).

The ultimate goal of many MSOs is to also offer long-distance IP telephony over their packet backbone networks. For example, a residential cable IP telephony customer served by Comcast in Philadelphia might call another cable IP telephony customer served by MediaOne in Los Angeles. The packet calls could be carried nationwide at very low cost without ever touching a telephone company network. MSOs are currently evaluating options to enter into backbone interconnection arrangements that would make such a solution viable.

Service Strategies

Cable operators have different IP telephony service strategies, ranging from plans to offer competitive lifeline phone service to simply selling second phone lines to families or remote PBX access for corporate telecommuters. After acquiring TCI, AT&T used cable IP telephony to compete with ILECs for primary line service, but not every MSO will follow this approach.

A key service most MSOs say they plan to pursue is offering corporations an integrated telecommuting service for their workers, including both remote LAN and private branch exchange (PBX) telephone access. In this way, employees could access both their e-mail and voice mail at home and answer their corporate telephone extension as if they were in the office.

Of course, by incorporating IP telephony functions into different devices, such as TV set tops and cable modems, MSOs could offer a range of new service options. For example, using an interactive set top, MSOs could offer directory services, caller ID, and other features on the TV. While service specifics are still sketchy, it is becoming clear that wireless broadband packet networks will operate with vastly different economic assumptions than the public switched telephone network (PSTN), resulting in different pricing and packaging models.

Wireless Broadband Fundamentals and Fixed-Wireless Broadband Systems

Our appetite for bandwidth is insatiable. And now, just as wireline modems are topping out at 56 kbps and ISDN service is finally available in most locations, new technologies, such as DSL (Digital Subscriber Line) and cable modems that offer transmission speeds of megabits per second, are beginning field trials. Meanwhile, old standbys, such as corporate T1 connections at 1.54 Mbps, are being upgraded by many companies to fiber connections. As quickly as LECs (local exchange carriers) and competitive access providers lay new fiber, however, many companies are finding high-bandwidth connections difficult to obtain or prohibitively expensive. Wireless broadband has always been an alternative for high-speed connections, but never has the range of choices been as great or the rate of innovation as rapid. This part of the chapter delves into the world of wireless broadband networks and other fixed-wireless broadband connections that deliver data rates from T1 to 155 Mbps. These wireless broadband connections serve the same function as a wireline—interconnecting private networks, bypassing an LEC, or connecting to the Internet.

This part of the chapter also focuses on communications that are fixed and at higher data rates. A simple form of such a system might involve a private microwave point-to-point connection. A more complex system might involve a carrier that has deployed a complete network using sophisticated point-to-multipoint hubs. A LEO (low-earth-orbiting) system of satellites would be even more complex. There are as many variations in high-speed wireless broadband systems as there are variations in wireline broadband systems.

Fixed-wireless broadband systems have a long history. Point-to-point microwave connections have long been used for voice and data communications, generally in backhaul networks operated by phone companies, cable TV companies, utilities, railways, paging companies, and government agencies, and, will continue to be an important part of the communications infrastructure[8] (Figure 1-4). Frequencies used range from 1 to 40 GHz. However, technology has continued to advance. This has allowed higher frequencies and thus smaller antennas to be used. The result has been lower costs and, easier-to-deploy systems for private use for a whole new generation of carriers that are planning to use wireless broadband access as their last mile of communication.

NOTE   The terms *wireless broadband* and *broadband wireless* are not used consistently, but generally, both apply to carrier-based services in which multiple data streams are multiplexed onto a single radio-carrier signal. Some vendors also use the terms to refer to privately deployed networks. Generally, the technical definition of *broadband* is a system that operates at speeds in excess of T1/E1.

NOTE   A backhaul connection is a company's internal infrastructure connection. For example, a phone company's backhaul might be from one central office to another.

Thus the goal of this part of the chapter is to show how fixed-wireless broadband systems are no longer a communications tool restricted to large or specialized organizations. They are available to almost any size company in a variety of ways for a variety of purposes. You will find that you have a wide

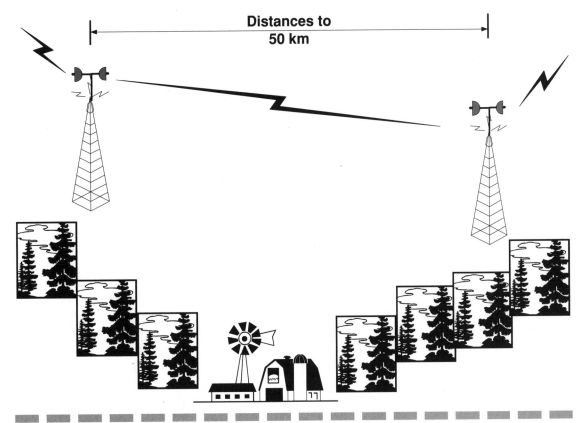

Figure 1-4   Fixed-wireless broadband system.

range of choices, including whether to use licensed or unlicensed spectrum, whether to deploy a private network or use a carrier network, and whether to use a terrestrial network or a satellite network. In some cases, you may not even know that your service provider is using wireless broadband technology. This part of the chapter also briefly discusses the options available, how the various technologies work, and how to go about implementing a fixed-wireless broadband solution. See Chapter 14, "Implementing Terrestrial Fixed- Wireless Broadband Networks," for a thorough discussion of how to implement fixed-wireless broadband networks.

Fundamental Concepts and Issues

Before briefly delving into the types of fixed-wireless broadband systems (see Chapter 2, "Wireless Broadband Networks Platforms") and how to use them, let's look at some of the fundamental concepts and issues involved. These include

- Fixed-wireless broadband applications
- Wireline versus broadband wireless
- Private versus carrier
- Unique aspects of wireless broadband
- Radio spectrum

Fixed-Wireless Broadband Applications

Fixed-wireless broadband systems can be used for almost anything that a wired network is used for, whether the network is a T1 circuit, a cable television cable, an Ethernet cable, or a fiberoptic cable. Fixed-wireless broadband systems are designed so that they emulate cable connections, and they use the same type of interfaces and protocols, such as T1, frame relay, Ethernet, and ATM. For this part of the chapter, it is assumed that your application is data, with emphasis on wireless broadband systems designed for data communications. Keep in mind that fixed-wireless broadband systems are also used for voice communications as well as for carrying television programming. However, most new development in fixed-wireless broadband systems is data-centric, such as for Internet access, or is flexible in supporting both voice and data communications. Fixed-wireless broadband systems match cable-based systems for all important parameters, including delay, bit-error rate (1 in 100 million or better), and throughput (1 to 155 Mbps). Consequently, any application that operates over a cable should be able to operate over a fixed-wireless broadband system. The only exception is communication involving geosynchronous satellites, where delays can exceed a quarter of a second.

Wireline versus Wireless Broadband

In some cases, a fixed-wireless broadband system is the only wireless broadband option. Thus you must decide if a fixed-wireless broadband connection is practical and if it is competitive with available wireline connections. Today, fewer than 14 percent of buildings have fiber to them, and only about 54 percent are close enough to a central office (12,000 ft or 3.5 km) to take advantage of DSL technology. Thus, in many cases, a wireless broadband connection could be the only option for high-speed communications. This is especially true in more remote areas. In some areas, the only option for communications will be by satellite.

NOTE The availability of satellite services is the only option in some areas. A favorable geography factor could help promote the growth of broadband satellite business.

When both wireless broadband and wireline options exist, the potential reasons to consider wireless broadband include lower costs, faster deployment, greater flexibility, and better reliability. Unfortunately, costs and deployment have to be evaluated on a case-by-case basis, and actual costs will depend on the particular circumstances. In developed countries, a wireless broadband system will not be more reliable than wireline options, but in developing countries, wireless broadband communications may be much more reliable.

Private versus Carrier

A fundamental distinction is whether you deploy your own wireless broadband connection or it is supplied by a wireless broadband carrier. In the past, most fixed-wireless broadband connections were private, but with new spectrum licenses, a number of companies are deploying or planning to deploy networks in most major metropolitan areas. Do not think of these companies as *wireless* broadband companies, though. Think of them as CLECs or ISPs that happen to be using wireless broadband technology. Instead of running fiber to a building, they are using wireless broadband links that may be less expensive to deploy than fiber.

Once one of these companies, Winstar[9] and Advanced Radio Telecom[10] are two examples, has a wireless broadband connection to a building, often to the roof, it can then market its communications services to the tenants of the building. These services look like standard networking services, and interfaces include frame relay, ATM, T1, and Ethernet using the same connectors, such as BNC and RJ-45. These services also can include value-added services, such as network management, Internet access, Web hosting, and e-mail. The fact that these carriers use wireless broadband technology will be transparent[11] (Figure 1-5).

NOTE You should ask questions to ensure dependable service. For instance, terrestrial wireless broadband carriers only have regional licenses, so you should ask whether the carrier can provide service to all your locations.

Satellites are another form of carrier service. They offer broadband services using geosynchronous satellites today and higher capacity LEO satellites in the near future.

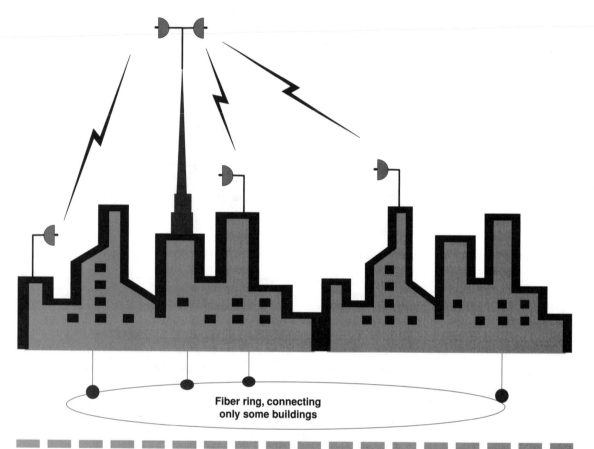

Figure 1-5   *Wireless broadband providing last mile of connectivity to buildings not having fiber connections.*

Unique Aspects of Wireless Broadband

Fortunately, you do not need to be a radio engineer to take advantage of fixed-wireless broadband communications. However, it is helpful to understand what makes wireless broadband different from other forms of communication, particularly when qualifying and specifying service parameters.

Wireless broadband communications offers tremendous flexibility and ever-improving performance, but it does have some limitations. First and foremost, wireless broadband uses radio spectrum, a finite resource. This limits the number of wireless broadband users and the amount of spectrum available to any user at any moment in time. The amount of spectrum available equates almost directly to data bandwidth, with 1 Hz of spectrum typically yielding between 1 and 4 bps of throughput depending on various factors, such as the type of modulation used and environmental factors. The amount of spectrum actually available varies from radio band to radio band, but suffice it to say that fiberoptic cable offers far greater overall capacity. Despite this capacity limitation, wireless broadband offers more than sufficient bandwidth for many applications. However, it is important to know the capacity of a particular wireless broadband system in order to understand how it can satisfy your requirements if they should expand in the future. Another limitation is that fixed-wireless broadband systems operate at frequencies that almost always require line of sight and that are restricted to distances that vary from a few miles to tens of miles. It is no mystery why microwave dishes are located at the tops of towers, hills, and buildings. Unlike cellular and other mobile wireless broadband systems, fixed-wireless broadband systems use fixed antennas with narrowly focused beams. A 3- to 4-degree beam is not uncommon. And unlike cellular systems, in which base stations communicate with dozens of mobile stations, broadband systems usually operate in a point-to-point manner, although a number of point-to-multipoint systems are in development.

Very few standards exist for fixed-wireless broadband systems. Chances are you will have to purchase equipment from the same vendor for both sides of the connection to ensure interoperability.

Radio Spectrum

Fixed-wireless broadband systems use frequencies allocated for such use from about 900 MHz to 40 GHz. The number of different bands can be bewildering, with multiple frequency bands assigned for private use and multiple bands assigned for carrier use. In addition, some bands are designated for licensed use, whereas others can be used without a license.

Should you care what frequency you use? Yes, but only in a general sense. Higher frequencies have some advantages over lower frequencies but also suffer some drawbacks. The principal advantage of higher frequencies is that there is more spectrum available for broadband applications. Most higher bandwidth systems use frequencies above 10 GHz. Antennas at these frequencies are smaller due to the smaller wavelengths, making systems easier to deploy. With higher frequency, however, components demand more sophisticated technology, so systems cost more. Also, propagation distance for reliable communications decreases, and the signal is more susceptible to weather conditions such as rain and fog. Higher frequency systems, those above about 30 GHz, are sometimes referred to as *millimeter wave* because the wavelength of these signals is on the order of 1 mm.

Both private and public carrier systems have a choice of using a licensed or unlicensed spectrum. The main advantage of an unlicensed spectrum is being able to deploy a system without applying for a license from the FCC (or equivalent body in other countries). The disadvantage is that you could experience or cause interference, although the type of technology used in these frequencies minimizes this possibility. The principal frequencies of interest are

- *900 Hz, 2.4 GHz, and 5.8 GHz.* Unlicensed systems using spread-spectrum techniques.
- *2.5 GHz.* Licensed to carriers for MMDS (Multichannel Multipoint Distribution System).
- *5 GHz.* New unlicensed band referred to as the UNII (Unlicensed National Information Infrastructure) band.
- *23 GHz.* Commonly used for microwave LAN systems.
- *28 GHz.* Licensed to carriers for LMDS (Local Multipoint Distribution Service).
- *38 / 39 GHz.* Licensed to carriers for general-purpose communications services.[12]

Fixed-Wireless Broadband Systems Types

Many different types of fixed-wireless broadband systems are available. Let's concentrate on the most important ones. Radiofrequency systems are emphasized in this part of the chapter, although optical systems are also available. The discussion includes both private and carrier systems:

- Private licensed links (microwave)
- Private unlicensed links (spread spectrum)
- 38-GHz carrier service
- LMDS (Local Multipoint Distribution Service)
- Satellite systems
- Others

Private Licensed Links (Microwave)

Microwave links are the traditional workhorse of fixed-wireless broad-band systems and were around long before the term *wireless broadband* was coined. These connections are point to point and require licenses. Frequencies available range from 1.7 to 40 GHz, with most of the lower frequencies being used by carriers for backhaul networks, such as T3 connections at 45 Mbps. Many of these are multihop systems and commonly operate at 2, 4, and 6 GHz. A 155-Mbps connection (OC-3) represents the high end for microwave communications today, but there is no inherent upper limit.

If you are not a telephone company with a backhaul network or a PCS carrier connecting thousands of base stations and instead are looking to bridge a LAN between two points, the FCC has allocated a frequency band specifically for private use: the 21.2- to 23.6-GHz band. The license-application process is streamlined, affordable products are available, and systems are relatively easy to deploy. For about $30,000 you can purchase a fully installed 10-Mbps connection with a 5-mile (8-km) range.

NOTE Ethernet type of bridging is less expensive than deploying T1 links because it can operate in a half-duplex asynchronous manner. Of course, if you need to carry voice or video, you may need a T1 or other form of synchronous connection.

Microwave links are very reliable and, using licensed frequencies, virtually eliminate any potential of interference. Unlike spread-spectrum connections, they offer considerable head room for increasing throughput if your requirements expand in the future.

NOTE Spread spectrum is a communications technique in which the modulated information is transmitted in a bandwidth considerably greater than the frequency content of the original information.

Private Unlicensed Links (Spread Spectrum)

An alternative to a microwave link is to use spread-spectrum bridging products. Many wireless LAN vendors offer such products because they incorporate much of the required technology within their access points. These wireless bridges, mostly operating in the 2.4-GHz band, offer rates of 1, 2, 3, 4, and 10 or 11 Mbps and distances up to 10 or 25 miles (16 to 40 km) depending on the type of antenna used. For longer distances, you may not be able to achieve as high a throughput. Some products also operate in the 5.8-GHz band.

Government regulatory agencies, including the FCC, mandate the use of a spread-spectrum radio technique that minimizes interference by making radio signals appear like background noise to unintended receivers. Spread spectrum can employ frequency hopping or direct sequence. These bridges offer the same types of features offered by wireline bridges: interconnection with Ethernet or Token-Ring networks; Spanning Tree Protocol support; remote configuration via telnet, File Transfer Protocol (FTP), Simple Network Management Protocol (SNMP), and HTML; automatic configuration using Bootstrap Protocol (BOOTP) or Dynamic Host Configuration Protocol (DHCP); and SNMP compliance supporting standard management information bases (MIBs).

38-GHz Carrier Service

Between 38.6 and 40.0 GHz, the FCC has made 14 pairs of 50-MHz-wide channels available for carriers to offer wireless last-mile communications. This band is also referred to as the 39-GHz band. The primary license holders of this spectrum at this time in the United States are Advanced Radio Telecom, Teleport, and Winstar. Forthcoming auctions for this spectrum inevitably will produce new wireless broadband competitors as well. These carriers manage the entire wireless link themselves, using the wireless broadband connection to extend the reach of their fiber networks. By placing wireless broadband hubs centrally in higher-density population areas, the carriers then make wireless broadband connections to other buildings with which they have a line of sight. This involves securing roof rights and installing antennas, radios, and interface equipment. The carriers usually target buildings that do not have fiber available. The carrier can then market high-speed connections to tenants of the building. The protocols and interfaces are standard communications interfaces such as T1, E1, frame relay, Ethernet, and ATM. To the customer, the service is indistinguishable from a wireline service. All he or she sees is a jack in the wall.

Different carriers emphasize different services. One approach is to offer basic telephony services to end users, bypassing the LEC. Another approach is to offer Internet access and associated services, such as Web hosting and mailboxes. Another approach is to sell connectivity to existing LECs, competitive LECs (CLECs), interexchange carriers (IXCs), long-distance service providers, and Internet service providers (ISPs), essentially being a carrier's carrier. Although service is available on a limited basis in dozens of cities in the United States, this market area is so new that no dominant business model has emerged.

LMDS (Local Multipoint Distribution Service)

As discussed previously, LMDS, another type of wireless broadband system, recently has received tremendous press attention, and for good reason. The FCC recently auctioned a larger block of spectrum than ever before in history: 1.3 GHz. The specific bands include 27.5 to 28.35 GHz, 29.1 to 29.25

GHz, and 31 to 31.3 GHz. One band, called the A^2 *band*, is 1150 MHz wide, and the other, the B^2 *band*, is 150 MHz wide. The smaller *B band* is available to any company, but restrictions on the *A band* have prevented incumbent LECs and TV operators from obtaining the spectrum. Although actual LMDS service is extremely limited at this time, it is projected to become a multibillion-dollar industry within 5 years, with nearly every large telecom and networking vendor having some involvement today.

The services planned for LMDS are quite similar to those of the 38/39-GHz band, namely Internet access, telephony, CLEC services, and resale via LECs, CLECs, long-distance service providers, and ISPs. The proposed architecture is point to multipoint, with centralized hubs communicating to fixed antennas and radios on neighboring buildings. Effective range is about 3 miles (5 km). Downstream radio channels typically will be 20 or 40 MHz wide and upstream channels 10 MHz, resulting in about 20 to 50 Mbps of downstream bandwidth and 10 Mbps of upstream bandwidth. The carriers will be able to reuse frequencies efficiently in a cellular fashion. Using a Time Division Multiple Access (TDMA) approach, multiple customers will be able to share the same radio channel. Like 38/39-GHz service, carriers will support standard networking and telephony.

Satellite Systems

Why include satellites in a discussion of fixed-wireless systems? Satellites are anything but fixed, but the ground stations are. Satellites were first used for intercontinental telecommunications before undersea fiber was available and for communications in remote areas, including to remote islands and ocean-going ships. By the end of 1999, more than 200 communications satellites were deployed, and today, satellite systems represent a sizable industry. A variety of new LEO systems are in development and deployment, and they will result in an estimated 2400 additional satellites by 2008. These new satellite networks will vastly increase the types of services available for both mobile and fixed use, but even now there are many instances when a satellite connection is the best option.

From a broadband perspective, companies such as Comsat[13] in the United States already offer flexible service ranging from 56 kbps to 155 Mbps with E1/T1, frame relay, and ATM interfaces operating via a geosynchronous Intelsat satellite. For example, 2-Mbps service requires a 1.8-m dish antenna that is relatively easy to install. Connection reliability matches landline quality, although there is a somewhat greater delay of about a quarter of a second for the signal to travel to and from the satellite. This delay can affect protocols, such as TCP at data rates exceeding 1 Mbps.

The Others

If all the systems described in the preceding subsections were not enough, a number of other systems, both private and carrier-oriented, are offering or are about to offer wireless broadband service. Let's quickly survey these, first private systems and then carrier solutions.

LASER   Laser technology can be used for reliable point-to-point communications. Like all the other systems discussed in this chapter, they require line of sight. For just a little more than $10,000, you can purchase a link offering 10 Mbps and a range of 1 km. Much higher data rates (45 Mbps) are also available. Lasers offer the advantage of not requiring licensing anywhere in the world. They also can be extremely secure because any interception of the beam will block the transmission, which can instantly be detected. No wonder lasers are sometimes used by financial institutions. However, because of the small lens size and tightly focused beam, lasers are sensitive to moisture on the lens, although this can be solved by heaters. They also are subject to vibration, and the signal can easily be blocked momentarily by birds. Finally, direct sunlight also can affect signal reception and must be factored into the deployment.

UNII (UNLICENSED NATIONAL INFORMATION INFRASTRUCTURE) BAND   The FCC recently allocated 300 MHz of spectrum for unlicensed use from 5.15 to 5.35 GHz and from 5.725 to 5.825 GHz, a swath of spectrum far larger than all the other unlicensed bands combined. Alhough no products are yet available, intended uses include wireless LANs as well as community-wide networks thanks to the higher power of 4 W effective isotropic radiated power (EIRP) allowed in the 5.725- to 5.825-GHz portion of the band. Expect both private-link UNII products and carrier-based UNII services in the future.

MMDS (MULTICHANNEL MULTIPOINT DISTRIBUTION SYSTEM)   This is a carrier service, initially intended for broadcast of television, and is commonly referred to as *wireless cable*. In the United States, this service is available at 2.5 GHz. MMDS service is usually analog and one way (transmit only), with a range of about 30 miles (50 km), and has been deployed in the United States, the Middle East, Latin America, eastern Europe, and the Asia-Pacific area.

Carriers have not been widely successful with television programming, and some have obtained waivers from the FCC to be able to offer two-way service for Internet. Others offer Internet service by using a hybrid approach with a PSTN connection for the return path. Meanwhile, the

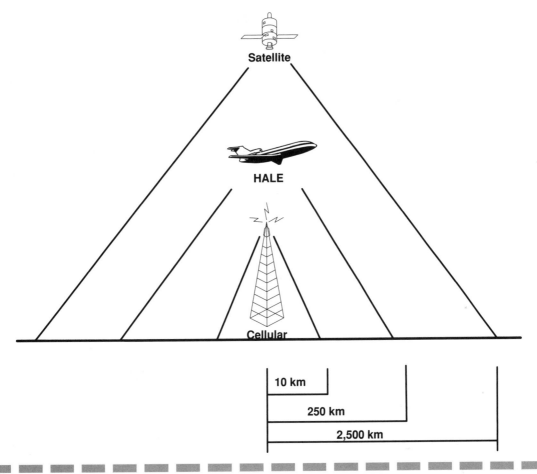

Figure 1-6 High-altitude long-endurance system with airplane as base station.

FCC is in the process of relaxing rules to allow two-way use of the band, which will facilitate data services. Two-way service reduces the effective range of MMDS to about 6 miles (10 km).

HIGH-ALTITUDE LONG-ENDURANCE (HALE) SYSTEMS So far we have seen radio transmitters and receivers on buildings and towers and on satellites. Why not put them on specially designed aircraft that can fly in a circle above a coverage area for a long period of time, as shown in Figure 1-6?[14] This is exactly what some companies are planning, including Angel Technologies Corp.[15] Such systems will offer broadband services with comparable protocols and interfaces as 38-GHz and LMDS carriers.

Wireless Broadband Market Demand and Projections

In the next 4 years, the Internet wireless broadband access market is going to see dramatic changes. The Internet will continue to grow rapidly, as affordable and attainable access solutions will be the driving need. High-speed access is expected to create demand for more multimedia content, virtual reality, multiplayer games, and IP voice and videoconferencing applications. The evolution of higher speeds also should make always-on connectivity, bandwidth-on-demand, and mobility norms rather than exceptions.

Most of all, the Internet wireless broadband access market will see a change in the way access is most often provided. Wireless will slowly become the top broadband access platform, due to faster service, better cost efficiency of point-to-multipoint operation, and continuous upgrades to the infrastructure. As shown in Figure 1-7, the users of wireless broadband high-speed access should outnumber their wireline counterparts in the year 2003.[16]

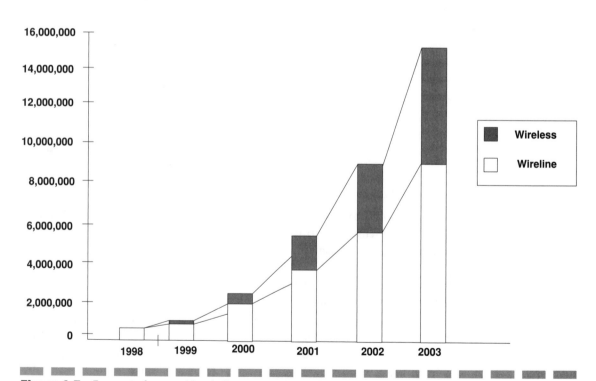

Figure 1-7   Forecast of users with wireline versus wireless broadband high-speed (individual) access, North America, 1998–2003.

However, speed also will take center stage in the market. Predictions say that cable modems should deliver a knockout blow to xDSL early in this century. Nevertheless, many studies show cable modems winning until around 2004 and then DSL taking off. However, both cable modems and xDSL are expected to lose big time to wireless solutions. And digital cellular and PCS operators will be the ones to provide mobile and fixed access at 64,000 bps and faster. Wireless broadband LAN technology should be the dark horse in the high-speed race.

NOTE Industry analysts predict that Teligent and WinStar will finish as the winners in wireless broadband networks. Companies in digital cellular/PCS, entrepreneurs using wireless broadband LAN technology, and sky-based solutions such as the Teledesic broadband satellite enterprise also will prosper.

Conclusion

This introductory chapter explored the wide-scale deployment of broadband wireless systems, networks, and services and concludes that wireless broadband is still somewhere in the very near future. However, short- to long-term prospects for these networks, systems, and services may be brighter than ever. A worldwide push toward spectrum licensing for Local Multipoint Distribution Service (LMDS) and other high-frequency spectrum technologies for terrestrial delivery of voice, data, and video services promises to deliver a much larger potential market for broadband wireless than was anticipated as recently as 6 months ago.

Currently, a handful of providers in the United States and abroad has begun commercial rollouts of new wireless broadband services. The equipment is now ready, and the new services have already had a market impact, according to those closest to the service development and planning process.

According to two U.S. wireless providers (Teligent, Inc., and WinStar Communications, Inc.), ongoing technology trials are yielding positive results for point-to-multipoint services. These services, which enable providers to deliver high-speed fixed-broadband wireless links to thousands of sites, will be the prime application driver for emerging wireless broadband technology.

The delay in implementing wireless broadband in the past may have worked in favor of service providers on two counts. First, equipment makers have more time to better tune their gear to the data-centric broadband market of the future. Second, the global expansion of interest in broadband wireless could bring down technology costs faster if its interest translates into strong equipment sales.

Teligent[17] and WinStar have an early lead in delivering broadband wireless offerings, mainly because they are not relying solely on LMDS technology, which operates at the 28-GHz spectrum tier. Both companies hold licenses for other high-frequency spectra that were issued prior to the federal government's decision to allocate airwaves via auction. Teligent is licensed to operate digital electronic messaging services (DEMS) at the 24-GHz tier. WinStar is now the largest U.S. provider of wireless service at the 38-GHz tier.

The two providers are pushing forward with expansion plans pegged to use point-to-multipoint technology that did not exist when they obtained their licenses. Teligent and WinStar say that their current point-to-multipoint technology trials are delivering results that square with expectations. Teligent launched point-to-multipoint as well as point-to-point services in 10 markets in 1998: Austin, Chicago, Dallas, Denver, Houston, Los Angeles, Orlando, San Antonio, Tampa, and Washington, D.C.

Meanwhile, in its Washington trial, WinStar is delivering what it calls the first use of interactive broadband wireless technology in an up-and-running environment. In this trial, WinStar deployed a two-transmitter system, with radio technology supplied by Northern Telecom, Inc., and telecommunications components from Siemens Telecom. WinStar is using Asynchronous Transfer Mode (ATM) over-the-air interfaces to deliver a full slate of wireless broadband services over multiple channels operating at up to 155 Mbps per second to each of four buildings on a bandwidth-on-demand basis (see Chapter 2 for more information on this topic).

An earlier technical test in Florida that measured performance under severe weather conditions proved that wireless broadband technology can meet the performance specifications set by WinStar for point-to-multipoint services, including 99.999 percent reliability and 10- to 13-bit-error-rate parameters.

Based on the success of its trials to date, WinStar is moving to expand its spectrum base, which now averages 750 MHz in the top 70 markets of the United States. The provider picked up licenses in the recently completed LMDS spectrum auctions and has bought 850 MHz of the 1300 MHz of spectrum held by LMDS pioneer CellularVision USA in the New York market for $32.5 million in cash.

The Big Apple spectrum acquisition gives WinStar 1750 MHz to work with in New York, by far the largest amount of spectrum held for terrestrial use by any provider in any market. In New York and other markets in which WinStar holds licenses both in the 38-GHz and LMDS tiers, the company operates point-to-multipoint radios at both frequency levels from the same hubs. This strategy has enabled WinStar to cover most of its initial market base in each area with about a dozen hubs. WinStar would have liked to have been able to move quickly to commercial rollout of point-to-multipoint service, but equipment makers are taking longer than expected to bring commercially deployable gear to market.

The availability of more equipment is a gating factor in WinStar's plans to move ahead with additional commercial deployment. Anyone who says they are ready to supply additional equipment now is providing misleading information.

One reason for the additional equipment delay is the slow-moving LMDS authorization process at the FCC. The FCC[18] began its LMDS licensing initiative in 1993, but spectrum auctions were not completed until 1998, and the agency still is sifting through license applications from many of the leading bidders, including top bidder WNP Communications, Inc.[19]

According to the FCC, they granted 75 percent of all the applications, representing 690 of the 1075 licenses won in the auction. These licenses include the 150-MHz (B-block) licenses as well as the 1150-MHz (A-block) licenses for the basic trading areas (BTAs) in which at least one qualifying bid was made. The FCC hopes to complete the licensing process in 2000 but could take longer because some applications are more complex than others.

For WNP, the licensing wait may not be a big problem, given the size of the task the company faces in putting together a business plan and infrastructure financing for its newly won empire. WNP ended up winning licenses in 39 BTAs, representing 41 percent of the nation's population. WNP did not expect bidding for the LMDS spectrum to be so low that it would end up with so much territory.

However, even with the larger operational issues with which it must deal, WNP is concerned that the equipment it needs will not be available when it is ready to begin deployments. If it takes a little longer than expected, so be it; the company wants to be able to deploy gear that will meet the demands of the emerging wireless broadband data market over the long haul. WNP and other providers want vendors to deliver products that are finely tuned to the dynamic bandwidth allocation and feature-rich possibilities of the latest developments in data communications.

The ability to merge multiple services into data streams can put providers of LMDS and other point-to-multipoint wireless broadband services in a strong position to exploit different market niches. Broadband wireless providers will be in a position not only to sell services directly to end users but also to meet the broadband access and backhaul needs of local and long-distance telecom providers, cable operators, and cellular and personal communications services providers. LMDS is going to be looked on as a technology that enables much faster deployment of full-service networks, whether it is used on the access side to reach customers or as a link that facilitates getting to end users with technologies like Asymmetric Digital Subscriber Line (ADSL) and cable.

The need for flexibility extends beyond the market conditions of the United States. In the United States and Canada, the market opportunity is more focused on being able to provide support for sophisticated new data applications, whereas in many other countries, it is more a matter of addressing a basic shortage of E1 (2-Mbps) connections.

For example, Alcatel [20] initially will use the ATM quality-of-service standard known as Multiprotocol over ATM (MPOA) to create IP service classes, but it plans to move to the more efficient Cisco-pioneered Multiprotocol Layer Switching technology once it is finalized as a standard. Actually, MPOA is a standard for routing over ATM, not QoS. And MPLS came out of early work from Cisco called *Tag Switching*, a proprietary form of an MPLS-like protocol.

Equally important to efficiency is the degree of integration between ATM and radiofrequency (rf) components. On this front, Alcatel has integrated rf modulation and customer interface technology from Stanford Telecommunications, Inc., directly into the ATM radio interface card that plugs into the MainStreetXpress 36170 ATM switch sold by Alcatel and Siemens. This system will allow LMDS providers to offer IP services as opposed to the services that are common over wireline networks today.

Alcatel also is developing interfaces for ADSL and Wave Division Multiplexing (WDM) technologies. The ADSL product will allow service providers to use existing wiring to distribute services within buildings served by broadband wireless links, whereas the WDM interface will extend the functionality of a base station to remote nodes connected via fiber.

In any event, the next 29 chapters will thoroughly discuss in finite detail all the topics examined in this chapter and much much more. Have a good read, and enjoy!

Endnotes

1. "BWA," Belstar Systems Corp., 4225 Executive Square, Suite 1550, La Jolla, CA 92037, 2000.
2. *Ibid.*
3. Nancy Gohring, "Broadband Wireless Operators Build Their Case," Intertec, A Primedia Company, 9800 Metcalf, Overland Park, KS 66212, 2000.

4. "HFC Broadband Technology," Suscom-Maine, Susquehanna Communications, 336 Bath Road, Brunswick, ME 04011, 2000.

5. Michael Arellano, "Broadband's Present Sense," tele.com, CMP Media, Inc., 600 Community Drive, Manhasset, NY 11030, 2000.

6. "Overview of Wireless Broadband Technology and Services," Kinetic Strategies, Inc., P.O. Box 59026, Phoenix, AZ 85076, 2000.

7. *Ibid.*

8. Peter Rysavy, "Wireless Broadband and Other Fixed-Wireless Systems," Network Computing, CMP Media, Inc., 600 Community Drive, Manhasset, NY 11030, 2000.

9. WinStar Communications, Inc., 685 Third Avenue, New York, NY 10017, 2000.

10. ART, 500 108th Avenue NE, Suite 2600, Bellevue, WA 98004, 2000.

11. Peter Rysavy, "Wireless Broadband and Other Fixed-Wireless Systems," Network Computing, CMP Media, Inc., 600 Community Drive, Manhasset, NY 11030, 2000.

12. *Ibid.*

13. COMSAT Headquarters, 6560 Rock Spring Drive, Bethesda, MD 20817, 2000.

14. Peter Rysavy, "Wireless Broadband and Other Fixed-Wireless Systems," Network Computing, CMP Media, Inc., 600 Community Drive, Manhasset, NY 11030, 2000.

15. Angel Technologies Corporation, 1401 S. Brentwood Blvd., Suite 760, St. Louis, MO 63144, 2000.

16. Phillips International, Inc., Corporate Headquarters, 7811 Montrose Road, Potomac, MD 20854, 2000.

17. Teligent, Inc., 8065 Leesburg Pike, Suite 400, Vienna, VA 22182, 2000.

18. Federal Communications Commission, 445 12th St. SW, Washington, DC 20554, 2000.

19. WNP Communications, Inc., 4420 Van Ness Street NW, Washington, DC 20016, 2000.

20. Alcatel, 54 Rue La Boétie, 75008, Paris, France, 2000.

CHAPTER 2

Wireless Broadband Networks Platforms

Standards-based technology has finally enabled full entry of the wireless broadband industry into the mainstream data/Internet services space. The critical remaining challenge for the industry is to endow its service offerings such that it has the opportunity to enjoy prosperous longevity in that space.

The bandwidth appetite of a growing number of applications enabled by today's cable modems (CMs) and digital set-top boxes (STBs) is already a concern in some broadband systems. Operators are frequently hearing wireless broadband network platform performance complaints from subscribers, especially in markets boasting a high penetration of data services. As Internet Protocol (IP) telephony, various streaming applications, Internet television, and numerous other Internet appliances find their way into subscriber homes and offices, wireless broadband network platform performance issues will become even more acute.

NOTE   The vertical blanking interval (VBI) is a portion of a television signal that can carry information other than video or audio, such as closed-caption text and stock market data. The interval in sending a video signal is required for the time it takes the electron gun in a television monitor's cathode-ray tube (CRT) to move back up to the top of the tube. VBI data can be inserted by a cable TV provider and transmitted to a special receiver that connects to a computer's RS-232 port. VBI data transmission is described in an open standard, the North American Basic Teletext Specification (NABTS), which is used in Europe, South America, and the Far East, as well as in North America. Other, similar standards, both open and proprietary, are WST (European), Gemstar, and Nielsen.

The rate of Internet growth suggests that wireless broadband operators will not have the luxury of waiting until wireless platform performance issues become critical to address them. In addition, the growing intensity of competition in wireless broadband from incumbent local exchange carrier (ILEC)–based and competitive local exchange carrier (CLEC)–based online services is sure to expose and exploit any performance impediments in hybrid fiber-coax (HFC)–based services.

A few of the largest multiple system operators (MSOs) already recognize the looming performance issues of HFC-based services. Market trials are already underway with wireless broadband network platforms that reduce the number of homes served from a single fiber node, as well as eliminate actives beyond the node. While no firm conclusions have been reached regarding the viability of these platforms, they are addressing the problem head-on. Cost-effectively minimizing the size of contention networks is the key to optimal performance in HFC-based networks.

NOTE A contention-based network is where two or more nodes attempt to transmit a message across the same wire at the same time. It is a type of network protocol that allows nodes to contend for network access. That is, two or more nodes may try to send messages across the network simultaneously. The contention protocol defines what happens when this occurs. The most widely used contention protocol is CSMA/CD, used by Ethernet.

Current trial wireless broadband network platforms achieve this contention network minimization through extending fiber further into the neighborhood while eliminating active electronics and reducing related points of failure and maintenance. With this in mind, the following wireless broadband network platforms will be examined in this chapter:

- Enhanced copper
- Fiberoptics and HFC
- Third-generation (3G) cellular
- Satellites
- ATM and relay technologies

Enhanced Copper

Does the humble telephone line, the Victorian technology that transformed the world, have a major role to play in shaping the third millennium? Can a mere pair of thin enhanced copper wires (see sidebar, "Twisted Pair") twisted around each other transmit Internet data reliably and securely at blazing speed, making it possible to view high-fidelity moving images, sound, and vast amounts of data on your personal computer (PC) screen or television? The answer is yes, as the growing success of Digital Subscriber Line (DSL) technology abundantly demonstrates.

Twisted Pair

Twisted pair is the ordinary copper wire that connects home and many business computers to the telephone company. To reduce crosstalk or electromagnetic induction between pairs of wires, two insulated copper wires are twisted around each other. Each connection on the twisted pair requires both wires. Since some telephone sets or desktop locations require multiple connections, twisted pair is sometimes installed in two or more pairs, all within a single cable. For some business locations, twisted pair is enclosed in a shield that functions as a ground. This is known as *shielded twisted pair* (STP). Ordinary wire to the home is *unshielded twisted pair* (UTP).

Twisted pair is now frequently installed with two or more pairs to the home, with the extra pair making it possible for you to add another line (perhaps for modem and fax machine use, in addition to a second phone line) when you need it. Twisted pair comes with each pair uniquely color coded when it is packaged in multiple pairs. Different uses such as analog, digital, and Ethernet require different pair multiples.

Although twisted pair is often associated with home use, a higher grade of twisted pair is often used for horizontal wiring in local-area network (LAN) installations because it is less expensive than coaxial cable. The wire you buy at a local hardware store for extensions from your phone or computer modem to a wall jack is not twisted pair. It is a side-by-side wire known as *silver satin*. The wall jack can have as many as five kinds of hole arrangements or pinouts, depending on the kinds of wire the installer expects will be plugged in (e.g., digital, analog, or LAN). This is why you may sometimes find when you carry your notebook computer to another location that the wall jack connections will not match your plug.

These trusty copper wires, installed in more than 700 million phone lines worldwide, provide high-quality, dependable voice service, but for a century most of their transmission capacity has lain dormant. DSL technologies exploit this resource, bringing a 60-fold increase in speed to millions of modem users, accelerating the growth of electronic commerce and changing the nature of communications.

Increasing the Speed Limit

The capacity of a communications channel depends on its bandwidth (the range of frequencies it uses) and its signal-to-noise ratio (which depends on the quality of the connection). Once these are fixed, it is physically impossible to exceed the fundamental limit. A voice connection through a conventional phone network uses a bandwidth of about 3000 Hz, from about 300 to 3300 Hz. An analog modem operating at 33.6 kbps requires a slightly wider bandwidth (3200 Hz) and needs a very good connection, one with a high signal-to-noise ratio. This type of modem is very close to the channel's theoretical capacity, about 35 kbps, a feat that has taken 30 years of modem circuit development. Modems operating at 56 kbps achieve their rates by taking advantage of digital connections that circumvent some sources of noise in transmissions toward the end user.

NOTE   They are still limited to 33.6 kbps for signals sent toward the service provider by the end user.

However, these bit rates are far from the maximum possible on a twisted pair alone. One process that limits bandwidth and signal strength is the steady attenuation of the signal as it travels down the line, with the higher frequencies being affected more severely. Greater capacity therefore is available if the lines are kept short.

NOTE   Joseph W. Lechleider, an engineer recently retired from Telcordia (previously Bellcore), proposed in the 1980s using an ordinary phone line as a very high bandwidth channel, over the short distance from the end user to a telephone central office. He also proposed multilevel coding of the signal to further enhance performance. This transmission technique was dubbed the *Digital Subscriber Line* (DSL). By the early 1990s, several firms, led by California-based PairGain Technologies, had developed high-bit-rate flavors of DSL (known as *HDSL*) that could transmit almost 800 kbps over a distance of 4 km.

Concurrent with the development of symmetric HDSL, John Cioffi of Stanford University demonstrated a signal coding technique called *discrete multitone*, using it to send more than 8 million bps through a telephone pair more than 1.6 km in length. The technique divides an overall bandwidth of about 1 MHz into 256 subchannels of about 4 kHz each. In essence, it creates 256 virtual modems operating simultaneously over the same line.

Originally, the discrete multitone approach was intended for sending entertainment video over telephone wires. Because such use relies principally on one-way transmission, most of the subchannels were devoted to the *downstream* signal (flowing toward the consumer), carrying about 6 Mbps, with about 0.6 Mbps available in the other direction. This asymmetric form of DSL has become known as *ADSL*, and the signal coding is now a worldwide standard[1] (Figure 2-1).

Although the video application has not yet borne fruit, asymmetric transmission fortuitously lends itself to browsing on the World Wide Web. Over the past 2 years, ADSL has begun to be widely installed in telephone networks for always-on Internet access, typically operating at several hun-

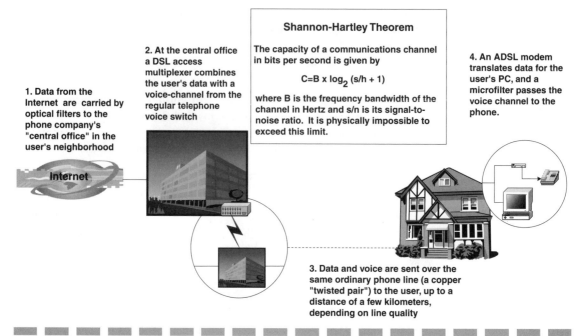

1. Data from the Internet are carried by optical filters to the phone company's "central office" in the user's neighborhood

2. At the central office a DSL access multiplexer combines the user's data with a voice-channel from the regular telephone voice switch

Shannon-Hartley Theorem

The capacity of a communications channel in bits per second is given by

$$C = B \times \log_2 (s/h + 1)$$

where B is the frequency bandwidth of the channel in Hertz and s/n is its signal-to-noise ratio. It is physically impossible to exceed this limit.

4. An ADSL modem translates data for the user's PC, and a microfilter passes the voice channel to the phone.

Internet

3. Data and voice are sent over the same ordinary phone line (a copper "twisted pair") to the user, up to a distance of a few kilometers, depending on line quality

Figure 2-1
How ADSL sends broadband data and voice over a phone line.

dreds of kilobits per second or higher over phone wires up to about 5.5 km in length. The beauty of ADSL, unlike the multilevel coding used in HDSL, is that the data can use channels operating above the voice frequency band, so a single phone line can transmit voice and high-speed data simultaneously.

The future of ADSL for the masses lies with G.lite (see sidebar, "G.Lite"), a global standard that limits the data rates to 1.5 Mbps downstream to the consumer and about 0.5 Mbps upstream. Truncating the speed lets G.lite operate reliably on more than 70 percent of unaltered phone lines and lowers cost and power consumption. Home computers containing G.lite-ready circuitry are already being sold.

G.Lite

G.Lite is the informal name of what is expected to be the standard way to install Asymmetric Digital Subscriber Line (ADSL) service. Also known as *Universal ADSL*, G.Lite makes it possible to have Internet connections to home and business computers at up to 1.5 Mbps (millions of bits per second) over regular phone lines. Even at the lowest downstream rate generally offered of 384 kbps (thousands of bits per second), G.Lite will be about seven times faster than regular phone service with a V.90 modem and three times faster than an ISDN connection. Upstream speeds from the computer will be up to 128 kbps. Theoretical speeds for ADSL are much higher, but the data rates given here are what are realistically expected.

With G.Lite, your computer's analog-to-digital modem will be replaced with an ADSL modem, and the transmission from the phone company will be digital rather than the analog transmission of plain old telephone service (POTS). G.Lite is also known as *splitterless DSL* because, unlike other DSL technologies, it does not require that a technician come to install a splitter, a device that separates voice from data signals, at the home or business (sometimes referred to as *the truck roll*).

NOTE You should be aware, though, that DSL is an analog technology. The encoding scheme is analog (the DSL devices are inherently modems); the data, however, may be digital. This is a common misconception.

The G.Lite standard was developed by the Universal ADSL Working Group, whose members included major phone companies in the United States and globally, including Ameritech, Bell Atlantic, BellSouth, GTE, MCI, USWest, Sprint, SBC Communications, Deutsche Telekom, France Telecom, British Telecommunications, Singapore Telecom, and Nippon Telegraph and Telephone. Microsoft, Intel, and Compaq are also represented in the working group. The group voluntarily disbanded itself in 1999, announcing at SuperComm in June 2000 that its work was completed.

The telephone companies and ADSL are competing with the cable TV companies and the cable modem to capture the market for fast Internet access. While phone companies concede the lead to the cable TV companies, a number of them will be launching new services during 2001 that will bring the G.Lite standardized version of ADSL to millions of homes and businesses. For example, SBC Communications plans to provide service to as many as 7 million homes and over 1 million businesses in California by the end of 2001 through their Pronto initiative. Yearly rates will be as low as $37 a month including the Internet connection.

The G.Lite standard (officially, G.992.2) was formally approved by the ITU-T in June 1999. Meanwhile, ADSL modems are currently being built and will cost the end user about $180.[2]

ADSL has a number of advantages over systems that use a cable television network. With ADSL, the signal on your line is not shared with other users. Cable modems work over what amounts to a giant party line; when someone else is receiving data, the available bandwidth is shared among all users—although you (and everyone else) can listen in on each others' data signals, albeit without the key to decode them if they are encrypted. Telephone wires, on the other hand, that are used for DSL are physically secure.

The backbone networks for ADSL carry composite signals for a few hundred consumers at 155 Mbps and up. A television channel has an effective throughput of only about 27 Mbps, greatly limiting its effectiveness under heavy use by hundreds of cable modems. The ADSL traffic also benefits from a statistical economy of scale—for example, 1550 people sharing a backbone of 155 Mbps will experience better performance than 240 sharing 24 Mbps.

Although cable networks cover 91 percent of the homes in the United States, they do not serve many businesses. Telephone networks are ubiquitous. Moreover, for effective use of cable modems, the cable operator must invest billions to upgrade the cable network with fiberoptics and two-way transmission equipment. ADSL, on the other hand, takes advantage of the same kind of telephone pairs that Alexander Graham Bell used in the nineteenth century.

> **NOTE** Cable companies have attempted to attract businesses with the promise of speed, but they do not seem to be making any progress in their efforts.

Cable modems have roughly a 2-year head start on DSL. It is not enough. Projections show that the number of DSL users will surpass those of cable modems within the next year or so. There is still plenty of life (and capacity) left in the old enhanced copper phone line.

The next part of this chapter explores an alternative approach to traditional node splitting for improving service performance on HFC systems (fiberoptics). It describes a distributed wireless broadband network platform (fiberoptics and HFC) that achieves the ultimate reduction in the scope of contention networks in an HFC environment. Other benefits of the platforms, including its flexibility and how wireless broadband operators might leverage that flexibility in a rapidly evolving online services marketplace, are also examined. Finally, a rough cost estimate for implementing such a platform is provided, as well as speculation on how the inherent efficiency of such an implementation could increase the revenue potential of HFC-based online services.

Fiberoptic and HFC

It is not difficult to identify and characterize the fundamental challenges facing cable television operators for the foreseeable future—they are distributed wireless broadband network platforms in nature. Wireless broadband operators need a scalable, robust, manageable, affordable, reliable, and future-proof service delivery platform. This part of the chapter explores a platform that employs the concepts of overlaying distributed traffic switching/routing onto a parallel spectral transport environment. This distributed-spectrum parallel HFC platform exhibits the key attributes discussed in the preceding sections, as well as other inherent benefits.

Platform Background

We have all heard the preceding attributes applied to platforms before. But what do these attributes really mean in the context of a wireless broadband network platform that is designed to sustain the performance edge of wireless broadband? Since a platform, by definition, frames the execution relationships of a variety of cooperating functions, a specific definition of its primary attributes merits examination.

NOTE   A platform represents a particular implementation framework for deploying systems infrastructure designed to accomplish a specific function or group of functions within a defined environment. A systems infrastructure represents the instantiation of a platform; it is the deployed infrastructure, naturally, in which the attributes of a platform manifest. The words *platform* and *infrastructure* are used interchangeably in this part of the chapter.

Scalability

The scalability of a wireless broadband network platform is a measure of its physical (scope) and logical (service suite) extensibility while maintaining stable and consistent service performance. This kind of scalability is critical to profitability, responsiveness, agility, and operational efficiency over the long term. Scalability also speaks to flexibility with regard to the ease at which new services can be deployed in response to market needs and/or competitive strategies.

Robustness

The robustness of a platform ensures stable and consistent service performance across a dynamically variable service portfolio. Service stability and consistency are critical to customer acceptance and related penetration levels of online services. With the system valuation numbers characterizing the recent industry consolidation, a rich services portfolio will be needed to capture the incremental $29 or so from 40 percent of the subscriber base that Wall Street needs to see. Without a robust platform, the introduction of new services may compromise the stability and consistency of existing services, creating support challenges and introducing customer doubt about the utility and future viability of the total service delivery platform.

Manageability

The manageability of a wireless broadband network platform is a measure of the meaningfulness of the operational status information it is capable of reporting, together with the degree to which it can be manipulated in support of system objectives. The fundamental challenge in creating a robust service delivery infrastructure that is also optimally manageable is primarily the uncertainty associated with future service requirements. The concurrency, load, and load characteristics (latency) of future services, as well as the extent and nature of their relationships with infrastructure functions, can complicate correlation functions, status reporting frequencies, performance tuning, and the proper interpretation of signal characteristics. This uncertainty makes it especially difficult to anticipate the manageability needs of future services. This complicates the development of automated infrastructure management capabilities and, as a result, depresses profit margins through higher support costs.

Affordability

Affordability is critical to competitiveness and system valuations and must enable granular growth consistent with market demands for services. However, the cost of implementing a well-architected service delivery infrastructure should be rationalized against the entire suite of services such an implementation is designed to support.

Reliability

The reliability of a service-delivery infrastructure is essentially a measure of its availability. This characteristic is essential to sustaining growth in penetration and service consumption. Superior service performance alone will not sustain growth in penetration unless service availability is at least at parity with competing service-access approaches available through local telephony, satellite, and terrestrial wireless platforms. Reliability is primarily a function of the cost of redundancy and the effectiveness of network monitoring and management at enabling proactive maintenance of the infrastructure.

Future-Proof

Finally, and probably most important, is the concept of a future-proof wireless broadband network platform. But isn't this what any good platform should do anyway? What is the purpose of a platform if not to provide a service-delivery platform capable of evolving with the demands of the market? Any wireless broadband service-delivery infrastructure deployed today not only must accommodate existing popular services (high-speed Internet access, broadband dialtone and/or packet telephony, intranet applications, and so on) but also must anticipate future services. Services still under development, services yet to be created, and the myriad of bandwidth-consuming appliances certain to arise within the home must all be considered in the design of any forward-looking service-delivery infrastructure.

The Platform Design

The approach used in the design of a wireless broadband network platform should be unique in that it is conceived without regard to any particular suite of services, related bandwidth requirements, concurrency scenarios, or other criteria. Instead, the design of the platform should be driven by the need to accommodate inherent wireless broadband transport characteristics and a multiplicity of services and traffic load characteristics without compromising optimal service-performance potential and efficiency.

Assumptions

The design baseline of a wireless broadband network platform should assume that most broadband networks will evolve to be hybrid fiber-coax (HFC) in nature (with increasing capacity) and also anticipate the continued evolution of Wavelength Division Multiplexing (WDM) and the emergence of Dense Wavelength Division Multiplexing (DWDM). The platform design also should assume continued movement toward digitization, a continued integration of greater functionality in silicon [as manifested in current cable modem (CM) and cable modem termination system (CMTS) chipsets], as well as the growing importance of service performance to end users of online services. All these baseline assumptions have since been proven valid.

Wireless Broadband Network Platform Attributes

The fundamental functional characteristics of a wireless broadband network platform should define an infrastructure that

- Bounds the context of collision domains.

- Maintains these bounded domains on a systemwide basis.

- Leverages fiber capacity that can be realized using parallel fiber channels enabled through WDM/DWDM and/or frequency-stacking techniques.

- Minimizes unnecessary systemwide traffic through network segmentation (maximum bandwidth availability for each user).[3]

Platform Design Goals

The design goals of a wireless broadband network platform should be to

- Optimize service performance and efficiency (robustness).

- Optimize and simplify flexibility and extensibility (scalability).

- Minimize cumulative noise funneling and bound the background noise floor [service reliability (stability and consistency)].

- Simplify service delivery domains (manageability).[4]

The affordability aspect of a wireless broadband network platform always should be considered within the context of an evolving service portfolio, combined with the cost attributes of the evolving technology assumptions discussed in the preceding sections.

Rationale

The underlying premise of a wireless broadband network platform should be based on a simple argument. This argument should suggest that while the future technical details of individual infrastructure component implementations are largely uncertain, the functional roles of these components will remain reasonably consistent over time. This is so because these components must continue to adhere to standard interfaces and protocols dictated by their platform role, whereas details of future implementations depend largely on the evolution of a variety of technologies. The strategic case for deploying a wireless broadband network platform–based service-delivery infrastructure is highlighted next.

The Trouble with the Future

With the present uncertainty surrounding the evolution of cyberspace, anticipating which online services will capture the imagination of the marketplace is a daunting if not impossible task. To further complicate service-delivery infrastructure planning, a number of Internet appliances will emerge soon that will at least introduce new traffic patterns and possibly even new wrinkles in bandwidth provisioning requirements (latency management). Currently deployed services, and those under consideration, easily can overwhelm HFC bandwidth—especially in the return spectrum. For example, capacity could be overstressed as a function of spikes in service load (concurrency) norms.

There is also no end in sight to online services, with new ones being introduced frequently—some developed specifically for wireless broadband environments. Not only is it impossible to predict the future network demands of yet-to-be-defined online services, their popularity (and related concurrency scenarios) also cannot be predicted.

Broadband operators are always free to decide what services will be offered on their networks (absent any unbundling regulations). However, a platform designed to maximize the efficiency and performance of wireless broadband networks will give operators the flexibility necessary to deploy the most lucrative service packages.

Clearly, the uncertainty surrounding future services complicates not only service-delivery infrastructure planning but also the introduction of new services. There appears to be precious few options available that result in a strategically balanced technical posture for the cable MSO. A strategically balanced technical posture is one that has the service-delivery capability in place or instantly deployable, whereby important service opportunities can be embraced quickly as they arise, and does so without incurring unreasonable costs that might depress existing and/or near-term value propositions.

NOTE One way to ensure adequate bandwidth is to withhold the availability of new services, but it is doubtful that Wall Street will approve, and it sends an awkward message to the subscriber base—especially if local competitors are making such services available.

Alternative Strategies

One way to approach this uncertainty, naturally, is to deploy an infrastructure that can adequately support existing services and those (presumably) popular services already visible on the near-term horizon, reacting to future service opportunities as they arise. This approach, however, has significant drawbacks. Responsiveness (time to market) and leadership (in the eyes of the market base) are put at risk with this wait-and-see approach. In the fast-moving Internet/online services space, sluggishness tends to concede market share to better-prepared competitors and seriously erodes subscriber perception of leadership.

In addition, MSOs may be forced to sacrifice entire wireless broadband network platforms in order to maintain access to the same scope of market/opportunity as their competitors who were more forward thinking. Starting over to accommodate every new wave of service opportunities can be very expensive.

Another common approach is to deploy extra fiber capacity today that can be leveraged when necessary through common node splitting. This approach, however, consumes fiber quickly and requires the replication of optics at both the fiber node and the hub/headend. It also imposes limitations on architecturally hierarchical functions an MSO may want to deploy. Another approach is one that leverages not only the uncertainty of the future but also the diversity of the subscriber base and the steady evolution of information and telecommunications technologies.

NOTE *Headend* is the electronic control center—generally located at the antenna site of a CATV system. It usually includes antennas, preamplifiers, frequency converters, demodulators, and other related equipment that amplify, filter, and convert incoming broadcast TV signals to cable system channels. *Fiber nodes*, on the other hand, are mininodes that perform the same function that traditional nodes do in that they convert signals from the optical domain to electrical (and vice versa in the upstream direction). These nodes, which are housed in bridger-sized packages, often can replace as many as two or three conventional radiofrequency (rf) amplifiers. The network from the mininodes to the customer premises becomes entirely passive.

Wireless Broadband Network Platform Details

The concept underlying a wireless broadband network platform is to maximize service performance and consistency through minimizing the scope of shared (contention-based or dedicated-circuit) networks. This is accomplished by isolating each rf coaxial network segment at the fiber node level (where switching and routing are defined by the platform). This isolation is maintained systemwide by using frequency-stacking and/or WDM/DWDM techniques to assign each coaxial segment to its own channel (frequency/lambda) on both forward and return fiber lines. This effectively transforms the F component of HFC networks into a marketwide non-contention-based bus.

The fundamental design philosophy behind a wireless broadband network platform is to deploy a service-delivery infrastructure that is performance optimized to begin with, thereby avoiding potential platform obsolescence (and related enhancement costs) that will likely accompany future services. In other words, deploy the most efficient platform possible up front, reducing future concerns to those having to do with managing the dynamics of concurrent services deployment and operations (bandwidth management—but at a neighborhood versus systemwide granularity).

The recent reduction of CMTS and other switching fabric functions to silicon levels (layer 2 switching and layer 3 routing), combined with the increased functionality of those application-specific integrated circuit (ASIC) packages [high-performance microprocessors, on-chip caches, sophisticated interfaces (universal serial bus or USB), and miniature form-factor storage], makes implementing a wireless broadband network platform now technically feasible. These advancements essentially allow key components of the headend- and/or hub-resident data service solution (CMTS, router, switches, and servers) to be shrunk and relocated to the fiber-node level. Additional benefits of a wireless broadband network platform are

- Greater granularity of service areas (and lower related service-enabling infrastructure costs).

- Increased service availability through reliance on smaller network segments.

- Improved overall (systemwide) network efficiency through node-level (neighborhood-level) routing and switching.

- Reduced rise in return-path noise floor due to a reduced number of potential contributing cable modems.

- Potentially higher physical-level efficiency gains through improved encoding techniques [denser constellations such as Quadrature Amplitude Modulation (QAM) 1024] for each isolated coaxial segment.[5]

By segmenting an HFC network into a collection of distributed LANs that also enjoy systemwide isolation of contention domains, the services suites within each LAN can be customized to meet the unique needs of subscribers on a neighborhood LAN level. This approach constrains the costs of specific service-enabling infrastructure and potential related complexities to only those network segments where demand for that service is high. Thus these are the fundamental attributes of a wireless broadband network platform.

Strategic Implications

Probably the more interesting strategic implications of a wireless broadband network platform are reflected in its potential fit with mainstream developments in the evolution of the Internet (its future proofing). One such mainstream Internet development is the evolving structure of the switching/routing functions of the Internet cloud.

According to some Internet experts, the Internet backbone structure will evolve to an electrooptical or all-optical switching fabric, thus pushing packet processing to the edge. This is in response to anticipated traffic loads and the performance bottlenecks associated with packet processing. The trend here is toward fewer layers with a switched optical core to accommodate anticipated loads at acceptable performance rates. Traffic flows will be managed at the edge of the network through techniques like multiprotocol label switching (MPLS), with diffserv or diffserv-like processing at the core.

NOTE   Diffserv (differentiated services) is a standard that purports to help solve the IP quality problem. Diffserv takes the IP TOS (type of service) field, renames it the DS byte, and uses it to carry information about IP packet service requirements. It operates at layer 3 only and does not deal with lower layers. So what does this all mean in terms of costs and compatibility? Diffserv relies on traffic conditioners sitting at the edge of the network to indicate each packet's requirements.

Currently, packet processing occurs on a networkwide basis, including telephone central office and cable headend facilities. However, as the all-optical switching fabric emerges, interexchange carriers (IXCs) and/or local exchange carriers [competitive (CLECs) or incumbent (ILECs)] may elect to deploy fiber from central office to cable headend facilities. Should this occur, then the potential exists to expand the Internet's anticipated all-optical switching fabric core to include cable HFC networks. This would place managed traffic flows (packet processing) somewhere within the HFC infrastructure. The question then becomes where, within the HFC network, is the optimal location for the packet-processing interface? The wireless broadband network platform suggests that this optimal location should be the neighborhood node, where fiber meets coax.

Industry fiber experts describe the current state of the art in DWDM technology as transporting 40 or more optical wavelengths, over more than 100 km, with 32 256-QAM channels per wavelength, after taking into account all fiber nonlinearities and dispersive effects over standard single-mode fiber. It is possible, with further effort, to reduce this spacing to 100 GHz, thereby increasing total capacity to a 40-wavelength DWDM system. Actually, Lucent is already doing 50-GHz spacing on commercial deployments.

NOTE   In addition, the industry experts state that this capability is based on 200-GHz spacing on the ITU raster and is effectively limited by the gain bandwidth of the EDFAs in use.

In addition, some IXCs are beginning to offer managed-wavelength services, enabling customers to manage their own wide-area bandwidth on their own terms. Still in the development stage, some carriers are using custom optical cross-connects to accomplish managed-wavelength services today. The standards community has already agreed on Lucent's Wave Wrapper approach, a digital wrapper/header attached to every wavelength, for adding the cross-connect intelligence necessary to route wavelength-provisioned traffic.

This wrapper/header contains information about traffic types (IP or ATM) and device-specific *infrastructure-conditioning* commands. These headers/wrappers could, for example, identify the information stream being carried as a specific IP packet type and also instruct an intelligent optical cross-connect

- To divert this traffic to lambda N and predistort/bias the transmit laser *if*.

- That the bit stream represents a TCP packet type.

- The bit stream is logically within a particular layer 4 session type.

- That it is between 9:00 P.M. and midnight Friday evening on a particular date.

- That another bit stream of type *SEC* (representing *security*, for example) is present in the cross-connect.

- That a broadcast bit stream of type X is also currently being routed to lambda N.[6]

These wrappers/headers could just as easily

- Indicate that a particular lambda is carrying a packet of type *CTL* (representing *control*, for example).

- Instruct the optical cross-connect to reduce power on all lasers of type M that are also engaged in layer 4 session type Z.

- Forward this wrapper/header and associated bit stream to each laser that actions the power reduction command.[7]

This wrapper/header structure containing bit-stream descriptors and related device commands essentially enables the practice of real-time device physics on a live infrastructure. The primary benefit of being able to perform live infrastructure physics is the ability to dynamically optimize infrastructure performance based on knowledge of particular content characteristics. Of course, if truck rolls are reduced and/or eliminated because of the preceding, cost savings will add up quickly. Another inherent benefit of intelligent optical cross-connects is the opportunity at each cross-connect to dynamically trigger different security/encryption schemes based on content.

Through basic neural net knowledge constructs (level 0 intelligence in artificial intelligence parlance), whereby specific configuration routines can be recorded, labeled, and made available for wrapper-initiated execution, the door is opened for the evolution of a content-shaped cyber infrastructure. Switching ASICs already exist that could function as the nucleus of a basic wrapper processor, and efforts are underway to enable the use of low-cost Fabry-Pérot (FP) lasers [versus distributed feedback (DFB)] for 1550-nm (network module) DWDM applications within HFC networks.

NOTE Time Division Multiplexed (TDM) lasers currently in production include 1.3- and 1.55-µm-wavelength Fabry-Pérot (FP) lasers, as well as 1.55-µm-distributed feedback (DFB) lasers. The 1.55-µm DFB lasers are used for the longest-distance links where both fiber loss and dispersion are factors, such as undersea links. The narrow linewidth of the DFB limits the effects of dispersion, and the fiber loss is minimal at 1.55 µm.

It is a short few steps from this point to implementing feedback mechanisms that allow the service infrastructure to also be shaped by service options and related user behaviors. Of course, this assumes that these wrappers are appropriately granular and functionally scoped consistent with the capabilities and configure ability of optical cross-connects and potentially other intelligent infrastructure devices.

Market reception to managed-wavelength offerings have been encouraging, with about twice as much demand as anticipated initially. According to this reference, the cost of optical components dropped by approximately 40 percent in 1998 and 40 percent in 1999, and another 40 percent is anticipated in 2000. These economics and other drivers surely will compel the introduction of managed-wavelength offerings by all major carriers.

Other experts suggest that even the issue of powering requirements in a deep fiber HFC wireless broadband network platform, which the platform design advocates, is not a problem. According to these experts, only 3 dB of extra fiberoptic broadcast optical power is required to support an order of magnitude increase in the number of nodes in a deep fiber network (see sidebar, "FTTC").

FTTC

Fiber to the curb (FTTC) refers to the installation and use of optical fiber cable directly to the curbs near homes or any business environment as a replacement for plain old telephone service (POTS). Think of removing all the telephone lines you see in your neighborhood and replacing them with optical fiber lines. Such wiring would give us extremely high bandwidth and make possible movies-on-demand and online multimedia presentations arriving without noticeable delay.

The term *fiber to the curb* recognizes that optical fiber is already used for most of the long-distance part of your telephone calls and Internet use. Unfortunately, the last part (installing fiber to the curb) is the most expensive. For this reason, fiber to the curb is proceeding very slowly. Meanwhile, other less costly alternatives, such as ADSL on regular phone lines and satellite delivery, are likely to arrive much sooner in most homes.

Fiber to the curb implies that coaxial cable or another medium might carry the signals the very short distance between the curb and the user inside the home or business. *Fiber to the building* (FTTB) refers to installing optical fiber from the telephone company central office to a specific building such as a business or apartment house. *Fiber to the neighborhood* (FTTN) refers to installing it generally to all curbs or buildings in a neighborhood. Hybrid fiber-coax (HFC) is an example of a distribution concept in which optical fiber is used as the backbone medium in a given environment and coaxial cable is used between the backbone and individual users (such as those in a small corporation or a college environment).[8]

The key point of the preceding discussion is that even the current state of the art in DWDM technology offers an abundant concentration of bandwidth capacity to facilitate the entry and exit of packets in and out of an expanded (HFC-inclusive) optically switched Internet network core. With all the uncertainty surrounding the future of cyberspace, one hesitates to attempt to put a value on an HFC located in a packet-processing interface for cyberspace. However, it is doubtful that it is insignificant, especially considering the increasing appetite for performance that online users are demonstrating as they migrate to broadband access.

Implementation

Of course, the implementation of a wireless broadband network platform can be a phased approach. For example, until penetration (and related traffic loads) warrant, simple Time Division Multiple Access (TDMA) techniques can be employed to multiplex individual coaxial-segment (rf) traffic streams onto a single wavelength connecting to higher level multiplexing hubs. These streams can then be transformed into packets (via CMTS function) and processed normally, being assigned to a unique lambda for transport to any destinations beyond the routing/switching domain of the multiplexing hub. However, this approach moves the packet-processing interface inward, and care must be exercised in the TDMA function not to corrupt the integrity of the Data Over Cable Service Interface Specification (DOCSIS) access methodology. Finally, if FP lasers can be adapted to drive DWDM capability using International Telecommunications Union (ITU) standard wavelengths, the cost of the lowest-level fiber nodes should compare favorably with nonwireless broadband network platform approaches (approximate 40 percent cost savings).

NOTE Lucent's LambdaRouter, Agilent's Bubblejet switch, and the new acoustooptical techniques are some of the successful optical cross-connect devices in use today.

Now, let's look at the next wireless broadband network platform: the evolution of cell phones on the road to 3G.

Third-Generation (3G) Cellular

Wireless broadband phone use is taking off around the world. Many of us would no longer know how to cope without our cellphones. Always being connected offers us flexibility in our lifestyles, makes us more productive in our jobs, and makes us feel more secure. So far voice has been the primary wireless broadband application. However, with the Internet continuing to influence an increasing proportion of our daily lives and more of our work being away from the office, it is inevitable that the demand for wireless broadband data is going to ignite. Already in those countries which have cellular data services readily available, the number of cellular subscribers taking advantage of data has reached significant proportions. We want wireless Internet, we want our organizational data from anywhere, and we want it now.

To move forward, however, the question is whether current cellular data services are sufficient, or whether the networks need to deliver greater capabilities. The fact is that with proper application configuration, use of middleware, and new wireless-optimized protocols, today's cellular data can offer tremendous productivity enhancements. For those potential users who have stood on the sidelines, however, subsequent generations of cellular data should overcome all their objections. These new services will roll out both as enhancements to existing second-generation cellular networks and an entirely new third generation of cellular technology. The job in this part of the chapter is to describe this road to the third generation (3G), as well as to show you how these services will allow new applications never before possible.

The World Today

Before we peek into the future, let's quickly look at where we are today. In 2000, the primary cellular-based data services are Cellular Digital Packet Data (CDPD), circuit-switched data services for Global System for Mobile (GSM) communications networks, and circuit-switched data service for Code Division Multiple Access (CDMA) networks (see sidebar, "Brief Overview of Other Primary Cellular-Based Service Technology Standards").

> **Brief Overview of Other Primary Cellular-Based Service Technology Standards**
>
> There are other primary cellular-based data service technology standards, and they will be covered extensively in Chapter 17, "Wireless Broadband Access Implementation Methods," and Chapter 28, "Next Generation Wireless Broadband Networks," as well as later in this chapter. For now, however, it is appropriate in this part of the chapter and book to briefly mention their existence.

General Packet Radio Service (GPRS)

General Packet Radio Service is a standard for wireless communications that run at speeds up to 150 kbps, compared with current GSM (Global System for Mobile) communications systems' 9.6 kbps. GPRS, which supports a wide range of bandwidths, is an efficient use of limited bandwidth and is particularly suited for sending and receiving small bursts of data, such as e-mail and Web browsing, as well as large volumes of data.

UMTS

Universal Mobile Telecommunications System (UMTS) is a third-generation (3G) mobile technology that will deliver broadband information at speeds up to 2 Mbps. Besides voice and data, UMTS will deliver audio and video to wireless devices anywhere in the world through fixed, wireless, and satellite systems. UMTS services will launch commercially some time in the year 2001.

CDMA2000

The design of CDMA2000 allows for deployment of the 3G enhancements while maintaining existing 2G support for CDMAOne in the spectrum an operator has today. Operators are presented with a number of options for using spectrum to combine CDMAOne and CDMA2000 on 1.25-MHz channels within 5-MHz blocks of spectrum.

Both CDMA2000 phase 1 and CDMA2000 phase 2 can be intermingled with CDMAOne to maximize the effective use of spectrum according to the needs of an individual operator's customer base. For example, an operator that has a strong demand for high-speed data services may choose to deploy a combination of CDMA2000 phase 1 and CDMAOne that uses more channels for CDMA2000. In another market, users may not be as quick to adopt high-speed data services, and more channels will remain dedicated to CDMAOne services. As the CDMA2000 phase 2 capabilities become available, an operator has even more choices on how to use its spectrum to support the new services.

Flexibility for CDMA2000 extends to the spectrum bands that can be used for its deployment. According to industry analysts, CDMA2000 appears to be the only 3G technology that can be deployed by operators in all of today's cellular and PCS spectrum bands for mobile and fixed wireless systems. It is also compatible with IMT-2000 spectrum bands, so operators who do acquire new spectrum will be able to experience the benefits of CDMA2000 as well.

Operators around the world are announcing their plans to evolve their networks to the first phase of CDMA2000. Ease of migration and the cost-effective manner in which CDMAOne supports 3G services are continually cited by industry executives as advantages they are realizing from their CDMAOne investment.

The CDMA2000 solution takes advantage of the existing CDMAOne format and combines radio spectrum to create a larger *pipe* for voice and data transmissions, allowing the 3G enhancements to coexist with the current CDMAOne network.

EDGE

EDGE stands for enhanced data rates for global evolution. EDGE is the result of a joint effort between TDMA operators, vendors, and carriers and the GSM Alliance to develop a common set of third-generation wireless standards that support high-speed modulation. EDGE is a major component in the UWC-136 standard that TDMA carriers have proposed as their third-generation standard of choice. Using existing infrastructure, EDGE technology enables data transmission speeds of up to 384 kbps.

Some brave souls connect their PC card modems to their analog cellphones, but this approach is not very popular because it is tricky to configure. All these services offer speeds in the 9.6- to 14.4-kbps range. Why such low speeds? The basic reason is that in today's cellular systems, data are allocated to the same radio bandwidth as a voice call. Since voice encoders (vocoders) in current cellular networks digitize voice in the range of 8 to 13 kbps, this is about the amount available for data. Remember, too, that today's digital and PCS technology designs started over 6 years ago. Back then, 9.6 kbps was considered more than adequate. Today, it can seem slow with graphic or multimedia content, although it is more than adequate for text-based applications and carefully configured applications.

NOTE *Encoder* is a device used to electronically alter a signal so that it can only be viewed on a receiver equipped with a special decoder. *Vocoder* is a device to convert speech into digital signals.

There are two basic ways that the cellular industry is currently delivering data services. One approach is with "smart" phones, which are cellular phones that include a microbrowser. With these, you can view specially formatted Internet information. The other approach is through wireless modems, supplied either in PC card format or by using a cellphone with a cable connection to a computer[9] (Figure 2-2).

Both approaches can give you access to Internet sites and corporate systems, including e-mail, databases, and host-based systems. However, both approaches also require that the user take throughput and latency of the network into account. In contrast, next-generation networks promise throughput, global coverage, and ease of use that will greatly expand your mobile computing options.

The World Tomorrow

Before diving into details of different network technologies, we need to realize that from a user perspective, the offerings from all these networks will be largely comparable. Introduction dates of services may vary by up to a year, and exact data rates may differ by 30 or 40 percent. However, just as voice users today may be hard-pressed to distinguish between the quality of an IS-136 call using AT&T's wireless network, a GSM call using

Smart phone

**Laptop attached to phone
operating as a modem**

Figure 2-2
"Smart" phone versus a phone connected to a laptop.

Omnipoint's network, or a CDMA call using the Sprint PCS network, data users will notice great similarity between the new cellular data services.

In thinking about the rollout of next-generation services, consider what features can be added to existing networks and what features will require vastly new network infrastructure. Since this part of the chapter refers to the current generation of cellular as second generation, new feature advancements to the current network are sometimes called *2.5G*. Generally, 2.5G technologies have been developed for 3G networks, but they are applied incrementally to existing networks. This approach allows carriers to offer new high-speed data and increased voice capacity at much lower cost than deploying all new 3G networks. In addition, they can do so using their existing spectrum.

Let's consider data rates in more detail. The global standards body for communications is the International Telecommunications Union (ITU). The 3G standards effort is called International Mobile Telephone 2000 (IMT-2000). IMT-2000 mandates data speeds of 144 kbps at driving speeds, 384 kbps for outside stationary use or walking speeds, and 2 Mbps indoors. Does this mean that we will all be using our cellphones at 2 Mbps? No. The indoor rate will depend on careful frequency planning within buildings and possibly an organization's commitment to work closely with a carrier. However, since high-speed services such as wireless LANs already offer speeds of up to 11 Mbps, it is difficult to predict the expected market demand for 2-Mbps indoor service when 3G networks roll out.

What is of much greater interest is the 384-kbps data rate for outdoor use, since this IP-based packet service will be available over wide areas. This service is the one that will let us extend our office to any location. And the good news? The technology that will provide 384 kbps in 3G networks is the same technology that will be deployed in 2.5G networks, albeit at slightly lower data rates in the 50- to 150-kbps range. However, this is still some 10 times faster than most options today. More good news? Most 2.5G services have been released well in advance of 3G networks, which will not start rolling out until 2002 at the earliest[10] (Table 2-1).

How the three major cellular technologies will provide these services varies, but all have a similar roadmap. In fact, these technologies are slowly converging beginning with a convergence of IS-136 and GSM data services and followed by a harmonization of the 3G versions of GSM and CDMA. By *harmonization* it is meant that while differences will continue to exist, the systems will interoperate more readily.

There are some other important trends to note. The first is that standards bodies are working not just on radio technologies but also on the networking infrastructure. One objective is to allow users to seamlessly

TABLE 2-1

Summary of
Forthcoming
Cellular Data
Services

Core Technology	Service	Data Capability	Expected Deployment
GSM	Circuit-switched data based on the standard GSM 07.07	9.6 or 14.4 kbps	Available worldwide now
	High-speed circuit-switched data (HSCSD)	28.8- to 56-kbps service likely	Limited deployment 2000 and 2001 because many carriers will wait for GPRS
	General Packet Radio Service (GPRS)	IP and X.25 communications over kbps	Trial deployments in 2001, rollout of service in 2002
	Enhanced data rates for GSM evolution (EDGE)	IP communications to 384 kbps, roaming with IS-136 networks possible	Trial deployment in 2002, rollout of service in 2003
	Wideband CDMA (WCDMA)	Similar to EDGE but adds 2 Mbps indoor capability, increased capacity for voice	Initial deployment in 2003 or 2004
IS-136	Circuit-switched data based on the standard IS-135	9.6 kbps	Some carriers may offer service, but not expected on widespread basis because key carriers already offer Cellular Digital Packet Data (CDPD)
	EDGE	IP communications to 384 kbps, roaming with GSM networks possible	Initial deployment 2003 or 2004
	WCDMA or wideband TDMA (WTDMA)	Similar to EDGE but adds 2 Mbps indoor capability	No stated deployment plans
CDMA	Circuit-switched data based on the standard IS-707	9.6 or 14.4 kbps	Available by some carriers now
	IS-95B	IP communications to 64 kbps	Expected in Japanese markets by early 2001
	CDMA2000 1XRTT	IP communications to 144 kbps	Trial deployment in 2002, rollout of service in 2003
	CDMA2000 3XRTT	IP communications to 384 kbps outdoors and 2 Mbps indoors	Initial deployment in 2003 or 2004

roam from private networks (Ethernet, WLAN) to public networks. Such roaming will require the implementation of standards such as Mobile IP. Another goal is to simplify the connection between mobile computers and wireless devices through personal-area network (PAN) technologies such as Bluetooth. Yet another trend is voice over IP. As terrestrial networks start using IP for voice and multimedia, it will be important for such IP communications to extend all the way to the wireless device.

NOTE   *Bluetooth* refers to a short-range radio technology aimed at simplifying communications among net devices and between devices and the Internet. It also aims to simplify data synchronization between net devices and other computers. Products with Bluetooth technology must be qualified and pass interoperability testing by the Bluetooth Special Interest Group prior to release. The Bluetooth 1.0 specification consists of two documents: the Foundation Core, which provides design specifications, and the Foundation Profile, which provides interoperability guidelines. Bluetooth's founding members include Ericsson, IBM, Intel, Nokia, and Toshiba.

Perhaps the most important trend of all is for ubiquitous coverage. This will be achieved not just by converging wireless standards but also by sophisticated new devices that operate in multiple modes and at multiple frequencies. This is the world of tomorrow. To understand how we will get there, let's look first at GSM and IS-136 networks and then at CDMA networks.

GSM and IS-136

GSM dominates the world today, with over 300 million users in over 100 countries. As the most mature digital cellular standard, GSM networks offered circuit-switched data services well in advance of other networks. Now in trials is a service called *High-Speed Circuit-Switched Data Service* (HSCSD), which combines two to four of the time slots (of a total of eight in each frame) to provide service from 28.8 to 56 kbps. HSCSD is attractive to carriers because it requires minimal new infrastructure. Nevertheless, most GSM carriers are putting their bets on a service called *General Packet Radio Service* (GPRS), a 2.5G technology. GPRS can combine up to eight (of eight available) time slots in each time interval for IP-based packet data speeds up to a maximum theoretical rate of 160 kbps. However, a typical GPRS device may not use all eight time slots. One proposed configuration is four time slots (80 kbps maximum, 56 kbps typical) for the downlink and one time slot (20 kbps maximum, 14.4 kbps typical) for the uplink. GPRS supports both IP and X.25 networking. Entering field trials in 2001, GPRS service should start rolling out in 2002.

GPRS can be added to GSM infrastructures quite readily. It takes advantage of existing 200-kHz radio channels and does not require new radio spectrum. The principal new infrastructure elements are called the *Gateway GPRS Support Node* (GGSN) and the *Serving GPRS Support Node* (SGSN). The GGSN provides the interconnection to other networks such as the Internet or private networks, whereas the SGSN tracks the location of mobile devices and routes packet traffic to them. GPRS capability will be added to cellphones and also will be made available in data-only devices such as PC card modems. Pricing will be either flat rate or based on the volume of information communicated. Services such as GPRS are exciting not only because of their higher data rates but also because packet service allows constant *virtual* connections without the need to constantly *dial* into the network.

NOTE   GPRS refers to a high-speed packet data technology, which is expected to be deployed in the next 2 years. It is expected to profoundly alter and improve the end-user experience of mobile data computing by making it possible and cost-effective to remain constantly connected, as well as to send and receive data at much higher speeds than today. Its main innovations are that it is packet based, that it will increase data transmission speeds from the current 9.6 kbps to over 100 kbps, and that it will extend the Internet connection all the way to the mobile PC—the user will no longer need to dial up a separate ISP. GPRS will complement rather than replace the current data services available through today's GSM digital cellular networks, such as circuit-switched data and Short Message Service. It also will provide the type of data capabilities planned for 3G cellular networks, but years ahead of them.

The phase after GPRS is called *Enhanced Data Rates for GSM Evolution* (EDGE). EDGE, generally considered a 3G technology, introduces new methods at the physical layer, including a new form of modulation (8 PSK) and different ways of encoding data to protect against errors. Meanwhile, higher-layer protocols, such as those used by the GGSN and SGSN, stay the same. The result is that EDGE will deliver data rates up to 500 kbps using the same GPRS infrastructure. Keep in mind, though, that 500 kbps represents a best-case scenario, with a strong signal, no interference, and a user device accessing the entire 200-kHz radio channel. In addition, this radio channel also must be shared by multiple users in that sector of the cell site. Consequently, practical throughputs may be only half the maximum rate. EDGE data services could start rolling out in 2003, depending on market demand and actual carrier deployments.

Although developed initially for GSM, the Universal Wireless Communications Consortium (UWCC), an organization that represents IS-136 carriers and vendors worldwide, has decided to embrace EDGE for IS-136 networks. The tricky part of adopting EDGE is that IS-136 networks use 30-kHz radio channels. Deploying EDGE will require new radios in base stations to support the 200-kHz data channels. The GGSN and SGSN will be virtually the same for both GSM and IS-136 networks. EDGE data users eventually will be able to roam between IS-136 and GSM networks around the world. EDGE data services for IS-136 networks probably will roll out shortly after EDGE for GSM networks, possibly in 2003 or 2004. Figure 2-3 shows the common network technology used by both GSM and IS-136 networks.[11]

IS-136 networks also will converge with GSM for voice-related functions. For instance, the same vocoder technology eventually will be used by both networks. Meanwhile, in advance of common vocoders, multimode

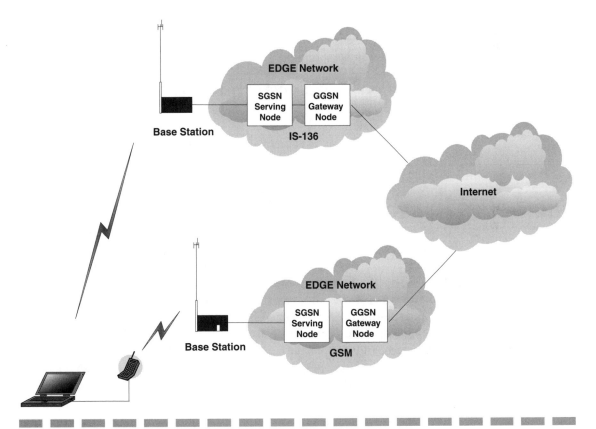

Figure 2-3
The same EDGE wireless device will be able to communicate across both IS-136 and GSM networks.

cellphones are planned that will allow voice operation across IS-136, GSM, and Advanced Mobile Phone Service (AMPS) networks worldwide.

The 3G version of GSM, Wideband CDMA or WCDMA, is based on CDMA technology. This version of CDMA deviates from American standards, although it uses the same spread-spectrum principles. For data, WCDMA adds the capability for 2-Mbps data rates indoors. The airlink, using either 5-, 10-, or 20-MHz radio channels, will be completely different from GSM's current 200-kHz channels. However, the data networking for WCDMA likely will be based on EDGE/GPRS infrastructure protocols, such as the GPRS Tunneling Protocol. The earliest WCDMA deployment is expected in Japan in 2003. IS-136 carriers eventually may use WCDMA technology, although a wideband TDMA (WTDMA) approach also has been proposed.

CDMA

CDMA network deployment and subscriber growth have developed considerable momentum, and data services are now available from a number of carriers. Currently, these carriers use circuit-switched technology operating at 14.4 kbps. As with GSM, CDMA requires a handset that specifically supports data. Connect the phone to a laptop, and the phone operates just like a modem, enabling you to establish dialup connections to the Internet, your corporate remote access server (RAS), and so on. Wireless Application Protocol (WAP)–based microbrowser applications are also being made available. Another service for CDMA networks is called QuickNet Connect. By eliminating conventional modem connections, this service allows fast connections (of approximately 5 seconds) to the Internet[12] (Figure 2-4). To the user, the carrier appears like an ISP offering dialup Internet service.

Today's CDMA service is based on the IS-95A standard. A refinement of this standard, IS-95B, allows up to eight channels to be combined for packet-data rates as high as 64 kbps. Japanese CDMA carriers, IDO and DDI, are planning on deploying this higher-speed service by early 2001.

Beyond IS-95B, CDMA evolves into 3G technology in a standard called CDMA2000. CDMA2000 comes in two phases. The first, with a specification already completed, is 1XRTT, whereas the next phase is 3XRTT. The *1X* and *3X* refer to the number of 1.25-MHz-wide radio-carrier channels used, and *RTT* refers to radio-transmission technology.

CDMA2000 includes numerous improvements over IS-95A, including more sophisticated power control, new modulation on the reverse channels, and improved data-encoding methods. The result is significantly higher capacity for the same amount of spectrum and indoor data rates up

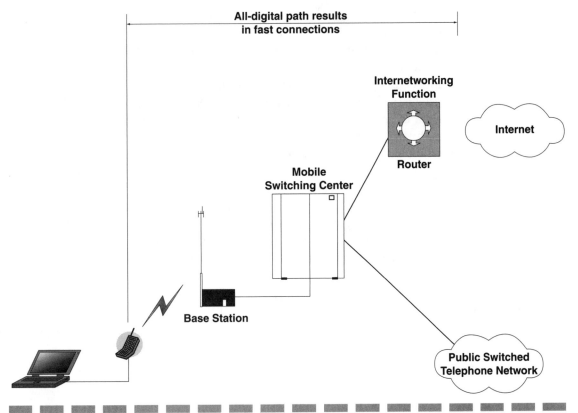

Figure 2-4
QuickNet Connect for CDMA.

to 2 Mbps that meet the IMT-2000 requirements. The full-blown 3XRTT implementation of CDMA requires a 5-MHz spectrum commitment for both forward and reverse links. However, 1XRTT can be used in existing CDMA channels because it uses the same 1.25-MHz bandwidth.

1XRTT technology is thus a convenient stepping stone for CDMA carriers moving to 3G, and it also can be thought of as a 2.5G technology. 1XRTT can be deployed in existing spectrum to double voice capacity and requires only a modest investment in infrastructure. It will provide IP-based packet-data rates of up to 144 kbps. Initial deployment of 1XRTT is expected by U.S. CDMA carriers in 2002, with 3XRTT following a year or two behind, depending on whether new spectrum becomes available.

However, what about the differences between CDMA2000 and WCDMA? If the goal of IMT-2000 is a single worldwide standard, can these two versions of CDMA be harmonized into a single standard? This is the very question being addressed by the CDMA Operators Harmonization Group that is developing the Global 3G CDMA standard (G3G). Since there are some irreconcilable differences between CDMA2000 and WCDMA in the radio portion, the approach is a modular architecture, as shown in Figure 2-5.[13] This approach allows any of three airlink technologies to be used in a network, including WCDMA, 3XRTT, and a time-division duplex form of spread spectrum. In addition to the three types of airlinks, the architecture recognizes that network infrastructures may be based on either GSM-MAP protocols or ANSI-41 protocols. G3G will give operators flexibility in choosing the airlink and network infrastructure that best addresses their particular needs.

One issue in harmonizing CDMA data is that WCDMA is based on GPRS protocols, which use the GPRS tunneling protocol (GTP) to forward IP packets to the mobile station. Mobility management is also handled by specific GPRS protocols. CDMA2000, however, is based on the Mobile IP

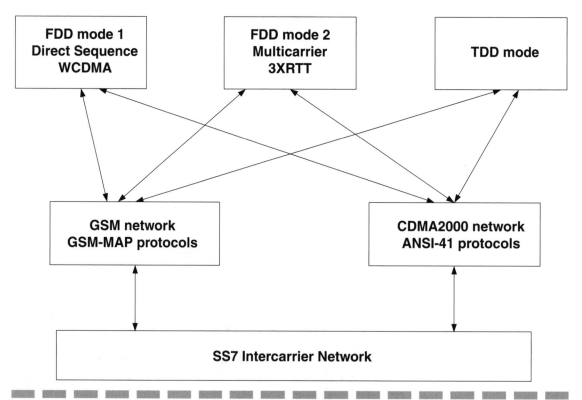

Figure 2-5
Modular approach used in the Global 3G CDMA architecture.

standard. Any harmonized CDMA standard ideally should be based on the same set of tunneling and mobility standards. For this reason, the European Telecommunications Standards Institute (ETSI), responsible for GSM and GPRS, has started an investigation of how GPRS/EDGE could integrate Mobile IP.

3G in Context

3G cellular technology is a huge technological and market phenomenon, but it needs to be understood in the context of other developments. One development is that there will be other high-speed wireless broadband data solutions available. For instance, do not overlook Metricom's Ricochet network. Although service is restricted to just several cities today, significant new investment from MCI WorldCom, combined with a new high-speed service at 128 kbps, will propel this service to much wider availability in 2001.

Consider also the Personal Handyphone System (PHS) deployed widely in Japan, a form of cellular technology limited to pedestrian use. PHS will soon offer 64 kbps data service. Nextel also has recently unveiled a new data service for its Integrated Dispatch Enhanced Network (iDEN)–based technology. This service uses Mobile IP to provide both WAP service and IP-based packet data at about 20 kbps. Also, some companies are planning on deploying wireless LAN technology in public places such as airports. Will all these developments stifle the demand for cellular-based data? Probably not, but they will offer options, increase competition, and help drive down prices.

Finally, some market developments will both shape the nature of wireless data networks and increase the demand for such services. These include the following:

- The control network used in telephone networks today is called *Signaling System 7* (SS7). This system will evolve into an IP-based system, increasing the importance for IP-based control mechanisms in wireless broadband networks.

- IP will be used increasingly for voice communications, so delivery of IP-based voice to cellphones will be critical. This will require resolution of difficult quality-of-service issues in wireless broadband networks.

- As e-commerce becomes more and more common, users will want to conduct transactions safely from their mobile terminals. Such use will make robust security protocols a must for wireless broadband networks.

- Mobile users will want to access private information from anywhere, driving the demand for secure communications and related technologies such as virtual private networks (VPNs).

- As a huge population of mobile data users emerges, content developers will start producing material specifically for these users, including items related to travel, entertainment, news, weather, and recreation. Although such developments are already underway, they are still in their infancy.[14]

There is no question that a myriad of new applications will be possible with next-generation wireless broadband data networks. However, keep in mind that these are massively complex networks, and it will take both time and large investments to develop and deploy the technology. Many of the advantages that these networks will offer are already available using existing data services. Organizations that gain experience with wireless broadband technologies today will be the ones best positioned to take advantage of new networks tomorrow.

Now, let's explore the world of satellite broadband networks: the next wireless broadband network protocol installment. On the agenda will be very small aperture terminals (VSATs), direct broadcast satellites (DBSs), and broadband satellite geostationary orbits (GEOs) and low-earth orbits (LEOs).

Satellites

Several different types of global satellite communications systems are in various stages of development. Each system, either planned or existing, has a unique configuration optimized to support a unique business plan based on the services offered and the markets targeted.

In the last few years, more than 60 global systems have been proposed to meet the growing demand for international communications services. More are being planned, and these are in addition to a large number of new regional systems.

Some of the global systems intend to provide global phone service, filling in where ground-based wireless systems leave off or providing seamless connectivity between different systems. Others intend to provide global data connectivity, either for low-cost short message applications such as equipment monitoring or for high-speed Internet access anywhere in the world.

The global phone systems will target two very different markets. The first is the international business user, who wants the ability to use a single mobile wireless phone anywhere in the world. This is impossible today on terrestrial systems because mobile phone standards are different from region to region. The second market is unserved and underserved communities where mobile and even basic telecommunications services are unavailable. Because global and regional satellite systems are relatively new in nonmilitary communications, these market approaches still are untested, and it is likely that economics, user acceptance rates, technical difficulties, and other factors will cause adjustments in the business plans of many of these systems.

VSATs

A VSAT is a remote terminal in a satellite communications network. The term *VSAT*, which stands for very small aperture terminal, refers to the smaller size of the antenna dish, normally 2.4-m or smaller in diameter[15] (Figure 2-6). This size is small when compared with larger earth station antennas, which can run 11 m or more in diameter. In other words, VSATs are effective tools for LAN internetworking, multimedia image transfer, batch and interactive data transmission, interactive voice, and broadcast data and video communications.

Figure 2-6

VSAT terminal with antenna and outdoor unit electronics mounted on antenna boom.

The satellite is essentially a repeater, or mirror, that reflects transmissions from the terminal back to earth. This enables one terminal in the network to communicate with another terminal hundreds of miles away. Furthermore, it also enables broadcasting information from one terminal to many others because the retransmission of the signal from the satellite back to earth normally covers a large geographic area.

Why Use VSATs and What Equipment Do I Need for My VSAT Network?

VSAT networks provide rapid, reliable satellite transmission of data, voice, and video to an unlimited number of geographically dispersed sites or from these sites to headquarters. Each site is equipped with a VSAT terminal consisting of an antenna, outdoor electronics mounted on the antenna for signal reception/transmission, and indoor electronics for connection to customer computer, telephone, and video equipment.

Typical VSAT Architectures

The VSAT network architecture can be star, full-mesh, or hybrid. *Star* means that one central site communicates with all the remotes. This is the architecture of satellite TV broadcasting, in which one large central antenna transmits to many small remote antennas. However, VSATs can offer two-way communication, with the remotes also transmitting to, as well as receiving from, the central site. If two remotes communicate, the sending remote transmits to the central site. The central site retransmits the message to the intended remote. This means two trips to the satellite.

Full-mesh means that any terminal in the network can communicate with any other with only one trip to the satellite. There is no intermediate stop at a central site. *Hybrid* means the network architecture employs both star and full-mesh. An example of this is a network that uses star for data transmissions to a central site and also provides voice communications between all remote terminals (full-mesh).

VSATs for Wireless Broadband Access

Currently, there are more than 500 million PCs in the world with about 60 million added each year. Experts estimate that roughly 36 percent of these are connected to the Internet. An increasing number of users, in either the residential or business market, are not satisfied with the data rates of a common dialup telephone modem. Different technologies are competing to provide high-bandwidth access. The main competitors are digital subscriber line (DSL) technologies, which use the existing local loop copper infrastructure and cable modems via the cable TV network. Upcoming wireless broadband technologies include LMDS or MMDS and satellite access. Each of those technologies has its strengths and weaknesses. For example, Bell Atlantic admits that it may never be able to serve 50 percent of its lines with DSL service due to technical limitations and limitations in reach. Cable modem networks are labor intensive in installation and have limited throughput when the last coax section is oversubscribed. But what are your options when you are too far away from the central office for a DSL service, a cable provider does not serve you, and there is no line of sight for an LMDS technology? This is where satellites come in.

A satellite can fill in pockets where other technologies cannot reach. It provides global coverage in a single network by its very nature. Quality of service and reliability are high. Furthermore, a satellite is unequaled for broadcast applications, such as the delivery of the same information to a large group of users. A majority of the Internet applications in the future will be streaming, broadcast, and multicast services such as playing audio or video.

In addition to providing fast access to the Internet for the individual user, a satellite also can provide reliable two-way Internet backbone connectivity, entirely bypassing local infrastructure. For regions of the world that lack affordable high-bandwidth terrestrial links, Internet via satellite can be the fastest economical means for an Internet service provider (ISP) to gain high-bandwidth access to the Internet.

VSATs and Rural Telephony

It is a well-accepted fact that there is vast potential for providing basic telephony to large areas of the world. The rural areas of developing countries in particular present a situation with a very low ratio of telephone lines to population. Often, large distances separate villages with hills and other features that make cable solutions expensive to install. Typical microwave and cellular solutions are also expensive because of the terrain features and dispersion of the population, which require the construction of many towers and base stations.

Satellite extensions of national phone networks can be the most cost-effective means of providing service in these cases. The small size of the remote terminals keeps installation costs down in even the most difficult locations. As the signal is received from the sky, mountains and trees have no impact on quality and reliability. The small integrated electronics of the terminal are suitable for solar power and other alternative power sources. Wireless local loop (WLL) extensions of the satellite terminal enable fast, cost-effective distribution of telephone access from the satellite terminal to individual subscribers throughout a village.

VSATs for Corporate Networks

VSATs provide wide-area network (WAN) connections for corporations and dispersed organizations in locations for which terrestrial connections are too expensive or do not exist. An example is a satellite WAN for a manufacturing concern in a developing country. The satellite WAN provides reliable, high-bandwidth links between the corporate local-area network (LAN) and the LAN at the manufacturing plant. Furthermore, there is a satellite WAN between the corporate LAN and each village distributor in the rural areas. The distributors use the remote terminal to order parts and update financial transactions. The terminals also can include voice links to other distributors and the corporate office.

DBS

Yankee Group predicts that Direct Broadcast Satellite (DBS) will have 17.6 million subscribers in the United States by the end of 2004 (Table 2-2) as DBS continues to make inroads into cable markets as well as expanding the market for multichannel video programming.[16]

According to Yankee Group, DBS penetration will continue to grow, particularly in areas not passed by cable or those areas serviced by cable systems with more antiquated plant and limited channel capacity. In addition, DBS will continue to see slow but steady growth in urban and suburban markets particularly as technological, operational, and marketing advancements create new opportunities in multi-dwelling units (MDUs) containing five or more residences. Key findings from consumer research conducted by the Yankee Group in conjunction with the SBCA relating to the DBS industry included the following:

TABLE 2-2

Year-End DBS
Subscriber Statistics

Year End	DBS Subscribers
2000	13,000,000
2001	14.550,000
2002	15,700,000
2003	16,500,000
2004	17,600,000

- Median household income for new DBS subscribers fell nearly 8 percent, from $48,360 in 1998 to $44,600 in 1999. However, it still remains significantly above the national median income of $37,005.

- The average cost of a DBS system (including installation) declined 39 percent from $429 in 1998 to $260 in 1999.

- Sixty percent of new DBS subscribers say they have access to cable television, and 17 percent of those with access subscribe to cable.

- Forty-nine percent of households in the United States know someone with a DBS system. Eighty-seven percent of DBS subscribers would likely recommend their system to a friend, and 45 percent of new DBS subscribers consider friends and family to be the most influential source of information when deciding to purchase a DBS system.[17]

The DBS consumer is changing. Much of this transformation can be traced to aggressive pricing by DBS service providers. As prices for hardware and installation continue to fall, DBS becomes more appealing to the average basic cable customer. This is particularly true in rural areas when they factor in the increased number of programming options, improved sound and picture quality, and expanded premium and pay per view (PPV) choices. As DBS penetration continues to grow, a number of trends are becoming evident:

- Subscriber demographics are beginning to more resemble the national averages, although at this point they remain slightly higher.

- New subscribers paid less for their system, are spending less per month on programming, and are less likely to maintain a cable subscription than the previous year. Due to a lower barrier to entry and increased price sensitivity of new subscribers, DBS service providers will have to be more conscious of managing retention in the future.

- DBS's strong points, more channels and picture and sound quality, continue to drive penetration in areas where cable is weakest or not available. Twenty-two percent of rural households indicated subscribing to DBS compared with 5 percent of urban households and 10 percent of suburban households.

- The majority of new DBS subscribers are interested in DBS for the programming options and the benefits that it provides, not because they are anticable.[18]

Wireless Broadband Satellite GEO and LEO

The design of a satellite system is closely tied to the market it is intended to serve and the types of communications services it is intended to offer. There are four general system designs, which are differentiated by the type of orbit in which the satellites operate: geostationary orbit (GEO), low-earth orbit (LEO), medium-earth orbit (MEO), and highly elliptical orbit (HEO). Each of these has various strengths and weaknesses in its ability to provide particular communications services.

Outside the well-defined GEO universe, the differences between these systems is often not absolute, and the acronyms applied to a system can be confusing and sometimes misleading. Several systems, for example, are variously described as LEOs and MEOs. Constantly evolving technology and newly developing markets and service definitions combine to blur the lines between one satellite system and another.

The definitions below are meant to describe the general characteristics of GEOs, MEOs, LEOs, and HEOs. Although examples of commercial systems employing these satellites are given, keep in mind that each system has unique characteristics that may not match precisely the general descriptions. The same caution should be applied to ascribing a particular satellite type's limitations to any one commercial system, since each uses several strategies for minimizing or overcoming the limitations inherent in satellite designs. For example, some systems may employ more than one type of satellite.

For the purposes of this chapter, GEOs and LEOs only will be discussed here. See Chapters 10 and 20 for further discussions about GEOs, MEOs, LEOs, and HEOs.

Geostationary (GEO)

GEO systems orbit the Earth at a fixed distance of 35,786 km (22,300 miles). The satellite's speed at this altitude matches that of the Earth's rotation, thereby keeping the satellite stationary over a particular spot on the Earth[19] (Figure 2-7). Examples of GEO systems include INTELSAT, Inmarsat, and PanAmSat.

Geostationary satellites orbit the Earth above the equator and cover one-third of the Earth's surface at a time. The majority of communications satellites are GEOs, and these systems will continue to provide the bulk of the communications satellite capacity for many years to come.

GEOs support voice, data, and video services, most often providing fixed services to a particular region. For example, GEO satellites provide backup

Figure 2-7
GEO satellite orbital
configuration.

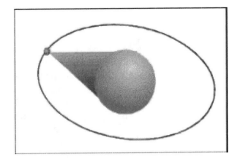

voice capacity for the majority of the U.S. long-distance telephone companies and carry the bulk of nationwide television broadcasts, which commonly are distributed from a central point to affiliate stations throughout the country.

Until recently, the large antennas and power requirements for GEO systems limited their effectiveness for small-terminal and mobile services. However, newer high-powered GEO satellites using clusters of concentrated spot beams can operate with smaller terrestrial terminals than ever before and can support some mobile applications. GEO satellite coverage typically degrades beyond 20 degrees north latitude and 20 degrees south latitude.

GEO systems have a proven track record of reliability and operational predictability not yet possible for the more sophisticated orbital designs now being deployed. GEO systems are also less complicated to maintain because their fixed location in the sky requires relatively little tracking capability in ground equipment. In addition, their high orbital altitude allows GEOs to remain in orbit longer than systems operating closer to Earth. These characteristics, along with their high bandwidth capacity, may provide a cost advantage over other system types.

However, their more distant orbit also requires relatively large terrestrial antennas and high-powered equipment and results in transmission delays. In addition, since only a few large satellites carry the load for the entire system, a GEO satellite loss is somewhat more consequential than for the systems described in Table 2-3.[20]

TABLE 2-3

GEO Pros and Cons

Pro	Con
GEO systems have significantly greater available bandwidth than the LEO and MEO systems described in Chapters 10 and 20. This permits them to provide two-way data, voice and broadband services that may be impractical for other types of systems.	GEO systems, like all other satellite systems, require line-of-sight communication paths between terrestrial antennas and the satellites. But because GEO systems have fewer satellites and these are in a fixed location over the Earth, the opportunities for line-of-sight communication are fewer than for systems in which the satellites travel across the sky. This is a significant disadvantage of GEO systems as compared with LEO and MEO systems, especially for mobile applications and in urban areas where tall buildings and other structures may block line-of-sight communication for hand-held mobile terminals.
Because of their capacity and configuration, GEOs are often more cost-effective for carrying high-volume traffic, especially over long-term contract arrangements. For example, excess capacity on GEO systems often is reserved in the form of leased circuits for use as a backup to other communications methods.	Some users have expressed concern with the transmission delays associated with GEO systems, particularly for high-speed data. However, sophisticated echo cancellation and other technologies have permitted GEOs to be used successfully for both voice and high-speed data applications.

Low-Earth Orbit (LEO)

LEO systems fly about 1000 km above the Earth (between 400 and 1600 miles) and, unlike GEOs, travel across the sky[21] (Figure 2-8). A typical LEO satellite takes less than 2 hours to orbit the Earth, which means that a single satellite is in view of ground equipment for only a few minutes. As a consequence, if a transmission takes more than the few minutes that any one satellite is in view, a LEO system must hand off between satellites in order to complete the transmission. In general, this can be accomplished by constantly relaying signals between the satellite and various ground stations or by communicating between the satellites themselves using intersatellite links.

In addition, LEO systems are designed to have more than one satellite in view from any spot on Earth at any given time, minimizing the possibility

Figure 2-8
LEO satellite orbital
configuration.

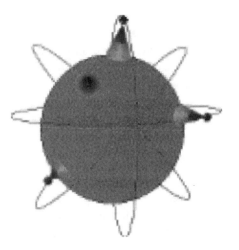

that the network will loose the transmission. Because of the fast-flying satellites, LEO systems must incorporate sophisticated tracking and switching equipment to maintain consistent service coverage. The need for complex tracking schemes is minimized, but not obviated, in LEO systems designed to handle only short-burst transmissions.

The advantage of the LEO system is that the satellites' proximity to the ground enables them to transmit signals with no or very little delay, unlike GEO systems. In addition, because the signals to and from the satellites need to travel a relatively short distance, LEOs can operate with much smaller user equipment (antennas) than can systems using a higher orbit. In addition, a system of LEO satellites is designed to maximize the ability of ground equipment to see a satellite at any time, which can overcome the difficulties caused by obstructions such as trees and buildings.

There are two types of LEO systems, big LEOs and little LEOs, each describing the relative mass of the satellites used as well as their service characteristics.

Little LEO

Little LEO satellites are very small, often weighing no more than a human being, and use very little bandwidth for communications. Their size and bandwidth usage limits the amount of traffic the system can carry at any given time. However, such systems often employ mechanisms to maximize capacity, such as frequency-reuse schemes and load-delay tactics.

Little LEO systems support services that require short messaging and occasional low-bandwidth data transport, such as paging, fleet tracking, and remote monitoring of stationary monitors for everything from tracking geoplatonic movements to checking on vending machine status. The low bandwidth usage may allow a LEO system to provide more cost-effective service for occasional-use applications than systems that maximize their value based on bulk usage. Examples of little LEO systems include Orbcomm, Final Analysis, and Leo One.

Big LEO

Big LEO systems are designed to carry voice traffic as well as data. They are the technology behind satellite phones or global mobile personal communications system (GMPCS) services now being developed and launched.

Most big LEO systems also will offer mobile data services, and some system operators intend to offer semifixed voice and data services to areas that have little or no terrestrial telephony infrastructure. Smaller big LEO constellations also are planned to serve limited regions of the globe. Examples of big LEO systems include Globalstar and the regional Constellation and ECO-8 systems.

An emerging third category of LEO systems is the so-called super LEOs or mega LEOs, which will handle broadband data. The proposed Teledesic and Skybridge systems are examples of essentially big LEO systems optimized for packet-switched data rather than voice. These systems share the same advantages and drawbacks of other LEOs and intend to operate with intersatellite links to minimize transmission times and avoid dropped signals[22] (Table 2-4).

Quick Comparison for Future Global Voice and Data Applications: GEO and LEO Broadband Satellite Architectures

The next generation of GEO (geostationary earth orbit) and LEO (low-earth orbit) satellite systems will provide new voice and data services on a global basis, and such systems are projected to become the dominant global broadband data providers by 2008. Rather than try and differentiate GEO from LEO, let's compare satellite to terrestrial, because any satellite Internet system has major advantages over terrestrial, be it wireline or wireless broadband. Among them are much lower capital cost per

TABLE 2-4

LEO Pros and Cons

Pro	Con
The transmission delay associated with LEO systems is the lowest of all the systems.	The small coverage area of a LEO satellite means that a LEO system must coordinate the flight paths and communications handoffs of a large number of satellites at once, making the LEOs dependent on highly complex and sophisticated control and switching systems.
Because of the relatively small size of the satellites deployed and the smaller size of the ground equipment required, the little LEO systems are expected to cost less to implement than the other satellite systems discussed here.	LEO satellites have a shorter life span than other systems mentioned here. There are two reasons for this: (1) the lower LEO orbit is more subject to the gravitational pull of the Earth, and (2) the frequent transmission rates necessary in LEO systems mean that LEO satellites generally have a shorter battery life than others.

potential user, seamless global coverage, faster to deploy global connectivity, lower end-user costs, the ability to connect both mobile and fixed sites equally, and no need for costly unsightly repeater antennas every 2 miles, etc. Given that the market for global broadband satellite systems is estimated at approximately $300 billion by 2006, it is expected that all the satellite systems, whether LEO or GEO, will most likely make significant global revenues and pay excellent dividends.

The inherent differences in LEO and GEO systems make them well suited to different applications, representing different business markets[23] (Tables 2-5 and 2-6). Specifically, the two major application groups (narrowband voice/paging and broadband data) are currently different services that will be used initially by a very different set of customers and later merged as LEO systems expand global bandwidth availability to probably eventually dominate the market. In the interim, GEO systems have an important place in developing global satellite Internet availability, albiet with antenna and delay problems inherent in the 22,000-mile orbit of GEO satellites.

TABLE 2-5

Quick Comparison Reference of the Relative Strengths and Weaknesses of GEO-LEO Satellite Architectures: Side-by-Side Comparison for Voice and Data Applications

	Geostationary Earth Orbit (GEO)	Low-Earth Orbit (LEO)
Applications	Preferred for TV broadcasting to fixed homes, has uses for corporate broadband data applications (broadcasting, data transmission, Internet connectivity), since high-speed connections can be made through fairly small, fixed antennas—easily, reliably, and cost-effectively. Works for corporations and ISPs. No uses for mobile and harder-to-install larger antennas makes LEO systems more attractive for individual consumers and the third world.	LEO is being deployed to deliver everything! No restrictions like GEO. Use for narrowband and broadband mobile voice and video-conferencing applications, with no delays or jitter, lightweight, cheap low-power, hand-held user terminals; smart, cheaper, no fixed pointing problems, wafer array antennas will work easily for broadband data applications, using sophisticated electronic satellite tracking by smart dual antennas technology.
Coverage	Only near global using first four satellites, prone to complete, disastrous long service outages if a single $500 million satellite is hit by micrometeorite or other failure; see recent pager service loss; one satellite can cover almost a third of Earth's surface, with near global coverage through four satellites; continuous regional coverage can be provided with a single satellite; can try to concentrate satellite power over markets where coverage is intended, although signal is weaker by a factor of 14, requiring larger antennas; satellite power is wasted on 75 percent of the Earth's surface, over oceans, deserts, jungles, and sparsely populated areas.	Global and easily expandable total bandwidth; requires full constellation (minimum 40 to 60 satellites) for continuous service; single satellite failure does not cause service interruption due to dual satellite signal coverage and cheap in-orbit spares; satellite power on beams is lowered when over 75 percent of the Earth's surface, over oceans, deserts, jungles, and more sparsely populated areas.

TABLE 2-5

continued

	Geostationary Earth Orbit (GEO)	Low-Earth Orbit (LEO)
Satellite tracking	GEO needs a single large, fixed, and pointed antenna, which must remain fixed (no satellite tracking required), since satellites appear stationary above the Earth; usually results in $100 to $200 costs of specialist installation; small dish antennas ideal for fixed broadband installations only, no mobile available.	New "Smart Wafer" phased-array antennas will be small, from pocket-sized up, and cheap for narrowband mobile and broadband data; very good for narrowband mobile voice, using a small handset with patch antenna; no need for expensive antenna pointing installation.
Technology	Based on old generation, expensive ($500 million per satellite), 30-year-old geostationary satellite technology, but potentially unreliable recent launch failures increase risk of failure and 2-year delays; 10- to 15-year lifespan for satellite unless hit by micrometeorite; GEO bandwidth cannot be expanded quickly.	Better, proven new-generation NASA-developed battery and solar power technology enables much more power and thus bandwidth, with minimal technological challenges to be overcome; 5- to 7-year lifespan for satellite; LEO constellation can be expanded and upgraded rapidly and inexpensively.
Cost comparisons	Similar initial cost for near-global coverage of GEO total coverage; cost for replacement of one failed GEO satellite is approximately $500 million each; GEO claims less expensive fixed "dumb" dish antennas for broadband applications.	Lower initial per-satellite and overall costs for space segment; incremental cost for replacing failed satellites is much lower, and system can be upgraded for less; not vulnerable to long service outage due to satellite failure; new user terminals with dual tracking patch antennas will be smaller, mass produced, and less costly to install.
Transmission delay	Much longer than LEOs—delays are significant for audio and videoconferencing applications.	LEO is shorter, faster than fiber; delay for interconnection traffic of GEOs is an annoying 0.25 to 0.5 second.

TABLE 2-6

LEO and GEO Broadband Satellite Architectures: Side-by-Side Comparison for Voice and Data Applications

	Geostationary Earth Orbit (GEO	Low-Earth Orbit (LEO)
Reliability	Excellent; a reliable data transmission method, providing high security and system reliability.	New IP technology just beginning to be used for voice-video communications; capable of providing very reliable data transmission, providing high security and system reliability.
Usefulness for voice and videoconferencing	Not really viable for voice and videoconferencing due to annoying echo caused by 0.25- to 0.5-second delay.	Excellent for voice and videoconferencing applications; provides cellular mobile connections for people and vehicles as well as fixed connectivity; can provide all of a consumer's private and business voice-video-data needs in one simple connection.
Overall complexity	Dumb; 30-year-old technology; minimum complexity in the sky and on the ground, given proven technology and fixed communications links.	Smart; higher complexity in the sky but gives global anywhere-to-anywhere real-time communications; uses frequent transmission handoffs like cellular; higher complexity on the ground but uses available off-the-shelf tracking and management facilities costing only a few million dollars more than GEO.
Link availability	99.5 to 99.9 percent.	99.5 to 99.9 percent, depending on location.
User terminals	Larger, fixed, pointed dish-style antennas for broadband data (0.7 to 2.0 m diameter); remains stationary because it does not need to track satellite but must be pointed accurately; usually requires expensive professional installation.	Can be pocket-sized; broadband applications require wafer "smart" array antennas to track moving satellites; technology has been around for years; small, low-power handsets are excellent for voice and videoconferencing communications, and use of Ka band frequencies allows lower-power handsets.

Narrowband voice and paging services will be used largely by people in developed markets fed up with overpaying for service, emerging country customers (80 percent of whom do not own a telephone today), and global business and recreational travelers carrying portable computers, palm-tops, and small, mobile IP-organizer handsets. Wireless broadband data services initially will be used by corporate customers, ISPs (large and small), and the military—via GEO and LEO systems. The GEO systems require larger, *fixed* antennas, requiring more precise pointing.

NOTE The real showstopper in the long run, though, is a nagging half-second time delay for GEO orbit signals. Bad enough for voice, a half-second is near eternity for computer communications; for the living-room and desktop supercomputers of 2002, a half-second delay would mean gigabytes of information to be stored in buffers. While companies across the country, from Intel to Digital Equipment, are rushing to market with cable modems to allow computer connections to CATV coax, geosatellites remain mostly computer-hostile. Even with the new digital cosmetics of DBS, geosynchronous satellites are a last vestige of centralization in a centrifugal world. With other link features equal, however, between 1226 and 3545 times more power is needed to communicate with a geostationary satellite than with a LEO.

GEO Architecture

GEO systems are dumb bent pipes, whereas LEO systems will be more likely to be smart with on-board routers switching data from anywhere to anywhere at the speed of light. GEO systems—like Cyberstar Loral-Orion and recently Astrolink—should have provided advantages over planned LEO systems in cost but most likely will fail to do so because of the high cost of the large GEO satellites and expensive, unreliable launches, as well as the use of expensive-to-install VSATs. Even though, only three or four GEO satellites are needed to provide complete Earth coverage, the cost of Astrolink alone will still be $3.6 billion for a total of 22.4 Gbps of bandwidth. GEO systems, while also inherently dumber and simpler, have far higher per-satellite costs and risks of failure that contribute to overall higher costs and quality-of-service risks.

Because of the GEO's greater distance from the Earth (approximately 22,000 miles versus 200 to 900 miles for LEOs), there is a far greater data propagation delay of 0.25 second involved in a point-to-point connection using a GEO satellite, creating annoying echos in voice or videoconferencing conversations and interactive data sessions. There is no escape from this inherent GEO delay problem.

LEO constellations have anywhere-to-anywhere data transfer rates faster than terrestrial fiber, allowing real-time voice conversations, video-conferencing, interactive multimedia games, and instant data transfer responses. LEO systems also allow operators to avoid costly terrestrial connections, thus lowering service costs and giving LEO operators a decisive technological and pricing advantage in the long term.

At each LEO satellite, switching and buffering will take place; this adds only 5 ms per hop of latency to the communications link. Thus, when the overall latency comparison of actual cases has been made by NASA and other researchers, taking into account all contributions, the overall latency in a GEO architecture always will be much higher. The latency of GEO systems (typically a quarter second) is only insignificant for broadband data applications such as TV broadcast or large file transfers. The delay always will be an issue for voice, videoconferencing, Internet, and multimedia use.

LEO Architecture

Finally, LEO systems hold many benefits, including lower per-satellite failure risk, lower per-satellite launch failure risk, no potentially disastrous service-failure problems, and smaller and cheaper mobile user terminals for voice, videoconferencing, Internet, and paging applications. Because of their lower orbits and lower operating frequency, LEOs can pick up narrowband voice signals from small hand-held terminals using patch antennas.

Last but not least, let's look at the last of the wireless broadband network protocols: ATM and Frame/Cell Relay technologies.

ATM and Relay Technologies

Several prominent wireless broadband ATM and relay technologies (Frame and Cell) research projects [including the European Community (EC)–financed wireless ATM network demonstrator (Magic WAND) and the Advanced Technology Program's (ATP's) Mobile Information Infrastructure project] are in the fifth year of their 6-year life spans. Participants in these endeavors are optimistic that a core set of technologies will be available soon on which to build commercial wireless broadband—ATM and relay products.

NOTE *Asynchronous Transfer Mode* (ATM) is a high-speed multiplexing and switching method utilizing fixed-length cells of 53 octects to support multiple types of traffic. ATM, specified in international standards, is asynchronous in the sense that cells carrying user data need not be periodic. *Frame Relay* is a networking technology that uses a form of packet switching with variable-length frames over a shared data network and is protocol-independent. *Cell Relay* is a statistically multiplexed interface protocol for packet-switched data communications that uses fixed-length packets (cells to transport data). Cell Relay transmission rates usually are between 56 kbps and 1.544 Mbps (the data rate of a DS1 signal). Cell Relay protocols (1) have neither flow control nor error correction capability, (2) are information content independent, and (3) correspond only to layers 1 and 2 of the ISO Open Systems Interconnection Reference Model. Cell Relay systems enclose variable-length user packets in fixed-length packets (cells) that add addressing and verification information. Frame length is fixed in hardware, based on time delay and user packet-length considerations. One user data message may be segmented over many cells. Cell Relay is an implementation of fast packet technology that is used in (1) connection-oriented broadband integrated services digital networks (B-ISDN) and (2) connectionless IEEE 802.6, switched multimegabit data service (SMDS). Cell Relay is used for time-sensitive traffic such as voice and video.

ATM

While many established players took the long view on wireless broadband ATM and partnered with both government, corporate, and academic entities, at least one company, Broadband Networks, Inc. (BNI),[24] struck out on its own and developed the front end needed to bring ATM to mobile users in fixed environments. BNI recently teamed with Siemens AG and Newbridge Networks (NN) to integrate its broadband wireless technology with the Siemens/Newbridge MainStreetXpress family of ATM carrier switches.

The Magic WAND program began trials and demonstrated the use of wireless ATM operating in the 5-GHz range, delivering 20 Mbps of bandwidth to hospital and office environments. The project is now complete and a success. Corporate participants included Nokia Mobile Phones, Ascom Tech, IBM France, Lucent Technologies WCND (LU), and Bosch. The project was funded through the European Community's advanced communications technologies and services program.

One of the few U.S.-based participants in Magic WAND is Trillium Digital Systems, Inc.[25] This company was chosen to provide the ATM signaling stack, LAN emulation stack, and a Window's NT software solution.

There was a fair amount of work involved in enhancing and modifying the software to work in the wireless broadband ATM environment, and part of the project was just to understand the protocol changes needed to make it work well.

The noisiness of the rf environment requires modifications to deal with the higher error rates. As a result, there are changes needed to the signaling protocol itself for actually establishing connections.

The mobile information infrastructure program, being performed by Lucent's Bell Labs and Sun Microsystems Federal, Inc. (SUNW), has entered the final phase. This project also is investigating wireless broadband ATM connections at up to 20 Mbps.

Network Simulations

The preceding companies have created a demonstration test bed in the laboratory that can provide multiple cells to simulate a WAN environment. The first step, however, is to transmit in an indoor LAN environment. Initially, the team is using a 10-Mbps infrared link to transmit digital video using real-time MPEG-2 transmitting over wireless broadband ATM. By the end of the project, the team hopes to have established enough technology so that people who are interested in pursuing product development can do so without significant technical risk.

The most consistent feature of ongoing wireless ATM projects is flexibility in spectrum use. The only thing that actually changes in the equation is the microwave transmission environment and the network architecture the rf transmission environment sits in.

However, some of these projects are constrained by government regulation and what frequency bands will be allocated. There are many possibilities.

Broadband Networks currently has customers trialing its wireless broadband ATM products. One of the trials involves embedding MPEG-5 video on ATM from a compression suite and moving it onto wireless ATM.

The preceding companies are working to harness the value of ATM as a backbone and move it further and further down the access chain. Their view is that over the next 5 years, wireless broadband ATM will grow into a multibillion-dollar market in North America. The value of putting discretionary fiber into the ground in the hope that someone will use it will wane.

Frame Relay

Frame Relay is a high-speed frame-switching protocol that moves frames over virtual circuits to connected network devices. A Frame Relay connection lets you establish a cost-effective virtual private network (VPN) between dialup users and corporate networks.

NOTE Frame Relay is a layer 2 protocol; packets occur at layer 3.

ISPs use a Frame Relay network to achieve speedy LAN-to-LAN or WAN-to-LAN internetworking data transfer and to connect multiple points of presence (POPs) in a geographic area. Frame Relay allows an access switch to connect to multiple sites using a single physical connection.

Frame Relay is a link-layer protocol (layer 2 in the OSI Reference Model). Each frame has a header (it is more than two octets) that contains a virtual circuit number (data link connection identifier, or DLCI) and some control bits (see sidebar, "Frame Relay" for details on headers).

Frame Relay

The Frame Relay packet contains flag fields to indicate the beginning and end of a frame, a 2-byte header field, the payload, and a frame check sequence (FCS) field, as shown in Table 2-7.[26]

The header field contains Frame Relay header fields, as shown in Table 2-8[27]:

- *Data link connection identifier (DLCI).* A 10-bit number that identifies the permanent virtual circuit (PVC) a packet should be sent on. Switches use DLCI numbers to route packets through a Frame Relay connection.

- *Command response (C/R).* This is application specific and is conveyed transparently.

- *Extended address (EA).* A bit indicating the end of the header field.

- *Forward explicit congestion notification (FECN).* A bit indicating to the receiving data terminal equipment (DTE) that the packet has experienced congestion.

■ *Backward explicit congestion notification (BECN).* A bit indicating to the receiving DTE that packets sent in the opposite direction may experience congestion.

■ *Discard eligibility (DE).* A bit indicating that this packet has low priority and should be discarded when congestion exists on the circuit. The Frame Relay DCE may set the DE bit to one in any frame that is above the configured committed information rate (CIR). For information on CIR, see sidebar, "Frame Relay: Handling Congestion."[28]

TABLE 2-7

Frame Relay Packet

Flag	2-byte header	Payload	FCS	Flag

TABLE 2-8

Frame Relay Header

Byte 1			Byte 2				
Upper DLCI (6 bits long)	C/R	EA	Lower DLCI (4 bits long)	FECN	BECN	DE	EA

Frame Relay: Handling Congestion

The level of data throughput and the quality of service that you can expect from a permanent virtual circuit (PVC) on the Frame Relay network depends on the configured committed information rate (CIR), the committed burst (Bc) size, and the excess burst (Be) size parameters.

Committed Information Rate
The committed information rate (CIR) is the data throughput rate that the Frame Relay provider commits to providing on the Frame Relay PVC. This means that if you set this parameter to 64,000 bits per second, the Frame Relay provider guarantees that, under normal conditions, the Frame Relay network has the ability to transfer an average of 64,000 bits of Frame Relay payload over a PVC every second. If the network receives more than 64,000 bits, it may or may not send the bits, depending on whether there is extra bandwidth

available at the time. If any congestion occurs, the extra bits may be dropped and only the first 64,000 bits moved through the PVC.

Burst Size

Determining the burst size a network can accept on a PVC is based on the settings for the committed burst size (Bc) and the excess burst size (Be) parameters;

- Committed burst (Bc) size is the maximum number of bits a Frame Relay network agrees to transfer during a measured interval, under normal conditions. This burst may be composed of one or several frames.

- Excess burst (Be) size is the maximum number of bits a Frame Relay network tries to deliver during a measurement interval, in addition to the committed burst size. This burst may be composed of one or several frames.

Congestion

The total number of bits the network will transfer over a PVC with extra bandwidth available is equal to Bc + Be. The network typically sets the discard eligibility (DE) bit to 1 for any frames transmitted in excess of Bc but not in excess of Be. If congestion exists on a PVC, the network discards packets with the DE bit set to 1. Then the higher level protocols are responsible for retransmitting the packets.

When a Frame Relay switch detects congestion over a PVC, it sets either the FECN or the BECN bit on all outgoing Frame Relay packets to 1. It sets FECN on packets that experience congestion and BECN on packets traveling in the reverse direction to indicate that further sent packets also may experience congestion. These bits are in the Frame Relay header.

If configured to do so, the access switch monitors the FECN bit. When it detects that more received frames have FECN set than not set in a measurement interval, it reduces the rate of transmission by one-eighth the current value per interval. When the congestion subsides, frame transmission gradually returns to the configured CIR level. When stepcount consecutive frames are received with BECN set, the transmission rate is reduced to five-eighths the maximum. The step-count is configurable in the FRInterface section. If this is greater than the old rate, it tries one-half and then finally one-quarter. When step-count/2 consecutive frames are received without BECN set, the rate increases by one-eighth until the CIR is restored.[29]

A Frame Relay frame moves along a permanent virtual circuit (PVC), which is a logical path through a Frame Relay network between frame DTEs. A Frame Relay network uses the DLCI information specified in the header of the Frame Relay frame to route it to its destination. The DTE uses the IP address in the body of the packet and in its routing tables to route packets to and from the Frame Relay network.

NOTE Currently, the Frame Relay implementation on the access switch only supports Internet Protocol (IP) packets. Nevertheless, Frame Relay is used for the transport of many different protocol types, including SNA, LAN traffic, and others, as well as IP.

Frame Relay Components

You connect to a Frame Relay switch (DCE) over the user-network interface (UNI), which is provided either by contracting with a Frame Relay provider (such as Sprint) or by a local connection to a Frame Relay switch in a proprietary Frame Relay network. To connect to a Frame Relay switch, you need the following:

- A device functioning as a Frame Relay DTE at the ISP's, telco's, or corporate site.

- One or more logical channels or permanent virtual circuits (PVCs) that carry a Frame Relay frame through the Frame Relay network to its destination.

- A dual serial card for a V.35 or X.21 connection (running between 64 bps and 8 Mbps) from your WAN to a Frame Relay network or a T1/E1 PRI card for a T1/E1 serial connection (running at 64 kbps) from your device to a Frame Relay network.[30]

Setting Up a Frame Relay Gateway

To create a Frame Relay gateway, install a Frame Relay card and software in the device. The Frame Relay gateway moves IP packets received from a dialup user through a Frame Relay PVC and on to its destination. You should then configure your device for IP routing over Frame Relay by setting either the Routing Information Protocol (RIP) parameters or the static route parameters.

To set up a Frame Relay connection, your Frame Relay service provider must set up a link between your device and their Frame Relay network. This link usually will be a dedicated line that connects the device to the nearest Frame Relay point of presence. Data traveling between two specific devices always will take the same virtual path.

The service provider also will set up PVCs between your device and other DTE devices attached to the network. For each PVC you request, your service provider will provide you with a DLCI. Each frame sent between the device and Frame Relay switch contains a DLCI—this is used by the service provider's switch to identify each PVC and the frame's destination. This number only has significance when the frame moves between the device and its local switch. To set up the device to work on a Frame Relay interface, your service provider should provide you with the values it uses for each interface:

- Line speed
- Frame Relay standard
- N391
- N392
- N393

You also need the values for the following for each circuit:

- Committed information rate (CIR)
- Committed burst size (Bc)
- Excess burst size (Be)[31]

Cell Relay Transmission

Finally, in Cell Relay systems, data are broken up into basic units (called *cells*) and transported through the wireless broadband network. A standard cell size is defined as consisting of 53 eight-bit octets. These 53 octets consist of 48 octets of payload (data) and 5 octets of header (routing) information.

Cell Relay operation is somewhat analogous to a processor bus. Instead of a 32-bit data buss, there is a 53-byte data buss. Instead of a 64-bit address buss, there is a 5-byte address buss. While the buss operates synchronously, under control of a buss clock, the buss function itself is asynchronous (similar in operation to an ordinary microprocessor bus). However, instead of the transfer being parallel, a high-speed serial ATM facility is used. This is Cell Relay!

As mentioned in the preceding paragraph, the buss function is asynchronous. This means that the I/O data (CPU modules in the preceding example) will immediately arbitrate for the facility (processor bus) when there are data destined for it. If there is a conflict, somebody loses, and data are lost. It is up to the application to recover (or not!) from the error condition.

Cell Relay operation can be summarized as being similar to conventional TDM, except that it has properties of asynchronous transfer. When operating with very high speed facilities, Cell Relay has the ability to integrate LANs and WANs through the use of protocols called LANE (LAN Emulation) and MPOA (Multiprotocol over ATM). Thus some Cell Relay transmission services are now under development or available on a limited basis [like Asynchronous Transfer Mode (ATM)].

Asynchronous Transfer Mode (ATM)

As mentioned previously, ATM is a cell-based transport mechanism that evolved from the development of the broadband ISDN (B-ISDN) standards. ATM does not stand for automatic teller machine or Ascom timeplex multiplexers (although this might apply); rather, it defines the asynchronous transport of cells (Cell Relay). Perhaps even more important, ATM is associated with a process known as the *ATM adaptation layer* (AAL). AAL describes how various I/O traffic types are converted into cells.

The adaptation process and the serial transport of cells are commonly referred to as fast packet multiplexing (FPM). While similar in concept, FPMs do not necessarily conform to ATM standards or switching conventions.

Conclusion

The substantial uncertainty surrounding future service types and related demand levels creates an atmosphere where wireless broadband network protocols become key. Design decisions made today will have far-reaching consequences with regard to an MSO's responsiveness to market demands and the expense of evolving HFC networks to stay at parity with online service opportunities as well as competing access approaches. Several protocol alternatives exist for embracing this uncertain future. These include simply designing for existing and near-term services and reacting to future service opportunities as they arise. A variation on this theme is to deploy latent excess bandwidth capacity that can be activated later through common node-splitting techniques. Drawbacks associated with these approaches were discussed earlier in this chapter.

Another approach, embodied by wireless broadband network protocols, is to deploy a performance-optimized infrastructure up front where efficiency/performance can only be improved marginally as a function of the evolution of individual components. The essence of protocols is the creation and systemwide sustaining of optimized collision domains (rf segments) using neighborhood-level traffic routing/switching, with each domain enjoying dedicated channels (wavelengths) on a systemwide basis (in both forward and return directions, if appropriate). Numerous technical experts espouse the benefits and feasibility of distributed protocols. The protocol approach allows operators to focus primarily on service packaging and related bandwidth-management issues in the last mile.

Implementation of wireless broadband network protocols primarily involves the use of highly integrated ASICs to accomplish a downscaling of standard DOCSIS CMTS and routing/switching capabilities that can be combined with DWDM techniques to maintain segment-level performance on a systemwide basis. Promising efforts are also underway to enable the use of low-cost FP lasers for the DWDM application. Additional powering requirements for the increased number of fiber nodes defined in a protocol are nominal.

Wireless broadband network protocols offer a variety of tactical and strategic advantages not available with other approaches. These advantages include

- Promotion of HFC-resident neighborhood switching nodes as the ideal locations for housing the packet-processing interface to a potentially all-optical Internet switching core.
- Deploying fiber is from interexchange points of presence (POPs) to cable headend facilities.
- Enabling the F component of HFC networks to be incorporated within the emerging all-optical switching fabric of cyberspace.
- Enabling the possibility of further increasing performance at the neighborhood level through improved PHY-level encoding methodologies (denser constellations).
- Reduction of unnecessary systemwide traffic through neighborhood-level switching/routing.
- Reduction in noise floor rise due to the abandonment of return combiner networks in favor of allocating parallel channels (wavelengths) to segment-specific data streams.
- Improved service reliability and consistency through reliance on smaller network segments.
- Simplified bandwidth management due to smaller contention domains.

- More cost-effective deployment of new service-enabling infrastructure through creation of separate system domains for each neighborhood.
- Potentially greater security through implementation of different encryption schemes wherever packet-to-lambda or lambda-to-lambda transforms exist.[32]

Combining the existing uncertainty of future service deployment scenarios with the threat of further complications due to potential unbundling requirements makes wireless broadband network protocols even more attractive. This is due to the inherent segmentation approach and the service-area granularity made possible by the protocols. With key headend equipment essentially downscaled, repackaged, and redeployed at the neighborhood level, a serious argument can be made against the need for systemwide unbundling. This would enable cable operators to price any unbundling-imposed access fees on a neighborhood-by-neighborhood basis.

Finally, in the increasingly competitive and high-stakes arena of advanced telecommunications services, the issues of responsiveness to market demands and cost of new service introduction loom large as other wireless broadband access technologies rally to preserve their once-dominant posture in the space. Wireless broadband network protocols address these and other issues with a rational, forward-looking approach to sustaining the performance advantage of wireless broadband HFC networks in an uncertain and increasingly competitive environment.

Endnotes

1. George T. Hawley, "DSL: Broadband By Phone," *Scientific American*, 415 Madison Avenue, New York, New York 10017 [High Speed Access Business Unit, Nokia Group (Finland) Corporate Communications, Keilalahdentie 4, FIN-02150 Espoo, P.O. Box 226, FIN-00045], 2000.
2. "G.Lite (Universal ADSL)," TechTarget.com, Inc., 113 Kendrick St., Suite 800, Needham, MA 02494, 2000.
3. Terry L. Wright, "Advanced Transport Architectures: Sustaining the Broadband Performance Edge," C-COR.net, 3950 Johns Creek Court, Suite 300, Suwanee, GA 30024-1265 (Kinetic Strategies, Inc., P.O. Box 59026, Phoenix, AZ 85076), 2000.
4. *Ibid.*
5. *Ibid.*
6. *Ibid.*
7. *Ibid.*

8. Harry Newton, "FTTC (Fiber to the Curb)," *Newton's Telecom Dictionary*, Flatiron Publishing, New York, 1997 (TechTarget.com, Inc., 113 Kendrick St., Suite 800, Needham, MA 02494, 2000).

9. Peter Rysavy, "The Evolution of Cellular Data: On the Road to 3G," Intel Network Systems, Inc., 28 Crosby Drive, Bedford, MA 01730-1437, 2000.

10. *Ibid.*

11. *Ibid.*

12. *Ibid.*

13. *Ibid.*

14. *Ibid.*

15. "Why VSAT?" STM Wireless, Inc., One Mauchly, Irvine, CA 92618-2305, 2000.

16. "DBS Is a Growing Business in the US," *SatNews Online Magazine*, Design Publishers, Inc., New York, 2000.

17. *Ibid.*

18. *Ibid.*

19. "Introduction to Global Satellite Systems," CompassRose International, Inc., 888 17th Street NW, Suite 900, Washington, DC 20006, 2000.

20. *Ibid.*

21. *Ibid.*

22. *Ibid.*

23. Quick Comparison for Future Global Voice and Data Applications, GEO and LEO Broadband Satellite Architectures," Sterling Satellite Communications LP, American S2COM, Inc., Australian S2COM, Pty., Ltd., US: P.O. Box 10904, Marina Del Rey, CA 90295, 2000.

24. Broadband Networks, Inc., 2820 E. College Ave., Suite B, State College, PA 16801-7548, 2000.

25. Trillium Digital Systems, Inc., 12100 Wilshire Blvd. Suite 1800, Los Angeles, CA 90025-7118, 2000.

26. "Frame Relay: Packet Format," Intel Network Systems, Inc., 28 Crosby Drive, Bedford, MA 01730-1437, 2000.

27. *Ibid.*

28. *Ibid.*

29. *Ibid.*

30. *Ibid.*

31. *Ibid.*

32. Terry L. Wright, "Advanced Transport Architectures: Sustaining the Broadband Performance Edge," C-COR.net, 3950 Johns Creek Court, Suite 300, Suwanee, GA 30024-1265 (Kinetic Strategies, Inc., P.O. Box 59026, Phoenix, AZ 85076), 2000.

CHAPTER 3

Services and Applications Over Wireless Broadband Networks

The ubiquitous role/nature of the Internet is enabling new consumer devices, applications, and services that are being developed to take advantage of the high-speed wireless broadband network that will link every home. Some examples that are discussed herein (but not all) include:

- *Internet phone.* This device functions as a regular phone, but instead of connecting to a public switched telephone network (PSTN), it transmits voice messages through Internet Protocol (IP) packets and is connected to an IP data wireless broadband network.

- *IP fax machine.* Analogous to an IP phone, this device transmits fax messages over an IP wireless broadband network.

- *Image server or mixed-media server.* These devices can provide a family or business with access to home-made videos, photo albums, personal recordings, etc.

- *Wireless broadband access devices.* These devices enable wireless broadband Internet access over cable TV systems, existing phone lines, or wireless technologies at speeds up to 40 Mbps.

- *Yuppie appliances.* These appliances could be devices such as the "pet tracker," which is a collar that goes on a pet that is tracked by a wireless application server to indicate the location of the pet. Some folks are also suggesting the use of "kid trackers" that would be tied into the home server, allowing instant messaging and Global Positioning Satellite (GPS) tracking of kid location.

- *Set-top box.* This device sits on top of a TV and provides a variety of services such as digital TV, Internet access, and gaming (interactive video games).

- *Residential gateway.* A residential gateway (Figure 3-1) is an intelligent gateway between wireless networked broadband information appliances inside the home and an intelligent wireless broadband

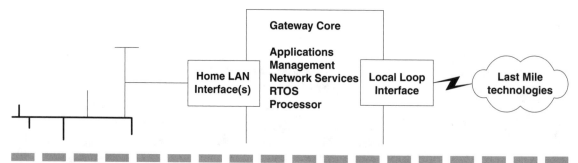

Figure 3-1   The residential gateway.

access network.[1] The residential gateway provides services such as file/applications sharing, Internet sharing within a home, and networked game play. It also may look up services on the Internet on behalf of in-home appliances. The in-home wireless broadband network that connects residential gateways and information appliances may be built using the existing telephone wiring, alternating-current (ac) electrical wiring, or new wireless broadband systems.

- *Video-on-demand.* Two-way residential wireless broadband networks will allow true interactive video-on-demand that did not live up to expectations a few years ago.

- *Work at home (telework).* Employees will be able to connect securely to their corporation's wireless broadband networks over high-speed Internet connections.

- *In-home wireless broadband networking.* A local-area network (LAN) using the existing home infrastructure will allow home automation and sharing of resources between information appliances and personal computers (PCs) within a home.

- *Control wireless broadband networks.* These devices enable secure remote utility meter reading; control of in-home devices such as burglar alarms, sprinkler systems, pet feeders, plant watering systems, humidity and temperature monitoring control system, and devices that add a bit more glamour to the usage; and so on.[2]

NOTE Many large and small businesses will benefit from the application services model. We will also see the emergence of the wireless accessible home and small office application and storage server. SAN technology also will be in the mix. The local (in-home or office) wireless server combined with a hardy 1-terabyte server to store applications, calendars, video, and music that is purchased and served up locally will help drive the application demand.

In the future, home entertainment equipment such as TVs, VCRs, and stereo systems also will be connected to a wireless broadband network along with PCs, telephones, thin displays on refrigerators, and even light switches. Figure 3-2 shows a possible scenario for future homes.[3]

In the middle of the wireless broadband network is a device called the *home gateway*, or *residential gateway*, that connects the in-home network and an external high-speed wireless broadband network (see Figure 3-1).

In other words, this chapter describes wireless broadband network software technologies, their functional components, and intended use. In addition, this chapter provides descriptions of the application-specific technologies required for residential gateways, IP phones, and IP fax devices.

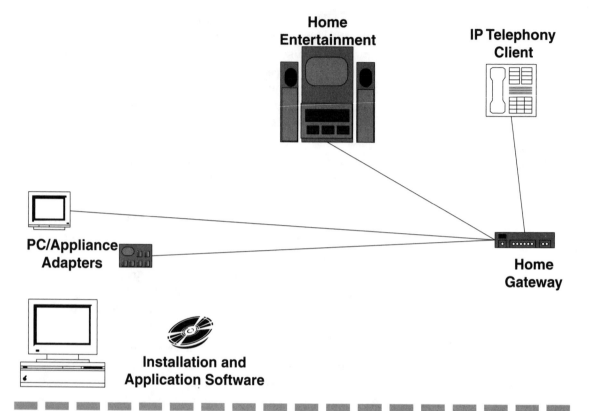

Figure 3-2 Home of the future.

What Is Required to Support Consumer Wireless Broadband Internet Devices?

Four layers of software components are needed for these emerging wireless broadband Internet device applications:

1. At the network level, an infrastructure is needed that allows these wireless broadband networked devices to behave in a manner that consumers have come to expect from electronic devices—devices that are easy to set up and use, require little or no training, are self-managing, and so on.

2. At the application level, enabling technologies are needed for IP telephony, IP fax, IP video, and other applications.

3. High-speed broadband access technologies are needed, such as cable modems and digital subscriber line (DSL) and wireless broadband devices.

4. Security and access control is needed to keep the home systems from being monitored or manipulated by outside parties.[4]

Many existing protocols and services can be used to support these new wireless broadband Internet devices. However, currently, the interoperability of devices on the wireless broadband network is problematic. Wireless broadband networks are growing so fast that the overhead for configuring devices is high. Existing protocols and policies must be enhanced and new ones developed to support the specific requirements of Internet devices. Dynamic wireless broadband network configuration, security, service location, network performance, device management, and so on are all required for the successful deployment of these new devices. In addition, technologies are needed to allow Internet devices to be largely self-managing and self-configuring.

General Applications and Services

Based on demographics, it is probable that all incumbent local exchange carriers (ILECs) and most other local exchange carriers (LECs) in the United States will deploy the advanced intelligent wireless broadband networking capabilities described earlier in this chapter nearly ubiquitously over the next 5 to 7 years. Some carriers have already made these services widely available. These services will represent to telecommunications subscribers what the advent of the PC represented to its user community. Users will be able to define and obtain customized call processing capabilities to support both voice and data/multimedia applications such as customized screening and routing of calls, automated media conversion to facilitate the delivery of messages, personalized telephone/network numbers, and access-control (security-related) services. These will be provided in a way that is easy to use, reliable, affordable, and capable of interworking with a wide variety of appliances and terminals, ranging from simple telephones to personal digital assistants (PDAs). Advanced intelligent wireless broadband networks will enhance multimedia communications by enabling users to control multiple channels in a single communications session and by interfacing with a variety of user terminal devices in a user-friendly way.

Integrated Services Digital Network (ISDN)

ISDN is widely deployed and available today. ISDN is a major step forward in enabling two-way interactive access to multimedia information, multimedia messaging, and multimedia teleconferencing and collaborative work. It will be the backbone of the transition of residential access toward wireless broadband over the next 20 years. Along with today's dialup modem-based access, ISDN will be a principal access technology for residential and small business users accessing the Internet over the next 20 years. ISDN, in both its basic rate (two 64-kbps B channels) and primary rate (twenty-three 64-kbps B channels) forms, will be used by businesses to meet their traditional telecommunications and Internet access needs, and it will be used by cellular and emerging personal communication service (PCS) providers to connect into the core telecommunications wireless broadband networks. ISDN will be a principal access mechanism for K–12 schools, libraries, and community centers to connect to the national information infrastructure (NII) and global information infrastructure (GII).

Higher-Speed Switched and Nonswitched Services

Until recently, the primary method by which businesses and institutions obtained nonswitched private-line connections between their locations was to use dedicated 1.5-Mbps T1 lines and dedicated 56-kbps digital private lines rented from telecommunications carriers, including the LECs. Some larger businesses and institutions have used higher-speed 45-Mbps private-line for point-to-point connections. Recently, new types of digital services, including Frame Relay and ATM Cell Relay, have been introduced by telecommunications carriers, including LECs. Frame Relay and ATM are currently nonswitched services that use predetermined destinations for traffic; switched versions of these services are under development. All these services offer the advantages of improved sharing of facilities (fibers, terminations on electronic equipment, etc.) through statistical multiplexing. These new services, particularly ATM, also can support advanced multimedia applications that require high data rates and low delay variability between communicating end points. These higher-speed services are being deployed in concert with market demands and are expected to be widely deployed and available over the next 5 to 7 years.

Cellular Wireless

Cellular wireless broadband networks are widely deployed in urban and suburban population centers, and coverage and connectivity are steadily improving. These networks are being expanded to meet the growing user base with the deployment of smaller cells and newer technologies. Low-power cellular (PCS) to support people on the move is being implemented and will be widely deployed over the next 5 to 7 years. Wireless networks are being upgraded to employ digital technologies that support data and multimedia applications. In addition, these digital technologies enable the incorporation of encryption methods to improve the resistance of wireless broadband services to eavesdropping. The use of advanced intelligent wireless broadband network functionality and services will allow for improved roaming and mobility for wireless users and will enable access to multiple wireless networking services (cordless telephony, high-power cellular, low-power cellular, and satellite-based services) from a single telephone handset. Such multitiered applications are being deployed now by some LECs, and they are expected to be widely available over the next 5 to 7 years.

Internet

The Internet, as it exists today, is built on services provided by LECs and interexchange (long-distance) carriers. Users access Internet routers (switches) through dialup telephone lines and 56-kbps or 1.5-Mbps T1 private lines leased from telecommunications network carriers, primarily LECs. Routers are interconnected with 56-kbps T1 and 45-Mbps private lines typically leased from telecommunications carriers. Increasingly, fast packet services (such as Frame Relay and SMDS) are being used to replace point-to-point links.

Recently, several LECs have announced offerings of complete Internet Protocol (TCP/IP) capabilities, including routing functionality, mail boxes, and support services. It is likely that most LECs will offer complete Internet service product lines in the next several years. However, there are regulatory issues that can delay the ILECs' offerings of Internet services. The Modified Final Judgment (MFJ) prohibits the ILECs from carrying traffic that crosses local access and transport area (LATA) boundaries.

Such traffic must be handed off to a long-distance carrier selected by the consumer. It is not clear whether, and if so, how, the restriction applies to the provision of Internet service.

In other words, offering a ubiquitous Internet access service with the burden of the long-distance restriction would increase capital costs by 75 percent and expenses by 100 percent. The following factors contribute to these additional costs:

- LATAs in which there is low customer demand cannot be served from other sites in other LATAs.

- Customers of switched data services frequently demand redundancy within the wireless broadband network to ensure service availability. Because of the long-distance restriction, sites in other LATAs cannot be used to provide redundancy.

- Current Internet routing technology requires the dedication of a router to each long-distance provider in each LATA.[5]

At this point, some ILECs are interpreting the MFJ restrictions to apply to their Internet service offerings. This is an area where regulations need to be changed to allow the ILECs to compete on an equal basis with other carriers that are not subject to MFJ restrictions.

Wireless Broadband Access

As described in the preceding sections, the provision of ubiquitous, affordable wireless broadband access to residences is one of the most difficult challenges facing telecommunications carriers. All ILECs have expressed a commitment to deploy wireless broadband access services as quickly as the market demand, technology cost trends, and regulatory and legal environments permit.

The ILECs have collectively invested approximately $80 billion per year in upgrades to their networks since divestiture in 1984. They have committed to increase their investments substantially if regulatory reforms are enacted that enable them to be full-service providers of telephony, video, and multimedia interactive services in an environment that is conducive to the high-risk investments required to deploy wireless broadband access networks. Several of the ILECs and other LECs have market trials of wireless broadband access under way or planned.

The deployment of symmetric two-way capabilities that permit residential users to originate individualized very high speed (greater than several hundred kilobits per second) upstream communications is a major challenge. One must differentiate between the concept of symmetric two-way access, which has been raised as an issue by the government and other stakeholders, and the concept of two-way capability. The most demanding two-way capability that has been identified in the context of wireless broadband networks that serve residences is two-way multimedia collaborative work, also called *multimedia teleconferencing*. Research has shown that two-way multimedia collaborative work can be supported, to a large extent, by basic-rate ISDN and that nearly all needs can be met with a two-way capability of 256 to 384 kbps. Most wireless broadband access network architectures being considered for deployment by the ILECs can support this capability on a switched basis for all subscribers. At issue is whether there is demand for still higher speed two-way capabilities, comparable in speed to the one-way capability needed to deliver entertainment-quality video to residential customers. The data rate associated with entertainment video ranges from 1 Mbps for VHS quality to 20 Mbps or more for high-definition TV (HDTV) quality. The ability to deliver entertainment-quality video both downstream to residential users and upstream from residential users is what is called *symmetric two-way access*.

Although a large number of alternative architectures have been studied extensively from a capability and cost perspective, it appears that in many situations substantial incremental investments are required to provide symmetric two-way capabilities. It is unlikely that these incremental investment costs will be recovered in a competitive marketplace if they are made many years ahead of the demand for such high-speed upstream services. The details of the tradeoffs among alternative broadband architectures vary from ILEC to ILEC depending on such things as the density of housing units.

Dependable, Usable Wireless Broadband Networks

The tradition of the telecommunications industry has been to provide network services that are highly reliable, secure, and usable by the widest possible range of telecommunications services customers. As new, interactive (education and video games), multimedia networking services and applications are deployed, using a wide range of new and heterogeneous technologies, it will be a great challenge for all industry participants to maintain this tradition in the context of the national information infrastructure (NII) and global information infrastructure (GII). If individuals, corporations, and institutions are to reengineer themselves to become dependent on wireless broadband networked applications, then those individuals, corporations, and institutions must be provided with wireless broadband network-based services and applications that are even more dependable than today's telephony services. They will expect these services and applications to be easy to use, to work all the time, and to be secure from intrusions and other security threats. The ILECs are committed to maintaining their tradition of reliable, secure, and easy-to-use services through a combination of technological and operational methods. In particular, the use and sharing (in public forums such as the National Security Telecommunications Advisory Committee) of best practices among network providers are essential to help prevent and minimize such threats. Cooperative testing between networks to detect incompatibilities, particularly of management protocols that protect faults from propagating into large outages, is an essential ingredient of this process.

As we move into the future, the role of telecommunications wireless broadband networks in facilitating interoperability and ease of use will become increasingly important to consumers. While early adopters and those who create new technologies have a relatively high tolerance for complexity and unreliability and are willing and able to invest substantial amounts of time in learning to use applications and in resolving problems, mass market users expect their applications and services to be extremely dependable and intuitive. In theory, software-based functionality can be placed in end users' terminals to enable interoperability, to resolve incompatibilities that would be perceived by customers as application failures, and to make complexity transparent to end users. In reality, this is achieved today by forcing end users to be systems administrators of their complex terminal software or to engage others to administer their systems for them. Traditionally, the telephone networks have hidden complexity from end users and have resolved incompatibilities among end-user terminals by employing middleware in the networks. For example, an end user in New York can make a call from an ISDN telephone to an analog cellular phone in London. As applications such as multimedia teleconferencing, multimedia messaging, and remote access to multimedia information become increasingly important in mass market applications, telecommunications wireless broadband networks will play a critical role in resolving incompatibilities between different types of user terminals and between user terminals and servers, in facilitating the location of resources, in helping users manage their communications services, and in providing capabilities such as multimedia bridging.

Conclusion

The objective of broadband wireless access (BWA) technology is to allow today's fast desktop computers to rapidly communicate with high-speed Internet servers, data servers, and other network services. By breaking the bottleneck at the final mile, broadband wireless access (BWA) could allow emergent as well as developed markets around the world to participate more fully in the global economy.

Today, the mission statement of most ILECs is to provide high-quality, cost-effective wireless broadband communications services. To provide these services, ILECs must accurately and efficiently transport information from one location to another as their customers' needs demand it. There are several network technologies that could be employed to transport this information, ranging from fiberoptic cable to satellite transmission to broadband wireless technologies. A number of ILECs believe that the most effective technology to employ is a reliable wireless broadband network for their customers. This technology is referred to as *broadband wireless access* (BWA). While other technologies may be employed where specific conditions suggest that they would be beneficial, BWA will be ILECs' primary technology.

NOTE   The U.S. Federal Communications Commission (FCC) calls the BWA technology LMDS (local multipoint distribution service).

Advantages of BWA Technology

Although not yet commercially deployed on a large-scale basis, ILECs believe that wireless broadband technology can offer the most cost-effective means of providing high-capacity, high-speed data, audio, voice, video, and Internet connectivity services. BWAs also can provide specialized applications such as interactive education, interactive video games, e-commerce, telework, "edutainment," and telemedicine. For example:

- BWA systems can provide massive capacity, optimized for two-way communications. For instance, a single BWA cell can support the equivalent of 128 E1 lines or the equivalent of over 3800 telephone lines for each assigned 56-MHz channel pair.

- The infrastructure is scalable and can be built to serve specific demand. Unlike wireline broadband networks, the amount of capital required is more closely matched to demand.

- Ease of network deployment allows ILECs to initiate service in the space of a few months from startup and deliver services to customers within days following an order.

- BWA could provide high-quality digital transmission with signal quality and reliability comparable or superior to other broadband technologies.

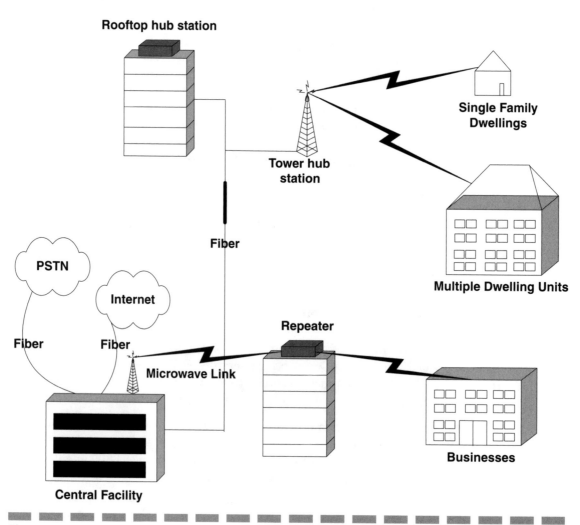

Figure 3-3   Diagram of a BWA system.

- BWA networks can extend to areas where fiber-based alternatives may never be economically feasible.[6]

System and Technology Description

BWA systems (Figure 3-3) are based on a fixed (as opposed to mobile) wireless technology, which uses 28-GHz frequencies in the United States.[7] Some other countries also use 28 GHz, and still others use frequencies ranging from 22 to 42 GHz. BWA systems use digital technology and frequency reuse within a cellular configuration to deliver high-speed data service, voice, and video. BWA systems transmit and receive digital signals between radio node facilities and customer locations. Optimal broadcast distances between each radio node are from approximately ½ to 3 miles. The number of radio nodes required in any area varies, depending on the size of the geographic area being covered, its topology, environmental factors, and capacity requirements. Radio nodes are typically installed on tall office buildings or could be on a freestanding tower[8] (Figure 3-4).

Recommendations

Finally, most of the technology-related challenges in creating applications and services to run over wireless broadband networks can be best addressed by the private sector, with the cooperation of the public sector. From the point of view of local exchange network providers, the regulatory

Figure 3-4
Example of BWA equipment.

impediments discussed in the preceding sections must be addressed to enable an investment climate that is appropriate for the high risks associated with the large deployments of network infrastructure needed to provide wireless broadband access. The public sector should work with the private sector to address issues related to universal access, applications, and service and to promote open systems and interoperability among networks, systems, and services. The public sector should remove barriers to full and fair competition, such as the MFJ restrictions and the network interface device requirement discussed in the preceding sections, and should avoid creating new barriers in the future. For example:

- The public sector should use wireless broadband networks provided by the private sector rather than building networks in competition with the private sector's commercial service providers.

- The public sector also must address the myriad legal issues related to intellectual property, liability, application-specific law (practicing medicine across state lines), and other issues that are impediments to the emergence of new applications. Many of these issues have been identified in forums such as the National Information Infrastructure Advisory Council and the private-sector Council on Competitiveness.

- The public sector should be a role-model user of the emerging NII and GII and should continue its initiatives to create a broad awareness of the potential of the NII and GII to address many of society's challenges in education, health care, criminal justice, telemedicine, facilities security such as airports, stadiums, public buildings, and government.

- The public sector should support and fund precompetitive research and development targeted toward enabling NII dependability, interoperability, and ease of use by the broad population. The public sector also should support and fund precompetitive research and development on advanced technology for next-generation wireless broadband networks and advanced applications and services.

- The public sector should collaborate with the private sector on programs that will lead to the realization of the goal of having K–12 schools and libraries connected to the NII and GII by the year 2006.

- Finally, the public sector should work with the private sector to protect U.S. interests in matters related to the global information infrastructure (GII), with particular emphasis on intellectual property protection and trade reciprocity.[9]

Endnotes

1. "Networking Technologies Incorporated in the Cisco Networks Product Development Kit." Some of the material in this book has been reproduced by McGraw-Hill with the permission of Cisco Systems, Inc. Copyright © 2000 Cisco Systems, Inc. All rights reserved, 170 West Tasman Drive, San José, CA, 95134-1706, 2000.

2. *Ibid.*

3. *Ibid.*

4. *Ibid.*

5. Stewart D. Personick, *Trends in Deployments of New Telecommunications Services by Local Exchange Carriers in Support of an Advanced National Information Infrastructure*, National Academy Press, 2101 Constitution Avenue NW, Lockbox 285, Washington, DC 20055, 2000.

6. Formus Communications, 720 South Colorado Blvd., Suite 600 North, Denver, CO 80246, 2000.

7. *Ibid.*

8. *bid.*

9. Stewart D. Personick, *Trends in Deployments of New Telecommunications Services by Local Exchange Carriers in Support of an Advanced National Information Infrastructure*, National Academy Press, 2101 Constitution Avenue NW, Lockbox 285, Washington, DC 20055, 2000.

CHAPTER 4

Wireless Broadband Marketing Environment

The markets for fixed and mobile broadband wireless networks have been evolving at a rapid pace. This chapter will enable you to understand where the major opportunities in these markets will arise.

Mobile Broadband Wireless Communications

Analysis in this chapter is based on projected subscriber numbers. Revenues are forecast for the three core market segments:

- Basic mobile data services
- Advanced second-generation-plus (2.5G) data services
- Third-generation (3G) data services[1]

Fixed Broadband Wireless Access

This chapter sets out projected subscriber numbers (Figure 4-1) and revenues.[2] Subscriber numbers use personal computer (PC) penetration as the chapter's base reference point. Revenues are split into implementation revenues (cost of installation and customer premise equipment) and usage revenues. Subscriber and revenue projections are provided for the following market sectors:

- Households
- Small businesses
- Medium-sized businesses
- Large enterprises[3]

Mobile Application Evolvement?

The world of mobile communications is going through a period of unprecedented change. Evolution is the name of the game, and in the mobile sector this is described in terms of *generations:* from first-generation (1G) analogue through second-generation (2G) digital systems to third-generation (3G) advanced high-speed interactive digital networks[4] (Table 4-1).

Figure 4-1

Total fixed wireless small business subscribers, 1999–2004.

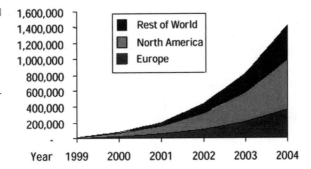

Broadband wireless opportunities in global markets provide a comprehensive view of the mobile evolution. Key issues include hybrid and third-generation systems.

Hybrid Systems

High-speed circuit-switched data (HSCSD) and general packet radio service (GPRS) or 2.5G hybrid systems are coming to market. Originally designed for voice and short message service, these digital systems can now handle medium-speed data services such as e-mail, limited Web browsing, and low-quality video. See sidebars, "HSCSD" and "GPRS" for more information.

TABLE 4-1

Mobile Application Capability Thresholds

	1G	2G	2.5G	3G
Voice	****	****	****	****
Short message service		****	****	****
E-mail		*	****	****
Web browsing			**	****
Intranet access			***	****
Document transfer			***	****
Low-quality video		*	***	****
High-quality video			**	****

HSCSD

Mobile data systems are already showing strong growth. And this is just the beginning. With the launch of high-speed data services, mobile usage will grow as never before. And this is why operators need to start now to be certain of winning their share of the opportunity that is mobile data.

With high-speed circuit-switched data (HSCSD), an operator can begin the transformation to become a true mobile data service provider. With HSCSD, you can prepare not only your organization but also your subscribers for the exciting future of third-generation services. An added attraction of this route is that HSCSD networks can be implemented with a surprisingly small investment.

With Acceptance Comes Opportunity   With HSCSD services, subscribers will start to learn about the possibilities of high-speed data over mobile. People's mobile data behavior will develop, and use patterns will become clear. As an operator, you are perfectly placed not only to learn from these early trends but also to influence how subscribers use the many new applications.

First to pick up the benefits will be business users who are willing and able to pay for high-quality services that they are comfortable using each day during their travels. This segment will quickly recognize and rapidly come to depend on the exciting new applications made possible by HSCSD.

With HSCSD, fast access to the Internet will become the norm. Other technologies, such as general packet radio services (GPRS), will complement and enhance the value of HSCSD. There are applications for both circuit-switched and packet-switched worlds. For instance, if the user needs to make PSTN/ISDN connections (toward corporate modem pools), only HSCSD can be used. HSCSD is ideal for real-time applications and GPRS for *always connected* applications. For example, HSCSD connections provide *active* e-mail and file transfer, whereas GPRS will run in the background for wireless broadband data networking.[5]

GPRS

Wireless broadband data usage is doubling every year in advanced markets. Many cellular operators already earn over 6 percent of their revenues from data traffic. In addition to income from traditional service subscription and use, wireless data systems bring new ways to generate revenue. Like content provisioning (value-added services, Internet access and services, advertising, and vertical services for specific market segments), successful operators will be the innovators and market makers for these new applications.

General packet radio service (GPRS) is the best platform for mobile data networking services. GPRS is also an essential stepping stone to third-generation personal multimedia services. For mobile operators and service providers, however, GPRS revolutionizes business and working practices, a trend that is both driven and reinforced by the convergence of telecommunications and data networking. GPRS opens up new opportunities but also introduces challenges, the most significant of which are changes in the tariff model and introduction to the new Internet Protocol (IP) infrastructure. To support users in this task, a complete GPRS solution features both comprehensive charging facilities and a best-in-class GPRS core IP network.[6]

Third Generation

UMTS (a 3G system) will deliver higher bandwidth. The company also will offer a much fuller range of services, including multimedia, high-quality real-time video, fast Intranet; database access, and other data-intensive applications.

Advantages of Fixed Wireless Broadband Over Wireline Network Options

Where do the inherent strengths of fixed wireless broadband systems lie? Wireless systems are being deployed to fulfill a number of functions. On a network level, they are suitable for both access and backbone infrastructure. It is generally agreed that it is in the access market where key advantages are held over wireline alternatives[7] (Figure 4-2). These include

- Rapid network deployment
- Simple and cost-effective upgrading of network capabilities
- Variable bandwidth on demand

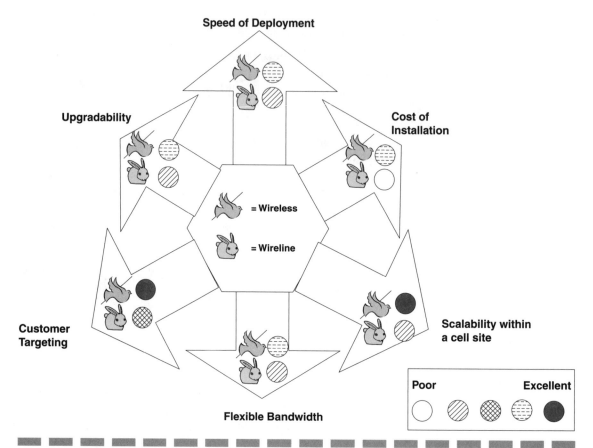

Figure 4-2 Key advantages of fixed broadband wireless (Datamonitor).

- Incremental targeted network deployment that can generate immediate returns on investments[8]

This chapter also provides essential information for decision makers. Key issues covered include

- What is driving the market forward?
- Who is going to be involved in equipment manufacturing and service provision?
- Where are the opportunities likely to arise?
- How large are the markets going to be?
- How fast will the market unfold?[9]

Market Penetration Development

As we move through 2.5G to 3G systems, the charge to sign up will be led by business users and high-end, more affluent consumers. Early adopters are likely to be attracted by the functionality of the technology. With growth of the Internet and the ability of new handsets to access it, the migration of these systems toward the mass market is likely to be more rapid than seen with earlier generations of mobile technology[10] (Figure 4-3). Given that price elasticity of demand for mobile phones is relatively high, the level of uptake will be very much determined by tariff plans. Broadband wireless opportunities in global markets also quantify important

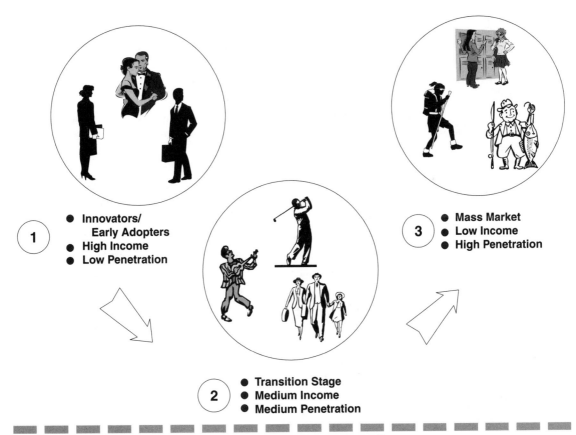

1
● Innovators/
   Early Adopters
● High Income
● Low Penetration

2
● Transition Stage
● Medium Income
● Medium Penetration

3
● Mass Market
● Low Income
● High Penetration

Figure 4-3   Mobile market evolution: Who will be the target audiences?

issues for players operating in or thinking of entering the broadband wireless markets, including

- Who will be the primary audience(s)?
- Who will be the secondary audience(s)?
- How will the market evolve and continue to do so?
- How many subscribers will there be, and how large are the revenues streams likely to be for various segments of fixed and mobile wireless markets?[11]

Wireless Broadband Access Markets

Wireless broadband access markets are on the verge of tremendous growth. Demand is high, and supply is growing. Within this escalating wireless broadband market, fixed terrestrial wireless systems are expected to generate global service revenues approaching $20 billion in 5 years and $39 billion in 10 years. Cumulative end-user equipment sales are projected to approach $5 billion by the end of 2009.

Global interest in wireless broadband is really taking off, with potential in both developed and developing telecom markets. In developed markets, the technology holds benefits for new competitive operators seeking to enter the local access market. For developing countries, wireless broadband offers state-of-the-art, cost-efficient, flexible networks that can be deployed quickly without the high cost and time involved in wireline infrastructure projects.

In 2001, early adopters such as the United States, Canada, and Argentina are rolling out commercial networks in major cities. Other large markets, including Japan and Germany, are conducting trials and issuing licenses. By 2003, it is likely that close to 70 countries will have licensed or be moving toward licensing broadband wireless networks.

As discussed in earlier chapters, *wireless broadband* refers to technologies that use point-to-point or point-to-multipoint microwave in various frequencies between 2.5 and 43 GHz to transmit signals between hub sites and end users. The technology can be used to provide voice, data, and video services and requires line of sight between the hub site and the end-user receiver. *Local multipoint distribution service* (LMDS) is the term used in the United States for 28 GHz.

Global Markets and Trends for Fixed Wireless Broadband: LMDS, MMDS, and ISM 2000

Global markets and trends for fixed wireless broadband include

- Subscribers to wireless broadband systems are expected to grow at over 120 percent per year through 2007.
- Unlicensed and narrowband spectrum will be converted into broadband systems.
- Broadband wireless subscriber revenues are expected to exceed $8 billion by 2007.
- Wireless broadband systems will be deployed by competitive local exchange carriers (CLECs) to avoid the plant of incumbent providers.
- Incumbent service providers will deploy wireless broadband systems to address dark spots in their network.
- Wireless will be used to provide digital subscriber line (DSL) to fiber speeds.
- Multichannel multipoint distribution service (MMDS) is expected to account for over 70 percent of broadband wireless subscribers by 2007.
- Service providers will no longer rely on just one platform. They will use a collection of wired and wireless technologies to maximize coverage area and expand their service offerings.

The arrival of wireless broadband technologies to the neighborhood has been delayed by problematic rollouts, raising the potential value of the wireless broadband market. The limits of conventional wired broadband technologies have become evident. Line congestion and slow deployments of DSL and cable modems have proven to be constant hurdles faced by many service providers, consultants, and their customers.

As a result, service providers are turning to wireless technologies: local multipoint distribution service (LMDS), multichannel multipoint distribution service (MMDS), and personal communications services (PCS) systems operating in the various industrial, scientific, and medical (ISM) bands (900 MHz and 2.4, 5.1, and 5.8 GHz). These technologies are expected to gain over 11 million broadband subscribers by 2007. They will be used to provide fiber and high-speed copper equivalents to otherwise underserved customers.

MMDS, including the 3.4- to 3.7-GHz worldwide standard for fixed wireless access, is expected to lead the market with a 90 percent share in 2007, largely in the residential and small office/home office (SOHO) sectors. LMDS will continue to make inroads into the market for high-value customers, accounting for 80 percent of subscriber revenues in 2007.

Meanwhile, traditional wireline and wireless carriers will join small Internet service providers (ISPs) in using a collection of bands (largely unlicensed) and technologies to address dark spots in their coverage areas. Because of its generous spectrum allotment, the 5.8-GHz band is receiving the most attention as an unlicensed broadband local loop. Systems operating in this band are expected to account for close to 700,000 subscribers in 2007. Total shipments of customer premises equipment for high-speed wireless technologies are expected to reach 5.8 million units in 2007.

Trends and Developments in the Wireless Broadband Market

Depending on the level of competition, mobile subscribers are set to grow to between 9.4 million and 10 million by the end of 2001. Mobile communications will replace fixed-line telephony (70 to 80 percent of traffic by 2002). Mobile phone data, including Wireless Application Protocol (WAP) and GPRS, will remain a niche market—the future is in wireless broadband data to the home. (See Chapter 28 for a detailed explanation of WAP.)

The Mobile Data Hype   The mobile industry would have us believe that it also will become a dominant player in this broadband market— maybe even take the market over[12] (Table 4-2). Based on their current business models, many industry experts do not share this view.

TABLE 4-2

Mobile Subscriber Forecast for 2001

Operator	Total	Market Share, %
Telstra	5,000,000	44
Optus	3,900,000	34
Vodafone	2,600,000	22
TOTAL	11,500,000	100.0

In the first place, there is a difference between mobile networks and wireless broadband networks. The current mobile networks are poised to take over the telephony market from the fixed-line operators—a trend known as *substitution* (as opposed to *convergence*). As soon as serious competition exists in Australia, for example, mobile call charges will drop, and the rates will at least equal and may even drop below call charges on fixed networks. Once this happens, over 70 to 80 percent of all voice traffic will move to mobile.

The preceding trend is already evident in a dozen countries around the globe, led by Scandinavia. Value-added voice services, like call waiting, on-hold, messaging, etc., also have increased in popularity on the mobile networks in these countries. However, this is where it stops—there is no interest in full-blown mobile data.

Mobile data service has been around for well over a decade, via dedicated services from Telstra and United Wireless and paging companies such as Hutchison and Link and Short Messaging Services (SMS) on the mobile networks themselves. Every application promoted in the WAP hype is available on at least one of these services at a fraction of the cost. Yet less than 30 percent of mobile users have shown any interest in full-blown mobile data. There might be some niche markets, such as the downloading of MP3 music and some of the other teenage video-based applications in Japan, but these are not cash-rich markets. Nevertheless, a few more niche markets can be developed around WAP and GPRS, especially in the business sector, but there will never be the mass market that the industry would like us to believe in.

In a desperate move to protect their lucrative mobile profits, operators are trying to upgrade their mobile services to avoid the inevitable decrease in call charges, and they hope that by adding WAP and GPRS they will be able to do this. Since most operators still sell mobile call/handset packages, they aim to bundle WAP into such packages, charge more, and maintain their revenues and profits. Manufacturers are more than happy to fuel this by trying to sell as many WAP phones as possible to the carriers for them to bundle into these packages. The reality is that people will not be prepared to pay more for these packages, and the ploy will fail.

To Wireless Broadband   Wireless broadband is a different conceptual approach. Once the mobile phone has replaced fixed telephony, many users will find themselves in a situation where the mobile phone is the only phone in the house. And anyone who has tried to connect their laptop to the Internet via a mobile phone knows that this is not a satisfactory option.

Therefore, mobile phone technology will have to be expanded into a wireless broadband access technology. Using the new Bluetooth technology, a simple wireless connection box in the house will link a variety of appliances, such as the phone, PC, and TV, to the outside world. Developments here are concentrated around the so-called third-generation (3G) technology. While the industry is promoting this as the *Internet-on-your-mobile phone*, it is more like having a new access technology for homes and businesses. Like LMDS and other wireless broadband technologies, it will offer an alternative choice for connection to the information superhighway. This development, however, will not reach mass-market potential before the middle of the present decade, and in this respect, the future of 3G looks shaky. It is too remote, whereas other technologies, such as LMDS, GPRS/EDGE, and digital multipoint distribution service (MDS), are reaching market maturity now.

Trends and Developments in the Wireless Broadband and High-Speed Markets

The success of rural information highways depends to a large extent on the removal of obstructive regulations by the government that support such inequities as the content monopoly by Foxtel and Optus, no roaming between wireless networks, limited video services over datacasting/digital TV, and after 10 years of debate, still no decision on the opening up of the universal service orders (USOs). There is an unmet demand for high-speed Internet (860,000 users), valued at $746 million.

There will be no stopping the Internet now. With over 350 million users and more than 15 million Web sites, sufficient momentum has been gained to keep the tsunami rolling. The synergy between these two groups will see more content, more services, and new, yet to be invented business models.

Another key driver is the community Web, where people form "e-tribes" and "e-communities" to communicate, exchange ideas, perform, listen, argue, vote, and socialize around ideas, personalities, etc. Everyone can be an Internet star, replacing the current cult of Hollywood stars. Over the next decade, this content-rich highly personalized and *always-on* medium will become the preferred option, overtaking (but not replacing) the roles of the traditional media, which are mainly broad-based and impersonal, with no direct input from the users/customers.

More and more, people and businesses are becoming comfortable with the online process and are beginning to see the potential of the Internet. For example, between 30 and 35 percent of Internet users in Australia (and

TABLE 4-3

Potential Market
High-Speed
Broadband,
2001–2002

Users	Internet Subscribers	High-Speed Potential	Revenue Potential
Residential	2.8 million	460,000	$360 million
Business	600,000	500,000	$496 million
TOTAL	3.4 million	960,000	$856 million

close to 90 percent of businesses) have recognized the possibilities and are keen to gain high-speed access and thus to experience more of the Web.

Rapid growth in high-speed services (mainly cable modems and DSL) within individual homes will be driven by the increasing demand of consumers looking for faster connection speeds that will enable them to experience the burgeoning quantity of high-bandwidth entertainment and information online. At a maximum price of $40 a month for residential users and $70 per month for business users, more than $600 million would be spent by these users on high-speed services if they were available. This could easily double in the following year and double again the year after that[13] (Table 4-3).

The next development will be that once such networks become available, many of the 2 million global Internet businesses will produce new video-based content. Video-based content providers, such as the Hollywood studios, will soon see this potential and will make special arrangements for Internet-based releases. One of the major casualties here will be the traditional free-to-air broadcasting companies.

Conclusion

The year 2000 held a lot of promise. But 2001 and 2002 are when things will really heat up in the wireless broadband Internet and data market, analysts predict.

Most wireless broadband Internet service runs on a spectrum called *local multipoint distribution service* (LMDS), using an architecture called *point to multipoint*, a kind of network of data receivers and transmitters. A unique system for sending and receiving data called *time division duplexing* (TDD) also can be used—which sends twice as much data across millimeter-wave radio signals, as did its predecessor, called *frequency division duplexing* (FDD).

Analysts predict that the market for wireless broadband data services in general will heat up starting next year. The future of Internet access is very much wireless.

While wireless broadband is barely in the picture at the moment, it is apparent that the wireless sector will benefit from the Internet and data movement. To date, the key word has been *wait*, as in hurry up and wait.

Telecommunications companies have been slow to integrate wireless broadband products in their networks because of a natural hesitance that precedes adoption of new technology. Whenever you think about the early days of new, complex technologies like land-line and cell phones, they are always slow in the first couple of years because there are so many issues to be resolved. It is the gap between where the technology has obvious utility and working out all the kinks to make it commercial. It is typical of big markets (to be hesitant) because the stakes are so high and people are careful about making decisions.

Of all the broadband technologies, LMDS is expected to take 15 percent of the market in the next 3 to 5 years, analysts predict. The U.S. wireless broadband market is expected to jump from revenues of $667 million in 2000 to $2.2 billion in 2001, doubling each year to reach $24.7 billion by 2006, according to forecasts by Stamford, Connecticut–based technology research group Dataquest, a division of Gartner Group. Wireless broadband technology is clearly something a lot of people believe in now.

3G Mobile Communications

How many of you are going to walk around with your mobile phone, watching TV or accessing the Internet? If you have the choice, you would pick a device other than your mobile phone for this purpose. Furthermore, you would do it from your desk or at home, safe and relaxed in front of the TV—not walking on the footpath or sitting in the car.

This response springs from industry analysts' overall predictions on trends and developments in the voice and data services, these being voice telephony will move to wireless broadband networks (70 to 80 percent by 2002), and data will dominate the fixed network (96 percent of all traffic by 2004).

There are some great opportunities for enhanced voice services over the current cellular mobile network. However, at the same time, analysts do not think that more than 30 to 35 percent of all mobile phone users will be interested in data services such as Internet access, etc. Current technologies such as GPRS and WAP are able to satisfy at least 90 percent of this demand. Over time, analysts do see these technologies becoming seamlessly included into the digital networks. This will allow the operators and service providers to develop new applications (and charge for them).

However, an element that analysts have addressed several times previously (e.g., in relation to LMDS) but not directly in connection with 3G is wireless broadband in the local loop. This is something that analysts believe the industry has not examined sufficiently in its quest for quick media coverage based on mobile Internet applications, as described in the preceding sections. The industry does talk about the importance of the development of content applications for 3G but still treats this as being very much within the parameters of the current cellular mobile situation. If it wants to become successful, 3G will have to make the quantum leap from its current environment into the "Brave New World" of wireless broadband.

NOTE   3G in the local loop (with speeds of up to 2 Mbps) basically will be able to replace your fixed phone in the house/office with, for example, an identical looking phone—but it will be linked in a wireless way.

Manufacturers of wireless local loop [WLL (narrowband)] technologies, based on current technologies such as global system for mobile (GSM) communications and code division multiple access (CDMA), are first of all going to make sure that the transition from fixed to wireless calls, as mentioned in the preceding sections, can be done in a more appropriate way. For instance, you will need cheap cordless phones, not the current *expensive* mobile phones, and wireless calls will, of course, have to be priced at or below fixed telephone charges.

Once this WLL technology is in place, the move from voice calls to data calls over such networks is an easy next step. However, at this stage, some other technologies (such as LMDS, because of its high capacity features) are better suited than the current cellular mobile networks.

Analysts also have great expectations of GPRS and WAP as transition technologies in this respect. They are looking very promising and are available. While 3G will be able to fully address this broadband market, it is still several years away (3 to 5 years). A lot of technical issues still need to be addressed, and the spectrum allocation also has not been sorted out.

The risks for 3G, therefore, are further delays and new technologies that may creep into its window of opportunity. Threats include currently available LMDS technologies and further upgrades of the cellular networks. Another wild card is the fourth-generation (4G) wireless technologies, based on the millimeter-wave band with speeds of up to 10 Mbps—currently planned for 2009 to 2011.

Analysts see 3G as an effective and efficient way to facilitate in a seamless way the transition from narrowband WLL to broadband WLL. Analysts are also sure that if this is indeed the case, telecom engineers will build this as an overlay on top of the current wireless broadband networks, since it will save time, money, and resources for their companies. However, such a development will be nearly invisible to the end user because it will be done in an evolutionary rather than a revolutionary way.

However, in the opinion of industry analysts, the window of opportunity for 3G is 2 to 3 years. After that, 2 Mbps may no longer be sufficient for the applications that will have been developed by that time. Digital TV, LMDS, and other broadband wireless technologies might then offer a more compelling proposition.

Endnotes

1. "Broadband Wireless: Opportunities in Global Markets," Global Information, Inc., Asahi Bank Bldg., 4th floor, 1-5-1 kamiasao, Asao-ku Kawasaki 215, Japan, 2000.
2. *Ibid.*
3. *Ibid.*
4. *Ibid.*
5. "Nokia HSCSD—Take the Lead with High Speed Data," Nokia Group (Finland) Corporate Communications, Keilalahdentie 4, FIN-02150 Espoo, P. O. Box 226, Finland 00045, 2000.
6. *Ibid.*
7. Global Information, Inc., 2000.
8. *Ibid.*
9. *Ibid.*
10. *Ibid.*
11. *Ibid.*
12. "Wireless Market 2000," Paul Budde Communication Pty. Ltd., 2643 George Downes Drive, Bucketty NSW 2250 Australia, 2000.
13. *Ibid.*

CHAPTER 5

Standards for Next-Generation High-Speed Wireless Broadband Connectivity

The need for high-speed wireless broadband communication equipment has been rising constantly. New user-friendly technology such as graphics-based documents and program interfaces have strained many existing wireless infrastructures, and the emergence of real-time high-definition video transmissions is sure to strain these infrastructures further.

A new standard for broadband wireless communication also had to address these challenges. The new technology not only had to be exciting but also had to be able to meet tomorrow's needs for bandwidth. For example, the emerging standard on compressed progressive digital video (MPEG3) currently requires individual data streams of 18 Mbps. This cannot be accommodated in any commercially available broadband wireless equipment.

With the need for bandwidth in wireless communications also comes the need to address the problems of quality of transmission service, especially video signals, which are very prone to drastic reductions of quality once the bandwidth drops even if only momentarily. Once the bandwidth drops, the video frame can freeze, and the sound and the video signals may loose their synchronization.

With this in mind, telecommunications industry leaders teamed up to drive the adoption of standards for next-generation high-speed broadband wireless connectivity. World leaders in communications and technology (Bosch, Dell, Ericsson, Nokia, Telia, and Texas Instruments) have joined to form a consortium to promote the HiperLAN2 standard worldwide. Hiper-LAN2 is a technical specification that provides high-speed connectivity for next-generation mobile communications in corporate, public, and home environments.

HiperLAN2 Standard

The HiperLAN2 Global Forum is fully committed to the adaptation of Hiper-LAN2 as the global broadband wireless technology in the 5-GHz band. It has brought seamless connectivity between communication devices and networks including third-generation (3G) cellular systems and will provide mobility, flexibility, and quality of service (QoS) for future multimedia and real-time video applications.

The consortium (which represents major suppliers of wireless broadband local-area networks, terminals, and semiconductors) is working closely with the European Telecommunications Standards Institute Project BRAN (Broadband Radio Access Networks), which is continuing to develop updated versions of the standard. The consortium also supported plans that established HiperLAN2 as the global standard of choice for the wireless local-area network (LAN) industry. With completion of the standard, the telecommunications industry has seen a major shift in the development of mobile technologies. Together with the massive growth in mobile communications and the emergence of multimedia applications, completion of the HiperLAN2 standard has enabled the success of wireless LANs on a global basis.

The customers of HiperLAN2-compliant products are confident about the safety of their investment. In addition to being compatible, these products will be quick to install and have high performance. HiperLAN2 provides the means for broadband wireless technology on a scale that is comparable with the performance of wired LANs.

It is also worth noting that the 5-GHz band to be exploited by HiperLAN2-compliant products will be allocated to wireless LANs worldwide. The band will have a large capacity, which in turn makes HiperLAN2 an essential standard for wireless broadband networking. Another important advantage of HiperLAN2 is its unique features, for example, a high security level, extensive mobility support, and equipment interoperability.

Publication of the HiperLAN2 standard has just been completed. The first products supporting the standard will be available commercially in 2002, with the majority on the market early in 2003.

Now, let's look at another major and very important standard that has just been agreed on: the G3G CDMA Standard.

Global 3G (G3G) CDMA Standard

Recently, many global broadband wireless operators have been meeting to determine how the various code division multiple access (CDMA) proposals for the International Telecommunications Union's (ITU's) IMT 2000 System for third-generation (3G) wireless could be harmonized. At the first full-fledged meeting, held in Beijing, the members approved two documents, an open letter to the ITU on intellectual property rights (IPR) issues and the *Harmonized Global 3G (G3G) Specification Framework for ITU IMT-2000 CDMA Proposal*. Subsequently, the participants held three other meetings in London, Tokyo, and Toronto to discuss key parameters—chip rate, pilot structure, and synchronization method.

NOTE Third-generation (3G or IMT-2000) is the next generation of wireless technology after personal communications services (PCS). 3G is characterized by high-speed, high-bandwidth services that support a variety of applications, including wireline-quality voice and high-resolution video, wirelessly. 3G or IMT-2000 is an initiative of the International Telecommunication

Union (ITU) that seeks to integrate the various satellite, terrestrial, fixed, and mobile systems currently being deployed and developed under a single standard or family of standards to promote global service capabilities and interoperability after 2000.

As a result of these efforts, the Operators Harmonization Group (OHG) has now agreed to a harmonized G3G CDMA standard framework. This agreement represents a major achievement for the global wireless industry. The harmonized G3G CDMA standard should have a positive impact on growth of the broadband wireless industry and should serve its customers well. It is anticipated that additional operators and manufacturers will respond very shortly in support of the standard as they complete their internal assessments. See sidebar, "CDMA Development Group (CDG)," for more information.

CDMA Development Group (CDG)

The CDMA Development Group (CDG) recently released a statement applauding Japan's Ministry of Posts and Telecommunications' (MPT) recommendation to adopt all modes of the global third-generation (G3G) CDMA standard for IMT-2000 systems. The recommendation gives operators the flexibility to deploy 3G systems using either the multicarrier mode or direct-spread mode of the global 3G CDMA standard being finalized in the International Telecommunications Union (ITU). Although TDMA was an option, the MPT did not include the standard in its recommendation.

Whereas it appears that Europe has locked down on the direct-spread mode and will mandate this solution for 3G, Japan recognizes the benefits of flexibility in deployment and the value of multicarrier. Japan continues to take a leadership position in the global efforts to develop 3G standards, and the CDG encourages governments and ministries worldwide to adopt a similar policy. This decision will allow operators flexibility in deploying 3G and indicates the global interest in G3G Multicarrier (MC). Operators will be able to reap the benefits of *cdmaOne* while protecting their investments.

The *cdmaOne* standard was created with the future in mind, and *cdmaOne* operators, such as DDI and IDO, are well positioned to be the first companies in Japan to offer 3G service. With phase one of *cdma2000* now standardized, *cdmaOne* operators will be able to cost-effectively upgrade their wireless data and voice services to keep pace with Japan's rapidly growing appetite for advanced wireless services. This demand is reflected in the country's impressive *cdmaOne* subscriber figures. Within just 17 months of the country's nationwide commercial *cdmaOne* launch, DDI and IDO are already serving more than 3.3 million subscribers.

Using *cdmaOne* today, DDI Corporation and IDO Corporation have introduced Web browsing services that enable subscribers to access e-mail and more than 200 Web sites directly from a mobile handset equipped with a microbrowser. To date, 300,000 subscribers are enjoying these wireless data services as well as two-way short messaging and laptop connectivity. To augment the high-speed data available today at 14.4 kbps, DDI and IDO have announced plans to upgrade to IS-95B, allowing for 64 kbps data rates.[1]

Operators Harmonization Group (OHG) Technical Framework Document

The Operators Harmonization Group (OHG) Technical Framework document outlines the key technical parameters that can meet the requirements of commercial broadband wireless operators from around the world who desire a common global specification for 3G CDMA systems. The harmonization framework draws heavily on the wideband code division multiple access (WCDMA) and *cdma2000* submissions made to ITU for IMT-2000 and described in an earlier OHG document entitled *Harmonized Global 3G (G3G) Specification Framework for ITU IMT-2000 CDMA Proposal* (Beijing output 2).

The majority of operators and manufacturers worldwide support this goal. The technical framework proposed for achieving a common global specification seeks to provide the foundation for accelerated growth in the mobile industry in the 3G millennium and to create a single integrated 3G CDMA specification and process from the seperate WCDMA and *cdma2000* proposals being developed by 3GPP and 3GPP2.

The technical parameters contained in this chapter build on the very successful CDMA harmonization activities undertaken to date between the Telecommunications Industry Association (TIA), the Association of Radio Industries and Business (ARIB), the European Telecommunications Standards Institute (ETSI), the Telecommunications Technology Association (TTA) and the Telecommunications Technology Committee (TTC). However, the proposal contained herein is strongly focused on a solution that would meet operators' needs based on available technical information on the merits of the various techniques without regard to intellectual property rights (IPRs). The wireless broadband operators have been assured that the manufacturing community will cross-license intellectual property on fair, reasonable, and nondiscriminatory terms for the good of the wireless broadband industry. This assurance was exemplified by the recent agreement on IPR cross-licensing between Ericsson and Qualcomm.

Greatest care has been taken in selecting technical parameters that protect every operator's present infrastructure investment and enable their 2G systems to evolve toward 3G services to the greatest extent possible. It is recognized that high-speed multimedia services will place different requirements on the infrastructure that will drive the development of new capabilities in both the radio access and core network systems.

The philosophy behind the development of this OHG technical proposal is to allow each operator the choice of implementing a subset of a harmonized global specification depending on its market and business needs. This chapter specifies several key radio parameters that form the basis for a harmonized global 3G (G3G) CDMA standard.

This chapter does not address either the UWC-136 or DECT IMT-2000 RTT submissions. Their architectures are significantly different as to fall outside the scope of harmonization addressed in this chapter. Their omission should not be construed as reflecting negatively on their suitability for IMT-2000 systems.

Technical Parameters

The operators are interested in having a harmonized global 3G (G3G) CDMA standard consisting of three modes: multicarrier (MC), direct spread (DS), and time division duplex (TDD).

Global 3G CDMA Specification   A harmonized G3G specification should

1. Be focused on customer needs for widespread availability of voice and high-speed nonvoice services
2. Maximize the ability of customers to roam with their services across regions, countries, and systems
3. Minimize 3G CDMA costs for the mobile industry
4. Maximize the ability of the information technology (IT), Internet, and personal computer (PC) industries to provide mobile applications, solutions, and subscriber devices
5. Provide a smooth and compatible evolution path from existing infrastructure

6. Be completed in time to meet the commercialization plans of all countries/regions

7. Recognize that there are two well-established core network architectures

8. Minimize the IPR impact on the industry

9. Promote the free flow of IPRs to accelerate innovation and create greater customer choice

10. Accommodate regional needs for different spectrum allocations

11. Use technical approaches and parameters that meet customer requirements[2]

Global 3G (G3G) CDMA Technical Specification   The key parameters are outlined below:

- The harmonized standard for DS will be based on the W-CDMA proposal.

- The harmonized standard for MC will be based on the *cdma2000* proposal.

- The key parameters for the harmonized standard for the TDD mode have not been considered in detail with the exception of a recommendation on the chip rate.[3]

INTER-BASE STATION SYNCHRONIZATION   The inter-base station synchronization will be as follows: The W-CDMA asynchronous and synchronous approaches shall be used for the DS mode. These approaches use different codes to identify base stations. The *cdma2000* approach should be used for the multicarrier mode.

FORWARD LINK PILOT STRUCTURE   The structure for the MC mode should be as defined in *cdma2000*. The operators support the harmonized forward link pilot structure described next for the DS mode.

Common Pilots and Common Channels   Figure 5-1 presents the common channel structure.[4] The objective is to introduce a common CDM pilot in the current W-CDMA channel structure and in particular to multiplex the pilot primary common control channel (PPCCCH) and synchronization channel (SCH) streams. Consensus was reached on the following structure:

- 100 percent duty cycle common CDM pilot channel (CPICH) on one code

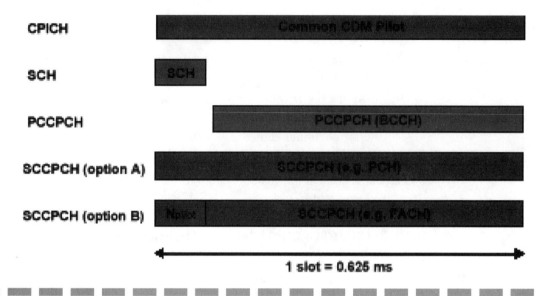

Figure 5-1   *Proposed common channel structure (position of pilot bits to be in accordance with WCDMA requirements).*

- 90 percent duty cycle PPCCCH on a separate code without TDM pilot symbols

- 10 percent duty cycle SCH codes transmitted during the PPCCCH idle period

Owing to the revised chip rate, some parameters indicated in Figure 5-1 may need to be adjusted, for example, the slot time.

Common CDM Pilot   A common CDM pilot is broadcast throughout a cell or sector on a code multiplexed channel with 100 percent duty cycle. Additional common CDM pilot channels may be broadcast, also with 100 percent duty cycle, to support scenarios where multiplexing shall also be specified as that share of an additional pilot reference. These additional common CDM pilots could be used to support transmit diversity techniques and spot beams.

SCCPCH Structure   Because of the common CDM pilot, the synchronization common CDM pilot channel (SCCPCH) requires modification. At this time, there are two cases to consider: The SCCPCH does not always require time division multiplexing (TDM) pilot bits, and the SCCPCH requires TDM pilot bits when beam-forming techniques Forward Access Channel (FACH) are employed.

Thus the recommendation is for optional insertion of TDM pilot bits, where the pilot bits (when applied) are to be used for support of beamforming techniques. Consequently, the SCCPCH would support 0 to 16 pilot bits ($N_{pilot} \in (\{0, 2, ..., 16\})$).

Dedicated Pilots In order to efficiently support low-rate-data services [8 kbps voice services, with a rate of one-third forward error correction (FEC) code and a spreading factor of 256 bits], the number of pilot bits that is to be applied to the dedicated traffic channel is still under consideration. Two proposals are under consideration: The Dedicated Channel (DCH) shall support insertion (TDM) of 0 to 16 pilot bits ($N_{pilot} \in (\{0, 2, ..., 16\})$), and the DCH shall support insertion (TDM) of 2 to 16 pilot bits ($N_{pilot} \in (\{2, 4, ..., 16\})$).

Two potential issues have been raised regarding the case of no pilot bits ($N_{pilot} = 0$). One possible issue regards the power-control algorithm design, and another regards timing. The operators supporting this standard request that 3GPP and 3GPP2 resolve this issue.

NOTE The chip rate will be 3.84 Mcps for direct spread, 3.6864 Mcps for multicarrier, and 3.84 Mcps for time division duplex for the CDMA radio-access modes.

NOTE The radio frequency (rf) parameters should be harmonized between the modes to the greatest extent possible to encourage economy of scale in rf components that could significantly reduce overall costs.

CDMA Harmonization (G3G) Proposal for Protocol Layers

The first Operators Harmonization Group (OHG) meeting agreed to the modular system block diagram shown in Figure 5-2.[5] This modular system also was supported subsequently by the Trans-Atlantic Business Dialogue (TABD) meeting held in Washington, D.C., during February 1999.

A 3G operator may select one or more radio access modules together with one or more core network modules to implement a G3G system subject to the regulatory requirements of its nation or region.

The global ITU specification for G3G must be sufficiently detailed to enable 3G operators to implement systems incorporating various harmonized radio access modes and core networks. As a consequence, it will be necessary to define the protocol layers associated with interconnecting the

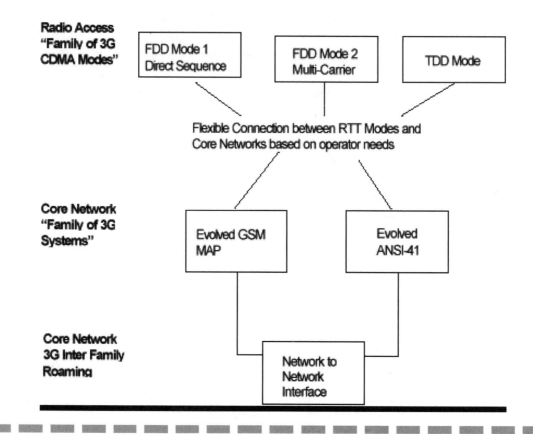

Figure 5-2   Modular 3G harmonization proposal.

radio access modes and core networks. Each community of interest will determine combination(s) in which they are interested and take on the task to specify them.

Harmonization Requirements

The requirements for harmonization are listed below.

1. ANSI 41 and GSM manufacturing replication protocol (MAP)-based services should be fully supported in the radio access network associated with all three 3G CDMA modes.

2. The harmonization should support functionality based on synchronous operation such as location calculation, etc.

3. The harmonization should support seamless handoff between the harmonized DS and MC, including IS-95 for ANSI 41 and the equivalent to this for UMTS/GSM.

4. The harmonization should minimize the complexity of dual-mode and multiband terminals and equipment.[6]

Harmonization Approach

A conceptual diagram of the harmonization required to achieve these requirements for the DS and MC modes is shown in Figure 5-3. Note that this figure includes potential changes to the physical layer L1 needed to support the requirements outlined in the preceding section. The harmonization approach shown in Figure 5-3 has the following components[7]:

- For the DS mode the baseline starting point for supporting both core networks is
    - L1 as per section 2.
    - W-CDMA L2.
    - W-CDMA L3 radio resource control (RRC).
- For the MC mode, the baseline starting point for supporting both core networks is

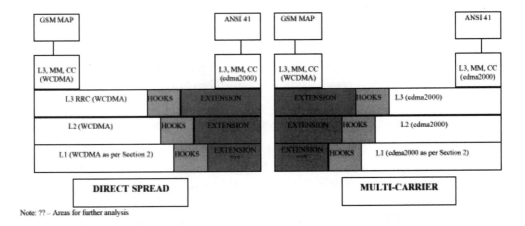

Figure 5-3 Protocol structure for implementing the modular concept.

- ▪ L1 as per section 2.
- ▪ *cdma2000* L2.
- ▪ *cdma2000* L3 radio resource control (RRC).

- ▪ For the TDD mode, the baseline starting point for supporting both core networks is
  - ▪ TDD mode L2 as per 3GPP.
  - ▪ TDD L3 radio resource control (RRC) as per 3GPP.

- ▪ The concept of *hooks* as shown in Figure 5-3 is defined as any functionality that is specified for the initial release of the standards so that the extensions needed to satisfy the requirements in the preceding section can be defined in detail.

- ▪ The concept of *extensions* as shown in Figure 5-3 is defined as any additional functionality at any layer that needs to be specified in detail to meet the preceding requirements, assuming the appropriate hooks are in place to enable the extensions to be defined without major changes to the baseline protocols.[8]

Phased Approach

Given the events to date and the current commercialization time schedule, it is not possible to completely harmonize all aspects of the upper layers for a unified global specification. Protocol layer 2 and 3 for direct spread, multicarrier, and TDD will be developed in two phases outlined below (including any consequential impacts on the physical layers). The timing of phases 1 and 2 may be different for a particular mode depending on market requirements

- ▪ *Phase 1* The baseline parameters in all three radio layers, including the hooks, as defined in the preceding, will be completed to meet the release 2001 timeframes of 3GPP and 3GPP2.

- ▪ *Phase 2* Completion of all the detailed specification of all the extensions to phase 1 is necessary to fully support ANSI 41 and GSM core networks.

A more detailed view of the protocol architecture for the DS mode connected to an ANSI 41 network based on the principles of Figure 5-3 is shown in Figure 5-4.[9]

A 3G operator may select combinations of the preceding protocol stacks subject to the requirements of its nation or region. The global specification for G3G must be sufficiently detailed to enable operators to flexibly choose between the various harmonized radio access and core networks.

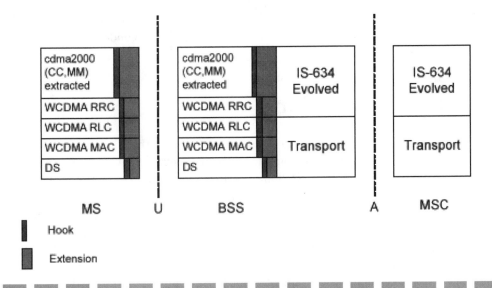

Figure 5-4 Detail of direct spread protocol stack.

ITU and Standards Developing Organizations (SDOs) are advised that maximum commonality is required between these protocols. The mobile terminal will have the ability to determine the network environment it is accessing or operating in.

Guidelines and Principles

In developing the harmonized global 3G CDMA standard, the following principles and guidelines must be followed:

- 3GPP and 3GPP2 shall maintain their 1999 release schedules.
- The hooks required to implement the harmonized CDMA standard must be identified as soon as possible to allow prioritization of work for inclusion in release 2001 and to ensure that completion of the work in phase 2 is facilitated.
- The objective is for all hooks to be specified by the end of 2001.
- All hooks specified by the end of 2001 should be included in release 2001.
- Changes to L1 should be minimized.
- Changes to the core networks (see Figure 5-4) should be minimized.

- The location of each change should be based on engineering judgment on a case-by-case basis taking into consideration the full set of guidelines.[10]

Conclusion

The objective of the process is to ensure that the OHG harmonization agreement can be implemented in a timely manner. OHG requests that layers 1 to 3 experts within 3GPP and 3GPP2 jointly determine the hooks in the 2001 release of the 3GPP specifications needed for the extensions to meet the service requirements specified in the OHG technical framework document. A similar process should be carried out for multicarrier. It also will help the valuable human resources of 3GPP and 3GPP2 to work together to achieve a common goal as opposed to working on two separate directions.

OHG further requests that there should be minimal delay in achieving this goal. To support these efforts, the OHG and the manufacturers are willing to host extra 3G standard meetings and provide the necessary resources. Progress reports should be given to OHG after every 3GPP/ 3GPP2 meeting.

OHG has carried out its primary mission and therefore does not see a need for further meetings at this time. However, operators want to ensure that their recommendations are implemented in 3GPP and 3GPP2 in a timely fashion.

The OHG and MHG (Manufacturers Harmonization Group) Ad Hoc plan to form transition teams to support this standard and navigate it through the standard bodies. OHG also feels that for complete harmonization, 3GPP and 3GPP2 should consider merging into a single body no later than December 2001. This merger will provide focus in developing a unified core network for the future as well as ensuring that air interfaces and the associated protocol layers in the future will be completely harmonized. To achieve this goal, the OHG will assist in the merger process. OHG is willing to sponsor a meeting between the two 3GPP leadership groups to facilitate the merger discussions.

Endnotes

1. "CDMA Development Group Applauds Japan's Recommendation for 3G Wireless," CDMA Development Group, 575 Anton Blvd., Ste. 560, Costa Mesa, CA 92626, 2000.

2 "Harmonized Global 3G (G3G) Technical Framework for ITU IMT-2000 CDMA Proposal," 3rd Generation Partnership Project 2, 2000.

3. *Ibid.*

4. *Ibid.*

5. *Ibid.*

6. *Ibid.*

7. *Ibid.*

8. *Ibid.*

9. *Ibid.*

10. *Ibid.*

PART **2**

Planning and Designing Wireless Broadband Networks Applications

CHAPTER 6

Planning and Designing Wireless Broadband and Satellite Applications

Applications for wireless broadband and satellite-based communications can be found in both the enterprise and consumer markets. Wireless broadband and satellite planning and designing solutions apply mostly where wireline solutions are not available either at the present time or for the foreseeable future.

Data Applications

Data applications are key to the business cases of almost all the new technologies, systems, and services discussed in this chapter. In many cases, voice and video are secondary considerations.

NOTE Traditional data applications are key to the business case, but video can become data, as can voice, in that video and voice applications can be key to mission-critical business applications.

For the time being, the satellite industry is responding to the changing applications needs of customers both by offering somewhat higher speeds on traditional products and by diversifying the markets it serves. The first of these strategies has been exemplified by the very small aperture terminal (VSAT) business, with VSATs gradually growing from a system that could support data rates in the tens of kilobits per second to one that can support data rates at T1/E1 and above. In addition, the continued viability of the current business satellite sector seems assured by its increasingly proven ability to support popular protocols including Asyncronous Transfer Mode (ATM), Frame Relay, and especially Internet Protocol (IP).

Some of the wireless broadband satellite planning and designing schemes appear to be predicated on the notion that they can steal very-high-bandwidth access and backbone implementations from fiber solutions. In fact, the history of the satellite industry has been that in a given era its spacecraft may be able to support the broadest of wireless broadband applications, but only until a wireline solution has caught up.

One of the biggest self-proclaimed advantages of wireless broadband is its ability to offer an attractive price/performance point to other last-mile access alternatives, that is, a fat communications pipe to businesses or homes at a much lower price than a wireline equivalent. In other words, wireless broadband access for data will be most attractive and successful in grabbing the attention of small and medium-sized businesses with T1, fractional T1, and/or Frame Relay–based data access requirements.

In addition, the time-to-market issue is of some importance. Because wireless broadband planning and designing are a local solution, there will be many areas (especially outside the United States) where wireless may be the first wireless broadband physical layer communications architecture to appear. In some cases, it may be the only such infrastructure to appear for quite a while.

NOTE Because of the favorable economics of wireless, it may be the only solution to ever appear in some geographic locations.

Voice Applications

The voice market is huge, and despite its apparent maturity, it continues to grow at a moderate rate each year. Voice has grown at more than a moderate rate when you look at minutes consumed versus dollars paid for those minutes—the minutes have soared while the dollars of revenue have grown modestly. This means that even for wireless broadband and satellite ventures that are more data-oriented, there could be many voice-oriented opportunities.

At least some of the wireless broadband satellite ventures are intended to provide multipurpose wide-area network (WAN) backbone facilities that would certainly include voice in the traffic they carry. Two applications areas where wireless broadband satellite capacity may make a difference in a voice environment are on enhanced submarine cable backup and on providing connectivity for remote call center facilities. Another voice application of wireless broadband (and perhaps even satellite networks) is cellular backhaul and other voice traffic backhaul needed for carrier networks. This has been mentioned consistently by local multipoint distribution service (LMDS) service providers as a *killer application* for their wireless broadband networks. However, although voice applications offer opportunities for wireless broadband service providers, few such service providers will offer voice alone.

Video Applications

Video is the definitive wireless broadband application—even the term *broadband* has a video-oriented history. It was used originally to describe cable television technology. However, most high-quality video transmissions to date have been analog. This is true particularly in the television sector, but corporate news and training wireless broadband networks also have frequently used analog feeds. Until quite recently, digital video meant low-quality video. However, it now seems certain that even the television sector will move toward a digital format.

Satellites play a key role in the television industry, where they are and will remain the primary means of distributing video to cable television headends and television stations. The big change here is that the mode in which such distribution occurs will shift from analog to digital. There has been some discussion in the trade press and in the technical literature of replacing satellites with fiberoptics for this application. However, in practice, this has not occurred, nor does there seem any likelihood of its doing so.

Where fiber is taking some business away from cable is in the area of video backhaul of production-quality video among studios and between major permanent news locations (stadiums, convention centers, etc.) and studios. The other important role for satellites in the television industry is for the distribution of entertainment video directly to homes. This area has received new respectability as a result of the emergence of direct broadcasting services, such as DirecTV.

Satellites can be expected to continue to account for a major part of the high-quality video business for the foreseeable future. The situation is somewhat different for video in the enterprise, although broadband satellites may have a direct role to play in the training and news-distribution applications within the enterprise. Video also may play a large role in interorganizational communications such as supply-chain applications and extranets.

As with satellites, wireless broadband has played an important traditional role in the television industry. Broadband analog wireless has been used for newsgathering, video backhaul, and even distribution to homes (*wireless cable*), and in all these cases, wireless broadband is making the transition from analog to digital.

Need for Perspective Planning and Design for Wireless Broadband Applications

Wireless broadband is now accepted as a basic infrastructure along with power and transportation for growth of global economies. Wireless broadband is also recognized as the means for accelerating the distribution of the fruits of economic growth to all countries, including remote and inaccessible areas in the world. Wireless broadband applications in the modern world are expected to usher in a concept of global economy and a single world marketplace. Thus wireless broadband applications have become part of the modern global wireless broadband network—providing access to anyone in the world for transporting information in the form of voice, data, or video anywhere.

Studies conducted on an international basis show a definite correlation between economic growth and the availability of wireless broadband facilities. Wireless broadband applications are also an eco-friendly means of meeting the communications needs of the people. They cut down travel cost and save natural resources such as fuel and forests (paper). It is in this context that during this decade wireless broadband applications have been recognized by the governments of almost all countries as a thrust area in their development plans and design.

Now let's look at a blueprint of what an efficient wireless broadband network application should look like.

Blueprint of an Efficient Wireless Broadband Network Application

If you are planning and designing a global wireless broadband network application, it should include the following:

- *Adequate availability.* This implies extensive distribution of wireless broadband network nodes from which subscribers could be provided telephone and data communications facilities as far as possible on demand.
- *Good accessibility.* Since it is not possible for everyone to have a personal telephone, there should be an extensive network of public pay phones (both rural and urban) from which occasional users of telephones or those who are traveling and are away from their own telephones could have access to both voice and nonvoice services.
- *Adequate connectivity.* A worldwide wireless broadband network of trunk switching centers suitably interconnected by transmission media capable of handling the anticipated level of traffic.
- *Business wireless broadband network.* A modern digital wireless broadband network capable of providing telematic/multimedia services, for example, mobile telephone service, radio paging, and value-added services required by business and industry.
- *Messaging facilities.* A network of telegraph and bureaufax offices from which the public could transmit its urgent messages and which could be delivered by messengers anywhere in the world.[1]

Need for Perspective Plan and Design

A perspective plan and design for the development of a wireless broadband network application are essential to establish necessary production facilities in a country. It is also essential to plan and execute time-consuming project elements such as land acquisition and construction of buildings well in advance in accordance with a well-laid plan and design and within the financial resources that are available. Wireless broadband technology has been undergoing change at a tremendous pace. In early eighties, satellite and microwave technologies were considered the most cost-effective means of providing modern communication facilities. In midnineties, fiberoptics were all the rage. Similarly, the digital switches with narrowband ISDN capabilities have now come into the wireless broadband network, and in the near future, broadband Integrated Services Digital Network (ISDN) facilities with compatible switches are likely to be introduced. In view of this fast-changing scenario, even a 10-year period appears to be quite difficult to attempt realistic detailed planning and design.

Objectives of a Perspective Plan and Design

Consolidation of the wireless broadband network and maintaining a high quality of service comparable with international standards are the key aims of planning and design. Other objectives of the perspective plan and design are as follows:

- The telephone connection should be provided on demand.
- ISDN services to be extended throughout the country to meet the demand of all value-added services.
- The wireless broadband network should be fully digital. All the electromechanical exchanges and life-expired analog exchanges will be replaced with digital exchanges.
- Digital transmission links should be provided up to all single device channel adapters (SDCAs).
- Digital connectivity should be provided to most of the exchanges by 2008.
- Extensive use should be made of optical fiber in the local, junction, and long-distance wireless broadband network.
- Life-expired analog coaxial and radio systems should be replaced.

- Broadband wireless technology and optical fiber technology should be introduced gradually in the subscriber loop.
- The latest telecommunications service computerization, etc. should be introduced.[2]

Demand Forecast

Demand for telephone depends on various parameters, such as the economic growth of the country, tariffs, etc. Based on the present trend of global telephone wireless broadband network growth over the period from 1993 to 2000, the average growth rate is 27.6 percent. At this growth rate, to meet the objectives of providing telephone on demand, there will need to be additional demand during the period of 2000 to 2010. As the basic services are being opened to the private sector, it is assumed that additional demand will be met by the private sector. Based on this assumption, the department of telecommunications will have to provide direct exchange lines during 2000 to 2010 to keep providing telephone on demand.

Presently, the average global telephone density is about 2.6 telephones per hundred population. Assuming that a country's present gross domestic product (GDP) growth will continue to be maintained, as well as the population growth rate, the average global telephone density will reach around 4 per hundred in 2001 and 10 per hundred in 2008. In global rural areas, it may cross the 2 per hundred population mark by the year 2008.

Correlation Between Actual and Projected Demand

The global telecommunications demand projection should be based on the trend where time plays a proxy for variables like increases in population, increases in the economic and industrial activity, etc. This method has been observed over the last few years to give quite accurate projections for a time frame of 2 to 5 years. Presently, a perspective plan should deal with a longer time frame of 10 years. It is expected that some deviations in telephone demand projections may accrue toward the end of a perspective plan's time frame (2005–2007, etc.). This is evident from an analysis of actual global demand and projected demand for the last 10 years.

New Services and Technologies

During the 2001 to 2005 time frame, hybrid switches with the capability of supporting both narrowband and wireless broadband services (STM and ATM switch block) are likely to be available. These switches will provide both narrowband and wireless broadband termination capability. With the advantages offered by synchronous digital hierarchy (SDH) technology in terms of larger capacity, higher reliability provided by self-healing rings, and efficient performance monitoring and measurement, SDH technology should be used in your wireless broadband network. Systems of up to STM-16 (capacity of 30,000 channels), will be introduced in the wireless broadband network toward the 2001 time frame, and STM 64 (capacity 120,000 channels) will be introduced by the 2006 time frame.

The use of optical fiber and optical repeating is likely to become more popular in the next decade. As a policy objective, fiber to the home (FTTH) can be projected to all subscribers in countries with a medium-sized population by 2008.

The customer premises equipment will be fully liberalized by then. The emphasis will be more on providing a wireless broadband network interface terminal at subscriber premises and leave the subscriber free to connect his or her own standard communication equipment.

Value-Added Services

The following global value-added services are likely to be introduced during the plan and design period:

- Intelligent wireless broadband network
- Global mobile satellite services
- ISDN
- Value-added services in rural areas
- Personal communications services
- Payphone services
- Home banking/telebanking
- Automatic teller machine (ATM)
- Internet
- Global information infrastructure
- Telemedicine

Intelligent Wireless Broadband Network Intelligent wireless broadband networks (IWBN) is a global platform to create various services for subscribers by using a computer database, called the *service control point* (SCP). This obviates the need to modify the software of each and every switching node in the network. IWBN is widely recognized as a network concept for easy creation, operation, and management of new services.

For implementing IWBN services, some additions in Common Channel Signaling 7 (CCS7) are necessary. These are mainly in the form of software modifications in new technology exchanges.

NOTE With the increasing demand for advanced IWBN services, CCS7 messaging capabilities for both wireline and wireless broadband networks become critical. Seeking greater control of this vital signaling function, service providers are looking for a cost-effective, reliable signal transfer point (STP) that can grow in both capacity and function as their networks expand.

Furthermore, computer databases will be required at a few places. The requirement of databases for providing intelligent network (IN) services is also being worked out globally. Certain IN services have been identified based on customer needs. The following global IWBN services would be introduced in a phased manner.

FREE PHONE SERVICE Free phone service permits subscribers to make free calls to companies' trading houses. Payment for these calls is made by the companies because this helps them to advertize and sell their products.

ACCOUNT CARD CALLING Account card calling is yet another useful service where the caller can make calls using a personal account number. These calls are not charged to the telephone from which the call is made, but the charge is debited from the caller's account number.

PREMIUM-RATE INFORMATION SERVICES Premium-rate information services enable customers to obtain a variety of information by dialing specific telephone numbers. The information is provided by service providers who may specialize in specific areas. Examples are stock market trading information, marketing information, sports, etc.

VIRTUAL PRIVATE NETWORKS (VPNS) VPNs are private networks that are built using public network resources. A virtual private automatic branch exchange (PABX) is created using different switches. A private numbering plan (PNP) can be incorporated on those numbers. Facilities such as call transfer, call hold, dialed restrictions, and other supplementary services can be provided within the wireless broadband network. Each line or user is assigned a class of service and specific rights in the wireless broadband network. To access the VPN from the outside, a VPN user is required to dial a password. A screening feature can be used to put restrictions on outgoing and incoming calls. Call charges are assigned to a VPN service subscriber. Additional account codes are assigned to service subscribers to analyze the cost linewise.

UNIVERSAL ACCESS NUMBER (UAN)   A UAN is a national number that can be published by a subscriber. The subscriber may specify the incoming calls to be routed to a number of different destinations based on geographic locations.

OTHER IN SERVICES   Apart from the preceding five services, which are likely to be available globally shortly, the following services also can be offered using the IN platform:

1. Automatic alternative billing (AAB)
2. Call distribution (CD)
3. Called rerouting distribution (CRD)
4. Completion of calls to a busy subscriber
5. Conference calling (CON)
   - *CON-Add-on.* Conference calling
   - *CON-Meet-me.* Conference calling meet me
6. Credit card calling (CCC)
7. Destination call routing (DCR)
8. Follow me diversion (FMD)
9. Mass calling (MAS)
10. Split charging (SPL)
11. Televoting (VOT)
12. Universal personal telecommunications (UPT)
13. User-defined routing (UDR)[3]

Global Mobile Satellite Services   Mobile satellite technology is aimed at the introduction of a range of affordable, portable, and convenient global personal mobile satellite communication services. Compared with cellular systems, the cost will be considerably more in terms of equipment and usage, and the systems will not offer equal penetration inside buildings. They provide a line-of-sight voice to and from hand-held terminals on or above the surface of the Earth. Within buildings, voice service may be possible close to windows.

The primary use of this technology (taking into account the various characteristics of satellite hand-held phones), is for the international business traveler, national roamer, and cellular extensions to cover geographic areas outside cellular coverage. In addition to this, applications with regard to maritime, aeronautical, and transport businesses are also expected. World over, various operators have three major options for selection of the satellite orbit:

- *Geostationary Earth orbiting (GEO).* Satellite system orbiting at 36,000 km above the Earth's surface.
- *Medium-Earth orbiting (MEO).* Satellite system of between 9 and 15 spacecrafts orbiting at about 10,000 km.
- *Low-Earth orbiting (LEO).* Satellite system comprising around 50 to 60 satellite systems at about 1000 km above the surface of the Earth.

At present, the following mobile systems are expected to be available during the same time frame:

- lnmarsat-P
- Global Star
- Odyssey
- Teledesic[4]

ISDN The ISDN is a network that has evolved from the telephony integrated digital network. It provides end-to-end digital connectivity to support a wide range of services, including voice and nonvoice services, to which the users have access by a limited set of standard multipurpose customer interfaces.

The services of ISDN are classified in three categories, namely, bearer services, supplementary services, and teleservices. A *bearer service* is a simple information carriage service. It specifies the bandwidth with mode of switching such as 64-kbps, 8-KHz structured speech or 64-kpbs packet, etc. *Teleservices* are basic telecommunication services such as telephony, fax, data, etc. The supplementary services are provided in conjunction with one of the bearer services/teleservices.

Examples of *supplementary services* include call diversion, calling line identification, call completion when free, call waiting, call forwarding on busy, call forwarding on no reply, user-to-user signaling, sending of short messages within a call or even during call setup and advice of charge, etc.

Some of the sophisticated and powerful services that can be used by ISDN subscribers include the following:

- ISDN subscribers can establish two simultaneous independent calls.
- G-4 fax can be connected.
- Up to 8 terminals can be connected in parallel, with a separate number allotted to each terminal to ensure easy access.
- A PC add-on ISDN card can be used for data transfer at 64 kbps. One can transmit the complete information on a 4-MB floppy disk in just 4 minutes.
- Video conferencing is possible among ISDN subscribers.
- Video phones can be installed, where images and speech can be transmitted at 128 kbps.
- Services such as video conferencing can be used for teleeducation and telemedicine.[5]

Value-Added Services in Rural Areas with Special Reference to Telemedicine, Health Information Services, and Teleeducation Telemedicine service involves sending of medical images such as x-rays and computed tomographic scans, etc. This allows specialists in different locations to compare and confer over the basic diagnostic information. The service will cater to the health care sector by use of databases, teleradiology (transmission of x-ray images or CT brain scans via telephone wireless broadband network), and electronic data interchange.

DISTANCE EDUCATION SERVICES Information technology (IT) may provide an aid for education. The benefits of IT can be achieved from off-line systems by making information available on a CD without requiring upgraded communications links. High-capacity communications links could be considered for open-access learning and virtual universities offering interactive or responsive education anywhere at any time.

Personal Communications Services Personal communications service (PCS) is an emerging concept in the area of telecommunications. PCS has been conceived as a superset of fixed and mobile network services with wide access and coverage—using hand-held portables with an access number independent of terminals or geographic locations. The PCS concept is to provide the communication anywhere, any time, to anyone in any form—where the origination, termination, and associated features of the calls are controlled by the subscribers. It has an end-user value like universal services, transparent movability, and low-cost and user-friendly interfaces. It is envisioned that services such as telepoint, cordless technologies, and cellular mobile will merge with the PCS using digital wireless access technology. Most of the functions will be determined by the wireless broadband network, such as where to reach and in what form to the subscribers.

PCS will offer users the ability to configure telecommunications services in a manner that best meets their individual needs at any time in any location. It will provide transparency of service, regardless of location and time across multiple wireless broadband networks, and be available to the user at any access point. PCS will permit the user to take advantage of the ever-increasing set of services that modern communications technology can provide.

Payphone Services   Payphones allow access to a telephone. Existing public coinbox payphones pose a lot of problems to customers. Customers are inconvenienced by the need to search for the right coin, while operators are faced with the cost of collecting and counting large amounts of coinage. To overcome these problems and provide satisfactory service to customers, the present trend is to move toward cashless payment through cards.

Various types of cards are available, and they are listed below. In each case, the tradeoffs among cost, convenience, security, and other features can be met by more than one technology.

- Magnetic cards
- Optical cards
- Chips cards: memory chip cards/"smart" cards
- Contactless cards[6]

The present trend is the disposable-chip card—which in the near future may move on to processor-based "smart" cards supporting multiple applications. The chip-card-based payphones can be managed centrally by a multilevel payphone management system at local, regional, and national levels.

For payphones, another strong contender is the credit card. Payphones that support chip cards and credit cards are available in the market. In mobile environments, payphones compatible with GSM systems, offering fixed telephone service, are another area of interest.

NOTE   One clear advantage of wireless to payphones is that it is easier to install a wireless payphone because you do not have to run wire (obviously), but the installation of payphones could drop considerably if they were wireless.

Home Banking/Telebanking   This service is offered by financial institutions to allow private customers to make transaction or arrangements over the telephone or via computer or videotext. Many of the normal banking transactions are possible, including transferring funds between accounts, bill payments, requesting up-to-date statements, and other general inquiries.

Automatic Teller Machines (ATMs)   This service provides for withdrawal of money from bank accounts through teller machines as well as account statements. These machines are located at convenient places and are connected to a host computer at a bank through a wireless broadband data network, leased line, or dial-up modem. In other words, wireless ATMs are pretty popular in rural areas at this point.

Internet   The Internet is a worldwide network of computer networks. It is a conglomeration of smaller computer networks and other connected machines spanning the entire globe. Around the world, each country has at least one backbone wireless broadband network that operates at very high speed and carries the bulk of traffic. Other smaller wireless broadband networks connect to that backbone. The Internet, once available to the government and academic and research communities, is today increasingly being commercialized.

Global Information Infrastructure   The convergence of telecommunications and computer technologies in the early 1980s has had a profound impact on telecommunications networks. The predominantly analog network of the 1970s started to evolve toward an all digital wireless broadband network of the 1980s.

The present decade is witnessing the evolution of the integrated digital network (IDN) toward the narrowband integrated services digital network (ISDN). As a result of the accelerated developments taking place in core technologies such as microelectronics, software, wireless broadband, and optical, a large number of wireless broadband network technologies such as synchronous digital hierarchy (SDH), asynchronous transfer mode (ATM), broadband integrated services digital network (B-ISDN), personal communication network (PCN), virtual private network (VPN), intelligent network (IN), telecommunciations management network (TMN), and multimedia are now ready for introduction in public wireless broadband networks.

With these wireless broadband network technologies, network administrations/operators are creating new information highways for high-speed electronic data exchange, mobile telephones, satellite television, and video-on-demand (VOD). These are just a few examples of the types of applications customers desire from the emerging technologies. Videoconferencing can provide an alternative to long-distance travel by saving time, energy, and cost. ISDN will provide very interesting applications such as telemarketing, teleworking, teleeducation, and telemedicine. The applications of ISDN are expected to have a profound impact on the quality of life of individuals. The telecommunication technologies are now poised to provide information highways.

The information highways will provide the means of exchanging vast quantities of information globally. Countries thus will make a transition from the industrial to the information society on a global scale. This globalization of the information society and management of the transition to this society constitute two of the most important tasks to be undertaken by the telecommunications sector of the last decade of the twentieth century. The evolving information society will have a fundamental impact on the way people interact.

Communications between individuals will involve a multiplicity of media mixes ranging from conventional telephony to the most interactive multimedia. The technological complexity of the information telecommunications wireless broadband networks will be immense. Whereas interactive multimedia services and applications appear to be the most visible component of the information society in the short run, in the very near future, entertainment and broadcasting also will be provided through information superhighways. Thus convergence of telecommunications and information technology is poised to bring greater social and economic development.

A number of new value-added services are likely to become available with the availability of low Earth-orbiting (LEO) satellite networks. These services are called personal communication services (PCS) and geographically independent numbering schemes (GINS).

Service Parameters

Fault rate on the telephone wireless broadband network should be brought to a level of around 1 fault per 100 telephones per month in line with the international level. Also, the call-completion rate should be around 70 percent in live-traffic conditions. Finally, staff standards should be revised and modified to take into account the reliability of the technology employed, and efforts will be made to improve the productivity. Emphasis should be placed on retraining and skill upgradation of available staff rather than attempting to retrench them.

Now, let's look at the connectivity/transmission factor when planning and designing wireless broadband and satellite applications.

The Connectivity/Transmission Factor

Diverse characteristics of the service areas where the connectivity is to be provided pose a complex problem. In suburban and urban areas, wireless broadband networks of densities between a thousand or several thousands of lines per 2 km have to be built that are characterized by the following factors:

- Short to medium distances between local exchanges and subscribers
- Inadequate existing infrastructure
- Difficulties in carrying out civil works
- Difficult terrain
- Time pressure due to high demand and the competitive environment
- Disaster and emergency needs[7]

In contrast to the preceding, a *rural area* can be defined loosely as an area comprising scattered groups of potential users. Of course, this also would include areas where there would be an immediate requirement to provide only one telephone initially in a cost-effective manner via public telephones in remote and isolated villages. The service providers are faced with most of the following difficulties that make the use of traditional systems time-consuming and, most important, expensive:

- Lack of reliable infrastructure
- Low economic activity and consequently poor returns expected on investment
- Lack of availability of reliable electric power supply
- Tough climatic and topographic conditions
- Long distances between local exchanges facilities and potential customers
- Clusters of subscribers separated by long distances

Requirements

Broadly, the requirements for planning and designing wireless broadband and satellite applications can be categorized as follows: trunk and junction traffic and local-access wireless broadband network including personal communication services (PCS).

One of the major needs of a public telecommunications operator is the ability to extend its service rapidly and economically to new geographic areas. Requirements for local-area wireless broadband networks, video-conferencing, video services, and high-speed data links between computers are spurring the rapid increase for trunk traffic. While the capability for wireless broadband in trunk and junction networks is no longer a major technological issue, its extension to local access poses an extremely challenging task.

Cable

When planning and designing wireless broadband and satellite applications, a brief overview of cable technology trends is in order so as to put everything into perspective:

- Digital subscriber line (DSL) and versatile multiplexer (VMUX) technologies
- Optical fiber amplifier
- Passive optical network (PON)
- Synchronous digital hierarchy (SDH) technology

Digital Subscriber Line (DSL) and Versatile Multiplexer (VMUX) Technologies   High-bit-rate digital subscriber line (HDSL) provides a 2-Mbps symmetrical stream over two or three pairs of coppers and covers a distance of 4 to 4.5 km on the existing copper plant. It offers a variety of services via voice interface, ISDN interface, payphone interface, 64-kbps data interface, and $n*64$ kbps data service for videoconferencing. The future trend is likely to be a single pair working. The equipment will provide excellent service in the wireless broadband access network for ordinary as well as premier customers. The products in the point-to-multipoint configuration may be used in the rural wireless broadband network as well. The application of this technology for junction working between two exchanges is also possible, thereby eliminating pulse code modulation (PCM) regenerators. This application also can be deployed for providing services to the customers in configuration of either 10 subscribers per pair or 15 subscribers per pair of copper.

Asymmetric digital subscriber line (ADSL) technology offers asymmetric services [it offers different bandwidths from exchange to subscriber (downstream) and from subscriber to exchange (upstream)]. The downstream bandwidth can be up to 8 Mbps and upstream to 640 kbps over a similar pair of copper. It also covers a distance of 3.5 km approximately, and it also carries one conventional voice channel besides the asymmetrical services. It can cater to video services or high-speed data. Worldwide trials of this technology are going on, and international standards are in the final stages of preparation.

A further enhancement to the DSL technology is a variable-bit-rate digital subscriber line—wherein there is a flexibility of bandwidth via the distance to be covered. The higher the bandwidth, the shorter is the distance, and vice versa.

Optical Fiber Amplifier   To increase the optical budget, optical fiber amplifiers (OFAs) can be used in optical-line systems. Optical amplifiers (erbium-doped fiber amplifier) have now been developed and are available commercially. OFAs with a nominal gain of 30 dB have been designed to work at 1550-nm wavelength. Amplification of signals at 1310-nm wavelength is also possible by using neodymium-doped optical fiber amplifiers, but the gain is limited to 10 dB nominal. Optical amplifiers are classified into the following categories:

- *Preamplifier.* The preamplifier is a very-low-noise optical device for use directly before an optical receiver to improve its sensitivity.

- *Booster amplifier (power amplifier).* The booster amplifier is a high-saturation-power OFA device to be used directly after the optical transmitter to increase its signal power level.

- *Line amplifier.* The line amplifier is a low noise OFA device to be used between a passive fiber section to increase the regenerator spacing. The target spacings between the in-line optical amplifier are nominally 80 and 120 km, with total target distances before requiring regeneration of nominally 360 and 600 km on ITU-T G.652 and G.653 type of fibers.[8]

An unrepeatered 263-km-long submarine link using an optical amplifier and a dispersion-shifted fiber has been achieved, and the 565-Mbps link is working successfully. This field trial was conducted in Italy in 1991. However, the technology is being introduced by other advanced countries in submarine and terrestrial links to avoid the regenerators and increase the repeater spacing.

Passive Optical Network (PON)   Passive optical network systems may be deployed up to the subscriber premises of fiber to the home (FTTH). The inherent wireless broadband capability and very high reliability of optical fiber allow network operators to combine existing narrowband services with future broadband services on a single wireless broadband access network using optical fibers as transmission media. The PON system should be capable of handling the following type of services:

- Plain old telephone service (POTS)
- Distributed telephony
- ISDN
- 64-kbps data
- Cable TV
- Video-on-demand
- LAN interconnection
- Videoconferencing[9]

In the wireless broadband access network, distances are short, and the requirements of present-day subscribers are high. The passive optical network is basically an optical splitter. The optical fiber is split in 16 or 32 ways. This increases the capacity of a single fiber for distribution of signals in many directions. It is very useful for point-to-multipoint information transport to a remote site. The subscribers located in remotely scattered sites can be served easily for all types of services.

The optical power is split at a node in different directions by an optical power splitter. The PON system may use single-fiber or two-fiber lines depending on the electronics used.

This technology is being implemented in a number of countries worldwide. It is also being evaluated by a few wireless network administrators in attempts to find solutions to meet wideband requirements. Germany, the United Kingdom, and Japan are introducing this technology in their wireless broadband networks to increase the capacity of local loops and to provide broadband services.

Through the use of this technology, there will be tremendous increases in servicing the lines from main telephone exchanges to remote subscribers. The remotely located subscribers will enjoy the full facility of wireless broadband services. Such remote subscribers can be connected to a main telephone exchange, since subscribers up to 20 km away can be served easily. Service provisioning can be simplified, and changes to meet demands can be made from a remote center without actual physical intervention. In addition, the transmission capacity of optical fiber can be shared by many subscribers. Demand for new wideband/wireless broadband services can be met, thus generating revenue without risk.

Synchronous Digital Hierarchy (SDH) Technology   The demand for very large bandwidth on the trunk routes, as well as in the long-distance wireless broadband network of metropolitan districts, has made the introduction of SDH technology an imperative need. With the proliferation of the wireless broadband network increasing at a rapid pace, system manageability through network management has become the accepted trend. The protection features support a high degree of reliability in fault restoration processes. Developments in the 1550-nm window of the optical fiber band, with respect to wavelength division multiplexing (WDM) systems, along with advancements in optical amplifiers, soon will make it possible to have enormously large communication superhighways within the existing optical fiber cable system. Wideband digital cross-connects (4/4 and 4/1 DXCs) provide the much-required flexibility at nodal intersections where several rings meet. With all these new SDH technologies, the quality of end-to-end user signals has improved so fast that bit-error-ratio (BER) figures of 10 to 11 have become possible.

Radio

Radio can be used to complement fiber in the wireless broadband network over adverse terrains, for spur routes, and where fast deployment or lower initial cost is required. Over adverse terrain, radio construction costs (using existing tower structures and feeders) can be substantially lower than the costs of aerial or buried fiber. *Adverse terrain* includes geographically difficult routes as well as routes with costly or unavailable rights of way. Since vast areas of the world are either sparsely populated or difficult to provision, radio in this environment becomes the economic vehicle of choice. Radio can be used to build hugely reliable spur and feeder routes—improving overall wireless broadband network availability and reducing overall costs.

The world of wireless broadband telecommunications is clearly diverse, with dozens of types of operational services now being offered and many more yet to be developed. Despite this diversity, the entire field of wireless broadband telecommunications can still be described as having the following characteristics:

- Frequency-demanding and spectrum-hungry
- Increasingly digitally driven
- Significantly constrained by standards
- Consumer-driven

- Demand-elastic in terms of price and in terms of new value-added services
- Well-suited to competitive markets
- Chaotically organized with overlapping services, regulatory regimes, standards, and operating systems
- Adept at being added as an adjunct to conventional wire-based systems to form potentially seamless hybrid networks
- Limited in its ability to compete with high-density fiberoptic cable in providing heavy interurban and intraurban services, but well suited to complement such services
- Driven heavily by the high-end business use (but entertainment and consumer-defined applications are still important)
- Well suited to implementation in societies at all levels of economic development and within geographic regions at all levels of population density
- Constrained in its deployment by considerations of health-related issues and power-level limits, quality and error control needs, and multipath scatter[10]

The list of technologies that will be developed and deployed in the next decade is long and impressive. The broad level of market support for developments in the wireless broadband field can be expected to promote rapid progress in the following areas.

- Advanced digital modulation and encoding will help accelerate advances with regard to many areas such as spread spectrum (CDMA), advanced codec designs for imaging and video, and improved interface protocols and error control techniques. Software advances, in general, will lead hardware advances for some years to come.
- Advanced digital compression techniques will likewise generate major gains not only in terms of performance and quality but also in terms of cost reductions.
- Microcellular and picocellular systems within advanced digital mobile networks will create significant increases in frequency-reuse and operational capacities. This trend is likely to be slower in coming than was first projected—as PCS cell sizes are adjusted to accommodate vehicular traffic. Specialized mobile radio (SMR) digital services also will prove capable of serving over 20 million subscribers.

- Advanced node interconnection systems for PCS networks, particularly within cable television and wideband telephone systems, will create new types of networks capable of providing broadband wireless services.

- Active reclamation and reallocation of frequencies for new, higher-value, and consumer-defined applications will proliferate. This may be in terms of reallocation and spectrum auctions, or it may be accomplished by indirect means, such as the case of enhanced specialized mobile radio services.

- Advanced satellite systems design concepts will include onboard signal regeneration, signaling, switching, and cellular beam systems with active phased-array antennas ("smart" antennas).

- Advanced intersatellite links with high-speed throughput and multiple satellite interconnection will be achieved with optical-link telescopes and millimeter-wave systems.

- Advanced hand-held and compact ground transceivers will begin to use the latest in strip, patch, and phased-array antenna systems. MMIC technologies and digital processing techniques will become operational, and the price of these devices should drop dramatically over the next decade.[11]

In many ways, the boom years of microwave sales in the developed countries during the 1970s and 1980s preceded the explosive growth of wireless broadband communications systems today—and for many of the same reasons. Most important, microwave transmission permits the construction of a modern, fully digital wireless broadband network without laying cable—saving up to 80 percent of all public network construction costs. Thus, as telecommunication service markets were opened to competition in the United States and the United Kingdom in the 1980s, operators such as MCI and Mercury used microwave to construct independent networks that allowed them to compete with established carriers without having to borrow circuit capacity from their rivals. Microwave has been the medium of choice for large companies that have constructed their own wireless broadband network carrier infrastructure, in countries where this is permitted.

These twin drivers (competition and telecommunications operator bypass) propelled the microwave market in the developed countries through much of the 1980s. Today, these carrier markets have shifted largely to fiberoptic transmission systems. However, microwave is finding a resurgence today as deregulation and privatization are sweeping public wireless broadband networks worldwide.

With a microwave backbone wireless broadband network, a competitive provider can be up and running over a wide geographic range within a matter of months of obtaining a networking right of way and frequency spectrum. It is easier to put up a microwave tower than it is to dig ditches, obtain rights of way, and lay cable.

More fundamental shifts may occur in the long term. These may include the migration to even higher frequencies, such as the extensive use of infrared transmissions for intraoffice communications or substantial use of millimeter waves for satellite services. The most radical change of all could be in the entire area of frequency use for wireless broadband telecommunications. It has been suggested that the technology now exists for dynamic ranging over many megahertz of frequencies and for choosing temporary frequencies for use on demand. This new technology would allow the practical expansion of total telecommunications capacity over existing static allocation procedures by perhaps two orders of magnitude.

NOTE   A process whereby the entire available spectra, perhaps segmented in two or three parts, is available for dynamic assignment on demand could encourage new applications, lower the cost of telecommunications services, and reduce regulatory processes to a minimum.

Wireless Broadband Access System   Common wireless broadband network elements should be able to provide virtually any desired future service combination between wired or wireless access links. The move from a wide range of market-specific products toward common standardized flexible platforms that meet the basic needs of most major public, private, fixed, and mobile markets around the world should allow a much longer product life cycle for these core wireless broadband network and transmission components and offer increased flexibility and cost-effectiveness to network operators, service providers, and manufacturers.

The global telephone system evolved under the guidance of ITU recommendations (voluntary standards) to provide the essential backbone for worldwide communications. The globalization trends in all forms of communications, business, and even entertainment require global standards that have sufficient flexibility to meet local needs and to allow regional/national systems to evolve smoothly toward future global and integrated wired/wireless broadband telecommunications. ITU initiated studies for defining services and radio transmission technologies needed for the International Mobile Telecommunication—2000 (IMT-2000) that was discussed in Chapter 5.

The IMT-2000 system provides access, by means of one or more radio links, to a wide range of telecommunication services supported by fixed telecommunications wireless broadband networks (PSTN/ISDN) and to other services that are specific to mobile users.

A range of mobile terminal types is encompassed, linking to terrestrial and/or satellite-based networks. And the terminals may be designed for mobile or fixed use. Key features of IMT-2000 (see Sidebar, "Services Supported by IMT-2000" for more information) are:

- High degree of commonality of design worldwide
- Compatibility of services within IMT-2000 and with the fixed networks
- High quality
- Use of a small pocket terminal with worldwide roaming capability
- Capability for multimedia applications and a wide range of services (video teleconferencing, high-speed Internet, speech, and high-speed data)[12]

Services Supported By IMT-2000

Services supported by IMT-2000 can be categorized as follows:

Speech Service   This service is to be considered a toll quality voice service.

Simple Messaging   This type of service is characterized by user bit rates of up to 14 kbps.

Switched Data   This type of service is characterized by user bit rates of up to 64 kbps. The service may be either circuit- or packet-switched.

Asymmetrical Multimedia Service   This type of service is characterized by more traffic flowing in one direction than in the other. It is assumed that the higher rate of flow is to the terminal, whereas the lower rate is from the terminal. Some examples of such services include file download, Internet browsing, full-motion video, and non-interactive telemedicine. Two types of asymmetric services are being considered:

- *High multimedia (HMM).* A user bit rate of 2000 kbps in one direction and 128 kbps in the other.
- *Medium multimedia (MMM).* A user bit rate of 384 kbps in one direction and 128 kbps in the other.

Symmetric Multimedia Services   Multimedia services generally are considered to be voice and/or high-speed data and/or video and/or image services. Symmetric multimedia service is characterized by an equal amount of traffic flowing in both directions. An example of such service is high-fidelity audio, video conferencing, telemedicine, and various video conferencing applications (including but not limited to interactive services such as telemedicine) and two-way image transfer. These services are circuit switched to accommodate the real-time constraints of the applications. Two types of symmetric multimedia services are a user bit rate of 128 kbps in each direction and a user bit rate of 384 kbps in each direction. However, on the first 128/128, service will be used and denoted *high interactive multimedia* (HIMM), considering that the second one can be handled appropriately being several times the first one.

Phase II   The current plan for IMT-2000 services is that they are to be implemented in phases. Phase I IMT-2000 includes those services supported by user bit rates of up to 2000 kbps. Phase II IMT-2000 services are envisioned as augmenting phase I services, some of which may require higher bit rates with user bit rates greater than 2 Mbps and less than 10 Mbps. An example of this service would be high-resolution video.

Three environments are considered representative:

1. High-density in-building also generally known as *central business district*
2. Urban pedestrian
3. Urban vehicular

These three environments are in fact representative of the deployment in cities, where they correspond to superposed layers. It should be noted that no user should occupy two operational environments at a time. In the first phase, the data rate supported is

- Stationary: 2 Mbps

- Pedestrian: 384 kbps
- Mobile: 144 kbps

Fixed wireless access (FWA) applications of IMT-2000 are considered to be important. Various proposals for radio transmission submitted to the ITU are expected to be finalized by 2001. In order to accommodate various frequency bands and interoperability with various existing technologies, multiband, multimode, and multichip-rate handsets may be designed. The economics of volume may bring the cost down. Once radio transmission technology is finalized, backward compatibility would work out with existing technologies and systems.[13]

Broadband Access   Most established multichannel multipoint distribution system/local multipoint distribution service (MMDS/LMDS) systems worldwide transmit at 2.5 GHz. A few systems in Latin America operate in VHF-TV (54 to 88 MHz and 174 to 216 MHz) and UHF-TV (470 to 806 MHz). Some systems also use 12 and 18 GHz, but the future thrust is expected to be in 27.5 to 29.5 GHz and 40.5 to 42.5 GHz—since these would be the harbinger of wireless broadband services. Higher-frequency bands are especially useful because the antennas are a small 15 by 15 cm panel that can be merged aesthetically with walls, windows, and facades of buildings.

NOTE   Unlike MMDS, LMDS is not a true line-of-sight system. In fact, buildings and other structures that normally would obstruct signals act as active or passive repeaters because the signals are bounced off or around them. This unique trait makes the LMDS system particularly suited to densely populated urban areas with tall buildings and skyscrapers, especially since LMDS signals can be bounced off brick or glass.

The MMDS/LMDS technology provides a market opportunity to offer wireless broadband services for the public telecommunications operators, in view of the evolution of this technology from analog to digital. The use of digital compression technology will increase the capacity of the system to 120 TV channels, and this would be a quantum jump in capability because the existing cable systems in third-world countries deliver only 10 to 12 TV channels. Furthermore, this would enable a vastly more competitive product in terms of cost and signal quality.

The limiting factors resulting from the evolution of technology should be removed. For example, the LMDS/MMDS technology would be an enabling factor for the merger of diverse services. The new technology also provides a cutting edge to the later entrant, unless the existing operator takes care to meet the challenges of new threats.

Furthermore, conventional telecommunications needs symmetric media architecture, whereas TV distribution needs an asymmetric media. Development of a new system architecture to provide two-way interactive wireless broadband broadcast architecture has been initiated by some companies. These companies expect to design a system capable of supporting fully interactive video, data, and telephony—potentially at both MMDS and LMDS frequencies.

Wireless Data   Most important mobile data systems operate in various mobile bands from 100 to 200 MHz. Specialized mobile radio operates in 900 MHz, and cable modem termination system (CMTS) bands operate at 824 to 894 MHz. The simplest application for wireless broadband data communication is using facsimile or terminal voice band modems available at transmission rates of 9.6 or 14.4 kbps. The error-correction modem protocols MNP-10, V.34 and V.44, are used for providing reliable data delivery in an error-prone wireless broadband transmission environment.

Mobile data systems provide a variety of services to business users and public safety organizations. The basic services supported are electronic mail, enhanced paging, modem, facsimile, remote access to host computers, and LAN and information broadcasting services. The work currently in progress in various countries is presented below:

- ARDIS
- Mobitex
- Cellular digital packet data (CDPD)
- Digital cellular data service
- Trans-European trunk radio (TETRA)

ARDIS   ARDIS is a two-way radio service joint venture between IBM and Motorola that was implemented in the United States in 1983. The service is suitable for two-way transfer of data files less than 10 KB in size. Much of its use is to support computer-aided despatching. The operating frequency band is at 800 MHz, with 45 MHz as a transmitter-receiver (TX-RX) separation. The system was implemented initially with 4.8 kbps of data per 25-kHz channel using the MDC-4800 protocol. The system has been upgraded to 19.2 kbps using the RD-LAP protocol. The modulation technique is frequency shift keying, and the access method is frequency division multiple access (FDMA). Transmission packet length is 256 bytes.

MOBITEX   The Mobitex system is a nationwide interconnect trunk data network developed by Ericsson and Swedish Telecom. This has been in operation in Sweden since 1986 and is being deployed in 13 other countries. Mobitex is designed to carry both voice and data services. However, in the United States and Canada, networks are used for providing data service only. The network architectureis designed with the same frequency band in mind that's allocated for cellular telephone networks. The system operates in 896 to 901 MHz and 935 to 940 MHz and uses a full- or half-duplex gaussian filter and data recovery for a minimum shift keying (GMSK) modulation technique at 8 kbps half-duplex in 12.5-kHz channels. The service is suitable for file transfer of up to 20 KB.

CELLULAR DIGITAL PACKET DATA (CDPD)   Cellular digital packet data are designed to provide packet data service on an existing cellular telephone network. The basic goal of the CDPD system is to provide data services on a noninterfering basis using existing cellular telephone service with 30-kHz channel spacing. This can be achieved by devoting some of the existing channels to the CDPD service. Second, CDPD is designed to make use of cellular channels (temporarily not being used for voice traffic). Basically the system is used along with the advanced mobile phone service (AMPS) system, and possible application is for digital advanced mobile phone service (DAMPS). The 30-kHz channel with the CDPD channel supports transmission rates of up to 19.2 kbps. The degraded radio channel condition, however, limits actual information payload throughput rates to lower levels such as 5 to 10 kbps. This will introduce additional time delay due to the error-detection and transmission protocol in the CDPD radio link physical layer by using GMSK modulation at standard cellular frequencies at both forward and reverse links.

DIGITAL CELLULAR DATA SERVICE   Digital cellular systems based on GSM, PDC, IS-136, and IS-95 standards have all the capability of supporting transparent and nontransparent data rates of up to 9.6 kbps. In the case of cordless technologies such as DECT, PHS, PACS, etc., voice-band data rates of up to 9.6 kbps are feasible. These technologies are also demonstrating 32-kbps and higher data rates of 64 kbps.

The PCS-1900 standard already can provide bit rates of 115.2 kbps using general packet radio service (GPRS) and high-speed circuit-switched data

(HSCSD). HSCSD uses multiple TDMA time slots per user. For IS-95, higher bit rates beyond 9.6 kbps are standardized. The first step in phase I provides bit rates of up to 64 kbps and in phase II of up to 144 kbps. IS-36 is currently supporting bit rates of 14.4 kbps. Further evolution is expected to bring them up to 57.8 kbps.

TRANS-EUROPEAN TRUNK RADIO (TETRA) The European Telecommunication Standard Institute (ETSI) has developed public standards for trunk radio and mobile data systems. The TETRA is a family of standards. One of the branches is for radio, and there is a network interface standard for trunked voice and data services. The other branch is an air interface standard optimized for wide-area packet data service for both fixed and mobile subscribers. Both these standards will use a common physical layer based on p/4-DQPS modulation and channel rates of 36 kbps on 25-kHz channels. TETRA will provide both connection-oriented and connectionless data services. The physical data port at the mobile station will be an X.25 interface. It will provide peer-to-peer communication between the mobile and fixed ends of the communication link. The system operates in 400- and 900-MHz bands.

The phenomenal growth of PCs, laptops, and notebook computers has created a market potential for wireless broadband data services. The mobile data communication services provide low-speed solutions for wide-area coverage. A horizon is opening up for new applications (based on the capacity of large computers for short periods of time) that require high-speed and local communication portable terminals with wireless broadband access to process data. Some of the applications could be a portable terminal in a classroom for instructional purposes or a hospital bed for medical diagnosis.

Wireless Broadband LANs (WBLANs) These systems have emerged only in the recent past for the purpose primarily of addressing business applications. WBLANs mainly are aimed at data transactions rather than video or voice and are most efficient at connecting portable computers and data-entry systems to local networks via a high data rate (typically a few megabytes per second over typically few tens of meters). Wireless broadband access supports transmission rates of from 2 Mbps to over 50 Mbps and low coverage of tens of meters in the majority of applications. Wireless broadband LAN networks are used as an extension or replacement of wired LANs. Spectrum allocation of LANs occurred initially in the industrial, scientific, and medical (ISM) bands at 900 MHz. Subsequently, spectrum at 2.4 GHz also has been used for these systems. IEEE standard

802.11 has provided impetus to the wireless broadband industry—resulting in widespread deployment of these systems. The main impetus has come from the computer market, where the user needs mobility and portability of the computer for daily work. The system provides sustained transmissions across the coverage area and supports handover (making the connectivity of LAN transmission to the users). The Ethernet package data transfer is connectionless, and the handover measure is easier to achieve in data network than in voice systems. The speed of movement typically is restricted to walking speed or indoor vehicle speeds. A maximum speed of m/s covers most of the in-building applications.

The growth of the WBLAN is driving data rates higher, and as a result, spectrum has been allocated for HI-PERformance Radio LAN version 1 (HIPERLAN 1), which is focused on the ad hoc networking application. It supports higher data rates and U-NII (unlicensed national information infrastructure)—formerly called SUPERNet—which provides connectivity at 5 GHz. These wireless broadband LANs support data rates of 20 to 25 Mbps and at much higher frequencies such as 40 and 60 GHz (with the LAN approaching current throughputs of 100 Mbps). The higher frequencies offer a large amount of spectrum. The radio systems require directional antennas for a robust link. Thus these are mostly suited for fixed links.

Wireless Broadband ATM   WBLANs and wireless broadband Asynchronous Transfer Mode (WBATM) provide wireless broadband local access. As mentioned in the preceding section, WBLAN is a mature technology with quality products available in the market, whereas WBATM is an evolving technology. WBATM is expected to provide end-to-end connectivity and quality of service in wireless broadband channels. In the recent past, several manufacturers and projects have developed infrastructure-based prototypes to implement WBATM technology. Three major prototypes have been developed by Lucent, NEC, and Magic WAND (project of ACTS Research Programme). The WAND project aims to develop and evaluate a wireless broadband ATM transmission facility at 52 GHz in a realistic user environment. The WBATM Working Group in the ATM Forum have been formed to define standards for wireless broadband local access using WBATM technology. The work has started, and there are plans to develop specifications for radio access MAC (media access control) and mobility support for WBATM. The standard is expected to be completed by 2001, and product availability should occur by 2003. The products under development are

- MIIBahama in 900-MHz and proposed 5-GHz U-NII bands. The modulation technique is OFDM or GMSK with data rates of 2 to 20 Mbps between laptop and PDS and a few gigabytes per second between BS.
- NEC in 2.4-GHz ISM bands with p/4GPSK modulation and data rates of 8 Mbps.
- Magic WAND in 5.2-GHz bands with 16-channel OFDM modulation and data rates greater than 24 Mbps.[14]

Because of the wide range of services supported by the ATM network, ATM technology is expected to become a dominant technology for transmission of both infrastructure wireless broadband networks and LANs. The ATM infrastructure can support all types of services, such as voice communication, desktop multimedia, desk multimedia conferencing, and a bursty transaction LAN traffic. Extension of ATM infrastructure to wireless broadband access will meet the needs of those users and customers who require end-to-end network infrastructure with high performance and consistent service characteristics.

Intelligent Transportation System (ITS)   Two main wireless broadband schemes in intelligent transportation systems (ITS) have emerged: One is *vehicle-to-vehicle link*, also known as *intervehicle communication* (IVC), and the other is *roadside-vehicle-roadside link*. Both these links serve complementary roles. Whereas a vehicle-to-vehicle link is necessary for safety reasons (toward accidents), a roadside-to-vehicle link is necessary for broadcasting information useful to the drivers of the vehicles.

Vehicle information and communication systems in Japan use a 64-kbps radio beacon that has a transmission range of about 70 m. The beacons are located 2 to 4 km apart along sections of highways, as well as at junctions, entries, and exits. The transmission frequency is 2.4997 GHz ± 85 kHz. Manchester coding is applied, and GMSK modulation is used.

A second wireless broadband beacon is used at 1 Mbps to transmit 80 KB of information each time a vehicle passes by. The transmission range is approximately 3.5 m, and transmitters are hung above major intersections on arterial roads. There are about 12,000 such beacons already in service. The modulation method is pulse amplitude modulation (PAM), and Manchester coding is employed. The infrared wavelength is 850 ± 50 nm.

The third wireless technology uses FM multiplex and a frequency of 76 kHz to broadcast informatio n over a range of 20 to 50 km. About 50 KB of information is permitted every 5 minutes. The speed of transmission is 160 kbps, and the modulation method used is level-controlled minimum shift key (L-MSK). With the popularity of the car navigation system in Japan, car manufacturers are incorporating navigation units in the new models.

The intervehicle communication (IVC) vehicles share data about their progress, speed, solution, and intention to turn to other vehicles to avoid possibly dangerous situations. Side or rear collisions can be avoided. The IVC is different from wireless broadband local-area networks or cellular communication. Unlike the cellular systems, movement of a vehicle from one direction, the predictable nature of movement, and slow variations of speed offer a simplified system. Infrared and millimeter bands are primary candidates for IVC medium. Infrared is popular because of the lack of regulations (a licence is not required), and the equipment is inexpensive. Since infrared links are basically line-of-sight links, interference by other vehicles is minimized. However, in rain and snowfall conditions, transmission rates fall dramatically. Furthermore, infrared systems are sensitive to alignment when transmitting to receiver. The millimeter band around 60 GHz also has been proposed as one of the leading candidates. One of the reasons that a maximum absorption rate is experienced in oxygen at this frequency is because it allows reuse of a particular frequency at a particular distance. Availability of adequate spectrum makes the millimeter band an alternative choice for an IVC system. Trials are in progress in Japan under the automated highway system.

In Europe, one-way traffic information is provided by FM relay by using automotive road information (ARI) and the radio data system traffic measurement channel (RD-TMC). This system transmits at 1.2 kbps using FM modulation. Use of infrastructure such as Moditex, GSM data service, and Tetra traffic management can be improved without the need for expensive infrastructure. Vehicle-to-vehicle experiments as part of the PROMETHEUS program have been carried out. Two wireless broadband IVC systems developed by MANET and Thompson use dynamic TDMA/CSMA at frequencies of 2.45 and 57 GHz and a bandwidth of 3 and 2 MHz, respectively, with a transmission coverage area of 500 m. Europe is moving toward a single integrated system, but the difficulty in many countries regarding the use of a single standard seems to be far away. However, GSM packet data services will be able to fill up the gap because the infrastructure is already in position. One of the well-known programs in the United States is the California PATH (Partner for Advanced Transit and Highways). The ITS models have separate links; the first link controls IVC, the second controls maneuvers among a group of vehicles, and the third controls the communication advisory vehicle (vehicle-roadside communication). The PATH program envisions a group of up to 20 vehicles transferring through less than 2 m, whereas each group is separated from other groups of vehicles by more than 50 m. The main motivation for the PATH program stems from congestion experienced on highways—particularly in southern California.

The PATH program has chosen an infrared system in the 830-nm band with on/off keying. It has a useful range of 30 m and data rates varying between 19.2 kbps and 1.2 Mbps. Maximum channel bandwidth is 3 MHz. The two systems under consideration for maneuver communications are both omnidirectional broadcasting radio systems. Pulse rate radio channels use frequency hopping spread spectrum modulation and provide data rates of 1 Mbps at 500 m. The waveLAN radio channel uses spectrum modulation at data rates of 2 Mbps and a maximum packet length of 100 bytes at a relative velocity of 30 m/s. The specifications for roadside wireless broadband links have now been finalized and implemented.

Satellites Let's look at the following emerging trends in broadband satellite communications and their impact on the planning and design of wireless broadband applications. The trends are as follows:

- Digital techniques
- Deployment of high-power satellites with steerable narrow beams
- Higher-frequency bands
- Onboard processing
- Evolution of MICROSATs
- Mobile satellite services
- Global mobile personal communications by satellite (GMPCS)

Digital Techniques The techniques of enhancing the capacity of satellite systems at lower cost and reducing bandwidth requirements are being adopted worldwide in lieu of the digitalization of switching and the transmission of wireless broadband networks. The digital techniques applied in the ground-segment equipment will increase the channel capacity and reduce transponder power requirements.

For example, low-bit-rate voice coding techniques to reduce bit rate from the conventional 64-kbps pulse code modulation (PCM) coding to a lower coding rate of 8 kbps have been adopted in fixed satellite systems and in the digital satellite phone terminal (DSPT). Mobile satellite systems are adopting a coding bit rate on the order of 4.8 to 6.4 kbps, which results in a further reduction in bandwidth and transponder power—with acceptable voice quality. The codecs at 6.4 kbps will be used in the INSAT-MSS system.

In addition, digital circuit multiplication equipment (DCME) using digital speech interpolation in conjunction with low-bit-rate encoding of 8 kbps provides 5 to 20 times enhanced capacity. These systems are used on trunk routes taking M inputs of 2 Mbps PCM from the exchange junction and reducing to N numbers the 2-Mbps PCM—where a ratio of M/N is up to 20. This DCME equipment enhances the capacity of the wireless broadband transmission network.

Also, forward error correction technique, in addition to Reed Solomon coding, improves the bit-error-ratio (BER) performance. Error coding techniques are being used in all satellite systems.

DEPLOYMENT OF HIGH-POWER SATELLITES WITH STEERABLE NARROW BEAMS   The high-power satellite with steerable narrow beams will facilitate use of low-power solid-state receive amplifiers with small Earth station antennas. This will provide wide coverage of the Earth's surface. The coverage of the Earth's surface can be selected by a beam-steering arrangement, whereas a high-power satellite facilitates use of smaller antennas. The steerable multibeam configuration reduces interference with other wireless broadband networks. However, it results in small ground coverage areas and requires more powerful satellite launch vehicles and complicated onboard controls.

Higher-power transponders being proposed on the INSAT 3 series could provide higher-capacity traffic even with smaller Earth stations. Shaped beams with wide coverage are proposed for multiple applications.

HIGHER FREQUENCY BANDS   With the full exploitation of conventional C and extended C bands, it has become very difficult to meet the ever-increasing demands for fixed satellite service, as well as for line-of-sight radio systems and interference coordination. Use of higher-frequency bands is inevitable to mitigate these problems. Ku band is being used extensively worldwide. Ku band is also used to a great extent for direct-to-home (DTH) broadcasting applications as well as for customer premises business wireless broadband networks.

The Ka band is used in high-capacity GMPCS, where the bulk of data transfer is satellite-to-satellite, feeder links, and VSATs for meeting the requirement of bandwidth on demand. Such systems are currently in the research, planning, and design stage, and it is expected that the terminal size will be very small. However, rain attenuation is prominent in this band.

The use of a high-frequency band should provide an advantage to miniaturization of Earth station antennas and equipment, with the possibility of locating an Earth station on the customer rooftop or in the backyard, thus obviating the last-mile problem, availability of larger bandwidth, and ease in coordination with terrestrial systems. This also will result in cost reduction and improvement in reliability.

Ku and Ka bands will open up a very large market for VSAT-based wireless broadband networks in third-world countries for business communications. However, INSAT 2C spacecraft have limited Ku band capacity. INSAT 3 satellites have been planned with more transponders in the Ku band and multiple beams for better coverage of a country.

NOTE Improvements in satellite and Earth station technology, coupled with use of higher-frequency bands (providing more bandwidth), inevitably will lead to the realization of much higher throughput, thereby reducing the operational cost of the wireless broadband network.

ONBOARD PROCESSING Significant increases in satellite channel capacity can be obtained by using regenerative repeaters onboard the satellite. This technique is also known as *baseband processing*. Onboard processing (OBP) also facilitates transfer to signals from one beam to the other depending on traffic and coverage requirements. With onboard processing, more effective use of bandwidth is possible. Onboard processing makes the spacecraft design more complicated, however.

Use of onboard processing requires complicated spacecraft technology and also requires high-power spacecraft launchers. Many of the satellite systems now have multibeam capability with beam switching and onboard processing. These techniques are used widely in global mobile personal communications services (GMPCS) systems. High transponder output power coupled with the introduction of systems having several spot beams leads to the possibility of using smaller Earth station antennas. Complexity in the space segment and increased costs are compensated by increased effective isotropic radiated power (EIRP) and G/T (G is the net gain of the system, and T is the noise temperature of the system) of the satellite, thereby facilitating smaller Earth station antennas and low-power transmitters, which are both major contributors to the cost of the Earth station terminal.

Although onboard processing satellites are cost-effective and have many advantages from the ground segment point of view, experimental studies may be useful to gain experience before these are planned for implementation. At present, onboard processing has not been planned in the INSAT system. However, in the future, this technology will provide a severalfold increase in channel capacity.

EVOLUTION OF MICROSATS   Use of 16, 8, 6.4, or even 4.8 kbps voice codecs via conventional 64-kbps PCM will provide 4, 8, 10, or 11.3 times the increase in channel capacity or reduction in satellite power and bandwidth at the expense of a slight degradation in voice quality and complexity. However, with more powerful microprocessors and DSPs becoming available, near-toll-quality low-bit-rate codecs, with a reduction in design complexity, have been achieved. The advantage in terms of reduction in Earth station size without a penalty on the space segment is tremendous. Low-bit-rate codecs (LRE) have led to the realization of handheld terminals.

Use of such low-bit-rate coding, high-power satellites, and higher-frequency bands permits reduction in Earth station antenna size. Very small aperture terminals (VSATs) or micro Earth stations can be used for voice and data communications.

Antenna costs are proportional to 2.5 times the antenna diameter. Reducing antenna size therefore reduces the costs substantially and facilitates quicker installation.

MOBILE SATELLITE SERVICES   Mobile satellite services (MSS) were started by INMARSAT for communications for distress, search, and rescue operations over the high seas. Soon the potential for use of mobile terminals over land was foreseen. Some domestic mobile satellite broadband networks are also operational. The frequencies used for feeder links (gateways to satellites) generally are in C band and for service links (customer terminals to satellite) in L/S bands.

For wide-area mobile communication in third-world countries, MSS is really the only choice because terrestrial communications are inadequate and mobile cellular services have barely covered urban areas so far. MSS will be highly useful for

- Maritime, train, aircraft, and trucking operations
- Military applications
- Remote area communications such as required at project sites and mines
    - Emergency and short-term requirements
    - Inaccessible areas[15]

MSS has been planned on INSAT 2C, but transponder power is fluctuating. The service is likely to start with the launch of INSAT 3-B in the year 2001.

GLOBAL MOBILE PERSONAL COMMUNICATIONS BY SATELLITE (GMPCS)
Mobile cellular communications are growing worldwide at an exponen-

tial rate. However, sparsely populated, remote, and less developed areas may not be covered by cellular services for a long time. Coverage of the entire Earth is feasible with satellites. To provide mobile satellite services with handheld sets, it is necessary to reduce space path loss. Low-Earth-orbit (LEO) satellites with an altitude below 1000 km and medium-Earth-orbit (MEO) satellites with altitudes of around 10,000 km, respectively, therefore have been proposed. Transmission delays also get reduced in lower orbits, although a large number of satellites are needed to obtain worldwide coverage.

ITU has defined the global mobile personal communication by satellite (GMPCS) system as any satellite system (fixed or mobile, broadband or narrowband, global or regional, geostationary or nongeostationary, existing or planned) providing telecommunication services directly to end users from a constellation of satellites on a transnational, regional, or global basis. The GMPCS user can make or receive calls using handheld, fixed, and application-specific terminals from anywhere and at any time. The calls are relayed to another GMPCS user directly or to a public switched telephone network/public land mobile network (PSTN/PLMN) subscriber through a constellation of satellites and ground stations connected to terrestrial telecommunication networks. GMPCS systems consist of a center for operation and control for a constellation of satellites, a network management center, gateways for regional operation, and handheld (application-specific) fixed terminals. The GMPCS system, apart from providing roaming facility for terminals around the globe, also has a facility to locate the terminal, authenticate the terminal, debar the service, and debar the area of operation, providing a monitoring facility. The GMPCS provides telephone, fax, and data services. GMPCS is now realizable with LEOs and MEOs. A number of satellite broadband networks are planned to provide worldwide service. The GMPCS service provides handheld terminals that are compatible with the cellular system (GSM, AMPS) to operate in dual mode. These handheld terminals are expected to be operated with cellular systems when they fall in the coverage area of a cellular system. Most of the operators are planning such an operation in their second phase.

Meteor Burst Communications System (MBCS)

A meteor, as it enters Earth's upper atmosphere (traveling at speeds of 10 to 75 km/s), possesses a large amount of kinetic energy. When the meteor collides with air molecules, kinetic energy is converted into heat, which vaporizes atoms from the surface of the meteor. These vaporized atoms, which are traveling with approximately the same speed as the meteor, collide with the air molecules in the process stripping away electrons—leaving a trail of positive charged ions and free electrons. It is these electrons that reflect or reradiate radio waves. Typical trails are 25 km in length, last 250 ms, and are formed by meteors the size of a grain of sand (0.5 cm radius).

Meteors are random, but they are very predictable. The intersections of the meteor's orbit with the Earth's orbit are not uniformly distributed but are concentrated so as to produce a maximum of intersections in August and a minimum in February—with about 3:1 variation. The rate of incidence of sporadic meteors is further dependent on the time of day, with the morning hours being more active. On the morning side of the Earth, meteors are swept up by the forward motion of the Earth in its orbit around the Sun. Meteor scatter link budgets are designed to provide acceptable performance at the worst time of the day and the worst time of the year.

The primary propagation mechanism used by the wireless broadband network is an extended-range line of sight at short ranges out to about 150 km and meteor scatter use for long-range coverage out to 800 to 2000 km. In areas where the nodal density is sparse, this technology represents a very cost-effective alternative to expensive satellite systems. For links used for intermodal communication, the average waiting time to communicate to a vehicle via meteor scatter will be on the order of 3 to 8 minutes. In the line-of-sight mode, it will be close to instantaneous. The arrival of meteor trails follows Poisson statistics so that there is a very high likelihood of being able to communicate in the required time.

Meteor communications systems generally operate using probe-and-listen types of protocols. In this mode of operation, centrally located master stations broadcast a probing signal consisting of some overhead information and who should respond, along with differential global positioning system (GPS) update information. If a unit receives the probe signal and it is part of the group of units that have been allowed to respond, it will transmit its position information and any message information located in its message queue.

After transmitting a probe signal, the master station listens to see if anyone has transmitted before it repeats the probe. How often units are allowed to respond is determined by the grade of service required. Complicated wireless broadband network protocols control network operation, thus minimizing the number of retransmissions due to collision. The output of the meteor scatter base stations then interfaces into conventional packet network systems.

Meteor scatter has the interesting property that the ground illumination footprint of individual meteors is very small. Thus, at any one time, only a very small subset of the wireless broadband network could respond, and with sufficient randomization, the probability of collision is very low. In line-of-sight mode, carrier sense multiple access (CSMA) protocols will prevent message collision.

The ionized trails of meteors entering the atmosphere can reflect VHF radio waves out to ranges of 1000 km or more. This has been known for close to half a century. It is only recently with an improved understanding of the propagation mechanism and development of inexpensive digital hardware that the full potential of this medium has been recognized. For more than a decade, the U.S. military has recognized the reliability of the medium and has depended on meteor scatter communication for some of its most important message traffic. The demand for meteor burst communications has gained strong momentum as a direct result of the technology being validated through the successful operating systems that have been installed since 1970s. Increased interest has resulted from the heightened user awareness of the benefits that can be derived from using a meteor burst communication system for either military or commercial applications. Continued technological advances have led to the development of products and systems that are user friendly and versatile and have improved life-cycle costs. System applications extend from water resource management and data acquisition to environmental monitoring and message communications—both commercial and military. These systems have been implemented in Alaska, Canada, Italy, Philippines, the United Kingdom, and the United States. These wireless broadband networks provide data acquisition and data communication services to government, military, and commercial users. The services include electronic mail, fax, remote monitoring/supervisory control and data acquisition (SCADA), orderwire for satellite or high frequency (HF), emergency communications, and vessel position monitoring and communications.

High-Density Fixed Systems (HDFS)

The vast majority of current worldwide HDFS deployments are in the 38 GHz band, with a primary focus on urban and suburban business and industrial areas. Future HDFS deployment is expected to extend to residential areas, spearheaded by local distribution of television programs in competition with cable TV and other new wireless broadband fixed services offered to the home. The variety of possible current HDFS wireless broadband network configurations includes conventional point-to-point (P-P) systems, conventional point-to-multipoint (P-MP) systems, and combinations thereof (P-P systems deployed in multisectored P-MP configurations). High-density deployment of independent P-P links similarly results in clusters that assume the essential characteristics of P-MP deployment. The densest HDFS deployment cases have reached the range of 1 to 10 stations per square kilometer and are expected to increase severalfold within a few years. Tables 6-1 and 6-2 summarize the trend for equipment in various frequency bands.[16]

TABLE 6-1

Equipment
Summary Trends
in Various
Frequency Bands

Frequency Band	Use and Room for Growth
30–36 GHz	Light to moderate use due to limited available allocations; contingent on future availability of sufficient spectrum for HDFS.
36 to about 50 GHz	Local access intercell links for mobile and wireless local loop networks.
About 40 GHz	Optical fiber backup, local TV distribution, wireless broadband GII access, intelligent transport, SDH access, RLANSs, ATM-compatible transport, substantial 38-GHz deployment in several countries; bands below antenna sizing are currently preferred to satisfy HDFS hop length, reuse, objectives, and uses proposed in other bands.
	HDFS in these bands could be subject to constraints resulting from future sharing with coprimary space and satellite service systems.

TABLE 6-2

Equipment
Summary Trends
above 50 GHz

Frequency Band	Use and Room for Growth
Above about 50 GHz	Technically similar to 30 to 50 GHz, but over shorter hop lengths, thus limiting services offered as compared with lower HDFS bands; HDFS deployment in progress in 55 to 58 GHz.
	Expanding HDFS uses in this and other bands planned.
	Limited availability of equipment and coprimary sharing considerations are the principal restrictive factors.
	High absorption losses in short hop lengths but very high frequency reuse.

High Altitude Platform Station (Stratospheric System)

The payload of the stratospheric relay station consists of separate transmit and receive beam-forming phased-array antennas, separate transmit and receive dish antennas for feeder links with ground switching stations, and a very large bank of regenerative processors that handle receiving, frequency conversion, demodulation, decoding, data multiplexing, switching, encoding, and modulating and transmitting functions. The station payload is expected to reliably receive, regenerate, switch, and retransmit stratospheric transmissions for a period of not less than 10 years before user-transparent replacement occurs.

Both transmit and receive antennas used on the stratospheric relay station will have 32- to 45-dBi gains, and a millimeter waveguide feed array will project a large number of cellular coverage areas on the surface of the Earth. The precise power allocated to each cellular coverage area and the area's boundaries will be capable of being changed via commands from the ground control center.

NOTE dBi stands for the decibel power relative to an isotropic source.

At a distance of 40 km from the nadir location along the surface of the Earth, each stratospheric relay station will be at a position in the sky 30 degrees above the horizon. At this radial distance (which includes 5000 km²), the cell size will be approximately 1.6 × 3.2 km with a corresponding coverage area of 16 km². As one extends further from the zenith point to the horizon, the elevation angle for communication continues to decrease, and hence the cell size continues to increase. For operational purposes, three regions have been defined and broadly categorized: urban area coverage (UAC), suburban area coverage (SAC), and rural area coverage (RAC). The communications performance is based on the general principle that users in the UAC zone would use small terminal units with a minimum of a 3-dBi antenna gain. SAC users would have units with 23-dBi antenna gain, and users in the RAC area would have units with 36-dBi antenna gain supplemented with higher transmit power. Transmissions from the stratospheric relay station to users in the RAC zone also would have increased transmit powers.

The stratospheric relay station transmit and receive systems consist of approximately 2100 cells that share the bandwidth in a hexagonal frequency-reuse pattern. The assigned bandwidth is divided into seven segments, and each segment is applied to 300 cells. The pattern is arranged so that separation between beams using the same frequency is sufficiently large to minimize any mutual interference.

The approximately 700 cells in the UAC region will each cover an average size of 7.2 km². The average cell size will be 63 km² in the SAC region and 1300 km² in the RAC region—these regions also include approximately 700 cells each.

Stratospheric relay stations use solar panels to provide all the necessary power. At night or during solar eclipses, the solar power must be supplemented by fuel cells. Onboard and remote power management can automatically change the power mix to meet the ever-changing demands from the ion engine module, the communications modules, and the control module.

A station-keeping ion-type engine requires no fuel except electricity. Ions used by the engine are generated through field emission, ionization, and charge-transfer processes involving air molecules in the stratosphere.

Stratospheric relay stations rely on multiple redundant GPS receivers and ion engines to remain fixed in positions to within 40 m in all three dimensions and further enable the antenna assemblies to remain accurately oriented with a deviation of no more than 0.1 degree in any direction. The main position-disturbing force in the stratosphere is the wind, which averages around 15 m/s but can gust to 40 m/s. However, the air is only about 4 percent the density at sea level, greatly reducing the drag.

The stratospheric relay stations employ both passive and active thermal controls to limit the temperature variation to within a few degrees, thus providing a protective environment for the payload. The stratospheric relay station has a predicted life span of more than 10 years. However, it is deemed necessary to replace and retire stratospheric relay stations after 10 years of service. The reasons for this include decomposition of gas-storage modules, decreased solar panel output, and structural fatigue. In addition, rapid advances in high-strength, lightweight, UV-resistant composite materials and compact, high-speed electronic/photonic switches will likely result in their use in a newer generation of stratospheric relay stations.

NOTE   The stratospheric relay station communications system consists of the stratospheric communications payload, ground switching systems, and user terminals.

The stratospheric relay station payload consists of separate wafer-scale integrated optically controlled and optically delayed beam-forming phased array antennas for transmission and reception, two dish antennas for feeder links with ground switching stations, and a large bank of TDMA, FDMA, or CDMA transceiver modems to communicate with fixed transportable user units on the ground. The incoming communications stream is frequency downshifted, and digital filter banks are used to segment the resulting signal stream based on phase, time, and/or frequency information.

Photonic amplifiers and fiber channel switching fabrics are used for high-speed same-cell switching. For connections between different cells within the service area of a single stratospheric relay station, ATM switch fabrics are used. A special access channel shared by all callers within a single cell is used as the out-of-band signaling channel for call setup, store and forward, paging, caller ID, and power control. For communications between different stratospheric relay station service areas, the call is routed to a feeder link down to a switching center that provides interface to a ground gateway station within the overlapping coverage area of an adjacent stratospheric relay station or, for communications to distant coverage areas, to the PSTN and other public networks. The signals are automatically converged into ATM cells where the callers can request either a higher bandwidth or a lower one by changing the quality-of-service (QoS) index freely. The very short time delay (<200 ms) allows the bandwidth to be managed efficiently for better traffic flow of congestion control.

At an average of 64 kbps per user terminal (half-duplex), with $k = 3$ hexagonal-pattern frequency reuse for TDMA/FDMA, and k 5 1.33 hexagonal-pattern reuse with $S = 3$ sectorization for CDMA, a theoretical maximum of 3 million simultaneous communications can be served with TDMA/FDMA. Slightly more communications can be served with CDMA.

Customers communicating with stratospheric relay stations are not restricted to the B-ISDN bandwidth of 64 kbps. Up to 2.048 Mbps (E1) of bandwidth is available to user terminal customers, and gateway customers can request a bandwidth of 34 Mbps (E3) or higher.

Stratospheric relay station systems will provide wireless broadband digitally switched fixed, portable, and gateway services worldwide, especially in areas of high population density. The system has been designed to provide e-mail, FTP, and World Wide Web (WWW) services at data rates from 64 kbps (B-ISDN) to E1 speed, as well as improved wireless broadband videophone and full-motion/full-screen video teleconferencing services. Depending on the user's location in the coverage area, the stratospheric relay station services may be accessed from a portable PDA-like device (UAC), from a small notebook-like device (SAC), or from a soup-bowl-sized satellite dish (RAC).

For voice-only communications, voice activity detection can further increase the capacity by roughly a factor of 3. For data traffic, the factor will be even greater because of the inherent bursty nature of the multimedia data traffic and the efficiency of the cell-switching technique in dealing with such traffic. If one assumes that at any given moment 20 percent of the subscribers are online, then one stratospheric relay station will be able to serve a high-density population area with approximately 4.7 million subscribers.

There will be one or more switching centers within each stratospheric relay station service area on the ground to serve as base stations for each system. To reduce cost, power requirements, and communications payload complexity of the stratospheric relay stations, communication traffic between different stratospheric relay station service areas, the PSTN, and other networks will be redirected to the switching centers from the stratospheric relay station in a *bent-pipe fashion*, with most of the switching done at the switching center. The switching centers are not designed to handle the maximum bandwidth needed in the worst-case scenario. However, the maximum bandwidth (half-duplex) of 1.2 Gbps (using polarization and space diversity and 300-MHz carrier bandwidth) should satisfy typical communications needs. In addition to the switching centers, other gateways can be set up to provide connectivity to the PSTN, VANs, etc., which usually do not have the bandwidth and the switching power of the switching centers. The switching centers also serve as the ground control centers.

Security features, such as password protection for access to the Internet/WWW services, public-key cipher for user and server (challenge/response) authentication, and end-to-end or link-to-link encryption of phone messages, will be implemented to prevent theft of service and password. Both the stratospheric relay stations and the switching stations are protected by multilayer firewalls to prevent tampering.

To manage worldwide portable subscribers, the home location register (HLR) database is maintained by all stratospheric relay station ground switching centers and is updated constantly. A visiting user must periodically inform the stratospheric relay station system about its geographic location by updating the contents of the HLR. The visitor location register (VLR) is a temporary database that maintains the information about a visiting user operating outside the area of its HLR. The visitor is automatically registered at the nearest switching center, and the VLR is informed of the arrival of the visitor. A roaming number is then assigned to the visiting unit to enable calls to be routed to it. A central wireless broadband network management and administration authority is responsible for the monitoring, control, and maintenance of the global stratospheric relay station network.

NOTE   The relatively high cost of a stratospheric relay station necessarily limits its likely use to high-density fixed-service routes.

Nongeostationary Earth Orbit Satellites

Satellites will play a major part in untethering computer and communications users—allowing them mobility and communications capabilities that were previously inconceivable. Perhaps we are already well on the road to a previously inconceivable future.

However, while potential customers might welcome a liberalized and competitive environment, it is fair to ask whether a half-dozen largely similar operators might be a few satellites too many. Naturally, the operators themselves would argue that each of their individual systems offers exclusive benefits. Because people will discover they have access to technology they simply cannot do without, the optimistic view is that the market will be big enough for all the systems. By thinking of one another by our personal phone number (not by a half-dozen numbers one might have to use today), ultimately, everyone will have individual communication devices (much as one wears a wristwatch). Since the bill for an hour of long-distance telephony is currently more than the cost of a one-night stay in a five-star hotel, a robust market with high demand coming from the international business traveler and a high priority target for each operator is predicted.

A total projection for voice usage of some 22 million subscribers is predicted by looking at the state of the mobile satellite market, examining in some considerable detail what everyone will be doing in 5 years, and factoring in other elements. However, the potential operators have to build successfully and on time. This alone can be a nightmare, with almost every satellite program in the world running 1 to 4 years behind schedule. The other nightmare (before getting to market distribution) comes from authorization agreements with different countries, plus the not inconsiderable challenges of setting up any marketing effort and customer proposition. There is, therefore, a need for each of these companies to complete each and every stage correctly—if they are to have any real chance of moving forward.

Motorola's Celestri and Teledesic   Teledesic is planning to launch a global/mobile super LEO system based on 399 satellites at a cost of $10 billion. Boeing has paid $200 million for a 20 percent stake in Teledesic. Boeing expects the relationship to be the perfect logical catalyst for saving satellite manufacturing costs, launch costs (on Boeing's Sea Launch), and generally taking the project to the next level.

NOTE   Too bad Boeing couldn't have done this with the International Space Station—where they took a $30 billion project in 1988 to well over $140 billion in cost overruns in 2000.

On June 17, 1997, an unexpected announcement was made that brought Motorola into play as a direct competitor to the Bill Gates/Craig McCaw–backed Teledesic system. This announcement called for a satellite constellation of 63 LEOs (dubbed *Celestri*), with a total project cost of $23 billion, scheduled for service availability in 2003. Motorola plans to target wireless broadband local networks with a $640 dish and a receiver and software package that will appeal to small businesses and direct-to-home users. Motorola's aim is to provide satellite-based data services ranging from 64 kbps to 51.84 Mbps. It is too early to state how one competitor will affect another. Furthermore, the number of satellite filings misrepresents the number of competitors in the market, and it is believed that many licenses will not be pursued seriously.

Teledesic and Celestri are targeted at different markets than those of Iridium; Globalstar and other big LEOs have been designed to reach the handheld telephony segment. Teledesic is the first proposed broadband LEO that would be the satellite equivalent of fiberoptic access. If it is accepted that cellular and fiber as not being real competitors on the ground, then the same may hold in the sky.

Globalstar   Globalstar, while targeting the international businessperson with its big LEO (designed for cellular/satellite telephony services), is of the view that this audience is smaller than that suggested by Iridium. Consequently, Globalstar also has a strategy to aggressively pursue users who have no telephone service at all. Systems such as Globalstar will make it easier for people to visit their local general store or post office and make a telephone call, which addresses the local payphone environment with a phone box served by solar panels. In addition to this market, the company plans on targeting mobile automobiles and/or trucks where the satellite is the backup service for the user who is out of cellular range.

Globalstar's strategy is diversified to target shares of several different market segments. Globalstar's biggest potential market is serving customers who would normally use a cellular phone but live outside the cellular coverage area (or frequently roam beyond it) and thus use a satellite phone instead. In addition, Globalstar has identified what it calls the *cellular extension customer*, who continuously roams in and out of cellular coverage areas. Cellular providers working with Globalstar can extend global roaming capabilities to their customers. If the Globalstar system is used in this way, Globalstar will bill the cellular provider, who will include this cost as a roaming charge in the standard customer billing procedure.

Globalstar predicts approximately 447,000 subscribers by the end of the first year of service and 800,000 to 900,000 by the end of second year, which is the number needed for Globalstar to break even. According to studies of over 200 countries, Globalstar estimates that the top 27 countries represent over 80 percent of the business for the Globalstar system.

Globalstar's strengths include relatively trouble-free licensing (because the system works with local terrestrial infrastructures) and being fully financed. Globalstar's pricing, not surprisingly, is a key element of its strategy to succeed. The pricing strategy allows the service providers to price the retail cost at a level that will be competitive in their region and does not set a fixed tariff that must be supported worldwide. The space-segment charge is already variable, based on volume and location. In developing nations, a different, regionally competitive price will be adopted compared with a market where a cellular system is already built out.

ICO Global Communications   ICO Global Communications, another big LEO competitor, was established in 1995 to provide communications coverage around the globe. ICO expects to provide satellite-enabled global mobile personal communications services for consumers worldwide as well as digital voice, data, facsimile, messaging, and information services through a global distribution system. Currently, ICO claims that it is on target for service a rollout in 2001 after completing satellite launches and system testing.

ICO has secured working capital of $2.5 billion from investors in more than 55 countries worldwide. Many of these investors represent some of the top 30 telecommunications operators globally, as well as satellite and mobile telecommunications organizations, including Inmarsat, Hughes Space and Communications, Comsat, NEC, and Ericsson, among others.

The ICO wireless broadband network will operate through 20 operational satellites (23 will be launched) in medium-Earth orbit (MEO) at an altitude of 10,355 km. The ICO satellite constellation, with a lifespan of 13 years, will operate in two orthogonal planes. The orbit will be inclined at 45 degrees to the Equator, with each plane having five operational satellites plus one spare. The orbital pattern is designed for significant coverage overlap, ensuring that at least two satellites will be in view of a user and access node at any given time. Each satellite will cover close to 40 percent of the Earth's surface at a given time. When determining the orbit for its satellites, ICO examined the benefits and consequences of the MEO, LEO and GEO orbits. Not wanting the technical complexities and costs of constructing and launching numerous satellites to operate in LEO, nor wanting the common voice delay of the GEO, ICO found the MEO to be the system's most beneficial orbital altitude.

Hughes Space and Communications was awarded a contract from ICO to design, develop, and construct the 13 satellites and associated telemetry, tracking, and control equipment. The satellites are versions of the popular HS601 model, with selected subsystems modified for the special requirements of the MEO. Hughes Space and Communications also has won the contract from ICO to supply launch and manage services for the 13-satellite system. The satellites will be launched during a 30-month period. Initial selections of launch vehicles include the Atlas 2AS (Lockheed Martin), the Delta 3 (McDonnell Douglas), the Proton (U.S.-Russian Launch Services Joint Venture), and the Zenith Sea Launch (Boeing-led Sea Launch Co.). Once in orbit, ICO satellites will communicate with 13 satellite access nodes (SANs) located around the globe. The SANs will provide the primary interface with the satellites for routing traffic and maintaining data. They also will link with gateways that will serve as the primary interface with public-switched telephone, mobile, and wireless broadband data networks. Each SAN complex will include five high-performance tracking antennas and associated control and switching equipment to provide the space-to-Earth interface. These 13 SANs, along with two network management centers and other related ground facilities, make up ICO's ground segment, or ICOnet.

The ICO system is designed to use preexisting terrestrial switching and routing whenever possible. ICO services are designed to complement cellular coverage, provide service where terrestrial systems do not reach, and provide an alternative when fixed systems are incompatible. ICO's satellite systems and Earth stations, coupled with partnerships with local cellular service providers and fixed network operators, will provide global roaming options to cellular customers worldwide. The consumer requires a service agreement with its local cellular provider (not ICO) and a dual-mode handset to have access to the ICO satellite system. The ICO service will be arranged and paid for through local service providers—thus keeping life simple for the consumer. Currently, ICO has signed service agreements covering more than 100 countries worldwide. ICO investors such as Hughes also have the options to be ICO service providers.

The ICO handsets are being designed and manufactured by such telecommunications equipment manufacturers as Mitsubishi, NEC, and Panasonic, among others. The handset, similar in size and weight to current mobile phones, will be compatible with satellite, cellular, and PCS systems based on U.S., Japanese, GSM, and other cellular standards. The dual-mode handset will select either satellite or terrestrial modes of operation automatically. Or, if under user control, it will be subject to the availability of satellite and terrestrial systems and the consumer's service arrangement. Consumers also will be able to communicate via satellite using specially designed equipment in automobiles, maritime vessels, and aircraft.

One problem common to all MEO operators is the radio interface with the handset. All satellite systems are characterized by low receive signal strengths when compared with cellular systems. For this reason, along with the need to clear the receiver's head to avoid signal blockage, the antenna must be bigger. Therefore, it will most likely be a foldable antenna and will require some interesting mechanical solutions. An additional problem being faced by MEO operators in the 2-GHz spectrum, is the regulatory affairs (relocation of systems) currently in operation in this spectrum that will be necessary. The estimated costs and work are gigantic.

Like the other big LEOs, ICO has received a warm reception from the financial community. ICO even found itself in the enviable position of turning away excess investment when it was funded initially. A total expected end-to-end requirement is $5.6 billion. The remainder of the funding is expected to come from additional equity from shareholders, an IPO, high-yield debt, and project bank debt.

More Players to Come   In July 1997, two more big LEO operators, Constellation Communications, Inc., and Mobile Communications Holdings, Inc., were announced. The funding behind Constellation comes from Verizon Communications (formally Bell Atlantic), Raytheon E-Systems, Spacevest, vendors, and a group of strategic investors from key markets within its equatorial service area. Constellation has a two-phased approach to implementing its LEO system. Phase I, dubbed *ECCO* and costing some $701 million, involves 12 operational satellites and one spare in equatorial orbit. ECCO is a merger of U.S. and Brazilian plans for a LEO system for voice, data, and paging services—principally to rural areas throughout the world's tropical regions, where telephone service is currently nonexistent. ECCO is sponsored in part by the Brazilian government, and the scheduled operational date for service is 2001. Constellation also will proceed with its phase II plans, calling for an additional 56 spacecrafts, 7 in each of eight planes (although one craft in each plane will be an in-orbit spare). Constellation's satellites are relatively light at 500 kg, orbiting at 2000 km, and scheduled for launch on a choice of LMLU, Taurus, Sea Launch, Shavit, or Ariane rockets. Constellation will sell wholesale space-segment capacity to existing terrestrial service providers with emphasis on the provision of rural fixed-wireless services and as a services complement to terrestrial cellular.

Mobile Communications Holdings' (MCHI) license covers its $1.2 billion big LEO Ellipso system of 28 satellites in highly inclined and elliptical equatorial orbits. There are a number of investor/partners, including Orbital Sciences, Aon Risk Services, L-3 Communications, and Israel Aircraft Industries. Also involved are U.S. technology companies such as

Harris Corp., Lockheed Martin Management and Data Systems, and Arianespace, as well as Vula Communications of South Africa and Spectrum Network Systems of Australia. Ellipso comprises two constellations of craft: Borealis, with two planes of five satellites apiece in inclined elliptical orbits over the Northern Hemisphere, and Concordia for the tropics and southern latitudes. MCHI expects 20 satellites in elliptical orbit (at 7846-km apogee, 520-km perigee) in two inclined planes with 3-hour orbital periods that will be sufficient to cover the Borealis service region above the Tropic of Cancer. Concordia will contain six crafts at a circular equatorial orbit (at 8040 km) that will be supplemented in time by four additional craft in a complementary elliptical orbit to increase daytime capacity. Service is scheduled to begin in 2001.

Little LEOs   The so-called little LEOs will provide lower-rate data services than their big LEO counterparts. Little LEOs are designed to provide store-and-forward data as well as paging services. One system, Orbcomm, has begun launching its little LEO constellation. Other systems are in various stages of development.

Leo One is a 59-satellite little LEO system that will target vehicle tracking, status monitoring, data acquisition, paging, e-mail, security monitoring, and emergency alerting. The Leo One system will provide high-quality store-and-forward coverage to all points on Earth between 73° North and 73° South latitudes. The overlapping coverage footprints ensure that satellites are always visible to users between 30° and 60° North and South latitudes—assuming a conservative 15° mask angle. This enables Leo One to offer near-real-time service for a region. Using the more standard 5° mask angle, the band of near-real-time service availability extends from 65° North and South—nearly to the Equator.

Leo One is the only little LEO capable of near-real-time service. All the other little LEOs experience significant gaps in availability that prevent them from serving those applications and markets which require near-real-time service. Based on independent studies, the company suggests a worldwide demand of 150 million subscribers by the end of 2010, with perhaps 119 million subscriber terminals in the United States alone. Part of Orbcomm's strategy is the new world of low-cost supervisory control and data-acquisition (SCADA) terminals. Available spectrum may be a challenge, but applications involving the automatic reading and reporting of utility meters via satellite could save electricity, gas, and water companies hundreds of millions of dollars. The little LEO data services could grow to more than 31 million by 2005. To address this market, Orbcomm is adding new gateways and new satellites. The complete system will be a 39-satellite constellation, with 9 as backup—which can be deployed to a new plane if there is a coverage hole or capacity needs augmentation.

NOTE The new-generation Orbcomm satellites are suitcase-sized, 95 lb in weight, and launched by Orbital Sciences Pegasus rockets, with the complete constellation costing about the same to launch as a single conventional communications satellite.

Volunteers in Technical Assistance (VITA)[17] reports to be the first private voluntary organization to bring what it calls the privileges of affordable Internet and e-mail to the developing world. VITA is a low-cost twin-satellite LEO system, partly based on amateur and experimental satellites first launched back in 1984. New license applications call for a single craft (VITAsat 1R), of which 60 percent of the operational capacity would be allocated for commercial use. VITAsat 1R will operate at a 1000-km height in a near-polar orbit, allowing users twice-daily access. VITA plans for up to 2000 Earth stations (costing $4600) to provide Internet access that will have special gateways in Norway, South Africa, Australia, and Chile.

Conclusion

As this chapter has clearly pointed out, planning and designing wireless broadband network applications are much more than the study of how to do it. The many different elements that constitute the field of planning and designing wireless broadband network applications interact in highly complex ways, with technology being only a part of the process. In any prediction of the trend of deployment of technology, it is useful to understand the process of these interactions.

The information environment of the twenty-first century seems very likely to be increasingly *hybrid*. This is to say that virtually every message, call, or transmission on future wireless broadband networks will be routed through links that are part wire and part wireless—sometimes changing back and forth several times. This is what the new future-oriented concept known as the *universal personal planning and designing of wireless broadband network applications* is all about.

This is so because the future of planning and designing wireless broadband network applications seems likely to represent a merger of the two basic technologies into complex interlinked networks. This trend is projected on the basis of the need to combine the broadband throughput and performance of fiberoptic with the flexibility, mobility, and accessibility of wireless.

Planning and designing wireless broadband network applications are heavily affected by the factors of technology standards, services and applications, management, tariffs, finance, policy, and regulation. All these factors interact within the broader marketplace. In short, this model suggests that attempting to understand planning and designing wireless broadband network applications by considering only technology, or only pricing concepts, or only regulation simply will not work. The key to addressing a complex field such as planning and designing wireless broadband network applications is thus seen as being at once multidisciplinary and interdisciplinary in scope. It requires understanding of the entire field with a synoptic overview. An integrated set of legal, regulatory, economic, marketing, business, and technological skills is needed to understand this rapidly evolving field.

The market that is defined by global planning and designing of wireless broadband network application products and services is expected to reach about $2 trillion by the year 2002, and the wireless broadband component of this market is estimated to be 30 to 35 percent of the total. The scope and size of the wireless broadband market will change rather dramatically over the next decade. This is particularly so in terms of shifts in the relative standing of the services provided within this high-growth industry. The sectors projected to grow the most are personal communications service, cellular, specialized mobile service (including enhanced SMR), wireless broadband LANs and PABXs, and personal digital assistants. Some studies have even suggested that cellular and PCS services alone will capture at least 35 percent of the total wireless broadband telecommunications market by 2006. These projections may seem to be overly optimistic at this time. Significant growth is also projected for wireless broadband cable television, mobile and direct broadcast satellite systems, and fixed and navigational satellite services.

In a general sense, those wireless broadband technologies which provide mobility, flexibility, and compact transportability will likely thrive and prosper in the marketplace. This is most likely to be so when these wireless broadband systems are also designed to connect to wire-based terrestrial systems in a seamless and highly cost-effective fashion. In short, an information megatrend is that both communications and entertainment will be increasingly mobile and personally interactive.

Wireless broadband services that compete directly with wire-based services for delivery of wireless broadband telecommunications to fixed locations likely will experience little growth. Those which supplement and augment fiberoptic cable systems, on the other hand, can be expected to expand rapidly. The only issue is the speed and dimension of the transformation.

Hybrid systems—those which merge or combine wire and wireless broadband technology—rather than outright substitution (or a dramatic flipflop), seem likely to be the predominant trend for perhaps some decades to come. By the end of 2010, there will be an era of air and glass as hybrid systems grow and mature.

The world of wireless broadband technology will be driven heavily by the rapid developments in fiberoptic cables. The development of solution pulse technology, the so-called repeaterless cable, advanced optical repeaterless cable, and advanced optical switching systems, not only will create a surge in the overall field of wireless broadband telecommunications but also will challenge the future development of wireless broadband technology as well. We may well see fiberoptic cables capable of transmitting a terabit per second by 2011. This suggests that communications satellites likely will need to achieve data rates of at least 100 Gbps by that time if they are to stay reasonably competitive. Mobile systems to vehicular, maritime, or aeronautical traffic also will likely need to achieve something on the order of 1.5 Mbps for voice/data/video links to keep pace with projected growth in wireless broadband services.

Two factors can contribute most to reducing costs. These are technological innovations and economies of scale or scope. Fortunately for the field of wireless broadband telecommunications, both forces are very active. The new technologies, coupled with the rapid growth of the subscribers base, certainly should continue to push the cost of cellular radio telephones downward. The same is true for CMTS services for at least the European and Asia-Pacific markets. Soon PCS services should be following the same trend line of reducing costs and prices. The area of satellite services (including fixed, mobile, broadcast, and navigation) also will show cost and price reductions. These reductions, however, may be more driven by technological innovation than by rapid market growth or major new economies of scale. In fact, it will most likely be a combination of the three.

The other major factor affecting the pricing of wireless broadband telecommunications is that related to competitive forces in the marketplace. In many parts of the world, the wireless broadband telecommunications market is being opened to competitive forces. In Europe, the licensing process for competitive VSAT terminals is now being opened to competitive suppliers. In many countries, such as New Zealand, the United States, and Hong Kong, competitors for cellular or PCS services are being allowed to compete with one another and, in effect, to purchase their frequencies on a competitive basis as well. Some believe that these combined processes, including new satellites for personal communications services, will produce a mobile service for under $0.25 per minute within 5 years and that, ultimately, the price differential for both long-distance communications and mobile services may become very small indeed. This is to say that only value-driven considerations will tend to keep mobile and long-distance service priced significantly above conventional services.

This strong pattern of innovation and competition likely will create a dilemma for the field of wireless broadband telecommunications. The potential problem would be that of declining price structure, which without rapid market growth could easily result in lower revenues. This suggests that new services, and especially important new value-added services, will need to be constantly added to the marketplace if net revenues are to continue to increase. Wideband mobile services for videoconferencing and imaging, enhanced GPS controls for "smart" highways, mobile telecommunications service for the distribution of electronic newspapers, and high-service/high-performance virtual offices will be among these new value-added services that will fuel new market growth. These high-value and high-productivity services seem to be a predictable part of the future. The highly competitive market for wireless broadband service also could lead to a continuing pattern of merger and acquisition.

A final issue is that of financial equilibrium on a global scale. The discrepancy in tariffing of wireless broadband telecommunication services worldwide is enormous. The high rates charged for wireless broadband telecommunications services in countries where there are still monopolies reflects a viewpoint that these markets and services are inelastic. Increasingly, however, call-back systems of other international carriers and competitive satellite systems are serving to provide competition, and rates are being driven downward.

The result over the next decade seems likely to be a downward movement of tariffs and greater parity or equilibrium between and among all service providers. In short, satellite, cellular, wire, or other forms of telecommunications will tend to reach common or at least comparatively equal cost and price levels without major discrepancies among them. This will be due in part to the overall driving force of digital processing in all these transmission technologies. This also should serve to equalize the current discrepancies in wireless broadband telecommunications rates, which give rise to serious problems and inequalities in the international collections and settlements process. Those entities or countries which seek to hold out against this overall macrolevel trend may very well find themselves losing businesses, investment, and even international standing as a progressive or enlightened nation.

NOTE Innovations in business practices to allow global decentralization of major international corporations as well as broad acceptance of concepts in total quality management and time-based management will allow progressive corporations to achieve a strategic advantage based on consumer satisfaction, rapid innovation and prototyping, and employee responsiveness.

The currently confused state of international, regional, and national standards making is not likely to resolve itself quickly. The "balkanization" of the standards-making process, if anything, continues to accelerate. The combination of business-based, professional, society-based, national and regional government-based, and international organization–based (UN and non-UN) standards-making organizations has proliferated greatly. Furthermore, the spread of these entities also has led to the spread of special joint technical working groups and committees, whose mission is to try to coordinate the work of their constituent groups.

When there are increasing numbers of joint committees whose responsibilities are defined by coordinating the efforts of standards committees and groups, one senses that the entire process is in trouble. The examples of PCS standards for the United States and the modulation standards for the so-called big LEO system illustrate the serious nature of the problem.

In the first case, the number of options being considered by PCS standards has been painstakingly narrowed from 20 to 7, but then no further resolution among the options proved possible, and thus all 7 were *accepted as standards*. This complicated process has already involved many thousands of weeks of activities, and the chances of a uniform global standards for PCS is today almost nil.

In the second case, deciding on the approved multiplexing technique to be used in the so-called big LEO satellite systems of the United States (in a process known as *negotiated rule making*) took over 1 year of effort that involved expenses to government and industry in the millions of dollars. Amazingly, this process, despite earnest and well-meant negotiations and technical discovery, ended without a clear-cut result. Some favored TDMA, and others, CDMA. The FCC thus was finally forced to segment the band between the two techniques.

The implication of these two examples, plus dozens more that also could be cited, is that both the regulatory and standards-making processes regarding existing and future wireless broadband telecommunications are inefficient, overlapping, and clearly handicapped by too many entities being involved. The processes are also greatly burdened by a high level of overhead, expense, highly legalistic processes, and sometimes strong political pressures as well. When it is realized that a measurable percentage of the cost of wireless broadband telecommunications is attributable to standards making and that this cost is now in billions of dollars, it seems clear that reforms are needed.

The rise of national and regional standards-making bodies as well as numerous international and regional bodies representing professional engineers, industry, and trade-based groups not only has eroded the former strength of the ITU in this area but also has created a process of multiple appeal. If one is not successful in one standards group, then one frequently can try again in another forum. If one is a multinational firm operating in many countries, the possibilities in terms of promoting one's own approach to a new or revised standard can go on for a very long time. Today, there seems to be no easy way to move from regional groups back toward a more integrated international approach or even to reduce the international participants to a smaller and more focused number.

The most significant development in worldwide wireless broadband telecommunications over the last decade is not a new technology or a service but rather the creation of a competitive marketplace. The move away from the monopolized provision of wireless broadband telecommunications services is gathering momentum the world over. The importance of natural monopolies and economies of scale has proved to be much less than thought. Today, many regulators are content to say that if a de facto monopoly cannot win out over its new competitors through fair competitive practices, then it was not really a *natural* monopoly with true economies of scale after all. Rapid technological innovation makes it truly difficult for any one established entity with a large investment in plant and equipment to dominate any market for any length of time.

The rapid spread of deregulation and competition within the wireless broadband world seems easily explained as simply part of a broader industry trend. The characteristics of wireless broadband telecommunications, however, also make it particularly well suited to deregulation. This is so because new entrants can enter the market without massive capital investment or long-term implementation schedules. The flexibility of coverage of wireless broadband systems allows customers to be easily aggregated from different locations, and capacity can be reallocated to meet emerging market needs. This can, for instance, allow a competitive cellular system to overlay an existing urban terrestrial network as new competition. It also can supplement the existing system or act as a hybrid of an operationally integrated, fixed, and mobile service provider. In contrast, terrestrial networks involve much larger investments and longer-term implementation. The basic need to try to achieve economies of scale, often associated with monopolistic terrestrial systems, do not necessarily apply to wireless broadband systems.

These changes are also frequently accompanied by streamlined or reduced regulatory control. In particular, entities such as OFTEL in the United Kingdom or AUSTEL in Australia, have been created to control violations of the framework that allows open and fair competition. This can result in heavy penalties and substantial fines, but it also allows a small and streamlined entity to monitor the industry rather than a detailed oversight group to review every service and every tariff—as is the case with the FCC in the United States. It is now felt in these countries that they have graduated to reregulation from the previous deregulation regime and that the new setup is more stringent than the one existing before deregulation.

However, this market and the financially driven regulatory environment can have its difficulties in that they are not well equipped to address technical, standards, interoperability, and interconnection issues. The problem of subscriber privacy and encryption cannot be handled easily by this minimalist approach. Likewise, the issue of control of children's television and the issue of convergence of wireless broadband telecommunications, broadcasting, consumer electronic goods, software, and content sectors simply cannot be handled by market forces alone. Social issues that do not easily translate into economic equations cannot be handled easily or even addressed adequately by a regulatory regime whose only responses to marketplace problems are economic equations. Nevertheless, social intervention that runs counter to market demand and economic forces is usually also doomed to failure. Balance between all the drivers within the regulatory process is thus often the key to success.

Finally, these factors represent an interesting and, at times, even contradictory list of considerations. They could, on the one hand, accelerate the rapid growth and development of wireless broadband telecommunications while inhibiting it, on the other. Although not every possible aspect of planning and design of wireless broadband network applications has been covered in this chapter, it is hoped that every major aspect of the relevant market, service, technology, finance, management, standards, policy, and regulation issues has at least been addressed in a useful and meaningful way.

Endnotes

1. "Need for a Perspective Plan for Telecommunications," VSNL, Videsh Sanchar Bhavan, M. G. Road, Fort, Videsh Sanchar Bhavan, Mumbai, India 400 001, 2000.

2. *Ibid.*

3. *Ibid.*

4. *Ibid.*

5. *Ibid.*

6. *Ibid.*

7. *Ibid.*

8. *Ibid.*

9. *Ibid.*

10. *Ibid.*

11. *Ibid.*

12. *Ibid.*

13. *Ibid.*

14. *Ibid.*

15. *Ibid.*

16. *Ibid.*

17. Volunteers in Technical Assistance, 1600 Wilson Boulevard, Suite 710, Arlington, VA 22209, 2000.

CHAPTER 7

Local Multipoint Distribution Service (LMDS) Design Technology

The demand for affordable, fast data connections is increasing both in the United States and around the globe. There are several reasons why faster connections are not readily available and affordable. They are a complex mix of entrenched interests of the incumbent connection providers, the high costs of wireline upgrades and the associated slow pace, cumbersome regulations, and tariffs; and the difficulty of forcing more data through already crowded data pipes.

A new wireless broadband point-to-multipoint microwave technology called *local multipoint distribution service* (LMDS) stands ready to bypass those barriers to readily available broadband connections. In the United States, incumbent connection providers were prevented from owning or controlling the large block of LMDS microwave spectrum in their territory for a period of 36 months (from the auction); consequently, the chances of entrenched interests limiting bandwidth availability are small. In Canada, local multipoint communication service (LMCS) applications from entrenched landline providers were not accepted (see sidebar, "More Communication Choices for Canadians"). The 1 GHz of LMCS spectrum was awarded to newly established companies and consortiums.

More Communication Choices for Canadians

Local multipoint communication systems (LMCS) is a wireless broadband system that is capable of carrying basic and advanced communications services. LMCS licensees provide competition to cable, telephone, and satellite distribution systems. This technology touches all three objectives set by the government for building the information highway: creating jobs through innovation and investment in Canada, reinforcing Canadian sovereignty and cultural identity, and ensuring universal access at reasonable cost.

LMCS applicants have invested over $5 billion and created up to 12,000 new jobs over the last 5 years in the wireless industry. Licenses were awarded for 1 GHz for 44 markets each to CellularVision Canada, Ltd., and Digital Vision Communications, and a similar license for service in 138 small communities was awarded to Regional Vision, Inc., to ensure that the expanding information highway continues to reach Canada's remote communities.

It is through the introduction of new and innovative products and services such as LMCS that Canadians will benefit from increased employment opportunities, a stronger economy, and more consumer choice. Thirteen detailed submissions were received and evaluated. The criteria for the awarding of the licenses, as outlined in the policy and call for applications, were competitive strategy, innovation, economic benefits and research and development, coverage, and demonstrated competencies.

What Is LMCS? Local multipoint communication systems (LMCS) is a broadband wireless telecommunications common carrier service in the 28-GHz range that is capable of carrying basic and advanced communications services such as *wireless* cable TV, Internet access, video teleconferencing, and various other multimedia.

Signals from a central transmitting/receiving station are sent to and received from homes and businesses within a 4- to 5-km radius. Several such stations are required in each city to service the total geographic area. Homes and businesses send and receive the signals through equipment consisting of a small, unobtrusive antenna plus the associated electronics, which are about the size of a television converter. The frequency band for LMCS consists of six spectrum blocks of 500 MHz each.

Competition in Telecommunications With advancements in the technologies used by each industry to deliver their services and ongoing change in the regulatory framework, each is now able to provide the other's core services, thereby offering a full range of services to consumers on a competitive basis.

A key aim of the policy measures adopted by the industry is for Canada to foster diversity of choice for consumers and businesses. These independent local networks for telecommunications services are fully competitive with existing networks.

Why License LMCS in Canada? Consumers have been asking for more choice in the provision of telecommunications and broadband distribution services in the home and workplace. Canadians also have embraced the use of personal computers and require cost-effective alternatives for the provision of high-capacity links to the outside world. LMCS are able to deliver on both these points.

Field trials and experimentation have been carried out in various Canadian cities as well as in the United States and Brazil. The United States government has recently introduced LMCS on a wide scale, and both Russia and Chile now have LMCS operations in their countries. The United States authorized at least 1 GHz to LMCS. Canadian interests will be served best by staying at the forefront of this technology.

Originally designed for wireless digital television transmission, LMDS and multipoint microwave distribution system (MMDS) were predicted to serve wireless broadband subscription television needs. MMDS is also a broadband wireless communications service that operates at lower frequencies. Usually, LMDS operates at frequencies above the 10-GHz range and MMDS at frequencies below the 10-GHz range. Later on they were extended to offer other interactive services.

NOTE Multipoint microwave distribution system, also known as multichannel multipoint distribution system and wireless cable, is another wireless broadband technology for Internet access. MMDS channels come in 6-MHz chunks and run on licensed and unlicensed channels. Each channel can reach transfer rates as high as 27 Mbps (over unlicensed channels: 99 MHz, 2.4 GHz, and 5.7 to 5.8 GHz) or 1 Gbps (over licensed channels). MMDS is a line-of-sight service, so it will not work well around mountains, but it will work in rural areas, where copper lines are not available.

Before discussing LMDS, it is necessary to understand the importance of using wireless broadband technology for local-area networks (LANs) first and then to look at the different methods available for wireless broadband communications.

Using Fixed Wireless Broadband Technology

Until about 1996, the only economical way to connect LANs was through a wired infrastructure. In the last 5 years, several new wireless broadband LAN infrastructures have been proposed and built. Wireless local loop is a new wireless broadband option and comes under fixed wireless broadband as opposed to mobile. *Fixed* here refers to a fixed location. It means that the data transmission is wireless and that the stations are fixed, unlike in mobile, where the stations could be moving (assuming that a station is a subscriber). Here, the stations communicate at a very high speed. Dense modulation schemes are also required, and a higher signal-to-noise ratio is required in the fixed wireless broadband scheme.

Advantages of Using Fixed Wireless Broadband Technology for LANs

Some of the various advantages of adopting a fixed wireless broadband paradigm are

- The entry and setup costs are very small (setup cost is very low, and expansion can always be opted on demand).

- Systems can be set up with great ease and speed. All equipment can be carried and installed with great ease.

- Equipment can be set up only after a customer signs up. This is different from wired systems, because for wired LANs, a complete infrastructure has to be built even before the customers show up.

- The buildout becomes *demand-based*, which is a major advantage when compared with wired architectures.

- The cost of upgrading can be substantially less, since there is no other infrastructure other than the end equipment. Once the equipment is designed to be upgradable, upgrading becomes very easy.

- There is less overhead for changing the transmission equipment, and many problems of wired LANs, such as damage tracking in transmission equipment, do not exist at all.

- Once the basic infrastructure is handled, quality of service can be achieved.

- Bandwidth reuse is very high because of the cell structure used.

- Network management, maintenance, and operating costs can be very low. However, it is believed to be low at this time, but as the number of users grow, network management and operating costs will increase. Nevertheless, there is no real evidence that in the long run it will be less expensive to manage the networks (software and personnel costs). Maintenance, on the other hand, is definitely lower because there is less physical plant.[2]

Thus the recent wireless broadband networks have the ability to offer a wide range of one-way and two-way voice, data, and video service transmission capabilities with a capacity many times larger than any current wireless or nonwireless service.

Different Methods Available for Fixed Wireless Broadband Communications

In order to achieve fixed wireless broadband communications, various physical media and equipment can be used—ranging from infrared, to microwave, to radiowave. A major problem with using an infrared signal is that it can be obstructed by physical objects. It is also likely that it can be affected by extreme weather conditions such as heat. Thus there should be an unobstructed path between the communicating equipment, which is not always possible. Microwave systems operate at less than 500 mW of power. For fixed service, broadband wireless access systems are of particular interest. The reasons for this are that they are very quick to install and are economical and cost-effective. Moreover, interconnection of the base station to fixed public switched telephone network (PSTN) is also possible and easy. In using the wireless broadband signal, there are various issues that need to be discussed, one important one being the spectrum that can be used.

Spectrum Allocation and Partitioning

The primary issue that needs attention is the spectrum in broadband that is best suited for fixed wireless needs and the bandwidth required for achieving a high data transmission rate. The FCC made several new bands of wireless spectrum available. In order to create viable opportunities for wireless broadband competition to incumbent local exchange carriers (ILECs) (they built a wired high-speed infrastructure for data transmission), the FCC enhanced the capacity of the existing spectrum licenses. It started a host of omnidirectional wireless high-speed-access (HSA) networks. The new allocations promote bidirectional transport with no receive-site license required.

Now let's discuss the new omnidirectional transmission bands. There are many bands other than the ones just discussed but none with exclusive licensing structure and bandwidth.

Integration with Existing Technology

The FCC has started a host of different omnidirectional high-speed access broadband networks that can be integrated with existing wireless broadband technology. They are

- The 38-GHz band
- The 28-GHz or LMDS band
- The DEMS band
- The MMDS band

The 38-GHz Band   The 38-GHz band is licensed primarily to WinStar. Winstar uses asynchronous transfer mode (ATM)-based equipment and provides plain old telephone service (POTS) and high-speed data. From a cost point of view (starting with point-to-point links and then as the network size increases), switching to an omnidirectional cell site is advisable. However, for a particular network, the shifting overhead is more, so it is better to start with omnidirectional networks.

The 28-GHz or LMDS Band   The 28-GHz band was regulated in 1998, with only a few major companies participating (see sidebar, "Propagation Impairment"). This is called the *LMDS band* because LMDS operates in this band in the United States.

NOTE   It could be different for different countries; for example, in Europe, it is the 40-GHz band.

The 28-GHz band has different blocks of bandwidth: the *A* block with 1150 MHz of bandwidth and the *B* block with 150 of MHz bandwidth. A high degree of *cellularization* is required with this band. Cell size is about 2 miles in radius. Various new proposals have been made about the band, and some of these will be discussed later in this chapter.

Propagation Impairment

Radio transmission at microwave frequencies (900 MHz to 60 GHz) has been used extensively for more than 50 years for a variety of applications, including long-haul transmission services for major carriers, backhaul transport, video distribution, cell-site interconnect, and private transmission (bypass).

One key issue that has challenged the radio design engineer is, *How far can you go with a microwave link?* While availability criteria, equipment specifications, and climate and terrain factors all affect the length of microwave paths, this part of the chapter specifically addresses the high-frequency bands, where rain is the controlling factor.

The frequency spectrum allocated by the FCC for local multipoint distribution services (LMDS) amounts to a total of 1150 MHz. The allocation is partitioned into three blocks of spectrum, with two located in the 28-GHz band (27.5–28.35 GHz and 29.1–29.25 GHz) and one located in the 31-GHz band (31.075–31.225 GHz). This massive amount of frequency spectrum will be used to supply broadband services such as voice, high-speed data, Internet, and video to subscribers that will include businesses of all sizes, school campuses, apartment complexes, and residential homes.

Service will be supplied via transmission from centralized hub locations transmitting via omnidirectional or broadbeam sector antennas with beamwidths of 45, 90, or 180 degrees. The hub transmitter will link to subscriber locations that will be equipped with roof-mounted 10- to 12-in directional antennas. To ensure that a link with acceptable availability is established between the central hub transmitter and each subscriber location, careful rf planning must occur. In some cases, the engineering approach in the LMDS frequency bands differs from the traditional approach taken when designing point-to-point microwave radio links in the lower part of the frequency spectrum between 2 and 11.2 GHz.

The part of the frequency spectrum between 30 and 300 GHz is referred to as the *millimeter-wave band* because the wavelengths vary from about 1 to 10 mm. At these wavelengths, the propagation impairments that control link availability differ from the controlling impairments in the S and X bands. While free-space loss between radiating elements is still the greatest common contributor to signal loss, the controlling propagation impairments at millimeter wavelengths include

- Attenuation by atmospheric gases
- Attenuation by precipitation
- Attenuation by foliage
- Attenuation by diffraction
- Attenuation due to reflection/signal scatter
- Attenuation due to heat

Engineering each hub-to-subscriber link with at least 60 percent of the first Fresnel zone clearance over terrain obstructions can mitigate losses from foliage, diffraction, and signal scatter. Losses due to signal absorption by water vapor and oxygen are significant and should be included in link budget calculations. Absorption losses are a function of path length and can be determined along with free-space loss provided the water vapor content is known. The remaining impairment is attenuation from rain, which is the greatest contributor to signal degradation at millimeter wavelengths. The elements of predicting attenuation from rain are encompassed in four quantities:

- Losses due to water being in or on an antenna
- The effective path length

- The rain rate distribution
- The specific attenuation

Losses due to water being in or on the outside of an antenna can be considerable depending on the characteristics of the radome or painted surface of the radiating element. Depending on the hydrophobic nature of the radiating element's exterior, during a period of rain, water will either form a film over the surface or bead in small droplets.

Studies have shown that a water film thickness ranging from 8 to 12 mm will cause 7 to 9 dB of attenuation, whereas beads of water droplets cause only 1 to 1.5 dB of attenuation. This wet radome loss degrades the rain attenuation margin such that outages from rain-induced fading will be greater than expected. The rain attenuation margin is simply the thermal fade margin adjusted by the wet radome losses of the hub and subscriber antennas. If a radio link is engineered with a 40-dB thermal fade margin and antennas are used that produce sheeting of water during rain (or snow or hail), at millimeter wavelengths the rain attenuation margin will be degraded as much as 8 dB per antenna such that a rain shower producing only a 24-dB fade would result in an outage.

The effective path length takes into account the nonuniform profile of the rain cell along the radio path. The effective path length is the length of a hypothetical path obtained from radio data dividing the total attenuation by the specific attenuation exceeded for the same percentage of time. Most rain attenuation models are based on a direct empirical relationship between a surface rain rate and an effective path length, which, when multiplied by the specific attenuation value for the surface rain rate, produces the desired attenuation value.

Recording the highest 1- or 5-minute average rain rate accumulated per year at a specific measurement site provides data from which rain rate distributions can be produced. By grouping measurement stations with similar distributions, it is possible to produce a climate region map. Rain region maps have been proposed by the International Telecommunications Union-Radiocommunications (ITU-R (CCIR)). Rain region maps traditionally are used as a matter of convenience when actual measured rainfall rate data are unavailable.

When determining outage time due to rain attenuation, Alcatel uses 5-minute rain rate distributions developed from data recorded at 263 weather stations across the United States. Using techniques developed by Bell Laboratories, 5-minute rain rate distributions were constructed using data that were collected over a period of 50 years.

By grouping cities with similar rainfall intensities, Alcatel devised seven rain regions in the United States that parallel the ITU-R rain regions. These seven regions are shown in Figure 7-1.[3] While Alcatel uses rainfall intensity curves for determining rain-induced outages, for the sake of comparing how far a path can reach, the seven rain regions are used in the examples that follow.

The specific attenuation is the loss per kilometer along a radio path and is a function of the rain rate, drop size distribution, drop shape, drop temperature, and velocity. These components have been

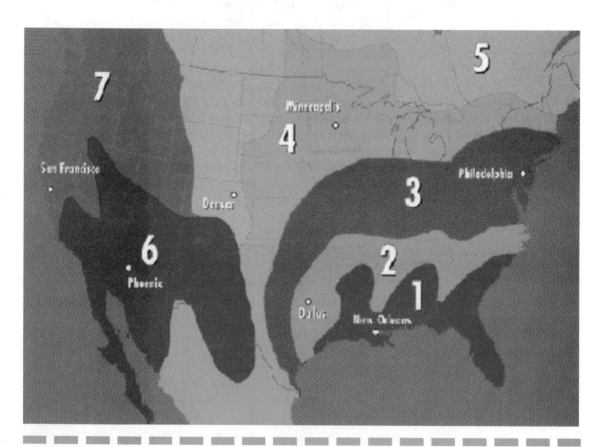

Figure 7-1   Rainfall intensity regions in the United States.

combined into rain attenuation models. The models take into account variations in the rain cell diameter depending on the rain rate, as well as the oblate spherical shape of rain drops and the correlated impact on signals of horizontal polarization compared with vertical.

The size of the LMDS cell depends on the system gain of the rf equipment, the gain of the hub and subscriber antennas, the rain region within which the LMDS system is located, and the acceptable level of path availability. Assuming that the rf system provides 104 dB of system gain and hub and subscriber antenna gains of 15 and 35 dB, respectively, Figure 7-2 shows how far a cell radius can extend in each of the seven rain regions for path availability figures ranging between 99.9999 to 99.9 percent.[4] Larger radii are possible by increasing the total gain of the system through

- Increasing the system gain of the rf equipment
- Increasing the gain of the hub antenna by using a high-gain antenna (21 dBi)

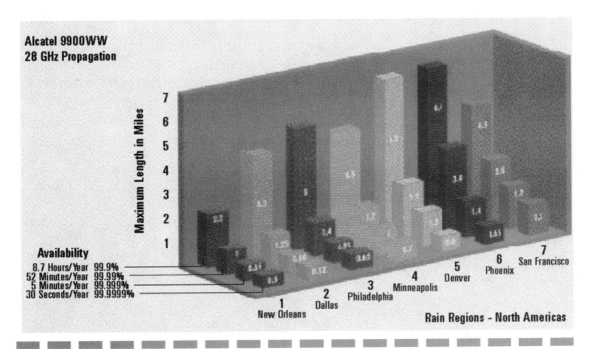

Figure 7-2 How far can you go?

- Increasing the directivity of the antenna by reducing the beamwidth from 90 to 45 degrees
- Increasing the size of the subscriber antenna

The results shown in Figure 7-2 illustrate further how millimeter wavelengths are affected by the lower rain rates. The higher availability figures (99.9999 percent) correspond to Figure 7-2. The 104-dB system gain corresponds with occurrences of higher rain rates, whereas lower availability figures correspond with lower rain rates. The higher frequency of rain showers that produce lower rain rates in regions 4 and 7 result in reduced cell radii in the case of 99.9 percent path availability. This result is somewhat unexpected because traditionally outages are expected to occur only during infrequent heavy downpours.

For the higher path availability cases, the additional path length that can be realized is only 2/10 or 3/10 of a mile. For lower path availability cases (99.9 percent), the additional path length is close to 1 mile. While the additional path length may not seem worth the expense of 6 dB of additional gain, it should be noted that the increase in square mile coverage ranges, on average, between 45 and 55 percent.

External interference also must be considered in outage calculations. Properly coordinated systems using receivers with reasonable selectivity will have no or very limited degradation due to external interference. While rain outage will limit path distances at higher frequencies, these same frequencies propagate considerable distances in the absence of rain and may degrade a path's availability.

External interference is site-dependent and not included in these calculations. Therefore, when designing a system with adjacent and overlapping cells, it is crucial to consider conditions that contribute to external interference and the effect on path availability.

It is important to understand that these results predict outages based on average rain rates. They do not represent a best- or worse-case scenario.

Due to the long-term variability of the statistical data required to accurately describe average conditions, the actual outage in a short period of time (less than 1 year) may vary dramatically from the calculation. Variations from predictions by a factor of 10 (better or worse) are possible.[5]

The DEMS Band The DEMS band was allocated originally at 18 GHz. It has 100 MHz of bandwidth.

The MMDS Band The FCC allocated about 200 MHz of spectrum at 2.1 and 2.5 to 2.7 GHz for television transmission. In 1995 and 1998, the FCC allowed for digital transmission with CDMA (code division multiple access), QPSK (phase shift keying), VSB (vestigial side band), and QAM (quadrature amplitude modulation) modulation schemes. This band is licensed primarily to such companies as SpeedChoice and Wavepath.

LMDS: The Technology for Fixed Wireless Broadband LANs

LMDS has proven to be a cost-effective technology that has no hassles of physical connections and can do two-way wireless broadband microwave transmission of mixed video, audio, and data. LMDS, the 28-GHz band in the United States (Europe uses the 40 GHz for LMDS), is the one that is being used for the wireless broadband LANs. Basically, it is a wireless broadband service that transmits fixed broadband microwave signals in the 28-GHz band of the spectrum within small cells roughly 2 to 3 miles in diameter. It offers a wide range of one- and two-way voice, video, and data service transmission capabilities with a very large capacity—better than what many current services offer. With millpond radio technology combined with an appropriate protocol, access method, and speed, LMDS is given the potential to transform society. When implemented with a multiservice protocol such as Asynchronous Transfer Mode (ATM), LMDS can transport among others, voice, data, and even video. As a transport system, LMDS can be engineered to provide 99.999 percent availability. A few of the various advantages of LMDS for local loops and LANs are as follows:

1. Overall, it is very cost-effective.
2. A major percentage of investment is shifted to customer premises equipment (CPE), which means that the operator spends money on equipment only if a customer signs up. Equipment cost can be shifted entirely to the customer in this model.
3. It has a very scalable architecture, and it uses open industrial standards—ensuring services and expendability.
4. Network management and maintenance are very cost-effective.[6]

Emergence of LMDS and Its Specifications   The advent of the LMDS channel was driven initially by digital TV applications. Standardizing for the digital TV was first initiated in Europe with the establishment of the Digital Video Broadcasting (DVB) project by the European Broadcasting Union. The technical specifications given by the DVB project were passed over to the European Telecommunications Standard Institute (ETSI) for the publication of standards. Focus on microwave transmission was then begun. The DVB created the standard for short-range millimeter-wave radio systems. Initially, it was called the *multipoint video distribution system* (see the sidebar, "MVDS") by the DVB.

MVDS

Multipoint video distribution system (MVDS) over the ETSI-recommended and CEPT-designated frequency bandwidth of 40.5 to 42.5 GHz has been used to deliver terrestrial digital video distribution services over small to moderately sized coverage areas. Compared with alternative distribution technologies, MVDS presents unique features, such as fast and low-cost deployment, regional programming, and interactivity that increase the competitiveness with CATV or satellite distribution. Moreover, MVDS at millimeter-wave frequencies offers a completely *transparent* interface with other distribution techniques and full compatibility with MPEG2 digital compression coding systems.

    A single omnidirectional transmitter or a group of sectoral broadcasting equipment constitutes a base station (BS). Generally, a BS converts a digital modulated multicarrier baseband signal to the millimeter frequency range in order to be a wireless broadcast over a coverage area with a radius of some kilometers. In this territory, several receiving units typically are placed on the roofs of buildings in line of sight (LOS) with the BS itself. Each customer-based remote terminal (RT) is implemented by a directional antenna (whose dimensions depend on the site distance from the BS and on service availability), a low-noise downconverter, and a standard decoder (or set-top box, STB). The RT receives and recovers the original digital signal bandwidth.

Compared with cable technology, MVDS offers fast installation/immediate coverage approach with low startup and maintenance costs. MVDS allows wireless broadband service provider business (against the monopoly of CATV networks), and at the same time it offers a suitable complementary solution to cabled distribution networks.

On different scenarios, MVDS permits the rebroadcasting of satellite distribution services together with local programming and advertising over profitable areas, full compliance with digital video satellite standards is accomplished, and compatibility with MPEG2 digital compression is guaranteed. Insertion of the hardware necessary to accomplish a return connection from the RTs toward the BS makes MVDS systems suitable to provide interactive services (video-on-demand, pay per view, etc.) and multimedia applications including the Internet.

Two classes of 42-GHz MVDS products have been developed: CATV-compatible equipment [suitable to implement alternative or extension of hybrid fiber coax (HFC) TV], distribution networks, and satellite-standard-compliant systems. Service provider requirements, different geographic area field-trial performances (cell size, service availability, BER, etc.), service distribution versus system implementation, and the approaches for asymmetrical interactivity through return channel capability all depend on multiple factors such as transmitted signal format, transmitter output power, transmitting and receiving antennas, receiver noise figure, requested service availability, geographic zone, etc.

Basic MVDS Configurations In order to minimize cost, volume, and outdoor unit (ODU) weight and increase system performance, a single multichannel transmitter configuration has been selected for this design. The basic transmitter characteristics are wide bandwidth approach [a single transmitter for 1-GHz (or more) broadcasting] and full solid-state power amplification.

The individual 42-GHz MVDS transmitter broadcasts a multicarrier input signal (generally 1 GHz wide and composed of a large number of multiple digital video programs) to the subscribers' RTs. The multichannel signal can be sent to the transmitter input already composed or, alternatively, formed at the BS site through suitable multiplexers. Generally, a single or double conversion step provides the translation into either the 40.5- to 41.5-GHz or the 41.5- to 42.5-GHz frequency range. A single power amplifier (selectable between a 1-, 5-, and 10-W configuration) and an individual antenna (single polarization) sustain the terrestrial broadcasting of the whole bandwidth. Sector coverage, with different azimuth angles, is used when a link budget requires a higher antenna gain. At each RT, the multicarrier signal is low-noise-amplified and downconverted by the receiver in order to provide at its output the original baseband signal.

Solid-state power amplification guarantees superior operating life. Moreover, multiple-parallel-module configuration increases transmitter mean time between failure (MTBF) performance with soft degradation of characteristics in case a failure occurs. Nevertheless, protected configurations with standby transmitter and switchover unit also have been developed for particular service provider requirements. The full-protected transmitting station has been implemented by using a dual indoor unit (IDU) and ODU setup. A millimeter-wave transfer switch, controlled by the transmitter control unit, provides the immediate switchoff of faulty equipment.

Receiver units have been designed and implemented through single or double low-noise downconverters, a pencil beam receiving antenna, and one or more set-top box decoders. Different receiving antenna sizes have been adopted from a small-diameter lensed-horn or patch antenna up to 60-cm parabolas. The receiving antenna typically is mounted on the building roof or on a wall. The receiver is enclosed in a weatherproof case located behind the antenna reflector in order to ensure the maximum grade of protection to the device.

MVDS systems can be alternative or complementary to two distinct terrestrial digital transmitting technologies: digital CATV broadcasting standard (DVB-C, digital video broadcast—cable for most of Europe and other countries) and digital satellite broadcasting standard (or DVB-S, digital video broadcast—satellite for most of Europe and other countries). In the first case, multiple 8-Mhz, 64-QAM modulated channels can be broadcast at 42 GHz—received and decoded by using standard CATV decoders. Alternatively, a satellite group of several bouquets can be retransmitted locally at 42 GHz, with the addition of regional programming and advertising, by using 39-MHz spaced QPSK-modulated channels and standard satellite decoders.

MVDS Compatible with DVB-C Standard In order to interface CATV networks as a wireless broadband complement to the last miles of HFC connections, specific 42-GHz MVDS equipment has been designed. DVB-C–compatible MVDS represents a *transparent* broadcasting system that directly takes the 54- to 860-MHz CATV input baseband, upconverts it at millimeter frequencies, and delivers it to customer RTs. In this case, a group of as much as 100- to 8-MHz, 64-QAM DVB-C channels in FDM format can be interfaced directly at a local node or fiber node from a single coaxial cable (or fiber), upconverted (all together), and then broadcast through an omnidirectional or a sector antenna. The advantage of this system is that once the multichannel baseband has been created, this can be delivered via HFC network to different hub stations, in which a single transmitter provides wireless broadcasting at 42 GHz. At each building terminal (BT), a low-noise downconverter unit transfers the original multicarrier signal to CATV set-top boxes (STBs). The advantages of the DVB-C–compliant MVDS system are best spectrum use (number of available broadcast channels) and direct interface with the CATV-HFC network.

With reference to the functional block diagram shown in Figure 7-3, a base station sector transmitter (DVB-C–compatible) is composed of an indoor unit (IDU) that operates a first frequency conversion into a 2.3- to 3.3-GHz through an AM SSB modulation.[7] This process includes

Figure 7-3
DVB–C–compatible MVDS sector transmitter.

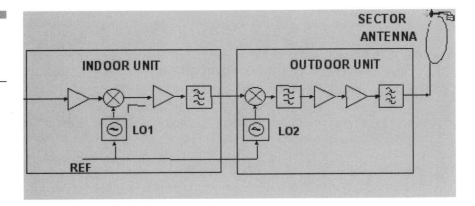

the insertion of a pilot tone to be used as a reference for the remote terminal PLL circuit. The local oscillator (and pilot tone) is phase locked to a high-stability internal reference. A personal computer (PC) control unit monitors and controls the fault and the configuration of each IDU and ODU transmitter subunit.

Through a 100-m-long coaxial cable, the 2.3- to 3.3-GHz multicarrier signal and the frequency reference are fed to the outdoor unit (ODU), which provides the second upconversion via an AM SSB modulation process and solid-state power amplification. Finally, different transmitting antenna sensor types can be used in order to provide the best coverage tradeoff in terms of range and area.

The MVDS-40C receiver is a double downconversion unit composed of an ODU and an IDU connected by a coaxial cable. With reference to Figure 7-4, the ODU includes a low-noise downconverter that translates the millimeter bandwidth into the 2.3- to 3.3-GHz frequency band.[8] The IF signal is then sent to a second downconverter that operates a further frequency translation in order to obtain the output signal in the 54-channel, 1000-MHz frequency band. Such a converter is provided by a phased-locked oscillator (PLO) circuit locked to the pilot tone and inserted at the transmitting site in order to compensate the millimeter-wave local oscillator frequency drifts. The indoor unit includes an N-way distribution unit (where N is the number of connectable DVB-C STB decoders) and a power supply unit providing the dc voltage to both the outdoor and the indoor units. The IDU is enclosed in a wall-fixed case.

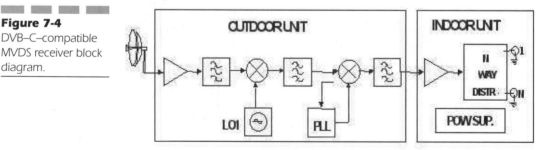

Figure 7-4

DVB–C–compatible MVDS receiver block diagram.

MVDS Compatible with DVB-S Standard Alternative 40.5- to 42.5-GHz MVDS systems have been developed in order to be compatible with the DVB-S standard. A single MVDS-40 wide-band transmitter for DVB-S can handle 24 (or 30) digital channels—generally an FDM mixture between locally generated bouquets and satellite-received programs. The individual transmitter directly upconverts the entire 1 GHz (or 1.2 GHz) of bandwidth at 42 GHz through a single AM SSB modulation and provides the terrestrial broadcasting. Satellite set-top boxes (STBs) are used at each customer remote terminal.

The corresponding receiver is a single conversion device with a low-noise amplifier at the input and output in the 950- to 1950-MHz (or 2150-MHz) frequency bandwidth. In this case, a single ODU is used, and the output signal is compatible with DVB satellite decoders. The power supply is provided by STB.

Comparison Between the Two MVDS Configurations The MVDS coverage area extension and system performance depend also on the kind of MVDS standard adopted. Considering a service availability of 99.7 percent over CCIR (E-zone) H polarization and a 72-degree sector transmitter with a 5-W power amplifier, a comparison between DVB-C or DVB-S standard–compatible MVDS can be achieved. Each system is dimensioned to carry on the maximum number of digital channels (30 channels to cover the 1.2-GHz bandwidth of satellite STB for MVDS-40S and 100 channels for MVDS-40C). Under these conditions, the satellite configuration allows a coverage radius of 10 km, with 25-cm receiving horn antennas, whereas the CATV-compatible configuration permits a maximum 4.5-km-radius coverage by using 60-cm receiving antennas. Despite the reduced system capacity, satellite configuration provides larger coverage areas with smaller receiving antennas. On the other end, the possibility of transmitting some hundreds of digital programs directly interfacing with HFC networks makes MVDS-40C more appropriate for applications such as near video on demand (NVOD).

Field Trial Results An DVB-C–compatible 42-GHz MVDS system has been installed and field tested for over 5 months by Telecom Italia, in the Roma-Ostiense (I) area (see Figure 7-5).[9] The sector antenna, a 72-degree shaped reflector (both in azimuth and in elevation) with

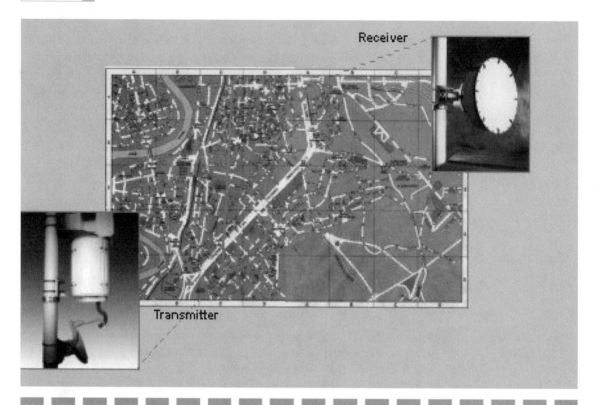

Figure 7-5   Telecom Italia field trial.

a minimum gain of 24 dBi over the 2-GHz bandwidth, has been housed externally to the Tx ODU in order to simplify the maintenance process without affecting antenna alignment. A suitable mount allowed full adjustment of the antenna's elevation and azimuth.

A system availability in excess of 99.9 percent has been demonstrated with more than 20 contiguous digital channels and over a 72-degree 2.2-km coverage sector in the K zone—in terms of rain intensity according to CCIR Recommendation 837. Each channel (64-QAM modulated) contained a different *bouquet* of MPEG 2-compressed video programs. A digital video analyzer R&S EFA QAM test receiver, interfaced with a PC for data storage, has been used to control bit error rate (BER), C over I ratio, jitter, symbol rate, and constellation spreading. The radio-link measurements, collected over the 5-month time frame, have been correlated with different environmental conditions (measured and recorded by a remote weather station placed in the middle of the covered area).

A 5-W sector DVB-S–compliant transmitter has been installed since January 1998 over the PTT tower in The Hague (The Netherlands). The MVDS transmitter rebroadcasts several satellite digital programs in the 40.5- to 41.5-GHz bandwidth over a 72-degree sector of more than 50 km². This area was extended to 250 km² when the installation of the other four adjacent sector transmitters was completed. Figure 7-6 shows the base station ODU transmitter (right) and the antenna (below the ODU), together with the satellite dish receiver (left).[10]

Some 42-GHz satellite standard–compatible MVDS receivers have been located within the coverage area with different antenna types according to the installation range from the PTT tower. This unit also has been connected to a Prolink analyzer in order to collect BER, *C/I*, and received power measurements. The MVDS system has been controlled remotely via modem, and all the operating data have been collected at the Technosystem Operations Center in Rome. A service availability of better than 99.9 percent has been demonstrated over The Netherlands E zone according to a CCIR 837 Recommendation. Figure 7-6 presents The Hague installation setup.[11]

Another international body called the *Digital Audio Video Council* (DAVIC) has come into existence. This body groups major network operators, service providers, and consumer electronics, telecommunications, and computer industries. Though DAVIC is not a part of any official standard making body, it is very powerful.

DVB Specifications In order for LMDS to benefit from the mass market of broadcasting satellites, specifications for LMDS downlink channels are the same as those of direct-to-home satellite services. Both use quarternary phase-shift key (QPSK) modulation and a concatenated forward error correction (FEC) coding scheme with a convolutional inner code and a Reed Solman (RS) outer code. The transmission frame is based on MPEG2 transport data stream.

The outer code carries 188 information bytes. It has a block length of 204 bytes and can correct up to 8 byte errors per each block. This code is obtained by shortening the RS (255,239) code. A convolution interleaver

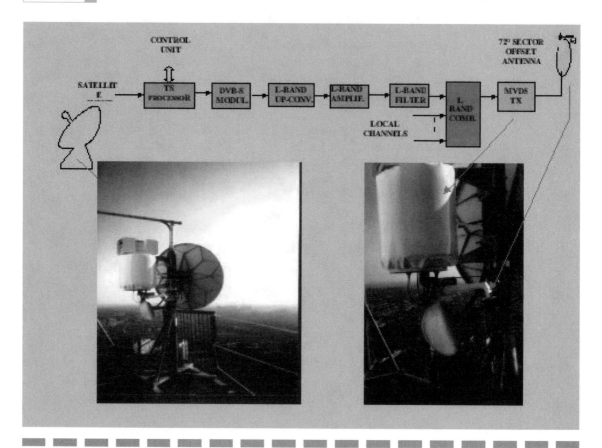

Figure 7-6   The Hague (NL) field trial.

(see Figure 7-7) with interleaving depth of $I = 12$ is inserted between inner and outer encoders.[12] This is done in order to uniformly distribute errors that occur by bursts at the VD output in the receiver. The interleaved and deinterleaved block diagram is sketched in Figure 7-7.

The input data bytes in the interleaver are fed in a cyclic fashion to the 12 parallel branches that consist of simple first-in, first-out shift registers. Starting from 0, the delays are increasing by multiples of 17, with the second branch having a 17-byte delay, and so on. It is given that a convolution interleaver of length N and depth I comprises I branches and that the Ith branch includes a delay of $(i \sim 1)N/I$ units. The output switch moves cyclically with the input switch. Except for the reverse order of the delays, the deinterleaver also has the same structure. The DVB specifications give all the transmission and receive functions and system parameters, except for the symbol rate of modem operation. This was so because no frequency planning was readily available.

Figure 7-7
Convolution
interleaver.

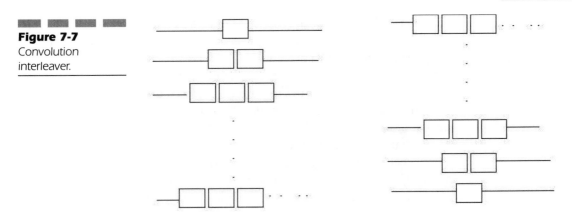

DAVIC Specifications   The DAVIC specification for LMDS basically is the same as the DVB specification except for an option of alpha values for channel filtering and either QPSK or 16 QAM for modulation. Basically, there is a lot of similarity between DAVIC and DVB specifications. DAVIC also seems to define future extensions. Along with the MPEG2 scheme use for detail video broadcasting (as discussed in the preceding section), a mapping function to the ATM data in the downstream channel is also made. Two 187-byte packets are formed when 3 control bytes are appended to 7 consecutive 53-byte ATM channels. A description of this is provided in Figure 7-8.[13]

Figure 7-8

Mapping of MPEG2
scheme to ATM cells.

Control Byte	ATM Cell 1 53 Bytes	ATM cell 2 53 Bytes	ATM cell 3 53 Bytes	ATM cell 4 53 Bytes

Control Byte	Control Byte	Cell 5 contd	ATM cell 5 53 bytes.	ATM cell 6 53 Bytes	ATM cell 7 53 Bytes

The specification of the return channel was done primarily by DAVIC because DVB was interested in broadcast services in its first phase. The return channel that has been designed by DAVIC for LMDS is a multiple-access channel, and it uses TDMA. The medium access control (MAC) protocol allocates time slots to different users. Each user can transmit only if he or she has been given a time slot. The time slots as per the specification consist of 68 bytes, which include a 4-byte preamble and a 1-byte guard. The remaining 63 bytes include 53 bytes of information and 10 bytes for parity check. Clearly, each time slot carries an ATM cell. Error protection on the upstream channel is not as efficient as it is on the downstream channel. However, compensation can be made at the design of the transmit and receive functions.

The MAC protocol is used to allocate resources to various user terminals. Both the downstream and upstream frames are encapsulated as one ATM cell. Each frame on the downstream frame includes two slots. There is a frame start slot, followed by a random access slot. The upstream frame has three slots, namely, the polling response slots, the contention slots, and the reserved time slots. The polling response slots are obviously used to respond to a poll message. The contention slots are shared and used by more than one terminal and may result in a collision. The contention when a collision occurs can be resolved in numerous ways—one by waiting for a random amount of time before retransmitting. Reserved time slots are reserved for use by the terminal. The terminal transmits on these slots whenever it has data, and when it does not have any data, it transmits an empty cell. The MAC protocol also has an option for a combination of circuit mode reservation for constant-bit-rate services, and it also has a dynamic reservation for variable-bit-rate and unspecified-bit-rate services. Polls are repeated periodically at intervals of less than or equal to 2 seconds. If a new user comes in, it listens to the downstream channel to find a message sent to it. If it does not find the message for 2 seconds, then it switches to the next downstream channel and listens. This goes on until the terminal finds the message transmitted to it.

LMDS Technical and Design Issues

A normal LMDS setup has a central facility with a fiber-linked PSTN and Internet connections that relay a signal via point-to-point microwave links, which in turn pass the signal along to hubs located on rooftops or as stand-alone towers for point-to-multipoint (PMP) transport to the end site. Basically, the four parts in the LMDS architecture are

1. Network operations center (NOC)

2. Fiber-based infrastructure

3. Base station

4. Customer premises equipment and NOC designs[14]

The network management equipment for managing regions of the customer network come under the NOC. Multiple NOCs can be interconnected. The fiber-based infrastructure basically consists of SONET, OC-12, OC-3, and DS-3 links; the ATM and Internet Protocol (IP) switching systems; interconnections with the PSTN; and the central office equipment.

The conversion from fibered infrastructure to a wireless broadband infrastructure happens at the base stations. Interface for fiber termination, modulation and demodulation functions, and microwave transmission and reception equipment are a part of the base station equipment. Local switching also can be present in the base station. If local switching is present, then customers communicating in the same base station can communicate with each other without entering the fiber infrastructure.

The customer premises equipment varies widely from vendor to vendor. All configurations include indoor digital equipment and modulation and outdoor mounted microwave equipment. The customer premises equipment may attach to a network using time-division multiple access (TDMA), frequency-division multiple access (FDMA), or code-division multiple access (CDMA). Different customer premises equipment requires different configurations. The customer premises will run the full range from DS0, POTS, 10baseT, unstructured DS1, structured DS1, Frame Relay, ATM25 serial, ATM over T1, DS-3, OC-3, to OC-1. And the customer premises locations can range anywhere from malls to residential locations.

Architectural Options　　There is one commonly discussed architecture with rf planning. Typically, the rf planning for these networks uses multiple-sector microwave systems. In this transmit and receive sector, antennas provide service over a 90-, 45-, 30-, 22.5-, or 15-degree beam width. The idealized circular coverage area around the cell is divided into 4, 8, 14, 16, or 24 sectors. Alternative architectures include connecting the base station indoor unit to the multiple remote microwave transmission and reception systems with an analog fiber interconnection between the indoor data unit and the outdoor data unit.

Manufacturers such as Ensemble Communications have come up with different approaches. One idea from Angel Technologies is to have an aircraft transmitting signals from overhead. The company called it HALO

Figure 7-9
The invisible fiber unit
(IFU) connecting the
buildings as a virtual
network.

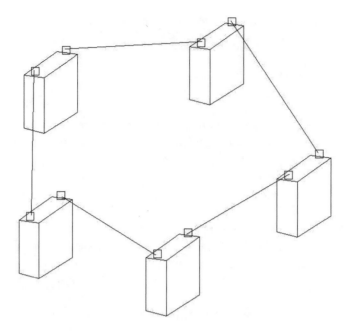

(high-altitude long-operating). This idea has various problems ranging from air traffic control to cost for medium-sized cities.

When developing an architecture, a standard issue that is considered is point-to-multipoint (PMP) communication. The question that arises is whether PMP is actually required. PMP allows multiple microwave paths—allowing spectrum and capacity to be shared as needed. Thus, when high bandwidth is required, the PTP (point-to-point) connection may be the best; otherwise, however, if a bandwidth on demand is the case, then PMP is well suited. A new model that is ramping up quickly is called *invisible fiber unit* (IFU) (see Figure 7-9).[15] Two IFUs are set up in a line-of-sight link and placed back to back with other links. Thus, in an IFU transmit and receive, a link should be created between source and destination.

Receiver Design   The customer premises equipment has one outdoor unit with a transmitter and receiver antenna and an indoor unit, which, in turn, communicates with subscriber equipment such as telephones and PCs. The indoor unit accepts the signal from the outdoor unit, demodulates and demultiplexes it, and then interfaces with the connected subscriber equipment. The downstream intermediate frequency in LMDS is the satellite intermediate frequency (950–2050 MHz). A major design issue for a receiver could be to achieve a large frequency-acquisition range in the carrier recovery loop.

Various Options in Access Methodologies   For any wireless broadband upstream link, there can be three access methodologies: TDMA, FDMA, and CDMA. In the downstream direction from base station to customer premises, most companies supply time division multiplexed (TDM) streams either to a particular user (PTP) or shared among various user sites (PMP). Figure 7-10 shows both the TDMA scheme and the FDMA scheme.[16]

The FDMA schema allows a fixed bandwidth or a bandwidth varying slowly over time. FDMA access links fit in well if the user requirement is a constant bandwidth (a dedicated one), especially when expecting continuous availability, such as a wireless DS3 or a multiple structured DS1 connection. FDMA links terminate in a dedicated FDMA demodulator, which, as it should be, is in the base station. When the customer does not have very heavy upstream traffic and just needs a 10baseT port, TDMA makes sense. Thus, the choice is based on customer requirements and system design.

Figure 7-10

The TDMA and FDMA access methodologies.

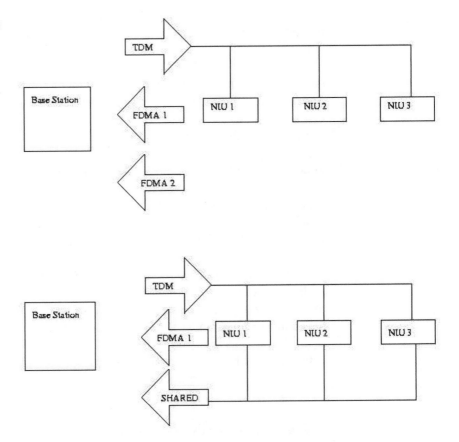

Code division multiple access (CDMA) supports a significantly smaller number of users than TDMA. Two classes of CDMA are available; one is orthogonal CDMA (OCDMA), and the other is the nonorthogonal CDMA. Systems often use a combination of the two. OCDMA is said to have identical capacity with TDMA. OCDMA allocates using a mutually orthogonal spreading sequence. The other class of CDMA, which is pseudonoise CDMA (nonorthogonal), is where all users interfere with each other, and the capacity depends on how much interference one is prepared to tolerate. Both CDMA and TDMA once again have case-based advantages, and both can be shown to be good in particular situations. When "smart" antennas are used, TDMA has an advantage.

"Smart" antennas use an adaptive array to cover a sector instead of fixed-beam antennas. With the help of sensor locations, the beam can be moved dynamically in the direction of the user. By changing the coefficients in the adaptive array, the beam can be moved horizontally or vertically. These "smart" antennas implement what is called *space division multiple access* (SDMA). Since the users in the TDMA are sequentially using the channel, it is well suited for the SDMA and "smart" antennas—whereas in CDMA the simultaneous access makes this complicated.

In discussing the data-rate capacity in both the access methods, you should use the bits per second per hertz measurement unit. For the various modulation schemes, this rate varies. Two areas where comparisons can be made would be data-rate capacity and the maximum number of customer premises sites.

MAXIMUM DATA RATE   The FDMA bandwidth spectrum efficiency is 1.5 bps/Hz for a 4-QAM modulation. For 16-QAM and 64-QAM modulation, the bandwidth spectrum efficiency is 3.5 and 5 bps/Hz, respectively. The TDMA band does not use 64-QAM modulation. For the other modulations, it has a reduced data rate.

MAXIMUM NUMBER OF CUSTOMER PREMISES SITES   In FDMA (assuming an x-MHz spectrum with a reuse frequency of r), the LMDS system provides an x/r-MHz usable spectrum per sector. If we assume the downlink spectrum to be d times the uplink spectrum, the downlink will have a $d(x/r)/(d + 1)$ spectrum, and the uplink will have an $(x/r)/(d + 1)$ spectrum. If the channel bandwidth is assumed to be b, then the maximum number of customer premise equipment would be

$$(x/r)/(d + 1)b$$

The TDMA for a given $(x/r)/(d + 1)$ spectrum assumes about 16 DS0 connections possible with 1 MHz. The total number of simultaneous users would then be $16(x/r)/[(d + 1)b]$. If the values of concentration over the entire sector and cell are assumed to be in the ratio $1/s$, then the total connections would be $s16(x/r)/[(d + 1)b]$—which would be very high when compared with what is possible with FDMA.

Network Planning Network planning for LMDS includes a cell design, where the design of an LMDS cell is discussed. Then the issue of planning the frequency comes in. After planning the use of a frequency (a very major issue, which could make a very big difference when it comes to data transmission speeds), the issue of cell reuse and reuse optimization should be discussed. Each of the preceding issues are discussed briefly next.

CELL DESIGN ISSUES The attributes that require attention while designing an LMDS cell are

- *Cell size selection.* Based on the desired reliability level, the cell size has to be decided.
- *Cell overlap.* This is an issue that has to be taken into consideration while designing the cells.
- *Subscriber penetration.* This is the number of subscribers having the required signal level to achieve quality of service.
- *Number of cells.* The number of cells in a sector depends on the cell size decided.
- *Traffic capacity.* Based on the traffic capacity of the area, the cell size and properties are fixed.
- *Quality of service.* Cell overlaps that exceed the allowed normal cell area (ca) affect the quality of service.
- *Link budget.* This is an estimation of the maximum distance that a user can be located from the cell while the cell is still achieving an acceptable service reliability.
- *Capital cost per cell.* This is used to estimate the network capital requirement.[17]

Telcordia Technologies, Inc. (formerly Bellcore), published a study of LMDS prior to the LMDS auction and concluded that only 25 cells covering only 2 percent of the land area should be built to yield an economical business. This may sound very attractive to the CLECs (competitive local exchange carriers).

Frequency Planning The channel spacing that is usable by the operators in Europe is 112, 56, 28, 14, 7, and 3.5 MHz. These are obtained by successive division of 112 by 2. The capacity in upstream and downstream locations usually differs because even if the bandwidth allocated is the same, the physical layer functions of both the channels are different. Thus, even if the bandwidth is equally distributed among the upstream and downstream channels, it is not possible to get the same capacity. Therefore, physical layer issues such as channel coding and filtering have to be taken into consideration when planning channels, especially if equal capacity for downlinks and uplinks is desired.

REUSE SCHEMES   A very important issue that can substantially change the speed of transmission and use of bandwidth is frequency reuse. In a given geographic area, how effectively can the frequencies be reused? The first possibility is to use a hexagonal cellular pattern (same old mobile cells). As illustrated in Figure 7-11, this frequency-allocation scheme requires three times the bandwidth allocated to one cell.[18]

Figure 7-11

The hexagonal cell reuse pattern.

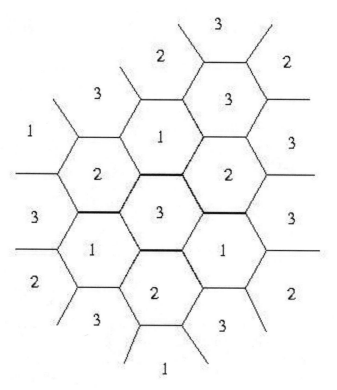

Figure 7-12
The rectangular-cell frequency reuse pattern.

d	c	c	c	d	c	c	d
b	a	a	b	b	a	a	b
b	a	a	b	b	a	a	b
d	c	c	c	d	c	c	d
d	c	c	c	d	c	c	d
b	a	a	b	b	a	a	b
b	a	a	b	b	a	a	b
d	c	c	c	d	c	c	d

Another possibility is to use rectangular cells. Each quadrant of the cell in Figure 7-12 is labeled with a digit that indicates the frequency or group frequencies used in that sector.[19] This frequency reuse pattern reduces the bandwidth requirements by 2 by using two orthogonal polarizations. This is shown in Figure 7-12. This is also the initial state. After optimization, the distribution is made with only two colors.

Antenna sectoring within a cell has the advantage of reducing the maintenance costs. A few techniques to optimize frequency reuse are

- Maximization of isolation between adjacent sectors through the use of polarization
- Maximization of the directivity of the cell antennas by sectoring the distribution system
- Minimization of cross-polarization and multipathing[20]

MODULATION SCHEMES Modulation schemes can tune the data rate to some extent. Low-density modulation allows greater distance at a given power but sacrifices data throughput rates. LMDS, however, uses QPSK;

therefore, it realizes about 1.8 Gbps of raw capacity even though it has five times the MMDS bandwidth.

NOTE   MMDS can give 1 Gbps using 64-QAM for its downstream links.

Recently, broadband developers have been taking more risk in employing advanced coding methods to achieve efficient use of bandwidth. Thoughts of using coding techniques such as orthogonal frequency division multiplexing (OFDM) for LMDS have been put forth. Another new coding scheme, called *frequency-domain reciprocal modulation* (FDRM), has been proposed as an alternative to OFDM.

Finally, the use of turbo product codes for LMDS applications is also feasible. Radio developers could cut the number of base stations necessary for the LMDS Internet access system potentially by reducing the rain fade common to such broadband systems and by using their turbo product codes.

The FCC and its auctions were mentioned briefly in the preceding section. Now let's talk about them a bit.

The FCC and Auctions

After several delays and protests over who would be allowed to participate, the auctions of broadband spectrum for local multipoint distribution services (LMDS) have been over for quite a while. Now the wireless industry is watching as licensees begin the next major step of trying to put in place viable commercial services. This part of the chapter takes a look at some of the significant challenges and opportunities facing licensees.

The Process

LMDS uses millimeter-wave signals in the 28-GHz spectrum to transmit voice, video, and data signals within cells 3 to 10 miles in diameter. The FCC will allow license holders to use up to 1.3 GHz of wireless spectrum in the 28-GHz Ka band.

In 1997, the FCC released the service and competitive bidding rules for LMDS spectrum in the 27.5- to 28.35-GHz, the 29.1- to 29.25-GHz, and the 31.0- to 31.3-GHz bands. The FCC's rules are summarized as follows [and in the sidebar, "Auction Rules for LMDS (Cc Docket 92-297)"]:

- 1300 MHz of LMDS spectrum was split into two licenses, one for 1150 MHz and one for 150 MHz. They are licensed in basic trading areas.

- Over their strong protests, the ILECs and cable TV (CATV) companies were prohibited from obtaining LMDS licenses in their regions for 3 years.[21]

Auction Rules for LMDS (Cc Docket 92-297)

The FCC established service and competitive bidding rules for a local multipoint distribution service (LMDS), new service using spectrum in 27.5 to 28.35 GHz, 29.1 to 29.25 GHz, and 31.0 to 31.3 GHz. The FCC's hope was that the decision opened the door for a new broadband wireless service that provides meaningful competition to cable and local exchange services and allocates adequate spectrum for the development of new services to be available to consumers throughout the nation.

LMDS licenses have afforded the licensees the opportunity to offer a variety of services such as multichannel video programming, telephony, video communications, and data services. The technology developed for use in this frequency band provides very high subscriber capacity for two-way video telecommunications. Thus there is sufficient capacity in the proposed LMDS system design to provide wireless competition to both local exchange carriers and cable television systems, even in urban areas.

LMDS Service Rules and Related Decisions The following rules were adopted:

- The LMDS spectrum is licensed by basic trading areas (BTAs) for a total of 984 authorizations and 1300 MHz of spectrum.

- Two licenses, one for 1150 MHz and one for 150 MHz, have been awarded for each BTA.

- All licensees have been permitted to desegregate and partition their licenses.

- There are no restrictions on the number of licenses a given entity may acquire.

- Incumbent local exchange carriers and cable companies may not obtain in-region 1150-MHz licenses for 3 years.

- LMDS may be provided on either a common-carrier or a non-common-carrier basis, or both.

- Licensees will be required to provide *substantial service* in their service areas within 10 years.

- Incumbents in the 31-GHz band are able to continue their operations; however, they receive protection from LMDS operations only in the outer 75 MHz (31.0–31.075 and 31.225–31.300) of the band. Incumbents have been given 75 days from the date of the publication of this item in the *Federal Register* to apply to modify their licenses to operate in the outer 75 MHz of the band and an additional 18 months to implement those modifications.

- Bidding credits and installment payment plans will be available to small businesses and entities with average annual gross revenues of not more than $75 million.

The ILECs also will be allowed to hold in-region 1150-MHz licenses after that 3-year period. Within 10 years, licenses will be required to provide substantial service, in their service areas. LMDS is to be provided on a common-carrier and/or a non-common-carrier basis.

Participants took 5 weeks and 128 rounds of bidding to claim the broadband spectrum in auctions. Two spectrum blocks were assigned in 493 markets, the *A* block containing 1150 MHz and the *B* block containing 150 MHz.

The Winners

The top 10 winners and additional information about them are listed in the sidebar, "The Winners." Both licensees and equipment vendors were happy with the way the auctions turned out.

The Winners

The local multipoint distribution services (LMDS) auctions closed on March 25, 1998, assigning licenses to 104 companies and raising $578 million for the U.S. Treasury. As explained previously, LMDS is a fixed broadband point-to-multipoint microwave service that, because of the amount of spectrum that will be licensed, will offer more capacity than is currently available from existing wireless services. LMDS has the long-term flexibility and the potential to promote competition in the local telephone and cable television marketplaces. It may be used, for example, for wireless telephony, data, Internet access, and video.

The Top 10 Winners
WNP Communications
Based in Earlysville, VA
Bid: $186 million
Acquired: 80 licenses

This group is composed of seven venture capital funds. Many of these funds had invested money with entrepreneurs in previous auctions, but this time they avoided the middleman and bid directly. They include former U.S. Senate candidate from Virginia, Mark Warner's Columbia Capital Corp., Madison Dearborn, Norwest Capital, ALPA Communications, Columbia Capital, Centennial, Chase Manhattan Venture Fund of New York, and Providence Ventures of Rhode Island. Principals include former MFS Communications Co., CEO Royce Holland, as well as media magnate Trygve Myhrem, the former CATV executive, and president of the Providence Journal Co.

NEXTBAND Communications LLC
Based in Bellevue, WA
Bid: $134.7 million
Acquired: 42 licenses

A startup affiliate of Nextel Communications, Inc., of McLean, VA, and NextLink Communications, Inc., of Bellevue. Craig McCaw, a cellular industry pioneer, is the dominant shareholder in both companies. Chief Officer: Wayne Perry, formerly vice chairman of McCaw Cellular Communications, Inc. (now AT&T Wireless Services, Inc.)

WinStar LMDS LLC
Based in New York
Bid: $43.4 million
Acquired: 15 licenses

Subsidiary of New York City–based WinStar Communications, Inc. Providers of local and long-distance telecommunications and Internet and information services. The company offers broadband wireless connections as well as customized, value-added information content to business and schools via fixed wireless technology.

Baker Communications L.P.
Based in Coudersport, PA
Bid: $25.6 million
Acquired: 232 licenses
Also known as Adelphia (ADLAC). ADLAC owns, operates, and manages CATV systems and other related telecommunications businesses. ADLAC operations consist primarily of selling video programming.

Cortelyou Communications Corp.
Based in New York
Bid: $25.2 million
Acquired: 15 licenses
A wholly owned subsidiary of CoreComm, Inc. CoreComm, through its subsidiaries, owns, operates, and markets cellular and paging systems in the Commonwealth of Puerto Rico and the U.S. Virgin Islands. Formerly Cellular Communications of Puerto Rico. In 1997, the company created CoreComm as a holding company and announced that it would begin pursuing communications-related opportunities outside the Caribbean.

BTA Associates
Based in Denver
Bid: $16.9 million
Acquired: 7 licenses
According to the FCC application filed by the company, BTA Associates is an unincorporated group of Colorado-based electric cooperatives: Consumer Services Associates, Inc., Holy Cross Electric Association, Inc., Mountain Park Electric, Inc., and Yampa Valley Electric Association.

ALTA Wireless, Inc.
Based in Denver
Bid: $15.1 million
Acquired: 4 licenses
Backed by EchoStar of Englewood, CO, a direct-to-home (DTH) satellite television company founded in 1980 by Chairman Charles Ergen and Cantey Ergen and James DeFranco. The company, one of the pioneers in the DTH television products, grew into a leading supplier of DTH hardware and services worldwide. Also part of the venture is Denver business owner Phanie Sundheim. EchoStar is a minority in the company.

Eclipse Communications Corp.
Based in Issaquah, WA
Bid: $14.3 million
Acquired: 51 licenses

Parent company is Western Wireless Corp., which owns or controls more than 20 different subsidiaries. The company provides an array of wireless telecommunications services, including cellular, paging, microwave, and personal communications services throughout the western United States.

ARNet, Inc.
Based in Amarillo
Bid: $11.6 million
Acquired: 16 licenses

An Internet provider corporation.

CoServ L.L.C.
Based in Corinth, TX
Bid: $10.3 million
Acquired: 6 licenses

A subsidiary of the 60-year-old Denton County Electric Company. The company provides retail electric distribution service to 46,000 businesses and residents within its area certified by the PUC.[22]

Future Auctions and Such

Certainly the wireless broadband technology and spectrum give service providers an incredible amount of bandwidth to deal with. Also, several major vendors are stepping up to the plate to provide the hardware, software, and other key needs of licensees. Vendors considered as the most likely to carve out significant market shares are Nortel, Lucent Technologies (Murray Hill, NJ), Alcatel Telecom (of France with U.S. offices in Richardson, TX), and Bosch Telecom (of Germany with U.S. offices in Irvine, TX). In addition, Sweden's Ericsson and Germany's Siemens also may become significant players.

Unproven? Vendors strongly dismiss the idea that LMDS is an unproven technology. Instead, they point out that it is based on very well established microwave radio and other telecommunications systems. This technology has been proven to work and to work well.

In the United States, CellularVision has been quietly operating an LMDS system. CellularVision is currently providing high-speed Internet service and 49 high-definition TV channels. It also provides telephony services. In fact, LMDS was once seen as a competitive alternative to CATV. However, none of the new LMDS licensees are currently talking about offering entertainment services to the mass market. Instead, industry executives say they see a migration period. First, they will offer high-speed data services to businesses in concentrated service areas, notably core business districts. In many cases, these businesses also may be competitive local exchange carriers (CLECs) seeking to extend their services the *last mile*. This would allow the fastest, lowest cost of deployment and a quick return on investment.

NOTE   The FCC granted CellularVision the only U.S. license as a *pioneer's preference*.

Buying into the Market   Bosch sees LMDS as a chance to establish a beachhead in the North American market. The company purchased the radio business of Texas Instruments (Dallas) as a launching pad. As part of that deal, Bosch acquired all assets and technology associated with multipoint systems and hired its 90 employees. The TI unit was one of that company's attempts to create commercial business from its defense group in the early 1990s. Bosch also has set up a shop in Silicon Valley to be closer to the small companies that are developing enabling technology for an array of products and services.

There is no question that LMDS is going to be a major business. The customer demand is proven. While the ramp-up may be a little slower than some are forecasting because of various complexities, 2001 is seen as the year of major commercial rollouts.

LMDS/LMCS Buildout Strategies and Opportunities

Revenues from competitive local exchange carrier (CLEC) business services topped $5.3 billion in 1999, according to Frost & Sullivan, of Mountain View, California. The consulting firm believes that such soaring revenues (combined with opening of the local market) will prompt CLECs to strive to become one-stop shops for an array of telecommunications services. The aspect of having a single service provider for all the telecommunications needs of an organization is attracting the attention of business customers who are constantly searching for ways to improve operational efficiency.

Other strategies being employed by CLECs to improve business include adding access lines to their networks and allowing provisioned services to an increasing number of business customers, exploiting interconnection agreements to enter the local market quickly, and promoting the increased use of the Internet, high-speed data transfer, and enhanced voice services.

Frost & Sullivan predict that business data services will grow extensively as a large number of businesses turn to Internet-related offerings. Currently, there are more than 180 CLECs operating in the United States. However, 83 percent of the market is controlled by a handful of large, nationwide facilities-based CLECs: Teleport Communications Group, Intermedia Communications, McLeod USA, GST Telecommunications, and ICG Communications.

LMDS/LMCS Applications/Services

This part of the chapter presents a telephony solution for local multipoint distribution service (LMDS) using technology for personal communications services (PCS). An actual system based on digital enhanced cordless telecommunications (DECT) has been implemented as an example. The system architecture of the DECT-based LMDS telephony system is discussed. Performance measurement results show that a DECT-based system does not have stringent frequency stability requirement and therefore can allow low-cost implementation.

Telephony   As explained previously, local multipoint distribution service (LMDS) is a broadband wireless distribution technology at the millimeterwave frequency band. The U.S. FCC has approved over 1000 MHz of spectrum for LMDS near 28 GHz. Approximately 850 MHz of the spectrum is assigned for downstream communications (from network to customers), and about 150 MHz of the spectrum is dedicated for upstream communications (from customers to network). With the large available bandwidth, LMDS is capable of providing two-way broadband network access to the home. It can support integrated applications such as telephony, high-speed data, and video services.

The deregulation of the telecommunications industry, through the 1996 Telecommunications Act, has opened up opportunities for competitive local exchange carriers (CLECs) to enter the local telephony service market. In the highly competitive telecommunications world, time to market and cost of deployment are critical factors when it comes to choosing the appropriate infrastructure technology for any service. LMDS is an attractive communications technology that can be used to deploy telephony service to the home. Because of its wireless nature, LMDS can offer fast and low-cost deployment by avoiding the need and the cost of installing underground cables or fibers and their associated right-of-way problems. Another advantage of LMDS is that it is a broadband infrastructure. Therefore, even with an initial deployment of only telephony service over LMDS, any service provider can expand to provide other broadband services with minimal additional infrastructure cost. Much of the LMDS equipment at both the network and customer sides can be reused.

In this part of the chapter the support of telephony over LMDS using existing technology for personal communications services (PCS) is presented. The rest of this part of the chapter is organized to follow a design approach and system architecture for a telephony solution. In particular, the overall system does not have a stringent frequency stability requirement and therefore can allow low-cost implementation of the LMDS millimeter-wave equipment.

DESIGN APPROACH AND SYSTEM ARCHITECTURE   Figure 7-13 shows the architecture of a telephony system over LMDS.[23] LMDS uses a cellular architecture with a typical cell size of about 2 km in radius. Due to antenna

Figure 7-13
LMDS system
architecture.

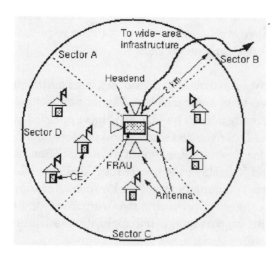

Figure 7-14

LMDS/PCS WLL block diagram.

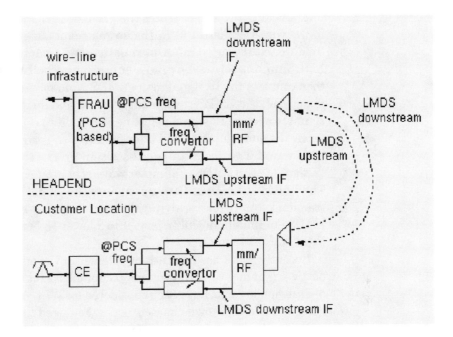

and other system design tradeoffs, each cell can be divided into different sectors. At each headend location, an antenna is used to transmit/receive signals to/from the customers within its sector. Correspondingly, each customer has an antenna to transmit/receive signals to/from the headend. Figure 7-13 shows that each cell is divided into four sectors. At the headend, equipment can be connected to the wide-area communications infrastructure via fiber links. The downstream path (headend to customers) is a broadcast channel in which the headend broadcasts information to the customers within the cell. This feature distinguishes LMDS from the traditional point-to-point microwave technology. In the upstream direction (customer to headend), each customer communicates with the headend using a point-to-point link.

A wireless local loop (WLL) architecture is used to deliver voice services to customers. Compared with other approaches, the advantage of using LMDS to build WLLs is that other services, such as video and high-speed data, can be integrated easily into the same broadband LMDS infrastructure. In this WLL architecture, fixed radio access units (FRAUs) are placed at headend locations, and customer equipment (CE) is placed at each customer location. Figure 7-14 further illustrates the WLL architecture.[24] The FRAU has an interface to the existing wire-line telecommunications infrastructure. It also executes the protocol to coordinate customer access to the wire-line network. In the downstream path, it delivers a properly conditioned IF signal (after modulation and frequency conversion) to the LMDS millimeter-wave/rf radio equipment. The LMDS radio equipment then converts the IF signal to the LMDS band for transmission. At the customer end, the LMDS equipment receives and downconverts the received signal to a lower IF signal before delivering it to the CE. The CE then performs the demodulation and later produces the original transmitted baseband signal. The upstream process is similar. The CE delivers a modulated IF signal to the LMDS millimeter-wave/rf equipment at the customer side. The LMDS equipment then upconverts the signal to the LMDS band for transmission. After receiving the signal at the headend, the headend LMDS equipment downconverts it to a lower IF before delivering it to the FRAU for demodulation.

Recently, there has been strong interest in various WLL applications. In particular, many communications techniques, ranging from analog FM to digital mobile radio, have been considered for WLL deployment. These technologies have their own characteristics. You need to choose an appropriate technology that can achieve the following in your LMDS telephony solution:

- *Voice quality.* As mentioned in the introduction, it is envisioned that LMDS can be used to deploy telephone service to the home. As a result, the voice quality of the telephony solution must be comparable with that of existing wired service.

- *Time to market / costs.* We would like our telephony solution to be based on proven technology to reduce development cost.

- *Tolerance to frequency drifts.* LMDS operates at millimeter-wave frequency band near 28 GHz.[25]

At such a high frequency, current millimeter-wave component technology cannot provide a stable frequency source at low cost. In order to avoid expensive millimeter-wave equipment, particularly for CE, the LMDS telephony solution must be able to tolerate frequency drifts without incurring severe impairment to voice quality.

Because of time-to-market/cost considerations, existing wireless broadband mobile telephony technology has been found to be most suitable for the WLL application in LMDS. Existing wireless broadband mobile telephony technology can be classified into two categories: high-tier cellular systems and low-tier personal communications services (PCS) systems. Unfortunately, all existing high-tier cellular technologies, such as analog FM, IS-54, and global system for mobile communications (GSM), employ narrow frequency channels (channel bandwidth less than a couple hundred kilohertz). The narrow frequency channels mean that these technologies require strict frequency stability, which is hard to achieve at low cost in the LMDS frequency band. Furthermore, the digital cellular technologies, such as IS-54, IS-95, and GSM, employ speech coding to reduce their bandwidth requirements. Their voice quality is generally inferior to that of wire-line voice because their speech rates are usually more than four times slower than the wire-line 64 kbps. As a result, high-tier cellular technologies are not applicable for integration to LMDS.

One approach is to base your LMDS WLL application on the low-tier PCS technology that is available in the market today. Due to the PCS design philosophy, all these systems support wire-line speech quality using 32 kbps ADPCM speech coding. Currently, there are three different low-tier PCS systems: digital enhanced cordless telecommunications (DECT), personal access communications system (PACS), and Japanese personal handiphone system (PHS). DECT is a European standard (Table 7-1), whereas PACS and PHS are U.S. and Japanese standards, respectively.[26]

Integrating with the LMDS system can be accomplished by building frequency converters to translate their respective operating frequency to the LMDS IF frequency (see Figure 7-14). Other system components, such as network interface and multiple access protocol, are already supported by the hardware developed for these systems. While these PCS technologies have been proposed to support WLL by themselves, the drawback of these systems comes from the fact that they were designed originally for low-power operations with long battery life. Consequently, they have only a limited practical coverage range of several hundred meters. The main advantage of the LMDS/PCS WLL approach is that coverage can be extended to about 2 km for each antenna tower, thus saving the infrastructure cost to provide service for a certain area.

As mentioned already, the LMDS/PCS WLL approach is satisfactory in terms of voice-quality and development-cost considerations. The remaining issue is whether these PCS technologies can tolerate the frequency

TABLE 7-1 DECT System Parameters		
Frequency (MHz)	1880–1900	
Multiple access	TDMA/TDD (10 carriers)	
Modulation	GMSK	
Raw bit rate (Mbps)	1.152 per carrier	
Speech coding	ADPCM	

drifts expected in LMDS radio equipment. This approach has been proven by developing a telephony solution based on DECT. DECT was chosen because it has the highest channel bandwidth (more than 1.5 MHz) among all the PCS candidates. As a result, it is expected to have the best frequency tolerance. Table 7-1 shows the system parameters for DECT.

Now let's look at the measurement results—showing the bit error rate (BER) and frequency tolerance performance of a DECT-based LMDS telephony system.

PERFORMANCE   This part of the chapter presents actual measurement results showing the performance of DECT when combined with LMDS radio equipment. The goal of the experiment is to study the actual BER performance and frequency tolerance of the integrated system. Figure 7-15 shows the setup for the reference experiments, which consist of connecting the DECT modulator and demodulator back to back without going through the LMDS system.[27] The BER analyzer generates pseudorandom data. The data from the BER analyzer are modulated and then subsequently demodulated by the DECT demodulator. The demodulated data are then fed back to the BER analyzer. Figure 7-16 shows BER versus frequency offset over selected received power levels.[28] As expected, it can be seen that frequency offset tolerance is higher for a higher received power level. For voice applications, a BER of better than 10^{-3} is appropriate. Figure 7-16 shows that the frequency tolerance ranges from 30 kHz at a received power of −69.3 dBm to approximately 100 kHz at received power of −57.3

Figure 7-15

Reference experiment block diagram.

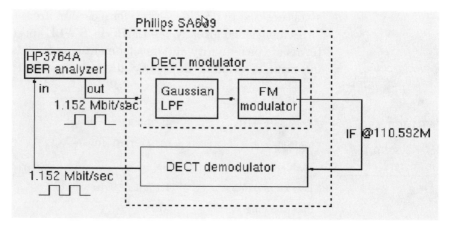

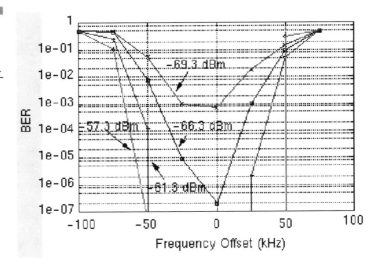

Figure 7-16
BER versus frequency
offset for various
received power levels.

dBm. This result indicates that an expensive frequency drift compensation circuit is not needed.

In addition to the frequency tolerance measurements, you also should verify the performance of DECT after it has been integrated into the LMDS system. In particular, you should verify that indeed the special frequency drift compensation circuit is not needed. Figure 7-17 shows block diagrams for the downstream and upstream paths for the integrated system, respectively.[29] These block diagrams are simply the reference block diagrams (see Figure 7-14) added to the appropriate frequency trans-

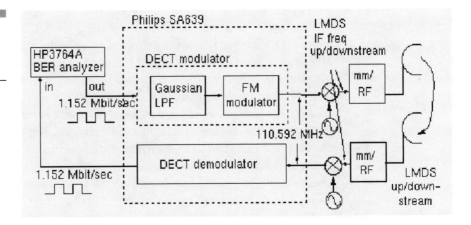

Figure 7-17
Block diagrams for
upstream/down-
stream experiments.

Figure 7-18
Performance
over LMDS.

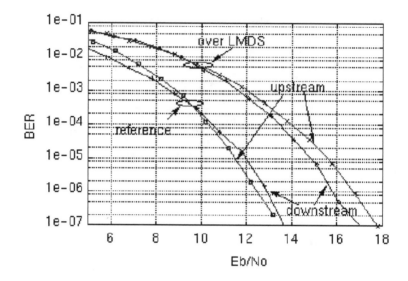

lators for downstream and upstream operations. The LMDS mm/rf system employs a free-running DRO with no phase lock loop to covert signal to/from the LMDS frequency band. Figure 7-18 shows the BER performance of the integrated system for various values of Eb/No.[30] The reference curves are obtained using the reference setup in Figure 7-14. It was found that the performance degradation is acceptable. There were 3 and 4.25 dB of degradation at a BER of 10^{-6} for the downstream and upstream paths, respectively.

An approach to provide telephony over LMDS was presented in this part of the chapter. The telephony solution is designed using current PCS technology. A product based on the European DECT standard was presented. The advantage of the proposed telephony solution is that by using DECT or other existing PCS technology, the cost of product development and time to market can be reduced. In addition, the LMDS architecture effectively can extend the range of existing PCS systems while integrating them to a wireless broadband infrastructure. A service provider therefore potentially can reduce infrastructure cost by using only one tall antenna tower at the headend to deliver integrated services (telephony, high-speed data, and video) to customers within a 2-km radius at the LMDS frequency band as opposed to delivering only voice services at the PCS band using several other antenna towers.

LMDS/LMCS Market Drivers

Since completion of the FCC spectrum auctions, local multipoint distribution services (LMDS) have been proposed for the delivery of a wide range of services. A point-to-multipoint radio access system is capable of providing services ranging from voice to high-speed data (up to 155 Mbps) and serving customers ranging from small to large businesses. In this brief overview, let's take a look at the LMDS market drivers, where it can satisfy a market need, the characteristics of the market, and its impact on the technology.

LMDS: A Transport System As mentioned previously, LMDS differs from ordinary transport systems in the way a train differs from a pipeline. Both are transport systems, but a pipeline can transport only one product from one place to another. A train, on the other hand, can transport many different products over the same infrastructure. LMDS, implemented with a multiservice protocol such as Asynchronous Transfer Mode (ATM), can transport, among others, voice, Internet, ethernet, video, computer files, and transaction data.

It is the multipoint radio technology, combined with the appropriate protocol and access method, that gives LMDS the tremendous potential to transform society. With transport technologies such as fiber in place, how can a newcomer compete? LMDS has some overwhelming advantages: reliability; as a transport system, LMDS can be engineered to provide 99.999 percent availability, rivaling that of the best fiber backbones; and speed of deployment. Once a hub is installed (a matter of days), new customers can be added in a matter of hours, future proof that LMDS provides data rates from T1 to OC-3c per user interface.

Managed Investment An LMDS hub can provide service to all buildings *visible* from the hub site. Physical technologies such as copper or fiber require individual rights of way to each building, as well as physical placement of the transport medium.

Market Need In today's networks, we have a mixture of twenty-first-century demand and 1950s infrastructure capability[31] (Figure 7-19). The huge capacity of the fiberoptic backbones is part of the twenty-first-century demand. The backbones have grown from the initial few installed by the major common carriers for long-distance traffic to many new miles of fiber not only for long-distance voice but also predominantly for data. In

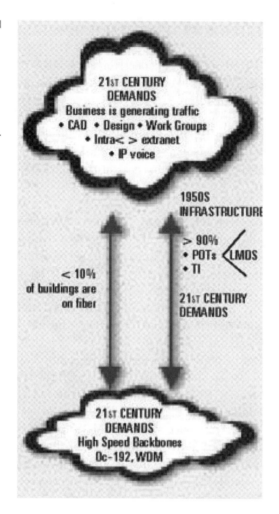

Figure 7-19
High-speed data network and computers connected to high-speed backbones with low-speed copper.

fact, it is the data load from business and the Internet that is driving the tremendous increase in backbone traffic. Wave division multiplexing (WDM) using different *colors* of light in the fibers came along just in time to rescue the major fiber backbones from being completely out of capacity.

The other twenty-first-century demand is seen in computers, workstations, and local-area networks (LANs) that are proliferating in quantity and capability. The latest outage of a Frame Relay backbone network underlined the fact that data communications are the lifeblood of today's business. We are using electronic data communications to submit our income tax forms, communicate with suppliers for just-in-time inventory, send bills, transmit design drawings to suppliers, utilize video teleconferencing, collaborate in work groups, and so on.

Dataquest (San Jose, CA), in one of its market reports, projected that the number of T1s in the United States will increase from about 2.8 million to more than 5.1 million by the year 2004. With voice traffic growing at about 5 percent per year, most of this increase is driven by the bandwidth needs of the computer age.

However, connecting these two marvels of technology is good old twisted pair. This intersection is where the incompatibilities of the 1950s meet the twenty-first century. Our blazing fast 600-MHz Macintosh computers are connected to the multigiga-bit-per-second fiber backbone with 28.8-kbps modems, 64-kbps ISDN (where available), or 1.5-Mbps T1s—all part of the 1950s technology.

This is a need LMDS can fill easily. LMDS can fill this need and provide high-speed, highly reliable connections from the workstation or LAN to the high-speed backbone. The traffic that LMDS can transport is not only computer data. LMDS also can and will transport voice as well as video.

It is ideal for transporting voice over IP and switched video as well as computer data. This reliable, high-speed technology is best suited to provide the interconnection through the twenty-first century.

Market Characteristics   Understanding the market requirements and needs constitutes the first steps in implementing an LMDS system. The next step is to understand the characteristics of these needs to provide the appropriate implementation of LMDS. To do this, we must examine who the users are and how they use the current technology.

Table 7-2 shows typical characteristics from various business segments.[32] On the left are large businesses that generate aggregated data.

TABLE 7-2

Various Business Segment Characteristics

FDMA (Large)	FDMA (Medium)	FDMA-TDMA (Small)	TDMA (SOH)	TDMA (Resident)
Aggregated-PBX	Aggregated-PBX	Semiaggregated-KEY	Nonaggregated	Nonaggregated
T1s	Trunks, T1s	Bus, lines, CO trunks	POTS, ISDN, T1	POTS
Proxy servers	Proxy servers	Low–medium speed, some firewall capability		Internet access
Steady traffic	Steady servers, some burstiness	Intermittent traffic, increasing burstiness	Sporadic, medium to long holding time	Sporadic, short to medium holding time

These are data (voice can be thought of as data even if it is not over IP) that are output from the trunk side of a PBX or the network side of a LAN. For security, most businesses permit access from workstations to the outside world only through a defensive mechanism such as a firewall. All the off-premises traffic is routed through this device. This traffic is relatively constant. PBX trunks are engineered for 90 percent occupancy. The output of a proxy or bastion server is also relatively constant with some burstiness.

Traffic Characteristics If the traffic is steady or bursty with a steady nonzero component, then the best access method is to assign a segment of spectrum to the user—frequency division multiple access (FDMA). If, on the other hand, the traffic is sporadic with periods of no access, then the best access method is one where the spectrum is shared among several users—time division multiple access (TDMA). When one user is not using the spectrum, another one can use it. In effect, the spectrum and the LMDS hub are acting as the aggregators of the traffic[33] (Figure 7-20).

The individual traffic patterns of the different users are not very different. It is how the traffic is offered to the LMDS system that governs the best access method.

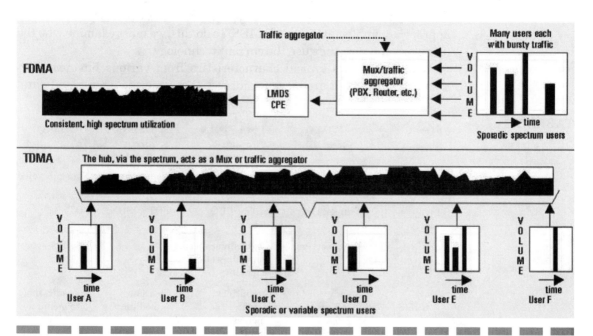

Figure 7-20 Spectrum users that are sporadic or variable.

The choice of access method is important—if the users offer steady traffic and you have provided a TDMA access method, there may be no time slots for other users. This results in a blocking situation. For sporadic users, a TDMA system is best. For steady traffic, an FDMA system works best. It is imperative that both types of access methods can coexist on the same LMDS hub.

The mix of users and their traffic patterns on the hub is not known and will change over time. The system must offer and support both access methods so that the hub can be optimized and the most efficient use of spectrum (your scarce resource) can be guaranteed.

Rain Fade   At 28 GHz, rain will decrease significantly the radio energy that the receiver gets. With this, the link must be engineered to achieve the link availability that customers need by including provision, as established by the ITU, for rain fade in the operating region. It is also important for LMDS system design to consider the radio environment. Some of the techniques that can be used are

- Forward error correction
- Dynamic power adaptation
- Dynamic modulation adaptation[34]

These techniques increase the robustness of the LMDS system.

Transport Protocol   The radio provides the physical link. The choice of transport protocol is very important because it will determine the operational characteristics of the system as well as the types of services that can be offered to the user. The important characteristics are support for all types of cargo (time-sensitive cargo such as real-time video and voice as well as time-insensitive cargo such as e-mail), avoidance of error bursts (system performance must be maintained), and standards that promote availability of low-cost silicon. ATM meets these requirements. It easily supports all types of data and even permits classes of service within the groups of data. All types of legacy traffic as well as currently anticipated traffic can be accommodated readily.

The short (53-byte) packet size enables inexpensive wire-line-speed forward error correction and minimizes the throughput penalty that longer packet sizes impose. An error burst during a 64,000-byte packet transmission will necessitate the retransmission of all 64,000 bytes. With an ATM-based system, retransmission can occur in 53-byte increments.

Modulation   Modulation is the conversion of bits to hertz. Several methods can be used. One of the more popular is quadrature amplitude modulation (QAM). This comes in several flavors—4 QAM, 16 QAM, 64 QAM, and higher. The higher the QAM, the more bits that can be transmitted in a hertz of spectrum. The price for more bits per hertz is the need for a much cleaner signal at the receiving site so that the more tightly packed bits can be recovered. With an FCC limit on the radiated power, this means reduced range. Thus the tradeoff becomes either lots of data-carrying capacity or longer range—which should not be a problem if the LMDS system supports multiple modulation methods in the same sector.

Preliminary market research will show the location of high-speed data sources. Locating the hub within the high QAM range will permit serving customers at the most efficient modulation. Lower modulation methods will serve customers located farther away. This allows the advantages of both to be utilized.

One marketplace certainty is the ever-growing need for bandwidth. With the growth in data, faster processors, video conferencing, data sharing, and distributed offices, the one component that is missing is high-speed access to the desktop. The LMDS marketplace has the spectrum and the technology available today to deliver on this need. The wish here is to never have to see the hourglass symbol pop up on computer screens. Instead, with LMDS technology, the industry can offer instant access to meet all information and telecommunications needs.

LMDS/LMCS Obstacles to Growth

As mentioned previously, local multipoint distribution services (LMDS) auctions were completed on March 25, 1998. The 128 rounds of bidding resulted in sales of 864 licenses for a sum of $578,663,029.

According to the rules set by the FCC, cable TV (CATV) operators and ILECs were not allowed to bid on *A* licenses in their territory, and their participation was light. US West was the only ILEC to bid, acquiring eight *B* licenses for $10 million. Auctions raised considerably less than the $3 billion that was expected, causing some parties to label it a failure and dampening enthusiasm on Wall Street.

However, the limited amount of revenues that was earned may be more of an indication of the size of the bidders than of the actual potential of the technology. It also may be evidence that bidders learned a lesson from previous personal communications services (PCS) auctions.

With LMDS auctions finally behind them, license winners and industry watchers now need to focus on a new set of problems and unknowns. LMDS proponents are not alone in their quest to bring wireless broadband and bundled services to businesses and consumers, and the fate of the spectrum that has been awarded is up in the air. Auction winners may opt to wait 3 years until they can sell these licenses to local exchange carriers (LECs) or cable providers. Questions also linger regarding the financing of many license winners and their ability to establish an LMDS network within a short period of time. Time to market could become very important because there are several other options that could fill the same void that LMDS carriers seek to address within the next 2 years. Background LMDS is essentially a fixed cellular network that operates at millimeter-wave frequencies. The system overcomes the challenge of signal attenuation, which can be a significant factor at millimeter-wave frequencies, by limiting the distance that signals must travel. Cell sizes in LMDS systems are on the order of 2 to 5 km, whereas cell sites in analog cellular systems are spaced 2 to 3 miles apart in metropolitan areas. As a result, reliable service can be obtained with relatively low output power. Communications are two way, and systems will be digital for the most part in order to maximize bandwidth efficiency and service quality. Perhaps the most intriguing aspect of LMDS is its wide bandwidth and capability. A-block license holders will have a 1150-MHz slice in the 28- and 31-GHz bands, which is large enough to support CATV, local telephony, and wireless broadband access simultaneously to users in each cell.

The cellular architecture also will enable providers to tailor CATV programming and advertising on a cell-by-cell base if desired. Yet, despite its many capabilities, the technology's success is likely to depend on provision of broadband and bundled services around data rather than voice or CATV. Why?

The latter market is already overcrowded with several alternatives, including traditional cable operators, whereas competitive local telephone service in itself is unlikely to justify the cost of LMDS customer premises equipment (CPE) for residential customers and many businesses. The ILECs' record for reliable service also will be a difficult obstacle to overcome in the telephone market. LMDS telephony is likely to be used for additional telephone capacity and sold to existing users.

Data, on the other hand, offers LMDS providers a golden opportunity. Bandwidth-hungry Internet and intranet content is pushing the telecommunications backbone to its limits and hampering the effectiveness of existing corporate and consumer data connections. Integrated services digital network (ISDN) basic rate interface (BRI) service is proving to be inadequate, and T1 services are too expensive for most users. Meanwhile, digital subscriber line (xDSL), cable modems, and satellite broadband programs still lack low-cost CPE and wide deployment. LMDS service providers could obtain a significant share of the burgeoning demand for low-cost, high-bandwidth data services in the business market if they can deploy a reliable network around major telecommunications users in a timely fashion. However, this may prove to be more difficult than originally anticipated. Stalls in FCC auctions have given 38-GHz radio, cable modem, and xDSL providers a head start over LMDS operators, and many questions remain about the ability of LMDS providers to build up a network quickly. As a result, LMDS will face some level of competition. An important question, then, is how does LMDS fare against competing options.

Competitors   Asymmetric digital subscriber line (ADSL), the xDSL front runner, will be able to provide from 1.5 to 7 Mbps downstream and from 200 kbps to 1 Mbps upstream of data to customers using the existing telephone company's twisted pair copper wires. Approximately 60 to 90 percent of U.S. access lines will be able to receive ADSL service with little or no upgrade to existing infrastructure, but ADSL solutions still cost from $900 to $2200 per line, significantly more than consumers or ILECs care to pay. Competing standards (CAP) and discrete multitone (DMT) have injected uncertainty in the market and slowed its progression, as has lack of interoperability between modems made by different manufacturers. Resolution of these problems may be forthcoming, however. Low-cost application-specific integrated circuits (ASICs) from leading semiconductor houses promise declines in the price of second- and third-generation ASDL modems. In addition, the Universal ADSL Working Group (UAWG), which is backed by a who's who of the networking, telecommunications, computing, and semiconductor industries, is working toward resolving lack of interoperability. The UAWG's work, if successful, also should help bring about lower-cost modems.

The other leading technology in the race to bring broadband capacity to users, cable modem service, can provide data rates of up to 36 Mbps downstream. However, because the medium is shared, experts consider speeds of 10 Mbps downstream and 200 kbps to 2 Mbps upstream (for two-way modems) more realistic. Cost per home passed is about $700 to $800, and interoperable multimedia cable network system (MCNS)–compliant modems are expected to be widely available for $400 to $500 by year end 2001. Two-way service is available to approximately 20 million U.S. households and businesses today, but support for the service has waxed and waned in recent years, depending on the provider. Some major cable providers appear to be more interested in digital CATV and telephony rather than in upgrading infrastructure to be two-way cable-modem-capable. Regardless, the technology is available today, and it works. Expansion is expected in coverage as well, although it is unlikely that more than

60 percent of U.S. homes will be passed by two-way cable-modem-ready infrastructure within the next 5 years.

In addition to ADSL and cable modem providers, satellite system operators and visionaries such as Kirkland, Washington–based Teledesic are now offering two-way data services to users around the world. Published expected data rates of the various satellite constellations vary between 200 kbps and 2 Mbps downstream/upstream for residential users and between 10 and 30 Mbps for corporate users. Production of CPE is limited to a few players per constellation, and online dates are in the year 2002 at best. Satellite systems are best suited for providing access to areas that are sparsely populated and which lack other alternatives. The cost per home passed for satellite systems can be below $30, but CPE exceeds $1700 in cost.

The other land-based alternative, fiberoptic cable to the home or curb, is prohibitively expensive and is deployed only to heavy business users. Full installation of fiber in the U.S. local loop would require at least 20 to 25 years to be completed at full speed, and the ILECs have done little to suggest that they are in fact pursuing fiber to the home or curb at full speed. Competitive local exchange carriers (CLECs), including long-distance giants, and the ILECs continue to establish fiber in densely populated areas, and these systems are already operational. However, extension of this capability beyond heavy business users is unlikely.

Despite a pipeline of several hundred megabits or even gigabits to each user, the cost of fiber deployment to the home (well over $3000 per home passed) will preclude widespread installation for some time. Sometimes referred to as a *fiber pipeline in the sky*, 38-GHz radio is operating successfully in several major metropolitan areas. To date, it has been used primarily to provide other telecommunications carriers with additional capacity. However, a shift to point-to-multipoint networks and the resulting use of low-cost CPE (less than $4000) should translate into a rapid customer expansion. Most important, 38-GHz radio is operational today.

LMDS   By comparison, initial tests by Hewlett Packard (HP, Palo Alto, CA) suggest that average residential users of LMDS will be able to receive data rates of 35 to 58 Mbps downstream, whereas commercial users will be able to attain rates of 51.84 to 155.52 Mbps (Sonet OC-1 to OC-3). Only a fiberoptic link to the home has greater capacity than LMDS, and deployment of that technology is unfeasible in the short term. At peak capacity, each subscriber to an LMDS system is expected to obtain results of at least 7 Mbps downstream and 1 Mbps upstream. Actual performance will be lower than quoted because these tests were based on full use of the 1300-MHz spectrum, but holders of A-block licenses (1150 MHz) will still be able to provide blistering data rates, CATV service, and telephony to their customers. LMDS will be relatively inexpensive to install at a cost of about $150 per premise passed, but infrastructure must be built from scratch, and attractive sites for towers may be difficult to come by. Basic CPE is expected to cost about $900 initially.

Evaluation   Overall, LMDS compares favorably with competing options on both a performance basis and a cost basis, but it lacks the wide support and financial backing that other platforms possess. This could prove to be significant.

Industry support has flooded behind cable modem and ADSL technologies. Low-cost chipsets and ASICs are available for platforms, and the technologies boast an impressive list of supporters, including Lucent Technologies (Murray Hill, NJ), 3Com (Santa Clara, CA), Analog Devices (Norwood, MA), Compaq (Houston, TX), Intel (Santa Clara, CA), Microsoft (Redmond, WA), Motorola (Schaumburg, IL), Ericsson (Sweden), NEC (Japan), and so on. Members of the computing industry in particular seem to be supporting ADSL, and to a lesser extent cable modems, as a means of delivering multimedia content to homes and businesses (a vehicle to justify the purchase of faster processors, greater storage capacity, and new software). This multibillion dollar industry has a lot to gain from the success of broadband delivery, and logic suggests that its members will go to great lengths to bring the most probable broadband technologies to the mass market. ADSL seems to be that technology.

LMDS is not as fortunate. Only a few companies have publicly committed to supporting the platform, and those which have, with the exception of HP, lack the distribution, name-brand awareness, and financing that supporters of ASDL and cable modems possess. The difference is likely to result in LMDS CPE that cost more than and lacks the distribution of cable and ADSL modems. In addition, there will be lower visibility for LMDS. Time also could be an issue. If cable modem and ADSL services become widely accessible within the next 2 years, then deployment of LMDS could prove unattractive in areas that already possess other alternatives. The cost per actual subscriber of LMDS infrastructure would shoot to over $3000 if penetration falls below 17 percent, and high levels of penetration could be tough to come by if 38-GHz radio, ADSL, fiberoptic links, satellite systems, and cable modems are already in place.

Thus, what will happen to LMDS? Only time can really tell. There are a number of variables that could drastically alter the market and the fortunes of LMDS providers. ADSL and cable modem deployment could lag considerably behind expectations, and satellite and many LMDS operators may not even build out their networks.

However, developments in the market today suggest that leading LMDS auction winners will deploy networks and that these service providers will concentrate their efforts on business and well-to-do residential customers. The high cost of CPE will preclude deployment to other residential areas, at least initially.

LMDS will face stiff competition from established and incipient technologies. And this is anticipated to cause LMDS to fall considerably short of the FCC's vision of it as a universal high-powered competitor to existing cable operators and ILECs.

It is unlikely that LMDS will come close to the FCC's mandate for significant coverage of operating areas in the short term, and this decree could prove to be unfeasible even in the long term. Yet, despite this, LMDS operators could be very successful in their own right. It is not LMDS's ability to succeed that really needs to be questioned but rather its ability to live up to the hype that surrounds it. In all, the technology's greatest shortcoming could prove to be the unrealistic expectations that have been cast on it.

Competing Technologies   One of the most promising great equalizers in the access network is wireless local loop technology, also known as *broadband wireless access* (BWA). Think about it: New competitive carriers can deploy wireless networks in a fraction of the time it takes to build wired infrastructures. And the availability limitations of DSL and cable modem services are not an issue in wireless broadband networks. BWA holds the promise of getting high-speed, competitively priced services to enterprise sites, remote offices, and, well, just about anybody really fast.

Two primary technologies are being rolled out to enable BWA. The first has been discussed in this chapter quite extensively: local multipoint distribution services (LMDS), a line-of-sight technology running in the 28-GHz band. LMDS is most suited for densely populated urban areas, where it is difficult and expensive to deploy additional or new wired infrastructures. Typical speeds are 45 Mbps downstream in a point-to-multipoint configuration. However, LMDS has the potential to exceed OC-3 (155 Mbps) speeds. Distances between sites are limited to 4 km.

The second primary technology—multichannel multipoint distribution service (MMDS)—operates in the 2- to 3-GHz band, is less susceptible to interference than LMDS, and has no line-of-sight requirements. MMDS can support greater distances than LMDS—up to 30 miles between sites. The tradeoff is that MMDS is slower, delivering downstream speeds in the neighborhood of 10 Mbps.

With both technologies, an antenna and radio are installed on the roof of a business site and are connected by coaxial cable to customer premises equipment in the LAN wiring closet. Also, commercial service availability is imminent. WorldCom has been conducting MMDS service trials with schools and residential and business customers in Boston, Dallas, Jackson, Mississippi, Baton Rouge, and, Memphis using equipment from Cisco and Motorola. Meanwhile, Cisco has said it plans to begin commercially shipping LMDS and MMDS interfaces for its routers by midyear—which sounds like any day now. The move could prove to be a major stepping stone for service provider deployments.

BROADBAND SATELLITE TECHNOLOGY Broadband wireless access— LMDS/MMDS (also termed *wireless cable*)—is based on the generic wireless technologies for TV distribution (for signals received from satellite or other sources) in possible direct competition with cable TV. A standard wireless system simply has a tower and homes scattered around the tower, and there is nothing between the tower and the home antenna unless the system is cellularized. Furthermore, it is both flexible and affordable, and therefore, neither government nor investors have to make long-term commitments to a particular infrastructure or technology (see the sidebar, "Broadband Wireless Access").

Broadband Wireless Access

Most established MMDS/LMDS systems worldwide transmit at 2.5 GHz. A few systems in Latin America operate in VHF-TV (54–88 MHz and 174–216 MHz) and UHF-TV (470–806 MHz). Some systems also use 12 and 18 GHz, but the future thrust is expected to be in 27.5 to 29.5 GHz and 40.5 to 42.5 GHz because these would be the harbinger of broadband services. Higher frequency bands are especially useful because the antennas are smaller, *viz.*, 15 × 15 cm panels that can merge aesthetically with walls/windows/facades of buildings. It is important to note that unlike MMDS, LMDS is not a true line-of-sight system. In fact, buildings and other structures that normally would obstruct signals act as active or passive repeaters because the signals are bounced off or around them. This unique trait makes the LMDS system particularly suited to densely populated urban areas with tall buildings and skyscrapers, especially since LMDS signals can be bounced off brick or glass.

The MMDS/LMDS technology provides a market opportunity to offer broadband services for the public telecommunications operators in view of the evolution of this technology from analogue to digital. The use of digital compression technology will increase the capacity of the system to 120 TV channels, and this would be a quantum jump in capability because the existing cable systems in India deliver only 10 to 12 TV channels. Furthermore, this would enable a vastly more competitive product in terms of cost and signal quality also.

The limiting factors due to the evolution of technology will be removed: First, the LMDS/MMDS technology would be an enabling factor for the merger of diverse services. The new technology also provides a cutting edge to the later entrant unless the existing operator takes care to meet the challenges of new threats. Second, conventional telecommunications need symmetric media architecture, whereas TV distribution needs an asymmetric medium. Development of a new system architecture to provide two-way interactive wireless broadcast capability has been initiated by some companies. These companies expect to design a system capable of supporting fully interactive video, data, and telephony potentially at both MMDS and LMDS frequencies.[35]

COST BENEFIT ANALYSIS ESPECIALLY WITH REFERENCE TO COMPETING TECHNOLOGIES Synergy between telecommunications and TV distribution can lead to better penetration. In fact, the rollout for telephony would be considerably cheaper because resources can be shared. This is important because the cost of external infrastructure for suburban and rural scenarios is exorbitant and has been an inhibiting factor so far in the growth of telecommunications.

ADVANTAGES AND DISADVANTAGES The existing cable TV operators find it profitable to operate in densely populated areas, leaving the sparsely populated areas to other options. Either direct-to-home (DTH) satellite systems or LMDS/MMDS systems can fill in this void. The possible regulatory issues to be addressed are as follows: First, both cable and MMDS/LMDS systems would provide the regulatory authority to preview/censor undesired broadcasts/retransmissions as opposed to DTH systems using satellites. At this stage of development, the opportunity exists to get the option for DTH foreclosed, as already done by some countries in the Middle East.

Second, for example, the current business rules of the government of India do not permit the Department of Telecommunications (DOT) to do

TV signal broadcasting. However, the DOT had been providing long-distance links as well as local end links to Doordarshan. Therefore, the provisioning of the medium would still fall into the domain of the public telecommunications operators, and they should lobby for change in the existing regulations. This is important because there would be stiff competition between cable and public telecommunications operators for this market if and when the same is opened up.

Third, the most promising frequency band for LMDS is 27.5 to 29.5 GHz, which is presently sparsely used the world over. Of course, satellite operators are eyeing this band for mobile and fixed satellite services. The FCC (in the United States) is likely to allocate 1 GHz of bandwidth each to LMDS and satellite services. The review done in the Test and Experimentation Center (TEC) on the frequencies beyond 1 GHz also has recommended shared usage. An early resolution of this issue would be beneficial for long-term growth.

EXPECTED DEPLOYMENT PROFILE   Currently, there are 4.5 million subscribers in 70 nations all using analogue MMDS technology. For example, the TV market in India is projected to grow rapidly by the end of the year 2002 fueled by the following factors:

- TV advertisement to grow fivefold
- Number of TV channels expected in the range 70 to 85
- Number of TV households to increase by 10.4 percent
- Number of cabled households to increase by 6.9 percent
- Cable penetration to increase to 59 percent[36]

In contrast, it is important to note that the projected growth of demand for telecommunications in India falls far short of the preceding figures. There is therefore an anomaly in this because a telephone is still an inexpensive proposition for most households.

NOTE   The use of telephony in this area for India is driven in part by the fact that India has the second largest expatriate population in the world. That is, the number of India natives living outside India is second only to the number of Chinese living outside China.

The telecommunications market is normally bigger than the market for TV. In fact, in the United States, the household penetration is 64 percent for cable TV and 97 percent for telephony. This fact should galvanize the telecommunications operators into urgent action.

Already a number of operators in India have signed up for planning, installing, and operating extensive optical fiber networks for meeting the requirements of cable TV, *viz.*, Hindujas, Siti, and BITV in Bombay, RPG in Calcutta, and United Breweries Group in Bangalore. The initial objective is to provide larger numbers of quality TV channels to be followed up by teleshopping, telebanking, videoconferencing, video-on-demand, and educational programs. Some of the operators (Globe Satellite Communications) also have realized the importance of LMDS/MMDS technology, and they have approached the Ministry of Information and Broadcasting.

COMPATIBILITY WITH EXISTING PRODUCTS AND ISSUES CONCERNING PHASING OUT OF OLDER TECHNOLOGIES The most important threat to public telecommunications operators is the potential entry by cable operators into telephony. The best way to counteract this threat would be by the public telecommunications operators entering the domain of cable TV operators through LMDS/MMDS technology. The advantage of this approach would be that it ultimately could lead to full deployment of switched broadband services as well as interactive digital television.

The ultimate test for any technology is the acceptance by market forces as the demand for new services builds up. Various issues are as follows:

1. In the residential area, the data flow is asymmetric (primarily one way toward the customer). However, TV is expected to be followed by interactive video, Web browsing, and other needs. As the market grows up, the data flow would tend to become symmetric.

2. In the business areas, data flow is already near symmetric with emphasis more on file transfer, telecommuting, videoconferencing, and LAN access.

3. Initial costs for LMDS is estimated to be approximately $550 per customer, which is half that for MMDS and one-fourth that for a cable system.[37]

STANDARDS The mission of Working Group 802.16 is *to develop standards and recommended practices to support the development and deployment of fixed broadband wireless access systems.* 802.16 is a unit of the IEEE 802 LAN/MAN Standards Committee, the premier transnational forum for wireless networking standardization and the source of ethernet standards.

Thus IEEE standards are highly regarded throughout the world because they are developed in an open process with rigorous procedures to ensure that all voices are heard and heard again until the quality of the output is fully accepted. IEEE has shown that with the support of dedicated teams, this process can lead quickly to superb results that are accepted immediately in the global marketplace. As a result of this quality control process, the name *IEEE standard* is zealously guarded.

IEEE 802 strongly objects to ISTO's format of the Broadband Wireless Internet Forum (BWIF) and the associated press release because, first, the press release implies an accredited standards process. The word *standard* appears 16 times (and *IEEE* 34 times) in the press release. This confusion cheapens the value of the highly regarded IEEE standards process. The confusion is enhanced by mentioning (3 times) the affiliation between ISTO and the IEEE standards association. Nowhere does the announcement state the difference between specification produced by this forum and an authentic IEEE standard.

Second, marketplace confusion has resulted because of the direct conflict with the scope of an IEEE-SA standards board approved project (802.16.3) that has been authorized to develop a broadband wireless access (BWA) standard according to accredited IEEE-SA rules and due process. The IEEE 802.16 Working Group on Broadband Wireless Access developing these standards is open to full public participation. To date, well over 400 individuals from well over 200 companies have participated in the working group. The ISTO announcement of a single, unified broadband wireless access industry standard is in direct conflict.

IEEE 802 makes the following requests:

1. The IEEE Executive Director should act to ensure that the ISTO dissociates itself from the BWIF prior to the BWIF's meeting.

2. The ISTO policies should be modified to avoid projects competitive with IEEE Standards projects unless requested by the IEEE standards sponsor.

3. The terms *IEEE industry standard* and *IEEE-ISTO industry standard* should be eliminated in favor of the term ISTO industry standard.

4. IEEE policy and procedures should clarify the difference between an ISTO-generated industry standard and an authentic IEEE standard with a statement such as ISTO is not accredited to write standards. It is separate from, and its actions do not affect programs in, the IEEE standards association. IEEE should issue a press release clarifying these issues with regard to the BWIF announcement.

IEEE 802 will submit this posit on statement to the IEEE Executive D rector, the IEEE-SA Board of Governors, IEEE-SA Standards Board, the IEEE Computer Society SAB, and the IEEE Microwave Theory and Techniques Society for their information and action.

LMDS/MMDS Market Forecasts

For those telecommunications executives involved in the day-to-day tasks of selling and deploying ordinary telephone service, it can be difficult to step back and appreciate just how momentous the changes are that are occurring in this industry. We truly stand at the edge of a new world, a world in which the Internet will be used to facilitate e-commerce transactions and provide entertainment, videoconferencing, and a number of hitherto undreamed-of applications. After years of hearing about the holy grail of convergence (the blending of television, personal computers, and phones into one device and the blending of voice, data, and video onto one network), the Internet is finally pushing these changes with breathtaking rapidity.

It is now appropriate to point out one other important trend of convergence: the seamless blending of the wireline and wireless broadband networks. In the past, customers grew accustomed to *wireless* meaning either their convenient but sometimes unreliable mobile phones or maybe even a direct broadcast satellite connection for advanced TV service. On the other hand, customers expected that their phone and Internet service to their homes and businesses would always be provided by wires. It was just what people were accustomed to.

Today, a newly accepted definition for *wireless* is emerging. With Sprint and MCI WorldCom's major purchases of fixed wireless operators in the multichannel multipoint distribution system (MMDS) band and the emergence of Wall Street sweetheart startups such as Teligent and WinStar, service providers and customers alike are beginning to think of wireless as the primary method of providing all the voice, broadband data, and video services that one could ever want, straight to a home or a business.

The Access Problem   For years, a number of technical and business problems have prevented a widespread penetration of broadband connections between customers' premises and the service providers. Either it was too complicated or too expensive, and the benefits of deploying new networks combining just voice and video services seemed too low. With the rapid infusion of the Internet into our lives, the need for broadband capabilities has never been so pressing. Communications carriers can select from an ample number of broadband two-way wireline access architectures:

- Integrated services digital network (ISDN)
- Fiber-to-the-home (FTTH)

- Fiber-to-the-curb (FTTC)
- Hybrid fiber coax (HFC) with cable modems
- Digital subscriber line (xDSL)

Even further options are available in the wireless realm, including

- Wideband personal satellite communications systems
- The high-frequency fixed wireless systems dubbed local multipoint distribution system (LMDS), digital electronic messaging service (DEMS), and 38 GHz
- The lower-frequency MMDS systems38

Each wireline and wireless broadband method has its advantages and disadvantages. Yet breakthroughs in radio technology, along with increased industry confidence following the success of personal communications service (PCS) and cellular mobile services, have dramatically improved confidence in radio as a reliable local access technology. In addition, digital technology has greatly improved the signal quality of broadband wireless systems and permits operators to greatly increase the amount of data that can be sent across a particular amount of spectrum.

LMDS   Historically speaking, the radio industry has long been ruled by skeptics who believed that there would always be an acute spectrum shortage and thus little room for broadband spectrum allocation. However, most failed to see that the migration to digital radio and higher frequencies eventually would cause a spontaneous spectrum glut. This is what has happened today. LMDS is just one of several new allocations that will help make obsolete the old paradigm that claims that radio is only good for narrowband services.

LMDS occupies the largest chunk of spectrum ever devoted to any one service. Located in sections of the 27.5- to 31.3-GHz band, LMDS can consist of a bandwidth of up to 1.3 GHz. This is in stark contrast to cellular, which consists of 25 MHz, or PCS, which consists of 30 MHz. Via the transmission of microwave signals, LMDS networks can provide two-way broadband services, including

- Video
- High-speed Internet access
- Telephony services39

An LMDS network can be composed of a series of cells that each delivers point-to-multipoint services to subscribers. Each transmitter in a cell serves a relatively small area, about 2 to 3 miles in diameter. This small cell size means that the LMDS network requires a large number of antennas. As cellular and PCS industry experience has shown, this can be troublesome because there are only so many places where antennas and hub equipment can be installed.

Many vendors have developed a full portfolio of equipment for the LMDS band and are actively marketing it to service providers. Since there are no standards, vendors approach the market in very different ways. For example, while some vendors promote time division duplexing (TDD) as the best frequency-sharing scheme, others prefer frequency division duplexing (FDD). The lack of standards for equipment has been one of the worst problems in terms of ensuring interoperability and keeping costs down. It is expected that third-generation (3G) wireless system standards will be one influence on the development of standards for LMDS.

Even though high-frequency fixed wireless has had a limited impact on the telecommunications market thus far, INSIGHT expects the total revenue from data services over LMDS alone in the United States to be $787.9 million by 2005.

MMDS   The MMDS frequencies, located in the 2.1- to 2.7-GHz band, are another option to deliver broadband wireless services. The MMDS frequencies traditionally have been used to provide a one-way analog wireless cable TV broadcast service. As such, the MMDS industry has been more widely known as the *wireless cable* industry.

The history of the wireless cable industry has been rife with failure. The smaller operators have, for the most part, been unable to generate a profitable business using the frequencies for the transmission of analog video. Several ILECs boldly claimed that MMDS would be their avenue to effectively compete with the cable TV operators, only to sell their MMDS properties off and retreat back into their telephony shell. Only BellSouth remains a significant provider of MMDS video service alongside its landline cable service (though several ILECs have since built semisuccessful landline cable TV services). The U.S. markets for residential video are crowded by broadcast TV, direct broadcast satellite (DBS), and cable, and the limited channel capacity of analog MMDS simply could not compete.

Yet, all of a sudden, MMDS frequencies have become the hot properties of 2000. Why is this portion of the spectrum just now catching the attention of the telecommunications industry? The answer is that MMDS is seen as a viable broadband service delivery option. The Internet has changed everything. MMDS providers are establishing Internet-focused subsidiaries, feverishly upgrading their existing networks with digital compression capabilities, and moving rapidly to install a return channel to create interactive capability. Unlike their counterparts operating in the LMDS band, who mainly target businesses in metropolitan areas, the MMDS providers mostly want to tap the pent-up demand for broadband digital data and TV directly into the home. Advantages of using MMDS include

- It has chunks of underutilized spectrum that will, once completely digital, become increasingly valuable and flexible.

- System implementation, which is little more than putting an installed transmitter on a high tower and a small receiving antenna on the customer's balcony or roof, is quick and inexpensive.

- Moreover, since MMDS services have been around for 20 years, there is a wealth of experience—at least with respect to the one-way distribution technology.[40]

Conclusion

LMDS promises a wireless alternative to fiber and coaxial cables. It has the potential to replace the existing wired networks, and it may prove to be the easiest way to deliver high-speed data and two-way video service. Its capability of handling thousands of voice channels with the existing bandwidth makes it a good contestant in the voice industry. With current industry trends that are tending to merge the telecommunications and networking industries, LMDS seems to be a solution that suits all their needs. For the recent digital TV world, LMDS is a very good choice considering the fact that LMDS was designed with digital TV broadcast in mind.

Auctions

The LMDS auction ended on March 25, 1998, netting only $578.7 million after entrepreneurial discounts for the largest block of spectrum ever allocated and leaving even the winners stunned at how it all came out. The technology underlying what the FCC (*www.fcc.gov*) calls local multipoint distribution service (LMDS) originally was perceived by the commission to be a means of driving competition in the local telecommunications and cable markets. The outcome of the auction left in doubt the pace and scale of deployment and thus the impact this segment of the wireless broadband sector might have on competition in the United States

It is no longer a question of who owns the spectrum but of who the service providers will be. With much of the LMDS spectrum (which is located at the 28- and 31-GHz tiers) now in the hands of venture capital firms and entrepreneurs rather than established operating concerns, it will take some time to sort out the answer to this question. If you had to predict who would participate in use of the spectrum, you should not discount the interexchange carriers, the ILECs, cable companies, competitive local exchange carriers (CLECs), and personal communications services (PCS) providers—in other words, the people already in the business.

Executives masterminding the strategy at the leading auction winner, WNP Communications, Inc., made it clear that they were going to take their time figuring out where to go from here, especially since they never expected to win as much spectrum as they ended up with. After 128 rounds of bidding that began on February 18, 1998, WNP was top bidder for 39 *A*-block licenses (1.15 GHz) and one *B*-block (150 MHz), representing more than 91 percent of the population in the top 12 basic trading areas, two-thirds of the population in the top 75 markets, and 41 percent of the entire U.S. population. The company won 11 of the top 12 markets, excluding only Los Angeles.

Dodging Obsolescence   Under the FCC's liberal licensing rules, LMDS providers have up to 10 years from the point of getting their licenses to offer *substantial* amounts of service in their markets. While WNP believes first-to-market advantage is important, the firm will not be in a rush to build infrastructure, preferring instead to make sure it chooses a technical platform that will not be outdated soon after it is built.

WNP also must raise money to build the infrastructure and put together a full management and operations team, which it expects to do through direct hiring rather than partnering with outside entities. While the firm is likely to seek vendor financing, it also will rely on other sources to avoid being too much under the sway of manufacturers.

Because there is so much spectrum, licensees will have the opportunity to divide the larger piece up among multiple providers for various applications within geographic subsections of each of the 493 basic trading areas covered by the licenses. Yet, for all the flexibility to deliver voice, data, and video services at such scales, the auction failed to come close to the level of participation anticipated as the final preparations were being made at the commission. Overall, 181 basic trading areas (out of a nationwide total of 493) representing 77.4 million people, or 32 percent of the total, were won with a single bid. Another 109 markets representing 10 percent of the population received no bids at all. After discounts to designated entities, including WNP's 45 percent discount, the government's take in the LMDS auction netted out at just $1.85 per person in the A-block.

FCC officials termed the auction a success. The marketplace now has 104 new LMDS players. However, A-block licenses covering two-thirds of the population were held by only three companies—WNP with 41 percent share of the A-block, NextBand Communications LLC with 12 percent (including the Los Angeles basic trading areas), and WinStar LMDS LLC with 7 percent. No one else had more than 5 percent.

WinStar in some respects may have been the biggest winner, since it already holds considerable spectrum nationwide at the 38-GHz tier and can use both spectrum tiers for provision of point-to-multipoint services in its markets, although the propagation characteristics are such that 38-GHz transmitter cell radiuses are somewhat shorter, meaning WinStar's buildout in a given market will be denser than would be the case in a pure LMDS play.

With its A-block wins covering Greensboro, NC, New Orleans, Norfolk, VA, Oakland, San Francisco, San Jose, Orlando, FL, and Salt Lake City, WinStar's spectrum holdings now average more than 750 MHz in the top 30 markets and approximately 740 MHz in the top 50, according to officials. WinStar, like Teligent, Inc., which holds smaller spectrum blocks averaging less than 400 MHz at the 24-GHz tier, has already begun using the new point-to-multipoint technology underlying LMDS in some of its commercial operations and thus has a big head start over the LMDS players in bringing fixed wireless services to market.

Next Up   NextBand, the second biggest bidder in the LMDS auction, plans to use the spectrum to support the venture's two operating backers, mobile wireless operator Nextel Communications, Inc., and competitive local exchange carrier NextLink Communications, Inc. NextBand won 13 A-block licenses, which will be useful in NextLink's operations for point-to-multipoint connectivity, and 29 B-block licenses, which will be used to provide backhaul links for Nextel and to support point-to-point connections to NextLink customers.

NextBand itself may not become an operating entity, choosing instead to license its spectrum to its controlling partners. NextLink operates in 26 markets in eight states (many of them in the same localities where NextBand will have licenses), whereas Nextel operates nationwide.

Where Did Everybody Go?   A number of factors contributed to the low level of competition in the LMDS auction. After the disastrously high bidding and subsequent financial collapses of many participants in the

PCS auctions, investors were extremely wary of backing speculative bidding on airwaves. In part, WNP succeeded in raising funds because it offered investors protection against the type of bidding that went on in the PCS auction. Thus the government is better off getting close to $800 million in revenues from people who can pay the money and deploy the technology than it is getting billions in illusory sums that will never be spent.

LMDS now has the support of the major telecommunications suppliers, including Alcatel Network Systems, Inc., Ericsson, Inc., Lucent Technologies, Inc., Northern Telecom, Inc., and others. However, most of these companies only got into the game as it became apparent that breakthroughs in the manufacture of low-cost gallium-arsenide processors had made possible solid-state broadband wireless communications at ultrahigh-frequency levels.

Future Projections

By now, gee-whiz notions about local multipoint distribution services (LMDS) technology have pretty much gone by the wayside. U.S. spectrum allocations have been made, larger vendors who have entered the market have replaced early proponents, and we are down to the nuts and bolts of using the technology.

Businesses must now emerge from the morass of talk, technical jargon, and market projections being bandied about to prove the true value of LMDS. LMDS supports many possibilities, but most break new ground into the trodden clay of established thinking. We are entering a time when technology has become so diverse, with so many options and applications that new models become viable—yet caution is advised.

It is not enough to offer one great black box or fantastic service and know the world will beat a path to your door. A suite of products and services ultimately must, in concrete ways, answer the real problems of real people and real businesses. Forcing a solution by offering a no-choice, single-vendor package in what will become an increasingly distributed network architecture is counterintuitive to the *next generation network* paradigms at play. Many service providers have made decisions for core technologies that best serve their needs and are looking for flexible solutions that best enable their point of differentiation. Thus, what drives the need for LMDS and how will service providers position themselves?

The Need for Speed   There is no doubt that the PC has become a critical communications tool; it is now found in more than half of all U.S. households. Looking back to 1985, the PCs of the day seem almost laughable. Today's users have no use for boat anchors with 2-MHz/16-bit CPUs, 5-MB hard drives, and 300-bps modems. Today's standard has risen to 300-MHz/32-bit CPUs with 5-GB drives, yet the vast majority of us still waddle along at 33-kbps communication rates.

On the computer side, technology shows no sign of slowing this escalation of PC capability. By 2002, PCs will have 700-MHz/64-bit processors and 25-GB hard drives. The PC is the number one communications appliance generating new network traffic. The problem, however, is also the opportunity that great and profitable businesses can be built around increasing access speeds to the public network.

Though network backbones and large commercial sites have increased communications pipe sizes at tremendous rates, local access to smaller end users has not kept up and is, in fact, falling behind. Although the Internet contributes to total network traffic, plain old voice remains the "killer application" from a revenue-generation perspective. The right solution must reliably carry voice and data traffic. This has proven a difficult proposition to date given the high cost of past ubiquitous, application-specific networks. LMDS removes this restriction.

LMDS Breaks The Mold   LMDS technology is stepping into the access gap. LMDS provides a flexible, economical, and reliable source of nearly unlimited broadband communications capability in the local loop. The technology, inherently scalable and modular in nature, can provide significant cost advantages over an incumbent provider's network. Standard network interfaces are provided at the ingress/egress of an ATM- and/or PDH-based local access platform, which makes integration simple. Service providers can count on the technology for rapid deployment of multiple services in their targeted markets. LMDS end users will experience tremendous benefits.

Bandwidth availability will improve dramatically, and healthy price competition with the incumbents is always good news. Standard interfaces are provided, which means that there are no stranded costs for information technology managers looking to increase the performance of their service, and it all comes with reliability comparable with that of fiber.

So what is LMDS? Where does it make sense today, and what are the best applications for the use of its unprecedented spectrum allocation?

LMDS: A Review of the Facts   LMDS is a broadband fixed wireless system that operates at 28 GHz and occupies 1300 MHz of licensed spectrum. LMDS offers line-of-sight coverage over a 3- to 5-km range and holds within its reach the capacity to provide data and telephony service for up to 100,000 customers. A 360-degree transmission pattern, sectorized into four quadrants of alternating polarity, allows effective reuse of all spectrum resources and an overlapping node pattern that drastically improves coverage for a targeted customer base[41] (Figure 7-21).

LMDS is initially best for areas of concentrated traffic. It also supports low traffic scenarios as the network is deployed. Physically, a system consists of two primary functional layers: transport and services. The transport layer comprises the customer premises rooftop unit (RTU) and the node electronics. The RTU solid-state transceiver is approximately 12 in in diameter. The node includes solid-state transmitters, receivers, and other related elements located at the transmit site. The services layer comprises a network interface unit (NIU) at the customer premises and the base electronics. The NIU provides industry standard interfaces to the customer, and the base provides control and transport functions from the hub site or central office/traffic aggregation site.

LMDS reliability compares favorably with fiber. In high-rain areas, adaptive power control holds desired link margins. Occasionally, cell size

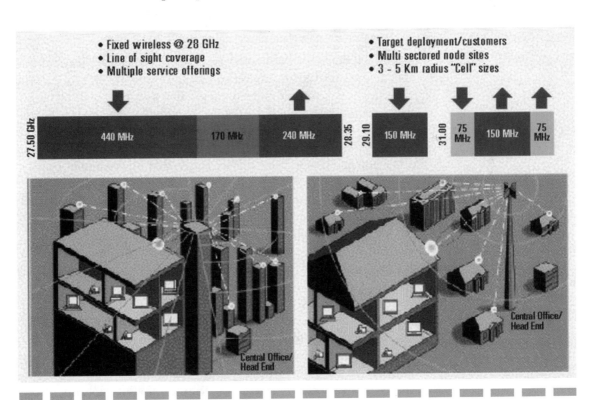

Figure 7-21   Local multipoint distribution services.

adjustments are required, but in areas with high rainfall such as Brazil and Mexico, economic 4 to 9 s of availability has proven achievable.

For service providers pursuing a competitive local exchange carriers (CLEC) business model, the technology is extremely cost-effective to implement. LMDS can be deployed in a matter of days and integrated with an existing network.

Incremental installation significantly improves the business case, allowing for additional implementation only as the customer base develops. As conditions change, LMDS is readily redeployable. So which end users should see the benefit of this technology first?

LMDS Product Opportunities   In the communications world today, significant opportunities are available in local access. Though the opportunities have been open to entrepreneurs since divestiture, the LECs have had a defacto monopoly. The multibillion dollar question has been how a CLEC can compete with thousands of miles of installed and paid-for copper. LMDS provides an extremely workable technology, which when planted in the fertile fields of explosive bandwidth requirements responds profitably.

Still, LMDS is no panacea and will see its widest deployment initially in the higher-traffic markets of businesses and multidwelling units (MDUs). The market segments and transmission speeds illustrated present the best opportunities for LMDS implementation.

Opportunity zones are not mutually exclusive but likely will be implemented differently because of the technical and economic issues associated with providing the most robust service. Each can, should, and will be deployed over time, and the proper technical architecture will provide a platform to support each of these service layers within a common point-to-multipoint rf system fabric.

Large and medium-sized businesses depicted in the red zone (Figure 7-22) call for supporting trunked telephony, private data circuits, remote access, and local-area network (LAN) interworking.[42] These are existing, high-traffic, and increasingly bandwidth-consumptive applications. Some are served by internal networks or incumbents, which can be challenged by lower-cost solutions. As bandwidth needs continue to expand, greater resources will be required. These subscribers, given their relatively small numbers but demanding purchasing criteria, are best served with dedicated point-to-point links operating in the LMDS band. The service provider also will use these links for internode distribution.

Medium-sized to small businesses and MDU-based residential tenants reflect the sweet spot for initial point-to-multipoint deployment. For medium-sized businesses, the economic threshold for private network implementation is harder to cross than for large businesses. Many of these

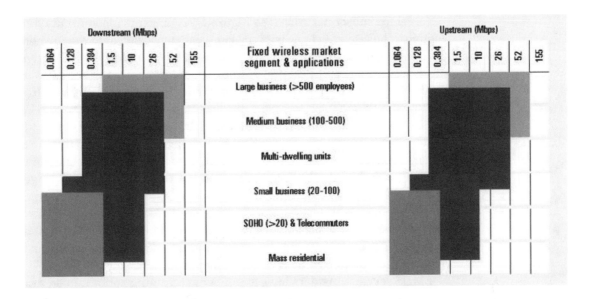

Downstream (Mbps)								Fixed wireless market segment & applications	Upstream (Mbps)							
0.064	0.128	0.384	1.5	10	26	52	155		0.064	0.128	0.384	1.5	10	26	52	155
								Large business (>500 employees)								
								Medium business (100–500)								
								Multi-dwelling units								
								Small business (20–100)								
								SOHO (>20) & Telecommuters								
								Mass residential								

Figure 7-22   Downstream (Mbps), upstream (Mbps).

entities clamor for advanced services but lack the internal staff and/or finances to specify and procure their solutions. Significant opportunities exist to offer previously unavailable high-capacity services to this segment or to replace higher-cost private solutions with lower-cost and more flexible shared services.

Residential bandwidth requirements constantly increase, but because of installed network insufficiency, MDUs presently emerge as an underserved segment, which holds great promise. The drift toward convergence (the ability of one network to serve all applications) is becoming a strong current with fax, entertainment video, videoconferencing, voice, and data transmission through the ubiquitous PC. LMDS is extremely effective in concentrated user locations that demand multiple integrated service offerings.

Small businesses have needs similar to their larger brethren but lack the economic clout to implement private networks that satisfy those needs. This is one of the most underserved market segments today. The capabilities of LMDS easily can serve this market, especially if the end users are geographically concentrated. This product opportunity zone will be best served with an architecture that blends the advantages of point-to-point's dedicated nature with the shared aspects of point-to-multipoint. A shared broadband downstream channel matched with frequency division multiple access (FDMA) uplinks is the most effective solution for this initial LMDS subscriber base.

The third subscriber zone (see Figure 7-22) presents a potentially huge customer base but brings with it some cautions for early deployment. Small office, home office, and work-at-home telecommuters are an increasingly growing segment of the business population. This segment poses concerns for service providers looking for high traffic and the resulting high revenues on which to base a new business venture.

The sporadic traffic patterns created by these entities beg for the deployment of a broadly shared access medium. In addition, these customers are often located in leased-site business parks or in single-family dwellings. As a result, the line-of-sight restriction for LMDS has its largest impact. Time division multiple access (TDMA) systems represent the most attractive means of achieving the economics necessary to address these subscribers. Still, the prudent service provider will use the TDMA systems to expand its initial network coverage based on the revenues reaped from a smaller but higher value core subscriber base.

LMDS service providers have a number of targeting options. In addition to the end-user market segments, tremendous opportunities for wholesale-type traffic arrangements exist, such as providing PCS or cellular backhaul for other wireless carriers looking to escape the grip of the incumbents for T1 links. This application puzzle is summarized in Figure 7-23.[43]

The best LMDS vendor partners will assist the service provider in prioritizing and providing the best technical solution for each application.

Figure 7-23
LMDS applications.

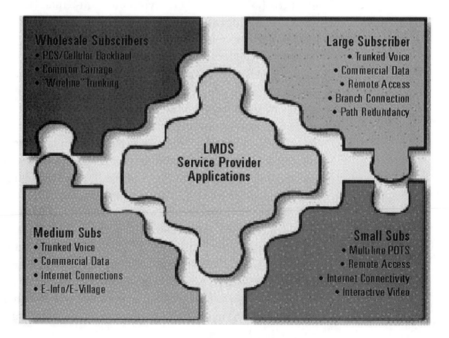

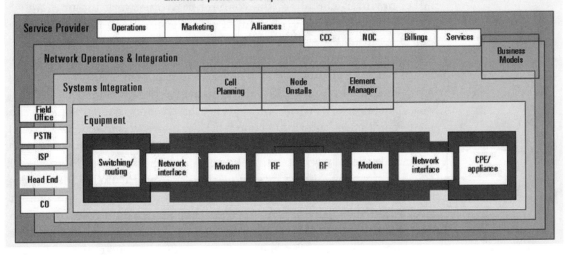

- New local access SP's have numerous challenges
- BBWL deployments will require wide skill sets
  - Robust RF and network planning competencies
- Extensible platforms and open interfaces needed

Figure 7-24　LMDS block diagram of a business.

A Broad Business Perspective　New local access service providers will have numerous challenges to overcome because no tried-and-true templates exist for this business. Those entering are truly on the leading edge of a new paradigm in communications. But therein also lies great opportunity.

LMDS deployments will require wide skill sets brought together in innovative ways and through creative partnerships. Figure 7-24 gives a graphic representation of what an LMDS business might look like.[44]

The service provider is the ultimate visible entity, providing operations and marketing and creating alliances with various partners (CLECs, IXCs, etc.). The structure on which the service provider sits will largely determine the possibilities of the business. If a choice is made to select a vertically integrated solution, certain limitations as to interfaces and platforms may dictate the eventual shape and customer set viable for the business.

Alternatively, if the choice is made to compile all the pieces from disparate vendors, the service provider risks venturing into uncharted territory unguided by know-how in the business. The preferred solution is a vendor team that provides the knowledge, experience, requisite technical solutions, and flexibility to support third-party choices made by the service provider. Look for vendors who have partnered with the best to address their noncore elements and have made the choices that grant the greatest customer effectiveness and flexibility.

To ensure that every aspect of deployment is accounted for, look for an LMDS provider who offers the comprehensive network integration service[45] (Figure 7-25). Each element of network integrations should be present to facilitate the seamless deployment of a successful enterprise.

Network engineering incorporates traffic and capacity engineering, selection of network elements based on service requirements, projected take rates, signaling system 7 (SS7) interconnection design, transport network design, and network operations planning. Interconnection agreements consist of coordinating interconnection to LECs; interexchange carriers (IXCs), and Internet service providers (ISPs) and facilitating the agreement process.

Central office site selection involves choosing the optimized location with regard to the proximity to interconnect points to LEC/IXC/ISP networks, building availability, price, and best value. Network integration and acceptance testing include management of issues related to data switching equipment, telephony switching equipment, video headend equipment, network operations software, multiplexing equipment, SONET and microwave transport equipment, and fiberoptics.

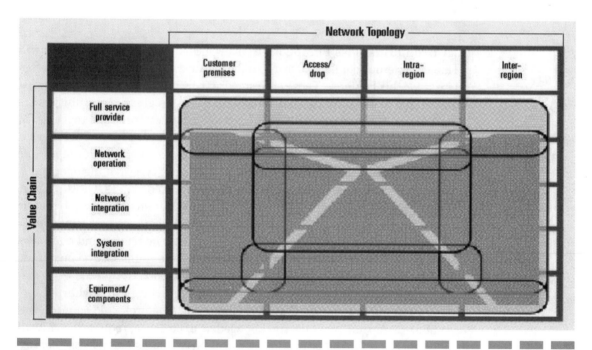

Figure 7-25   The strategic architecture model.

Training involves personnel concerned with installation, integration, maintenance and repair, and network management. Project management includes oversight of the turnkey project, contractor and vendor selection and management, master schedule and budget creation, adherence, quality control, and progress monitoring and reporting.

The LMDS access integration mosaic significantly eases the installation burden from the service provider and puts it squarely on the shoulders of the equipment supplier. Look for an rf system integrator vendor who provides all elements.

Again, project management entails developing the overall project plan and implementation schedule, coordinating with all suppliers for delivery of products and services, progress reporting, and adherence to budget, schedule, and quality specifications. Rf engineering includes site selection and design, propagation analysis, interference coordination, capacity planning, and loss-of-signal analysis.

Site acquisition is comprised of zoning analysis, property ownership due diligence, lease negotiations, municipal planning approvals, and assessment of existing rights of way. Construction consists of tower, structural and building code analysis, engineering design, tower and building site design, zoning and building permit approvals, and construction management.

Installation and integration relate to node and base station equipment, power systems, acceptance testing and commissioning, and interconnection to the network. Training involves classes for hub operations and maintenance, customer premises equipment installation, maintenance and operations, element management, operations, and administration.

The preceding discussions have presented an educated perspective on what LMDS is, where and when it makes sense to deploy, and what challenges lie ahead for new service providers.

A Strategic Model for Partnership

Finally, system vendors typically partner with the most effective equipment, knowledge, and support suppliers in the marketplace and provide an integrated face to their customers. Today, no one entity in the LMDS market can say that it excels in every component and every area of customer service. Therefore, it is necessary for a partnership to comprise sectors of core competency covering the entire picture.

Creative partnering, an integral piece of the groundbreaking, is key to providing the service provider and end user with optimal choices. The philosophy is simple in its presentation but certainly more complicated to implement. Suffice it to say that the unknown in this graphic is the triangle rising up the center area of the architecture most affected by the LMDS system integrator. Service providers should not lightly place their bets in the triangular region but rather must perform the requisite due diligence on those entities claiming to fill this area of responsibility.

The rf system integrator's relationships with the vendors who occupy the flanking areas on this strategic architecture are critical as well. Open interfaces afford the service provider greater options, but selected vendor integration options may provide significant performance, management, and cost advantages while not limiting total network architecture flexibility.

Endnotes

1. "LMCS," Canadian TELECOM, 145 Front Street East, Suite 201, Toronto, Ontario, Canada M5A 1E3, 2000.

2. Vinod Tipparaju, "Local Multipoint Distribution Service (LMDS)," Department of Computer and Information Science, The Ohio State University, 2015 Neil Avenue, DL 297, Columbus, OH 43210-1277, 2000.

3. Mike Mead, "Propagation Impairment at 28 GHz," America's Network, Advanstar Communications, 201 Sandpointe Ave., Suite 600, Santa Ana, CA 92707, 2000.

4. *Ibid.*

5. *Ibid.*

6. Vinod Tipparaju, "Local Multipoint Distribution Service (LMDS)," Department of Computer and Information Science, The Ohio State University, 2015 Neil Avenue, DL 297, Columbus, OH 43210-1277, 2000.

7. "42 GHZ Multipoint Video Distribution System," Technosystem S.p.A., Via Pietro Fumaroli, 14-00155 Rome, Italy, 2000.

8. *Ibid.*

9. *Ibid.*

10. *Ibid.*

11. *Ibid.*

12. Vinod Tipparaju, "Local Multipoint Distribution Service (LMDS)," Department of Computer and Information Science, The Ohio State University, 2015 Neil Avenue, DL 297, Columbus, OH 43210-1277, 2000.

13. *Ibid.*

14. *Ibid.*

15. *Ibid.*

16. *Ibid.*

17. *Ibid.*

18. *Ibid.*

19. *Ibid.*

20. *Ibid.*

21. Charles Mason, "LMDS: Fixed Wireless Wave of the Future?" America's Network, Advanstar Communications, 201 Sandpointe Ave., Suite 600, Santa Ana, CA 92707, 2000.

22. Cdebbie L. Sklar, "And the Winners Are . . .," America's Network, Advanstar Communications, 201 Sandpointe Ave., Suite 600, Santa Ana, CA 92707, 2000.

23. Lam, Derek, Elrefaie, Aly F., Plouse, Lynn, Chang, and Yee-Hsiang, "Telephony Solution for Local Multi-Point Distribution Service," HP Labs, 1501 Page Mill Road, Palo Alto, CA 94304-1126, 2000.

24. *Ibid.*

25. *Ibid.*

26. *Ibid.*

27. *Ibid.*

28. *Ibid.*

29. *Ibid.*

30. *Ibid.*

31. Ihor Nakonecznyj, "Marketplace Demand for Bandwidth Here and Now Gives LMDS Edge," America's Network, Advanstar Communications, 201 Sandpointe Ave., Suite 600, Santa Ana, CA 92707, 2000.

32. *Ibid.*

33. *Ibid.*

34. *Ibid.*

35. "Appendix III: Transmission," Telecommunication Engineering Centre, Department of Telecommunications, Government of IndiaKhurshid Lal Bhavan, Janpath, New Delhi 110001, India, 2000.

36. *Ibid.*

37. *Ibid.*

38. "LMDS and MMDS: Fixed Wireless Options in Telecom Networks 1999–2004," The Insight Research Corporation, Gatehall I, One Gatehall Drive, Parsippany, NJ 07054, 2000.

39. *Ibid.*

40. *Ibid.*

41. Tom McCabe, "What Lies Ahead for LMDS," America's Network, Advanstar Communications, 201 Sandpointe Ave., Suite 600, Santa Ana, CA 92707, 2000.

42. *Ibid.*

43. *Ibid.*

44. *Ibid.*

45. *Ibid.*

CHAPTER 8

Broadband Fixed Wireless Network Design

The arrival of broadband technologies to the neighborhood has been delayed by problematic rollouts, raising the potential value of the fixed wireless broadband market. For example:

- Subscribers to fixed wireless broadband systems are expected to grow at over 100 percent per year through 2006.
- Unlicensed and narrowband spectrum will be converted into broadband systems.
- Broadband wireless subscriber revenues are expected to exceed $7 billion by 2006.
- Fixed wireless broadband systems will be designed and deployed by competitive local exchange carriers (CLECs) to avoid the plant of incumbent providers.
- Incumbent service providers will deploy fixed wireless broadband systems to address dark spots in their network design.
- Fixed wireless will be used to provide DSL to fiber speeds.
- MMDS is expected to account for over 60 percent of fixed broadband wireless subscribers by 2006.
- Service providers will no longer rely on just one platform. They will use a collection of wired and fixed wireless technologies to maximize coverage area.[1]

Thus the limits of conventional wired broadband technologies have become evident. Line congestion and slow deployments of DSL and cable modems have proven to be constant hurdles faced by many service providers, consultants, and their customers.

As a result, service providers are turning to fixed wireless technologies: local multipoint distribution service (LMDS), multichannel multipoint distribution service (MMDS), and personal communications services (PCS) systems operating in the various industrial, scientific, and medical (ISM) bands (900 MHz, 2.4, 5.1, and 5.8 GHz). These technologies are expected to gain over 10 million fixed broadband subscribers by 2006. They will be used to provide fiber and high-speed copper equivalents to otherwise underserved customers.

NOTE   ISM stands for industrial, scientific, and medical applications (of radiofrequency energy). It has to do with the operation of equipment or appliances designed to generate and use locally radiofrequency energy for industrial, scientific, medical, domestic, or similar purposes, excluding applications in the field of telecommunications.

MMDS, including the 3.4- to 3.7-GHz worldwide standard for fixed wireless access, is expected to lead the market with an 80 percent share in 2006, largely in the residential and Small Ofice, Home Office (SOHO) sectors. LMDS will continue to make inroads into the market for high-value customers, accounting for 70 percent of subscriber revenues in 2006.

Meanwhile, traditional wireline and wireless carriers will join small Internet service providers (ISPs) in using a collection of bands (largely unlicensed) and technologies to address dark spots in their coverage areas. Due to its generous spectrum allotment, the 5.8-GHz band is receiving the most attention as an unlicensed broadband local loop. Systems operating in this band are expected to account for close to half a million subscribers in 2006. Total shipments of customer premises equipment for high-speed fixed wireless technologies are expected to reach 4.7 million units in 2006.

Underlying Technology

One cannot really overstate how important wireless broadband capabilities are for the U.S. and global market economies. Breaking the last mile bottleneck with fixed wireless broadband services is the cornerstone of this industry. Many consumers are unaware of their choice in Internet, telephony, and video television service. The common belief among consumers is that these services are provided only by traditional wired companies. Consumers, however, have many choices. With its relatively low cost and simple operational structure, fixed wireless (see the sidebar, "Fixed Wireless") is the preferred

Fixed Wireless

Sprint's recent announcement of its entry into the fixed wireless broadband market came as no surprise. The company was the last of the three major telcos to offer a fixed broadband service. With homes and small businesses hungry for high-speed access, fixed wireless will be giving cable modems and DSL a run for their money.

Although fixed wireless has not received nearly as much attention as its mobile counterpart, it is poised to take off. The telcos are betting that this innovative wireless technology can catch up and overtake DSL and cable modem services. Because the technology is wireless, providers do not have to sink time into running lines or maintaining a cable plant. Nor do they have to cut deals with intermediary "Baby Bells" for access. Consequently, these new wireless services should hit the market fast.

Sprint launched its Broadband Direct service in Phoenix, with an impressive initial coverage of 85 percent of the metropolitan area. Priced competitively at $39.95 a month, the service should supply customers within 35 miles of Sprint's transmission towers (and within line of sight) with average data rates of 1.5 Mbps.

MCI WorldCom debuted its WarpOne and Warp310 fixed broadband services in Jackson, Mississippi, Baton Rouge, Louisiana, and Memphis, Tennessee, using the same multichannel multipoint distribution service technology that Sprint is using. MMDS uses the 2.1- and 2.5- to 2.7-GHz range, previously a one-way band used by wireless cable companies. The Federal Communications Commission (FCC) put in place new rules in 1998 that allowed two-way transmission on this band, making it suddenly attractive for broadband data services.

AT&T unveiled its fixed wireless service, called AT&T Digital Broadband, in Fort Worth, Texas. AT&T has an important hook to its offering. It is the first to bundle standard telephone service along with wireless broadband data. For $34.95 a month, customers get high-speed, always-on Internet access, and for an additional $25.95, a single voice line is included with caller ID, call waiting, three-way calling, and unlimited local calls.

Sprint dismissed this advantage, noting that Sprint plans on adding voice services early next year. Sprint also claims that Sprint and MCI WorldCom's technology will help it serve far more users than AT&T. AT&T is using 10 MHz to offer fixed broadband service, and *will quickly run out of enough spectrum to serve customers*. Sprint and MCI WorldCom, by contrast, have 200 MHz of spectrum available for MMDS and can serve customers up to 35 miles away from their equipment, compared with approximately 3 miles for AT&T's service.

Once merged, MCI WorldCom and Sprint should have a jump on the market (but see note below). Both have been investing heavily in MMDS companies, each spending more than $1 billion to acquire access to this spectrum. The combined MMDS effort is one of the most frequently cited advantages of the proposed megamerger.

NOTE   Staff members at the Department of Justice's antitrust division have opposed WorldCom's $115 billion bid to buy Sprint, and this could deal a severe setback to a proposed merger that was designed to create a long-distance and Internet powerhouse. Assistant Attorney General Joel Klein formally decided to accept the staff recommendation and go to court to block the deal. Analysts and attorneys familiar with the case say the companies face an uphill battle to salvage the merger. In addition, officials at the FCC, which is also reviewing the deal, have suggested that opponents of the merger postpone making further presentations until after the Justice Department weighs in. This suggests that they expect the department to oppose the deal.

MCI WorldCom estimates that within 2 years the combined companies will cover 54 million households in 190 cities, nearly 60 percent of the country. While DSL and cable operators are scrambling to build out their networks, many consumers may find that their first broadband option is wireless.[2]

method for a growing number of satisfied consumers seeking data, telephony, and/or video television service in their homes and businesses.

Fixed wireless services have been available to consumers since the early 1980s, most notably as wireless cable. Many multichannel multipoint distribution service (MMDS) operators have been offering data services for a number of years, with a wireless downstream and telephone upstream path. The advent of new digital systems has greatly increased their capabilities and capacity. To illustrate the growth in this industry, 200,000 subscribers in the United States in 1992 have grown to over 3 million, with 11 million subscribers in 92 nations.

With its beginnings as an alternative to wired cable television in New York, local multipoint distribution service (LMDS) companies are developing standards for their growing menu of broadband wireless services. Following the much-anticipated completion of the U.S. auctions in the spring of 1998, these companies are gearing up, with 1300 MHz of spectrum in the United States to offer data, telephony, and video services. These efforts will serve as a showcase for similar expansion worldwide. In addition, other millimeter wave technologies are growing, proving that fixed broadband wireless networks are the most efficient and economical bridge for the last mile.

These systems, operating alone and in conjunction with others, are causing an explosion in the service offerings [see high-density fixed systems (HDFS) later in this chapter]. Given the rapid developments being made in technology and the associated expansion of wireless services, fixed broadband wireless will remain in the forefront of the communications industry.

Why? How is fixed broadband wireless so different from mobile wireless technology that it will remain in the forefront? Let's take a look. It is really all a matter of design, you see.

Fixed Broadband Wireless versus Mobile Wireless Technology in Wireless Local Loop Application Design

Wireless local loop (WLL) services may be defined as fixed broadband wireless services intended to provide primary access to the telephone network (wireless services supporting subscribers in fixed and known locations). A variety of recently designed fixed wireless broadband technologies and services can provide users with primary access to the public switch telephone network (PSTN), including point-to-point and point-to-multipoint microwave, cellular mobile radio, personal communications systems (PCS) or, equivalently, personal communications networks (PCN), and satellite systems.

A number of tradeoffs arise, however, when technologies developed to support mobile applications are used for fixed wireless broadband services without adaptation. This part of the chapter highlights such issues, addressing the distinctions between mobile technologies and technologies explicitly adapted for fixed wireless broadband services in the context of generic WLL services.

The Variety of Wireless Local Loop Services   To provide wireline telephone service, individual copper lines must be routed and wired to each subscriber from the PSTN central offices. By contrast, to provide wireless broadband telephone service, the wireless local loop infrastructure must first be deployed (the radio base stations and their link to the PSTN must be constructed in order to yield the geographic coverage and capacity required by the network). Telephone service is then available to all potential subscribers within range of each base station's radio signal, with individual service beginning on installation of the wireless local loop's subscriber terminal and on network authorization and activation. The first telephone service to tens, hundreds, or (depending on the subscriber density, the available bandwidth, and the particular radio technology that is employed) perhaps thousands of subscribers can thus begin with the installation of the first base station.

In comparison with the alternative of deploying copper lines, wireless local loop technology generically can offer a number of key advantages: faster deployment, sooner realization of revenues, and reduced time to payback of the design and deployment investment; lower construction costs; lower network maintenance, management, and operating costs; and greater flexibility to meet uncertain levels of penetration and rates of growth.

Different markets, however, make different demands on the capabilities expected of WLL services. In more mature markets, WLL systems may be designed and deployed as a means to bypass the existing wireline system or may be designed and deployed to provide advanced features above and beyond plain old telephone service (POTS). In industrializing nations, by contrast, WLL systems may be designed and deployed to provide only basic POTS (voice and, optionally, fax and data communications). The choice of technology used to address these different markets thus can vary considerably. And the choice of WLL technology has additional dimensions aside from the fundamental service capabilities offered. The subscriber density to be supported and the spectral efficiency required in a particular network design and deployment, for example, add another dimension to the choice of WLL technology.

Adaptation of Mobile Wireless Technology for Fixed Wireless Broadband Service   Many WLL systems are based on cellular or PCS technology, either analog (AMPS, TACS, ETACS, etc.) or digital (GSM, DECT, PDC, CDMA, etc.). These technologies have been designed and developed for mobile wireless communications, and to the degree that the corresponding mobile wireless systems are successful, WLL systems based on such technologies can benefit from the associated economies of scale and enjoy reduced costs.

At the same time, there are intrinsic characteristics of fixed wireless broadband service that are not fully addressed by mobile wireless technologies without explicit consideration. In other words, while mobile technologies can be used readily for WLL systems, the ideal WLL system for a given market will be designed and adapted for fixed rather than mobile services. The distinctions between fixed wireless broadband and mobile technologies are most clearly manifest in the WLL network design and deployment, the WLL subscriber terminals, and the WLL interface to the PSTN.

Network Design and Deployment   Because the subscriber locations in a WLL system are fixed and not mobile, the initial deployment of radio base stations need only provide coverage to areas where immediate demand for service is apparent. While a system supporting mobile communications would strive to provide coverage for an entire region before inauguration of service, fixed WLL systems can initiate service in stages. Service for a city, for example, can begin neighborhood by neighborhood as the WLL base stations are deployed. This distinction between fixed wireless broadband and mobile applications does not in itself imply any differences in the technology, but other dissimilarities associated with network design and deployment do.

For example, the capacity needed for a mobile system is different from that for a fixed WLL system. While a mobile system's base stations must provide adequate capacity to support worst-case (rush hour) traffic, a fixed system's base stations only must provide the capacity needed to support a known number of subscribers. This capacity may be greater than that needed by the same number of mobile subscribers. However, in a fixed WLL system as compared with a mobile system, the grade of service may be mandated to be better, and the traffic generated per subscriber may be higher due to lower tariffs than those charged for premium mobile service and the different use patterns of homes and offices. Consequently, the ideal fixed WLL system should be fully modular and scalable so that additional capacity can be added readily to base stations, so that network capacity can be redistributed among existing base stations, and so that base stations can be redeployed as needed to best meet changes in traffic demand.

The nature of coverage is also different in fixed wireless broadband and mobile applications. While a mobile system effectively must provide communications to all areas within signal range of the base station, a fixed wireless broadband system can assume that the subscriber terminal has been positioned to obtain the best possible signal. A fixed subscriber terminal will be oriented for the greatest signal strength on installation, and if necessary, a directional antenna pointing to the nearest WLL base station can be used to improve signal quality (in terms of the carrier-to-interference ratio) or extend the range.

Similarly, a fixed wireless broadband subscriber terminal will not experience the same magnitude of fading effects seen by a mobile terminal. Even fixed terminals will experience fades, however, due to local changes in the propagation environment. While mobile terminals can be expected to move out of such fades, a subscriber terminal adapted for fixed wireless broadband service should employ diversity receive antennas to counter the effects of whatever fades are present.

As a result of such differences between fixed and mobile propagation environments, the transmit power levels of a fixed WLL system can be reduced compared with those of a mobile system, assuming the same range of coverage and that all other variables are held constant. If the fixed wireless broadband subscribers are localized, moreover, then directional antennas may be used at the base station to further improve the system's link margins. Adapted for fixed wireless service in this way, reduced transmit power levels at the base station of a fixed WLL system imply reduced base station costs and improved reliability.

WLL Subscriber Terminals Subscribers in a WLL system receive phone service through terminals linked by radio to a network of base stations. The WLL terminals may be handsets that allow the subscriber some degree of mobility, they may be integrated desktop phone and radio sets, or they may be single- or multiple-line units that connect to one or more standard telephones. Terminals may be mounted indoors or outdoors, and they may or may not include battery backup for use during line power outages. These differences in WLL terminal designs reflect the use of different radio technologies in WLL systems and the varying levels of services that can be supported from plain old telephone service (POTS) to advanced broadband services. Such WLL subscriber terminal design variations highlight how mobile technology can be adapted to suit the variety of fixed wireless broadband applications. As mentioned previously, WLL subscriber terminals adapted for fixed wireless broadband service should incorporate antenna diversity to compensate for fading and should allow use of directional antennas to extend range.

Single- and multiple-line units that connect to standard wireline telephones are uniquely suited for fixed wireless broadband services. Unlike any mobile wireless unit, multiple-line subscriber terminals provide more than one independent channel of service, with each line routed as appropriate to support an office, an apartment complex, or a bank of payphones. With such single- and multiple-line designs, the WLL subscriber terminal effectively becomes the analog of a wireline phone jack—one connects a standard phone and receives standard phone service as if connected by copper lines to the telephone network. To truly deliver standard phone service however, requires WLL capabilities above and beyond those offered by many mobile systems. For example, the WLL and its subscriber terminal should support data and facsimile communications as well as voice without requiring any external digital modem adapters. Each line provided by a single- or multiple-line subscriber unit should provide the ring current needed to support multiple extensions. And, as required, the subscriber terminals should support the signaling needed for payphone service.

WLL Interfaces To The PSTN Subscribers to a WLL system are linked via radio to a network of radio base stations, which, in turn, are tied by a backhaul network to allow interconnection to the PSTN. In general, the WLL system's interface to the telephone network can be supported either by its own switch or through direct connection to the local exchange. The manner in which the WLL system interconnects to the PSTN, however, represents a key distinction between systems based on mobile wireless technology or adapted to fixed wireless broadband.

WLL systems are available that incorporate their own switch or that connect to only one or a few specific switch types. In part, this approach to WLL system architecture reflects the difficulty of supporting direct connection to the wide variety of switches globally deployed. It also can reflect a given WLL system's reliance on technology designed for the support of mobile services. Due to the history of mobile services as competitive independent networks distinct from wireline service providers, such systems have been developed for use with specific mobile switch centers. The requirement of mobile switch centers or specific switch types as part of a WLL system, however, represents additional cost to the network operator.

By contrast, direct connection of a WLL system to existing central office switches effectively makes the WLL network a direct extension of the wireline network and allows use of underutilized switching resources. The WLL system itself can rely on the PSTN to provide all primary switching functions. Ideally, a WLL network adapted to fixed wireless broadband services as a cost-effective extension of the wireline network should be able to connect to existing local exchanges in a cost-efficient manner that preserves the advanced features provided by the exchange and supports mixed-vendor networks.

Direct connection to PSTN switches can be through either analog or digital interfaces. Analog two- or four-wire interfaces are provided by all central office switches to support copper line local loops, and some WLL systems are able to use them effectively. Digital interfaces using 64 kbps PCM voice channels, on the other hand, can be more convenient and less expensive. In particular, the V5.2 landline digital interconnect standard has been standardized by the European Telecommunications Standard Institute (ETSI) as the recommended open digital interface between a landline switching office and WLL system, remote switch unit, or private branch exchange. Unfortunately, while V5.2 would allow interface across multiple switch and WLL vendors, its adoption and introduction by the world's local exchange switch manufacturers have only just begun. In the meantime, WLL equipment manufacturers have developed proprietary digital interfaces to suit specific switches as required by their specific markets.

Finally, the needs of WLL systems are different and distinct from those of mobile wireless systems, although aspects of the technology may be common.

To best suit fixed wireless broadband applications in WLL systems, mobile wireless technology should be adapted to directly address the requirements of fixed wireless broadband design. From the point of view of the network operator, the questions to ask any WLL system vendor must include

- Is the system modular, allowing cost-effective deployment of capacity, capable of future growth, and suitable for redeployment if needed?
- Is the system's underlying wireless broadband technology standardized and able to take advantage of economies of scale?
- Is the system spectrally efficient, especially for high-capacity needs or in regions with severely constrained access to bandwidth?
- Does the system take advantage of the differences between fixed wireless broadband and mobile propagation environments through directional antennas at the base station and lower transmit powers?
- Are single- and multiple-line subscriber terminals provided?
- Do the subscriber terminals support multiple extensions?
- Can directional antennas be used at the subscriber terminals to extend the range from the base station?
- Is antenna diversity used at the subscriber terminal to defeat the effects of fading?
- Are data and facsimile communications supported in addition to voice without external adapters?
- Can existing switch capacity be used by the WLL system by direct connection?
- Is the deployment and additional cost of a mobile switch center or specific switch type avoided?[3]

Now, let's take a brief but close look at the multipoint microwave distribution system. Also known as the multichannel multipoint distribution system and wireless cable, it is another wireless broadband technology for Internet access.

Multipoint Microwave Distribution System (MMDS)

MMDS channels come in 6-MHz chunks and run on licensed and unlicensed channels. Each channel can reach transfer rates as high as 27 Mbps (over unlicensed channels: 99 MHz, 2.4 GHz, and 5.7 to 5.8 GHz) or 1 Gbps (over licensed channels). MMDS is a line-of-sight service (see Fresnel zone definition), so it will not work well around mountains, but it will work in rural areas where copper lines are not available.

NOTE Fresnel zone is an area around the visual line of sight that radio waves spread out into after they leave the antenna. This area must be clear or else signal strength will weaken. Fresnel zone is an area of concern for 2.4-GHz wireless systems. Although 2.4-GHz signals pass rather well through walls, they have a tough time passing through trees. The main difference is the water content in each. Walls are very dry; trees contain high levels of moisture. Radio waves in the 2.4-GHz band absorb into water quite well. This is why microwaves (which also use the 2.4-GHz band) cook food. Water absorbs the waves, and heat from the energy cooks the food.

MMDS: Better than Sliced Bread

In the opinion of many, MMDS could be the best thing since sliced bread—maybe even better than sliced bread. Of course, bread is a bit easier to understand than advanced broadband wireless technology. So let's take a look at MMDS, what it is, and what it can mean for telcos as well as consumers.

MMDS stands for *multichannel multipoint distribution service* and includes wireless frequencies licensed by the FCC in the 2150- to 2162-MHz and 2500- to 2690-MHz spectrum bands. MMDS shares the 2500- to 2690-MHz band with ITFS licensees, such as colleges and universities, local school systems, and religious educational institutions, all of which use their spectrum to broadcast educational programming and lease their excess spectrum capacity.

MMDS service was licensed originally as a one-way service providing wireless video programming sometimes referred to as *wireless cable*. The wireless cable industry largely failed in its effort to compete with wired and satellite-based video programming providers. As a result, the FCC recently revised its service rules to permit the MMDS and ITFS spectrum to be used for bidirectional services, opening the door for the frequencies to be used as a transport mechanism for high-speed Internet access.

The technology behind MMDS will enable telcos to deploy a fixed wireless network providing broadband Internet and other data services. The timing could not be better for MMDS. Consumer demand for bandwidth is growing faster than the number of new TV quiz shows. The lines between home and business communications are increasingly blurred, and growing numbers of users are working away from the corporate office. MMDS effectively will meet the needs of residential consumers, work-at-home entrepreneurs and telecommuters, as well as small-sized businesses and remote-site offices.

Furthermore, fixed wireless service will cover rural, suburban, and other underserved areas that cannot receive service through wireline connections such as DSL because they are too far away from a central office or cable systems that either do not upgrade or choose not to serve such areas. As a result, telcos will bring broadband services to millions of residential consumers who otherwise would not have access to high-speed services.

With a single transmitter, the telco can serve customers within a 35-mile radius—a coverage area totaling more than 3000 square miles. For example, Sprint's MMDS service is delivered using land-based radio transmitters positioned at the tallest feasible location in a metropolitan area.[4] Sprint's transmitter in Chicago, for example, is atop the 1454-ft-tall Sears Tower; in Phoenix, the transmitter is on top of South Mountain.

Customers obtain the MMDS signal using a small 13.5 × 13.5-in diamond-shaped digital transceiver placed on their roof with line of sight to the transmitter. MMDS will provide access to a megabits-per-second (Mbps) downstream channel for Internet and/or data communications. The digital receiver receives the signal and transfers it to a wireless modem, which communicates with the individual PC or Macintosh computer or local-area network (LAN).

Advantages of MMDS   MMDS technology offers a broad spectrum (pun intended) of advantages for telcos, as well as potential residential and business customers. Some of the advantages are

- Spectrum
- Interference
- Coverage
- Infrastructure
- Availability
- Expandability

SPECTRUM   MMDS represents a new generation of an already established and proven wireless service. For over 30 years, radiowave wireless spectrum has been used to transmit television signals—now digitized, it has been adopted to beam data and Internet traffic.

INTERFERENCE   Using licensed spectrum, telcos can deploy high-speed wireless LANs on secure channels without interference concerns associated with using unlicensed spectrum from other users or other wireless signals. Moreover, unlike other wireless technology or satellite transmission, the signal performance of MMDS is very resistant to rain, snow, or fog.

COVERAGE   A single MMDS cell can serve a 35-mile-radius coverage area. Higher-frequency wireless technologies such as local multipoint distribution service (LMDS), in contrast, cover an area with only a 2- to 3-mile radius. Do the math and you will discover that it would take over 136 LMDS cells to cover the same area as just one MMDS cell.

INFRASTRUCTURE   Radiowaves are colorless, odorless, and most important, wireless. According to Motorola, it costs around $25,000 per mile to lay new two-way hybrid fiber coaxial cable. Other sources say that in New York City, the average cost of laying fiberoptic cable is $3 million per mile. Deploying a wireless solution is much more cost-effective. For example, Sprint's MMDS network does not rely on the large and expensive landline networks of cable/copper plant required by traditional cable/phone companies. The cost of installing a single tower is around $6 million. This provides a cost of roughly $2000 per square mile—significantly less than the cost of wiring a square mile. Not to forget, installation is easy, immediate, and not dependent on the quality and availability of phone lines.

AVAILABILITY   MMDS technology is available now, with a potential of reaching 30 million U.S. homes. In contrast, it will take years and billions of dollars for the ILECs and cable multiple system operators (MSO) to retrofit thousands of miles of outdated network cable plant, which requires removing line concentrators and loop conditioning.

EXPANDABILITY   To meet future growth of the customer base and bandwidth requirements, telcos can expand the already vast capacity of the MMDS network using two methods—by sectoring its transmitter antennas or reusing the same frequencies to different locations and by cellularization or reusing the same frequency with multiple transmission sites. It certainly sounds like the best thing since sliced bread.

Spectrum Analysis   Originally, the MMDS/ITFS wireless spectrum consisted of 33 analog video channels, each with a bandwidth of 6 MHz. The evolution of video technology from analog to digital enabled Sprint to convert the 33 analog MMDS/ITFS channels into 99 digital data streams, each transmitting at 10 Mbps. As a result, Sprint can deliver up to 1 Gbps of capacity from a single transmitter.

How Fast Is Fast High speed is among the primary advantages of MMDS fixed wireless broadband technology, with broadband Internet service delivering speeds over 100 times faster than traditional dial-up connections. To put that speed into perspective, a 10-Mbps wireless modem could download the 3¼-hour movie *Titanic* in 7 minutes and 23 seconds; a DSL or cable modem would take 9 minutes and 14 seconds at 8 Mbps; T1 would take 49 minutes and 20 seconds; ISDN would need 9 hours and 14 minutes; and a 28.8-K modem would need a whopping 42 hours and 30 minutes, or 13 times longer than the movie itself.

Vendors and carriers are falling over themselves trying to build out networks, forge partnerships, and land capital in the race to capture a piece of the fixed wireless broadband market. With this huge potential market on verge of a boom, it presents many commercial opportunities for telecommunications companies—even very small ones. Let's take a look at one.

Commercial Opportunities for Everyone

Compared with its larger telco siblings, Adaptive Broadband[5] is a small company. However, it has big ideas. The company is targeting fixed wireless broadband carriers that have extravagant plans and a slew of spectrum but little to show so far in commercial deployments. But awareness of these nascent services is on the rise, and with it comes demand for the products being touted. And this could make fixed wireless broadband the next big thing in the wireless industry.

Specifically, Adaptive Broadband has developed high-speed broadband two-way radios that function in frequencies ranging from 2 to 42 GHz. Branded under the name AB Access, Adaptive Broadband's equipment can provide 25 Mbps of two-way broadband to all kinds of businesses. You can do huge file transfers, video streaming, videoconferencing, surf the Web, and now the company is incorporating voice into it—simultaneously over one connection.

The big bonus of AB Access is that it can be deployed in so-called unlicensed bands such as 5.8 GHz. The band is like a frontier where quasi-squatters' rights apply. In other words, because few businesses are using

5.8 GHz right now, the band is wide open for companies such as Fuzion to claim turf—in this case, to launch a two-way broadband data service in the United States and Canada. To date, Fuzion has already acquired some revenue-producing customers. Thanks to AB Access, the company's future looks bright.

Given AB Access's ability to provide a high-speed last mile solution, it is not surprising that larger companies are eyeing this product as well. In fact, US West has even signed a master volume agreement with Adaptive Broadband and installed AB Access for a Denver-area trial.

Great things are expected by the telcos for fixed wireless broadband. It is the future—about a $100 billion market worldwide.

Lending Credibility

Adaptive Broadband is not the only fixed wireless broadband company to have reason to celebrate. WinStar Communications, Inc., which is launching broadband services in bands such as 28 and 38 GHz, has just scored a potentially fat contract with Microsoft.

NOTE   WinStar recently became the first U.S.-based carrier to offer fixed wireless broadband services to businesses in Europe, launching in Amsterdam. Recently, WinStar announced it would expand into 70 leading international markets within the next 5 years. The company has already acquired spectrum in four of its top ten targeted international markets. Furthermore, WinStar Communications, Inc., is a pioneer in providing business customers with broadband communications services, including local and long-distance phone service, as well as high-speed Internet access and data and information services. WinStar provides these Wireless FiberSM services in more than 50 U.S. markets over its own local broadband networks using its licenses in the 28- and 38-GHz spectrum, which are connected to the company's nationwide fiberoptic network. In addition, the company offers wireless fiber services in two markets outside the United States.

Under the deal, WinStar will provide Microsoft Office 2000 applications to customers via its wireless and fiberoptic networks. The concept: Rather than buy Microsoft Office themselves, businesses can *rent* it from WinStar. To do this, they tap into Microsoft Office software from WinStar's own servers as needed, just as if they were accessing a network server on their own LAN. WinStar is conducting a 6-month trial where it supplies Microsoft Office online to selected customers at no extra charge. After this, the company will consider offering Microsoft Office on a monthly rental basis.

Adaptive Broadband's and WinStar's good fortune is a good omen for the fixed wireless broadband industry. In fact, having endured some slow years—particularly in multichannel multipoint distribution services (MMDS)—fixed wireless broadband seems on the verge of a boom.

There are a number of reasons why this is happening, but the most important has to be American business's insatiable appetite for bandwidth. This is why fixed wireless broadband is suddenly such a hot commodity. First, it gives business a high-speed detour around the local loop's traffic jam, according to Teligent (see the sidebar, "Fixed Wireless Broadband Networks").

NOTE   Currently available in 34 U.S. markets, Teligent provides two-way broadband wireless at 24 GHz.

Fixed Wireless Broadband Networks

Teligent and REMEC, providers of broadband and wireless microwave and millimeter-wave systems, recently unveiled new antenna technology that will extend the reach of fixed wireless broadband networks by virtually eliminating the requirement for direct line-of-sight access. The active antenna repeater technology, developed jointly by the two companies, redirects microwave signals from a network base station to customer buildings that otherwise would not be accessible because they are not directly in the base station's line of sight. The technology will enable Teligent (TGNT) to reach more than 90 percent of all buildings within range of Teligent base stations. According to Teligent, by increasing the number of buildings that can be served by individual base stations, active antenna repeaters will lower network costs and expand Teligent's pool of potential customers.

The new technology is a major development for the fixed wireless industry that will allow Teligent to extend the reach of its SmartWave networks at a fraction of the cost of deploying additional base stations. The Teligent-REMEC active antenna repeater was developed from a Teligent design concept at REMEC's San Diego headquarters. The device was tested and evaluated at Teligent's Broadband Research Laboratory in Washington, DC. A patent is pending for the network application.

Under the joint development agreement, Teligent has an exclusive right to deploy the first generation active antenna repeater for

8 months. The first-generation repeater operates in the 24-GHz band and features vertical and horizontal polarized antenna ports, a signal level detector for precise antenna alignment, and an operational range from −40 to 140°F. The repeater is designed to operate at humidity levels of up to 100 percent.

The active antenna repeater is the latest in a series of devices and technologies that have been put through their paces in the multi-million-dollar state-of-the-art Teligent laboratory. In recent months, Teligent has conducted extensive research on nanometer, beam-bender, millimeter-wave, and other fixed wireless broadband technologies in the laboratory.

Completed in 1998, the Broadband Research Laboratory features a fully operational replica of Teligent's network. The network simulator includes working reproductions of a customer site, a Teligent broadband switching facility, and a Teligent base station.

The lab is used to evaluate installation procedures, enhance network architecture, and test new and leading-edge products and services. The live environment allows Teligent to fine-tune its communications networks in real time without affecting customers. The lab also is available for Teligent vendors to test their products and technologies.[6]

Second, fixed wireless broadband can provide customers with high-speed access within hours. In contrast, ordering a T1 (from an incumbent local exchange carrier) can take 3 to 6 months to get. The reason? Backhoes do not follow Moore's law. In other words, it takes time to arrange and lay new wireline networks. In contrast, fixed wireless broadband networks are quick to install, especially if the network hub is already in place.

MMDS Emerges

No wonder fixed wireless broadband is proving a great business proposition. This also explains why after all these years fixed wireless broadband is helping the 2.5-GHz MMDS band to take off (see the sidebar, "Cisco Extends Broadband Fixed Wireless Leadership Through Addition of New World Ecosystem Partners").

Cisco Extends Broadband Fixed Wireless Leadership Through Addition of New World Ecosystem Partners

To give service providers new options for providing broadband fixed wireless services to customers, Cisco Systems, Inc., the worldwide leader in networking for the Internet, recently announced four new broadband fixed wireless ecosystem partners. Bechtel, Fluor, and Getronics are focused on integration, deployment, and implementation of carrier-scale, complex networking and radio frequency (rf) solutions. Additionally, Netro Corporation's AirStar broadband wireless access system will be made available to qualified system integrator partners. These partnerships will extend Cisco's ability to satisfy growing customer demand for broadband wireless solutions.

With the addition of Bechtel, Fluor, Getronics, and Netro to the ecosystem, Cisco's customers have the flexibility to choose among best-of-breed solutions. The broadband fixed wireless market is rapidly emerging, and Cisco has taken this opportunity to focus on meeting customer demands and getting solutions to market quickly.

Bechtel, Fluor, and Getronics will integrate Cisco's MMDS broadband fixed wireless solutions and core infrastructure products to create New World wireless networks. Cisco's MMDS solutions implement vector orthogonal frequency division multiplexing (VOFDM) in order to overcome line-of-sight issues common to microwave radio networks. These solutions currently are in trials with MCI WorldCom and Nucentrix.

In addition, Cisco has reached an agreement with Netro Corporation in which qualified ecosystem system integration partners will have access to Netro's AirStar broadband wireless access system. Netro's leading millimeter-wave broadband wireless access equipment complements Cisco's Asynchronous Transfer Mode (ATM) and Internet Protocol (IP) core infrastructure solutions. The Netro AirStar system also extends Cisco's ecosystem offerings to the 10-, 26-, 28-, and 39-GHz LMDS ranges, complementing Cisco's 2.5-GHz MMDS and 5.7-GHz UNII solutions for the U.S. market.

As a significant element of the New World ecosystem, the Cisco-Motorola alliance has led to key wireless opportunities and successes in the mobile wireless market, including the first major deployment of integrated mobile data, voice, and video services in an all-IP-based cellular infrastructure. Cisco and Motorola have already successfully deployed the first live commercial general packet radio service (GPRS) network at customers BT Cellnet and T-Mobil and continue to drive other mobile wireless trials worldwide. Cisco and Motorola are also continuing the development of the centers of excellence that enable operators and service providers to experience the latest in IP-based networking technologies.[7]

MMDS's rejuvenation started when the FCC decided to allow two-way digital signals on this band. To say that this was a smart choice is an understatement: One-way TV delivery over MMDS had never caught on, and the spectrum was essentially lying fallow.

The second important factor was separate decisions by both Sprint and MCI WorldCom to seriously move into MMDS. Sprint spent $2.4 billion to acquire People's Choice TV, American Telecasting, Inc., Transworld Telecommunications Inc., Videotron USA, and WBS America. It put all these companies—and its 200 MHz worth of licenses—into a new broadband wireless group and then declared its intention to launch high-speed Internet and Sprint's integrated on-demand network over MMDS.

Were the MMDS purchases worth it? Perhaps! MMDS is much better suited for high-speed data than most people believe, particularly for PCS carriers.

On paper, this does not appear so. After all, MMDS was intended originally to provide single-tower coverage over areas 30 to 35 miles in radius—hence the TV broadcast model—whereas LMDS signals travel only about 2 miles in the 28- to 31-GHz frequency range. This is why LMDS is a natural for data transmission, since its short propagation range fits perfectly with a cellular model of transmission. Making LMDS an even better choice for fixed wireless broadband is that the FCC allocated 1.3 GHz of bandwidth for this purpose, as opposed to just 200 MHz for MMDS.

Given these factors, one has to wonder why Sprint or MCI WorldCom bought so many MMDS licenses. Currently, each owns about 40 percent of MMDS licenses in the United States, or 80 percent combined.

The answer lies in the hidden possibilities of MMDS. Just because this spectrum can cover up to 35 miles with a single tower does not mean that MMDS operators have to do so. Actually, they can build low-power MMDS transmitters within a few miles of each other, cellularizing the coverage area in order to boost its carriage capacity. In this configuration, MMDS is a perfect fit for Sprint, which has lots of PCS towers covering small cells. Obviously, this means that these same towers can be reused for MMDS, thus creating a really good synergy between Sprint PCS and MMDS operations.

MMDS will allow the merged company to break the local telephone monopoly that has frustrated public policymakers throughout the twentieth century—Sprint's fixed wireless broadband assets, when combined with WorldCom's, create a true broadband alternative. Telcos have the ability from an engineering perspective to add cell sites throughout the respective (MMDS) region and to increase the line of sight of the technology as well.

As for the impact of the Sprint–MCI WorldCom merger on MMDS fixed wireless broadband, it only adds *credibility* to deploying MMDS in this manner. It is a bullet-proof technology, and with companies like Sprint and MCI (buying into it), it lends itself to greater distribution at a much faster rate.

Nextlink: The Sleeping Giant

Meanwhile, things also are heating up on the LMDS front. In this spectrum, Nextlink is the undisputed king. Nextlink has bought up 97 percent of the licenses covering the top 50 U.S. markets. Add to this LMDS's 1.3 GHz of bandwidth, and one can see why Nextlink is poised to offer two-way fixed wireless broadband in a big, big way.

Still, to think of Nextlink as mainly an LMDS provider is to miss the total picture. This is so because the company also owns 44 local fiberoptic networks and will soon have access to a 18,000-mile network being built in the United States and Canada. In other words, what Nextlink is creating is a multilayered high-speed carrier able to operate with wires or without.

Ironically, Nextlink would prefer to use only fiberoptic landlines. However, since only 7 percent of all U.S. businesses have fiberoptic connectivity, fixed wireless broadband is the next best choice. As for tying Nextlink into the traditional phone network, only as a last resort do you rely on the facilities of the ILEC.

This said, Nextlink has yet to launch fixed wireless broadband. In contrast, Sprint has an MMDS system up and running in Phoenix, while HighSpeed.Com offers LMDS in Walla Walla, Washington, Bend, Oregon, Bakersfield, California, and Boise, Idaho. Thus, although Nextlink may claim it is the powerhouse of American fixed wireless broadband, this status currently only exists on paper.

Challenges Ahead

All told, it is clear that fixed wireless broadband is heating up MMDS and LMDS in the United States, as well as spurring new developments in the unlicensed bands. Thus, are there any clouds attached to this silver lining? The answer, unfortunately, is yes.

The first problem is rolling out these services: Building fixed wireless broadband systems takes time, even for the most cash-rich of companies. The second is that the local phone companies are not always keen to help. In fact, fixed wireless broadband's major challenges stem from the resistance of incumbent telcos in opening up their networks.

One reason established telcos are not aiding fixed wireless broadband providers is because they realize the potential of this medium. After all, why else would AT&T Wireless Services be conducting its own hush-hush fixed-wireless wireless trials? Called *Project Angel*, the 1.9-GHz trial is aimed at delivering voice and 384-kbps data to residential customers. If all goes well, there should be some sort of commercial deployment soon.

If there is a message to the preceding information, it is that fixed wireless broadband is definitely the coming thing. In fact, it may well be the last mile solution of the twenty-first century, given the limits of wireline networks, asymmetric digital subscriber line and cable modems notwithstanding. After all, you can only push the copper cage so far. Cable TV does not go everywhere. As a result, fixed wireless broadband may indeed be a killer application whose time has finally come.

Conclusion

The year 2000 will be remembered in telecommunications history as the year that marked the beginning of a dramatic growth period for fixed wireless broadband. Global service revenues from the technology are projected to reach US$16.3 billion by 2004, a compound annual growth rate of 140 percent over 1999 revenues.

Everything seems to be finally coming together for fixed wireless broadband. There is more frequency spectrum available, the equipment seems ready, and carriers, both big and small, are deploying systems in numerous markets. With these three elements converging, the global market is poised for tremendous growth, for both carriers and vendors, in the next couple of years.

While North America, with a larger potential market and earlier system rollouts, will represent 39 percent (US$6.4 billion) of the global market in 2004, significant increases are forecast throughout the world. In Europe and Asia, market activity is beginning to increase with more trials and a few commercial deployments. Within Latin America, all the major countries have made spectrum available for fixed wireless, and a few carriers have launched commercial systems. With these developments, Europe,

Asia, and Latin America are forecast to generate US$4.1 billion, US$3.0 billion, and US$2.7 billion in service revenue by 2004, respectively.

Because of their unique characteristics, such as a relatively quick deployment time and bundled service capabilities, fixed wireless broadband technologies are finding a place with established and new carriers in both developed and developing markets. In the United States, companies such as AT&T, MCI WorldCom, and Sprint are using fixed wireless broadband as a complement to other technologies to increase their market reach. Fixed wireless broadband is also an effective means to gain a foothold in a new market and quickly compete with the incumbent carrier. This has been the business strategy of companies such as Diveo in Latin America.

Finally, significant growth in fixed wireless broadband is imminent. Telcos are seeing tremendous opportunity and have invested billions of dollars to rollout services throughout the world. These investments are starting to pay off now and will accelerate rapidly in the future.

Endnotes

1. "LMDS, MMDS, and ISM 2000: Global Markets and Trends for Fixed Wireless Broadband," Global Information, Inc., 69 Overshore Drive West, Madison, CT 06443, 2000.

2. "Fixed Wireless Heats Up," The Industry Standard, Production, 315 Pacific Ave., San Francisco, CA 94111, 2000.

3. Alan Jacobsen, "Fixed versus Mobile Wireless Technology in Wireless Local Loop Applications," Diva Communications, Inc., 32930 Alvarado-Niles Road, Union City, CA 94587, 2000.

4. Sprint, 2330 Shawnee Mission Parkway, Westwood, KS, 66205

5. Adaptive Broadband, 1143 Borregas Avenue, Sunnyvale, CA 94089, 2000.

6. Thor Olavsrud, "Teligent and REMEC Extend Reach of Fixed Wireless Broadband Networks," Teligent, 8065 Leesburg Pike, Suite 400, Vienna, VA 22182, 2000.

7. "Cisco Extends Broadband Fixed Wireless Leadership Through Addition of New World Ecosystem Partners." Some of the material in this book has been reproduced by Osborne/McGraw-Hill with the permission of Cisco Systems, Inc. Copyright © 2000 Cisco Systems, Inc. All rights reserved. 170 West Tasman Drive, San Jose, CA, 95134-1706, 2000.

CHAPTER 9

Broadband Wireless Access Design

Broadband wireless access systems are emerging as a new and growing area of telecommunications. These systems have the capability to provide access without a need for a copper or fiber infrastructure. A form of broadband wireless access today is a geographic localized technology called a *wireless local-area network* (WLAN).

NOTE Broadband wireless access bypasses today's local-loop bottlenecks to provide multimegabit voice, video, and data communication.

The need for mobility of people at their workplaces is creating a market for broadband wireless access for computer and multimedia terminals. The evolved WLAN standards and evolving WATM standards are creating emerging markets. It is expected that such systems will find deployment in the near future.

So what is broadband wireless access? What are its advantages? Let's take a look.

What Is Broadband Wireless Access?

Broadband wireless access uses high-frequency, licensed spectrum to transmit voice, video, and data signals within cells several kilometers in diameter. It is a short-haul, line-of-site technology operating in the millimeter-wave frequency range (10–42 GHz). In the United States, LMDS (local multipoint distribution service) licensees control up to 1.3 GHz of spectrum at 28 and 31 GHz[1] (Figure 9-1). Over short distances, 1.3 GHz can carry a broad band of digital data at speeds in excess of 1 Gbps. LMDS is a *cellular* technology based on multiple contiguous or overlapping cells.

Objective of Broadband Wireless Access (BWA) Technology

The objective of broadband wireless access (BWA) technology is to allow today's fast desktop computers to communicate rapidly with high-speed Internet servers, data servers, and other network services. By breaking the bottleneck at the final mile, BWA could allow emergent as well as developed markets around the world to participate more fully in the global economy.

Figure 9-1
BWA operates in the millimeter-wave frequency range.

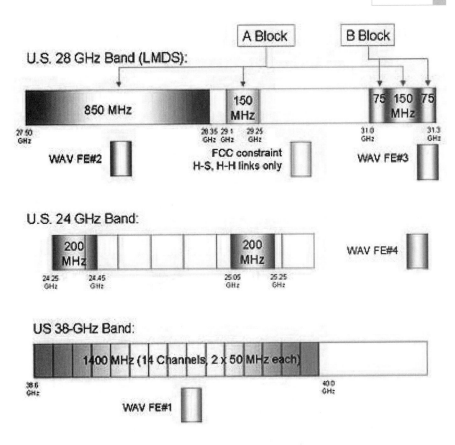

To paraphrase the telcos' mission statement, they intend to provide *high-quality cost-effective broadband communications services.* To provide these services, the telcos must accurately and efficiently transport information from one location to another as their customers' needs demand it. There are several network technologies that could be designed and employed to transport this information, ranging from fiberoptic cable to satellite transmission to broadband wireless technologies. Most telcos believe that the most effective technology to employ to design and build a reliable network for their customers is a technology referred to as *broadband wireless access* (BWA). While other technologies may be employed where specific conditions suggest that would be beneficial, BWA will be the telcos' primary technology.

NOTE   The U.S. Federal Communications Commission (FCC) calls this technology LMDS (local multipoint distribution service).

First, however, let's look at the ATM side of BWA: the ABWACS project.

ATM Broadband Wireless Access Communications System

The ATM Broadband Wireless Access Communications System (ABWACS) project's main objective is to design and develop a system concept and test-bed demonstration of wireless public access to B-ISDN services. The system operates in the 19-GHz band with user bit rates of up to 34 Mbps and radio transmission ranges between 50 to 100 m. The project supports limited slow-speed mobility as in line with expected use of high data services but with improved portability. The project builds on the use of an experimental prototype at a 19-GHz ATM wireless platform provided by a Japanese partner, which marks the significant importance of the establishment of working relationships throughout the worldwide mobile communication community. Figure 9-2 depicts a more humorous approach for the ABWACS project.[2] The demonstrator of ATM wireless access (AWA) preprototype equipment associated with channel sounder helps to provide propagation data, bit error rate (BER), and ATM performance at 19 GHz. Based on this information, enhancement techniques are to be investigated to support a fully integrated antenna solution, mobility, and spectrum- and power-efficient radio access technologies required to support ETSI-RES10 HIPERLAN specifications. These targets are to be supported further by the following subobjectives: cooperation with other wireless ATM-related projects in domains and chains in order to have close links concerning system development and strong commitment to contribute to standardization

Figure 9-2
The creation of a 19-GHz ABWACS bridge for ATM wireless access. Also, if you are not traveling as fast as an ABWACS radar airplane, the ABWACS project can provide you with wireless ATM access. Just connect your ATM pipe, and the sky is your limit!

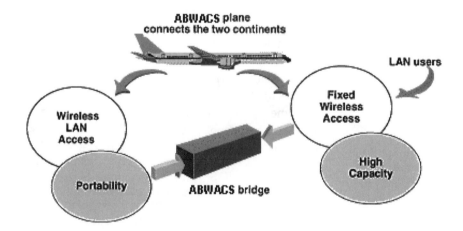

bodies such as ETSI-RES10, ITU, and ARIB in Japan via external liaison activities within the project.

Technical Approach

The ABWACS technical approach is centered around a testbed and associated trial campaign program. Trials were conducted using the existing ATM broadband wireless access platform made available to the project by one of its partners. Associated program work will then be directed at enhancing this current state-of-art system toward the final target features of the emerging ATM wireless specifications, in particular various HIPERLAN types as currently being defined by ETSI-RES10. Equalization, multicarrier techniques, and COFDM techniques are not being considered by the project; instead, a spatial filtering approach is to be pioneered by the project[3] (Figure 9-3), and therefore, enhancements to the existing demonstrator are considered in the following areas:

- Antenna system design and control (intelligent antennas)
- Application of channel coding
- Optimization of link-layer protocols to match ATM bearer types
- Feasibility of 40-GHz rf technology for ATM wireless local-area network (LAN) applications
- Mobility management techniques together with the impact on the radio bearer appropriate for high-bit-rate communications[4]

The ABWACS project will benefit from a wide range of available expertise and tools that have been brought into the project from members of the consortium (Alcatel CIT, Alcatel SEL, CSELT, Elektrobit, Ltd., NTT, and University of Bristol). These include an experimental ATM wireless access system, propagation modeling tools, system evaluation tools, software radio link simulation tools, antenna expertise, and millimeter-wave measurement systems (which are discussed in Chapter 10, "Designing Millimeter Wave Devices").

Summary of Trial

The ABWACS field trial included a concept of "virtual office" trials toward the end of project. This included three potential cases depending on the technical capabilities of the demonstrator:

Figure 9-3
Combating multipath
for wireless ATM
access.

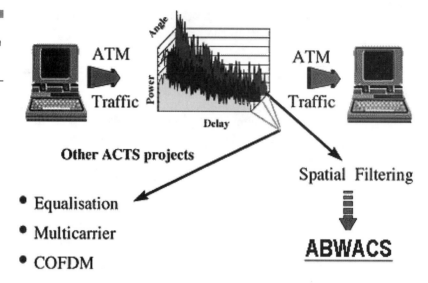

- Wireless multimedia communications link between an engineer at the production site and an expert at the office
- Video communications in meetings between physically separated sites
- Visual wireless network access to virtual office facilities at one of the partner's locations

The objectives of these trials can be summarized as follows:

- Improvement of communications between physically separated offices by telepresense technologies
- Reduction in the need for travel between geographically separated offices
- Improvement in the response time of expert advice in problem solving by visual communications
- Freeing of staff from fixed office hours[5]

Key Issues   Key issues to be considered include

- The performance evaluation of a 19-GHz ATM-compatible modem
- Identification of functional capabilities and limitations of the demonstrator
- Investigation of possible enhancements to the ATM-compatible modem (antenna design)

■ Preparation of strategic vision document resulting from ABWACS that contains possible upgrading techniques of the existing prototype, what is available in terms of rf technology at 40 GHz and above, long-term vision including market issues, market expectations in terms of technology, as well as implications on spectrum issues[6]

Achievements   During the first phase of the project, the AWA preprototype equipment from the Japanese partner was introduced successfully to the project. The equipment and channel sounder have been configured for 19-GHz propagation characteristics and propagation simulation techniques in order to measure the propagation data efficiently. The project has defined forecasted wireless ATM applications to be used for trials toward the final stage of the project, and the demonstration system has been configured for this purpose in order to achieve real-time experience for further ABWACS development.

In system studies, initial link-level simulations (BER performance of radio transmission chain) and system-level simulations (users, capacity, and coverage) have been conducted. Some preliminary statistical propagation models from ETSI-RES10 have been integrated for the simulations. Also, a spatial propagation model has been proposed for wireless ATM. Furthermore, reference models and performance parameter sets from ETSI-RES10 and the ATM Forum have been analyzed, and the first step toward a definition of MAC/LLC procedures for the project have been taken.

The real-time trials will be expected to indicate the capacity of the available system in a real user environment. The trial results will contribute to the development of common specifications and standards such as ETSI-RES10, HIPERLAN specifications, ITU, and ARIB in Japan.

Expected Impact   The objective of ABWACS is to ensure that manufacturers, operators, and users are able to realize maximum benefits of future technology—for example, by the introduction of new services. The project will then make a significant contribution to the emerging market of integrated fixed and mobile wireless broadband services. In addition, it will open new dimensions of mobile services in rural and less developed areas. The results are also expected to facilitate and promote the introduction of new specifications such as HIPERLAN types.

Next, let's look at ground-based wireless networks delivering the full range of broadband services that can be deployed quickly and inexpensively: LMDS. Yes, LMDS is covered quite extensively in Chapter 7, but it needs to be covered briefly here to support the BWA design technology.

LMDS: Broadband Wireless Access

The past decade has seen explosive innovation by the telecommunications industry as it strives to satisfy a worldwide appetite for greater bandwidth. Several developments are fueling this growth—proliferation of the Internet, increased dependence on data, and a global trend toward deregulation of the industry.

Nowhere is the phenomenon more evident than in the quest to alleviate the local-loop bottleneck. This constriction occurs where local-area networks (LANs), which link devices within a building or a campus, join to wide-area networks (WANs), which criss-cross countries and hold the Internet together.

Advances in fiber technology have extended the capacity of WANs to trillions of bits per second. Meanwhile, LANs are evolving from 10 Mbps to gigabits per second. The connections between these two domains have not kept pace, especially with the vast majority of copper-wire circuits being limited to about the 1.5-Mbps rate of a so-called T1 line. The typical home user faces a more extreme case of the same affliction—where data are crawling between computer and the Internet (at about 30 times slower) through a modem and phone line operating at a mere 56 kbps.

NOTE   A T1 line is a high-speed digital connection capable of transmitting data at a rate of approximately 1.5 million bps (bits per second). A T1 line is typically used by small and medium-sized companies with heavy network traffic. It is large enough to send and receive very large text files, graphics, sounds, and databases instantaneously and is the fastest speed commonly used to connect networks to the Internet. Sometimes referred to as a *leased line*, a T1 is basically too large and too expensive for individual home use.

Of the variety of technologies developed for high-speed wireless access, local multipoint distribution service (LMDS) offers an ideal way to break through the local access bottleneck. Like cellphone networks, LMDS is a wireless broadband system, but it is designed to deliver data through the air (Figure 9-4) at rates of up to 155 Mbps (typical cellphone voice calls use a mere 64 kbps, or 8 kbps in compressed digital systems).[7] LMDS may be the key to bringing multimedia data to millions of customers worldwide. It supports voice connections, the Internet, videoconferencing, interactive gaming, video streaming, and other high-speed data applications.

A major advantage of LMDS technology is that it can be deployed quickly and relatively inexpensively. New market entrants who do not have the luxury of an existing network, such as the copper wires or fiber of

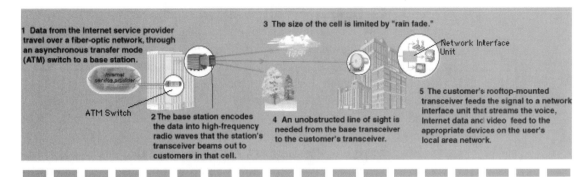

Figure 9-4   How a wireless system can send broadband data through the air.

incumbent operators, can build an advanced wireless network rapidly and start competing. LMDS is also attractive to incumbent operators who need to complement or expand existing networks. For example, operators who are setting up a service primarily based on digital subscriber lines but who want their service to be universally available could use LMDS to fill in gaps in their coverage. And while cable modems are making inroads in the residential and home-office markets, the business market (where little to no cable network exists) remains a prime niche for LMDS.

The higher capacity of LMDS is possible because it operates in a large, previously unallocated expanse of the electromagnetic spectrum. In the United States, the FCC has auctioned to LMDS operators a total bandwidth of about 1.3 GHz in the millimeter waveband (Figure 9-5) at frequencies of about 28 GHz.[8] In other countries, depending on the local licensing regulations, broadband wireless systems operate at anywhere from 2 to 42 GHz. Canada, which is actively setting up systems around the country, has 3 GHz of spectrum set aside for local multipoint communications systems, as it is called there. Regular digital cellphone systems operate at about 0.8 GHz with a typical bandwidth allocation of 30 MHz or less.

How It Works

Sending digital signals of the required complexity at 28 GHz is made practical by recent improvements in the cost and performance of technologies such as digital signal processors, advanced modulation systems, and gallium arsenide integrated circuits, which are cheaper and function much better than silicon chips at these high frequencies.

LMDS uses wireless cells that cover geographic areas typically from 2 to 5 km in radius. Unlike a mobile phone, which a user can move from cell to cell, the transceiver of an LMDS customer has a fixed location and remains within a single cell. A common design puts the customers' antennas on rooftops to get a good line of sight to the hub transceiver.

The LMDS cell size is limited by *rain fade*—distortions of the signal caused by raindrops scattering and absorbing the millimeter waves by the same process that heats food in a microwave oven. Also, walls, hills, and even leafy trees block, reflect, and distort the signal, creating significant shadow areas for a single transmitter. Some operators have proposed serving each cell with several transmitters to increase coverage; most will have one transmitter per cell, sited to target as many users as possible. Of value to operators in an industry with a high rate of turnover of customers is the ability to pick up the hub equipment and move it to a different location as market economics dictates—an impossibility with networks of telephone wires, television cable, and optical fiber.

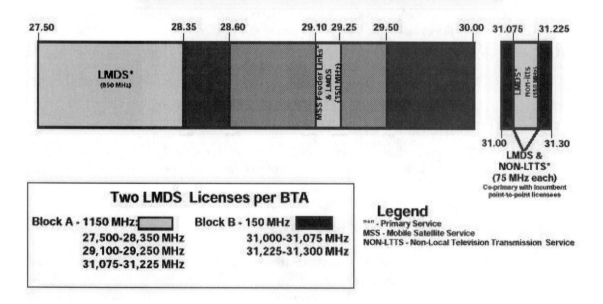

Figure 9-5   LMDS band allocation.

Most, if not all, LMDS systems send data using a technique called *Asynchronous Transfer Mode* (ATM), which is used extensively in WANs and allows a mixture of data types to be interleaved. Thus a high-quality voice service can run concurrently over the same data stream as Internet, data, and video applications. In summary, LMDS will be a versatile, cost-effective option for both providers and users of broadband services, with the rapid and inexpensive deployment being particularly attractive to the providers.

Now let's discuss some of the advantages of BWA technology.

Advantages of BWA Technology

Although not yet deployed commercially on a large-scale basis, most telcos believe that broadband wireless access technology can offer the most cost-effective means of providing high-capacity, high-speed data, voice, video, and Internet connectivity services. The advantages of broadband wireless access (BWA) make it a viable option for operators today and an excellent investment for the following reasons:

- Variable cost-driven architecture.

- Viable at low take rates.

- Rapid deployment.

- True multimedia (data, voice, video).

- BWA systems provide massive capacity, optimized for two-way communications. For example, a single BWA cell can support the equivalent of 128 E1 lines or the equivalent of over 3800 telephone lines for each assigned 56-MHz channel pair.

- The infrastructure is scalable and can be built to serve specific demand; unlike wireline broadband networks, the amount of capital required is more closely matched to demand.

- Ease of network deployment allows telcos to initiate service in the space of a few months from startup and deliver services to customers within days following an order.

- BWA could provide high-quality digital transmission with signal quality and reliability comparable with or superior to other broadband technologies.

- BWA networks can extend to areas where fiber-based alternatives may never be economically feasible.[9]

There Is No Real Alternative to Broadband Wireless Access

BWA's variable, cost-driven architecture lets operators compete effectively in the burgeoning broadband access marketplace. In fact, there is no real alternative to BWA. Because of its high cost of installation, fiber is an option for only a fraction of the marketplace. Fiber's inability to deliver on its original promise is demonstrated by the fact that even after many years of availability, less than 6 percent of business buildings in the United States are served by fiberoptic cable. Also, the number of fibered buildings actually has been decreasing since 1996, indicating that fiber deployments are reaching an addressable limit. xDSL technologies need access to copper local loops and operate at lower data rates. There are also significant technology issues associated with the quality of copper cable and distance limitations that impede DSL deployments. Cable modem service is highly asymmetrical, and there is a lack of cable plants in core business areas. With both cable and copper technologies, operators are dependent on the strength of incumbent providers to supply service.

System and Technology Description

BWA systems are based on a fixed (as opposed to mobile) wireless technology, which uses 28-GHz frequencies in the United States. Some other countries also use 28 GHz, and still others use frequencies ranging from 22 to 42 GHz. BWA systems use digital technology and frequency reuse within a cellular configuration to deliver high-speed data service, voice, and video. BWA systems transmit and receive digital signals between radio node facilities and customer locations. Optimal broadcast distances between each radio node are from approximately 1/2 to 3 miles. The number of radio nodes required in any area varies depending on the size of the geographic area being covered, its topology, environmental factors, and capacity requirements. Radio nodes typically are installed on tall office buildings or could be on a freestanding tower[10] (Figure 9-6).

Choosing Equipment

When choosing equipment (Figure 9-7),[11] service providers look for cost effectiveness, simplicity, flexibility, and scalability. First, service providers need a system that is flexible enough to operate across multiple millimeter-wave bands. This is so because most LMDS licensees will sell or sublicense their spectrum to service providers who may own or plan to acquire spectrum in multiple spectral bands. In fact, as discussed previously in Chapter 7, LMDS licenses in the United States were awarded in two blocks, A and B, at 28 and 31 GHz, respectively. The reality is that many licensees own spectrum in both blocks, sometimes in the same city. Service providers also need a simple hardware solution (one that is easy and quick to install), scalable for ease in supporting an expanding network and growing customer base, and one that offers efficient use of bandwidth for optimizing revenue per megahertz of spectrum.

Another factor influencing equipment choice is the nonuniformity of worldwide spectrum allocations. In the United States, A-block licenses are 1150 MHz of spectrum; B-block licenses are 150 MHz. Around the world, other millimeter-wave licenses are sized differently, and some are more restrictive. Many broadband wireless access systems are optimized for the A block only, so service providers in the B block will have to find other solutions. However, with the increasing trend toward sublicensing and acquisition of multiple spectral bands, the need for equipment to efficiently operate in multiple block allocations of varying sizes is of key importance.

Figure 9-6
Diagram of a BWA system.

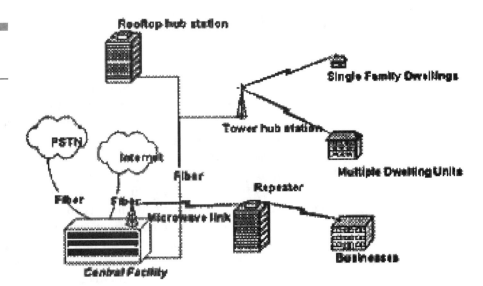

Figure 9-7
Example of BWA
equipment.

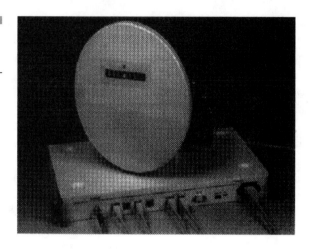

Broadband Wireless Access and Time Division Duplexing

Today's businesses are demanding higher-capacity communications networks to increase productivity and deliver goods and services more efficiently. LAN and WAN capacities are keeping pace with the tremendous growth in data traffic, but the *local-loop bottleneck* between them is getting worse. This is so because wireline technologies such as copper, cable, and fiber are not viable alternatives.

Attempts by phone companies to invigorate aging voice-grade copper lines using xDSL technology are plagued by limitations on distance, copper quality, and ironically, bandwidth. Cable modems are saddled with a legacy asymmetric network in residential neighborhoods. Businesses prefer more symmetric networks in business districts. And fiber, while offering plenty of bandwidth, is (at approximately $250,000 per mile to install) too expensive to justify trenching to any but the very largest commercial buildings. The solution to the local-loop bottleneck is point-to-multipoint broadband wireless access (BWA) extensions from existing high-speed fiber rings. Point-to-multipoint technology is an air link that provides two-way multimegabit voice/data connectivity to multiple remote units simultaneously. Traffic at the hub is multiplexed onto fiber. BWA links can be engineered for availability equal to that of fiber.

Two Approaches

The heart of any BWA system is its air-link technology, and in point-to-multipoint BWA, there are two basic approaches: time division duplexing (TDD) and frequency division duplexing (FDD). When TDD is used, occupied bandwidth is fixed, while the transmit/receive duty cycle varies in time. With FDD, bandwidth is variable, and the transmit/receive duty cycle is fixed. TDD and FDD consume equivalent spectrum for a given throughput. For example, the two advantages of TDD can be summed up like this: First, no minimum spacing is needed between transmit and receive bands. Put another way, no capacity is lost to the transmit/receive separation (guardband, typical of FDD). All spectrum can be allocated to revenue generation. Moreover, TDD allows network operators to leverage spectrum that is noncontiguous, limited (50 MHz), or lacking in any transmit/receive channel plan. Apart from the fragmented band plans that describe 38 GHz and LMDS in the United States, outside the United States (even among a small number of countries), band plans are not uniform.

Second, twice the number of frequencies are available for the *reuse pool*. FDD requires two frequencies (one for transmit and another for receive). TDD, therefore, offers higher frequency reuse than FDD.

Bandwidth-on-Demand

Bandwidth-on-demand uses a contention-based protocol to manage the bursty aspects of the asynchronous data, quality-of-service agreements, and the subscribers' need for bandwidth. The protocol determines how much data a subscriber sends and receives. Since all subscribers do not transmit and receive at the same time and their data rates vary, spare capacity can be given to additional subscribers. Oversubscription generates more revenue for the wireless network operator than giving each subscriber a specific bandwidth and not using the unused bandwidth.

Neither TDD nor FDD can claim an advantage over the other in transporting synchronous data such as voice. TDD, however, can claim an important advantage over FDD in transporting asynchronous data, such as ATM cells or Internet Protocol (IP) packets when bandwidth-on-demand technology is used. If more data are being sent than received, it is possible to *borrow* time from the receive side of the link to increase the transmit time.

For example, during time segment T0, both TDD and FDD meet the demand for delivering 20 Mbps on the forward link and 10 Mbps on the reverse link. During time segment T1, demand changes to only 15 Mbps on both forward and reverse links.

NOTE   TDD occupies a single frequency.

In this case, FDD wastes 5 Mbps on the forward link and comes up short 5 Mbps on the reverse link. By comparison, the single TDD frequency meets subscriber demand without waste or shortfall. FDD cannot *borrow* from the transmit side to give to the receive side, and vice versa.

TDD's capability to borrow time is significant given the runaway growth in asynchronous data traffic (100 percent per year) compared with synchronous voice (14 percent per year). Additionally, bandwidth-on-demand technology represents a network operator's principal lever for maximizing revenue because wireless links can be *oversubscribed*. Given that TDD can, in conjunction with bandwidth-on-demand, transport asynchronous data more efficiently and flexibly than FDD, it follows that TDD can support more subscribers than FDD in the same amount of spectrum.

Staying Flexible

Since broadband networks carry voice (synchronous and asynchronous) and data (asynchronous), it is very difficult to plan network capacities for future growth. Likewise, it is difficult to predict the nature (degree of asymmetry) and amount of bandwidth that the marketplace will require. TDD's flexibility allows the operator to easily adapt the forward and reverse links of the network. And since one TDD radio operates across an entire band allocation without having to buy new radios, changing usage patterns will not jeopardize the capital invested in existing equipment.

Conclusion

The tremendous success and exponential growth of the Internet, as well as novel applications such as data broadcasting and multicasting, have resulted in the requirement for significantly higher speeds in network access—especially in broadband wireless access. This increasing bandwidth demand cannot always be satisfied adequately with many of the traditional access techniques. Another element that has an important impact is mobility, manifesting itself in the widespread use of cellular telephony. Digital cellular systems have become a service and technology driver in many parts of the world. In some countries, more than half the population is already using cellular phones. The third generation of cellular phones will provide fairly high-speed access to the Internet and multimedia services. Broadband wireless access design techniques are therefore becoming increasingly important.

The new digital TV broadcasting standard (DVB) for terrestrial cable and wireless broadband, as well as satellite systems, provides an efficient means for TV distribution but also can support dissemination of Web content and interactive services at high speed. This is interesting not only for areas where the terrestrial infrastructure is less developed or cable is too expensive or impossible to install but also for new operators who wish to become independent from the copper cable or fiber infrastructure of traditional network providers.

Satellites have shown their benefit in providing high-speed services to large user communities. The most successful commercial application up to now has been TV distribution, but new systems (already in an advanced development stage) are geared at high-speed wireless network access, exploiting satellite technology.

Spectrum also has been allocated for these new systems, some of it in unlicensed bands. Among these, the local multipoint distribution system (LMDS) has emerged as a solution to the last mile problem. New spectrum allocation also has stimulated the deployment of a range of new wireless LANs delivering high-speed services to fixed, mobile, and nomadic users using novel technologies and improved protocols.

Endnotes

1. "Broadband Wireless Access," Harris Corporation Headquarters, 1025 West NASA Boulevard, Melbourne, FL 32919-0001, 2000.
2. "ATM Wireless Access Communication System," Acts Central Office, European Commission, Dir INFSO, ACTS Central Office, APRR Reception, BU9 5/60, Avenue de Beaulieu 9, B-1160 Brussels, Belgium, 2000.
3. *Ibid.*
4. *Ibid.*
5. *Ibid.*
6. *Ibid.*
7. John Skoro, "LMDS: Broadband Wireless Access," *Scientific American*, 415 Madison Avenue, NY, NY 10017, 2000.
8. *Ibid.*
9. "What We Do," Formus Communications, Inc., 720 South Colorado Blvd., Suite 600 North, Denver, CO 80246, 2000.
10. *Ibid.*
11. *Ibid.*

10

Designing Millimeter-Wave Devices

The market for millimeter-wave devices will grow tenfold by 2006, with the satellite end-user segment surpassing the Local Multipoint Distribution Services (LMDS) customer premise equipment market by that year, according to a new report from Allied Business Intelligence. Total shipments of millimeter-wave devices are expected to grow from 636,000 in 2001 to just under 5 million in 2006.

Traditional, point-to-point, point-to-multipoint millimeter-wave radio (12–40 GHz) and back-haul applications are expected to constitute the majority of the millimeter-wave shipments in 2001 with greater than 92 percent of the market. Less than 7 percent of the point-to-point millimeter-wave radios that are sold are expected to be used to provide access to end users in 2001. This ratio will change dramatically during network buildouts.

End users will drive the satellite side of the broadband market during the study period, with customer premises equipment (CPE) for the many broadband satellite constellations expected to take a lead in the market in 2006 with a 65 percent share. Despite the connotations of its name, early LMDS deployments are expected to be primarily point to point. Shipments of LMDS CPE during the period in question are expected to grow from 3 to 16 percent of the market, with most of the sales serving the business sector. Many users will share a CPE.

Automotive radar systems, which are expected to account for 7 percent of the shipments of millimeter-wave devices in 2001, continue to post strong results in the trucking industry. Migration of the technology to the mass market is expected within the next 5 years, and it is expected to account for 43 percent of millimeter-wave device shipments in 2006.

Cost continues to limit the ability of equipment builders and service providers to expand their potential market. Among the tools that will aid them in their quest for lower prices are the expanding number of discrete semiconductors and integrated circuits (ICs) that are becoming available for millimeter-wave applications. Total shipments of millimeter-wave semiconductors are valued at $40.3 million in 2001, with brisk growth expected in the oncoming years. Much of the development of these devices is targeted to LMDS, which is expected to account for 31 percent of the market in 2001.

With this in mind, this chapter discusses wireless broadband technology related to the design of integrated microwave, millimeter-wave devices and submillimeter-wave device (Terahertz) components. Very high level discussions include fundamental design analysis, modeling, and measurement of millimeter-wave devices and circuits that have applications ranging from commercial microwave-integrated systems to radio astronomy. Specific topics covered are

- Monolithic microwave and millimeter-wave IC (MMIC) device design

- MMIC packaging

- Wireless broadband cascaded reactively terminated single-stage distributed amplifier design

Monolithic Microwave and Millimeter-wave IC (MMIC) Device Design

The design of new sources and detection technologies in the millimeter- and submillimeter-wave device region includes picosecond pulse generation, which offers applications in a vast array of other areas such as all-weather radar for airplanes, radio astronomy, atmospheric radiometry, contraband detection, nondestructive testing, automotive collision-avoidance radars, and high-speed data communications. Millimeter wave device technologies include the theory and design of millimeter-wave device frequency multipliers, beam-control arrays (BCAs), high-speed switching arrays, hybrid and monolithic Schottky diode mixer arrays, subharmonic mixers, nonlinear transmission lines (NLTLs), and nonlinear delay lines (NDLs).

On the other hand, high-power millimeter wave and microwave source technologies (MMICs) include the development of wideband disk-loaded gyrotraveling-wave tube (TWT) amplifiers, gyroamplifiers, and gyrofrequency multipliers. In addition, programs exist to develop high-brightness radiofrequency (rf) guns, CsTe photocathodes, femtosecond laser technology, and chirped pulse free electron lasers (FELs).

There is also a need for extremely high power (1 kW–1 GW) microwave/millimeter-wave device sources. Applications include particle accelerators, deep-space communications, fusion plasma heating, radar, and material processing. Research in high-power millimeter-wave and microwave source technologies includes the design of wideband disk-loaded gyrotraveling-wave tube (TWT) amplifiers, gyroklystrons, gyrofrequency multipliers, multiple-beam klystrons, and high-current-density cathodes. In addition, programs also exist to develop chirped pulse millimeter-wave radars, solid-state device and material characterization, surface physics, and plasma diagnostics. Other projects involve the use of microfabrication techniques to make miniature field emitter arrays.

So what is a monolithic microwave and millimeter-wave IC (MMIC) device used for?

Why MMICs?

The enormous growth in the wireless communication industry and the need for low-cost, high-bandwidth data links have resulted in a demand for active circuits that operate at microwave and millimeter-wave frequencies. Systems operating at these frequencies are attractive because only a small fractional bandwidth is needed for a high-data-rate link. Also, they use antennas that can be both directive and small. Communications applications include cell phones, satellite communications, and deep-space probes. Other applications include radars (navigational, weather, automotive), radiometers, and global positioning systems.

The monolithic microwave ICs (MMICs) used in these applications are analog circuits that downconvert a modulated microwave signal to a baseband signal or upconvert a baseband signal to a microwave signal. The baseband signals are lower-frequency and can be processed by conventional ICs. Since MMICs run at very high frequency, they are, debatably, the most high-tech part of a cellular phone. Their performance sets the range of the wireless broadband link and is one of the most important factors affecting battery life and call quality. They must be sensitive (for increased range), efficient (less battery and weight), and linear (higher channel density). MMICs often consist of several subcircuit types: low-noise amplifiers, mixers, power amplifiers, oscillators, and switches.

MMIC Design

Microwave ICs typically are limited by the performance of the individual transistors they use, field-effect transistors (FETs) or heterojunction bipolar transistors (HBTs), for example. Microwave ICs operate at high enough frequencies that the circuit components on the surface of the chip must be modeled very carefully. The orientation of signal traces, the details in the structure of capacitors or inductors, and the types of junctions all add small, unavoidable capacitances and inductances that have important effects at high frequencies. It is therefore necessary that students have an exposure to electromagnetics in order to develop a feeling for the techniques used to model these features.

It is also essential that an MMIC designer understand how MMICs are used in larger systems. Very often an MMIC designer will work with a system designer to help determine what system specifications are possible and how these translate into IC specifications.

MMIC Design Project: A Compact Ku-Band Low-Noise Amplifier Using a Coplanar Circuit Medium

A compact 12- to 18-GHz gallium arsenate (GaAs) MMIC low-noise amplifier has been designed and constructed recently using the coplanar waveguide (CPW) circuit medium throughout, as shown in Figure 10-1.[1] The purpose of this work is to demonstrate that a CPW can be used at these frequencies for a low-noise design and still meet the size limitations necessary for low-cost production. Attractive features include reduced back-side processing, no bias, and suitability for flip-chip mounting.

The design process required topologic considerations and modeling procedures that are less well known for CPWs than for other circuit media. For example, an important consideration in choice of coplanar topology is the tradeoff between size and loss. This is especially important in the input-matching circuitry for a low-noise amplifier (LNA). Another consideration is the choice between lumped and distributed elements. A combination of electromagnetic simulation and measured test structures was used to determine accurate lumped-element models for coplanar structures such as T-junctions, bends, and spiral inductors.

Figure 10-1

A coplanar low-noise amplifier (LNA) designed in cooperation with M/A-COM's Microelectronics Division in Lowell, Massachusetts.

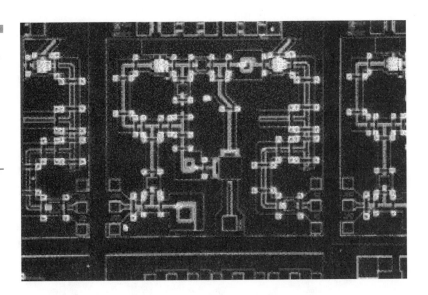

The 12- to 18-GHz design, constructed at M/A-COM's GaAs foundry, achieved first-pass characteristics of 12-dB gain, 2.5:1 voltage standing wave station (VSWR), and 4-dB noise figure in an area of 1.6 × 1.6 mm. Thus the modeling/design procedure has been verified. Further measurements and more detailed modeling show that a second-iteration design using the same process would achieve a 14-dB gain, 2:1 VSWR, and a 3.5-dB noise figure.

Now let's look at some MMIC package projects that are currently being designed at the University of Massachusetts. The following package design projects contain information relevant to MMIC package modeling.

MMIC Packaging

Currently, the main activity in MMIC package modeling is the simulation of electrical and thermal characteristics of packaging and the experimental verification of the models results. The following electrical models of microwave and millimeter-wave IC (MMIC) packaging topics are covered very briefly here:

- A circuit topology for microwave modeling of plastic-surface-mount packages
- Electromagnetic model for resonance frequencies in low-cost MMIC packages
- Circuit model for resonance coupling in grounded coplanar waveguide circuits
- The use of side-wall images to compute package effects in methods-of-moment (MoM) analysis of MMIC circuits
- A simple circuit model for resonant-mode coupling in packaged MMICs

A Circuit Topology for Microwave Modeling of Plastic-Surface-Mount Packages

A circuit topology is shown in Figure 10-2 for modeling a class of plastic-surface-mount packages.[2] The model consists of three pieces, each of which is circuit modeled based on an electromagnetic simulation.

▬▬ ▬▬ ▬▬ ▬▬

Figure 10-2
Modeling a class of
plastic-surface-mount
packages.

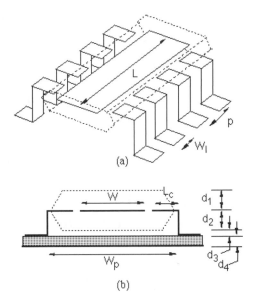

(a)

(b)

An Electromagnetic Model for Determining Resonance Frequencies of Low-Cost MMIC Packages

A simple model is presented (Figure 10-3) for approximate calculations of the lowest-order resonance frequencies of low-cost MMIC packages.[3] The model shows the effect of seal-ring characteristics such as dielectric constant and via holes. Experimental results confirm the usefulness of the model.

▬▬ ▬▬ ▬▬ ▬

Figure 10-3
Approximate calcula-
tions of the lowest-
order resonance
frequencies of low-
cost MMIC packages.

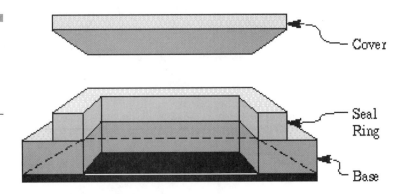

Cover

Seal
Ring

Base

Circuit Model for Substrate Resonance Coupling in Grounded Coplanar Waveguide Circuits

At high frequencies, grounded coplanar waveguide MMICs can be prone to destructive intercircuit coupling effects due to substrate resonances (Figure 10-4).[4] Analytic formulas for a simple circuit model of this coupling help solve the problem.

The Use of Side-Wall Images to Compute Package Effects in MoM Analysis of MMIC Circuits

This is concerned with a novel formulation for the method-of-moments (MoM) solution of the shielded enclosed microstrip of MMIC circuits. The technique involves computing a circuit's mutual impedance characteristics with no lateral enclosure.

Figure 10-4

Measuring a simple circuit model.

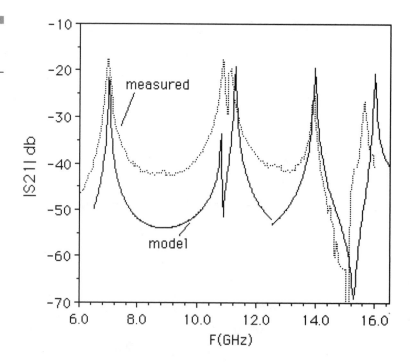

A Simple Circuit Model for Resonant-Mode Coupling in Packaged MMICs

Neglecting the effect of enclosing an MMIC in a resonant conducting package (Figure 10-5) can have undesirable consequences such as power loss, poor isolation, and circuit instabilities.[5] In principle, these effects can be predicted by currently available computer aided design (CAD) model packages.

Finally, the next part of this chapter presents a novel design technique and measured performance for a wireless broadband (2 – 18 GHz) amplifier using a cascaded reactively terminated single-stage distributed amplifier (CRTSSDA) configuration. The amplifier employs double-heterojunction pseudomorphic high-electron-mobility transistors (DPHEMTs). A commercially available CAD program was employed extensively to simulate and optimize the designs. A broadband (2–18 GHz) amplifier employing three CRTSSDAs was designed and fabricated. The amplifier achieved a gain level of 26 ±1.5 dB and input and output standing-wave ratios (SWRs) of better than 2. In addition, the amplifier also provided substantially improved efficiency performance by more than twofold compared with that obtainable by an equivalent-gain conventional three-stage traveling-wave amplifier configuration.

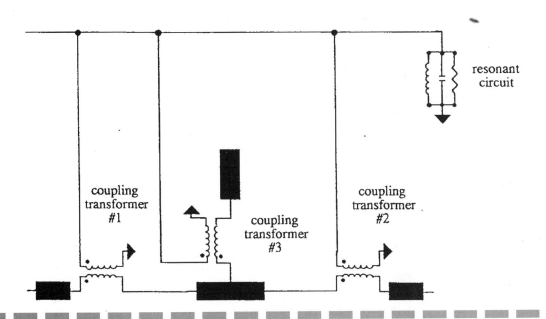

Figure 10-5 Resonant-mode conducting package.

Wireless Broadband Cascaded Reactively Terminated Single-Stage Distributed Amplifier Design

Distributed amplifiers have been investigated extensively and realized successfully in hybrid microwave integrated circuit (MIC) and monolithic circuit (MMIC) technologies. They have dominated wireless broadband amplifier design for the last two decades and provide an excellent method for realizing amplifiers for multioctave-band applications. Unfortunately, the gain performance of a single-stage traveling-wave amplifier comprising two active devices is limited to approximately 8 to 9 dB. In order to realize high-gain amplifiers, a number of single-stage traveling-wave amplifiers must be cascaded. However, the major deficiencies of the traveling-wave amplifier method are higher manufacturing costs and a substantial reduction in the amplifier power-added efficiency.

Wireless broadband amplifiers with high stability, gain, and efficiency characteristics are demanded for wireless broadband systems such as in electronic warfare applications (or information warfare). Other applications include ultra-wide-bandwidth preamplifiers for photodevices used in digital optical communications receivers and video detection. In practice, these amplifiers are also required to provide high production yields and reproductibility to minimize manufacturing costs. The advent of the DPHEMT with low associated device parasitic components enables the wireless broad bandwidth to be achieved. Major advantages afforded by the CRTSSDA configuration included the realization of high gain levels, a significant reduction in power consumption, and improvement in power-added efficiency. In addition, the amplifier can be realized in MIC or MMIC technologies and offers a cost-effective solution because the component count is significantly reduced in the realization of wireless broadband high-gain amplifiers.

Amplifier Design

The conventional traveling-wave amplifier uses the well-known properties of an artificial transmission line consisting of series inductors and shunt capacitors contributed by the active device parasitics. The amplifier circuit can be analyzed in terms of ¼ or T-sections and has a frequency-dependent characteristic impedance that becomes wholly imaginary at the cutoff frequency, at which point propagation down the artificial transmission line ceases. At frequencies below this cutoff frequency, a generator connected at one end of the line will dissipate all its available power into a load connected at the other end, provided that the generator and load have matched frequency characteristics and the line is loss-free.

Figure 10-6 shows a cascade of three traveling-wave amplifiers, each composed of two active devices.[6] Although not shown, the bottom artificial transmission lines have shunt capacitors connected to them resulting from the active device's gate-source capacitance (C_{gs}). The top artificial transmission lines have shunt capacitors connected to them due to the active device's drain-source capacitance (C_{ds}). The drain-source capacitances are also connected in shunt with the active device's current generator. The gate and drain lines are both terminated in their characteristic impedance Z_0, respectively.

A voltage wave from the gate generator propagating down the gate line (with a phase constant β_g), develops a voltage across each gate-source capacitor. Consequently, each of these voltage drops produces a corresponding current with an appropriate phase delay in the drain line. In addition, the current from each active device drain port propagates down the drain line in both directions (with a phase constant β_d). The total combined current at the output load therefore is determined by the vector sum of the individual currents. Hence the traveling-wave amplifier is designed in such a way as to equalize ($\beta_g - \beta_d = 0$) the phase velocity of the gate and drain transmission lines. The equalization causes the signals on the drain line to add in the forward direction as they propagate to the output.

The schematic circuit diagram of the proposed cascaded reactively terminated single-stage amplifier is shown in Figure 10-7.[7] The conventional traveling-wave amplifier configuration is based on the ladder network

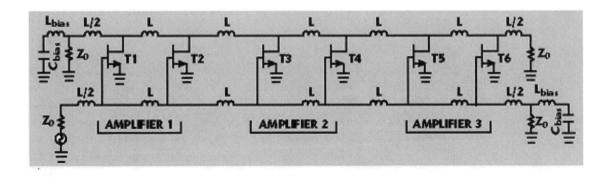

Figure 10-6   *Three-stage conventional traveling-wave amplifier circuit schematic.*

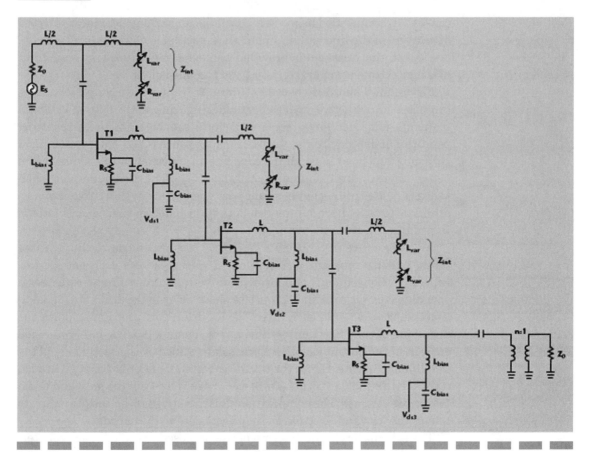

Figure 10-7   *Three-cascaded reactively terminated single-stage distributed amplifier.*

arrangement, whereas the CRTSSDA is based on the principle of cascading a T-section network of amplifiers in series. The signal power injected at the matched-input generator port is coupled and amplified by the transconductance of the active device at each stage and finally terminated by the matched-output load port. At each stage, the signal power can be improved by terminating with a properly matched load resistor. Unlike the traveling-wave amplifier, phase-velocity equalization is not required for the CRTSSDA configuration due to the fact that the total output current is not dependent on the phase coherence of the individual current generators. The only requirement is to equalize the characteristic impedance of the input gate and output drain port of the active devices employed. However, the gate and drain inductance present in the circuit limits the amplifier bandwidth performance. It is shown here (see Figure 10-7) that the bandwidth limitation can be compensated by the inclusion of the inductance L_{var} and resistance R_{var}. Selection of the bias components L_{bias} and C_{bias} also plays a critical role in optimizing the bandwidth. These components should be chosen to possess minimum intrinsic parasitic components in order to avoid in-band resonances.

The design process for the amplifiers covering the frequency range of 2 to 18 GHz began by initially characterizing the device to be used. The DPHEMT device selected was the state-of-the-art model LP6836 device manufactured by Filtronic Solid State, which has a gate length of 0.25 μm and a gate width of 360 μm. The device was characterized using the same mounting parasitic conditions that matched with the final amplifier construction. Small-signal S parameters were measured across 2 to 18 GHz. The measured S parameters were deembedded from the test fixture, and the CAD program LIBRA was then used to obtain the small-signal model. This small-signal model was fitted and optimized to the deembedded S parameters. Excellent agreement between the optimized and measured performance has been achieved, as shown in Figure 10-8, for S_{11}, S_{22}, S_{21}, and S_{12}.[8] Hence the small-signal model (optimized LP6836 DPHEMT) device selected was a state-of-the-art model derived using the preceding technique and provides an accurate model for subsequent circuit simulation using this device.

Circuit simulations and optimization of a three-stage traveling-wave amplifier and three-CRTSSDA device were performed using LIBRA. The traveling-wave amplifier design began with determination of the minimum number of devices required to achieve a gain level of 27 dB, since this was the optimal gain obtainable from the three-CRTSSDA device. A three-stage traveling-wave amplifier comprising six active devices was required to achieve the specified gain level of 27 dB.

Amplifier Fabrication

Fabrication of the amplifiers was carried out by employing conventional thin-film MIC technology. The three-stage conventional traveling-wave amplifier and three-CRTSSDA device were fabricated on 15-mil-thick alumina substrates ($\varepsilon_r = 9.8$) composed of nichrome and gold layers. The microstrip-matching circuits were etched into the gold layer. Thin-film resistors were realized by etching into the nichrome layer, which was

Figure 10-8
Measured and modeled (a) S_{11} and S_{22}, (b) S_{21} and S_{22}, and (c) S_{12} and S_{12}.

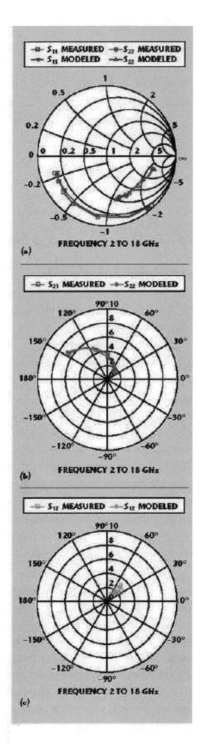

Figure 10-9
Fabricated three-stage traveling-wave amplifier layout.

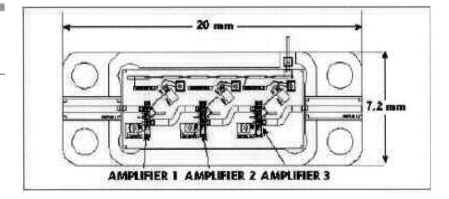

deposited below the gold layer. The alumina substrates were soldered onto the gold-plated tungsten-copper amplifier housings. The LP6836 DPHEMT devices and chip components were epoxied. All the electrical connections were carried out using 0.7-mil gold wires. All the high-value inductors were realized by fabricating miniature gold coils of the appropriate turns using 1-mil-diameter gold wire. In the fabrication of the gold coils, particular attention was paid to minimize any in-band resonances over the operating bandwidth. Figure 10-9 shows the fabricated three-stage conventional traveling-wave amplifier layout, and Figure 10-10 shows the fabricated three-CRTSSDA device assembly layout.[9]

Figure 10-10
Fabricated three-cascaded reactively terminated single-stage distributed amplifier layout.

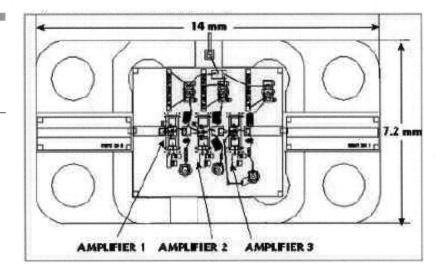

Figure 10-11
Measured small-signal
response of three-
cascaded reactively
terminated single-
stage distributed
amplifier.

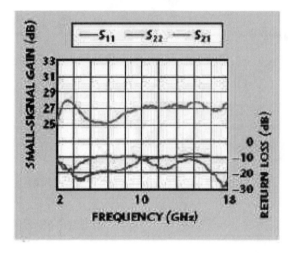

Figure 10-11
Measured small-signal
response of three-
cascaded reactively
terminated single-
stage distributed
amplifier.

Amplifier Performance

The measured small-signal gain and input and output return losses of the three-CRTSSDA device are shown in Figure 10-11 across 2 to 18 GHz.[10] The amplifier was operated in the self-bias mode of operation at 0.5 I_{dss}. The measured gain was 26 $\pm$ 1.5 dB, and the input and output return losses were better than 9.6 dB (SWRs of better than 2). A comparison of the measured results with the simulated response shows excellent agreement.

Figure 10-12
Measured
small-signal response
of three-stage
traveling-wave
amplifier.

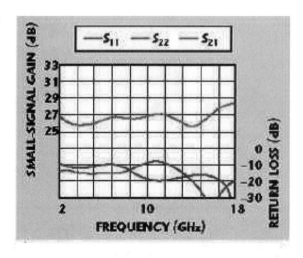

Figure 10-13
Measured power-added efficiency of three-cascaded reactively terminated single-stage distributed amplifier and three-stage traveling-wave amplifier.

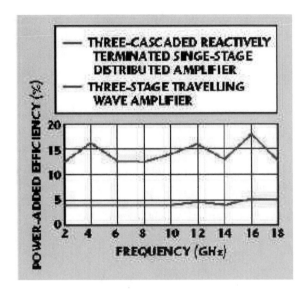

The measured small-signal gain and input and output return losses of the three-stage conventional traveling-wave amplifier are shown in Figure 10-12 across the 2- to 18-GHz frequency range.[11] The measured gain was 27 ± 2 dB, and the input and output return losses were better than 9.6 dB (SWRs of better than 2). Excellent agreement has been achieved with the simulated performance previously shown.

Finally, the measured power-added efficiency performances for both the amplifiers as a function of frequency are shown in Figure 10-13 for $V_{ds} =$ 7.6 V and 0.5 I_{dss}.[12] The power-added efficiency results demonstrate the substantial improvement in efficiency; that is, in excess of 12.6 percent across 2 to 18 GHz is achievable from the CRTSSDA compared with only 5 percent achievable by the optimized conventional traveling-wave amplifier design.

Conclusion

Design and fabrication of a novel high-gain wireless broadband amplifier have been described in this chapter by employing the CRTSSDA technology. An equivalent-gain three-stage conventional traveling-wave amplifier also was designed and fabricated to provide a performance measure to the novel CRTSSDA. The major advantages of using the CRTSSDA design approach were realization of compact design, achievement of excellent stability with frequency, achievement of high power-added efficiency performance when compared with a conventional traveling-wave amplifier, and significant reduction in component count of active devices employed.

Endnotes

1. John R. Lachapelle, Michael T. Murphy, and Robert W. Jackson, "A Compact Ku-Band Low-Noise Amplifier Using a Coplanar Circuit Medium," 201C Marcus Hall, University of Massachusetts, Amherst, MA (Trimble Navigation, Sunnyvale, CA and M/A-COM, Lowell, MA), 2000.

2. *Ibid.*

3. *Ibid.*

4. *Ibid.*

5. *Ibid.*

6. Avtar S. Virdee and Bal S. Virdee, "A Broadband 2 to 18 GHz Cascaded Reactively Terminated Single-Stage Distributed Amplifier," Filtronic Components, Limited, Milton Keynes, U.K. and University of North London, School of Communications Technology and Mathematical Sciences, London, U.K., 2000.

7. *Ibid.*

8. *Ibid.*

9. *Ibid.*

10. *Ibid.*

11. *Ibid.*

12. *Ibid.*

CHAPTER 11

Wireless Broadband Services: The Designing of the Broadband Era

The last mile as we know it may soon be a thing of the past. Historically, the market for broadband access has favored incumbent telephone companies (telcos) and cable concerns—companies that already boast a fixed network. Wireless broadband technology is on the verge of forever altering the dynamics of this arrangement. Indeed, with demand for bandwidth surging, many companies today are taking aim at alleviating the local-loop bottleneck by embracing alternatives, particularly wireless.

Wireless broadband technology wields several advantages over wired solutions. It is less expensive to deploy. It can be implemented much more quickly and, arguably, more efficiently. It can be configured for multiple applications. It is, bottom line, the source of cheap, high-quality, and high-bandwidth services (wireless broadband services). For many, it is frequently becoming the source of choice.

However, there are hurdles. Distance limitations, attenuation, inherent line-of-sight restrictions, and of course, the nagging problems associated with trying to launch a market into orbit are just a few. What is needed now is information.

This chapter shows you how to design wireless broadband services. It shows you how to fuse together all the different wireless broadband elements into a single sweeping strategic assessment and opportunity. Its insights and recommendations are exclusive, as are die models used to project growth into this. This chapter is essential reading for anyone involved in one of the most dynamic markets of this or any other industry—wireless broadband networks.

In view of this, let's begin the discussion with a look at the design of residential wireless broadband access services. A discussion of the design of competitive local exchange carriers (CLECs) wireless broadband services follows.

Residential Wireless Broadband Access Services Design and the Teleworker: Security Considerations for the IT Manager

The teleworker (the employee who performs a portion of his or her work duties from a residence) may be the fastest growing part of the corporate workforce. For some enterprises, connectivity needs for the majority of its teleworkers may be accommodated using the same technology and security measures used for roaming and remote access. For others, the emergence of residential wireless broadband services offers new opportunities for extending the corporate local-area network (LAN) to the residence-based employee. The high-bandwidth, low-latency, and *always connected* characteristics of services based on digital subscriber line (DSL) or cable modem technologies allow teleworkers access to corporate LANs using NOS (network operating system) file, session, and printer services, including AppleTalk, Microsoft Network, and UNIX/NFS/X. These NOS services generally are impractical to use over traditional dialup services because of dialup's low bandwidth, high latency, and intermittent connectivity. Thus the design of residential wireless broadband services allows for a qualitative difference in teleworker activities compared with dialup services by enabling teleworkers to use the corporate network at home in the same way they do at the office.

The characteristics of the design of residential wireless broadband services are similar to public switched data services such as Frame Relay and switched multimegabit data service (SMDS), with one noteworthy exception. Most Frame Relay and SMDS connections terminate at remote offices or corporate locations, where some site security policy typically is enforced: Employee identification is required, connectivity to the public Internet is restricted and protected by corporate firewalls, etc. Residential wireless broadband service, as the name implies, usually terminates in the home of a corporate teleworker. Because of this difference, the characteristics that make residential wireless broadband service attractive also may raise security concerns for some information technology (IT) managers.

Why is the design of residential wireless broadband access to a corporate network so different from modem and Integrated Services Digital Network (ISDN) dial access from a residence or hotel? Why are some IT managers cautious about bringing DSL or cable modem services into their enterprise? Are there ways to safely integrate residential wireless broadband into an enterprise network? Is one residential wireless broadband technology safer than the rest? Let's take a closer look.

Residential Wireless Broadband Services Design: Digital Subscriber Line and Cable Modem

Digital subscriber line (DSL) technology is used to provide layer 2 (data-link layer) access services. There are many different variants of DSL technology. For example, Covad Communications Company's[1] TeleSpeed service is offered using IDSL, ADSL, and SDSL (Figure 11-1).[2] The TeleSpeed service shares many characteristics with Frame Relay. Both are point-to-point services based on permanent virtual circuits (PVCs). A PVC is conceptually just a bidirectional pipe between two systems; data that are placed in one end of the PVC come out the other end unmodified. Customers can use any network protocol (AppleTalk, IP, IPX, etc.) over a PVC. PVCs transport data without examination; this means that the data can be encrypted, compressed, or otherwise transformed in ways agreeable to the systems using the PVC without affecting the PVC itself.

If your enterprise has already completed a risk assessment for Frame Relay, the security measures deemed appropriate for Frame Relay transport probably can be applied to DSL-based services. For example, if your enterprise uses encryption over Frame Relay links, you can do so over TeleSpeed service links as well. This is true for many configuration and management issues as well. Covad is an alternative public data service provider. The same third-party trust model that companies understand and accept when dealing with other telephone and Frame Relay providers applies to Covad as well. Basically, everything related to customer service is done at the customer's request. Covad sets up new PVCs only when the customer submits an authorized service order. Furthermore, Covad setting up a new PVC is not enough to create a new connection into the cus-

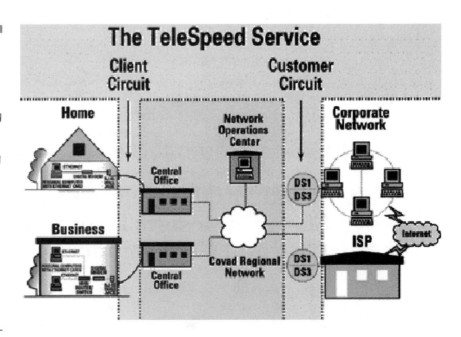

Figure 11-1

Covad's TeleSpeed service uses PVCs that originate at the teleworker's residence as a DSL circuit operating over a copper twisted pair. This copper pair is connected to Vocad equipment in physically secured Vocad facilities in the teleworker's serving central office. The PVC is relayed over the Covad regional network and then onto a dedicated circuit to the customer's enterprise network.

tomer's network. The customer also has to set up its own router or switch to handle the PVC. Like telephony providers, Covad facilities are physically secured, and only authorized Covad personnel monitor and administer Covad's equipment.

Cable modem technology offers another method for designing and providing residential wireless coax broadband services. Cable modems use two radiofrequency (rf) carrier signals (*channels*) from the CATV spectrum to provide high-bandwidth, low-latency, shared access service to residential customers. Cable modem operates a layer 2 service over a hybrid fiber-coax plant that passes residences in neighborhoods to reach a cable company's central office for relay to a distribution hub (the *headend*), as shown in Figure 11-2.[3] Cable companies often collaborate with (or franchise services from) public Internet service providers (ISPs) for layer 3 (Internet Protocol) service. Service offerings of this kind are best compared against Covad's small business Internet access service.

Whereas the DSL-based services offered by Covad are point-to-point services, services based on cable modems are multipoint services. Cable modem

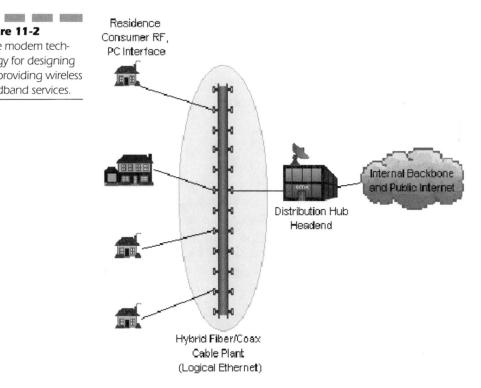

Figure 11-2
Cable modem technology for designing and providing wireless broadband services.

service is similar to LAN service provided by shared-medium (traditional, nonswitched) Ethernet. In security terms, shared-medium Ethernet and cable modem systems (in the most common deployment configuration) are promiscuous media: All stations sharing the same medium can read frames transmitted over the medium, and can write frames to the medium.

NOTE   Unlike PVC-based services, shared-medium services rely on stations to honestly identify themselves when transmitting data. Passive monitoring, forgery, and denial-of-service attacks are thus all greater risks with cable modem services than with DSL services.

When using cable modem services, data encryption is often warranted to ensure message privacy and integrity. Of course, this adds complexity and expense and can affect performance.

Residential Broadband Services and Security

During the design of residential wireless broadband services, the characteristics they share that may be associated with security risk are as follows:

1. The residence is not a physically secured premises, at least not in the same way as other corporate facilities.

2. The residence has an *always-connected* link to the enterprise network.

3. The connection from the residence to the enterprise network is a high-speed link.[4]

The first and second concerns are related, as are problems common to all communications services used by teleworkers and roaming employees who access corporate information resources remotely. Regardless of whether it is via analog modem, ISDN, or dialup bridge/router access, connectivity typically is automated. Because of this automated connectivity, the physical security of a teleworker's premises should be a concern for the IT manager regardless of whether access to the enterprise is achieved using on-demand or always-connected services.

For example, is DSL service a greater risk than remote LAN access using dialup ISDN service because DSL is always connected, given that ISDN router automatic dial-on-demand features generally are used by teleworkers? The answer, of course, depends on other factors, including the security measures in place at the corporate network and at the host computer(s) in the teleworker's residence. If all other factors are equal, the answer is usually *no, always-connected DSL service is no greater risk than automatic dial-on-demand ISDN service*. In many ways, in fact, always-connected DSL may be a lesser risk because it can only be used from a single premises. Dial-on-demand ISDN can be accessed from any ISDN-connected site anywhere in the world.

The third concern (that the connection from the residence to the enterprise network is a high-speed link) often proves to be the most troubling, especially in the case of remote or teleworker access to corporate servers. When corporate security is evaluated, the speed of a link is a weighting factor in determining risk. Simply put, if a low-speed link is compromised, information could be leaked from the enterprise network, but not nearly as fast as if a high-speed link is compromised. The rate at which a motivated intruder can access or collect sensitive information from a corporate server is more worrisome than whether the intruder is dialing in or is using facilities from a physically unsecured premises.

Let's examine several scenarios where these characteristics become issues for the IT manager and consider how they might be addressed. How an organization addresses security in these scenarios is greatly influenced by the perceived and real risks to corporate resources, the organization's financial and technological abilities to reduce or mitigate these risks, and the ability of an organization to implement and enforce the security measures chosen.

Scenario 1: The Teleworker Operates Systems That Do Not Fall under the Purview of Corporate Desktop Administration

By definition, teleworkers work outside the physically secured workplace. The IT manager may have little control over equipment at the teleworker's residence. The teleworker who runs unauthorized services (a Web, file, or mail server) and unapproved software may create vulnerabilities and compromise a secure perimeter established for an enterprise network. Network antivirus and intrusion-detection measures can be circumvented, and mail distribution, name resolution, or enterprise routing could be disrupted. Whether the result of accidental misconfiguration or malicious attack, activities initiated over the residential connection can interfere with or deny service to fellow corporate workers.

Recommended Policy and Best Practices for Desktop Security

It is easy to get caught up with concern over theft or modification of data transported over a network and overlook the more mundane issue of protecting stored information. Information is not any less sensitive because it is recorded on a removable medium (a Jazz drive) or hard disk of a laptop than if it is recorded electronically. A security policy for both teleworker and mobile employee should consider

- Desktop authentication
- Antivirus utilities
- Secure file storage and stored file encryption
- Desktop file security and access controls
- Unauthorized services

Desktop Authentication   This can be as simple as requiring that all PCs, irrespective of location, use login and screen saver passwords with a small idle timeout. It also can be as sophisticated as requiring a security token, key, or card to access a personal computer (PC) or a removable medium. For example, Cylink Corporation[5] offers products that require a physical token and password to access a PC. If you are interested in authentication based on biometrics, NEC[6] and others offer affordable fingerprint-recognition systems.

Antivirus Utilities   Teleworker PCs should run antivirus software to prevent the spread of email-borne viruses from the residential PC into enterprise networks. This is probably consistent with your corporate desktop security, but it is especially important if your network relies on network antivirus measures at your secure perimeter. MacAfee, Symantec, IBM Corporation, and several others offer fine antivirus products.

Secure File Storage and Stored File Encryption   There are a number of easy and effective applications for encrypting files stored on PCs and removable media. Often the same application provides file deletion that prevents recovery (*electronic shredding*). Pretty Good Privacy, Entrust Solo, and EMD Worldwide's Encryptor can be used for secure file storage and secure electronic mail. RSA SecurPC from Security Dynamics Technologies, EMD Worldwide, Software Shelf International, and Symantec offer products that are aimed at protecting enterprises from the loss or compromise of sensitive information resulting from the theft of laptops. And these alternatives are appropriate for teleworker PCs as well.

Desktop File Security and Access Controls   File (folder) sharing on Windows 2000 is simple to use but too often ignored. Insist that teleworkers assign passwords to network users, and discourage them from allowing full access privileges to entire disks and partitions. Consider a centrally administered user-level access control list for network domains that include teleworker PCs. Use third-party products (e.g., EMD Armor 97, which offers advanced access control features for Windows 2000). For increased file security, consider Windows 2000, directories, or other secured objects (devices, ports) that offer more effective and granular access controls.

NOTE   One way to motivate any worker to take file security seriously is to explain that personal or sensitive information stored on a PC in a residence or on a corporate LAN could easily be viewed by anyone in the corporation who sees that PC through Microsoft's Network Neighborhood.

Unauthorized Services   Consider a security policy that expressly prohibits services operating on desktop PCs that can expose the corporate network to attacks. It is not uncommon for IT managers to expressly prohibit FTP server applications or nominally prohibit anonymous FTP access from operating on all desktop PCs, including teleworker PCs. Web hosting applications present a number of security issues when operated on desktop PCs. Entire file systems can be browsed if file permissions on a Web server are not set appropriately, and the IT manager cannot exercise adequate control over the features, CGI scripts, and services operated. Nor can he or she control the use applets and downloadable programs.

The IT manager may wish to prohibit the operation of mail, telnet, tftp, route, and domain name servers on teleworker LANs. Consider blocking or filtering of routing protocol updates, name server announcements, and SMTP messages used between mail transfer agents emanating from a teleworker connection.

NOTE   This is only a partial list of servers that may be inappropriate for operation from an uncontrolled desktop.

Scenario 2: The Teleworker's Residence Has Multiple Physical Connections

Depending on how residential wireless broadband services are terminated at the corporate network, a second connection in the teleworker's residence can provide an unprotected access or backdoor into the corporation. There are several ways multiple physical connections can be introduced, as shown in Figures 11-3 and 11-4.[7]

Recommended Policy and Best Practices for Multiple Connections to the Residence

The most commonly encountered second or alternative connection a teleworker may have is an analog modem or ISDN terminal adapter (TA) on the teleworker's PC. An IT manager can expressly prohibit modems and

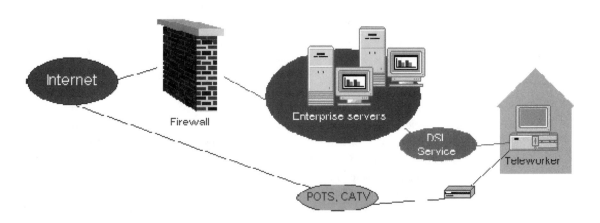

Figure 11-3   The teleworker has a PC with a modem, incoming calls are accepted by the modem, and software operating on the PC (PC Anywhere, Netopia Virtual Office, UNIX shell, telnet) is compromised to allow an outsider to gain control of the PC. An extreme case of this configuration is one in which the teleworker has a second LAN NIC and uses this to connect to the public Internet via the DSL or cable modem.

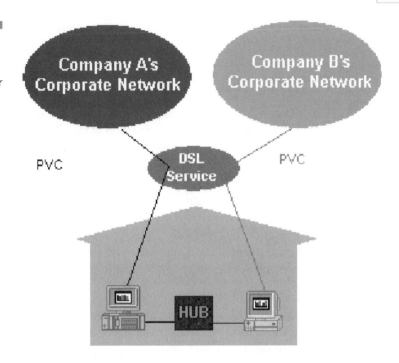

Figure 11-4
The teleworker of Company A operates a PC LAN at his or her residence, and a second system, for example, a house partner's host or router, is connected to both the PC LAN and the public Internet. In this scenario, anyone who gains access to the house partner's PC also may gain unauthorized access to Company A. An extreme case of this scenario is where Company A's teleworker and a housemate share a PC LAN in the residence, and where the housemate has a separate Internet connection or a connection to the housemate's corporate network (Company B).

TAs, but a less stringent but more readily enforceable alternative is to prohibit incoming (data) calls.

Even with incoming call handling disabled and with a security policy that prohibits server operation from a desktop [including routing services (UNIX gated, NT R&RAS)], the IT manager must consider the security implications of client applications, especially Web browsers. Executable programs carried over an HTTP stream are especially dangerous in those situations where a teleworker has multiple connections, because the teleworker may unknowingly download active content using a Web browser. The downloaded executable may contain code designed to circumvent firewall or Web proxy defenses and provide an intruder with access from the outside. It may contain a virus or other undesirable software, and this could be propagated onto the corporate network. One security measure to consider is to require that teleworkers disable the download of active content (Java, ActiveX) to browsers or require that they use antivirus software to filter it out. Disabling active content should include disabling download of executables and archive files containing executables. Seemingly harmless applications can contain "easter eggs" or other suspicious code. A better long-term policy and practice is to implement strong public-key-based authentication between servers and clients (see the section entitled "Universal Precautions" later in this chapter).

LANs in the teleworker's residence can pose additional security problems. Covad TeleSpeed service is commonly offered through a two-port router or bridge. One port is connected to the DSL service, and the other is connected to the Ethernet segment to which the teleworker's PC(s) and perhaps printers are connected. Ethernet is commonly implemented in a residence using inexpensive hub technology. Unauthorized equipment attached to the hub can be used to gain access to the corporate LAN through the DSL router or bridge.

This section has discussed how LANs shared between housemates are yet another form of multiple, unsecured connections in a residence. There are several ways to address this problem as a matter of policy or practice:

1. Do not permit the use of shared hubs; instead, use Ethernet crossover cabling between the DSL router and the teleworker's PC. This limits systems at the residence with DSL access to the router and the teleworker's PC.

2. Use managed hubs, port switching hubs, or workgroup Ethernet switches at the teleworker's residence. Disable all but the authorized number of Ethernet ports on the hub using administrative controls only accessible to authorized IT staff. SNMP-manage the hubs and enable traps so that unauthorized attempts to modify the hub configuration are forwarded to IT management systems.

NOTE   Think of an always-connected medium as an asset rather than a liability. You do not have to enable and manage incoming calls at the teleworker's residence to manage hubs remotely over an always-connected DSL service.

---

3. Consider hubs or switches that offer advanced security features. Some equipment (3COM port switch hubs and workgroup switches) has the ability to learn the MAC address of a station attached to one of its ports. Once learned, the hub or switch will disable the port and generate an alarm (to console or as an SNMP trap) should any address other than the learned address be seen on that port.

4. Use packet and MAC frame filtering. IT managers may wish to pre-configure network-level packet filters on routers or bridges to block

access to well-known services ports of teleworkers' PCs, to block traffic from unauthorized addresses originating at the teleworker's LAN, and to block network protocols other than authorized protocols. Where bridging is used, IT managers may wish to configure filters that only permit forwarding of LAN frames originating from authorized MAC addresses.

5. Restrict routing and bridging protocols. For the majority of teleworker environments, static routing is sufficient and should be the only routing used between routers at a teleworker's residence and corporate routers. Similarly, a static forwarding database can be configured in many bridges, and learning can be disabled.[8]

Scenario 3: The Teleworker Requires Access to Application Servers and NOS Services That Would Otherwise Be Blocked by a Corporate Firewall

The kinds and locations of enterprise servers and NOS services that a teleworker may need to access depend on the nature of the work the teleworker is expected to perform from a residence and include

- Intranet Web servers
- File and print servers accessed using Network Operating System (NOS) protocols
- Client-server remote login
- Internal database and other networked application servers[9]

In this scenario, the IT manager may have to terminate residential wireless broadband services behind the corporate firewall or make exceptions to an existing security perimeter to accommodate access to, for example, intranet file servers (Figure 11-5).[10] Such actions introduce vulnerabilities. Existing methods for compartmentalizing LAN communications within the enterprise may not be accommodated from a common termination point within the corporate network.

Figure 11-5
The IT manager may
have to terminate
residential wireless
broadband services
behind the corporate
firewall.

Recommended Policy and Best Practices for Teleworker Access to Enterprise Servers

AppleTalk, Microsoft Network (SMB/CIFS), and UNIX/NFS/X cannot be used effectively over traditional dialup services. However, residential wireless broadband services easily satisfy bandwidth and delay characteristics for teleworkers, so they naturally will want access to the same LAN environment from home as they have in the office. There are several ways to accommodate LAN access. These should be implemented in conjunction with the best practices already described and include the following techniques:

■ For teleworker access to intranets, consider products that allow you to build community-of-interest networks (COINs) based on strong user authentication.

■ For NOS protocol support, use Virtual Private Network techniques to securely extend file, print, and other NOS services from enterprise networks to the teleworker (see "Strong Authentication" and "Encrypted Data Transport" later in this chapter).

■ For client-server remote login, consider secure shell and secure telnet applications.[11]

Universal Precautions

The measures previously described can greatly reduce risks associated with common configuration scenarios associated with teleworker residences. They are largely based on security measures that generally are understood to be among the *best practices* in building secure networks. They are universal precautions and, where implemented, will be effective in mitigating and reducing certain risks, whether the user is a teleworker, mobile employee, or office employee. Let's examine these more closely.

Strong Authentication

Strong authentication is perhaps the most important security measure you can implement. Access controls, accounting, message confidentiality, and message integrity are all based on the ability to require a user to prove that he or she is who he or she claims to be. If a user's or server's authenticity can be demonstrated with a high degree of confidence (assurance), IT managers can control access to specific hosts, information, and applications. They can exercise considerable control over the kinds of actions users can perform on secured objects, and they can dictate when message exchanges between users and objects should be conducted using encryption for privacy and integrity.

There are a number of strong authentication systems to choose from, and you may have already implemented these over corporate LANs and for remote access. These include Kerberos, one-time passwords such as Bellcore S/Key or RSA SecurPC (SoftID), and authentication token systems from Security Dynamics Technologies (SecurID).

An increasing number of organizations that require strong authentication for Web-enabled applications make use of the Secure Sockets Layer (SSL) and Secure Hypertext Transfer (S-HTTP) protocols between Web servers and clients. SSL can be enabled on most commonly used browsers and servers to provide mutual, strong authentication between clients and servers. For applications that operate over transmission control protocol (TCP), strong end-to-end session encryption can be negotiated and employed as well. SSL uses public-key cryptography for strong authentication. Aventail Corporation main-tains a good reference site on SSL and SOCKS security resources. Secure HTTP (S-HTTP), an extension to HTTP, provides strong client-server authentication, *spontaneous encryption* and message integrity, and request/response nonrepudiation.

NOTE A good resource for information about S-HTTP is Terisa Systems.

The use of a public-key-based authentication requires an infrastructure [a certificate authority (CA) for assigning personal and server certificates]. A CA not only issues certificates but also is used to assert the trustworthiness and validity of certificates. You can outsource CA to third parties such as GTE, Verisign, CyberTrust, and Thawte Consulting, or enterprises can use certificate servers from companies such as Xcert, Netscape, or Entrust to implement private CAs. Once implemented, teleworkers (indeed, all workers) acquire personal certificates for use and configure their browsers to only permit downloads of active content from servers that present trusted and valid certificates.

Encrypted Data Transport

Certain organizations may find it necessary to use encryption over any communications link that is not physically secured, and security policy may dictate that any intraenterprise communications exchanged over unsecured links must be encrypted. Consider virtual private network (VPN) products based on IP Security (IPSEC) standards to fill this need. Layer 3 IPSEC tunnels provide IP-based virtual secure connections. In this IPSEC mode, normal IP packets are routed between tunnel end points. Host systems or IPSEC routers can terminate tunnels. Tunnel end points can operate over any intervening network topology. Encapsulated within tunneled IP packets are IETF-specified security protocol headers that provide packet-level authentication (AH, authentication header) and data integrity and confidentiality (ESP, encapsulating security payload). These protocol extensions are compatible with IPv4 and IPv6. When used in conjunction with an Internet Key Management Protocol (IKMP), IPSEC protocols can be used with any authentication or encryption algorithm (MD5, SHA1, RC5, DES, 3DES, etc.). Products based on draft standards for tunnel- or transport-mode IPSEC include the Cisco IOS routers, Compatible Systems IntraPort, RedCreek Ravlin, Timestep PERMIT, VPNet VSU-1010, and FTP Software Secure Client.

In situations where corporations wish only to encrypt certain data, application-specific or circuit-level encryption may be appropriate. The Aventail VPN server encrypts application data transmitted over TCP connections. InfoExpress offers a VPN solution that proxies Windows Internet Naming Service (WINS) and Microsoft File Sharing for Windows environments. InfoExpress recently added AppleTalk proxy support to its virtual TCP secure remote VPN product. Electronic mail applications from Microsoft, Netscape, Network Associates, and others support either Secure MIME or Pretty Good Privacy. These products let you digitally sign and encrypt mail and attachments.

Intrusion Detection, Attack Recognition, and Response

Where you terminate residential wireless broadband services in the corporate network and the services you expect to provide to teleworkers may change the way you proactively monitor for intrusions and attacks. If you are already performing monitoring, logging, and auditing activities on all internal segments, subnets, and systems, consider extending the practice to include teleworker connections. If you only proactively monitor systems on DMZ subnets or systems on subnets that can be accessed by outsiders or partners, consider how these same practices can be extended to subnets where teleworker connections are terminated.

Proactive monitoring systems and software products represent one of the fastest growing segments in the security industry. FireWatch from Bellcore and UNIX tcpwrapper and tcpdump provide administrative assistance in collecting logs and creating reports for network auditing purposes. PingWare from Bellcore, Internet Scanner from ISS and UNIX COPS proactively scan networks for known configuration flaws that are exploited by intruders. Products from Cisco Systems, Network Associates, and ISS take intrusion detection to the next level. These products scan networks searching for traffic patterns and content that match known attack signatures. NetSonarä from Cisco Systems, ISS SafeSuiteä, and Network Associates' (formerly TIS) Stalker3.0 or higher products can intervene and reconfigure firewalls, screening routers, and servers when they detect an attack or misuse of a network.

Network Antivirus Protection and Content Filtering

Blocking or intercepting executable code from sources outside the enterprise is a persistent concern for IT managers. Again, where you terminate residential wireless broadband services in the corporate network and the services you expect to provide to teleworkers may change the segments and subnets to which you choose to restrict downloads and filter content that were discussed previously.

Firewall-based VPN products from vendors such as Aventail Corporation, CheckPoint, Raptor, and Network Associates can monitor application data and can enforce security policies at a more granular level, for example, by blocking application protocol content such as Java and ActiveX. Products that focus entirely on Web security and management to provide URL and content access controls also can be obtained from companies such as Netegrity (SiteMinder) and Caravelle (Webwatcher).

Symantec's Norton AntiVirus for Firewalls and McAfee NetShield Security Suit work with any firewall that supports the Content Vectoring Protocol (CVP), a standard interface used by firewall clients to validate message content by passing requests to a scan server. The scan server checks HTTP, FTP, and SMTP requests for known virus signatures and repairs or deletes infected messages before they can be propagated inside the firewall. McAfee NetShield Security Suite performs similar security services from a Windows NT server or workstation.

Finally, let's look at how competitive local exchange carriers (CLECs) will change the face of the telecom industry. In other words, let's look at how the design of wireless broadband services by CLECs can dramatically alter and rejuvenate the telecom landscape.

CLEC Wireless Broadband Services Design

CLECs are changing the face of the telecom industry. The following topics will be discussed in reference to how the telecom industry is changing:

- The regulatory terrain as it stands today
- The current state of competition as described by the Federal Communications Commission (FCC)
- Issues facing CLECs as they enter the marketplace
- Challenges to building a company prepared for competition in the local loop
- Wireless broadband service design opportunities afforded CLECs (in particular, we'll look at traditional and not-so-traditional wireless broadband services design as well as complementing wireless broadband services for residential and business customers; see the sidebar, "Broadband Wireless Services.")
- Delivery options CLECs can consider

Broadband Wireless Services

Sprint is readying about 30 new services for broadband fixed wireless, targeting the high-bandwidth offerings at homes and small businesses along with large enterprises. Sprint Broadband also will soon be expanding beyond its initial service areas in Arizona into metro markets that include San Francisco, Detroit, Houston, and Denver.

Sprint will start rolling out the new services in early 2001. Plans call for Spectrum Management between Sprint, WorldCom, and

NuCentrix Networks to cooperate in building out new high-bandwidth wireless services within the United States. Sprint's new broadband wireless services will include Internet portals for consumers, along with wireless VLANs (virtual local-area networks) for businesses and integration with existing wired Ethernet LANs.

In Phoenix, Sprint Broadband has already launched a wireless telecommuting service. The telecommuting service is deployed during "Smog Days," when large businesses in Phoenix implement telecommuting among some of their employees.

Sprint Broadband instituted wireless broadband services in Phoenix in the spring of 2000, following up with a launch in Tucson, Arizona. Sprint also has already opened some broadband facilities in Detroit.

For consumers, Sprint's wireless ISP services will include features like personal Web pages and chat and newsgroups. Sprint also was careful to draw a distinction between fixed wireless services such as Sprint Broadband, which require installation of equipment in a home or other building, and narrowband wireless services such as Sprint PCS. For Sprint Broadband's customers, *mobility* will refer to the ability to use a device anywhere within the home, as opposed to when speeding down the highway, for instance.

Sprint plans to speed deployment and lower costs by developing systems that either do not need to be installed or can install themselves. Customers also will start to see *qualitative changes*, such as user-selectable wireless bandwidth, by the middle part of 2001.

Also in the future, Sprint expects to unveil additional Spectrum Management partners. The Spectrum Management plan is based on the Breckenridge Agreement announced in January 2000. The first three Spectrum partners are also the three largest providers of fixed wireless services in the 2.1- and 2.5- to 2.7-GHz bands. The new Spectrum Management plan sets up guidelines for cooperation among service providers when building in adjacent markets and operating in the multipoint distribution service, multichannel multipoint distribution service, and wireless communications service frequencies.

To comply with FCC rules on protected service areas, wireless broadband networks operating in these spectrums usually are built to cover a 35-mile radius from the transmission tower. But radiofrequency signals in this bandwidth actually can extend further than 35 miles.

Another potential source of interference is that the FCC now lets individual operators determine which frequencies to use for upstream and downstream communications. The new Spectrum Management plan recently announced raises the acceptable interference levels above those specified by the FCC while also outlining a preferred spectrum for carrying upstream and downstream traffic based on frequency availability and licensing factors in each market.[12]

Regulatory Terrain

The Telecom Act of 1996 was enacted by Congress in February 1996 "to provide for a pro-competitive, de-regulatory national policy framework designed to accelerate rapidly private sector deployment of advanced telecommunications and information technologies and services to all Americans by opening all telecommunications markets to competition."

What is noteworthy about the Telecom Act of 1996 is that it opens the telecommunications access market to anyone brave (or foolish) enough to believe that they can compete and distinguish themselves in local-loop services. It defines a framework in which competition will operate. It does not, however, describe in detail how competition will be implemented. This is a matter for both the FCC and state regulatory agencies to determine. Interpretations of the act and rule making by state agencies can lead to different implementations from state to state. The rule making by states and the FCC is guided by what have come to be known as the *competition trilogy*, which consists of

- The Local Competition Proceeding (CC Docket No. 96-98)
- The Universal Service Proceeding (CC Docket No. 96-45)
- The Access Charge Proceeding (CC Docket No. 96-262).[13]

Of these, the Local Competition Proceeding impacts CLECs most.

Local Competition Proceeding

The local competition proceeding considers all the following aspects:

- *Access to unbundled elements.* This includes access to local loops, local and tandem switches (including vertical features), interoffice transmission facilities, network interface devices, signaling and call-related database facilities, operations support systems (OSS) functions, and operator and directory assistance.

- *Interconnection.* This includes connection to the line and trunk sides of the local switch, trunk interconnection points of a tandem switch, central office cross-connect points, and out-of-band signaling points.[14]

The Local Competition Proceeding also addresses collocation of CLEC equipment in incumbent LEC central offices, resale of facilities, pricing of interconnection and unbundled elements, and access to rights of way.

Current State of Competition

The Telecom Act has had the desired effect of attracting competitors to the local-loop marketplace. In addition to the observations made on the slide, it is important to note that the actual number of CLECs is hard to estimate and changes frequently as new carriers are issued certificates. According to the FCC, several CLECs have already gone out of business. The actual number of applications for operating certificates is also difficult to collect because this is regulated at the state level and changes constantly.

The AOL and GTE DSL initiative notwithstanding, most CLECs hope to penetrate the enterprise and growing teleworker market. Access to the public Internet and online services is a secondary business because of the real versus perceived cost of DSL. Many telecommunications analysts are skeptical about the ability for any company to profitably offer bandwidth and online or Internet service at $50 to $60 per month. Given the cost of copper-tone, switching, field craft, support systems, and Operations Administration and Maintenance (OAM) associated with deploying DSL (and given that many ISPs lose money per subscriber at rates between $20 and $30), how much can be left for GTE and AOL to share? Price points in the $100 to $400 range for ADSL only at various rates seem more realistic, and this matches the business budget more so than the residential consumer budget.

CLEC Market Appeal

On-ramps to the Internet highway are congested. ISDN and 56K V.90 modems will improve this only marginally, but they do not exhibit LAN-like characteristics necessary for extending certain applications (SMB/Microsoft File Sharing, highly visual applications). DSL and transparent LAN services are the answer, and CLECs want to penetrate this business.

CLECs also will want to compete in dialtone, wireline and wireless, and of course, Internet voice. Consider the market size. Why wouldn't someone want to go after the local loop for voice? T-carrier will continue to be a lucrative business (not constrained by distances like DSL), and T1 competition undoubtedly will grow.

There are also intriguing voice arbitrage opportunities for CLECs that incorporate Internet telephony into their business (more on this later). How many PCs will there be by 2001, and how many will be able to answer the phone?

Issues: Tripwires for CLECs

It is tempting to ask, "So you want to become a CLEC? Have you considered . . ." The regulatory terrain is uncertain. Legal matters are as important as business and technology. It is also good to acknowledge early on that equipment and technology are first generation: Do not expect that any vendor will satisfy all your needs, and accept that vendor interoperability is not universal. You also may need to roll your own OSS systems.

Finally, there is the little matter of the incumbent carriers you must deal with. ILECs own the plant and COs. This may be the only business in history where your landlord is your competitor!

Challenges

The challenges most frequently mentioned include staffing and facilities development or maintenance. Finding staff who are competent in data and voice technology, telecom transmission systems, and network administration is hard; such folks are a scarce commodity. For those CLECs which are building facilities, duplicating the last mile is expensive, whereas for those leasing copper, maintaining the local loop means learning how to practice an old craft.

Learning with whom and how to deal with ILECs is critical. You may not be able to find a champion inside an ILEC, but you can still find staff who have a "do the best job possible for the customer" mentality from pre-divestiture days. These are the best folks to work with, and they are your best allies, whether you're delivering ISDN, ISDL, POTS, or DSL.

Pricing has multiple dimensions and issues. Your costs for cage space and copper, staff, and craft should be the basis for pricing. However, pricing competitors that promote in direct competition with your service will affect your ability to do business profitably. The things you should worry most about with pricing are the promotional and lowball pricing by the incumbents that you are intending to use—especially when the incumbent announces its intent to deploy. If you are deploying service now at $120 per month and the incumbent announces an intent to offer the same service in the fourth quarter of 2001 (4Q01) at half that rate, how many buyers could this affect? Come 4Q01, what is the guarantee that the incumbent will deploy, and how long will the rate be available? Meanwhile, your market share has suffered.

CLEC Wireless Broadband Service Models

The local-loop deployment and backbone (aggregation) alternatives for CLECs who enter the level 2 business are as follows:

- Digital subscriber line access multiplexers (DSLAMs) in multi-tenant businesses, coppertone from the landlord.
- DSLAMS in collocation arrangements at ILEC COs.
- Depending on bandwidth needs for regional data distribution, CLECs will buy FR, broadband ATM, and even SONET and will deploy their own switching and routing solutions.[15]

The local-loop deployment and backhaul/aggregation issues are the same. The big difference here is that the CLEC rolls out IP service and differentiated wireless broadband services.

Differentiated Wireless Broadband Services Design

There is a tremendous opportunity for a CLEC to either partner with ISPs or offer wireless broadband services itself that complement broadband with a differentiated wireless broadband services design. More than ever, just offering available bandwidth is no longer an option. Managing bandwidth and latency and providing application-specific bandwidth are critical factors for successful ISPs. Adding security for information transport using virtual private networking techniques is another means of service differentiation. Voice is an incumbent's cash cow, and there is no doubt a lucrative but challenging opportunity to provide Internet telephony using V.90 technology, or voice over frame, or lifeline voice using ADSL with POTS splitters, or Universal ADSL. Once you are offering voice, it is not that big a stretch to imagine, investigate, and experiment with virtual voice networks and features that allow the company PBX to extend to the teleworker's desktop.

VPNs and Security

Virtual private networking solutions provide promising and potentially lucrative wireless broadband service design opportunities for CLECs and ISPs. But do not limit your consideration to security over the wire. Security in other forms is also critical and will prove an especially significant hurdle to cross for the enterprise customer. And it is not just security over the wire. CLECs must be convinced that broadband to teleworkers does not introduce new security risks but rather that always-connected access makes it more important than ever to examine security policies and address security for remote access in more comprehensive ways. Your staff must be able to explain the kinds of technologies and practices that enterprise administrators can deploy to increase confidence in the evolving *security perimeter.* Biometric and other forms of strong authentication, physical lockdown of facilities, and personal firewalls are coming. CLECs who know how to explain these to their customers also can consider security consulting as yet another service to offer.

Delivery Options

Despite all the excitement over residential wireless broadband data design, opportunities abound to offer voice. Even data folks appreciate how enormous the voice market is. Voice can be offered as efficiently when packetized as when circuit switched. The voice fidelity you can now achieve with bandwidth management and V.90 modems, for example, is just the appetizer.

Conclusion

This chapter provided background information for IT managers who must maintain tight security while also introducing new wireless broadband access technologies into the enterprise. It explained how residential wireless broadband services based on digital subscriber line and cable modem operate. The chapter also identified potential vulnerabilities that are sometimes associated with DSL-based wireless broadband services but are in many cases vulnerabilities exposed by many, if not all, wireless broadband services used by remote workers and mobile employees. It discussed deployment scenarios you may wish to consider as you evaluate corporate security policies regarding remote access and teleworker arrangements. Through examples, the chapter described how risks can be mitigated or reduced using commercially available security products.

Passive Optical Network (PON)

Copper pairs are being used currently to cater to the needs of the subscribers in local networks. The local loop is a vital part of wireless broadband network service design. However, the copper technology has many limitations because it offers only a narrow bandwidth and is unable to handle wireless broadband services that are the need of the information age. With large bandwidth and high reliability, optical fiber has become an automatic choice for the local loop.

Expected Deployment Profile

Recent deployments in PONs offer the imminent possibility that fiber system can be deployed economically not only to small and medium-sized businesses but also to residential customers requiring wireless broadband services. Full-service (broadband service) access networks cover the following types of services:

- *Broadcast services:* cable TV, video on demand
- *Transactional services:* music, video, video games, electronic directories, home shopping
- *Communications services:* voice telephony, videoconferencing, distant learning, PC communication[16]

Radio

Reading the accounts of the ambitious network modernization projects underway around the globe, it is tempting to believe that radio is an outdated technology, bypassed by the limitless capacity and wireless broadband service options of optical fiber transmission. However, with the growing demand for wireless broadband services, speed of deployment, startup costs, and rapid revenue returns are significant factors in the selection of transport technology.

The complexity of wireless broadband telecommunications design seems undeniable. There are in excess of 30 clearly defined wireless services being provided worldwide. Some of these, such as troposcatter and short-wave radio communications, are being phased out of operation. Other, new and innovative services such as personal communications service (PCS), universal personal telecommunications (UPT), personal digital assistants (PDAs), low- and medium-earth-orbit mobile satellite communications, and direct broadcast satellite services are in various stages of being phased into service.

Some of these wireless broadband services are outside the *normal* commercial wireless marketplace in that they represent military services or federal, state, or local government services. These include public safety, search and rescue, or other governmental services. Finally, there are other *special* wireless broadband communications activities such as amateur radio, environmental monitoring, humanitarian relief work, and international peace-keeping operations.

New Wireless Broadband Services that Can Be Introduced

Since conventional telephony requires symmetric networking, the preceding evolution would meet its requirements, making the merger of diverse wireless broadband services possible and feasible. In fact, radio technology will have the edge in providing interactivity and making the network less asymmetric. The coverage can be effectively extended to urban, suburban, and rural areas, which is an important consideration in the national telecom policy. Furthermore, this will be an enabling technology for reaching the customer cost-effectively and quickly for provision of the emerging wireless broadband services.

NOTE   This chapter offered considerations for implementing security in enterprise networks where DSL-based services are applied. It did not profess to address every security issue for every enterprise IT manager. In the course of this chapter, security is mentioned with regard to products that may satisfy a security need for an IT manager and may direct the IT manager to a review of certain products. Any such mention does not represent an endorsement of any kind by this author.

Hopefully, this chapter has alleviated your concerns about radio and DSL-based services and security and has helped you move one step closer to a successful design and deployment of wireless broadband services. We are entering one of the most exciting times in the history of telecommunications. And we have not even begun yet.

Endnotes

1. Covad Communications Company, 2330 Central Expressway, Santa Clara, CA 95050-2516, 2000.

2. David M. Piscitello, "Residential Broadband Access and the Teleworker: Security Considerations for the IT Manager," Core Competence, Inc., 3 Myrtle Bank Lane, Hilton Head, SC 29926 and 344 Valley View Lane, Chester Springs, PA 19425, 2000.

3. *Ibid.*

4. *Ibid.*

5. Cylink Corporation, 3151 Jay Street, Santa Clara, CA 95054, 2000.

6. NEC USA, Inc., 8 Corporate Center Drive, Melville, NY 11747, 2000.

7. Core Competence, Inc., 3 Myrtle Bank Lane, Hilton Head, SC 29926 and 344 Valley View Lane, Chester Springs, PA 19425, 2000.

8. *Ibid.*

9. *Ibid.*

10. *Ibid.*

11. *Ibid.*

12. Jacqueline Emigh, "Sprint Readies 30 Broadband Wireless Services," Sm@rt Partner, 100 Quentin Roosevelt Boulevard, Suite 400, Garden City, NY 11530, 2000.

13. "CLEC Market Overview," Core Competence, Inc., 3 Myrtle Bank Lane, Hilton Head, SC 29926 and 344 Valley View Lane, Chester Springs, PA 19425, 2000.

14. *Ibid.*

15. *Ibid.*

16. *Ibid.*

CHAPTER 12

U.S.-Specific Wireless Broadband Design

With no need to bury new lines or fiber (implying a quick and inexpensive deployment), wireless technologies such as local multipoint distribution service (LMDS) and multichannel multipoint distribution service (MMDS) are being hailed as wireless broadband access saviors. Wireless competitive local exchange carriers (CLECs) have begun to deploy them. Companies such as MCI/WorldCom and Sprint are banking on their success. Federal Communications Commission (FCC) auctions of fixed wireless spectrum have fetched hundreds of millions of dollars.

The promise of wireless broadband access is indeed compelling: the ability to leverage broadband wireline access over a larger area, reach new markets, and provide everything from high-speed Internet to voice and video services. Yet this is increasingly the promise of wireless broadband connections in general. How and where wireless broadband competes with landline alternatives (such as fiber, cable, and DSL) ultimately will determine its success and place in the market.

With the preceding in mind, this chapter explores U.S.-specific wireless broadband design: LMDS, MMDS, and unlicensed spectrum and the vast potential of wireless broadband as a competitive local access technology in the voice, video, and Internet access markets. Following an extensive exploration of current trends in telecommunications demand and competitive broadband markets, the case for wireless broadband technologies is detailed and industry forecasts developed. Topics presented in this chapter include

■ Review of wireless broadband technologies, including vendor offerings and product comparisons

■ Current wireless broadband deployments, including LMDS, MMDS, and unlicensed spectrum operators

■ Indepth case study of major operating and future wireless broadband carriers

■ Overview of competitive service markets

■ Profiles of major wireless broadband carriers and vendors

Therefore, let's first look at how popular cable modem specifications become an important ingredient in the development of LMDS and MMDS system designs.

Adapting DOCSIS for U.S.-Specific Wireless Broadband Access Design

Although the data-over-cable service interface specification (DOCSIS) is designed for interoperability among cable modems and related products, with a few modifications, it also can be used in wireless broadband multipoint multichannel distribution service (MMDS) and local multipoint distribution service (LMDS) systems. Both LMDS and MMDS are on the rise as providers move forward with deployments, and MMDS in particular is being eyed as a *wireless DSL* of sorts.

The DOCSIS standard was developed initially by a consortium of equipment manufacturers and CATV operators. Now defined, this specification details the radiofrequency (rf) physical layer specifications, looking specifically at modulation types and symbol rates. Additionally, the DOCSIS protocol defines initialization, data control, and security aspects of CATV system development.

Although the DOCSIS specification was targeted initially at CATV applications, it is beginning to find a home outside the TV market. Specifically, a group of companies have banded together as a consortium, called the *Wireless Broadband DSL Consortium*, to produce an enhanced version of DOCSIS for wireless broadband applications. The new standard, dubbed DOCSIS+, builds on the original specification but adds specific extensions for the LMDS/MMDS market. These extensions have been proposed for a new standard (or an extension to the existing DOCSIS standard) and are currently under study by the IEEE 802.16 Committee.

A Look Behind DOCSIS

DOCSIS+ is an Internet Protocol (IP)–centric point-to-multipoint standard that was developed for wireless broadband Internet access applications (see the sidebar, "Despite Promises—Few Deliver High-Speed Wireless Broadband Internet") over cable TV networks. As such, the DOCSIS standard is designed to support all existing as well as future IP-based services.

Despite Promises—Few Deliver High-Speed Wireless Broadband Internet

Wireless broadband Internet companies promise the future but mostly deliver speeds out of the past. The mobile Internet is still largely a dream—and slow data rates are a large part of the problem. The net over cellular phones right now works at a relative crawl, maxing out at 19,200 baud—the speed of a state-of-the-art modem in 1995 and less than a third of the speed of the slowest modems included with today's computers.

A company called Metricom,[1] though, hovers above the fray, providing a real, fast solution by making an end run around the entire cell phone system. Metricom plants all over a city shoebox-sized radios, which relay signals to and from radio modems attached to laptop computers, as shown in Figure 12-1.[2]

The company's Ricochet service is fabulous. At 28 kbps, it is about three times the average speed of a telephone modem, but it is expensive and currently only works in 11 metropolitan areas. But the mobile Internet field will get much more crowded in the next 2 years, with a bewildering alphabet soup of new standards such as GPRS, HDR, and 3G offering users faster speeds.

For workers on the go, high-speed mobile net means popping open Web pages while working at a café or tapping into corporate networks during meetings. For consumers, it means downloading portable music at will or watching streaming movies on your handheld computer.

Alphabet Soup   One other company is trying to do what Metricom does, on a much more limited scale. Mobilestar, based in Richardson, Texas, provides high-speed service within 131 hotels and airport frequent flyer clubs around the country. At $40 per month for unlimited access, it is cheaper than Ricochet.

Mobilestar uses wireless broadband local-area network (LAN) technology similar to that used in offices. Its network runs at 1.6 Mpbs in some places, 11 Mpbs in others—an office network kind of

Figure 12-1
Shoebox-sized radios that can relay signals to and from Ricochet modems attached to laptop computers are strung from lampposts around a city.

speed. But the technology is relatively short-range, so a network transmitter must be installed in every building the company wants to serve. Right now, the service is only useful if you spend a lot of time in certain hotels or American Airlines Admirals' Clubs.

Within the next 2 years, though, the wireless broadband net arena will expand. General packet radio service (GPRS), which works with the cell phone system, potentially offers Ricochet-type speeds—though realistically users may be limited to about 50 kbps, according to a GPRS analysis from Mobile Lifestreams, Limited. GPRS networks will start appearing in the United States during the last half of 2001.

New Jersey–based Flarion Technologies, a spinoff of Lucent, is preparing Flash-OFDM technology, which promises data rates ranging from 384 kbps to 3 Mbps. The company will be testing out its technology next in 2002, but it has not officially lined up any service providers.

Flash-OFDM, like Ricochet, uses many small transmitters and is a data-only network. Invented by Bell Labs, the technology uses a large number of narrow frequency bands to transmit information very quickly.

Also for launch in 2002, Qualcomm is working on HDR (High Data Rate), a cellular-based data technology. It will have speeds up to 2.4 Mbps, but nobody has tested it on the market yet. Tantivy, a Melbourne, Florida–based startup, is currently testing a technology for reliable 368 kbps connections via existing cellular systems.

Farther down the road, third-generation cellular (3G) systems promise 384-kbps data rates and clearer voice calls throughout the cellular market—but they will not start appearing in the United States until 2002 or later. Third-generation cellular may be the first truly universal high-speed data solution, because it will eventually apply throughout the mobile phone world.

If You Build It, Will They Come?   But there are psychological as well as technological barriers to useful wireless broadband Internet, according to experts. Right now, wireless broadband Internet access comes in three distinct flavors: the slow, painful kind done through cheap and ubiquitous cell phones; somewhat more useful but still almost entirely text-only access through palmtops; and, the full-bore experience through powerful but bulky laptops.

For palmtop Internet to take off, it needs to be faster, but also you need the services that people want to use. This is a user who is mobile, distracted, and operating in an environment very different from an environment in which you would operate your laptop. Bandwidth is not going to help the user who needs to get at his or her data in less than three taps.

Right now, it takes up to three keypresses to type one letter on a cell phone Internet browser. More advanced palmtop technology certainly will help.

There's a paradigm shift still to happen—a graphics-rich microbrowser on a portrait display with a high-speed network. We are close, but we are not there yet.

New Paradigms   The entire structure of the mobile Internet industry needs to change to become useful. Vendors should focus on building a high-quality infrastructure rather than marketing inadequate services today. And service providers like Sprint and AT&T should be more open to partnerships with a wide range of content companies to build compelling mobile applications.

If they are open enough to incorporating new applications and letting consumers vote with their feet, they will compel the network builders to build out. Competition will bring down costs, but companies still need to find a way to pay for the huge expense of building the networks.

Metricom may find its niche with mobile professionals who need to work on their laptops while away from the office. But for the rest of us, mobile applications must be simple, location-based, and timely—*where's that ATM?* They've got to be easy to use and cannot be the kind of thing you can already do with a map in the glove compartment.

Finally, when true wireless broadband Internet (which requires those high-speed networks) appears on mobile devices, the killer applications finally will be able to appear. It is going to be great someday. It just is not very great today.[3]

The CATV-centric DOCSIS spec, also called DOCSIS 1.1, assumes that all the upstream and downstream channels are equally available to all users all the time. Hence all the upstream and downstream channels in use in a specific serving area support the performance requirements as set forth in paragraph 2 of the DOCSIS RFI specifications (SP-RFIv1.1-I04-000407) for all the users within the serving area all the time. As a result, the selection/assignment of a pair of upstream and downstream channels per user is relatively fixed in time and involves traffic balancing and quality-of-service (QoS) considerations rather than rf performance optimization.

The DOCSIS 1.1 specification contains features that are necessary for applications that require special treatment from the network. The specification enables system designers to develop products that offer ATM-like services via these additional features.

For QoS deployment, functions are included for data and hybrid voice-video applications, service flows, classifiers, scheduling types, and dynamic service establishment. Fragmentation features in the specification allow for segmentation of large packets, thereby simplifying bandwidth allocation for constant-bit-rate (CBR) services.

Likewise, concatenation support allows bundling of multiple small packets to increase throughput, while security enhancements support authentication and other security measures such as baseline privacy plus, which builds on the baseline privacy available in DOCSIS 1.0. Inline DES encryption/decryption is also possible through these improvements, as is encryption support for multicast signaling [Internet Group Management Protocol (IGMP)]. Additionally, the enhancements enable payload header suppression, which suppresses unnecessary Ethernet/IP header information for improved bandwidth utilization.

The key additions, therefore, are multiple service-class support, dynamic service establishment, support for real-time services, and cryptographic authentication of the modem. Let's look at these a little closer.

Service-Class Support

Multiple service-class support makes it possible to define more than one kind of network access for a wireless broadband modem. One can browse with predefined network settings and can use the modem to make phone calls at the same time. This was not possible under the DOCSIS 1.0 specification, since there was not enough detail to support multiple service classes in a vendor-independent way.

Dynamic service establishment offers a way to supply valuable services on demand. For example, in cases where one has a voice-over-IP (VoIP) telephone, bandwidth is reserved only when a call is to be placed.

Real-time support provides a consistent way to support time-critical applications. For example, in a VoIP application, it is possible to define how much delay and jitter is to be tolerated. Since the time-critical services are much more valuable than the usual Internet service provider (ISP) services, making sure that a modem is identified correctly becomes very important. DOCSIS 1.1 defines a cryptographic way to reliably identify modems. Applications that stand to benefit from DOCSIS 1.1 support include

- A mixture of transaction-processing or real-time traffic (both of which are sensitive to latencies), with low-priority Web browsing and bulk file transfer on a user-by-user basis. For example, DOCSIS 1.1 would allow a user's business-related data to be set at a higher priority than casual Web browsing. In general, situations like this require multiple service IDs (SIDs) stored within each modem—a defining characteristic of DOCSIS 1.1.

- Integrated enterprise backbones combining data traffic, teleconferencing, and telephony over a single channel. So-called network policy-management decisions are enabled via the DOCSIS 1.1 specification.

- A mixture of protocols that require short transit times to avoid protocol timeouts and retransmissions when intermingled with bulk traffic.

- Sharing of channel bandwidth by different organizations that want to apportion costs through service-level agreements (SLAs). CBR services are one example of this type of tiered bandwidth-allocation application.[4]

Support for Asynchronous Transfer Mode (ATM) cell transport is targeted to be available in DOCSIS 1.1. An ATM cell protocol data unit (PDU) has been reserved for ATM cell transport. This is not covered in the current DOCSIS 1.0 specification.

Table 12-1 shows how features in the DOCSIS 1.1 specification map compare with ATM features.[5] Each DOCSIS frame consists of a DOCSIS header and an optional PDU. The PDU types are variable-length PDU, ATM-cell PDU (not defined in current specifications), reserved PDU, and DOCSIS MAC-specific PDU.

TABLE 12-1

Mapping DOCSIS 1.1 Features to Their ATM Equivalents

ATM	DOCSIS 1.1
Virtual circuit	Service ID
Cell-based	Fragmentation
CBR-support	Unsolicited grant
Real-time VBR support	Real-time polling
Switched VC	Dynamic service establishment

Security Considerations

Security threats fall into two general categories: security of data-transport services and security of CPE (which uses wireless broadband modems to attach to public data networks). The DOCSIS 1.1 architecture includes security components that secure data-transport services across the shared-medium network.

In the DOCSIS+ version of DOCSIS 1.1 data transport, security will provide wireless broadband modem users with data privacy across the network by encrypting traffic flows between the wireless broadband modem and the wireless modem termination system (WMTS) located in the base station of the wireless network. Additionally, DOCSIS security will provide operators with protection from theft of service.

The new DOCSIS system prevents unauthorized access to these data-transport services by requiring that the WMTS enforce encryption of the associated traffic flows across the wireless broadband network and by employing an authenticated client-server key management protocol in which the WMTS (the server) controls distribution of keying material to client wireless broadband modems.

Wireless broadband systems use the DOCSIS key management protocol to obtain authorization and traffic encryption material from a WMTS and to support periodic reauthorization and key refresh. The key management protocol uses X.509 digital certificates, RSA public-key encryption, and triple digital encryption security (DES) to secure key exchanges between the wireless broadband modem and the WMTS.

Radiofrequency (rf) Impairments

Before discussing the modifications that are being employed in the DOCSIS specification to make it suitable for wireless broadband applications, it is best to review the rf impairments that wireless broadband links must face. As with any wireless broadband communication link, the key figure of merit is the signal-to-noise ratio (SNR) or carrier-to-noise ratio (CNR). The greater the signal (short of overloading, of course) and the less the noise (and distortion products), the better. Unfortunately, several rf phenomena work to reduce the signal and increase noise—not really the direction you may want to go.

At the LMDS frequencies, rf signal propagation is line of sight and is thus fairly short range. Lower frequencies do allow some refraction of the wavefront. Since these systems employ a line-of-sight transmission scheme, signals can be blocked (or partially blocked) by buildings, hills, and other structures. Rf signals also can be affected by foliage, as well as humidity or precipitation.

One of the most significant challenges is multipath fading. Unlike the situation in a cable environment, rf signal propagation in free space is three-dimensional. The signal will be reflected by buildings, aircraft, and any structures or surfaces that are large in relation to the signal's wavelength. The receiver will pick up not only the main signal (the *direct-path signal*) but also those which arrive on various other, longer reflected paths, as shown in Figure 12-2.[6] Because of the difference in arrival times for the various path lengths, these other signals may either add to or detract from the amplitude of the main signal. In fact, in a worst-case scenario, signals may arrive at the receiver 180 degrees out of phase and thus cancel each other completely (see Figures 12-3 and 12-4).[7]

Frequency offset also impedes proper operation of wireless broadband systems. In an ideal world, both the receiver and transmitter would be

Figure 12-2

Multipath interference occurs when a radio wave is reflected by buildings, structures, or topographic features. When this happens, the signal at the receiving point will consist not only of the direct signal (the signal that arrived on the most direct, straight-line path) but also of those which took more indirect paths.

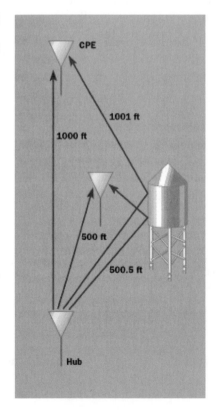

Figure 12-3
When the difference in arrival time between the direct signal and a reflected signal is a small fraction of a wavelength, the two signals will be nearly in phase with each other and thus will be mostly additive in amplitude.

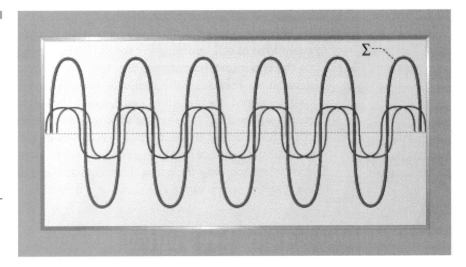

tuned to precisely the same frequency. In practice, there usually will be slight offsets between the transmitter and receiver. Crystal drift (due to temperature sensitivities, for example) can create frequency shifts, whereas crystal aging produces more long-term frequency variation.

Interference Headaches

A wide range of interference problems can occur in an rf environment. These interference issues can come from the communication system itself (known

Figure 12-4
When the difference in arrival times between the direct signal and a reflected signal is about one-half a wavelength, the two signals will be nearly out of phase with each other and thus will reduce the amplitude.

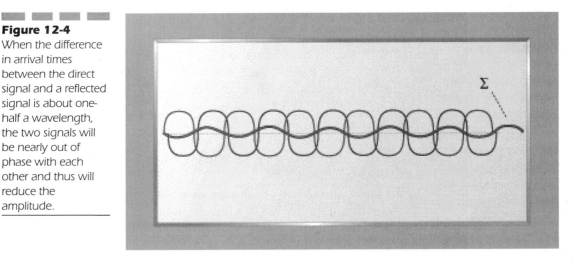

as *self-jamming*) or from other systems. One form of self-jamming occurs when the subscriber's transmissions interfere with the receiver section. Another type of self-jamming is caused by other users of the system.

Of the two interference types previously listed, interference from other systems causes the biggest headaches for today's wireless broadband systems developers. An rf system can create interference for other systems. Fortunately, the FCC offers rules to stop one system from interfering with another. Specifically, the commission requires engineers to keep the spurious emissions at 3-MHz offset of a system's transmitter to less than −60 dBc. Systems meeting these requirements are less likely to interfere with other systems operating in the same or adjacent bands.

DOCSIS Modifications

Engineers must consider the major assumptions made by cable DOCSIS with respect to the performance of the upstream and downstream channels when designing for wireless broadband systems. For downstream performance, the CNR in a CATV downstream 6-MHz channel should not be less than 35 dB, whereas the typical multipath (micro-reflections in the cable) should not be greater than 1.5 ms. The carrier frequency offset between head-end modulator and the CPE demodulator is negligible, but the receive power level at the CPE is relatively fixed (nonfading).

Upstream performance assumptions include an SNR in the cable upstream channel (including ingress noise) of greater than 25 dB and a typical multipath of less than 1.5 ms. The carrier-frequency offset is negligible, and the receive power level at the UMTS remains constant.

Wireless broadband network characteristics differ from cable deployments in some key areas. Regarding downstream performance, there is a limited SNR that is determined mainly by the transmit level, antenna gain, distance, link budget, and receiver noise figure. Narrowband and burst interference exists from other transmitters (harmonics and intermodulation of PCS, AMPS, TV, radar, and so on), as do interferences from cochannels and reused frequencies. Multipath may be higher than 5 ms. A higher carrier-frequency offset may exist between the modulators and demodulators, along with a higher dynamic range and more fading, which must be accommodated.

In the upstream portion of a design, wireless broadband designers normally encounter a limited SNR, which is mainly determined by the CPE transmit power, antenna gains, and narrowband and burst interference rates, as well as multipath values. The carrier-frequency offset between the head-end modulator and CPE demodulator ranges up to ±50 kHz. Fading receive power level at the base station may exceed 20 dB. There is a high dynamic range requirement from propagation-path losses.

The different characteristics of the wireless broadband network relative to the CATV network indicates that the existing DOCSIS standard limits large-scale wireless broadband deployment unless it is modified. Modifications are required at both the media access control (MAC) and the physical (PHY) layers.

PHY Changes

The PHY scheme should be robust enough to enable reliable operation over a wireless network. Designs need to address the SNR and multipath requirements in particular.

For the upstream channel, DOCSIS uses quadrature phase shift keying (QPSK) or 16-bit quadrature amplitude modulation (16-QAM) techniques. Either modulation scheme may be set by the system designer during equipment configuration settings. DOCSIS specifies five upstream symbol rates—160, 320, 640, 1280, and 2560 ksymbols/s. The lower symbol rates may be used to increase the robustness against multipath, since multipath has less impact on lower symbol rates than it does on higher symbol rates. The upstream frequently must be capable of power compensation.

The downstream direction also needs additional robustness. For the downstream, DOCSIS specifies 256-QAM and 64-QAM—giving high data rates but also yielding brittleness in the challenging rf environment. 256-QAM is not usable in a wireless application, and for 64-QAM, DOCSIS specifies a single symbol rate of 5.056 Msymbols/s. The system is made more tolerant with additional, more robust QAM constellations (QPSK and 16-QAM) and lower symbol rates. The addition of lower symbol rates on the downstream, together with a more powerful (~10 ms) equalizer, will provide the required multipath robustness in the downstream.

In addition to the single-carrier approach offered by QPSK or QAM, the multicarrier approach of orthogonal frequency-division multiplexing (OFDM) is another way to provide a more robust PHY. Due to its multi-carrier properties, OFDM has greater immunity to multipath interference. Another method to defeat multipath is that of antenna diversity. Incorporating this technology on the receive side of the WMTS will produce higher reliability. DOCSIS+ incorporates these features.

MAC Updates

The MAC scheme should support optimization of the upstream and downstream channels per user. It should allow for continuous monitoring of the individual CPE performance and dynamic modification of the upstream and downstream operational parameters of the CPE based on its performance.

There are several approaches to performing this dynamic modification of upstream and downstream communication parameters relative to the cable DOCSIS MAC. For dynamic modification of upstream operational parameters, the DOCSIS initialization process allows the modem to acquire an upstream channel from a list of available multiple upstream channels using a two-stage procedure.

First, in a temporary phase, the cable modem scans the upstream channel descriptor (UCD) messages that are transmitted in the downstream channel. The modem employs the first usable channel for which a UCD message was received. This upstream channel is used by the modem to complete the registration process. Next, the modem's permanent upstream channel assignment is defined in the configuration file that is downloaded to the modem.

However, following registration, the WMTS may direct the broadband DOCSIS+ wireless modem to change its upstream channel. This may be done for traffic balancing, noise avoidance, or any other reason. To accomplish this, the WMTS can use the DOCSIS upstream channel change (UCC) message procedure, which allows the modem to switch to the new channel by performing initial or station maintenance on the new channel or by using the new channel directly without performing initial or station maintenance.

The third alternative provides the fastest transition time but requires the ranging information to be known in advance. In the case of a CATV network, it can be assumed that the ranging parameters (time offset, transmit power level, and frequency offset) on the new upstream channel are quite similar to those of the previous channel. However, this is not likely to be the case in wireless broadband applications.

Finally, the MAC protocol therefore is required to support modem performance evaluation on other upstream channels in the background. Designers can accomplish this by adding a global periodic ranging procedure that will provide opportunities for the modem to perform ranging on all the available channels. The ranging parameters of the modem relative to each of the upstream channels can then be stored in the modem or in the WMTS. The WMTS will run an upstream performance table, which will be used by the WMTS to select the alternate channel for a modem if the performance on the current channel is not acceptable.

Conclusion

In order to achieve dynamic modification of downstream operational parameters, DOCSIS supports a multiple downstream channel scheme with fixed characteristics for downstream channels (such as modulation scheme) that will allow each modem to select the best available downstream channel. This may lead to a relatively high number of channels and the use of more bandwidth than is actually required.

Designers can reduce the number of channels, however, by permitting characteristics of the wireless broadband downstream channel to change to provide the best fit per modem. This will turn the DOCSIS+ downstream channel into a *bursty* channel with burst profiles similar to those used for the upstream channels.

Finally, a great deal of work has been invested in developing the DOCSIS standard for the transmission of data over CATV networks. This makes it an excellent foundation on which to build enhancements that permit use in a wireless broadband environment. The challenges that communications links face can be met by adding specific enhancements, such as extending frequency tolerance, adding more equalization, increasing the dynamic range, and supporting multiple modulation types and multiple modulation symbol rates. With these enhancements, DOCSIS has the potential to be as successful in the wireless broadband environment as it is proving to be in the wired CATV realm.

Endnotes

1. Metricom, Inc., Headquarters, 333 West Julian Street, San Jose, CA 95110, 2000.
2. Sascha Segan, "Untangling the Mobile Net," ABC News, 1399 Moffett Park Drive, Sunnyvale, CA 94089, 2000.
3. *Ibid.*
4. Eric K. Wilson and Chet Shirali, "Adapting DOCSIS for Broadband Wireless-Access Systems," *Communication Systems Design*, 525 Market St., Suite 500, San Francisco, CA 94105, October, 2000.
5. *Ibid.*
6. *Ibid.*
7. *Ibid.*

PART 3

Installing and Deploying Wireless Broadband Networks

CHAPTER 13

Deploying Wireless Broadband Satellite Networks

It is quite obvious from discussions in the preceding 12 chapters that broadband communications are no longer confined to wires. Venture capitalists are pouring money into local multipoint distribution service (LMDS). Giant communications companies are constructing the first satellite-based wireless broadband delivery systems. And point-to-point microwave systems are being built that operate at SONET speeds. This chapter is required reading if you want to know why broadband without wires is causing so much excitement and where the most profitable opportunities will arise.

In other words, this chapter will help you understand the business case for LMDS and the new satellite networks. You also will grasp how international markets for these new services differ from North American ones and which markets are ripe for penetration by wireless broadband and satellite services.

Furthermore, this chapter includes a detailed 10-year forecast of broadband satellite and wireless equipment and services of both industry giants and start-ups. You will learn how to distinguish between hype and reality and will discover who the market leaders will be in this exciting new business and what key strategies they will be following for success.

Now that you are an expert in how fixed wireless broadband communications work, here are some practical pointers on how to determine whether one of these systems is for you, which one to use, and the questions to ask your prospective vendors. Topics presented in this chapter include, but are not limited to,

- Choosing between wireless broadband and wireline
- Understanding geography and climate
- Choosing between private and carrier
- How to deploy a private connection
- How to use a wireless broadband carrier
- When to use satellites
- When to use meteor burst wireless broadband communications systems (MBCSs)
- When to use nongeostationary earth orbit satellites

Choosing Between Wireless Broadband and Wireline

In many instances, both wireless broadband and wireline alternatives will be available. Here are some guidelines for choosing which to use.

Remember Line of Sight

You must be able to see the point with which you wish to connect, whether it is your own site or a wireless broadband carrier. Depending on the technology used, effective range is from about 3 miles (5 km) to about 20 miles (30 km). Multiple hops also are an option but add complexity.

Consider Wireless Broadband if There Are No Good Wireline Options Available

Perhaps you are in a suburban area and need high-bandwidth connectivity, but no fiber runs to your building. Even if wireline options exist, the length of time to obtain wireline service may be prohibitive.

Consider Wireless Broadband if You Need to Bridge Local-Area Networks (LANs) in Two Buildings in Close Proximity

An unlicensed spread-spectrum or licensed microwave connection could be cost-effective, particularly if you have to pay $500 or more for a monthly T-1 connection. Wireless broadband equipment providers claim a typical payback of 2 years.

Consider Wireless Broadband if Crossing Wireline Service Boundaries

Wireline service might be exceptionally expensive if crossing different local exchange carrier (LEC) areas. Also, a wireless broadband connection could be cost-effective.

Consider Wireless Broadband for Temporary or Backup Connectivity

Wireless broadband might be your best option if you need a temporary connection between two nearby sites. It also might be your best option if you need a backup connection.

Compare Offerings Between Wireless Broadband and Wireline Carriers

If a wireless broadband carrier is offering service to your building, investigate its pricing, because it may be undercutting wireline providers to develop its business. Wireless broadband carriers also may have greater flexibility in their offerings, such as the ability to easily increase bandwidth on demand.

Understanding Geography and Climate

With most data communications you do not care if there is a hill between you and another location or whether it is sunny or raining. But with wireless broadband communications, you must consider both geography and climate. This applies both to private and carrier systems. First, the geography.

We have already emphasized line of sight. But what does this mean exactly? It means that the two antennas must be clearly visible to each other. So beware of items like foliage or future construction. If your sites are separated by miles, how can you even tell if you have line of sight? There are companies that specialize in wireless broadband integration that will be able to assist you with a site survey. Software packages that characterize the terrain of particular areas also may be helpful. Low-technology approaches, such as flashing a mirror, also work. The advantage of a carrier service is that the carrier does all this work as part of the deployment.

Weather should not be a factor for the unlicensed 2.4- and 5.8-GHz bands. However, it is a factor in the millimeter-wave bands of 28 GHz and higher. A 3-mile (5-km) link operating at 38 GHz in heavy rainfall of 1 inch per hour will suffer a degradation of 1000 times the received signal strength. Carriers design margin into their links to account for weather, but you should review their design parameters and ask what link reliability to expect over the course of a year.

Choosing Between Private and Carrier

This is relatively simple. If you need to interconnect your own sites and have line of sight, consider a private wireless broadband connection. If you want Internet or telephony services, consider a carrier solution. However, there are other topologies as well. For instance, the wireless broadband carrier might offer a cost-effective wireless broadband Internet connection to your site *A*. If your site *B* has an Internet connection, you could then consider a VPN (virtual private network) connection between the two sites. Another option is where the wireless broadband carrier provides coverage to both your sites. You could obtain a private virtual circuit between your two sites that never leaves the carrier's backbone network. Think of this as a public Frame Relay or Asynchronous Transfer Mode (ATM) network that happens to use wireless broadband links in its infrastructure. The bottom line is that you will need to research all the options available, including whether wireless broadband carrier service is even available. Service options are limited today but will be expanding rapidly over the next 2 years.

How to Deploy a Private Connection

If you have determined that a private fixed wireless broadband system addresses your communications requirements, there are a number of decisions you will need to make. One important decision is whether to use licensed or unlicensed bands. Table 13-1 summarizes the principal characteristics of each.[1]

You can think of microwave systems as offering higher performance with a lower potential for interference but costing more and being slightly more difficult to install.

In choosing a private link, you should have determined that you have line of sight. But you also will need to check vendors' specifications for tradeoffs between distance and throughput. For example, a spread-spectrum product might offer 4 Mbps at distances to 10 miles (16 km) but only 2 Mbps at 25 miles (40 km).

You also must decide where to mount your antennas and what type of antennas to use. Many types of antennas are available. At shorter distances of 1 mile (1.6 km) or less, when using spread spectrum, you may be able to use a patch antenna that mounts on the inside of a window (Figure 13-1). At even smaller distances of 100 m, you could use an omnidirectional antenna. For longer distances to 20 miles (30 km), you will need an antenna that needs to be aimed carefully, usually on a roof or suitable tower. Some products, for example, have a light-emitting diode (LED) that lights when the antenna is aligned correctly. Check with your vendor for its antenna options and installation procedures. In all

TABLE 13-1

Principal
Characteristics of
Unlicensed Spread
Spectrum and
Licensed
Microwave

	Unlicensed Spread Spectrum	Licensed Microwave
Ease of deployment	Simpler	More difficult
	No licensing required	License required
	Simpler antennas for shorter distances	Frequency coordination sometimes required
	End-user installable in many instances	Generally need services of integrator
Performance	1–11 Mbps Error rates match wireline	1–10 Mbps typical but higher rates to OC-3 (155 Mbps) available Greater flexibility for increasing throughputs Error rates match wireline
Interference	Potential for interference because bands are unlicensed, allowing multiple simultaneous users	Potential for interference very low
Costs	Equipment costs comparable to microwave, but installation costs can be lower	Slightly higher due to higher installation costs
Number of vendors	Greater Many wireless LAN companies offer bridge products	Fewer
Security	Spread-spectrum signal harder to eavesdrop, but proper security still requires encryption of the data	Easier to eavesdrop

cases, the antennas you will be working with will be compact, generally about a half meter in diameter or smaller.

Do not choose a wireless solution based just on distance and throughput. Make sure it provides the data interfaces you need, supports the protocols you need, and supplies suitable network management functions.

Various value-added resellers and systems integrators specialize in wireless broadband communications. Some of these offer both licensed and unlicensed products. They can help you choose which technology to use, obtain licenses, determine how to factor in local climate conditions, conduct site surveys, and install your equipment.

Figure 13-1
Proxim directional spread-spectrum antenna.

How to Use a Wireless Broadband Carrier

Using a wireless broadband carrier is easy. You may not even know that the carrier is using a wireless infrastructure. In many instances, the carrier will provide comparable services to a competitive local exchange carrier (CLEC) or an Internet service provider (ISP). Or their services might be resold by existing LECs, CLECs, or ISPs. Nevertheless, there are a number of questions worth asking if you are considering wireless broadband services:

1. What carriers are available? Since wireless broadband carriers are only now deploying service, you may not even be aware that a wireless carrier is offering service to your building or area.

2. Where does the carrier have licenses, and what is its deployment plan? Carriers only hold licenses on a regional basis. And most are deploying their networks building by building. Find out also what kind of license the carrier has. Is the carrier operating on the basis of a license waiver, and if so, what are the terms of that waiver?

3. Is the deployment on a network basis or customer basis? Some carriers have a rigid deployment plan. Others will respond to individual customer demand.

4. What value-added services does the carrier offer? Some carriers will be telephony-centric. Others are Internet-centric with Web hosting, mailbox services, network management, and so forth.

5. What interfaces, protocols, data rates, and error rates does the carrier support? Because wireless broadband services have an inherent upper end in throughput owing to the width of radio channels, find out what options exist for increasing your throughput.

6. What reliability does the carrier guarantee? Because wireless broadband signals at 28 and 38 GHz are affected by weather, ask to see an analysis of reliability that takes regional weather patterns into account.

7. What networks does the carrier interconnect with? If it connects to the Internet, who is its backbone provider? Does the carrier interconnect with existing frame networks?[2]

Thus the wireless carrier will provide services that look very much like wireline services, and the wireless broadband portion of its infrastructure should be mostly invisible to you. Nevertheless, obtaining answers to the preceding questions could head off potential difficulties.

When to Use Satellites

A number of satellite systems are available today for wireless broadband communications to 155 Mbps. Today these all involve geosynchronous satellites, but soon low earth orbit (LEO) systems also will be available, as shown in Figure 13-2.[3] Satellites today are not usually competitive when good land-line communications options exist. Rather, they make the most sense in the following types of situations:

- There are no good terrestrial options. This is especially true in developing nations or out at sea.

- You are deploying a mesh network of more than five or six nodes that spans a large geographic area (multiple countries).

- You are broadcasting data to a large number of locations.[4]

When to Use Meteor Burst Wireless Broadband Communications Systems (MBWBCSs)

With respect to deploying wireless broadband satellite networks, a meteor burst wireless broadband communications system (MBWBCS) uses ionized meteor trails as a means of radio signal propagation. Billions of ionized meteor trails are produced daily in the region of the earth's atmosphere from 80 to 120 km above the surface. These trails dif-

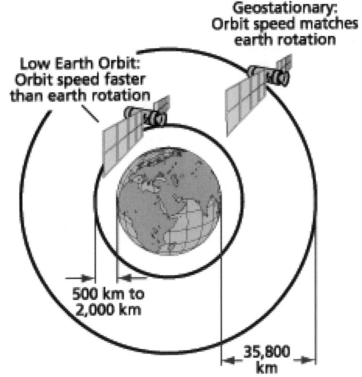

Figure 13-2
Geosynchronous
versus low earth
orbit satellites.

Low Earth Orbit:
Orbit speed faster
than earth rotation

Geostationary:
Orbit speed matches
earth rotation

500 km to
2,000 km

35,800
km

For any orbit, there is a speed where centrifugal
force matches gravitational force.

fuse rapidly and usually disappear within a few seconds. However, during their existence, they reflect VHF (very high frequency) radio waves and provide a reliable communications channel.

Cost-Benefit Analysis, Especially with Reference to Competing Technologies

Conventional telephone systems are currently circuit switched and designed for voice traffic. It is a very expensive way to send telex- or email-type data because a great deal of infrastructure is required. The current system does not serve a number of areas in third world countries, and the service may not be adequate for data communications. The cost of building the infrastructure may not support the level of use. In a common carrier data system using meteor burst technology, the cost of the central infrastructure is borne by the entire network rather than a single user, as in a dedicated system.

Conventional high-frequency (HF) communications reflect radio signals off the ionosphere and as such require a number of frequency allocations to adapt to the rapidly changing propagation conditions. The requirement of a number of frequencies in an already very crowded band makes the problem of network control and management very difficult, especially as the number of nodes moves into the thousands. HF is also very susceptible to both atmospheric noise due to lightning and artificial noise due to ignition and electrical power systems. In addition, due to the relatively large area on the ground that is illuminated, networks generally are limited to at most several hundred units. The greater the density of users, the lower is the cost, because the infrastructure cost is divided by the number of users. Since the network density is limited, the cost per user typically is high. For these reasons, HF is not an optimal technique.

Specialized microwave radio (900 MHz and above) propagates well over short ranges and can provide high-quality service over a limited area such as along a major highway route or in an urban area, but there is no mechanism that will provide the extended regional coverage required to cover remote areas. In remote areas, it is often not cost-effective to set up an extensive network of repeaters required to provide coverage. However, given the population density in third world countries away from major urban areas, there is room for low-cost technology to fill the gap in a conventional cellular system. Cellular telephony is a very expensive way to deliver packet data. The cost per message for cellular versus the common carrier network is close to an order of magnitude in difference.

Geosynchronous satellite communications systems are capable of providing coverage and a high quality of service, but the equipment is very expensive. Looking down the road, mobile LEO satellites will open up new possibilities, but this technology is still a few years away to prove itself for low-cost remote area communications. Meteor scatter technology costs approximately 1/5 to 1/20 that of satellite systems, and since meteors are in essence free natural satellites, the long-term life-cycle cost savings actually increase. Since meteor scatter operates in the low VHF band, the cost of the remote station radio system is approximately 1/2 to 1/5 that of satellite systems. Thus both the cost of the equipment and the operating costs of meteor scatter networks are significantly less than that of satellite-based systems for packet data applications.

Meteor scatter/extended-range VHF uses a combination of propagation mechanisms to provide seamless wide-area coverage with a minimum number of base stations. Because there are fewer base stations, the cost of the infrastructure is much less than that of conventional microwave cellular (both data and voice) systems. Meteor scatter has a unique property: The ground illumination footprint of individual meteor trails is very small. This provides an inherent spatial multiplexing in a large network that reduces the likelihood of message collisions. Thus meteor scatter networks can support a much larger number of users per base station, further reducing the total system cost. A network can be designed to provide multiple overlapping coverage of each remote station to enhance the robustness of the network to single-point failure. In total, a high grade of packet data service at less than 1/2 to 1/8 the cost of comparable satellite systems is possible with meteor scatter technology.

Advantages and Disadvantages

The use of meteor scatter for communicating data to both mobile and fixed users provides a number of significant advantages over other technologies for third world countries to fill a number of gaps in the conventional telecommunication system, such as:

- Performance
- Reliability
- Cost
- Frequency utilization
- Capacity
- Redundancy
- Maintainability
- Full coverage
- Terminals hardened against earthquakes and floods
- Hardened against electromagnetic pulse

Meteor scatter technology is proven and has been deployed in dozens of military and commercial remote communication systems worldwide. The conversion of this former military technology for low-cost packet data communication is natural.

Expected Deployment Profile

Base stations are designed to run autonomously or with minimal supervision. They consist of base station transmitter, receiver, computer, backup power units, and equipment to connect the output to an existing commercial data network. Antennas at the base stations can include sophisticated multiple-receiver/multiple-beam phased-array technology. Phased-array technology provides high performance at the least cost. Base station signal processing is more complicated than remote station signalling to make up for the lower transmitter power and reduced antenna gains. Typical base stations use 500- to 10,000-W transmitters depending on the system design and area of coverage.

Base stations include high-performance microcomputers to receive, route, and piece together messages. If the message is for a unit within the coverage area of the given base station, then it will be routed to the user; otherwise, the message is sent to a data center for routing to the appropriate base station and then to the user. The base stations can be connected to the data center via the telephone system, meteor scatter, or satellite link depending on the availability.

The data center consists of a computer system and radio/telephone interface circuitry for routing messages, monitoring system status, billing, and controlling the operation of the network. At the data center, messages can be routed over the network to the user or via one of many existing commercial packet data services, such as connections to Internet and other international services allowing a user to communicate with the world. Backup power systems allow the network to continue to operate through emergency conditions when commercial power is unavailable.

For example, India is a large country with many remote areas without any conventional telecommunications infrastructure. Since complete voice telephony coverage may not be possible for some time, there is a need to provide data messaging and electronic mail services to even the most remote villages and outposts. The key issue is to design and install a low-cost VHF packet data network designed to provide telex and electronic mail (email) types of service to remote areas not currently serviced by the public telephone network at a significantly lower cost than competing technologies. Each base station utilizes extended line-of-sight techniques to cover the 0- to 150-km range. Meteor burst techniques are used to cover the 150- to 2000-km range, although they provide the best performance from 400 to 1400 km. The system also can be used to monitor the position of mobile platforms or to provide messaging to mobile platforms. The system is hardened against earthquakes, floods, and other natural disasters and can be used to provide emergency communications when the conventional telecommunications system is not available.

By networking groups of base stations, complete national or regional coverage with a minimum infrastructure is possible. The coverage area of a single base station is much greater than that of conventional VHF or microwave radio systems that would require a large number of expensive base stations to cover the same area. This technique can rapidly and inexpensively provide advanced packet data communications to remote areas of India that currently do not have access to these services. The network can be implemented in stages, providing increasing coverage and quality of service.

As with other common carrier systems such as in Canada, Alaska, Italy, or the United States, the deployment of base stations can proceed in phases to match increasing user density and performance requirements. A first system could consist of four base stations providing nonredundant baseline coverage to the entire country. Operating in the telex/email mode, message throughputs would be on the order of 30 to 120 words per minute, and for telemetry collection, the waiting time with 90 percent confidence would be better than 15 minutes. The time required to send a 1000-character message would be on the order of 5 to 15 minutes depending on a number of factors. This network with four base stations would be capable of supporting up to 10,000 to 15,000 users without significant contention within the network. In the second phase, system capacity could be increased with augmentation of the number of base stations and provide both increased performance and redundant service to users.

New Services that Can Be Introduced

Depending on the application, the equipment configuration and the performance will vary. Applications can vary and typically include telex/electronic mail delivery, position monitoring and remote sensor monitoring, and control, among others.

For use in gathering remote sensing data, the equipment configuration is similar with several exceptions. A very low power communications unit is used, and the entire station is powered by solar cell–charged batteries. Data are relayed from the telemetry unit to a base station and then from the base station to a data center, where it is routed to the user's data collection facility for processing. The base station architecture is very flexible and can be designed to support different service classes ranging from telemetry to electronic mail.

When to Use Nongeostationary Earth Orbit Satellites

An opportunity has been opened up for meeting the new and latent communications needs using nongeostationary satellite systems. An attempt is made to describe the scenario that is evolving and the need for an early initiative to harness this technology.

Conventional geosynchronous earth orbit satellites (GEOs) orbit the earth 35,680 km above the equator, taking exactly 24 hours to complete one orbit—thereby holding themselves steady above a fixed spot. A constellation of three GEOs could provide coverage to the entire planet (due to which one of the popular uses is for broadcasting video programs). However, the inherent 0.25-ms signal delay each way, plus further delay involved in the ground-based switching, makes GEO use for mobile telecommunications awkward. In-orbit life is now tending toward 15 years, and recent Proton launches give some GEOs a theoretical life approaching 25 years.

The orbit of medium earth orbit satellites (MEOs) is significantly closer to earth than a GEO satellite at 2500 to 10,000 km. Although this reduces signal delays, it also means that a MEO's signal area is smaller than that of a GEO. In other words, more MEOs are needed to cover the same area as a GEO. However, due to the satellite's proximity to earth, MEOs life expectancies are on the order of 6 to 12 years. Thus a MEO-based system requires more launches to maintain a system than a GEO-based one, and users must redirect antennas as satellites enter and leave the orbit. Furthermore, complex tracking and coordination are needed.

There are three generally accepted categories of Low Earth Orbit Satellites (LEOs):

- Little LEOs
- Big LEOs
- Broadband or super-LEOs

LEOs operate 600 to 2500 km above the earth, and consequently, there are negligible transmission delays between end users and satellites. The advantage of LEO technology is that power requirements are relatively low, meaning that small, handheld cellular-type units can transmit signals to and from LEOs. LEOs also present a valuable savings to the satellite builder. Cell size on earth is determined by the size of the satellite antenna and the orbital height. The higher the altitude, the larger is the antenna needed to achieve the same cell size. And the antenna size can be about 3 percent of the GEOs.

Finally, satellite battery life also plays a major part in LEO, MEO, and GEO mission planning. The Globalstar LEOs orbit in about 100 minutes—requiring a consequent 5000 charge/discharge cycles each year for the onboard batteries. In GEO orbit, the batteries could be expected to easily last around 15 years, but this drops markedly in low earth orbit, with life expectations of only about 8 years.

Cost-Benefit Analysis, Especially with Reference to Competing Technologies

The market potential for mobile satellite services, both voice and data, is enormous. The lower the prices and the more accessible the equipment, the larger is the market.

However, one contender, GE Starsys, had already dropped from the race because the company did not meet internal deadlines of establishing global partners. This dropping out brings out the immense challenges. Although there may be enough room in the market for everybody, not everybody is going to get to market.

Expected Deployment Profile

The number of satellites in orbit is 1209, as estimated by the International Telecommunications Union (ITU) on September 2000, of which 1142 are in geostationary orbit and 67 in nongeostationary orbit. Another 762 GSO and 56 non-GSO satellites have been projected but are still to be brought into service.

Market predictions for the satellite industry are quite optimistic, and the investment per annum is expected to grow to US$79 billion by the year 2003. Tables 13-2, 13-3, and 13-4 give the breakdown of market growth as segregated on the basis of technology and regions.[5]

The perusal of these tables shows some trends—some of which are a cause of concern. For example:

- North America is taking the maximum initiative—perhaps they know something that the rest of the world does not know. The future lies in satellites.

TABLE 13-2

Geostationary
Orbit (GEO)

Region	2001	2002	2003	2004	2005	2006	2007	2008	2009	2010	Total
Africa/ Middle East	3	1	2	0	0	0	6	9	9	9	39
Asia Pacific	5	5	5	4	5	7	21	17	14	14	97
International	3	4	4	0	0	0	12	6	7	6	42
Latin America	2	0	1	0	1	2	7	8	8	7	36
North America	5	8	5	2	4	3	14	19	21	19	100
South Asia	2	1	2	2	1	0	7	6	8	7	36
Western Europe	7	5	3	1	2	3	14	12	12	10	69
TOTAL	27	24	22	9	13	15	81	77	79	72	419

- LEOs are likely to dominate in the future.
- The numbers of international LEOs and MEOs are going to be limited—thus disproving the often-held belief that these systems are for international operation only.

Nevertheless, the most disturbing part is that third world countries are yet to initiate a thrust in this area.

TABLE 13-3

Medium Earth
Orbit (MEO)

Region	2001	2002	2003	2004	2005	2006	2007	2008	2009	2010	Total
Africa/ Middle East	0	0	0	0	0	0	4	4	4	4	16
Asia Pacific	0	0	0	0	0	0	5	4	4	4	17
International	0	0	0	0	0	0	4	7	9	9	29
Latin America	0	0	0	0	0	0	4	4	4	4	16
North America	5	5	6	4	3	3	7	9	12	18	72
South Asia	0	0	0	0	0	0	4	4	4	4	16
Western Europe	0	0	0	0	1	0	5	4	4	4	18
TOTAL	5	5	6	4	4	3	33	36	51	47	184

TABLE 13-4

Low Earth Orbit
(LEO)

Region	2001	2002	2003	2004	2005	2006	2007	2008	2009	2010	Total
Africa/ Middle East	1	1	0	0	0	0	5	4	9	4	24
Asia Pacific	18	20	16	9	14	14	8	10	7	21	137
International	0	0	0	0	0	0	6	5	6	4	21
Latin America	9	0	2	0	0	0	8	5	13	10	47
North America	17	14	12	11	11	51	139	80	47	52	434
South Asia	3	1	2	1	1	0	6	5	5	8	32
Western Europe	38	42	15	12	2	5	8	8	8	6	144
TOTAL	86	78	47	33	28	70	180	117	95	105	839

Conclusion

The availability of the radio spectrum for the nongeostationary satellite system is limited, and a later entrant would not get a chance to start this service. In the mid-seventies, India was one of the few countries in the world besides Canada and Indonesia who initiated the action for setting up a geostationary satellite system. A similar opportunity has now been presented, and immediate action is called for.

Endnotes

1. Peter Rysavy, "Wireless Broadband and Other Fixed-Wireless Systems," CMP Headquarters, CMP Media Inc., 600 Community Drive. Manhasset, NY 11030, 2000.
2. *Ibid.*
3. *Ibid.*
4. *Ibid.*
5. Khurshid Lal Bhavan, Telecommunication Engineering Centre, Department of Telecommunications, Government of India, Janpath, New Delhi 110001, India, 2000.

CHAPTER 14

Implementing Terrestrial Fixed Wireless Broadband Networks

Implementing terrestrial fixed wireless broadband networks is now one of many options for small and midsized companies to help ease the communications process and lower the costs of networking. This chapter offers a brief but comprehensive look at the implementation of terrestrial fixed wireless broadband technologies. With the first local multipoint distribution service (LMDS) auction completed, license winners now are faced with the challenge of implementing and building out their systems. What strategy is best? Should your business plan exploit the full potential of the spectrum and offer voice, data, and video? Or would a gradual ramp-up of services be better? This chapter also examines the implementation of enterprise terrestrial fixed wireless broadband technology, services, and equipment.

This chapter also will answer the important questions facing the terrestrial fixed wireless broadband industry, including

- What can be learned from terrestrial fixed wireless broadband service providers such as WinStar, CellularVision, Teligent, and Teleport?

- What is the likely response from digital subscriber line (DSL), cable, Internet, and phone service providers?

Furthermore, this chapter offers an indepth look at the competition and the likely response to a new DSL operator. The chapter also examines the enormous potential for DSL licensees. The chapter offers an indepth look at the quality of services DSL can provide and probes the anticipated competition from existing local exchange carriers (LECs), cable television operators, and Internet service providers (ISPs). The chapter also examines the DSL equipment market and forecasts the market for equipment providers.

Implementing Fixed Terrestrial Enterprise Wireless Broadband Networks

Fixed terrestrial enterprise wireless broadband networks computing to date primarily has been a revolution for the consumer market. Hampered by a slow roll-out (likely an effort by providers to keep their ROI alive on heavily invested business products such as T-1 and ISDN), wireless broadband's potential impact on the business sector is finally being felt.

Less costly than leased lines and traditional data circuits, fixed terrestrial enterprise wireless broadband networks provide a new opportunity to efficiently extend networking resources through high-speed, low-cost wide-area network (WAN) options. With fractional T-1 lines starting at nearly $1000 per month, fixed terrestrial enterprise wireless broadband networks offer companies a means to reduce budgetary constraints with regard to Internet connectivity and at the same time provide improved speed and cost savings over ISDN.

On the downside, fixed terrestrial enterprise wireless broadband networks are still hampered by enterprise-level quality-of-service (QoS) concerns. Furthermore, Internet Protocol (IP) capacity restrictions on many fixed terrestrial enterprise wireless broadband network solutions make implementing more than 150 seats a costly proposition. In such instances, T-1 typically would offer a more cost-effective solution; broadband is best suited to small and midsized companies.

Because the inward-facing network topology for broadband will not differ notably from traditional connectivity pipes, the bulk of your effort toward implementing a broadband solution will be spent assessing availability and choosing the solution that fits your company's needs. For example, the following step-by-step procedure should be used when implementing fixed terrestrial enterprise wireless broadband networks:

1. Assess service availability in your area.

2. Select a service and provider and attempt to negotiate QoS baselines.

3. Expect to wait 1 month for installation.

4. Add router and firewall to maximize security.

5. Enjoy cost savings and speedy workgroup connectivity.[1]

DSL versus Cable

The first step in implementing fixed terrestrial wireless broadband networks in the enterprise involves spending some time investigating the suppliers and specific services available in your area (see the sidebar, "Terrestrial Fixed Service Loses Current Coprimary Status"). Availability of services is still sketchy in many regions.

Terrestrial Fixed Service Loses Current Coprimary Status

The Federal Communications Commission (FCC) recently issued an order in connection with the pending Notice of Proposed Rule Making (NPRM) proposing to redesignate the 17.7- to 19.7-GHz band among the various services that are allocated spectrum in that band (the 18-GHz Proceeding). Recall that in September 1998, the FCC proposed to provide primary designations for terrestrial fixed service use in the 17.7- to 18.3-GHz band, geostationary orbit fixed satellite service (GSO/FSS) use in the 18.3- to 18.55-GHz band, and nongeostationary orbit fixed satellite service (NGSO/FSS) use in the 18.8- to 19.3-GHz band. Coprimary designations would be retained for terrestrial fixed service use and GSO/FSS use in the 18.55- to 18.8-GHz band and terrestrial fixed service use and mobile satellite service feeder link use in the 19.3- to 19.7-GHz band.

Under this proposal, the terrestrial fixed service will lose its current coprimary status in the 18.3- to 18.55- and 18.8- to 19.3-GHz bands. The service will be reduced to a secondary service in those bands. This, of course, divides up the 18-GHz band (18,142 to 18,580) used by private cable operators for the distribution of video entertainment material to customers. Grant of the proposal will significantly affect the continued availability of the band for such use.

In its NPRM, the FCC proposed to grandfather terrestrial fixed service operations that were licensed or for which applications were pending as of September 18, 1998, the NPRM's release date. The FCC has now extended that date. Under the recently released order, the cutoff date for private cable operator applications in the 18.3- to 18.55-GHz band to be coprimary with future FSS operations in that band will be the release date of the report and order in the 18-GHz Proceeding.

Private cable operator applications for new authorizations in the 18.3- to 18.55-GHz band must provide sufficient documentation of plans for immediate implementation of the proposed facility, including, but not limited to, binding contracts for new equipment, binding contracts for new private cable operator services, and other documents the FCC may require to demonstrate a firm commitment to new and expanded video service. Applicants failing to provide such information will not qualify for coprimary status.[2]

Your ability to choose DSL service may be hampered by the proximity of your location to the central office of your telecommunications provider. With signal degradation proportional to the distance from the central office, your company's geographic location might limit service quality.

Specific distance requirements vary both by provider and by the version of DSL being implemented. Asymmetrical and symmetrical DSL (ADSL and SDSL) impose distance caps of 20,000 ft from the central office. Although effective data speeds can reach close to 7 Mbps at less than 10,000 ft, users will likely find speeds running closer to 1.5 Mbps and 512 kbps for ADSL and SDSL, respectively, as you move out into the service perimeter.

Cable, as an alternative, does not suffer from the same proximity pitfalls as DSL. Several modulation schemes for cable are available, providing downstream (from server to client) data rates of either 10 or 32 Mbps. Although 10 Mbps is currently most prevalent in the marketplace, cable still offers considerable speed benefits over DSL. But the problem with cable is that it does not currently run to most offices.

You likely will find that the hardest part of implementation is choosing a service provider. Pricing between options is fairly comparable from market to market throughout the country. Most have a variety of plans available, upload and download bandwidth options, and dedicated IP capacity limits that vary from vendor to vendor. Be certain your plan will accommodate your bandwidth and IP requirements.

When choosing a provider, base your decision on such criteria as backbone and infrastructure stability, number of static IP addresses provided, and price. It has been found that the initial experience with the provider often can be a good indicator of future service expectations.

Once you have made your decision on which platform to implement, be prepared to play the waiting game. If you have implemented a T-1 previously, you know the multistep process involved; now you are adding a DSL provider into the mix along with your ISP and local telecommunications company to bring the project to fruition.

Because many DSL providers do not act directly as ISPs, you also might have to choose from a selection of partnered ISPs. The ISP will then go back to the DSL provider and have it configure the local loop with your telecommunications company. In total, you can expect the process to take the better part of a month from the time of your initial order to completion, but it is otherwise a fairly effortless process.

Most providers' pricing includes the modem/router that sits between your in-house router/firewall and the provider's head-end router, as shown in Figure 14-1.[3] It is best not to replace this equipment. Although most of the

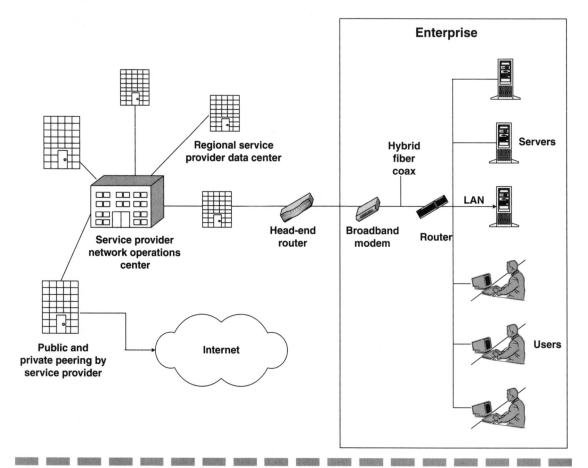

Figure 14-1 Anatomy of a fixed terrestrial enterprise wireless broadband network. Fixed terrestrial enterprise wireless broadband network solutions have matured to provide good availability and easy installation for small to midsized businesses.

equipment is standards-based, actual implementations can vary just enough between vendors to make updating equipment a frustrating endeavor.

Routing for Security

The final step after installation is configuring the router/firewall. This is comparable with any network installation. Your router should be capable of providing a 10-Mbps connection to the WAN side (to the cable/DSL modem) and a higher data rate internally (100 Mbps or higher). Many broadband-ready routers are fairly inexpensive and include features such as IP addressing with the Dynamic Host Configuration Protocol (DHCP) enabled and are fully capable of handling a sufficient number of IP addresses to manage the class C network running behind them. Most offer additional benefits such as user authentication and static port routing of services.

The setup and configuration of the WAN and local-area network (LAN) topology typically involve a Web-based utility, most of which supply graphic interfaces that will have you running with minimal effort. Security on broadband should be treated like any open door into your network. Preventing a breach will entail implementing the usual firewall and encryption standards.

Conclusion

Although QoS typically is seen as better on nonshared, business-grade DSL lines, few vendors currently deliver enterprise-level QoS guarantees. Although there have been improvements as services continue to mature, service quality remains a concern to enterprise availability when simple oversubscription on a DSL access multiplexer (DSLAM) can so easily affect performance.

You also might want to consider a service-level agreement (SLA). This is an option still rare for cable providers, as well as negotiate in advance a structure for refunds for issues of nonperformance and support.

Easy to install and quick to configure, fixed terrestrial wireless broadband networks skirt the hurdles in place for fat-pipe implementation. Although perhaps still a bit green for enterprise-level, mission-critical reliability, fixed terrestrial wireless broadband networks offer small and midsized companies a chance to save some money on Internet connectivity today.

Endnotes

1. James R. Borck, "Implementing Enterprise Broadband Is an Art," InfoWorld Media Group, Inc., 155 Bovet Road, San Mateo, CA 94402, 2000.
2. Howard Barr, "Proposed Redesignation of the 18-GHz Band," Pepper & Corazzini, L.L.P., 1776 K Street, N.W., Suite 200, Washington, D.C. 20006, 2000.
3. James R. Borck, "Implementing Enterprise Broadband Is an Art," InfoWorld Media Group, Inc., 155 Bovet Road, San Mateo, CA 94402, 2000.

CHAPTER 15

Implementing Broadband Wireless and Satellite Applications

Now that everyone is getting cable modems and digital subscriber line (DSL) service at home, no one wants to go to work. Implementing a wireless broadband satellite connection makes everything related to the Internet faster: surfing the Web, receiving large email attachments, downloading digital media files, and connecting to corporate resources via a virtual private network (VPN). With 3-Mbps cable modems and 6-Mbps DSL circuits, residential users (once the bottom feeders in the telecommunications food chain) have more juice than they get from their desktops at the office. The home bandwidth revolution is reshaping the modern workplace.

The burgeoning remote workforce is often cited as the key impact of residential implementation of wireless broadband satellite applications (data, voice, and video) in business. But it is not the only or even the most dramatic effect of home high-speed Internet access. The explosive growth of wireless broadband satellite users will exact a tremendous burden on Internet businesses. If you do business via the Web, you need to rethink your strategies with implementing wireless broadband satellite applications in mind.

Home Is Where the Circuit Is

Despite the hype of implementing residential wireless broadband satellite applications, only a few million homes (most of them in the suburbs of large cities) have access to them. However, like telephone service, residential wireless broadband satellite application access is on the verge of becoming a right.

How will homes not presently equipped for high-speed data services get wired? Some phone companies are going crazy over residential DSL expansion. SBC, the parent company of "baby bell" behemoths Pacific Bell and Southwestern Bell, is rapidly deploying remote DSL terminals in lucrative neighborhoods. Under SBC's Project Pronto, millions of homes in places such as Stillwater, OK, and Tomball, TX, which have been denied DSL because of distance or line-quality problems, suddenly will qualify for service.

SBC's Project Pronto is mirrored by other efforts to extend wireless broadband's reach. Verizon has purchased Northpoint Communications, a leading provider of symmetrical DSL (SDSL) service over wires leased from local phone companies. Sprint has a competing DSL service called ION and is also selling high-speed wireless broadband in Phoenix, Detroit, and San Francisco. AT&T Digital Wireless Broadband, another wireless contender, has completed its Texas trial and is being sold commercially (see the sidebars, "AT&T's Project Angel Wireless Broadband Data, Voice, and Video Goes Live in Texas" and "The Business and Technological Case for AT&T's Digital Wireless Broadband"). Smaller point-to-multipoint microwave carriers are popping up all over the country, taking advantage of the Federal Communications Commission's (FCC's) deregulation of low-power data transmission.

AT&T's Project Angel Wireless Broadband Data, Voice, and Video Goes Live in Texas

The vast majority of American homes lack access to DSL or cable modem data services. Except for those few million users lucky enough to live within narrow DSL/cable coverage areas, the dialup modem remains the best (and sometimes only) way to access the Internet. Users stuck in these telecom ghettos are shut out of tele-commuting, Web-based learning, and other opportunities available to those with wireless broadband connections.

In early 2000, AT&T unveiled its residential fixed wireless data service, AT&T digital wireless broadband. In development for several years as Project Angel, AT&T rolled out its initial commercial offering in the Dallas/Fort Worth region of Texas, the same area where AT&T conducted its pilot program. AT&T set up shop in Texas and tested its service for several weeks. AT&T rated its service *good* based on the comparable speed, reliability, and cost that DSL and cable modem subscribers currently enjoy.

AT&T digital wireless broadband's ingenious design places minimal strain on the remote computer user, and the service is priced competitively considering that the $61 monthly bill includes one voice line. Its performance places AT&T digital wireless broadband between ISDN and consumer satellite data services, both of which are more costly. Once AT&T increases its wireless broadband performance and pays attention to users' support needs, digital wireless broadband may be welcomed at even home work sites where DSL or cable is available. Until then, AT&T digital wireless broadband is best reserved for those remote workers who currently cannot do better than dialup.

AT&T also markets digital wireless broadband as a replacement for local phone service. To this end, AT&T connects its users to local 911 dispatchers and sells typical telephone services such as call waiting, three-way conferencing, caller ID, and voice mail. But the poor quality of AT&T's wireless broadband voice service makes it impractical. The wireless broadband voice channels will not carry fax or modem traffic reliably, and they cannot be used with most alarm system monitoring services. Still, at $25.95 for the first line and $7 for each additional line (up to four total), and, with an in-state and out-of-state long-distance flat rate of 7 cents a minute, it is very competitive for those home workers who need one or more extra voice lines.

A call to AT&T's digital wireless broadband sales office results in a quick appointment for installation. The order taker minces no words about service requirements: a PC running Windows 95 or 98, no existing LAN, access to the garage, and ownership of the home where the service will be installed. AT&T assembled a sacrificial Windows 98 PC for the installation, taking care not to install any Windows networking software.

AT&T's installation took several hours and a team of four people. AT&T permanently installs four major components: a receiver unit (RU), a telephone junction box, a power supply with battery backup, and a PCI network adapter. The RU is a flat, square antenna (Figure 15-1), about 1 ft^2, which installers bolt to the side of the house.[1] A swivel mount allows installers to point the RU at the nearest tower. In AT&T's case, the local tower is clearly visible from the side of the house, and the distance is less than one block. Line of sight between the RU and the tower is not required.

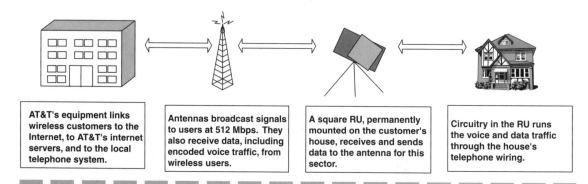

AT&T's equipment links wireless customers to the Internet, to AT&T's internet servers, and to the local telephone system.

Antennas broadcast signals to users at 512 Mbps. They also receive data, including encoded voice traffic, from wireless users.

A square RU, permanently mounted on the customer's house, receives and sends data to the antenna for this sector.

Circuitry in the RU runs the voice and data traffic through the house's telephone wiring.

Figure 15-1   *Getting connected means no more dialup. AT&T technicians quickly and efficiently come to users' homes to install its digital wireless broadband services. Once the cables are in place and the computer is configured, a user is ready for an Internet connection that is better than dialup.*

The RU's housing contains all the rf (radiofrequency), telephone, and networking electronics needed to access AT&T's voice, data, and video services. AT&T uses the 1.9-GHz band to send and receive data, voice, and video signals. The backup battery ensures that the wireless broadband voice service will remain available during power failures. The battery does not protect the Internet service, but you can install your own uninterruptible power supply (UPS) to keep surfing after the lights go out.

The effort expended by the AT&T installation crew (who were all impeccably professional) was astounding considering that there was no installation fee and no term of commitment. AT&T's installation involved drilling holes through heavy brick, and by the time the crew departed, all the cables were neatly tacked down and the holes were plugged with silicone.

Home Networking AT&T digital wireless broadband brings the data and voice service into the home using an ordinary telephone jack. If you replace your local phone service with AT&T, the installers connect the RU to your home's existing telephone wiring. The voice service works with ordinary telephones, answering machines, and caller ID equipment.

The data signal rides along with voice and video traffic, using the Home Phoneline Networking Alliance (HomePNA) standard. AT&T's equipment operates at 1 Mbps. Newer HomePNA network adapters run at 10 Mbps, but they lower their speed to communicate with slower devices such as AT&T'S RU. Through HomePNA, voice and data coexist on the same phone line without interfering with each other.

AT&T's installation includes a single HomePNA network card or USB adapter. The software bundle includes drivers for the network adapter and a VPN dialer. An installer configures your PC with the IDs and passwords required to access the Internet provider, World-Net, and to send and receive email. After that, you only need to double click on a desktop icon to connect to the service. You remain connected until you reboot the PC or leave the line idle for 24 hours.

For home workers, AT&T's approach is a mixed bag. You can connect as many as five PCs at no charge by equipping them with HomePNA adapters and AT&T's software. To use Ethernet, you will need to install a gateway between the HomePNA and Ethernet LANs. AT&T offers no assistance for this. AT&T created a gateway using the Windows 98 Internet Connection Sharing, but it was difficult. Minor changes to AT&T's standard software would make setting up such a gateway easier.

Lack of Performance   In its current state, AT&T digital wireless broadband falls a bit shy of minimum broadband performance. By convention, a wireless broadband service should be capable of downloads at a steady 384 kbps, the low end of DSL's performance spectrum. AT&T's performance immediately following installation was abysmal, with averages hovering around 100 kbps. Over several weeks of testing, performance improved steadily. Periodic tests run in the past 2 weeks clocked the service's average bandwidth at 332 kbps for downloads and 48 kbps for uploads. This seems appropriate given the 512-kbps stream rate between the tower and the RU. Subsequently, AT&T announced plans to upgrade users from 512 kbps to 1 Mbps. The company expects that this move will boost performance enough to meet users' broadband expectations.

An average download speed of 332 kbps is certainly better than the dialup maximum of 53 kbps, but users looking for DSL-class performance will be disappointed. We also found that performance suffers during peak Internet usage periods. The bottleneck did not seem to be in the rf link but in the routing through AT&T's busy WorldNet service. We hope AT&T follows through on its initial promise to allow digital wireless broadband users to choose their own Internet provider.

AT&T wireless broadband services have been criticized by digital wireless broadband users for poor support. The company's responsiveness in its Usenet support newsgroup has improved, but it is evident that AT&T needs to beef up its technical staff. AT&T's calls during business hours to digital wireless broadband technical support were answered by a recording admonishing its users to call back during business hours. AT&T was fortunate that its service worked relatively well; users had little reason to call support.

In areas not served by DSL or cable, fixed wireless service like AT&T's may be a remote worker's best option. AT&T digital wireless broadband costs less than ISDN and is easier to use than satellite Internet. AT&T needs to pay more attention to performance and customer service issues. Line quality for voice and fax traffic could stand to be upgraded. These improvements, combined with digital wireless broadband's price, will make AT&T competitive even where other wireless broadband options already exist, as shown in Table 15-1.[2,3]

TABLE 15-1 A Growing Wealth of Wireless Broadband Options (Residential Internet users will have a wealth of wireless broadband choices in the coming years, including newly introduced two-way satellite services that will bring high-speed data to even the most rural areas.)

Technology	Approximate Monthly Cost	Top Download Speed	Carriers	Coverage	Availability
Cable modem	$50	10 Mbps (2 to 6 Mbps common)	AT&T, Cox, Adelphia, Charter	Areas with large cable providers and updated infrastructure	Now
Copper DSL	$40+	8 Mbps (384 Kbps to 1.5 Mbps common)	Baby Bells, Northpoint, Covad, Sprint	Established neighborhoods with modern telephone switches	Now
FTTC-DSL (fiber to the curb)	Unknown	60 Mbps	Baby Bells (esp. Pacific Bell)	Newly built and upgraded neighborhoods	Currently in trials
Fixed wireless	$50–$100	10 Mbps with some systems (1 to 2 Mbps common)	AT&T, Sprint	Metropolitan areas and major suburbs; rural regions may be covered by smaller providers	Now in limited areas
Satellite	$70	2 Mbps	Starband, DirecPC (Hughes)	Nationwide	Now, with major expansion in 2001

The Business and Technological Case for AT&T's Digital Wireless Broadband

Business Case   In areas not served by DSL or cable modems, remote employees may be stuck with inadequate dialup service. AT&T brings combined voice, video, and data service to the employee's home for about $61 per month.

Technology Case   AT&T's wireless solution uses HomePNA to create a 1-Mbps data stream. The line quality is comparable with a digital cell phone and is not reliable enough to carry modem or fax signals.

Pros

- AT&T's installation team takes care of everything.
- No charge for as many as five computers sharing one connection.

- Line of sight to wireless tower not needed.
- Competitive local and long-distance rates.

Cons

- Performance and support problems.
- Must retain copper phone line for fax, modem, or alarm system.
- Download performance falls short of broadband levels.

Cost $61 per month for one voice line plus high-speed data.

Availability   Limited to areas of Texas and California; widespread rollout planned.

Service   Installation service was great, but high-speed connection was just one step above dialup service.

Supported Platforms   Windows PCs with PCI, USB, or PC Card Home-PNA adapter.[4]

In 2001, only the most secluded home will be outside the reach of fast Internet service. Satellite carriers Hughes, Digistar, and Starband are rolling out new services and beefing up existing ones. Download speeds as fast as 2 Mbps are promised, and Hughes and Starband are planning DSL-priced services that not only download via satellite but also upload data from PCs to the Internet by satellite.

The wireless broadband have-nots are about to ditch their modems. When they do, they could clobber your e-commerce site. One DSL user can consume the equivalent bandwidth of as many as 150 dialup users. Unfortunately, these DSL surfers will not increase your online revenue in proportion to their use of your resources. It is up to you to keep the wireless broadband stampede (see the sidebar, "Staving Off the Broadband Deluge") from overpowering your Web servers while balancing users' desires for responsive content.

Staving Off the Broadband Deluge

The following four tips will help you prepare your company's e-commerce Web site for the implementation of wireless broadband satellite applications and the resulting flood of its high-bandwidth users:

1. Tune your company's e-commerce site for maximum responsiveness so that all customers, wireless broadband and otherwise, spend less time waiting. A responsive site will make your customers less likely to get frustrated and jump to a competitor's e-commerce site.

2. Decide whether or not wireless broadband content (large audio, video, and software files) is vital to doing business on your e-commerce site. If it isn't, don't host it.

3. If you need wireless broadband content, consider moving large files to external servers. Use hosting or colocation providers, thereby increasing the responsiveness of your Web servers.

4. Do not accept long-term commitments with service providers on expensive data circuits. Affordable commercial connectivity will come, and you want to be ready to switch when the right high-speed service at the right price becomes available.[5]

The Few, The Wired, The Broke

The catalog shopping site, the portal that thrives on banner ad revenue, and the auto dealer that lets well-wired users bypass the showroom all have reason to dread wireless broadband ubiquity. Information technology (IT) management is used to sizing Internet service based on a maximum number of simultaneous users. A 1.5-Mbps T-1 line used to be enough to handle 50 to 200 surfers. Now, it is a joke: One residential wireless broadband user can gobble up every bit of your IT's capacity, often with enough spare bandwidth to surf two of your competitors' sites at the same time. If one of those sites is slow to respond, it is toast—you better hope it is not yours.

If T-1 is a joke, it is a costly laugh at corporate users' expense. By design, appealingly priced DSL and cable services are too slow to replace old-fashioned data lines. Providers have preemptively disallowed commercial use of wireless broadband connections unless the subscriber agrees to higher fees. The T-1 that should be outclassed by DSL is still a mainstay, even at $1600 per month. With prices for 48- and 155-Mbps service commanding into five figures each month, you can scarcely afford to size your circuits for a reasonable number of wireless broadband users.

Very large corporations and some Internet companies of scale can justify shelling out tens or hundreds of thousands of dollars monthly on data circuits (see the sidebar, "The Wireless Broadband Business and Technology Case"). When smaller companies learn that they have bought more bandwidth than they can afford, they become application service providers (ASPs) or hosting providers (see the sidebar, "New ASPs Get Web Apps Up Quickly"). Reselling bandwidth or buying it from another firm with an oversupply is one way to serve wireless broadband users while holding the line on costs.

The Wireless Broadband Business and Technology Case

Business Case   The proliferation of residential wireless broadband throughout the United States means that fewer users will consume more of your company's Internet resources. The increased burden on servers, applications, and bandwidth will affect the performance of e-commerce Web sites and possibly reduce site availability.

Technology Case   Internet business leaders need to restructure their companies' services with the burgeoning base of wireless broadband users in mind, accounting for much higher per-user bandwidth (as much as 150 times greater than with dialup).This requires performance-tuning existing Web content and possibly relocating massive files to off-site hosts.

Pros

- Users in underserved areas will soon have access to high-speed Internet.
- Remote workers have more wireless broadband choices.

Cons

- One user can consume the equivalent bandwidth of 50 to 150 dialup users.
- Wireless broadband advances are primarily targeted at residential users rather than business locations.
- Commercial high-speed telecommunications circuits are still too expensive.[6]

New ASPs Get Web Apps Up Quickly

Talk about a no-brainer. Well over a year ago, it was crystal clear that many users would jump at a chance to use cell phones and handheld devices for wireless online trading.

For brokers at the National Discount Brokers Corporation, the real questions were how many, how soon, and how much of their internal IT budget should they devote to making it happen? The 100-person IT staff at the company's NDB Division was already overwhelmed with hundreds of projects, including just keeping the e-commerce site up and running. Getting up to speed on wireless broadband Web technologies (and keeping up with the rapid changes in wireless broadband protocols, devices, and markup languages) would require a major investment. It was an investment that, without some wireless broadband Web experience under its belt, NDB was not quite ready to make.

So in 2000 the corporation opted to turn deployment of the first phase of NDB's wireless broadband trading initiative over to Aether Systems, Inc., one of a small but growing number of application service providers (ASPs) specializing in helping e-businesses go wireless (Table 15-2).[7] The result: NDB was able to get its first wireless broadband Web offering off the ground quickly, gaining valuable knowledge about what wireless broadband services brokerage customers want most.

This is the beauty of outsourcing. You do not have to worry about the technology and testing devices.

A growing number of e-businesses are turning to wireless broadband ASPs. Time- and cash-strapped companies such as NDB and CDNow, Inc., see outsourcing as the best way to get wireless broadband Web applications up quickly and to cut through complex and rapidly changing wireless broadband technologies, all without needing to invest directly in new hardware, software, or people.

Wireless broadband ASPs, however, are not necessarily the answer for every e-business. E-businesses dealing with sensitive customer data, for example, will want to carefully investigate outsourcers' security technologies and processes before turning data over to one of them.

At the same time, services from wireless broadband ASPs are not cheap. Many levy initial setup fees that can run from $100,000 to $200,000. And many charge monthly per-user fees on top of that.

TABLE 15-2   *A Sample of Some of the ASPs Hoping to Help e-Businesses Launch Wireless Broadband Services Quickly and Keep on Top of Rapidly Changing Wireless Broadband Technologies*

Name	Application/ Services Offered	Pricing	Customer Examples
Aether Systems, Owings Mills, MD	Middleware called Aether Intelligent Messaging that can be hosted or deployed internally; custom development of wireless broadband applications and services, including bundles of wireless broadband service and devices	Varies, based on monthly software hosting and service fees, software licenses, and custom development charges	Charles Schwab & Co., Inc., Office Depot, Inc., and the U.S. Navy
Air2Web, Atlanta, GA	Hosted platform called Always Interactive that transforms Web data into forms that can be accessed from wireless broadband devices	Per user per month; typical charge is $3000 per month for 750 users	United Parcel Service of America, Inc., NetBank, Inc., and SportsLine.com, Inc.
2Roam, Redwood City, CA	Desktop application called Nomad for application development; hosted middleware called Catalyst for transforming data for wireless broadband devices; a service that connects to online ad agencies such as DoubleClick, Inc.	$20,000 site license for Nomad and monthly subscription for Catalyst (average of $80,000 a year); ad service extra	eBay. Inc., Fogdog, Inc. and iWon, Inc.
ViaFone.com, Redwood City, CA	Hosted middleware called OneBridge Mobility Platform for making back-end data accessible through wireless broadband devices, customization, and integration services	$40,000 to $100,000 setup for customization and integration; $10,000 a month per data application, such as WAP	CDNow, Cnet's mySimon, and Obongo, Inc.

Still, using a wireless broadband ASP to get applications up quickly makes sense. You need a lot of financial commitment to do wireless broadband today if you do it yourself.

A New Market Takes Flight   Wireless broadband providers such as Aether, of Owings Mills, MD, represent the latest wrinkle in the ASP model. While ASPs' offerings vary, most wireless ASP services revolve around hosted applications that transform Web and legacy system content and data into formats such as wireless markup language and handheld device markup language that can be accessed by customers using a variety of wireless broadband devices, everything from WAP (Wireless Application Protocol) phones, Palm, Inc., PDAs (personal digital assistants), and Microsoft Corp.'s Pocket PCs to two-way pagers such as Research in Motion, Ltd.'s BlackBerry.

Some, like Aether, also help e-businesses build and host wireless broadband applications and even bundle those with wireless broadband devices that can be sold by e-businesses to their online customers. They also offer support for wireless broadband customers.

The field of wireless broadband ASPs today is small but growing rapidly. It includes start-ups such as ViaFone.com, Inc., and 2Roam, Inc., both of Redwood City, CA, and Air2Web, Inc., of Atlanta. Some wireless broadband ASPs, such as Aether, and competitors such as Toronto-based 724 Solutions, Inc., and New York–based w-Technologies, Inc., have targeted the financial services industry. Aether is also working in transportation, government, and health care. All these providers are chasing a market for wireless broadband ASP services that is expected to grow rapidly over the next few years, from about $14 million in 1999 to $732 million by 2004, according to IDC (Figure 15-2).[8]

In addition to the ASPs that have been launched to provide hosted wireless broadband Web applications, some existing ASPs are beginning to add wireless broadband capabilities on top of applications they were already hosting. They include UpShot, Inc., of Mountain View, CA, and Done.com, Inc., of Belmont, CA (see the sidebar, "Hosted Wireless Broadband Services from ASPs").

Figure 15-2

ASPs leave wires behind. The wireless broadband ASP market, although small today, is projected to grow at a compounded annual rate of more than 100 percent through 2004.

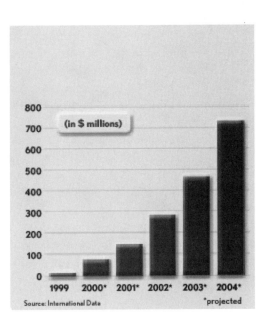

(in $ millions)

800
700
600
500
400
300
200
100
0

1999 2000* 2001* 2002* 2003* 2004*

Source: International Data   *projected

Using Aether so far has paid off for NDB. The broker was able to quickly dip its toe into the wireless broadband market, launching its initial service targeted at its more affluent, high-net-worth customers in 10 months.

The service, called Mobility, was launched in September 2000. For $49.99 a month, customers get a Palm V handheld with an OmniSky Corp. modem and access from the device to NDB stock quotes, news, and trading, plus email. Aether handles customer service and fulfills orders for the service and the devices along with hosting its middleware, which provides wireless broadband access to NDB's Web applications and trading system.

Now that it has used Aether to get some wireless broadband experience, NDB plans to expand its wireless broadband Web offering. One thing the company has learned: Customers want to use a wide range of wireless broadband devices, not just Palm handhelds. In the first quarter of 2001, NDB plans to launch services for a full array of devices, including WAP phones, Pocket PCs, and two-way pagers. The expanded service will be made available to NDB's overall customer base.

No Muss, No Fuss   While e-businesses such as NDB see using ASPs as a good way to get into wireless broadband quickly, others are motivated more by the opportunity to offload the hassle and expense of responding to lightning-quick changes taking place in wireless broadband technologies.

We are still in an era of competing standards, and who knows who the winner will be? For example, NetBank, which launched its wireless broadband offering in September 2000, wanted to deploy the service to as many of its 135,000 account holders as possible and to support a wide array of devices, including PDAs, WAP phones, and even non-WAP cell phones using short message service. Supporting this many wireless broadband devices, however, meant that NetBank would need to be ready to respond quickly when, say, the still-young WAP standard changes. So NetBank, which had experience outsourcing other operations to ASPs, decided to use an ASP for wireless broadband Web services.

Not all enterprises will be willing to rely on relatively young ASPs to support critical wireless broadband services or to protect sensitive customer data. Before signing on with a wireless ASP, IT managers should be satisfied that the service provider has a strong business plan and that it will not go away. IT managers also should ensure that their wireless broadband ASP has invested in creating a secure environment. Because they view wireless broadband as a competitive advantage, many larger enterprises in particular may choose to maintain control of their wireless broadband initiatives.

One company that has decided to develop wireless broadband Web systems and skills in-house is Excara, Inc. The company, which runs industrial goods e-marketplace PurchasingCenter.com, recently decided to deploy NetMorf, Inc.'s SiteMorf software to transform Web content (350,000 catalog items) into a form accessible by buying agents using WAP phones. Officials at Excara expect that NetMorf will help the company keep up with changes in wireless broadband technology standards by continuously upgrading the SiteMorf tool. Meanwhile, Excara gets to take direct responsibility for issues like security and reliability.

Not that e-business managers going the wireless broadband outsourcing route are not also concerned about controlling issues like security. NDB took pains to get their reliability and security questions answered before signing on with Aether. For example, they demanded contract language prohibiting Aether from making any use of NDB's customer information. In addition, NDB made sure that Aether's wireless broadband sessions are encrypted. NDB's IT department approved Aether's security before the implementation. And NDB, during its review of wireless ASPs, evaluated all providers' long-term viability, considering their financial backing and plan for growth.

While a wireless broadband ASP might not be right for everyone, it was a fit for music e-tailer CDNow. While other dot-coms have leapt into wireless broadband by spending millions of dollars on development and bleeding-edge features, CDNow could not afford this. Like a growing number of dot-coms, CDNow was running low on cash before being acquired in September 2000 by Bertelsmann AG.

The wireless broadband initiative started at the beginning of the year with pulling together a team from across the company that now numbers about four people focused on wireless broadband and another 10 who help out when needed. Few of them had much experience, however, with wireless broadband technology or strategy. So in May 2000, CDNow signed on with wireless broadband ASP

ViaFone. The company was able to launch its first WAP application 5 months later, on October 16, 2000.

The first iteration of CDNow's wireless broadband offering is what is called *bare bones*. Wireless broadband browsers can search CDNow, browse the music charts of top sellers, get recommendations, and order CDs. It does not yet allow consumers to purchase other products such as DVDs and videocassettes.

CDNow's plans call for adding access from Palm Vs and VIIs soon. Next will be two-way pagers and voice access.

Although its current wireless offering is minimal, the important thing is that, using ViaFone, CDNow was able to gain valuable wireless broadband experience quickly. This is critical because wireless broadband is expected to bring CDNow a new link to customers and potential sales increases. And for struggling dot-coms such as CDNow, this is crucial.[9]

Hosted Wireless Broadband Services from ASPs

In the market for hosted wireless broadband services but nervous about signing on with a new, untested wireless broadband ASP? Not to worry. Soon you may be able to get hosted wireless broadband services from the application service provider you are already using to run your enterprise applications.

ASPs that are already offering hosted sales force automation, workflow, and other applications are increasingly rolling out wireless broadband versions. Two smaller ASPs that have done so in the last 6 months are Done.com, Inc., and UpShot.com.

Done.com, of Belmont, CA, focuses on workflow management, while UpShot.com, of Mountain View, CA, has an SFA (sales force automation) application. For UpShot customers, adding wireless broadband to SFA means salespeople on the road can get instant access to contacts and leads. For customers of Done.com, knowing when a coworker or customer has made a change to a project, anytime, anywhere, can make projects go more smoothly.

At start-up Conduit, Inc., for example, the wireless broadband component of Done.com's workflow application has helped the company land some of its most important deals. Allowing salespeople to respond to customers quickly using wireless broadband devices has been a critical factor in Conduit's winning at least two of its five customers.

Conduit, of South San Francisco, CA, has been using Done.com for 6 months, first in managing recruitment. It added wireless broadband on Wireless Application Protocol phones and Palm VIIs, and four salespeople are now using it to receive alerts when customers have sent email messages about pending deals.

Using the wireless broadband feature to help close even one deal would more than pay for the service, which costs Conduit $500 a month. The bottom line is: When you send an email to someone and they respond back in 2 to 3 minutes, you increase the chances of getting the deal.[10]

But such stopgap measures may not work for long. Today's typical wireless broadband user cruises along at T-1 speed. "Baby Bell" copper DSL cranks up to 6 Mbps. Sprint's ION DSL service tops out at 8 Mbps. Cable and point-to-multipoint microwave raise the ante to as high as 10 Mbps. In addition, local telecommunications companies want to push category 5 and fiber into homes to carry voice-over-IP (VoIP) and multichannel video, with enough left over to support 50-Mbps to 60-Mbps Internet downloads. If you think you can keep up with the wireless broadband Joneses by buying ever-fatter telecommunication lines, forget it.

Play the Waiting Game

Finally, your smartest move may be to buy only as much bandwidth as you need today with the shortest possible commitment. The telephone giants are forced to share their circuits with competitors, and some of the wireless broadband and satellite technologies serving home users will find commercial applications. Wait it out by paying higher month-to-month rates for the freedom to move to a competing carrier later.

While you are waiting, you can prepare for the broadband onslaught. Start by squeezing the most from the bandwidth you have now. Optimize your Web content for responsiveness. Never leave users hanging, wondering if your server has gone to sleep.

You may be able to rework some processes to be asynchronous. Send users an automated email response rather than making them wait for an online answer. If you must make users wait, use an animated progress bar or another means of updating the display while you compute in the background.

The simplest way to avoid wireless broadband bottlenecks is to avoid wireless broadband content. If you run a lean mix of Web text and compact graphics, you can stretch a basic circuit (including the much maligned T-1) across a surprising number of users. The squeeze occurs when you host massive video, audio, or software files, now known as *wireless broadband content*, on the same servers and circuits that run your interactive content.

If you need those big files to grab the eyeballs of high-speed surfers, move your wireless broadband content to a server outside your primary network. Wireless broadband files are ideal candidates for hosting or colocation providers. For far less than the cost of a suitably fast circuit, you can rent an external wireless broadband repository.

Conclusion

Finally, if you put your ear to the ground, you can hear the coming stampede. You could mortgage your company's future to pay for circuits and service fast enough to feed all those hungry surfers. But it is smarter to hang back, optimize your existing content, and get ready to jump when the right ultrafast service at the right price makes its debut. In this way, when high-speed users get their first glimpse of your flashy, robust wireless broadband content, you will have had time to polish it. The companies that panic or fall in love with being first out the door with wireless broadband content will get flattened by the enormous cost. But this does not have to happen to you.

Endnotes

1. Tom Yager, "AT&T's New Service Brings Voice and Data," InfoWorld Media Group, Inc., 155 Bovet Road, San Mateo, CA 94402, 2000.
2. *Ibid.*
3. Tom Yager, "Prepare for a Broadband Assault," InfoWorld Media Group, Inc., 155 Bovet Road, San Mateo, CA 94402, 2000.
4. Tom Yager, "AT&T's New Service Brings Voice and Data," InfoWorld Media Group, Inc., 155 Bovet Road, San Mateo, CA 94402, 2000.
5. Tom Yager, "Prepare for a Broadband Assault," InfoWorld Media Group, Inc., 155 Bovet Road, San Mateo, CA 94402, 2000.

6. *Ibid.*

7. Matt Hicks, "Wireless without the Wait," *eWeek*, ZD, Inc., One Athenaeum Street, Cambridge, MA 02142, 2000.

8. Matt Hicks, "Service Providers Ease the Way to Wireless for e-Business," *eWeek*, ZD, Inc., One Athenaeum Street, Cambridge, MA 02142, 2000.

9. Matt Hicks, "Wireless without the Wait," *eWeek*, ZD, Inc., One Athenaeum Street, Cambridge, MA 02142, 2000.

10. Matt Hicks, "ASPs Tie Wireless into the Package," *eWeek*, ZD, Inc., One Athenaeum Street, Cambridge, MA 02142, 2000.

CHAPTER 16

Packet-over-SONET/SDH Specification (POS-PHY Level 3):

Deploying High-Speed Wireless Broadband Networking Applications

The call is out for a jack-of-all-trades that will be able to handle the sheer variety of services such as Asynchronous Transfer Mode (ATM), packet-over-SONET/SDH (POS), Frame Relay, and Gigabit Ethernet. The packet-over-SONET/SDH physical layer (POS-PHY) level 3 interface is a robust, nonblocking interface that is flexible enough to answer this call.

The unrelenting demand for Internet-based services is driving high-speed wireless broadband network equipment designers to develop an array of new switch and router port cards to support multiservice traffic and aggregate bandwidths up to OC-48 (2.488 Gbps) and beyond. These new products must support the existing Frame Relay and ATM infra-structure as well as emerging traffic types such as POS and Gigabit Ethernet. With this in mind, the topics presented in this chapter include, but are not limited to,

- Multiservice PHY-link interface evolution

- POS-PHY interface design requirements

- Simultaneous packet and cell support

- Simplifying link layer design

- POS-PHY appropriate for short-packet traffic

- Standardization activities

Furthermore, this chapter covers the building and deployment of next-generation multiservice switches and routers possessing attributes like Frame Relay, ATM infrastructure, as well as emerging traffic types such as POS and Gigabit Ethernet, and the requirement of a protocol agnostic physical to data link layer interface such as POS-PHY level 3 (PL3). The PL3 chip-to-chip interface has received substantial industry backing from the SATURN development group and semiconductor and equipment vendors because it provides a robust and efficient means to connect a variety of different physical layer devices to data link layer devices using a single common PL3 bus (Figure 16-1).[1] A more detailed technical description of the PL3 interface is presented in the sidebar, "PL3 Interface Overview."

NOTE   The PL3 interface defines operations between physical layer devices (such as ATM, POS, and Gigabit Ethernet framers) and link layer devices (such as ATM, IP, and Gigabit Ethernet forwarding devices) at OC-48 line rates.

Figure 16-1
The PL3 bus supports ATM, POS, Gigabit Ethernet, and multi-service port card designs.

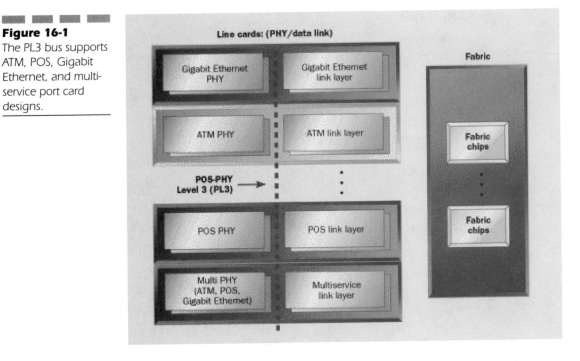

Line cards: (PHY/data link)

Gigabit Ethernet PHY

Gigabit Ethernet link layer

ATM PHY

ATM link layer

POS-PHY Level 3 (PL3) →

POS PHY

POS link layer

Multi PHY (ATM, POS, Gigabit Ethernet)

Multiservice link layer

Fabric

Fabric chips

Fabric chips

PL3 Interface Overview

The PL3 interface can transfer both fixed-length cells (ATM) and variable-length packets (PPP, Frame Relay, or Ethernet) at line rates up to OC-48. The receive/transmit end-of-packet (REOP/TEOP) signals enable the transfer of variable-length packets. A receive-enable (RVAL) allows the PHY device to indicate when valid data are not present (e.g., between packet transfers or when its FIFO is empty during a transfer). To indicate error conditions caused by FIFO overflows and to detect abort sequences, frame-check-sequence (FCS) errors, and other special conditions, receive/transmit error signals (RERR/TERR) are included. Byte lane enable signals (RMOD/TMOD) indicate the position of the last valid byte on end of packet for the 32-bit-wide bus. A listing of all PL3 interface signals is provided in Table 16-1.[2]

TABLE 16-1

PL3 Interface
Signals Defined

Signal	Description
TFCLK	Transmit FIFO clock
TADR[n:0]	Packet-mode transmit address
PTPA	Polled-PHY transmit packet available
TENB	Transmit enable
TDAT[31:0]	Transmit data, driven from link to PHY layer
TSX	Transmit start of transfer
TSOP	Transmit start of packet/cell
TEOP	Transmit end of packet
TMOD[1:0]	Transmit word modulo
TERR transmit error	TPRTY transmit parity
DTPA[3:0]	Direct-status transmit packet available
STPA	Selected-PHY transmit packet available
RFCLK	Receive FIFO clock
RENB	Receive enable
RDAT[31:0]	Receive data, driven from PHY to link layer
RSX	Receive start of transfer
RSOP	Receive start of packet/cell
REOP	Receive end of packet
RMOD[1:0]	Receive word modulo
RERR	Receive error
RPRTY	Receive parity
RVAL	Receive data valid

Multiservice PHY-Link Interface Evolution

When high-speed wireless broadband networkers and carriers became interested in creating systems capable of supporting mixed-media traffic at OC-48 line rates, the SATURN development group [see the sidebar,

"Next-Generation Packet and Cell Processor Device Supporting New Packet-over-SONET/SDH Specification (POS-PHY Level 3) for System Interfaces up to 3.2 Gigabits per Second"] realized the need to define an interface capable of interconnecting a variety of cell and packet-based media-processing devices. During the development of this agnostic interface, it became apparent that simply frame extending the UTOPIA-style interface to provide robust multiservice support was not satisfactory. A novel approach would be required to create an interface (Table 16-2) flexible enough to support both ATM cells and packets.[3] The SATURN development group spent considerable time and effort in developing the current PL3 interface bus specification.

NOTE SATURN is a communications industry group with a mandate to define and develop interoperable standards-compliant solutions for high-speed wireless broadband networking applications.

TABLE 16-2   The Attributes of Each Interface Including Those Supporting Lower Line Rates (A Summary of the Primary Advantages of the POS-PHY Interfaces)

POS-PHY (ATM Cell and IP Packet)	UTOPIA (ATM Cell Only)	Primary Advantages	Application	Bus	Clock Rate (Nominal)	Throughput
NA	Level 1	PL1 implemented as a subset of PL2	Single device Single channel	8 bit	25 MHz	200 Mbps
Level 2	Level 2	PL2 accomodates both ATM cells and packets	Multidevice Multichannel	16 bit 8 bit	50 MHz 33 MHz	800 Mbps 264 Mbps
Level 3	Level 3	PL3 accomodates both ATM cells and packets	Single device Multichannel	32 bit 8 bit	100 MHz 100 MHz	3.2 Gbps 800 Mbps

Note: The POS-PHY interfaces can be viewed as a superset of the UTOPIA interface.

Next-Generation Packet and Cell Processor Device Supporting New Packet-over-SONET/SDH Specification (POS-PHY Level 3) for System Interfaces up to 3.2 Gigabits per Second

The PM5357 S/UNI-622-POS is the first POS-PHY level 3 and ATM physical layer device sanctioned by the SATURN Development Group. PMC-Sierra (NASDAQ:PMCS) of Burnaby, BC, recently introduced a new packet-over-SONET/SDH physical interface specification that allows up to 3.2 Gbps throughput. The specification enables high-speed POS interfaces, such as OC-48 and multichannel OC-12, for the next generation of super-routers and layer 3 switches. The new SATURN-endorsed POS-PHY level 3 physical interface is an extension of the industry-standard POS-PHY level 2 interface announced by the company earlier. The company also announced the PM5357 S/UNI-622-POS, the industry's first framer to support the new specification.

PMC-Sierra's new S/UNI-622-POS is the industry's first PHY device to meet the SATURN POS-PHY level 3 interface specification. The highly integrated 3.3-V device is a dual-mode POS frame processor and ATM cell processor operating at 622 and 155 Mbps. The S/UNI-622-POS is the industry's first 622-Mbps packet-over-SONET/SDH PHY that integrates serializer-deserializer, clock recovery, and clock synthesis, together with a framer and cell processor to achieve the highest level of integration currently available.

The methods for transporting IP are evolving, and the POS-PHY level 3 interface enables the alternative packet-over-SONET/SDH method for direct mapping of IP into SONET/SDH. POS-PHY level 3 is developed and endorsed by the SATURN POS Subworking Group which is comprised of leading manufacturers of IP packet and ATM equipment. Packet-over-SONET/SDH optimizes the link bandwidth utilization by enabling Internet routers to connect directly to SONET/SDH rings without requiring an intermediate layer. The SATURN Subworking Group was formed in December 1997 to accelerate the adoption of POS standards and facilitate equipment interoperability. POS-PHY level 3 and POS-PHY level 2 have been submitted to the Optical Internetworking Forum for open standardization.

The SATURN POS Subworking Group includes PMC-Sierra and major network equipment suppliers such as 3COM, Alcatel, Ascend Communications, Cabletron, Cisco Systems, ECI Telecom, FORE

Systems, Hughes Network Systems, Lucent Technologies, NEC, Nokia, Nortel, Redstone Communications, Sumitomo Electric and Tellabs. The SATURN POS-PHY level 3 interface specification can be requested from PMC-Sierra at *POS-PHY@pmc-sierra.com*.

The PM5357 S/UNI-622-POS is characterized for the industrial temperature range operation from −40 to +85°C and supports all functionality required for WAN SONET/SDH applications. The device is sampling now in a 304 SBGA package and is priced at $481 in one-thousand-unit quantities.

For POS-based applications, the S/UNI-622-POS provides comprehensive SONET/SDH clock recovery and framing and includes the standard X43+1 payload scrambling, byte serial HDLC processing, and packet FIFO as defined by IETF RFC-1619 and RFC-1662. The device implements the POS-PHY level 2 interface and the 8-bit × 100-MHz POS-PHY level 3 mode of operation, enabling low-pin-count solutions for channelized OC-48 and multichannel OC-12c solutions. The device is feature and interface compatible with the quad-channel OC-3c PM5351 S/UNI-TETRA.

The S/UNI-622-POS enables enterprise and access systems to support packet-over-SONET/SDH or ATM-over-SONET/SDH, therefore preserving hardware and software investment. The industry standard POS-PHY system interface specification ensures interoperability among vendors for rates from OC-3 to OC-48.

For ATM-based applications, the S/UNI-622-POS connects directly to the PM7322 RCMP-800 ATM layer cell processor, with the PM73487 QRT/PM73488 QSE switching chip set over an industry standard UTOPIA level 2–compliant bus. The device is also compliant to the 8-bit × 100-MHz UTOPIA level 3 interface specification. The S/UNI-622-POS is pin-compatible and software-compatible with the PM5356 S/UNI-622-MAX device and software-compatible with PMC-Sierra's existing industry standard PM5355 S/UNI-622 device.

PMC-Sierra is a leading provider of high-speed wireless broadband internetworking component solutions emphasizing ATM, Ethernet, SONET/SDH, T-1/E-1 and T-3/E-3 applications. The company's quality system is registered with the Quality Management Institute to the ISO 9001 standard. As cofounder of the SATURN Development Group, PMC-Sierra works with over 30 other member companies to define and develop interoperable, standards-compliant solutions for high-speed wireless broadband networking applications.

Headquartered near Vancouver, BC, PMC-Sierra also offers local technical and sales support in California, Illinois, Ontario, Massachusetts, Texas, Europe, and Asia. In Beaverton, OR, the company has established an Ethernet products division focused on developing leading-edge Ethernet semiconductor solutions. PMC-Sierra is located on the World Wide Web at *http://www.pmc-sierra.com*.[4]

First-generation PBX systems lacked scalability, forcing customers to conduct expensive forklift upgrades. This led to new system design attributes like standard OSes (Windows NT), client-server control, mixed-media switching (circuit ATM and IP), and diversified desktop transmissions (analog, digital, and IP). Today's PBXs are designed for voice traffic and are not equipped to handle data, video, and image traffic. In adopting IP, PBX designers are forced to deal with performance problems caused by process-intensive protocols (H.323) that touch and shape the medium. OEMs have addressed these problem areas by offering patchwork solutions, a stop-gap strategy until next-generation designs are available.

Previously, proprietary-based legacy PBX systems used voice and control buses to process the call traffic. But with the advent of the PC and a little help from industry standards like H.100/110, CompactPCI (CPCI), the Ethernet, hot swap, and software like Windows NT, OEMs are migrating from proprietary to open systems. PBX equipment, once designed using proprietary components, architectures, and software, is now designed using standard, off-the-shelf PC technology adapted for the high-reliability requirements of today's telephone infrastructure. OEMs can begin to focus more of their efforts on developing the next generation of wireless broadband networking applications instead of worrying about integrating closed-system architecture from various manufacturers.

POS-PHY Interface Design Requirements

When designing a system's PHY link layer interface to support multiple services, three key factors must be considered. First, the interface must be able to transfer both packets and cells (ATM) to support a variety of multiservice port cards. Second, the simpler the PHY-link layer protocol, the less problematic it will be to interface the system's physical and link layer devices. Finally, widespread vendor support and standardization are important. The PL3 interface addresses all these design requirements.

Simultaneous Packet and Cell Support

PL3 can be used to design an agnostic interface to carry both packets and cells, or it can be used to develop separate packet or cell cards. As a result, the PL3 interface offers system developers a common line-card interface that yields considerable time-to-market and design reuse advantages. For example, if a first-generation switch only supports ATM (or only packets), the design can be easily iterated to provide multiservice capability, since the same PL3 interface can be used for packet, ATM, or mixed traffic. The PL3 interface can be viewed as a superset of UL3 in its ability to agnostically accommodate both ATM and packet traffic. Since UL3 does not define how to manage the transfer of variable-length packets, use of the PL3 interface is a necessity in these types of systems.

The transmit interface for PL3 can support both cells and packets. It is similar to UL3 in operation with the exception that PL3 employs a port address prepend that is inserted in the dead cycle used by UL3 to implement PHY selection. The timing diagram in Figure 16-2 illustrates the dual-mode PL3/UL3 transmit support feature.[5] The receive PL3 interface can be thought of as a UL3 interface with the polling/selection state machine disabled and replaced by a port address prepend reader.

Simplifying Link Layer Design

A simple polling and selection protocol can bypass the design complexities associated with interrupts, addressing, and scheduling. In the PL3 transmit interface, the selection of the PHY and polling of the PHY to determine its ability to accept a packet occur independently. In practice, the selection of the PHY is achieved by inserting an in-band PHY address. The in-band insertion of the prepend address uses a single clock cycle. This implementation simplifies the interface design of the link layer device by requiring a simple polling state machine.

The PL3 receive interface does not require polling or selection by the link layer device. Instead, the PHY device pushes data to the link layer device by sending a port address prepend. As with the transmit interface,

Figure 16-2

Timing diagram for transmit and receive interface operation (UL3/PL3-compliant).

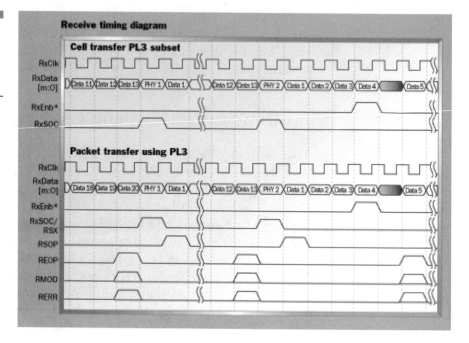

the port address prepend only consumes a single clock cycle. The *push* approach provides several advantages that simplify design of the link layer device. The design complexity of the receive data link is greatly reduced by the transfer of the PHY selection protocol to the physical layer device. Fewer device pins are required because there is no need to provision for address and receive packet-available signals. Finally, the architecture scales easily for a large number of ports because there is no need to poll a large number of PHY devices.

Implementing a UL3 extension-style transmit interface requires interrupts to the polling sequence to insert the selected PHY port address. This complicates the design of the link layer device and reduces the available polling bandwidth. In the receive mode, the extended UL3 interface polls and then selects the appropriate PHY. Aside from its complexity, this process also introduces a minimum latency of four clock cycles between packet transfers. To avoid this four-cycle dead period, the link layer device could absorb the first four cycles of the next packet in the same port before selecting another port. However, this proposal complicates the link layer device by requiring additional packet buffer management and overhead functions to handle the four-cycle fragments.

POS-PHY Appropriate
for Short-Packet Traffic

Short packets (ACK/RST/SYN, for example) comprise a significant amount of packet traffic on the Internet. The corresponding minimum bus clock frequencies for packet lengths around the short-packet peak of the bimodal distribution of Internet traffic are shown in Table 16-3.[6] The clock frequency is not monotonic with packet length because the number of valid bytes occupying the last cycle on an end-of-packet occurrence affects the utilization of the available bus bandwidth. To prevent packet blocking on the bus, the PHY device must be selected and written to as quickly as possible. The PL3 interface has a single cycle of overhead latency between back-to-back packet transfers. The minimum bus clock frequency associated with the single-cycle overhead of PL3 is well within maximum acceptable limits. As a result, the PL3 interface provides a nonblocking bus in multiservice applications like ATM, Gigabit Ethernet, and POS. Additionally, developers can either design to a lower bus clock frequency to simplify board implementation or design to a higher frequency when greater bandwidth is needed to carry application-specific overhead, with packets transferred over the interface.

With frame-extended UL3, there is a latency of at least four cycles between the end-of-packet and the start-of-next-packet transfer. At least two clock cycles are required for the link layer device to respond to an end-of-packet signal and select the next port. An additional two cycles are required for the PHY to respond to the link layer device. This implies a four-cycle dead time, which adds bus overhead and becomes significant for short-packet transfers. As a result, the minimum clock frequency typically runs very close to the maximum UL3 clock rate of 104 MHz, exceeding the

	Minimum Bus Clock (MHz)	
	4-Cycle Overhead	1-Cycle Overhead
Packet Length (Bytes)	**(as in the UL3 Extension)**	**(as in PL3)**
35	108.15	83.2
40	102.27	80.4
45	104.17	84.6
50	104.17	82.2

TABLE 16-3

Minimum Bus Clock Frequencies for Worst-Case Scenarios

maximum clock rate in some cases. This condition is undesirable because once the maximum clock rate is exceeded, blocking will occur on the bus. In addition, the significantly higher clock frequency of such frame-extended UL3 interfaces makes for a more complex circuit-board implementation.

Standardization Activities

The PL3 interface has been standardized by the SATURN Development Group and is publicly available at *www.pmc-sierra.com/posphylevel3*. While PL3 has gained de facto acceptance in the industry for interfacing 2.5-Gbps data link and PHY layer devices, it will benefit the industry to have PL3 adopted by an open standards body for further maintenance, dissemination, and reference for any subsequent work. Accordingly, the PL3 interface has been submitted to the ATM Forum and Optical Internetworking Forum (OIF) and is presently under review. In particular, the PL3 specification has been adopted as a baseline draft document for System Packet Interface Level 3 (SPI-3) for 2.5-Gbps aggregate bandwidths at the OIF. The PL3 specification also has been accepted and approved for straw ballot at the ATM Forum (Frame-Based ATM Interface Extension to UL3, STR-PHY-FATM-01.00).

NOTE   The ATM Forum Technical Committee is responsible for the disposition of POS-PHY level 3: A system of interface for cell and packet transfer for OC-48 aggregate bandwidth wireless broadband networking applications (ATMF 99-0421).

Conclusion

Finally, the POS-PHY level 3 interface is a technically superior solution to a frame-extended UTOPIA level 3 interface. It possesses both solid standards-body support and wide adoption within the equipment and semiconductor vendor community. Since next-generation equipment must support multiple services such as ATM, POS, Frame Relay, and Gigabit Ethernet, the sheer variety of services creates a significant challenge for designers. To achieve optimal performance in this class of systems and gain the most head room for future products and services, the PL3 interface is the logical choice. It provides a robust, nonblocking interface that is simple to implement and capable of processing cell and packet-based traffic up to OC-48 line rates. By providing a common interface for these multiple service types, the PL3 bus maximizes design reuse potential and offers system designers time-to-market benefits in the development of multi-service OC-48 high-speed wireless broadband networking equipment.

Endnotes

1. Jeff Camillo, "POS-PHY Level 3: Enabling High-Speed Networking Applications," *Communication Systems Design*, 525 Market St., Suite 500, San Francisco, CA 94105, 2000.
2. *Ibid.*
3. *Ibid.*
4. "PMC-Sierra Announces Next-Generation Packet and Cell Processor Device Supporting New Packet-over-SONET/SDH Specification (POS-PHY Level 3) for System Interfaces up to 3.2 Gigabits per Second," PMC-Sierra, Inc., 105-8555 Baxter Pl., Burnaby BC, V5a 4v7 Canada, 2000.
5. Jeff Camillo, "POS-PHY Level 3: Enabling High-Speed Networking Applications," *Communication Systems Design*, 525 Market St., Suite 500, San Francisco, CA 94105, 2000.
6. *Ibid.*

CHAPTER 17

Wireless Broadband Access Implementation Methods

Wireless broadband communications will be the next storm in the communication industry, and over $100 billion will be invested in the coming years. Wireless broadband is also at the edge of a significant revolution—broadband multidimensional wireless will emerge in all areas of our information society.

Convergence of wireless broadband and the Internet and of wireless broadband mobile and access will greatly improve the implementation methods as well as the quality of communications. Wireless broadband business will penetrate everywhere: mass market and specialized services, indoor and outdoor, local area and wide area, terrestrial and satellite. Wireless broadband mobile Internet applications surely will drive this boom.

The wireless broadband infrastructure is also becoming totally multidimensional, whether in technologies (diversified and harmonized), applications (free mobile, local, or global), or services (bandwidth on demand). Reconfigurable and adaptive wireless broadband systems will dominate this market in the very near future. With the recent takeoff of third-generation (3G) wireless in Europe, a new wireless race has just begun.

With this in mind, this chapter will discuss the new construction of an open wireless broadband core for the implementation of mobile and access applications. As wireless broadband goes multidimensional and the Internet goes wireless, this new compact architecture surely will trigger a new revolution in wireless broadband communications.

This chapter also presents an overview of packet mode data transfer in cellular networks. Leading second-generation (2G) plus cellular networks of GSM/TDMA GPRS and IS-95B are introduced. Architecture and protocol layers in two leading 3G cellular network proposals, cdma2000 and WCDMA, are presented. Mobile Internet Protocol (IP) support in various cellular networks is discussed next. With efficient support of mobile IP in cellular networks, seamless integration of cellular networks with the Internet is expected to be reached at a rapid pace.

NOTE   UMTS is the International Telecommunications Union's attempt to harmonize the U.S. and European approaches to 3G.

The Convergence of Wireless Broadband Mobile and Access Implementation Methods

The future of wireless broadband is not just wireless; it is a part of life. When we look back to the 1980s, everyone dreamed of having a nice mobile phone. However, if we dream of the wireless broadband picture in 2010, the story will be totally different. Why? Because at that time, the wireless broadband infrastructure (not just for communications) will be totally multidimensional, whether in technologies (diversified and harmonized), applications (free mobile, local, or global), or services (service/bandwidth on demand). Our wireless broadband personal communicator or assistant (the size of a wallet or up to a book with enough bandwidth and memory) can help us enjoy our lives. Wireless broadband becomes easy and affordable in the mass market; even when you are away from your office, your business will never be offline. Global roaming and a high-speed wireless broadband link (thanks to tremendous silicon advancements) will make our travels wonderful and make us feel at home anywhere.

The key applications evolved from the advancement of wireless broadband, and the underlying technologies, including wireless broadband mobile (3G wireless and 4G mobile), wireless broadband access, wireless broadband networking, as well as wireless broadband satellite solutions, surely will dominate the whole communications market and therefore improve the business model in many aspects (see the sidebar, "Wireless Broadband Access and VoDSL Solutions").

Wireless Broadband Access and VoDSL Solutions

Netopia, Inc. (Nasdaq: NTPA), a market leader in providing digital subscriber line (DSL) Internet equipment and e-commerce Web platforms to small and medium-sized businesses, recently announced its new contract with Ericsson (Nasdaq NM: ERICY) to develop business-class G.SHDSL voice and data solutions. Netopia will be the primary supplier in providing G.SHDSL customer premise equipment (CPE) and integrated access devices (IADs) into the Ericsson ENGINE access ramp next-generation access solution for both voice and data. The alliance will enable Ericsson to deliver complete end-to-end solutions to its telecommunications carrier customers worldwide.

G.SHDSL is a new technology standard that combines the benefits of symmetric digital subscriber line and high bit-rate DSL, allowing symmetrical data transfer over inexpensive dual copper lines at speeds of up to 2.3 Mbps. G.SHDSL enables users to take full advantage of applications that require high bandwidth in both directions such as video conferencing, LAN-to-LAN VPN connections, and large file transfers. The technology is also well suited for voice-over-DSL (VoDSL) applications.

> Netopia is very pleased to have been selected as a strategic part-
> ner by Ericsson to pursue international wireless broadband market
> opportunities. Ericsson has a long history of delivering leading-edge
> network solutions for the European, Latin American, and Asian mar-
> kets. As these markets begin to ramp up their wireless broadband
> deployments, Ericsson and Netopia are very well positioned to deliver
> products that meet both current and emerging market requirements.[1]

Convergence of wireless broadband mobile and access will be the next storm in wireless communications. Fueled by many emerging technologies, including digital signal processing, software-definable radio, intelligent antennas, superconductor devices, as well as digital transceivers, the future wireless broadband system will be much more compact with limited hardware and more flexible and intelligent software elements. Reconfigurable and adaptive terminals and base stations allow the system to be applied easily in the wireless broadband mobile as well as wireless broadband access applications. The compact hardware and very small portion of software (called the *common air interface basic input-output system*, or CAI BIOS) will go the way the computer industry did in the past. A compact multidimensional wireless broadband model will be adopted for system design and implementation.

Wireless broadband mobile Internet will be the key application of this converged wireless broadband system. The terminal will be very smart instead of dumb and compatible with mobile and access services, including wireless broadband multicasting as well as wireless broadband trunking. This new wireless broadband terminal will have the following features:

- Ninety percent of the traffic will be data.
- The security function will be enhanced (fingerprint chip embedded).
- A voice-recognition function will be enhanced; keypad or keyboard attachment will be an option, as will wirelessness.
- The terminal will support single and multiple users with various service options.
- The terminal will be fully adaptive and software-reconfigurable.[2]

As wireless broadband communications evolve to this convergence, fourth-generation (4G) mobile wireless broadband communications (4G mobile) will be an ideal mode to support high-data-rate connection from 2 to 20 Mbps based on the new spectrum requirement for International Mobile Telecommunications 2000 (IMT-2000), as well as the coexistence of current spectrum for broadband wireless access. This 4G mobile system's vision aims at

- Providing a technological response to accelerated growth in demand for wireless broadband connectivity.
- Ensuring seamless services provisioning across a multitude of wireless broadband systems and networks, from private to public, from indoor to wide area.
- Providing optimal delivery of the user's desired service via the most appropriate network available.
- Coping with the expected growth in Internet-based communications.
- Opening new spectrum frontiers.[3]

Figure 17-1 shows the convergence of wireless broadband mobile and access in one track, generating 4G mobile.[4] The next part of the chapter discusses some detailed implementation issues, including system architecture, the reference model, and the protocol stack, as well as system design.

Network Architecture

The future wireless broadband network should be an open platform supporting multicarrier, multibandwidth, and multistandard air interfaces with content-oriented bandwidth-on-demand (BoD) services dominant throughout the whole network. In this way, packetized transmission will

Figure 17-1

Convergence of wireless broadband mobile and access in one track.

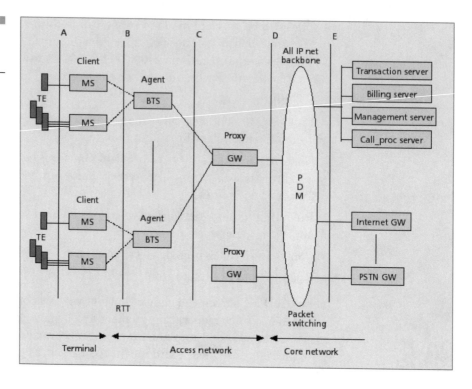

go all the way from one wireless broadband end terminal directly to another. Figure 17-2 shows this new wireless broadband network architecture.[5] The major benefits of this architecture are that the network design is simplified and the system cost greatly reduced. The base transceiver system (BTS) is now a "smart" open platform with a basic wireless broadband hardware pipe embedded with a CAI BIOS. Most functional modules of the system are software-definable and reconfigurable. The packet switching is distributed in the wireless broadband packet backbone (or core network, called *packet-division multiplex*, or PDM). The wireless broadband call processing, as well as other console processing, is handled in this network. The gateway (GW) acts as proxy for the core network and deals with any issues for the BTS, and the BTS is an open platform supporting various standards, optimized for full harmonization and convergence. The terminal (mobile station, or MS) can be single- or multi-user-oriented, supporting converged wireless broadband applications. Figure 17-3 illustrates unified wireless broadband networks based on this architecture.[6]

Figure 17-3
Unified wireless
broadband networks

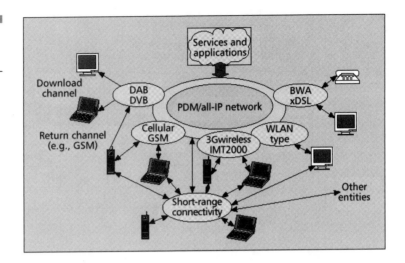

The Protocol Stack

Considering the signaling protocol in Figure 17-2, the client-server model is established between a wireless broadband terminal and the core network. The BTS becomes the agent in both directions. This end-to-end direct signaling can ensure that the wireless broadband terminal is intelligent rather than the dumb one in the current wireless broadband system. Figure 17-4a shows the system protocol stack.[7]

Different services [Asynchronous Transfer Mode (ATM), IP, Synchronous Transfer Mode (STM), MPEG] can be supported through a service convergence layer. To guarantee wireless broadband quality of service (QoS) and high spectrum utilization, dynamic bandwidth allocation (DBA) is required through the medium access control (MAC) DBA sublayer, which improves the conventional layer architecture. The DBA scheduler is the core of the MAC. To realize dynamic resource allocation, this scheduler is essential for the wireless broadband link, which in general helps

- Support class of service offerings.
- Provide agnostic support for all network protocols.
- Eliminate the need for traffic shaping and user parameter control.
- Eliminate end-to-end packet and/or cell delay variation.
- Increase spectrum utilization.[8]

The transmission convergence layer handles various transmission modulations, error corrections, segmentations, and interface mappings of wire-

Figure 17-4
(a) General protocol
stack; (b) protocol
stack examples.

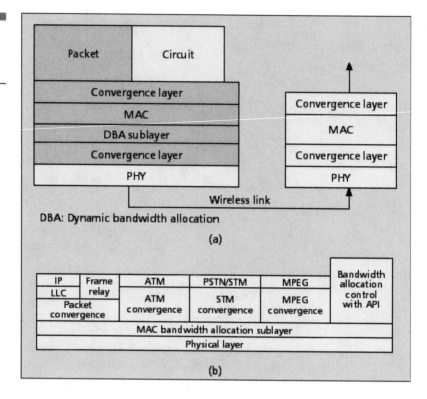

DBA: Dynamic bandwidth allocation

(a)

(b)

less mobile and access in the physical layer. Figure 17-4(*b*) presents an example of support for wireless broadband access applications.

Compact Open Core

As mentioned in previous sections, this converged wireless broadband system will have the following features:

- Multistandard: 3G wireless plus wireless broadband access
- High channel density with efficient resource utilization
- Dynamically scalable data rates: from 32 kbps to 20 Mbps
- Software-definable and over-the-air programmable modules
- Open core: various reconfigurable kernels and CAI BIOS[9]

Figure 17-5
Multidimensional and reconfigurable radio.

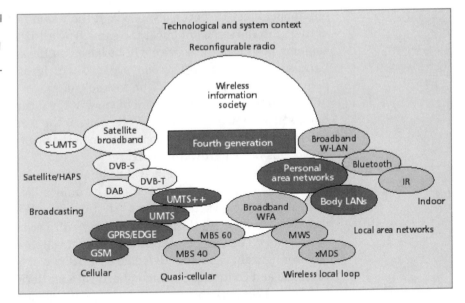

Figure 17-5 depicts this multidimensional and reconfigurable radio, whereas Figure 17-6 shows its open interfaces.[10] As wireless broadband goes multidimensional, different standards come out every day for differ-

Figure 17-6
Compact wireless broadband—open interfaces.

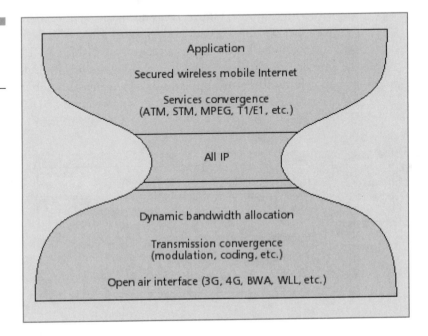

ent applications. However, if you look at their architectures in detail, most of them are the same or almost the same. The all-IP layer will become the common platform; the service will be based on the secure wireless broadband mobile Internet. The convergence will focus on variable service demands as well as transmission technologies.

From an implementation point of view, in the future, the wireless broadband software will take about 75 percent of the work, and the hardware will take only 25 percent for construction of the open platform. Figure 17-7 shows this basic hardware structure.[11]

The digital block eventually will be implemented in one system, and further on one chip (system on a chip). The analog block leaves there as an open module subject to various CAI standards. With superconductivity technology advances, this block probably will become a separate analog header only. The wireless broadband pipe throughout this hardware will be reconfigurable and adaptive. The CAI BIOS will be the software kernel to access and control the common hardware platform.

Figure 17-8 lists the major functions embedded in this compact hardware implementation, where minimum software control is required.[12] There are four key modules in the systems: the air interface module, the baseband processing unit, the digital broadband transceiver, and the smart antenna array. The detailed functional segments are required for the converged implementations of the proposed wireless broadband system.

As an example, Figure 17-9 shows the open terminal architecture of this compact wireless broadband system, where the DSP core, CAI BIOS and soft radio API, and main processor unit (MPU)/CPU are the three most important entities.[13] The RF/IF subsystem is an independent unit configurable to different applications of wireless broadband mobile or wireless broadband access. The digital downconverter (DDC), digital upconverter

Figure 17-7

An open platform for wireless broadband mobile and access.

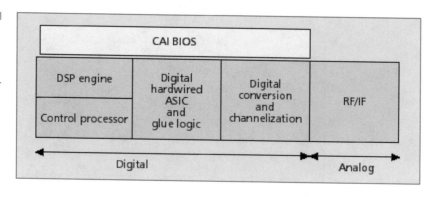

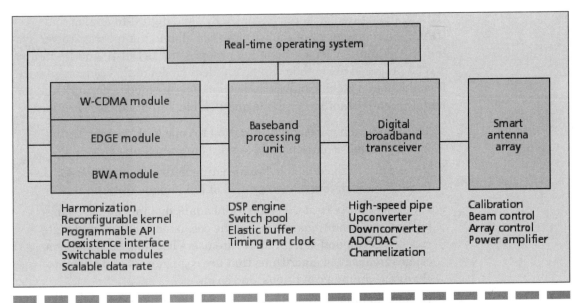

Figure 17-8 Functional segments of the converged wireless broadband systems.

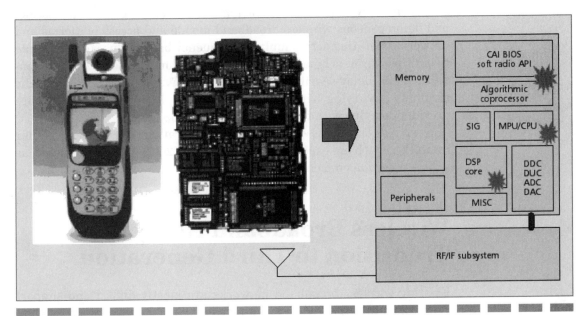

Figure 17-9 A compact wireless broadband open terminal.

(DUC), analog-to-digital converter (ADC), and digital-to-analog converter (DAC) are components of the wireless broadband digital transceiver system. SIG handles various signaling protocol stacks (all-IP and IP-on-air).

The proposed 4G mobile will be an ideal model of this converged wireless broadband mobile and access system. The 4G mobile network and terminal reconfigurability (scalable and flexible, self-organized) includes

- The adaptation of resource allocation to cope with varying traffic loads, channel conditions, and service environments.

- Integration of fixed/mobile/broadcasting networks and rules for distribution and decentralized control of functional entities.

- Protocols that permit the network to adapt dynamically to changing channel conditions and allow the coexistence of low- and high-rate users, handoff of high-data-rate users between base stations, congestion-control algorithms that are cognizant of and adjust to changing channel conditions, and so on.

- Development of system concepts for digital wireless broadband millimeter-wave capable of delivering higher bit rates for wireless broadband access applications.[14]

Therefore, 4G mobile will provide seamless high-data-rate wireless broadband service over an increasing number of integrated but distinct and heterogeneous wireless broadband mobile and access platforms and networks operating across multiple frequency bands. This service adapts to multiple wireless broadband standards (and multimode terminal capabilities) and delay-sensitive or delay-insensitive applications over radio channels of varying bandwidth across multiple operators and service provider domains with fully user-controlled QoS levels.

Next, let's look at 2G+ systems. Third-generation (3G) wireless cellular networks, which are expected to be deployed in 2001, are also discussed, as well as a section on mobile IP support.

Wireless Broadband Networks: Transition to Third Generation

Existing wireless broadband networks are mostly digital and support voice communications at a low bit rate of 9.6 to 32 kbps (see the sidebar, "Advanced Voice Services over Wireless Broadband"). Fueled by the explosive growth of the Internet, applications are demanding that higher capacity, higher data rates, and advanced multimedia services be supported in the near future. The evolution to higher data rates and more advanced services occurs in two steps. The first step is the emergence of 2G+ systems in which second-generation (2G) systems such as the Global System for Mobile Communications (GSM) and IS-95 are extended to provide high-speed data communications either without changing the air interface or by using improved coding techniques. The second step is to provide higher capacity, data rates, and multimedia services. Wideband code-division multiple access (WCDMA) standard proposals such as the cdma2000 system include a greatly enhanced air interface to support wider bandwidths for improved capacity and higher data rates.

Advanced Voice Services over Wireless Broadband

Flexion Systems, a provider of managed business solutions for the growing company, and Convergent Networks, a provider of wireless broadband voice infrastructure solutions for the new public network, have recently signed an agreement to jointly sell and market next-generation wireless broadband access solutions. By deploying Convergent Networks' Cohesion wireless broadband switching solution at the network edge and Flexion's BusinessGuardian family of integrated communications platforms on the customer premises, service providers can today offer high-value services over an efficient packet network.

In partnering with companies that deliver next-generation customer premises equipment like Flexion Systems, Convergent Networks expands service providers' options when deploying the network infrastructure they need to deliver on their business plans. With this joint solution, carriers not only address the ripe market opportunity created by the growing demand for wireless broadband services but also differentiate themselves in the marketplace with integrated service offerings that attract and retain customers.

The joint solution creates an architecture that allows service providers to enter new markets and offer cost-effective, revenue-generating services over unified wireless broadband access networks. Utilizing Convergent Networks' ICServiceWorks service creation softswitch and Flexion's BusinessGuardian family of solutions, service providers can deliver advanced communications offerings, such as centrex services, unified communications, and calling card services. By leveraging Asynchronous Transfer Mode (ATM) technology, the combined solution ensures voice quality of service (QoS) while leveraging the economic benefits of packet-switching technology.

The ability to provide interoperable, cost-effective, intelligent networking solutions is a must for service providers as they strive to meet the needs of the demanding small business. Flexion's partnership with Convergent Networks allows next-generation service providers to deliver advanced business applications as well as integrated wireless broadband voice and data services, going beyond just basic connectivity.

Carriers today need networking solutions that will help them show differentiation in an increasingly competitive market. The ability to deliver wireless broadband data services with high-quality voice communications is becoming more of a requirement as service providers look to grow their networks and deliver additional services to the small to medium-sized business.[15]

In a cellular network, there are radio ports with antennas connected to base stations (BSs) serving the user equipment, the mobile stations (MSs). The communication from the MS to the BS is the uplink and from the BS to the MS the downlink. The downlink is contentionless, but the uplink is accessed by several MSs; therefore, another important characteristic is the multiple-access technique used for its uplink. Frequency-division multiple access (FDMA), time-division multiple access (TDMA), and code-division multiple access (CDMA) are the most widely used physical-layer multiple-access techniques.

The infrastructure of cellular networks includes mobile switching centers (MSCs), which control one or more BSs and interface them to the wired public switched telephone network (PSTN), and a central home location register (HLR) and visiting location register (VLR) for each MSC. The HLR and VLR are databases that keep the registered and present locations of MSs to be used in handoffs (the process of handing a call over to the new cell when an MS moves).

2G+ Systems

Two examples of the macrocellular packet mode standards are Global System for Mobile Communications (GSM's) General Packet Radio System (GPRS), a TDMA-based system, and IS-95A's IS-95B, a CDMA-based system. Higher-capacity transmission is achieved with multislot mode in TDMA and multiple codes in CDMA-based systems. In some cases, a higher-level modulation format is used to increase the rate of transmission.

Evolution of GSM Packet Mode: GPRS

GPRS is the packet-mode extension to GSM. It uses the same air interface but with a new physical channel called a *52-multiframe*, which is made of two 26-control multiframes of voice-mode GSM. Packet-mode control and data channels are mapped into different slots of the 52-multiframe, which takes 240 ms. 52-Multiframe consists of 12 blocks (B0–B11) of four frames to which several packet-mode logical channels can be mapped and four additional frames.

The architecture of GPRS is shown in Figure 17-10.[16] The serving GPRS support node (SGSN) is in charge of one or more GPRS BSs. The base station controller (BSC) monitors and controls several BSs or base transceiver stations (BTSs). The BSC and its BTSs form a base station subsystem (BSS). A BTS and the MSs in its control form a cell. The gateway GPRS support node (GGSN) is for interconnection with the Internet. The registration of packet mode MSs is done with the architectural entities, the MSC/VLR and HLR.

Logical channels of GPRS are the packet common control channels (PCCCHs). They are comprised of logical channels for common control signaling used for packet data and a packet random access channel (PRACH)—uplink only, which is used by an MS to initiate uplink transfer for sending data or signaling information—a packet paging channel (PPCH)—downlink only, which is used to page an MS prior to downlink packet transfer—and a packet access grant channel (PAGCH)—downlink only, which is used in the packet transfer establishment phase to send

Figure 17-10
GPRS architecture.

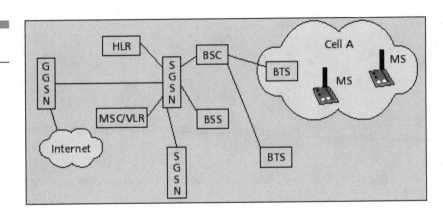

resource assignment to an MS prior to packet transfer. There is also a packet broadcast control channel (PBCCH)—downlink only, which is used to broadcast packet-data-specific system information. In addition, the packet data traffic channel (PDTCH) is a channel allocated for data transfer. It is temporarily dedicated to one MS. In multislot operation, one MS may use multiple PDTCHs in parallel for individual packet transfer. All PDTCHs are unidirectional, either uplink (PDTCH/U) for a mobile-originated packet transfer or downlink (PDTCH/D) for a mobile-terminated packet transfer. A packet associated control channel (PACCH) conveys signaling information related to a given MS. The PACCH also carries resource assignment and reassignment messages, assigning a capacity for PDTCH(s) and for further occurrences of the PACCH.

A multislot MS can be assigned up to eight slots in any frame of any of 12 blocks. In a given cell, up to four downlink-uplink pairs of 52-multiframes can be generated on four different pairs of frequencies.

Protocol layering in GRPS is as follows. The Subnetwork Dependent Convergence Protocol (SNDCP) does the convergence. Logical Link Control (LLC) is the upper layer of medium access control. Radio Link Control (RLC) and the Medium Access Control (MAC) protocols provide reliable access to the radio link.

Transmission/reception data flow is shown in Figure 17-11.[17] A temporary block flow (TBF) is a physical connection used by the two radio

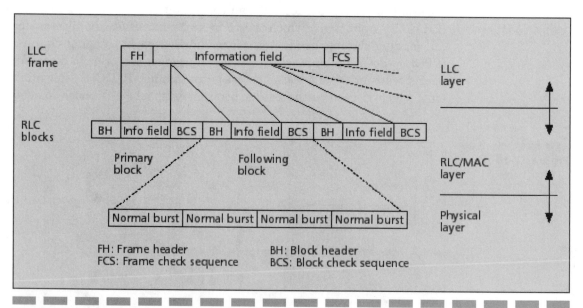

Figure 17-11   GPRS downlink-uplink segmentation.

resource (RR) entities to support the unidirectional transfer of LLC PDUs on packet data physical channels. The TBF is allocated on some radio resources on one or more PDCHs and comprises a number of RLC/MAC blocks carrying one or more LLC PDUs. A radio block consists of a 1-byte MAC header, followed by RLC data or an RLC/MAC control block and terminated by a 16-bit block check sequence (BCS). It is carried by four normal bursts (it is 57 bytes long). A TBF is temporary and is maintained only for the duration of the data transfer. Each TBF is assigned a temporary flow identity (TFI) by the network that is unique in both directions.

The GRPS allows a maximum of eight slots per frame to be allocated to the PDTCH on the downlink and uplink on all radio blocks B0 to B11. On the downlink, an IP datagram of 1500 bytes, to be transmitted as an LLC PDU, is fragmented into 29 RLC blocks. These blocks can be transmitted using a total of 116 consecutive bursts. During one 52-multiframe with an 8 slots/frame dynamic allocation scheme, 3.3 such IP datagrams can be transmitted, yielding a maximum data rate of 165.5 kbps for GPRS downlink.

On the uplink, an IP datagram of 1500 bytes, to be transmitted as an LLC PDU, is fragmented into 31 RLC blocks that can be transmitted in 124 slots. During one 52-multiframe with an 8 slots/frame dynamic allocation scheme, three such IP datagrams can be transmitted, yielding a maximum data rate of 154 kbps for GPRS uplink.

Evolution of IS-95 to Packet-Mode Data: IS-95B

IS-95B is the packet-mode version of direct-sequence CDMA standard IS-95A. IS-95B supports multiple codes per MS on both the downlink and the uplink.

Physical channels on the downlink are the pilot channel, paging channels, and traffic channels; and on the uplink, access and traffic channels. The BS always generates the pilot channel. One synchronization channel and up to seven paging channels can be generated, in which case 55 code channels to be used as traffic channels are generated. Up to 63 traffic channels can be generated on the downlink. Each traffic channel contains one fundamental code channel (FCC) and up to seven supplemental code channels (SCCs). The pilot channel provides CDMA infrastructural support such as demodulation and power control measurements. The sync channel provides synchronization information such as paging channel data rate and system time. It operates at 1.2 kbps.

On the uplink, the access channel, like the PACCH of GPRS, is used by an MS to initiate a call, to respond to a paging channel message from the BS, and for location updates. Each access control channel is associated with a downlink paging channel; therefore, there can be up to seven access channels. Access channels support 4.8 kbps data rate only. Traffic channels consist of a single FCC and up to seven SCCs per user. A total of 64 uplink physical channels can be generated in a cell on a given frequency. Downlink-uplink SCCs can use only the full rates of 9.6 or 14.4 kbps.

The data-link layer in IS-95B is organized as the multiplexing sublayer, layer 2 for primary traffic, e.g., the Radio Link Control Protocol (RLP) and upper layers for primary traffic containing the LLC Protocol. RLC provides reliable data-link control and stream-oriented delivery of LLC data. The radio link is divided into 20-ms time slots. During a time slot, an MS can transmit/receive packets containing 192 bits, of which 172 are information bits at the full rate of 9.6 kbps, or 288 bits, of which 267 are information bits at 14.4 kbps using one FCC and up to seven SCCs.

Packet-mode message exchange is originated by an MS using fundamental code channels. A BS may decide to assign some supplemental code channels during packet-mode communication. In this case, the BS sends a supplemental channel assignment message and then begins transmitting on the downlink SCCs. If the MS requires more bandwidth, it sends a supplemental channel request message to the BS on the reverse FCC. The BS replies with a supplemental channel assignment message, which is forwarded to the FCC. The MS then begins transmitting on the assigned reverse SCCs.

In IS-95B, the segmentation and reassembly of packet data are done at the RLP layer. For rate set 1 (9.6 kbps), the maximum length is 19 bytes, and for rate set 2, the maximum length is 31 bytes. Format B data frames have a sequence field of 8 bits and 20 octets of data for rate 1 and 32 octets of data for rate 2.

An IP datagram of 1500 bytes will be segmented into 79 RLP format A data frames at 9.6 kbps and 49 frames at 14.4 kbps. Assuming one FCC and seven SCCs are to be used, it takes 10 frames for 9.6-kbps and seven slots for 14.4-kbps rate sets to completely transmit this datagram. The resulting maximum downlink data rates are 60 and 86 kbps for rates sets 1 and 2, respectively.

In the uplink, the MS sends an access probe in one R-ACH. An R-ACH is organized in slots of a multiple number of 20-ms frames (5 frames or 100-ms slots). After transmitting the access probe, the MS waits a specified period, TA, which has a minimum value of 160 ms, to receive an acknowledgment. If an acknowledgment is received, packet transmission can start on the FCC and SCCs. The resulting maximum uplink data rates are 26

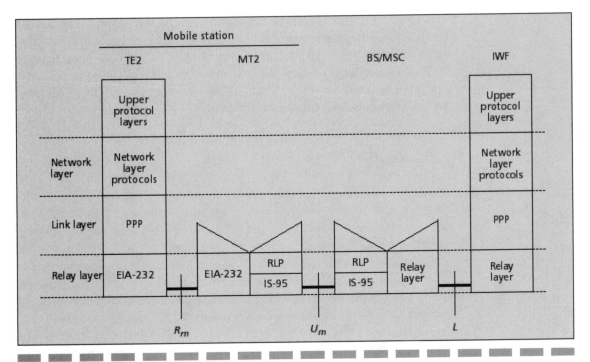

Figure 17-12 RLP high-speed packet data layering in IS-95B.

and 30 kbps for rates sets 1 and 2, respectively. These rates are extremely low compared with downlink rates. However, if the MS continues to send subsequent IP datagrams after the access probe, data rates close to the downlink rates of 60 and 86 kbps can be achieved.

During packet data communication between an MS and an Internet node, an interworking function (IWF) acts as a gateway, and the layering shown in Figure 17-12 is in effect.[18] The Internet's Point-to-Point Protocol (PPP) is used as the link layer. The network layer employs the Internet Protocol (IP).

Third-Generation Wireless Broadband Systems

Many 3G wireless broadband systems are expected to be based on WCDMA technology. Wideband CDMA is being standardized by a consortium of leading standardization organizations of the United States, Europe, and Asia, and the resulting standards are being harmonized by the International Telecommunication Union Radiocommunication Standardization Sector (ITU-R) in its International Mobile Telecommunications in 2000 (IMT-2000) harmonization initiative. Let's now discuss the two leading proposals: cdma2000, which is an extension of IS-95B, and WCDMA, proposed by several European institutions.

cdma2000

Main parameters of cdma2000 are (1) chip rates (Mchips/s) of $N \times 1.2288$ ($N = 1, 3, 6, 9, 12$), each corresponding to radiofrequency (rf) channel bandwidths (MHz) of $N \times 1.25$, (2) 0 or 1 SCC per service at 9.6 kbps to 2 Mbps, and (3) a frame length of 5, 10, 20, 40, and 80 ms.

Several reverse and forward link physical channels are supported. The reverse pilot channel (R-PICH) is an unmodulated spread-spectrum signal used to assist the BS in detecting MS transmission. The MS also inserts a reverse power control subchannel in the R-PICH. The reverse power control subchannel is used to transmit forward power control commands. The access channel (R-ACH) is used by the MS to initiate communication with the BS and to respond to paging channel messages. The enhanced access channel (R-EACH) is used by the MS to initiate communication with the BS or to respond to an MS-directed message. The reverse common control channel (R-CCCH) is used for the transmission of user and signaling information to the BS when reverse traffic channels are not in use.

The radio configurations (RCs) specify the data rates, channel encoding, and modulation parameters supported on the traffic channel. For spreading rates 1 and 3, there are six RCs for the reverse link and nine RCs for the forward link. RCs 1 and 2 are specified to provide backward compatibility with Telecommunications/Electronics Industries Association (TIA/EIA)-95B systems. RCs provide different rate sets obtained from the basic rates of 9600 and 14,400 bps. The reverse traffic channels with RCs 1 and 2 include the reverse fundamental channel (R-FCH) and the reverse supplemental code channel (R-SCCH). The reverse traffic channels with RCs 3 to 6 include the reverse dedicated control channel (R-DCCH), the R-FCH, and the reverse supplemental channel (R-SCH). The R-DCCH and R-FCH are used for the transmission of user and signaling information to the BS during a call. The RSCCH and R-SCH are used for the transmission of user information to the BS during a call. Up to seven R-SCCHs and up to two R-SCHs can be generated for each MS.

The forward pilot channel (F-PICH), the transmit diversity pilot channel (F-TDPICH), the auxiliary pilot channels (F-APICHs), and the auxiliary transmit diversity pilot channels (F-ATDPICHs) are unmodulated spread-spectrum signals used for synchronization by a mobile station operating within the coverage area of the BS. The sync channel (F-SYNCH) is used by MSs operating within the coverage area of the BS to acquire initial time synchronization. The paging channel (F-PCH) is used by the BS to transmit system overhead information and MS-specific messages. The broadcast channel (F-BCH) is used by the BS to transmit system overhead information. The quick paging channel (F-QPCH) is used by the BS to inform MSs. The common power control channel (F-CPCCH) is used by the BS to transmit common power control subchannels (1 bit per subchannel) for the power control of multiple reverse common control channels and enhanced access channels. The common assignment channel (F-CACH) is used by the BS to provide quick assignment of the reverse common control channel. The forward common control channel (F-CCCH) is used by the BS to transmit MS-specific messages. For RCs 1 and 2, the forward traffic channels include the forward fundamental channel (F-FCH) and the forward supplemental code channel (F-SCCH). For RC9, the forward traffic channels include the forward dedicated control channel (F-DCCH), the forward fundamental channel (F-FCH), and the forward supplemental channel (F-SCH). Up to seven F-SCCHs and up to two F-SCHs are generated.

Different state machines are kept for each active packet or circuit data at the MAC layer. The Link Access Protocol (LAC) sublayer supports highly reliable point-to-point over-the-air transmission of signaling and circuit-mode data traffic using automatic repeat request (ARQ) techniques. The logical channel structure of cdma2000 is based on the packet service state transitions. A forward/reverse dedicated MAC logical channel (f/r-dmch control) carries MAC messages. This channel is allocated in active and control hold states. A forward/reverse dedicated traffic logical channel (f/r-dtch) is used to carry user data. It is allocated throughout the active state. A forward/reverse common signaling channel (f/r-csch) and a forward/reverse dedicated signaling channel (f/r-dsch) are used to carry signaling information.

Forward and reverse physical channels may support 5-ms frames, 20-ms frames, or both 5- and 20-ms frames. The 5-ms frames are used to carry MAC messages, whereas the 20-ms frames carry upper-layer signaling and RLP frames. In the downlink, the forward common logical channels of f-csch are mapped to F-CCCH or F-PCH. The forward link logical channels f-dsch, f-dtch, and f-dmch are mapped to F-FCH. The forward link logical channel f-dtch is mapped to F-SCH, and f-dsch, f-dtch, and f-dmch are mapped to F-DCCH.

The reverse link logical channels r-dsch, r-dtch, and r-dmch are mapped to R-FCH; r-dtch also can be mapped to R-SCH or R-DCCH. r-dsch and r-dmch are mapped to R-DCCH. The reverse link logical channels r-csch, r-ctch, r-cmvch, r-cmsch, and r-cmdch are mapped to R-CCCH or R-ACH.

In order to gain access to one or more of the limited number of traffic channels, MSs use the multiple access channels of R-CCCH or R-ACH to make access probes or packet access requests. A 20-ms frame is divided into 5-ms access probe slots in which a short access request message can be transmitted by an MS. A traffic channel assignment normally should be received during the next frame. Failing that, the MS enters into an exponential backoff procedure in which the access probe is retransmitted after exponentially increasing the number of frame times.

Access probes are made by MSs on R-ACH in order to send either a response to transactions initiated by the BS or channel access requests autonomously. R-ACH is slotted, and there is an offset between the slots of different parallel R-ACHs. After an initial backoff, the MS sends a short message called an *access probe*. If no acknowledgment is received due to a collision, the MS waits for an exponentially increasing backoff period before sending the access probe again.

High-Speed Data Transfer   Let's take RC 6 on the reverse link and RC 9 on the forward link, which provide 2, 4, 8, 16, 32, and 72 times 14,400 bps (with the maximum rate of 1,036,800 bps) as an example. This maximum rate is possible at spreading rate 3 on a supplementary channel (SCH).

High-speed packet data communication is possible on the links between an MS and the packet data serving node (PDSN) using PPP as the link layer and IP as the network layer. The MS is connected to the BS over the U_m interface. The BS with packet control function (PCF) is connected to the PDSN over the A_{quater} interface. Once a PPP connection is established between the MS and the PDSN, the bandwidth (traffic channels) is allocated to the connection on a dynamic basis.

On the U_m interface, the Link Layer Protocol used is RLP type 3, which uses negative acknowledgments to provide a reliable link-layer packet-mode transfer. Twelve-bit sequence numbers are used, and the packet data are segmented into a maximum of 4096 octet segments, further divided into frames as units of transmission. Each frame can carry up to 256 octets of user data and a 4-octet header. Each 20-ms RLP can receive, at most, 17 RLP frames.

Consider IP datagrams of 1500 octets to be transmitted on a forward link logical channel f-dtch at the rate of 1,036,800 bps. The PPP layer adds a header of 8 octets. The resulting packets are transmitted by RLP in several fragments, with each frame carrying 256 octets of user data, each fragment to fit into 2592 octets, which is transmitted during one frame of 20 ms. This yields a maximum data rate of 1,020,800 bps without considering retransmissions. On a reverse link logical channel, the same datagram takes at least 20 ms longer to transmit due to multiple access on R-ACH, which reduces the maximum data rate. The reverse link rate increases if the MS continues to transmit without waiting for another access procedure while it approaches the rate of the downlink.

WCDMA

Support for high-data-rate transmission (384 kbps with wide-area coverage, 2 Mbps with local coverage), asynchronous BS operation, high service flexibility with support of multiple parallel variable-rate services on each connection and a 10-ms frame length, and a chip rate of 3.84 Mchips per second are the key features of wideband code-division multiple access (WCDMA), which has two versions: frequency-division duplex (FDD) and time-division duplex (TDD). The FDD version is designed to operate in either of the following paired bands:

- 1920–1980 MHz uplink; 2110–2170 MHz downlink
- 1850–1910 MHz uplink, 1930–1990 MHz downlink[19]

The European version of IMT-2000, the Universal Mobile Telecommunications System (UMTS), is composed of a core network (CN), connected with interface I_u to the radio access network, called the *UMTS Terrestrial Radio Access Network* (UTRAN), which is connected to the user equipment (UE) with interface U_u (Figure 17-13).[20] The UTRAN consists of a set of radio network subsystems (RNSs) connected to the CN through the I_u. An RNS consists of a radio network controller (RNC) and one or more node Bs. A node B is connected to the RNC through the I_{ub} interface. The RNC is responsible for the handover decisions that require signaling to the UE. Inside UTRAN, the RNCs of the RNSs can be interconnected through the I_{ur}. I_{ur} can be conveyed over a physical direct connection between RNCs or via any suitable transport network. Each RNS is responsible for the resources of its set of cells, and each node B has one or more cells.

Protocol layer 2 of WCDMA is split into the following sublayers: MAC, RLC, Packet Data Convergence Protocol (PDCP), and broadcast/multicast control (BMC). Layer 3 and RLC are divided into control (C-) and user (U-) planes. PDCP and BMC exist in the U-plane only. In the C-plane, layer 3 is partitioned into sublayers, where the lowest sublayer, denoted radio resource control (RRC), interfaces with layer 2 and terminates in the UTRAN. The next sublayer provides *duplication avoidance* functionality,

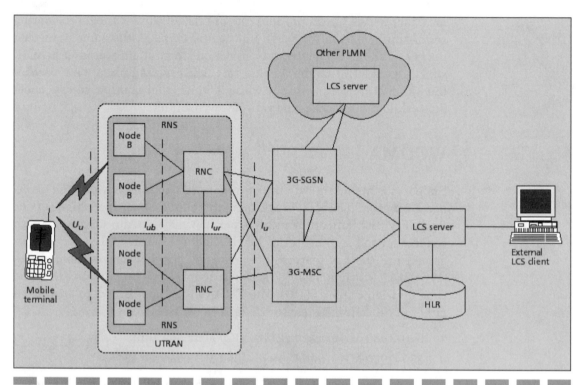

Figure 17-13   Third-Generation Partnership Project (3GPP) architecture.

which prevents loss of data in case handovers terminate in the CN. In case of no change to the I_u connection point, the RLC sublayer's ARQ functionality, which is closely coupled with the radio transmission technique used, prevents all loss of data.

Logical/Transport and Physical Channels   The characteristics of a transport channel are defined by its transport format (or format set), specifying the physical layer processing to be applied to the transport channel in question, such as convolutional channel coding and interleaving, and any service-specific rate matching as needed. Random access channel(s) (RACH, uplink), forward access channel(s) (FACH, downlink), broadcast channel (BCH, downlink), paging channel (PCH, downlink), synchronization channel (SCH, TDD downlink), downlink shared channel(s) (DSCH), common packet channel (CPCH, FDD downlink), and uplink shared channel (USCH, TDD) are common transport channels. The dedicated channel (DCH, uplink/downlink) and fast uplink signaling channel (FAUSCH) are dedicated transport channels.

Variable-bit-rate transmission in layer 1 is achieved by associating a transport format or format set to a transport channel. A transport block is a basic unit exchanged between layer 1 and MAC entities and typically corresponds to an RLC PDU. A transport block may be 20 bits of coded speech or 320 bits of RLC PDU. Layer 1 adds cyclic redundancy check (CRC) into a transport block. A transport block is transmitted during a transmission time interval that is 10 ms or a multiple of 10 ms. A set of transport blocks may be transferred during a transmission time interval. The transport format combination indication (TFCI) field uniquely identifies the transport format used by each transport channel within the current radio frame. The multiplexing and exact rate-matching patterns follow predefined rules and are encoded in the TFCI field by the transmitter. The receiver derives this information from the TFCI field without signaling over the radio interface.

WCDMA in FDD mode supports several physical channels that transmit the data in the transport channels. Physical channels typically consist of a three-layer structure of superframes, radio frames, and time slots. A superframe has a duration of 720 ms and consists of 72 radio frames. A radio frame has a duration of 10 ms and consists of 15 time slots. Physical channels are the uplink dedicated physical data channel (uplink DPDCH) and uplink dedicated physical control channel (uplink DPCCH). The uplink DPDCH is used to carry dedicated data generated at layer 2 and above (the dedicated transport channel, DCH). The uplink DPCCH is used to carry control information (pilot symbols, power control commands, TFCI field) generated at layer 1. The physical random access channel (PRACH) is used to carry the RACH. The physical common packet channel (PCPCH) is used to carry the CPCH. There is only one type of downlink dedicated physical channel, the downlink dedicated physical channel (downlink DPCH). The primary common pilot channel (CPICH) serves as the phase reference; the primary common control physical channel (P-CCPCH) is used to carry the BCH. The secondary CCPCH is used to carry the FACH and PCH. The SCH is a downlink signal used for cell search. The physical downlink shared channel (PDSCH), used to carry the downlink shared channel (DSCH), is shared by users based on code multiplexing. Depending on the symbol rate of the physical channel, the configuration of radio frames or time slots varies.

The random access transmission is based on a slotted ALOHA approach with fast acquisition indication. UE can start transmitting at access slots where there are 15 access slots per two frames. The random-access transmission consists of one or several preambles of length 4096 chips and a message of length 10 ms. The message has a data part to transmit layer 2 data and a control part to transmit pilot bits and the TFCI field. The data and control parts are transmitted in parallel. The highest RACH data transmission rate is 120 kbp/s.

The MAC layer provides data transfer services on logical channels that are divided into control channels (for the transfer of control-plane information) and traffic channels (for the transfer of user-plane information). The synchronization control channel (SCCH), broadcast control channel (BCCH), paging control channel (PCCH), common control channel (CCCH), dedicated control channel (DCCH), and shared channel control channel (SHCCH) are the control channels. A dedicated traffic channel (DTCH) is a point-to-point channel, dedicated to one UE, for the transfer of user information. A DTCH can exist in both uplink and downlink; it is a point-to-multipoint unidirectional channel for transfer of dedicated user information for all or a group of specified UEs.

High-Speed Data Transfer   The RLC layer performs segmentation/reassembly of variable-length higher-layer PDUs into/from smaller RLC payload units (PUs). The RLC PDU size is adjustable to the actual set of transport formats. RLC transfers user data, and the transfer may be unacknowledged on the control-plane logical channels of BCCH, PCCH, CCCH, SHCCH, and SCCH (downlink only) and on the U-plane logical channel of DTCH or reliably delivered with flow control on DCCH/DTCH logical channels. CCCH uses unacknowledged mode (segmentation/reassembly with sequence number checking), but only for the downlink, and transparent mode (only segmentation/ reassembly is performed) only for the uplink. Frames of 320 bits are used for segmentation/reassembly. In acknowledged mode, the first 2 octets contain the header fields such as 12-bit sequence number, and the rest is used for user data. In order to transmit at higher rates, the header compression procedure enables placing four 80-bit PUs, with only the first PU having a header.

In WCDMA, each slot carries 2560 chips. At a spreading factor of 4, each slot carries 640 bits and, with 15 slots in 10 ms, yields an uplink bit rate of 960 kbps. The downlink rate is twice the uplink bit rate because the symbol bit rate is half the channel bit rate. If burst type 1 is used, each slot can carry 488 data bits, which yields a data bit rate of 732 kbps for the uplink and 1464 kbps for the downlink. Higher rates can be obtained if multiple codes are used.

Consider IP datagrams of 1500 octets to be transmitted on the uplink. The RLC layer segments the datagram into 27 RLC PDUs and adds a 2-octet header into each. The MAC layer adds a 3-octet header if 16-bit UE-id fields are used and forms MAC PDUs. Each such PDU can be transmitted in one slot. This yields an uplink data rate of 672 kbps. The downlink data rate is 1344 kbps.

Integration with the Internet   Efficient support of mobile IP in wireless broadband networks is important for the integration of wireless broadband networks with the Internet. In the wired Internet, when a node moves from one network to another, mobile IP is used to correctly deliver the datagrams into the new network. Operation of mobile IP is as follows. A router called the home agent (HA) in the home network tunnels the datagrams to either another router, the foreign agent (FA), in the visited network or directly to the mobile host. The new location of the mobile host is made known to the HA using registration signaling. The HA and FA send periodic agent advertisements. The mobile sends a registration request to the FA that is relayed to the HA. Registration terminates with a registration reply sent to the mobile by the FA.

Cellular networks have built-in support for mobility in terms of registration, VLR/HLR, and handover procedures. The problem arises for incoming datagrams from the Internet that are routed according to the destination IP address. These datagrams will arrive at the BS in the home cell of the MS. If the MS is not at its home cell, mobile IP support is needed in order to route the datagrams to the destination cell. Supporting mobile IP requires HA and FA functionality in the cellular network infrastructure (PDSN, SGSN, GGSN, etc.).

Integration of mobile IP in cdma2000 is based on the PDSN supporting mobile IP FA functionality (Figure 17-14).[21] The PDSN is connected to the radio network via an R-P interface. A link layer connection is established between the MS and the PDSN after the MS connects to the CDMA network using PPP. After PPP initialization, the PDSN sends agent advertisements to the MS. The MS generates a mobile IP registration request, and the PDSN sends this to the HA using an authentication, authorization, and accounting (AAA) protocol. The PDSN extracts the mobile IP registration reply from the HA and forwards it to the MS.

Handoff between the RN within the same PDSN is handled by transferring the existing R-P link to the new RN and terminating the endpoint with the old RN. In case of handoff between PDSNs, the traffic channel is transferred to the new RN, a new packet service session ID is created between the new RN and the new PDSN, and the packet endpoint to the old PDSN is closed. Using the session ID, the PDSN realizes that this is a new R-P link and not an existing link. If mobile IP route optimization is

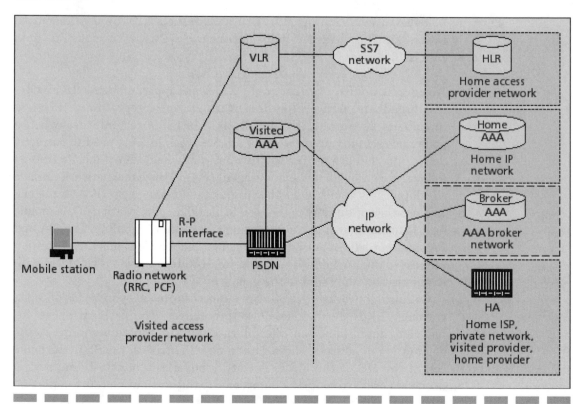

Figure 17-14 Mobile IP in cdma2000.

supported, binding update messages are sent to the corresponding hosts, and the corresponding hosts start to tunnel their datagrams to the new PDSN.

The Third-Generation Partnership Project (3GPP) approach to integrating mobile IP is based on CN nodes called *Internet GPRS support nodes* (IGSNs), to provide FA functionality with commonly deployed extensions such as identifying clients by using network access identifiers (NAIs). During PPP session establishment, the MS gets a care-of address (temporary IP address) from the IGSN and uses this address instead of its home IP address (Figure 17-15).[22]

The MS first performs the international mobile subscriber identity (IMSI) attach and PDP context setup procedures, which establish a link-layer connection to start using 3GPP services for packet data. Over this connection, the IGSN sends an agent advertisement message. The MS gets

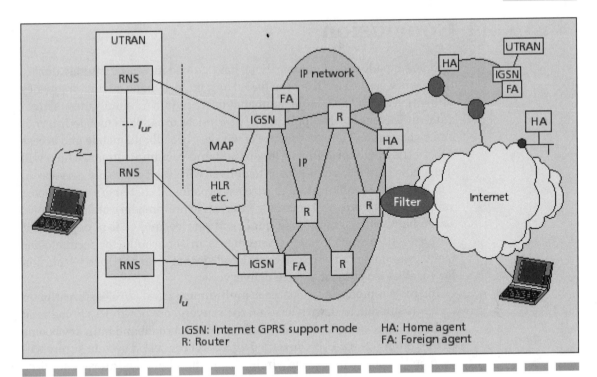

Figure 17-15   Mobile IP in 3GPP.

its care-of address and then registers with its HA. The HA intercepts the datagrams arriving in the home network and tunnels them to the care-of address, in this case the FA (IGSN). Before the IGSN can deliver the datagram to the mobile node, paging and other functions need to be performed according to general UMTS/GPRS procedures. During handoff, the MS may go to an area served by a different IGSN; then the MS, after establishing a link-layer connection with the new IGSN, goes through a new mobile IP registration process. After registering its new care-of address with the HA, the HA tunnels the datagrams from correspondent hosts to the new IGSN, which delivers them to the MS.

The model shown in Figure 17-15 assumes that the CN has native mobile IP support. The IGSN nodes support route optimization in which the correspondent nodes are notified of the new care-of address of the MS, and the correspondent nodes start tunneling the datagrams to the MS directly at its new care-of address.

Conclusion

Wireless broadband communications have gained increased interest during the last few years. This has been fueled by a large demand on high-frequency utilization as well as a large number of users requiring simultaneous high-data-rate access for the applications of wireless broadband mobile Internet and e-commerce. The convergence of wireless broadband mobile and access will be the next storm in wireless broadband communications, which will use a new network architecture to deliver wireless broadband services in a more generic configuration to wireless broadband customers and support value-added services and emerging interactive multimedia communications. Large bandwidth, guaranteed quality of service, and ease of deployment coupled with recent great advancements in semiconductor technologies make this converged wireless broadband system a very attractive solution for wireless broadband service delivery.

In this chapter, a new compact multidimensional wireless broadband core was summarized, with focus on the convergence of wireless broadband mobile and access technologies. As the wireless broadband industry booms in the coming years, this converged wireless broadband system surely will become the major player for wireless broadband mobile Internet services and applications.

This chapter also presented 2G+ systems GSM GPRS and IS-95B. Present cellular systems are based on TDMA and CDMA technologies and provide packet data transmission at low rates. GPRS is a TDMA- and IS-95B a CDMA-based system. Packet-mode data capabilities of these networks represent several improvements over 2G cellular networks.

Wideband CDMA is presently accepted as the technology for 3G cellular networks. This chapter discussed two proposals: cdma2000 and WCDMA. Both standards offer higher packet data rates and facilitate interconnection with the Internet.

It seems a challenge to reach worldwide consensus on a standard for 3G wireless networks. Similarities in the cdma2000 and WCDMA approaches indicate that such a consensus can be reached.

Finally, the International Telecommunications Union defined future wireless broadband systems beyond 3G wireless as 4G mobile, which actually outlines the key features of the proposed convergence of wireless broadband mobile and access systems. 4G mobile will present a beautiful wireless life in 2010, when wireless broadband will not just be a technology.

Endnotes

1. "Netopia Selected by Ericsson as Primary CPE Partner to Deliver Broadband Access and VoDSL Solutions," Technology Marketing Corporation, One Technology Plaza, Norwalk, CT 06854 USA, 2000.

2. Willie W. Lu, "Compact Multidimensional Broadband Wireless: The Convergence of Wireless Mobile and Access," *IEEE Communications Magazine*, IEEE Communications Society (Siemens-Infineon, AG), 305 East 47th Street, New York, NY 10017, USA, 2000.

3. *Ibid.*

4. *Ibid.*

5. *Ibid.*

6. *Ibid.*

7. *Ibid.*

8. *Ibid.*

9. *Ibid.*

10. *Ibid.*

11. *Ibid.*

12. *Ibid.*

13. *Ibid.*

14. *Ibid.*

15. "Flexion, Convergent Networks Partner to Deliver Advanced Voice Services over Broadband," Technology Marketing Corporation, One Technology Plaza, Norwalk, CT 06854 USA, 2000.

16. Behcet Sarikaya, "Packet Mode in Wireless Networks: Overview of Transition to Third Generation," *IEEE Communications Magazine*, IEEE Communications Society (University of Aizu), 305 East 47th Street, New York, NY 10017, USA, 2000.

17. *Ibid.*

18. *Ibid.*

19. *Ibid.*

20. *Ibid.*

21. *Ibid.*

22. *Ibid.*

Configuring Wireless Broadband Networks

CHAPTER 18

Configuring Wireless LANs

A wireless local-area network (WLAN) is a flexible data communication system implemented as an extension to, or as an alternative for, a wired LAN within a building or campus. Using electromagnetic waves, WLANs transmit and receive data over the air, minimizing the need for wired connections. Thus WLANs combine data connectivity with user mobility and, through simplified configuration, enable movable LANs.

Over the last several years, WLANs have gained strong popularity in a number of vertical markets, including the health care, retail, manufacturing, warehousing, and academic arenas, as shown in Figure 18-1.[1] These industries have profited from the productivity gains of using handheld terminals and notebook computers to transmit real-time information to centralized hosts for processing. Today, WLANs are becoming more widely recognized as a general-purpose connectivity alternative for a broad range of business customers. The U.S. wireless LAN market is rapidly approaching $2 billion in revenues.

With this in mind, this chapter introduces the benefits, uses, and basic technologies of configuring wireless LANs (WLANs). A WLAN is an on-premise data communication system that reduces the need for wired connections and makes new applications possible, thereby adding new flexibility to networking. Mobile WLAN users can access information and network resources as they attend meetings, collaborate with other users, or move to other campus locations. However, the benefits of WLANs extend beyond user mobility and productivity to enable portable LANs. With

Figure 18-1
Some popular WLAN applications.

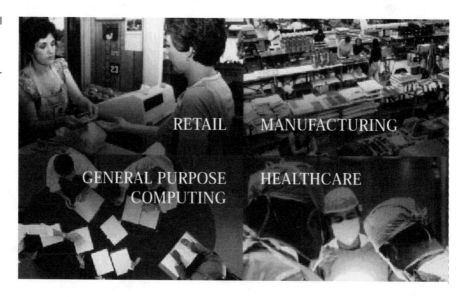

WLANs, the network itself is movable. WLANs have proven their effectiveness in vertical markets and are now experiencing broader applicability in a wide range of business settings.

This chapter also describes the business benefits and applications of configuring WLANs and explains how WLANs differ from other wireless broadband technologies (see the sidebar, "Differences in WLANs from Other Wireless Technologies" and Table 18-1).[2] It explains the basic components and technologies of configuring WLANs and how they work together. It explores the factors that customers must consider when evaluating and configuring WLANs for their business applications needs. Finally, it introduces the Wireless LAN Alliance (WLANA), a nonprofit consortium of wireless LAN vendors that provides ongoing education about specific applications, current technologies, and future directions of wireless LANs.

Differences in WLANs from Other Wireless Technologies

Wireless LANs provide all the functionality of wired LANs, but without the physical constraints of the wire itself. Wireless LAN configurations include independent networks, offering peer-to-peer connectivity, and infrastructure networks, supporting fully distributed data communications. Point-to-point local-area broadband wireless solutions, such as LAN-LAN bridging and personal-area networks (PANs), may overlap with some WLAN applications but fundamentally address different user needs. A wireless LAN-LAN bridge is an alternative to cable that connects LANs in two separate buildings. A wireless PAN typically covers the few feet surrounding a user's workspace and provides the ability to synchronize computers and transfer files and gain access to local peripherals.

Wireless LANs also should not be confused with wireless metropolitan-area networks (WMANs), packet radio often used for law enforcement or utility applications, or with wireless wide-area networks (WWANs), wide-area data transmission over cellular or packet radio. These systems involve costly infrastructures, provide much lower data rates, and require users to pay for bandwidth on a time or usage basis. In contrast, on-premise wireless LANs require no usage fees and provide 100 to 1000 times the data transmission rate.[3]

TABLE 18-1   *High-Level Differences Between WLANs and Other Wireless Broadband Technologies*

	Wireless Local-Area Network (WLAN)	LAN-LAN Bridge	Wireless Wide-Area Network (WWAN)	Wireless Metropolitan-Area Network (WMAN)	Wireless Personal-Area Network (WPAN)
Coverage area	In building or campus	Building to building	National	Metropolitan area	A few feet
Function	Extension or alternative to wired LAN	Alternative to wired connection	Extension of LAN	Extension of wired LAN	Alternative to cable
User fee	No	No	Yes	Yes	No
Typical throughput	1–11 Mbps	2–100 Mbps	1–32 kbps	10–100 kbps	0.1–4 Mbps

Applications for Wireless LANs

Wireless LANs frequently augment rather than replace wired LAN networks—often providing the final few meters of connectivity between a backbone network and the mobile user. The following list describes some of the many applications made possible through the power and flexibility of wireless LANs:

1. Doctors and nurses in hospitals are more productive because handheld or notebook computers with wireless LAN capability deliver patient information instantly.

2. Consulting or accounting audit engagement teams or small workgroups increase productivity with quick network setup.

3. Network managers in dynamic environments minimize the overhead of moves, adds, and changes with wireless LANs, thereby reducing the cost of LAN ownership.

4. Training sites at corporations and students at universities use wireless connectivity to facilitate access to information, information exchanges, and learning.

5. Network managers installing networked computers in older buildings find that wireless LANs are a cost-effective network infrastructure solution.

6. Retail store owners use wireless broadband networks to simplify frequent network reconfigurations.

7. Trade show and branch office workers minimize setup requirements by installing preconfigured wireless LANs needing no local IT support.

8. Warehouse workers use wireless LANs to exchange information with central databases and increase their productivity.

9. Network managers implement wireless LANs to provide backup for mission-critical applications running on wired networks.

10. Senior executives in conference rooms make quicker decisions because they have real-time information at their fingertips.

11. Rental car agencies check in returned rental cars and print customer receipts, which speeds up the process of rental car returns.

12. Package delivery services use metropolitan wireless LANS to track delivery of packages.[4]

Benefits of WLANs

The widespread strategic reliance on networking among competitive businesses and the meteoric growth of the Internet and online services are strong testimonies to the benefits of shared data and shared resources. With wireless LANs, users can access shared information without looking for a place to plug in, and network managers can set up or augment networks without installing or moving wires. Wireless LANs offer the following productivity, service, convenience, and cost advantages over traditional wired networks:

■ *Mobility.* Wireless LAN systems can provide LAN users with access to real-time information anywhere in their organization. This mobility supports productivity and service opportunities not possible with wired networks.

■ *Installation speed and simplicity.* Installing a wireless LAN system can be fast and easy and can eliminate the need to pull cable through walls and ceilings.

■ *Installation flexibility.* Wireless broadband technology allows the network to go where wire cannot go.

■ *Reduced cost of ownership.* While the initial investment required for wireless LAN hardware can be higher than the cost of wired LAN hardware, overall installation expenses and life-cycle costs can be significantly lower. Long-term cost benefits are greatest in dynamic environments requiring frequent moves, adds, and changes.

- *Scalability wireless.* LAN systems can be configured in a variety of topologies to meet the needs of specific applications and installations. Configurations are easily changed and range from peer-to-peer networks suitable for a small number of users to full infrastructure networks of thousands of users that allow roaming over a broad area. [5]

How WLANs Work

Wireless LANs use electromagnetic airwaves (radio and infrared) to communicate information from one point to another without relying on any physical connection. Radio waves are often referred to as *radio carriers* because they simply perform the function of delivering energy to a remote receiver. The data being transmitted are superimposed on the radio carrier so that they can be extracted accurately at the receiving end. This is generally referred to as *modulation of the carrier* by the information being transmitted. Once data are superimposed (modulated) onto the radio carrier, the radio signal occupies more than a single frequency, since the frequency or bit rate of the modulating information adds to the carrier.

Multiple radio carriers can exist in the same space at the same time without interfering with each other if the radio waves are transmitted on different radio frequencies. To extract data, a radio receiver tunes in (or

Figure 18-2
Typical WLAN configuration.

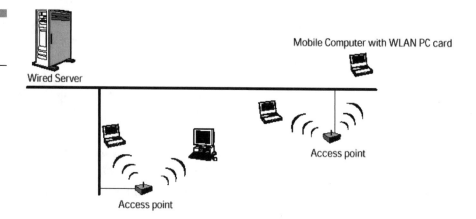

Wired Server

Mobile Computer with WLAN PC card

Access point

Access point

selects) one radio frequency while rejecting all other radio signals on different frequencies.

In a typical WLAN configuration (Figure 18-2), a transmitter/receiver (transceiver) device, called an *access point*, connects to the wired network from a fixed location using standard Ethernet cable.[6] At a minimum, the access point receives, buffers, and transmits data between the WLAN and the wired network infrastructure. A single access point can support a small group of users and can function within a range of less than 100 to several hundred feet. The access point (or the antenna attached to the access point) is usually mounted high but may be mounted essentially anywhere that is practical as long as the desired radio coverage is obtained.

End users access the WLAN through wireless LAN adapters, which are implemented as PC cards in notebook computers, or use ISA or PCI adapters in desktop computers or fully integrated devices within handheld computers. WLAN adapters provide an interface between the client network operating system (NOS) and the airwaves (via an antenna). The nature of the wireless broadband connection is transparent to the NOS.

Bluetooth

Bluetooth technology is a forthcoming wireless personal-area networking (WPAN) technology that has gained significant industry support and will coexist with most wireless LAN solutions. The Bluetooth specification is for a 1-Mbps, small-form-factor, low-cost radio solution that can provide links between mobile phones, mobile computers, and other portable handheld devices and connectivity to the internet. This technology, embedded in a wide range of devices to enable simple, spontaneous wireless broadband connectivity, is a complement to wireless LANs—which are designed to provide continuous connectivity via standard wired LAN features and functionality.

WLAN Configurations

WLAN configurations consist of the following:

- Independent WLANs
- Infrastructure WLANs
- Microcells and roaming

Figure 18-3
Independent WLAN.

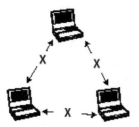

Independent WLANs

The simplest WLAN configuration is an independent (or peer-to-peer) WLAN that connects a set of PCs with wireless broadband adapters. Any time two or more wireless broadband adapters are within range of each other, they can set up an independent network (Figure 18-3).[7] These on-demand networks typically require no administration or preconfiguration. Access points can extend the range of independent WLANs by acting as a repeater (Figure 18-4), effectively doubling the distance between wireless PCs.[8]

Infrastructure WLANs

In infrastructure WLANs, multiple access points link the WLAN to the wired network and allow users to efficiently share network resources, as shown in Figure 18-5.[9] The access points not only provide communication with the wired network but also mediate wireless broadband network traffic in the immediate neighborhood. Multiple access points can provide wireless broadband coverage for an entire building or campus.

Figure 18-4
Extended-range
independent WLAN
using access point
as repeater.

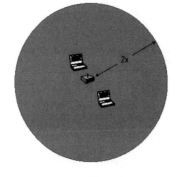

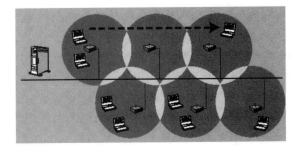

Microcells and Roaming

Wireless broadband communication is limited by how far signals carry for a given power output. WLANs use cells, called *microcells*, similar to the cellular telephone system to extend the range of wireless broadband connectivity. At any point in time, a mobile PC equipped with a WLAN adapter is associated with a single access point and its microcell, or area of coverage. Individual microcells overlap to allow continuous communication within the wired network, as shown in Figure 18-6.[10] They handle low-power signals and hand off users as they roam through a given geographic area.

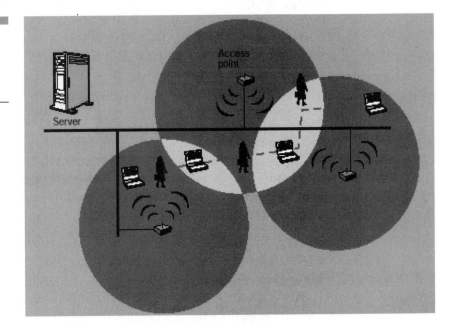

Wireless LAN Technology Options

Manufacturers of WLANs have a range of technologies to choose from when designing a WLAN solution. Each technology comes with its own set of advantages and limitations.

Spread Spectrum

Most WLAN systems use spread-spectrum technology, a wideband radiofrequency (rf) technique developed by the military for use in reliable, secure, mission-critical communications systems. Spread spectrum is designed to trade off bandwidth efficiency for reliability, integrity, and security. In other words, more bandwidth is consumed than in the case of narrowband transmission, but the tradeoff produces a signal that is, in effect, louder and thus easier to detect, provided that the receiver knows the parameters of the spread-spectrum signal being broadcast. If a receiver is not tuned to the right frequency, a spread-spectrum signal looks like background noise. There are two types of spread-spectrum radio: frequency hopping and direct sequence.

Narrowband Technology

A narrowband radio system transmits and receives user information on a specific radio frequency. Narrowband radio keeps the radio signal frequency as narrow as possible just to pass the information. Undesirable crosstalk between communications channels is avoided by carefully coordinating different users on different channel frequencies.

A private telephone line is much like a radio frequency. When each home in a neighborhood has its own private telephone line, people in one home cannot listen to calls made to other homes. In a radio system, privacy and noninterference are accomplished by the use of separate radio frequencies. The radio receiver filters out all radio signals except the ones on its designated frequency.

Frequency-Hopping Spread-Spectrum Technology

Frequency-hopping spread spectrum (FHSS) uses a narrowband carrier that changes frequency in a pattern known to both transmitter and

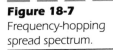

Figure 18-7
Frequency-hopping
spread spectrum.

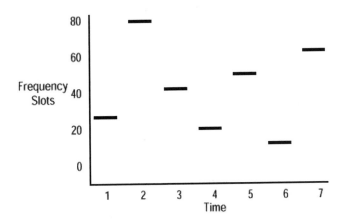

receiver (Figure 18-7).[11] Properly synchronized, the net effect is to maintain a single logical channel. To an unintended receiver, FHSS appears to be short-duration impulse noise.

Direct-Sequence Spread-Spectrum Technology

Direct-sequence spread spectrum (DSSS) generates a redundant bit pattern for each bit to be transmitted, as shown in Figure 18-8.[12] This bit pattern is called a *chip* (or *chipping code*). The longer the chip, the greater is

Figure 18-8
Direct-sequence
spread spectrum.

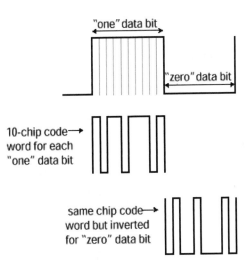

the probability that the original data can be recovered (and, of course, the more bandwidth required). Even if one or more bits in the chip are damaged during transmission, statistical techniques embedded in the radio can recover the original data without the need for retransmission. To an unintended receiver, DSSS appears as low-power wideband noise and is rejected (ignored) by most narrowband receivers.

NOTE   DSSS is sometimes referred to as "noise-modulated spread spectrum."

Infrared Technology

Infrared (IR) systems use very high frequencies, just below visible light in the electromagnetic spectrum, to carry data. Like light, IR cannot penetrate opaque objects; it is either directed (line-of-sight) or diffuse technology. Inexpensive directed systems provide very limited range (3 ft) and typically are used for PANs but occasionally are used in specific WLAN applications. High performance directed IR is impractical for mobile users and therefore is used only to implement fixed subnetworks. Diffuse (or reflective) IR WLAN systems do not require line of sight, but cells are limited to individual rooms.

WLAN Customer Considerations

Compared with wired LANs, WLANs provide installation and configuration flexibility and the freedom inherent in the network mobility. Potential WLAN customers also should consider some or all of the following issues:

- Benefits of WLANs
- Range/coverage
- Throughput
- Multipath effects
- Integrity and reliability
- Interoperability with wired infrastructure
- Interoperability with wireless broadband infrastructure
- Interference and coexistence
- Simplicity/ease of use

- Security
- Cost
- Scalability
- Battery life for mobile platforms
- Safety

Benefits of WLANs

The widespread strategic reliance on networking among competitive businesses and the meteoric growth of the Internet and online services are strong testimonies to the benefits of shared data and shared resources. With WLANs, users can access shared information without looking for a place to plug in, and network managers can set up or augment networks without installing or moving wires. WLANs offer the following productivity, service, convenience, and cost advantages over traditional wired networks.

Range/Coverage

The distance over which rf waves can communicate is a function of product design (including transmitted power and receiver design) and the propagation path, especially in indoor environments. Interactions with typical building objects, including walls, metal, and even people, can affect how energy propagates and thus what range and coverage a particular system achieves. Most WLAN systems use rf because radio waves can penetrate many indoor walls and surfaces. The range (or radius of coverage) for typical WLAN systems varies from under 100 ft to more than 500 ft. Coverage can be extended, and true freedom of mobility via roaming, can be provided through microcells.

Throughput

As with wired LAN systems, actual throughput in WLANs depends on the product and how it is configured. Factors that affect throughput include airwave congestion (number of users), propagation factors such as range and multipath, the type of WLAN system used, and the latency and bottlenecks on the wired portions of the WLAN. Typical data rates range from 1 to 11 Mbps.

Mulitpath Effects

As Figure 18-9 shows, a radio signal can take multiple paths from a transmitter to a receiver, an attribute called *multipath*.[13] Reflections of the signals can cause them to become stronger or weaker, which can affect data throughput. Affects of multipath depend on the number of reflective surfaces in the environment, the distance from the transmitter to the receiver, the product design, and the radio technology.

Integrity

Wireless broadband data technologies have been proven through more than 50 years of wireless broadband application in both commercial and military systems. While radio interference can cause degradation in throughput, such interference is rare in the workplace. Robust designs of proven WLAN technology and the limited distance over which signals travel result in connections that are far more robust than cellular phone connections and provide data integrity performance equal to or better than that of wired networking.

Figure 18-9
Radio signals traveling over multiple paths.

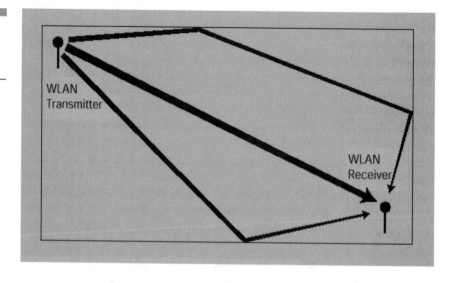

Interoperability with Wired Infrastructure

Most WLAN systems provide industry standard interconnection with wired systems, including CSMA/CD (802.3) and Token Ring (802.5). Standards-based interoperability makes the wireless broadband portion of the network completely transparent to the rest of the network. WLAN nodes are supported by network operating systems (NOS) in the same way as any other LAN node via network device drivers. Once installed, the NOS treats the wireless broadband nodes like any other component of the network.

Interoperability with Wireless Infrastructure

Several types of interoperability are possible between WLANs. This will depend both on technology choice and on the specific vendor's implementation. Products from different vendors employing the same technology and the same implementation typically allow for the interchange of adapters and access points. An eventual goal of the IEEE 802.11 specification currently being drafted by a committee of WLAN vendors and users is to allow compliant wireless broadband multimedia products to interoperate without explicit collaboration between vendors.

Today, everyone in the WLAN industry is focused on deploying products that deliver data rates at Ethernet speeds—11 Mbps. However, the next big WLAN design push is coming as engineers start eyeing 5-GHz operation.

IEEE 802.11a: Wireless Broadband Multimedia   By 2002, we can expect to see various semiconductor suppliers and OEMs debut plans for radio chipset and WLAN network interface card (NIC) product offerings that target the IEEE 802.11a specification. These products will feature data rates at blinding speeds of up to 54 Mbps and will operate in the 5-GHz frequency band. This technology is aimed at supporting a host of high-speed broadband wireless applications tailored to deliver streaming video for multimedia desktop applications in the office and home.

The IEEE 802.11 specification is a WLAN standard that defines a set of requirements for the physical layers (PHYs) and a medium access control (MAC) layer. For high data rates, the standard provides two PHYs—IEEE 802.11b for 2.4-GHz operation and IEEE 802.11a for 5-GHz operation. The IEEE 802.11a standard is designed to serve applications that require data rates higher than 11 Mbps in the 5-GHz frequency band. This part of the chapter explores the modulation techniques used in 802.11 for 5-GHz operation and some of the key features supported in the MAC layer.

FRAGMENTATION   The wireless broadband medium on which the 802.11 WLANs operate is different from wired media in many ways. One of these differences is the presence of interference in unlicensed frequency bands, which can affect communications between WLAN NICs. Interference on the wireless broadband medium can result in packet loss, which causes the network to suffer in terms of throughput performance.

Current 2.4-GHz 802.11b radios handle interference well because they support a feature in the MAC layer known as *fragmentation*. In fragmentation, data frames are broken into smaller frames in an attempt to increase the probability of delivering packets without errors induced by the interferer.

When a frame is fragmented, the sequence control field in the MAC header indicates placement of the individual fragments and whether the current fragment is the last in the sequence. When frames are fragmented into request-to-send (RTS), clear-to-send (CTS), and acknowledge (ACK), control frames are used to manage the data transmission. Therefore, using fragmentation, designers can avoid interference problems in their WLAN designs.

However, interference is not the only headache for today's WLAN designers. Security issues are also a major concern. To solve potential security problems, the IEEE has incorporated a MAC-level privacy mechanism within the 802.11 specification that protects the content of data frames going over a wireless broadband medium from eavesdroppers. The mechanism, dubbed *wired equivalent privacy* (WEP), is an encryption engine that takes the contents of the entire data frame and passes them through an encryption algorithm. The encrypted data frames are transmitted with the WEP bit set in the frame control field of the MAC header. The received encrypted data frames are decrypted using the same encryption algorithm employed by the sending unit.

The encryption algorithm used by 802.11 is RC4. RC4 is a symmetric stream cipher developed by RSA Data Security, Inc., that supports variable key lengths up to 256 bits. The standard specifies a 40-bit key, but many 802.11-compliant products being shipped today support key lengths of up to 128 bits.

SCANNING   In order for a mobile station to communicate with other mobile wireless broadband NICs in a given service area, it must first locate those wireless broadband NICs or access points. To enable communication between the mobile station and the NIC, active and passive scanning techniques are supported in the MAC.

Passive scanning involves listening for traffic only on an 802.11 network. Passive scanning allows a mobile wireless broadband NIC to find an IEEE 802.11 network while minimizing dc power consumption. In this mode, the wireless broadband NIC listens for special frames called *beacons* and probe responses while extracting information about the particular frequency channel. Although passive scanning expends minimal power, the cost is the time spent listening for a frame on a channel that is idle or may never occur.

Active scanning, on the other hand, requires the scanning of wireless broadband NIC to transmit and receive responses from 802.11 wireless broadband NICs and access points. Active scanning allows the mobile wireless broadband NIC to interact with another wireless broadband NIC or access point. The 802.11 standard does not specify a method for scanning. However, many WLAN OEMs support both methods and variants to differentiate their products in the market.

MOVING TO HIGHER FREQUENCIES When developing WLAN systems, choosing the right modulation and frequency band should be a priority in rf design, especially when designing IEEE 802.11a radios. For the past decade, WLAN systems have been designed to operate in the unlicensed 2.4-GHz frequency band. The 2.4-GHz band provides 83 MHz of total contiguous bandwidth, spanning from 2.4 to 2.483 GHz.

Moving to the 5-GHz band offers over three times the operating bandwidth over the available spectrum in the 2.4-GHz band. The 5-GHz band is also less susceptible to interference, unlike the 2.4-GHz unlicensed band, which shares spectrum with other wireless broadband appliances such as Bluetooth devices.

There are, however, a few things to consider when switching to 5 GHz. The first is that the frequency allocation is not contiguous across the band, and the transmit power levels are restricted depending on which block of frequency is occupied. Second, in order to achieve the same effective range as covered in the 2.4-GHz band, the transmit power of a 5-GHz system must be slightly increased. Designers of 5-GHz radios must carefully consider these issues in product development.

In the United States, 300 MHz of bandwidth is allocated in the 5-GHz band to WLANs under the rules of the Unlicensed National Information Infrastructure (U-NII). The bandwidth is fragmented into two blocks that are noncontiguous across the 5-GHz band.

In Europe, only Hiperlan WLANs are allowed to operate in the 5-GHz frequency band. A total of 455 MHz of spectrum is allocated for Hiperlan radios. The frequency spectrum allocations for each of the geographic regions are shown in Figure 18-10.[14]

It is important to point out that although the PHY specifications for IEEE 802.11a are similar to the Hiperlan2, radios compliant with the 802.11a specification are not allowed to operate in the 5-GHz band according to ETSI rules. Efforts are under way by IEEE 802 and ESTI together with the ITU-R to harmonize a global allocation of 5-GHz spectrum for WLANs. Global harmonization could occur by late 2002.

A COMMON APPROACH   When the IEEE 802.11 began evaluating proposals for 802.11a, the working group adopted a joint proposal from NTT and Lucent that recommended orthogonal frequency-division multiplexing (OFDM) as the baseline technology for 5-GHz WLAN systems. OFDM was chosen because of its superior performance in combating multipath. This battle is extremely important, particularly in applications that transmit streaming video.

NOTE   Orthogonal frequency division multiplexing (OFDM) is a digital modulation method consisting of a large number of equally spaced carriers, each modulated digitally. It is used as a channel modulation for digital terrestrial TV or digital terrestrial radio. It was invented by NTL in the United Kingdom and the French CCETT lab.

Figure 18-10
GHz frequency
spectrum allocation.

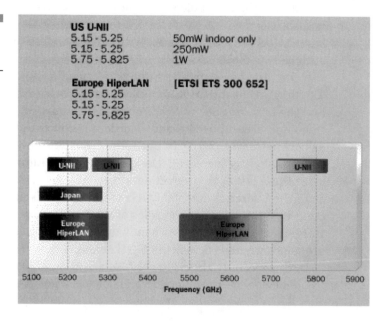

During the development of the 802.11a specification, ETSI was charging ahead with a 5-GHz WLAN project called Hiperlan2. They too adopted OFDM.

For the most part, the PHY for 802.11a is similar to Hiperlan2. The differences between the two standards are minimal and reside in the method by which convolution encoding is used to generate the OFDM symbols and data rates. However, it has been said that by making the convolution encoder a programmable feature in the baseband processor, the same silicon can be used to support both standards. This is an extremely attractive feature for those who want to develop products for both standards. Unfortunately, the MAC layers are very different. But that's a subject for later.

5-GHZ CHANNELS In the U-NII band, eight carriers are spaced across 200 MHz in the lower spectrum (5.150–5.350 GHz) and four carriers are spaced across 100 MHz in the upper spectrum (5.725–5.825 GHz). The channels are spaced 20 MHz apart, which allows for high bit rates per channel. The channel scheme used for 5 GHz is illustrated in Figure 18-11.[15]

As Figure 18-11 illustrates, there are 52 subcarriers per channel in the 5-GHz band. Of these channels, only 48 carry actual data. The remaining 4 subcarriers are used as pilot tones, which assist in phase tracking for coherent demodulation. The duration of the guard interval is 800 ns, which provides excellent performance on channels with delay spreads of up to 250 ns.

Figure 18-11
IEEE 802.11a frame format for 5 GHz.

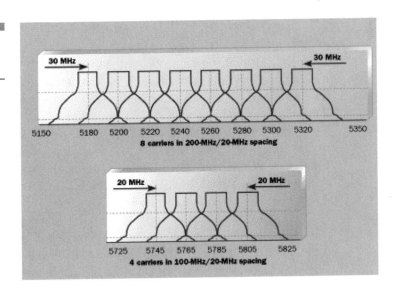

To efficiently use the spectrum provided in the 5-GHz range, designers of IEEE 802.11a systems use OFDM techniques. OFDM is a unique form of multicarrier modulation. The basic concept is to transmit high-data-rate information into several interleaved, parallel bit streams and let each of these bit streams modulate a separate subcarrier. In this way, the channel spectrum is passed into a number of independent, nonselective frequency subchannels for transmission between wireless broadband NICs and access points.

The OFDM modulation technique is generated through the use of complex signal-processing approaches such as fast Fourier transforms (FFTs) and inverse FFTs in the transmitter and receiver sections of the radio. One of the benefits of OFDM is its strength in fighting the adverse effects of multipath propagation with respect to intersymbol interference in a channel. OFDM is also spectrally efficient because the channels are overlapped and contiguous.

OFDM is well tested and has been adopted by a number of standards bodies for several applications, including a wired global standard for asymmetric digital subscriber line (ADSL) and for digital audio broadcasting (DAB) in the European market. To complement OFDM, the IEEE 802.11a specification also offers support for a variety of other modulation and coding alternatives. For example, the standard allows engineers to combine BPSK, QPSK, and 16-QAM modulations with convolution encoding ($R = 1\acute{U}2$ and constraint length seven) to generate data rates of 6, 12, and 24 Mbps. All other combinations of encoding rates, including $R = 2\acute{U}3$ and $R = 3\acute{U}4$ combined with 64-QAM, are used to generate rates up to 54 Mbps, which are optional in the standard.

PACKET DATA FRAME   During development of the 802.11a standard, the IEEE 802.11 working group carefully optimized the PHY for traffic transmitting multimedia content such as streaming video. The packet data frame defined in the 802.11a specification consists of the PHY header, the PHY convergence protocol (PLCP), and the payload (PSDU). This is similar to the structure used in the IEEE 802.11b specification.

The first field of the PLCP header is called the *preamble*. The preamble consists of 12 symbols, which are used to synchronize the receiver. The second field is the *signal field*. The signal field is used to indicate the rate at which the OFDM symbols of the PSDU payload are transmitted.

The PLCP header is always BPSK modulated and convolution encoded at $R = 1\acute{U}2$. The PSDU packet payload is modulated and transmitted at the rate indicated in the signal field. This rate is variable from 6 up to 54 Mbps. The structure of the packet data frame is illustrated in Figure 18-12.[16]

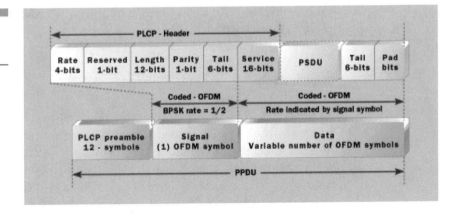

Figure 18-12
IEEE 802.11a
channel scheme.

Interference and Coexistence

The unlicensed nature of radio-based WLANs means that other products that transmit energy in the same frequency spectrum potentially can provide some measure of interference to the WLAN system. Microwave ovens are a potential concern, but most WLAN manufacturers design their products to account for microwave interference. Another concern is the colocation of multiple WLAN systems. While colocated WLANs from different vendors may interfere with each other, others coexist without interference. This issue is best addressed directly with the appropriate vendors.

Simplicity/Ease of Use

Users need very little new information to take advantage of WLANs. Because the wireless nature of a WLAN is transparent to a user's NOS, applications work the same as they do on tethered LANs. WLAN products incorporate a variety of diagnostic tools to address issues associated with the wireless elements of the system; however, products are designed so that most users rarely need these tools.

WLANs simplify many of the installation and configuration issues that plague network managers. Since only the access points of WLANs require cabling, network managers are freed from pulling cables for WLAN end users. Lack of cabling also makes moves, adds, and changes trivial operations on WLANs. Finally, the portable nature of WLANs lets network managers preconfigure and troubleshoot entire networks before installing them at remote locations. Once configured, WLANs can be moved from place to place with little or no modification.

Security

Because wireless broadband technology has roots in military applications, security has long been a design criterion for wireless broadband devices. Security provisions are typically built into WLANs, making them more secure than most wired LANs. It is extremely difficult for unintended receivers (eavesdroppers) to listen in on WLAN traffic. Complex encryption techniques make it impossible for all but the most sophisticated to gain unauthorized access to network traffic. In general, individual nodes must be security-enabled before they are allowed to participate in network traffic.

Cost

A WLAN implementation includes both infrastructure costs for the wireless broadband access points and user costs for the WLAN adapters. Infrastructure costs depend primarily on the number of access points deployed; access points range in price from $900 to $3000. The number of access points typically depends on the required coverage region and/or the number and types of users to be serviced. The coverage area is proportional to the square of the product range.

WLAN adapters are required for standard computer platforms and range in price from $300 to $800. The cost of installing, configuring, and maintaining a WLAN is generally lower than the cost of installing, configuring, and maintaining a wired LAN for two reasons. First, a WLAN eliminates the direct costs of cabling and the labor associated with installing, configuring, and repairing it. Second, because WLANs simplify moves, adds, and changes, they reduce the indirect costs of user downtime and administrative overhead.

Scalability

Wireless broadband networks can be designed to be extremely simple or quite complex. Wireless broadband networks can support large numbers of nodes and/or large physical areas by adding access points to boost or extend coverage.

Battery Life for Mobile Platforms

End-user wireless broadband products are capable of being completely untethered and run off the battery power from their host notebook or handheld computer. WLAN vendors typically employ special design techniques to maximize the host computer's energy usage and battery life.

Safety

The output power of WLAN systems is very low, much less than that of a handheld cellular phone. Since radio waves fade rapidly over distance, very little exposure to rf energy is provided to those in the area of a WLAN system. WLANs must meet stringent government and industry regulations for safety. No adverse health affects have ever been attributed to WLANs.

Conclusion

Flexibility and mobility make WLANs both effective extensions and attractive alternatives to wired networks. WLANs provide all the functionality of wired LANs but without the physical constraints of the wire itself. WLAN configurations include independent networks, suitable for small or temporary peer-to-peer configurations, and infrastructure networks, offering fully distributed data connectivity via microcells and roaming. In addition to offering end-user mobility within a networked environment, WLANs enable portable networks, allowing LANs to move with the knowledge workers who need them.

A wide range of WLAN products are now available. By evaluating the strengths and differences of each of these offerings, savvy network managers and users can choose a WLAN solution that best meets their business and application objectives.

Finally, on the 5-GHz front, we can expect to see first-generation 802.11a products enter the market beginning in 2002 in the form of chipsets, wireless broadband NICs, and access points, with infrastructure expanding in a manner similar to its predecessor IEEE 802.11b. Later in 2002, we can expect to see the Wireless Ethernet Compatibility Alliance (WECA) begin interoperability and compliance testing of 5-GHz 802.11a products.

Endnotes

1. "Introduction to Wireless LANs," Wireless LAN Association, 38083 West Spaulding, Suite 203, Willoughby, OH 44094, 2000.
2. *Ibid.*
3. *Ibid.*
4. *Ibid.*
5. *Ibid.*
6. *Ibid.*
7. *Ibid.*
8. *Ibid.*
9. *Ibid.*
10. *Ibid.*
11. *Ibid.*
12. *Ibid.*
13. *Ibid.*
14. Bob Heile, "IEEE 802.11a—Wireless Multimedia," *Communication Systems Design*, 525 Market St., Suite 500, San Francisco, CA 94105, 2000.
15. *Ibid.*
16. *Ibid.*

CHAPTER 19

Configuring Unlicensed-Band Systems to Enhance Wireless Broadband Services in Multichannel Multipoint Distribution Services (MMDS)

Wireless broadband services are being deployed rapidly using Multi-channel multipoint distribution system (MMDS) spectrum. For certain applications, license-exempt bands (also called *unlicensed bands*) used in conjunction with MMDS spectrum can provide better wireless broadband services more cost-effectively in areas where coverage otherwise is difficult due to terrain or other conditions. This chapter gives a few examples of scenarios where this concept of using multiple-frequency bands can be very effective, especially for second-tier markets. Generally, for first-tier markets consisting of large cities, a large number of minicells using the MMDS spectrum can address the capacity and coverage needs fairly well. This chapter also provides alternate system architectures and gives examples of

1. A point-to-multipoint system
2. A wireless broadband backhaul application
3. Building wireless local-area network (WLAN) applications using 2.4- , 5.8-, 24-, and 60-GHz license-exempt bands[1]

MMDS License-Exempt-Band Point-to-Multipoint System

High-speed data services using MMDS spectrum can be deployed today using a few large cells (>20 mile radius) or many small cells (<5 mile radius) or a combination of both. Deployment of many small cells offers advantages of higher capacity and better coverage than the large-cell approach but has significantly higher initial deployment costs. For rural areas with very low population density, a large-cell scenario is more applicable. For those areas of a given geographic region that do not meet the minimum number of potential subscribers to justify the expense of an MMDS base station, using license-exempt solutions in the ISM bands offers an attractive solution to the coverage problem. Whether it is an area over a hill, one blocked by tall buildings, or one simply beyond the range of the main MMDS site, wireless broadband routers operating in the ISM bands offer a cost-effective and easily integrated supplemental network.

NOTE   ISM refers to industrial, scientific, and medical (ISM) applications (of radio frequency energy). It also refers to the operation of equipment or appliances designed to generate and use locally radiofrequency energy for industrial, scientific, medical, domestic, or similar purposes, excluding applications in the field of telecommunications.

In this scenario, a remote MMDS unit is located where it can be colocated with the point-to-multipoint central site while still maintaining line of sight (LOS) to the main MMDS base station. *LOS propagation* here refers to an electromagnetic wave propagation in which the direct ray from the transmitter to the receiver is unobstructed (the transmission path is not established by or dependent on reflection or diffraction).

NOTE The need for LOS propagation is most critical at VHF and higher frequencies.

The diagram in Figure 19-1 illustrates the fundamental network topography being proposed.[2] This technique is especially useful if the rural area to be covered is very hilly. Even in large cities such as Pittsburgh with many hills, tests have shown that hills can cause significant blockage of signal, and the homes and businesses on the other side of the hill could not be served unless more MMDS hub sites were added. Detailed simulations with link budgets and coverage maps with EDX software for the Pittsburgh area where this approach is applicable are presented later in the chapter. In this manner, license-exempt-band systems extend the reach of the broadband MMDS wireless network. Figures 19-2 through 19-4 show

Figure 19-1

Network architecture showing use of unlicensed band for areas uncovered by MMDS band cell (due to hills, buildings, etc.).

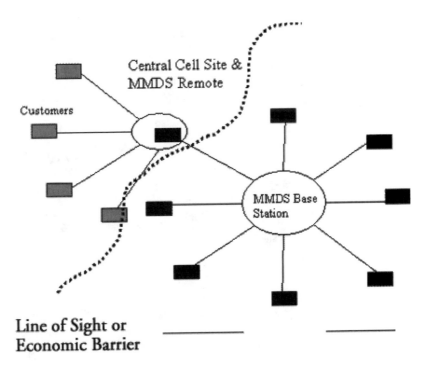

Figure 19-2
Service area covered
with MMDS and
unlicensed bands.
The map shading
reflects the MMDS
coverage only.

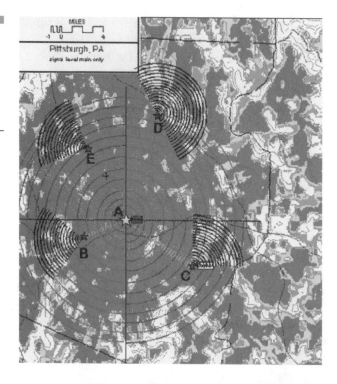

Figure 19-3
Zoom in of the area
covered by the U-NII
hub C.

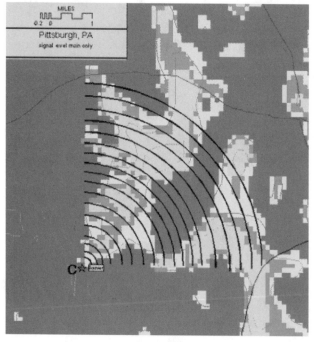

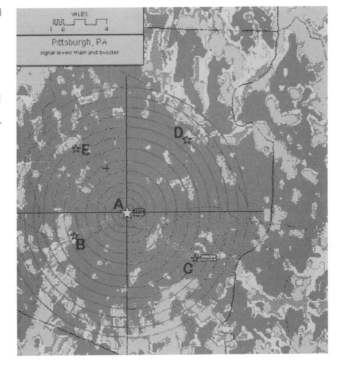

Figure 19-4
Service area covered by MMDS and the U-NII hub C. Shading reflects combined coverage, MMDS and unlicensed band.

the coverage maps for Pittsburgh using realistic link budget parameters for a large cell.[3] Since the terrain is very hilly, the coverage in many of the areas is poor. These are the areas where the coverage can be improved using the combined MMDS and unlicensed-band system architecture.

Architectures for Servicing Shadow Areas in the MMDS Coverage

A very important question when planning MMDS service coverage is how to provide high-speed service in areas where buildings and irregular terrain form shadow areas that cannot be covered from a central point. An operator is motivated to maximize the coverage in order to get the maximum return from initial investment in the base station, the tower real estate, and all the networking, modem, transmit, and receive equipment. Obviously, the solution of installing new cells in the shadow area is always available, but only when the number of subscribers in the area justifies the relatively higher cost of another wireless broadband MMDS base station.

This chapter thus analyzes solutions based on the use of an unlicensed-band system. The advantages of this choice are as follows:

- The unlicensed-band technologies are relatively mature, and several manufacturers offer relatively low cost solutions for both indoor and outdoor.

- For a low number of subscribers at relatively short to medium distances (2 to 10 miles), the unlicensed technologies offer solutions competitive with an additional MMDS base station.

- The use of a non-MMDS frequency spectrum in the shadow areas simplifies the MMDS interference scenario and reuse pattern.

- The unlicensed-band systems use spread-spectrum techniques and have built-in interference-mitigation techniques so that the interference between their different segments is generally negligible.

In a system involving the combined use of MMDS and unlicensed bands, one will need to analyze a number of system architecture parameters: capacity of the unlicensed band system covering the shadow and relevant MMDS frequency and capacity planning data interfaces and services.

Capacity of the Unlicensed-Band System

The capacity of the unlicensed-band cell is one of the determining factors in deciding whether to use an unlicensed band or an MMDS band minicell in the uncovered area. It is the number of subscribers and the data capacity of the shadow area that have to be estimated first. Depending on the subscriber type and number, the following unlicensed-band options should be considered:

- Outdoor wireless broadband access systems operating under 802.11
- Unlicensed point-to-point systems
- Unlicensed wireless access systems in the 5-GHz band

Outdoor Wireless Broadband Access Systems Operating under 802.11

This kind of solution may provide up to 3 Mbps total raw data rate per base station and serve several tens or even hundreds of thousands of subscribers. Lesser numbers would apply for higher-capacity subscribers such as businesses or SOHOs.

NOTE Small office/home office (SOHO) is the fastest growing market for computer hardware and software. So-called SOHO products are specifically designed to meet the needs of professionals who work at home or in small offices.

One such product is the BreezeACCESS, an outdoor FHSS system based on 802.11 from Breezecom. As a bridged solution, it is best suited for one customer or short-range campus-style networks. It will be available toward the end of 2001. Up to 15 hub stations can be colocated.

Another product with higher capacity is WaveNet IP 2400 and 2458 from Wireless, Inc., which provides coverage up to 20 mile. As part of a routed or layer 3–based network, these products are a good fit for multi-customer networks in applications such as Internet access.

Unlicensed Point-to-Point Systems

This kind of solution would apply when you want to serve a small number of high-capacity subscribers. These systems operate also with a PHY similar to 802.11 (compliant with FCC part 15) but provide communication only between two points. This is a quite established technology with products capable of providing one E-1/T-1 or even more, from companies such as Breezecom, California Microwave, P-Com, and others.

Unlicensed Wireless Access Systems in the 5-GHz Band

These are systems that operate in one or more of the U-NII bands (at 5.15 to 5.35 GHz and 5.725 to 5.825 GHz) or the ISM band at 5.775 to 5.850 GHz (see the sidebar, "Wireless Broadband Local Access in the U-NII Band"). Such systems are capable of providing between 10 and 25 Mbps. Wireless, Inc., offers systems with capacity in the range of 16 Mbps either as point-to-point or as point-to-multipoint systems. Wi-LAN has promoted the ambitious 802.11a standard using OFDM. Presently, this company offers a point-to-point system migrating toward an access system. Other companies offer more established technologies such as the point-to-point systems from RadioLAN (10 Mbps) and the adaptive Asynchronous Transfer Mode (ATM)–based TDD system AB-Access from Adaptive Broadband at 25 Mbps.

Wireless Broadband Local Access in the U-NII Band

During the past 15 years, high-frequency digital microwave radio has proven to be a cost-effective and quality solution for short-haul local-access applications. The high growth of cellular, PHS, PCN, and PCS networks has predominantly fueled the widespread use of wireless broadband solutions from 10 to 38 GHz for last-mile solutions.

Radio frequency allocation below 10 GHz continues to be used for wideband backbone traffic. The emphasis and requirement for microwave radio equipment operating below 10 GHz have been on new modulation techniques designed to squeeze more data into less bandwidth. Along with fiber networks, these *spectral efficient* backbone radios feed both wired and wireless broadband local-access applications.

Although technological advances continue to provide lower-cost high-frequency products and more efficient backbone solutions, these bands are often congested and still too expensive for the next wave of wireless broadband applications. As personal communications products and services evolve, faster and less expensive solutions are in high demand. One of the most exciting developments in the telecommunications industry has been the Federal Communications Commission (FCC) ruling 15.407 in favor of the U-NII frequency spectrum.

The FCC Allocates 300 Mhz of Spectrum for U-NII Use in the 5-GHz Band
In January of 1997, the FCC made available 300 MHz of spectrum for Unlicensed National Information Infrastructure (U-NII) products. The FCC believes that the creation of the U-NII band will stimulate the development of new unlicensed digital products that will provide efficient and less expensive solutions for local-access applications.

The U-NII band is divided into three subbands at 5.15–5.25/5.25–5.35/5.725–5.825 GHz, as shown in Table 19-1.[4] The first band is strictly allocated for indoor use and is consistent with the European High Performance Local Area Network (HIPERLAN). The second and third bands are intended for high-speed digital local-access products for campus and short-haul microwave applications.

Short-Haul Microwave Applications in the U-NII Band   The FCC rules for products operating in bands 2 and 3 of the U-NII band are best suited for digital microwave applications over distances in excess of 10 miles, as shown in Figure 19-5.[5] FCC spectral efficiency and maximum power requirements for these bands facilitate the deployment

	Band 1	Band 2	Band 3
	Frequency 5.15–5.25 GHz	5.25–5.35 GHz	5.725–5.825 GHz
	Power (max): 200 mW (EIRP)	1 W (EIRP)	4 W (EIRP)*
	Intended use: indoor use only	Campus applications	Local access, 10 miles

*A recent FCC Memorandum Opinion and Order (MOO) released on June 24, 1998 allows the use of directional antennas with 23 dBi gain and a maximum transmitter output power of 1 W in the 5.725- to 5.825-GHz U-NII band.

of highly reliable microwave links for both data and telephony transmission. Table 19-1 depicts the relationship between the maximum EIRP and occupied bandwidth of the transmitted signal in accordance with the regulations.

The most effective use of the band is by means of robust modulation schemes capable of carrying high-speed Ethernet or multiple DS-1/E-1 digital circuits. Modulation techniques such as binary phase-shift keying (BPSK), frequency-shift keying (FSK), or quadrature phase-shift keying (QPSK) are best suited to provide the most cost-effective and reliable interconnection solution.

Microwave Transmission in the U-NII Band The U-NII frequency band is an ideal solution for short-haul applications. Unlike high-frequency microwave links above 10 GHz, the U-NII band is not affected by outages due to rain attenuation. Above 10 GHz, rain is a considerable factor in determining the maximum distance of a properly engineered

Figure 19-5

Maximum EIRP in the FCC U-NII bands 2 and 3.

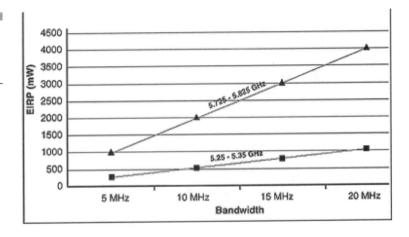

microwave path. High-power amplifiers and larger antennas help, but these solutions are expensive and often not applicable.

Microwave transmission is also less affected by free space loss at 5.25–5.825 GHz than high-frequency microwave. Even with FCC limitations on power output and antenna gain in the U-NII bands (5.3 and 5.7 GHz), microwave paths can operate full duplex, using both bands 2 and 3, over 10 miles with 99.995 percent reliability. Because the band is optimized for short-haul transmission, U-NII microwave paths are not adversely affected by microwaves.

The microwave system performance using both bands 5.3 and 5.7 is limited by the FCC transmitter and antenna rules for band 2. The use of dual-band operation, however, does have the benefit of separating the system transmitters and receivers by approximately 480 MHz. This significantly simplifies transmitter and receiver design, resulting in a lower-cost product. Dual-band operation also promotes frequency reuse, allowing the use of 200 MHz of bandwidth as opposed to 100 MHz in single-band operation.

The use of 2- or 4-ft highly directional parabolic antennas (with gains of approximately 27 and 33 dBi, respectively) in the U-NII band improves the overall performance of the system. As shown in Figure 19-6, a high level of availability is typical for paths in the 10-mile range while meeting FCC rules for maximum EIRP (equivalent isotropic radiated power).[6] Antenna gain can exceed 6 dBi as long as the peak power spectral density is reduced proportionately. Parabolic antennas also offer additional isolation from colocated or adjacent microwave signals.[7]

Figure 19-6

Typical microwave path performance in the U-NII bands 2 and 3.

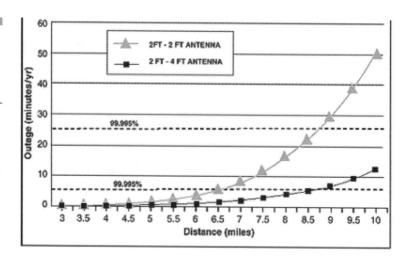

Relevant MMDS Frequency and Capacity Planning

The MMDS system acts as backhaul for the previously reviewed unlicensed systems. The interface with the MMDS system can be one of the following two options: When the area served by the unlicensed system has high capacity, on the order of more than 3 Mbps both ways, then the preferred option is the use of dedicated point-to-point links within the MMDS spectrum. Such links can be engineered with high-gain antennas and an adequate amount of power to create minimum interference and ensure high link availability. One channel for upstream and one for downstream have to be reserved for this purpose, and because of the narrow beam they can be reused several times in the service area. The data rate is 27 Mbps, so it can backhaul one U-NII hub station. Figure 19-6 shows such an MMDS deployment. The MMDS hub A (star) covers four sectors. Two sub-bands are reused in back-to-back sectors. Each subband has one or more channels. The MMDS coverage area is shown with a sufficient receive signal level and edging levels. The unlicensed band-hubs are shown as stars: B, C, D and E. They are on high points covering the MMDS shadow areas. Two of them, hubs B and C, are fed through point-to-point MMDS links that use different channels. Figure 19-3 is a zoom-in of the area covered by hub B and shows its 90-degree coverage over the shadowed area. Figure 19-4 shows the same area as Figure 19-1, but now the coverage given by hub B is taken into consideration. The simulation considers a 0.25-W transmission power at 5.8 GHz.

Other unlicensed hub stations with less capacity, hubs D and E, are connected not through point-to-point MMDS but through the basic MMDS access system, having a regular MMDS modem as its interface. In these cases, the upstream capacity is the limiting factor. For close, nonchallenging locations, upstream channels of 3.2 MHz can be used, providing approximately 3.4 Mbps. In most locations, however, the upstream channel's bandwidth is required to be down to one-quarter or even one-eighth of this.

Data Interfaces and Services

The unlicensed-band system is complementary to the MMDS system and will have to interface and to provide an extension of its services and functionality. Most of the unlicensed-band systems have a 10baseT or 100baseT interface. The most important service-related issues involve the extension of the following MMDS system features to the unlicensed point-to-multi-point access systems:

1. *QoS*. Short for quality of service, a networking term that specifies a guaranteed throughput level. One of the biggest advantages of ATM over competing technologies such as Frame Relay and Fast Ethernet is that it supports QoS levels. This allows ATM providers to guarantee to their customers that end-to-end latency will not exceed a specified level.

2. *VoIP*. Internet telephony products are sometimes called *IP telephony, voice over the Internet* (VOI), or *voice over IP* (VOIP) products.

3. *Security.*

4. *Remote management.* Either browser-based (SNMP) or both. SNMP is short for Simple Network Management Protocol—a set of protocols for managing complex networks.

5. *Bandwidth.*[8]

Some systems preserve the QoS in its native IP form, such as those based on 802.11. AB-Access, from adaptive wireless broadband on the other side, translates into ATM. Others, such as those developed by Wireless, Inc., incorporate the features in the base radio protocol. VoIP is also supported in both MMDS and the complementary unlicensed systems, but the exact characteristics of the interworking still have to be analyzed for every case. Security is implemented at the low-level MAC layer in the MMDS systems aligned with DOCSIS, as well as in 802.11. Since the interface is in nonencrypted mode, no particular problems are expected.

Interference Mitigation

One of the concerns with operation in a license-exempt or ISM band is that of interference from other unlicensed-band users. With proper use of the spread-spectrum technology and network planning, interference can be almost eliminated. There are four primary methods or factors that contribute to addressing these interference issues, and each is discussed briefly next.

Spread-Spectrum Technology

When deploying networks that are point to multipoint in nature in the ISM bands, there are essentially two choices or spread-spectrum technologies to be considered: direct sequence (DS) and frequency hopping (FH). It is generally acknowledged that DS systems can support higher bit rates than FH systems, but at the cost of reduced immunity to interference.

For resisting narrowband transient or even nontransient interference in point-to-multipoint networks, FH systems will have an edge over DS networks. If the FH system experiences a bad hop, or possibly even more, it will merely send the data out on the next clear hop. No data are lost. With a DS system, if the interference is high enough, the link will fail, and data transmission will be interrupted.

Split-Band Operation

The large majority of license-exempt equipment deployed today operates in the 2.4-GHz ISM band, with a small percentage in the 5.8-GHz ISM band. Wireless, Inc., uses both these bands to allow full-duplex operations and reduce the effects of interference as follows: When operating a point-to-multipoint wireless broadband network, the central units typically use an omni or sector antenna. The remote units will have a directional antenna pointing back to the central site. Thus it is at the central units where most of the interference occurs with the wide-beam antennas. The system is designed to transmit from the central to the remote at 2.4 GHz and receive data from the remotes at 5.8 GHz. Thus the band that has the greatest amount of potential noise, 2.4 GHz, is only seen through a narrowbeam directional antenna at the remote.

Locating the Central Sites

It is a common misconception that wireless broadband network providers want the highest point in town for their central site equipment. While this may be true to a limited extent, LOS issues almost always will result in several central sites being deployed. Once this is acknowledged, the question becomes where best to situate these central sites. Most of the interference that occurs in the 2.4-GHz band comes from dense urban areas with businesses that are being served by 2.4-GHz point-to-point equipment. This means that the 2.4-GHz radiation is emanating outward from the city center. With the split-band system, the central sites are located on the edges of the city. The remote units are situated facing outward to the central sites with the backs of their antennas exposed to the 2.4-GHz interference sources.

Rural or Edge Deployment

In the U.S. market, where wireless broadband access plays best is where the infrastructure is weakest. There is little need in downtown New York, for instance, for wireless broadband fractional T-1 connectivity because the fiber or copper is already installed and is easily obtained. Where wireless broadband networks can make the largest contribution and reach the "low hanging fruit" is in the second- and third-tier markets. These markets are typically less built out and, as a result, have far fewer ambient 2.4-GHz radio signals floating around. In these environments, coverage of up to 20 miles is easily achievable as a network-deployment strategy with the Wireless, Inc., system.

By employing these techniques, a service provider can be extremely successful in deploying license-exempt networks in a fashion that will provide the promises and benefits of these networks not only in the beginning but also for several years after installation.

Case Study: W-DSL in Las Vegas Using License-Exempt Bands

Unlicensed-band networks providing wireless digital scriber line (W-DSL) technology from Wireless, Inc., have been deployed in a number of areas. For example, one successful deployment in Las Vegas shows that this technology is realistic today. As development of W-DSL networks progressed in the spring of 1999, it became apparent that the final proof of concept was going to require a complete citywide network as a final test case. The city of Las Vegas was chosen as this test city for several reasons:

- There was a lack of adequate copper infrastructure. In Las Vegas, business customers had the choice of 128 kbps or 1.5Mbps, with nothing in between.
- There was a demand for these fractional T-1 services from the business community.
- The relatively nearby location made logistical support for installation and operation much less complicated.[9]

During the summer of 1999, Wireless, Inc., installed a W-DSL network in Las Vegas with the intention of operating as a wireless broadband competitive local exchange carrier (CLEC). As a wireless broadband CLEC, it would allow several Internet service providers (ISPs) to support customers on one wireless broadband network.

NOTE A competitive local exchange carrier (CLEC) is a telephone company that competes with an incumbent local exchange carrier (ILEC) such as a regional Bell operating company (RBOC), GTE, ALLNET, etc.

Basic Architecture

For a W-DSL network, there are three basic components:

1. The central cell sites. This is where the point-to-multipoint equipment is located.

2. The backhaul of the traffic from each cell site to a distribution node.

3. The distribution node itself, where all wireless broadband traffic is aggregated and then, based on which customer belongs to whom, that traffic is sent off to the proper ISP.

The diagram shown in Figure 19-7 is a logical description of this design.[10]
For the cell sites, point-to-multipoint routers are used to ensure adequate security and segregation of IP traffic from each customer. For mixed customer networks, it is acknowledged that a routed solution must be used, and thus it is of critical importance that these first-layer local-access devices be routed solutions.

With the advantages of using license-exempt point-to-multipoint routers as the first-layer wireless broadband access device, it is important for the same reasons to have the point-to-point backhaul solution be license-exempt as well. In the Las Vegas W-DSL network, this was accomplished by using a U-NII band Ethernet bridge, which had the ability of coexisting with the full-duplex 2.4-GHz/5.8-GHz wireless broadband routers.

At the distribution node, the point-to-point traffic comes into an Ethernet switch, which then passes it to a bandwidth manager to offer different classes of service. At the back end of the distribution node, another router with multiple T-1 ports segregates each customer's traffic based on the ISP to which the customer belongs, and then sends it out the appropriate port.

Central Cell Sites

The central cell sites can have from 1 to 12 central routers depending on market demand for that cell sector. In Las Vegas, the initial deployment has 6 central routers at each cell site. This equipment was mounted in a

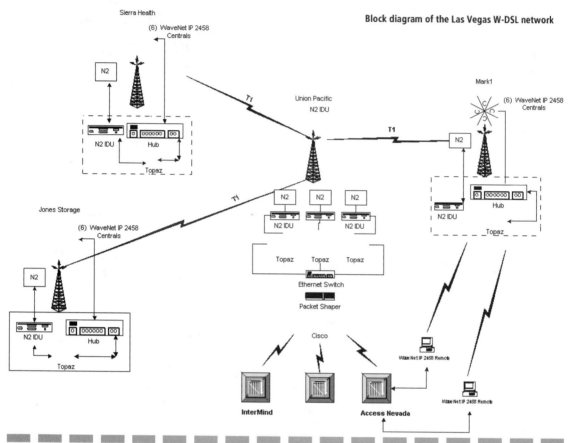

Figure 19-7 Block diagram of the Las Vegas W-DSL network.

variety of ways, some bolted to stairway walls and some using nonpenetrating roof mounts. Figure 19-8 shows the former method. [11]

> **NOTE** Figure 19-8 shows only three of the six central units; the other three are mounted on the opposite side of the roof.

With a scalable technology, more central routers or more cell sites can be added as the business warrants. The W-DSL network was to meet a market demand that copper just was not fulfilling. As a complete wireless broadband solution, the city of Las Vegas local ISPs can now offer fast Internet access without reliance on the local RBOC, which may be a competing ISP in the future.

Figure 19-8
Central-site antenna and other hub equipment.

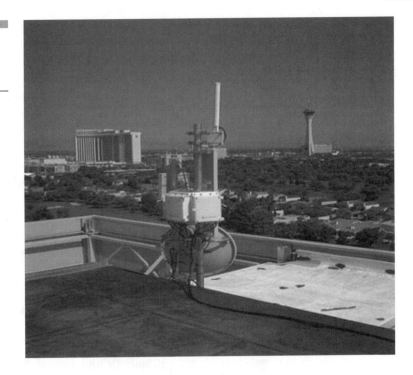

Wireless Broadband Backhaul Application

In a many-cell cellular MMDS architecture, the cells need to be connected together with a backhaul solution capable of high data rates. Many backhaul options are available for MMDS networks based on customer requirements, including backhaul capacity, cost, use of customer's existing fiber network, phased cellular deployment, etc.

There are many system tradeoffs in selecting an optimal backhaul solution. For small towns (of less than 100,000 population) with less data traffic, T-1 backhaul capacity may be enough. For larger towns with large numbers of subscribers with high data rate needs, OC-3 and higher capacity may be needed. For lower backhaul capacity needs, multiple T-1 connections or point-to-point radio link connections may be sufficient. Point-to-point microwave links are appropriate for backhaul when the required capacity is less than a few T-1s to DS-3 and the cost of fiber near the base station is too high. This is generally the case in rural and less populated areas. Also, frequently the base station hub is located on a ridge that may be inaccessible by fiber.

There are unlicensed-band (ISM and U-NII bands) products available for backhaul applications from a number of companies. The capacity of these products is generally low (16 Mbps) for MMDS cell backhaul applications. N2-X is one such product operating in the 5.3- and 5.7-GHz bands. This type of low capacity is only useful in cells in rural areas with less population. A typical MMDS cell in a larger city needs OC-3 or higher backhaul capacity.

In a combined MMDS/unlicensed-band system, an MMDS point-to-multipoint system can satisfy the backhaul needs of the unlicensed-band cells, as shown in Figure 19-3. In this scenario, the upstream link will be the limiting factor in terms of capacity because the MMDS system modulation rates in the upstream are typically QPSK and 16-QAM. Downstream capacity is generally higher due to availability of 64-QAM modulation.

In-Building Wireless Broadband LAN

Many applications in a building require portable wireless broadband connections to a notebook or a laptop PC. In-building WLANs at 2.4, 5.8, and 24 GHz are now available at multimegabit data rates. Integration of the MMDS network with the in-building WLAN will be required for many of these applications. Also, as Bluetooth and HomeRF technology is developed, a low-cost in-build network will provide an easier way for mobile computing and communications devices to communicate with one another and connect to the Internet at high speeds without the need for wires or cables. Bluetooth technology also will make it easier for users of mobile computers, mobile phones, and handheld devices to keep their data synchronized. The Bluetooth radio operates in a globally available 2.4-GHz ISM band, ensuring communication compatibility worldwide. Connections are instant, and they are maintained even when devices are not within line of sight. The range of each radio is approximately 10 m, but it can be extended to around 100 m with an optional amplifier. In Bluetooth technology, each channel supports 64 kbps synchronous (voice) link. The asynchronous channel can support an asymmetric link of maximally 721 kbps in either direction while permitting 57.6 kbps in the return direction, or a 432.6 kbps symmetric link. A broadband MMDS network in the future needs to be able to interface seamlessly in these advanced in-building wireless broadband networks.

Conclusion

Various architectures are proposed to use license-exempt bands to supplement and enhance broadband MMDS networks. Specifically, unlicensed-band networks can be used in conjunction with MMDS network to fill holes in coverage due to hills or buildings or extend the coverage of the MMDS network. MMDS and unlicensed bands also can be used for low- to medium-capacity backhaul requirements. As more devices become available that comply with Bluetooth and HomeRF and others in building networks, it makes sense to integrate these networks seamlessly with wireless broadband MMDS networks.

Finally, network providers and private users currently in need of cost-effective and reliable solutions for short-haul interconnect will find the greatest benefit of the U-NII band. Because the U-NII is an *unlicensed* band, the costs and time associated with frequency coordination and licensing are eliminated. Network providers, businesses, schools, and government agencies can install microwave links rapidly for high-speed digital local access. Operating in the 5-GHz band, the U-NII solution is both robust and cost-effective due to the technical characteristics and innovations in this band.

Endnotes

1. Sanjay Moghe (ADC Telecommunications), Vincent Roman (ADC Telecommunications), David Sumi (Wireless, Inc.), and Len Gee (Wireless, Inc.). "Use of License Exempt Bands to Enhance Broadband Services in an MMDS Network," Wireless, Inc., 5452 Betsy Ross Drive, Santa Clara, CA 95054-1101, 2000.
2. *Ibid.*
3. *Ibid.*
4. *Ibid.*
5. *Ibid.*
6. *Ibid.*
7. *Ibid.*
8. *Ibid.*
9. *Ibid.*
10. *Ibid.*
11. *Ibid.*

CHAPTER 20

Configuring Wireless Broadband Satellite Networks

By the year 2007, wireless broadband technology will serve more than 30 million customers worldwide, whereas wireless broadband satellite technology will serve almost 10 million customers. However, success in non-wireline broadband technology will require some careful configuring of wireless broadband satellite networks. Some companies are becoming dazzled by new technologies such as LMDS or wireless broadband low-earth-orbiting satellites (LEOs) and are not paying enough attention to configure these new high-speed unwired technologies.

Wireless broadband satellite and wireless broadband technology is very much a technology of the gaps. Satellite and wireless broadband will never be a serious contender where broadband wireline technology proves in, but the places where wireline will not work are common enough to make broadband unwired solutions quite viable. Careful configuration of wireless broadband satellite networks by Teledesic, Skybridge, and Hughes Spaceway Network Systems are seen as major opportunities for Local Multipoint Distribution System (LMDS) and new satellite systems, such as in rural Internet access, telemedicine, distance learning, desert start industrial and commercial developments, and rapid infrastructure deployment in developing nations. In addition to providing a penetrating configuration analysis of wireless broadband satellite and wireless broadband technology both in the United States and overseas, this chapter contains detailed configuration profiles of wireless broadband and satellite equipment, including customer premises equipment (CPE), cell site equipment, other microwave radios, and even the wireless broadband satellites themselves. The chapter also profiles the leading service providers, including both the emerging providers of high-speed wireless alternatives (companies such as WNP, WinStar, and Teligent) and wireless broadband satellite projects, such as those planned by Hughes and Alcatel.

Applications

Applications for wireless broadband and satellite-based communications can be found in both the enterprise and consumer markets. However, most of the discussion in this chapter is focused on where the configuration of wireless broadband and satellite lies. Wireless broadband and satellite configuration solutions apply mostly where wireline solutions are not available either at the present time or for the foreseeable future.

Data Applications

Data applications are key to the business cases of almost all the new technologies, systems, and services discussed in this chapter. In many cases, voice and video are secondary considerations.

For the time being, the satellite industry is responding to the changing application configuration needs of customers both by offering somewhat higher speeds on traditional products and by diversifying the markets it serves. The first of these configuration strategies has been exemplified by the Very Small Aperture Terminal (VSAT) business, with VSATs gradually growing from a business that could support data rates in the tens of kilobits per second to one that can support data rates at T-1/E-1 and above. In addition, the continued viability of the current business satellite sector seems assured by its increasingly proven ability to support popular protocols including Asynchronous Transfer Mode (ATM), Frame Relay, and especially the Internet Protocol (IP).

Some of the wireless broadband satellite configuration schemes appear to be predicated on the notion that they can steal very high bandwidth access and backbone implementations from fiber solutions. In fact, the history of the satellite industry has been that in a given era its spacecraft may be able to support the broadest of wireless broadband applications, but only until a wireline solution has caught up.

One of the biggest self-proclaimed advantages of wireless broadband configuration is its ability to offer an attractive price/performance point to other last-mile access alternatives, i.e., a fat communications pipeline to businesses or homes at a much lower price than a wireline equivalent. Wireless broadband access for data will be most attractive and successful in grabbing the attention of small and medium-sized businesses with T-1, fractional T-1, and/or Frame Relay–based data access configuration requirements.

In addition, the time-to-market issue is of some importance. Because wireless broadband configuration is a local solution, there will be many areas (especially outside of the United States) where wireless broadband may be the first broadband physical-layer communications architecture to appear. In some cases, it may be the only such infrastructure to appear for quite a while.

Voice Applications

The voice market is huge and, despite its apparent maturity, continues to grow at a moderate rate each year. This means that even for wireless broadband and satellite ventures that are more data-oriented, there could be many voice-oriented opportunities.

At least some of the wireless broadband satellite ventures are intended to provide multipurpose wide-area network (WAN) backbone facilities that would certainly include voice in the traffic they carry. Two applications areas where wireless broadband satellite capacity may make a difference in a voice environment are on enhanced submarine cable backup and on providing connectivity for remote call center facilities. Another voice application of wireless broadband (and perhaps even satellite networks) is cellular backhaul and other voice traffic backhaul needed for carrier networks. This has been mentioned consistently by LMDS service providers as a "killer application" for their networks. However, although voice applications offer opportunities for wireless broadband service providers, few such service providers will offer voice alone.

Video Applications

Video is the definitive wireless broadband application—even the term *broadband* has a video-oriented history. It was used originally to describe cable television technology. However, most high-quality video transmission to date has been analog. This is true particularly in the television sector, but corporate news and training networks also have frequently used analog feeds. Until quite recently, digital video meant low-quality video. However, it now seems certain that even the television sector will move toward a digital format.

Satellites play a key role in the television industry, where they are and will remain the primary means of distributing video to cable television headends and television stations. The big change here is that the mode in which such distribution occurs will shift from analog to digital. There has been some discussion in the telecommunications industry of replacing satellites with fiberoptics for this application. However, in practice, this has not occurred, nor does there seem any likelihood of its doing so.

Where fiber is taking some business away from cable is in the area of video backhaul of production-quality video among studios and between major permanent news locations (stadiums, convention centers, etc.) and studios. The other important role for satellites in the television industry is for the distribution of entertainment video directly to homes. This area has received new respectability as a result of the emergence of direct broadcasting services, such as DirecTV.

Satellites can be expected to continue to account for a major part of the high-quality video business for the foreseeable future. The situation is somewhat different for video in the enterprise, although wireless broadband satellites may have a direct role to play in training and news distribution applications within the enterprise.

As with satellites, wireless broadband has played an important traditional role in the television industry. Analog wireless broadband has been used for newsgathering, video backhaul, and even distribution to homes ("wireless cable"), and in all of these cases, wireless broadband is making the transition from analog to digital.

Orbiting Height

Information is becoming increasingly essential to all those things we associate with quality of life: economic opportunity, education, health care, and public services. Yet most people and places in the world do not now have access even to basic telephone service. Even those who do have access to basic phone service get it through 100-year-old technology (analog copper wire networks) that for the overwhelming part will never be upgraded or configured to an advanced digital capability. Even in the developed countries, there is a risk that whole areas and populations will be denied access to the powerful digital technologies that are changing the world.

The digital revolution is just as fundamental as the industrial revolution and the agricultural revolution before that. It will change all aspects of our societies. Previous changes took place over many generations—indeed, in parts of the world they are still ongoing today. Driven by advances in microelectronics technologies, where product generations are measured in months, the digital revolution is taking place at a breathtaking pace. The digital technologies that grow more powerful every day in our notebook computers will soon be exploding out through network connections. Yet outside the most advanced urban areas, most of the world will never get access to these technologies through conventional wireline means.

While there is a lot of fiber out there in the world (and the number of places is growing), it is used primarily to connect countries and telephone company central offices. Even in a country such as the United States, little of this fiber will be extended for local access to individual offices and homes, which represents 80 percent of the cost of a network. In most of the world, fiber deployment likely never will happen.

This is a big problem for all our societies. If these powerful technologies are available only in advanced urban areas, people will be forced to migrate to those areas in search of economic opportunity and to fulfill other needs and desires. Society now is organized around the economics of infrastructure. With the agricultural revolution, technology (seeds) tied people to the land and brought them together in towns and villages. With the industrial revolution, people came together in increasingly congested urban areas, all organized around the economics of industrial infrastructure—wires, rails, highways, pipes, machinery. To the extent that the digital revolution is tied to wires, it is just an extension of the industrial age paradigm. Like the highways and the railways before them, wires are rigidly dedicated to particular locations. If you live alongside the main line, you prosper. If you live a few miles distant, you are left behind.

It is no longer sound (economically or environmentally) to force people to migrate to increasingly congested urban areas in search of opportunity. The real potential of the information age is to find a means of allowing people to choose where they live and work based on such things as family, community, and quality of life rather than access to infrastructure. The United States has done a very good job of extending one-to-many communications to most of the world. But having created a means for everyone to see all the benefits of our societies, we also have created expectations (legitimate expectations) that will seek fulfillment. We need to provide the means for people to participate fully in the benefits of our societies where they are. We need to create and configure the two-way network links that allow people to participate economically and culturally with the world at large without requiring that they pick up and move to where the infrastructure is.

Moore's law, which says that a microprocessor will do twice as much for the same cost every 18 months, has correctly predicted the exponential growth of the computer industry for over 25 years. However, while computers today are tens of thousands of times faster than those available a decade or two ago, networking has shown only linear growth. Improvements in networking performance, which have required backhoes to dig up streets and replace antiquated copper with modern fiberoptic technology, have not come close to keeping pace. Backhoes do not obey Moore's law.

The solution we seek to bring into being is wireless broadband access to advanced network connections. Unlike wireline technologies, the cost of wireless broadband access is largely indifferent to location. But to get the bandwidth required for fiberlike service through wireless means, it is necessary to move way up into the millimeter-wave frequencies—in the 60- to 70-GHz range (the Ka band). However, sending signals horizontally, over the land, in these frequencies is problematic. They are subject to rain attenuation and blockage by terrain, foliage, and buildings. The solution being adopted is simple. Send the signals vertically. This lead us to a satellite-based solution.

The next issue that is being faced is: What kind of satellite system? Viewed from the turn of the century, it is difficult to predict with certainty all the advanced applications and data protocols that such a network will be called on to accommodate in the twenty-second century. However, it is reasonable to assume that these applications will be developed for the wireline networks in the advanced urban areas—in other words, the fiber networks.

To ensure seamless compatibility with those fiber networks, it is important that the satellite network have the same essential characteristics as fiber. Such characteristics include wireless broadband channels, low error rates, and low delay.

The advanced digital wireless broadband networks will be packet-switched networks in which voice, video, and data are all just packets of digitized bits. In these networks, you cannot separate out the applications that can tolerate delay from those which cannot. People will not want to maintain two networks, one for delay-sensitive applications and another for applications that can tolerate delay. Traditional geostationary orbit (GSO) satellites will never be able to provide fiberlike delays.

This leads us to a low-earth-orbit (LEO) network. To put this in perspective, the space shuttle orbits at about 290 km above the earth's surface. There is only one geostationary orbit, and this is over the equator at 40,000 km—almost 138 times further out than the space shuttle. By contrast, satellites would be configured to orbit at about 1100 km—36 times closer to the earth than geostationary satellites.

With the combination of a very high minimum vertical angle to the satellite (to overcome the blocking and attenuation problems associated with the Ka band) and the low altitude, geometry takes over, and a constellation of hundreds of satellites is required to cover the earth. The large number of satellites also allows economies of scale in manufacturing and creates a system with very large capacity that allows a low cost of service.

The concept of a network consisting of thousands of satellites may seem radical when compared with traditional geostationary satellites, but it is less radical when compared with the evolution of networks on the ground. Computer networks have evolved from centralized systems built around a single mainframe computer to distributed networks of interconnected personal computers (PCs). Similarly, satellite networks (for switched-network connections) are evolving from centralized systems built around a single geostationary satellite to distributed networks of interconnected

LEO satellites. The evolution in both cases is being driven by some of the same forces.

A decentralized network offers other advantages: A distributed topology provides greater reliability. Redundancy and reliability can be built more economically into the network rather than into the individual unit. Also, because a LEO satellite has a smaller footprint within which frequencies can be reused, it is inherently more efficient in its use of spectrum resources. Geostationary satellites will continue to have an important role to play, particularly for broadcast applications, where their large footprint is advantageous. Increasingly, however, geostationary satellites will coexist with nongeostationary orbit (NGSO) satellite networks.

This evolution toward NGSO systems has resulted in the configuration of three LEO system types, each focused on a different service segment and using a different portion of the radiofrequency (rf) spectrum. The best way to distinguish between these three LEO system types is by reference to their corresponding terrestrial services:

The so-called little LEOs are the satellite equivalent of paging. They operate below 1 GHz and provide simple store-and-forward messaging. These systems offer low data rates but can provide valuable services in a wide range of settings, such as remote monitoring and vehicle tracking.

The so-called big LEOs have received the most attention. They are the satellite equivalent of cellular phone service and operate between 1 and 3 GHz. For example, Teledesic was the first to propose a wireless broadband LEO. It provides the satellite equivalent of optical fiber. Because it operates in the Ka band, essentially line of sight from the user terminal to the satellite is required, which makes it more appropriate for fixed applications or mobile applications such as maritime and aviation use, where line of sight is not an issue. It will provide advanced digital wireless broadband network connections to all those parts of the world that are not likely to get such capabilities through wireline means.

Since the emergence of the World Wide Web, network-centric computing has provided a compelling configuration model for a different kind of telecommunications: switched wireless broadband services. Peer-to-peer networking, based on the ubiquity and exponential improvements of personal computing, is transforming the way individuals live and businesses create value. Switched connections communicate from anyone to anyone, and wireless broadband allows the transmission of all forms of digital information—voice, data, videoconferencing, and interactive multimedia.

The Internet today is still at a relatively primitive stage of development, comparable with the first personal computers in the late 1970s. At that time, it was difficult to imagine the pervasiveness and range of applications of personal computing today. By contrast, the World Wide Web already provides a revealing glimpse of the promise of the Internet, with hundreds of thousands of companies and millions of individuals exploring, publishing, and developing on this new medium. Any and all information can and will be digitized, uploaded, and transmitted anywhere.

Well, not quite anywhere. The promise of the information age is constrained by the lack of access to switched wireless broadband services in most of the developed and virtually all of the developing world. Recent developments in configuring wireless broadband satellites will provide a means to help extend these switched wireless broadband connections on demand anywhere on earth.

There is an important aspect of these NGSO systems that is worth noting. There have been a number of studies, many of them by the International Telecommunication Union (ITU), that show a direct correlation between economic prosperity and teledensity. In the absence of a high level of economic development, however, a country is not likely to attract the investment required for an advanced information infrastructure. NGSO systems can help developing countries overcome this "chicken and egg" problem in telecommunications development and configuration.

Once you come out of a geostationary orbit, then, by definition, satellites move in relation to earth. With an NGSO system, continuous coverage of any point requires, in effect, global coverage. In order to provide service to the advanced markets, the same quality and quantity of capacity have to be provided to the developing markets, including those areas to which no one would provide such capacity for its own sake. In this sense, NGSO satellite systems represent an inherently egalitarian technology that promises to radically transform the economics of telecommunications infrastructure. It is a form of cross-subsidy from the advanced markets to the developing world, but one that does not have to be enforced by regulation but rather is inherent in the technology.

Let's return to the issue of latency in satellite networks that was mentioned earlier as one of the reasons for adopting an NGSO approach. This point is probably worth some elaboration. Even at the speed of light, round-trip communications through a geostationary satellite entail a minimum transmission latency (end-to-end delay) of approximately 0.5 s. This latency causes the annoying delay in many intercontinental phone calls, impeding understanding and distorting the personal nuances of speech. What can be an inconvenience for analog voice transmissions, however, can be untenable for videoconferencing and many data applications.

Applications will be developed for terrestrial networks, not for special networks with nonstandard characteristics. Companies that build networks that are not compatible with the predominant data protocols and applications are taking a big business risk that their systems will be usable only for specialized, proprietary applications. History has not looked favorably on companies that have made big bets on low-quality service. And since telecommunications customers make purchasing decisions based on their most demanding (not their average) application, geostationary satellite systems may not be a feasible choice if even a relative minority of services are latency-sensitive. In fact, most switched data applications are adversely affected by high latency.

Excessive latency causes otherwise high-bandwidth connections to communicate at a fraction of their capacity. And these issues arise not with obscure data protocols or obsolete hardware but with almost all implementations of the only data protocol with which most people are familiar, TCP/IP, which connects the global Internet and is the standard for corporate networking.

For all lossless protocols that guarantee the integrity of the data transmission, latency is a constraining factor on the usable bandwidth. Since a data packet may be lost in transmission, a copy of it must be kept in a buffer on the sending computer until receipt of an acknowledgment from the computer at the other end that the packet arrived successfully. Most common data protocols operate on this principle. The data packet's trip over the geostationary connection takes 250 ms at best. And the acknowledgment packet takes another 250 ms to get back, so the copy of the data packet cannot be removed from the buffer for at least 500 ms. Since packets cannot be transmitted unless they are stored in the buffer, and the buffer can only hold a limited number of packets, no new packets can be transmitted until old ones are removed when their acknowledgments are received.

Specifically, the default buffer size in the reference implementation of TCP/IP is 4 kb, which is 32 kb. This means that at any given moment, only 32 kb can be in transit and awaiting acknowledgment. No matter how many bits the channel can transmit theoretically, it still takes at least half a second for any 32 bits to be acknowledged. Thus the maximum data throughput rate is 32 kb per half second, or 64 kbps.

To put this in perspective, if you take off-the-shelf hardware and software, hook up a wireless broadband geostationary link, and order a T-1 line (1.544 Mbps), you expect to be able to transmit about a T-1 line worth of data. In fact, any connection via a geostationary satellite is constrained to only 64 kbps, which is 4 percent of the purchased capacity.

Changing protocols is not a feasible solution in this situation. The trend in data networking is toward a single "pipe" carrying many types of data (including voice and other real-time data). It is therefore likely to be neither useful nor economical to transmit specific kinds of data using custom, proprietary protocols. In theory, the implementations of standard protocols, such as TCP/IP, can be modified to support higher buffer sizes. But these modifications are rarely simple or convenient, since computers on both sides of any connection need to be upgraded. Moreover, the maximum buffer size possible in TCP/IP is 64 kilobytes, which still only provides 1.024 Mbps, or 67 percent of a T-1 line, over a geostationary link.

Even worse, if the geostationary link is not at one of the end points of the data transmission but is instead an intermediate connection, there is no method to notify the transmitting computer to use a larger buffer size. Thus, while data packets can seamlessly traverse multiple fiber and fiberlike networks (such as Teledesic), geostationary links are unsuitable for seamless intermediate connections.

The interplay of latency and buffer sizes does not affect all data transmissions, only lossless ones. For real-time data, such as voice and video, where it is not essential that all data be transmitted, lossy protocols can transmit higher data rates with less overhead. Unfortunately, real-time applications, such as voice telephony and videoconferencing, are precisely the applications most susceptible to unacceptable quality degradation as a result of high latency.

Instead of attempting to modify the entire installed base of network equipment with which one might want to communicate, receiving seamless compatibility with existing terrestrial networks becomes increasingly attractive. As both bandwidth requirements and the use of real-time data accelerate, the benefits of fiberlike service are only growing in importance.

What all this discussion makes clear is that no one single technology or satellite system type is going to be appropriate for all communications needs in all settings. The capabilities of fiber cannot be matched for very dense traffic. For basic telephone service, the economics of terrestrial cellular systems are compelling, particularly where no wireline infrastructure exists. Geostationary satellites will continue to play an important role, particularly for video distribution and other broadcast applications, where latency is not an issue and a large footprint is desirable. And each of the LEO system types has an important role to play.

Each of these technologies should be given the opportunity to fulfill its potential without bias from the regulatory structure. However, international regulatory structures are not evolving as quickly as the technology. The period between World Radio Conferences (WRCs), for example (2 years), is longer than an entire generation of computer chip technology. In the past, the conservative nature of the WRC process actually served a positive function in helping to preserve options for the future. Today, however, there is a serious risk that the failure to take into account new technologies and new approaches actually could foreclose options for the future. It is important that the international regulatory process not be biased toward any particular technology or approach but rather that it preserve our options for the future.

For the past 35 years of satellite communications, geostationary satellites have been virtually the entire relevant universe, and the international satellite spectrum allocations and associated regulations reflect this. Geostationary satellites currently enjoy general priority status in all fixed satellite service frequency bands (see the sidebar, "Coexistence Between Fixed Service and High-Density Fixed Satellite Systems") by virtue of ITU Radio Regulation 2613. This subjects NGSO satellite systems to unbounded regulatory uncertainty, since their operation would be vulnerable to preemption by any and all geostationary satellites, even those deployed long after the NGSO systems. For those providers who propose a nongeostationary satellite system, special accommodation is required. By contrast, someone proposing a geostationary satellite system need only file the appropriate paperwork with the ITU.

Coexistence Between Fixed Service and High-Density Fixed Satellite Systems

In many frequency ranges, the terrestrial fixed service (FS) and the fixed satellite service (FSS) are coprimary. If both services are regulated by adequate technical and regulatory conditions, this will not constrain the development of both services and offer an efficient method of spectrum utilization.

During the last two WRCs, the discussions about the needs and requirements of new high-density fixed satellite service (HDFSS) systems were dominating all other topics and services. HDFSS systems are FSS networks operating with a high geographic density of user terminals. Whereas there is no doubt that these new satellite networks will offer new possibilities and advantages, they also have their limits and drawbacks, particularly as regards efficient use of spectrum. With the development of telecommunications deregulation and the explosion of mobile communications, it seemed important to the European Public Telecommunications Network Operators' Association (ETNO) to reassert the importance of terrestrial radio communication services. It is especially important to avoid the possibility that new HDFSS systems put new constraints on existing and planned FS systems.

Satellite networks are very efficient tools to provide seamless coverage of wide geographic areas and offer cost-effective solutions especially in sparsely populated regions. However, in densely populated areas like Europe, the FS is by far more frequency efficient and can offer much more capacity than any existing or planned HDFSS system. Therefore, ETNO is of the opinion that the FS should be given priority in Europe compared with HDFSS. HDFSS systems should be taken as a useful complement for the FS to provide efficient coverage in remote areas of Europe that cannot be covered efficiently with FS/HDFS.

ETNO therefore proposes that the FSS and the FS/HDFS should continue to share the same frequency bands. Segmentation of the spectrum should be avoided as far as possible. Priority for the FS means that the future development of the FS (including HDFS) is not hindered by the new HDFSS systems and that it might be necessary to take further steps to adapt the HDFSS accordingly. There should be, under no circumstances, any constraints on existing FS networks as a result of the implementation of new HDFSS systems.

For example, a very important band in this respect is the harmonized 18-GHz band, where many thousands of FS links already exist all over Europe and many more are being rolled out every month. The HDFSS has to accept the existing environment in the 18-GHz downlink band. Therefore, HDFSS terminals should not claim protection from the terrestrial FS stations.[1]

In bands such as the C and Ku bands that already are congested with geostationary satellite systems, it would not be appropriate to change this regime. To allow for the future development of both satellite system types, however, designated subbands in which nongeostationary systems would have priority status need to be established in the satellite service expansion bands.

In the Ka band, the WRC recently made provisions for nongeostationary satellite systems. This was an impressive example of the ability of the ITU to adapt to new circumstances and accommodate new technologies. But the Ka band is not the final frontier of satellite spectrum. To allow for the future development of both satellite system types, consideration should be given to the long-term spectrum needs for both geostationary and nongeostationary satellite systems. The ITU can play a constructive role in enabling all technologies and system types, preserving each country's ability to make its own choices of systems, services, and service providers.

With this in mind, the demand for advanced information services is growing in terms of both the number of users and the services to be supported. Voice and low-rate data services are insufficient for users in a world where high-speed World Wide Web access is taken for granted. The trend is toward global information networks offering flexible multimedia information services to users on demand, anywhere, anytime. Potential services include video-on-demand, interactive video, fast Internet access, telemedicine, tele-education, and large-file transfer. The need to support bandwidth-intensive multimedia services places new and challenging demands on satellite systems and networks. Flexibility, efficiency, mobility, and the ability to guarantee end-to-end quality of service are at a premium. Next, a survey of future wireless broadband multimedia satellite systems is provided.

Systems

Consistent with emerging third-generation (3G) communications systems, the focus is on multimedia information services over IP and IP/Asynchronous Transfer Mode (ATM). The implementation and configuration of future IP/ATM over satellite communications (SATCOM) networks can be divided into two fundamental cases: the bent-pipe satellite relay and the switch in the sky. The relative advantages and disadvantages of each architecture will be discussed. Key issues and trends also will be examined.

Future Broadband SATCOM Systems

Future wireless broadband SATCOM systems will offer high-speed Internet access and multimedia information services, such as multicasting and interactive video. Multimedia communication requires guaranteed quality of service (QoS), which differs by service class (voice and data) and may be complicated by increased errors, delay, and delay jitter over satellite links.

ATM was designed especially for multimedia information services and supports guaranteed QoS by service class. At present, IP supports only one service class, but work is in progress to enhance IP. Few current SATCOM systems employ ATM in a meaningful way; however, several major systems are in the planning stages, and others are envisioned. A summary of future broadband satellite systems is provided in Table 20-1.[2] Most plan to employ either IP, ATM, or a combination of both.

TABLE 20-1 Next-Generation SATCOM Systems

System	Operation	Satellites	Altitude (km)	Frequency	Access	Network	Capacity	Services
Astrolink	2003	9 GEOs	36000	Ka band	FDMA TDMA	IP/ATM, ISDN	6.5 Gbps	High-speed multimedia
Cyberstar	2001	3 GEOs	36000	Ka band	FDMA TDMA	IP/ATM, Frame Relay	9.6 Gbps	Internet access, VoD broadband services
Spaceway	2002	16 GEOs 20 MEOs	36000 10352	Ka band	FDMA TDMA	IP/ATM, ISDN, Frame Relay	4.4 Gbps	High-speed Internet BoD, multimedia
SkyBridge	2001	80 LEOs (Walker)	1469	Ka band	CDMA TDMA FDMA	IP/ATM	> 20 M users	High-bit-rate Internet access, interactive multi-media service
Teledesic	2002	28 LEOs 12 planes of 24	1375	Ka band 60 GHz	MF-TDMA ATDMA	IP/ATM, ISDN	10.0 Gbps	"Internet-in-the-Sky," ISDN high-quality voice, data, video
iSky (KaStar)	2001	2 GEOs	36000	Ka band	—	IP/ATM	—	Internet, DBS, PCS, BoD

Some systems, such as Teledesic, have constellations with many LEO satellites, whereas others, such as Cyberstar and iSky (KaStar), plan to operate with as few as two to four satellites in geosynchronous earth orbit. Broadband satellite architectures may be based on ATM with sophisticated onboard processing (OBP), onboard switching (OBS), and intersatellite links (ISLs), whereas others employ simple bent-pipe transponder relays. The system design choices depend on many factors, including coverage, cost, user service, and traffic.

Most of the systems in Table 20-1 operate in the Ka band. SkyBridge operates in the Ku band. The key reason for use of the Ka band is the availability of bandwidth to support wireless broadband multimedia communications (capacity). This is the common denominator. Each of these systems is designed to exploit the emerging market for high-quality multimedia information services on demand to users with relatively small terminals over wireless broadband wide-area networks.

Astrolink   The Astrolink satellite constellation contains nine GEO satellites. Astrolink is a Ka-band satellite system. The uplink is 28.35 to 28.8 GHz and 29.25 to 30.0 GHz. The downlink is 19.7 to 20.2 GHz. The system is designed to support high-speed multimedia communications. Astrolink employs OBP for increased efficiency and OBS for flexibility. Each satellite is an integral part of the communications network, as opposed to being a bent-pipe relay. Data rates range from as low as 16 kbps to 9.6 Mbps. Up to 384 kbps is supported to 90-cm dishes, which makes Astrolink potentially suitable for large mobile platforms.

Cyberstar   The Ka-band Cyberstar constellation consists of three GEO satellites. Cyberstar is designed to provide IP multicasting services to Internet service providers (ISPs), large and small business organizations, and multimedia content providers. The capacity of the Cyberstar network is 9.6 Gbps. IP multicasting is implemented based on Frame Relay and ATM technology.

Spaceway   The Spaceway (Hughes) constellation consists of 16 GEO and 20 medium-earth-orbit (MEO) satellites. The Ka-band system is designed to support high-speed data, Internet access, and wireless broadband multimedia information services. The Spaceway satellite architecture is based on conventional bent-pipe relay. It offers high QoS (bit error rate, BER $< 10^{-10}$) to users with terminals as small as 0.66 m at data rates starting at 16 kbps up to 6 Mbps. The Spaceway system is compatible with

ATM, Integrated Services Digital Network (ISDN), Frame Relay, and X.25 terrestrial standards.

SkyBridge The SkyBridge constellation consists of 80 satellites in circular LEOs at 1469 km. The orbital inclination is 53°s. The system is intended to support advanced information services (interactive multimedia) at data rates from 16 kbps to as high as 60 Mbps. SkyBridge satellite design is based on a bent-pipe relay architecture. Unlike the other systems in Table 20-1, SkyBridge is a Ku-band system. The uplink operates at 12.75 to 14.5 GHz, and the downlink is 10.7 to 12.75 GHz. The choice of Ku band is due to the availability of Ku-band technology.

SkyBridge gateway stations interface with terrestrial networks via ATM switches. The majority of services are expected to be IP-based. SkyBridge employs a combined code-/time-/frequency-division multiple access (CDMA/TDMA/ FDMA) waveform; however, the satellites themselves are transparent (bent pipe). Spot beams, with frequency reuse in each beam, are employed to enhance capacity. SkyBridge is designed to accommodate traffic from over 20 million simultaneous users.

Teledesic The Teledesic constellation consists of 288 satellites in 12 planes of 24 satellites. Teledesic is a Ka-band system with 60-GHz ISLs between adjacent satellites in each orbital plane. The uplink operates at 28.6 to 29.1 GHz and the downlink at 18.8 to 19.3 GHz.

Teledesic employs full OBP and OBS. The system is designed to be an "Internet in the sky." It offers high-quality voice, data, and multimedia information services. QoS performance is designed for a BER $< 10^{-10}$. Multiple access is a combination of multifrequency TDMA (MF-TDMA) on the uplink and asynchronous TDMA (ATDMA) on the downlink. The capacity of the network is planned to be 10 Gbps. User connections of 2 Mbps on the uplink and 64 Mbps on the downlink are possible. A minimum elevation angle of 40.25° enables the Teledesic system to achieve an availability of 99.9 percent.

iSky (KaStar) iSky, formerly KaStar, is focused on providing wireless broadband data and Internet services to North America. This Ka-band system is designed to support high-speed two-way Internet access, direct broadcast services (DBS), and future personal communications systems (PCS) to homes and offices via small-aperture (26-in) antennas. The initial constellation consists of two GEO satellites. The uplink frequency is 19.2 to 20.0 GHz, and the downlink is 29.0 to 30.0 GHz. Data rates up to 40 Mbps are envisioned, with typical rates in the range of 1.5 to 5 Mbps.

Future Trends and Issues:
Ka-Band and Higher Frequency

Many future satellite systems will operate at Ka band. Examples are provided in Table 20-1. A major reason is the availability of spectrum. Other frequencies also may be of interest, including V band (40–50 GHz) and millimeter wave (60 GHz). As the number of satellite systems and users and the bandwidth they demand increase, further pressure to consider higher frequencies is expected, despite the well-known problems associated with rain and atmospheric attenuation at such frequencies. Another reason for interest in Ka-band and higher frequencies is the potential for smaller antennas. However, this must be balanced against other factors, such as increased rain attenuation at these frequencies, which favors the use of larger antennas.

GEO versus LEO   Coverage is the primary advantage of GEO satellites over LEO systems. The wide-area coverage of GEO satellites makes them ideal for multicasting. However, the higher orbit means that the round-trip delay is much larger than for LEO or MEO systems. Longer delay means that GEO satellites typically are less suitable for applications such as voice or interactive video than LEO systems. Higher altitude also makes GEO satellites more expensive to launch (than LEOs).

LEO systems require frequent handover between the ground terminal and the satellites, which are in view for a relatively short period of time. Additionally, they also rely on crosslinks between neighboring satellites to increase coverage. This tends to increase the complexity of LEO systems (OBP in support of routing). It also leads to a problem with delay jitter, which can degrade voice performance. One way to address delay jitter is through buffering. This is the approach employed by Teledesic.

Enhanced TCP   Research is ongoing into various aspects of TCP implementation and performance of TCP/IP over satellite links. Issues include the slow start algorithm, the ability to accommodate large bandwidth-delay products, congestion control, acknowledgment, and error recovery mechanisms.

The slow start algorithm is especially inefficient for data transfers that are short compared with the delay-bandwidth product. Larger initial window sizes and byte counting are under investigation. Furthermore, when the product of the data rate over the TCP connection and the round-trip delay exceeds the available memory, performance degrades rapidly. This favors the use of LEO satellite systems over, say, GEO systems. There are several potential solutions. One involves *spoofing* TCP. In this case, premature acknowledgments are sent to trick TCP into continuing transmission. Another option is selective repeat acknowledgment (SACK), and a SACK version of TCP is under study by the Internet Engineering Task Force (IETF). SACK-based loss-recovery mechanisms can be employed to improve both protocol efficiency and congestion control over long-delay links.

IP, ATM, and Enhanced QoS Awareness   IP, ATM, or a combination of the two (IP/ATM) is expected to form the backbone of efficient future multimedia information networks. The trend is toward increasingly flexible, packet-oriented, quality-of-service (QoS)–aware networks. Multiple service and priority levels are expected in terms of both quality and speed. Guaranteed QoS is essential to multimedia communications. The ability to allocate exactly the necessary resources per service class is important in terms of efficiency (optimal use of resources).

ATM was designed to support guaranteed QoS per-service class. By comparison, IP currently supports only a single QoS via best-effort delivery; however, in the future, IP is also expected to support multiple QoS classes (IETF RFCs 2475 and 2216) and therefore multimedia services.

IP Security Over SATCOM   As e-commerce increases, the need for reliable Internet security does as well. The potential for interception and corruption may be increased by the wide-area coverage of satellite links. Internet Protocol security (IPSec) mechanisms must ensure confidentiality, authentication, integrity, access control, and key management. Confidentiality means that only the appropriate users have access to the information. Authentication requires verification of a user's identity and right to access. Integrity means that the information has not been corrupted. Access control ensures that the system cannot be compromised by unauthorized access (pirating a satellite). Key management is a key issue with respect to IPSec over multicast SATCOM. The problem is to provide an efficient means of dynamically generating and distributing keys. The problem may be further complicated by the routing technique (encapsulation of headers).

IP Routing and ATM Switching   IP routing is a logical option for networks that carry IP traffic. It is also of interest because it can support multicast transmission via the widely used Internet Group Management Protocol (IGMP) (RFC2236). However, IP routing presents new challenges over satellite networks, perhaps especially with respect to multicast routing in full-mesh LEO satellite networks.

The development of routing protocols capable of supporting multicast transmissions over wide areas with dynamic group membership and changing ISLs is simply more complex than for static SATCOM links. Topology information on which terrestrial Internet routing protocols, such as Open Shortest Path (OSPF) and Routing Information Protocol (RIP), rely can become obsolete rapidly.

Routing may be implemented on the ground or onboard the satellite (onboard routing, OBR). In either case, current information concerning the space segment (satellite ID and ISL interface) and the ground segment (geographic position, host ID, and MAC information, such as the CDMA code, TDMA time slot, or FDMA frequency) is required. Research is ongoing into various IP routing techniques for SATCOM, including tunneling, network address translation (NAT) (RFC2663), Border Gateway Protocol (BGP) (RFC1771), IP/ATM with Multi-Protocol Label Switching (MPLS), and proprietary constraint-based routing techniques tailored to the satellite network. In the future, IP routing for satellite networks may be implemented via a combination of tunneling, NAT, border routing, and MPLS, which appears to be well suited to support IP routing over ATM-SATCOM networks.

Most of the proposed wireless broadband commercial satellite systems are expected to be ATM-based. Switching/routing would be accomplished via proprietary protocols in combination with ATM, IP/ATM, encapsulation, and tunneling. For example, Teledesic is expected to employ its own proprietary protocols for both the ISLs and the space-ground links. Spaceway and Astrolink use ATM-based communication for the ISLs and earth-space links, as well as a custom MAC/LLC and custom signaling. SkyBridge employs ATM in the ground segment (there are no ISLs or OBP, OBS, or OBR). Each of these systems is expected to support IP via tunneling.

Bent-Pipe Satellite Relay versus the "Switch in the Sky"

In a bent-pipe satellite relay, the satellite transponder performs signal amplification and frequency translation (at 650 MHz). Signal detection, decoding, and protocol translation are not performed. The satellite is essentially independent of signal format and transparent to the protocol suite. In principle, any user with the appropriate terminal (power, bandwidth, and out-of-band radiation) could access the satellite. This case will be referred to as the *satellite relay ATM* (SR-ATM).

Implementation of a "switch in the sky" requires substantial onboard processing (OBP). The case of a satellite with a fully capable onboard satellite switch (SS) will be referred to as *satellite-switched ATM* (SS-ATM). Although rare today, the use of OBP, OBS, and OBR is expected to increase in the future, since they afford potentially superior performance and more sophisticated networking capabilities than the basic transparent pipe relay.

OBP, OBS, and OBR   One of the main goals of processed satellites is to provide single-hop connectivity to small earth stations. Examples of satellites with varying degrees of OBP, OBS, and/or OBR include the U.S. Milstar, the NASA Advanced Communication Technology Satellite (ACTS), and Italsat 2. There are many forms of OBP that may be applicable to the implementation of ATM-SATCOM networks. OBP may be divided into three classes, which roughly correspond to

- Class 1: Baseband OBP and OBS/OBR

- Class 2: Intermediate/radiofrequency (IF/rf) processing and switching

- Class 3: Support processing.[3]

Class 1 is commonly referred to as a *fully processed satellite*. It is exemplified by the case of the satellite "switch in the sky." Class 2 roughly corresponds to that of a *partially processed satellite*. It may include signal regeneration and rf or IF switching but does not include baseband OBS. Other forms of processing, not directly related to communications, but which support communications functions, are grouped into class 3. Only baseband OBP and OBS are considered in this chapter.

Baseband Processing   The goal of baseband OBP is to enhance link performance and efficiency. Enhancements may be applied to reduce cost or increase capacity, the latter favored by current trends such as wireless broadband communications. Perhaps most important, the combination of baseband OBP and OBS can enhance overall network efficiency and flexibility. OBS is the essential element satellite "switch in the sky" concept. In the case of SS-ATM, OBP enables cell-based OBS.

Baseband OBP involves much more than merely signal amplification and frequency translation. Key functions include demodulation, demultiplexing, error detection and correction, and removal of routing and control information. Examples of baseband OBP functions associated with signal regeneration and transmission are switching or routing of data, beam forming, data buffering, and data multiplexing.

Signal-regeneration techniques are usually employed to improve the signal-to-noise (S/N) ratio and reduce the BER. This may be especially important with respect to the operation of ATM over SATCOM, where the ability to achieve and maintain a BER of 10^{-8} or less may be required. A key point with respect to OBP is that the satellite is no longer a transparent repeater. This has implications in terms of interoperability (the waveform must be compatible in order to communicate).

In addition to signal regeneration and switching, baseband OBP can facilitate a wide range of techniques for optimizing system performance. Beam forming is a prime example. OBP can facilitate dynamic beam forming as well as nulling an interferer. Similarly, it may be possible to provide dynamic, on-demand allocation of antenna gain and coverage, which enables flexible allocation of satellite effective isotropic radiated power (EIRP).

Fully Processed Satellites

A conceptual illustration of a fully processed SS-ATM-SATCOM network is provided by Figure 20-1, from which it can be seen that the satellite is a node in the ATM network.[4] Dynamic OBS of logical connections is possible at the cell level, as opposed to slower, less dynamic switching at IF or RF, under ground control. All OBP processing is assumed to be performed at baseband in this example.

OBP and Satellite Resource Allocation   In principle, the combination of OBP and OBS enables resource allocation to be performed by the satellite. This is desirable because the satellite has direct first-hand knowledge of the available resources, unlike an injection terminal, and therefore, it can, in principle, more effectively perform access control. Ground-based estimates of the available capacity would not be required; as a result, power and delay uncertainty due to propagation over the satellite is removed.

Although the same argument could be made for satellites with non-ATM-based OBP and OBS, the potential benefit of, and sensitivity to, onboard resource allocation is arguably more significant with respect to an SS-ATM system, since ATM is uniquely designed to support flexible allocation of any amount of bandwidth, up to the full capacity, on demand, at the appropriate QoS. Not all services are treated alike. Resource allocation is more granular than over a conventional time-division multiplex (TDM)/FDMA link, where capacity is either available or not.

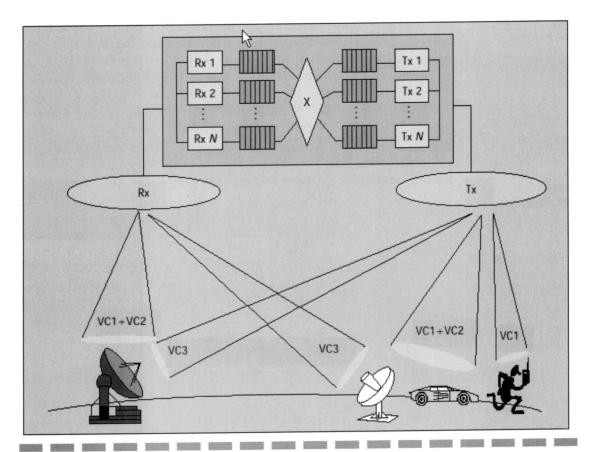

Figure 20-1   A fully processed satellite-switched ATM-SATCOM network.

Estimation of Resources   An issue with respect to ATM-SATCOM and resource allocation concerns identification of the available resources. An approximation of the available resources can be obtained using measurements of the queue lengths in the ATM switch, but this is only an estimate of the capacity based on delay. OBP makes it possible to more accurately assess the available capacity at the desired QoS, given direct knowledge of a user's requirements and signal characteristics, as well as all other frequency and power allocations onboard the satellite (the fully processed satellite controls WAN access and resource allocation).

Adaptive Beam Forming and Resource Allocation   The SS-ATM networking concept illustrated in Figure 20-1 also depicts dynamic beam forming and resource allocation. The use of phased-array (PA) or multiple-beam antennas (MBA) is envisioned. TDMA is considered in this example, where an association is made between ATM virtual circuits (VCs) and antenna beams in order to match the gain and EIRP as closely as possible to the requirements of user groups and to facilitate ATM-SATCOM-based multicasting. A proprietary medium access control (MAC) layer tailored to the topology and characteristics of the satellite network is envisioned.

The combination of SS-ATM and the ability to support flexible bandwidth allocation together with adaptive beam forming and the ability to focus precisely the required gain on the area(s) of interest allow bandwidth, power, and EIRP to be treated as a pool of resources. Ideally, the satellite would be able to allocate exactly the required capacity from this pool to any user or user group on demand, tailored to the service and QoS requirements and the capability of the terminal. In this way, OBP and ATM can enhance performance, given effective control.

Control may be either autonomous, in which case it is performed onboard the spacecraft, or performed on the ground. Although full OBP and OBS are not common today, they may be in the future as processing power and networking demands increase. Of the relatively few satellites with OBP today, most, if not all, are ground-controlled. The NASA ACTS and Italsat are examples of satellites with ground-controlled baseband OBS.

Service-Enabling Platforms

The ability to offer multimedia information services to users with small disadvantaged terminals requires the efficient integration of the service with the terminal (handset) and the network. An important issue in this regard concerns the role of service-enabling platforms, also known as *middleware*. Service-enabling platforms may be viewed as a layer of functionality between the transport system and the underlying network supporting distributed multimedia information services.

Middleware provides the basic mechanisms for sharing computing and communications resources. It supports adaptability and scalability and also provides mechanisms to support service management and delivery (multicast service, security, QoS management, synchronization, and error control). As such, it may affect many aspects of the communications system. In the case of a future system offering Internet services to SATCOM terminals via a processed satellite, the choice of service-enabling platform ultimately may have a role in the way in which the satellite network and communication resources are shared, as well as the integration of the satellite system into distributed multimedia networks.

Market Factors

A resounding theme throughout this chapter is that both the wireless broadband and satellite markets are quite immature, especially when compared with competing wireline copper and fiber-based infrastructure. As a result, it is important to look at the factors shaping and guiding the evolution of both these markets. Comparatively speaking, the satellite market is much more mature than the LMDS and related markets, despite the fact that satellite delivery and service dates are farther into the horizon.

The LMDS market still has much progress to make. The auctions themselves ended in March 1998 after much anticipation in 1997. From this point, those which have won licenses from the auction are planning their rollouts toward the end of 1998 and into 1999. Furthermore, they are also bound to the delivery dates imposed by the equipment vendors prior to offering service. Moreover, because of the gradual phase approach in setting up operation, there definitely will be distinct phases in the ramp-up of an LMDS service provider when offering service in a given locale. The actual turnaround time, however, from license acquisition to commercial service rollout can be as little as 11 months for a basic setup.

The satellite market, though, is quite mature by comparison with the LMDS and related wireless broadband markets. Not only has it been around for over 30 years, but much more attention has been given to it from the media and Wall Street. The $11 billion raised by Teledesic (primarily from Craig McCaw and Bill Gates) and Motorola's multiple satellite interests are evidence of this observation. Granted, this market also needs to grow between the equipment vendors and service providers; however, there seems to be more of a long-term focus and vision in its strategy.

No Cable and DSL: Try Satellite

For the past 5 years, wireless broadband access to the Internet via satellite has been the ugly stepsister to cable modem and DSL service. Downloading has been on a par with cable modem and DSL, but the uplink has been via a conventional dialup line. Not only does that slow things down, but it makes satellite service complicated and expensive.

Recently, however, at least two satellite companies have announced two-way satellite services designed to rival other broadband offerings more directly. These companies are betting that for the estimated 50 million households in the United States that cannot get cable modem or DSL service, satellite-based Internet access will prove to be the ideal solution (see the sidebar, "Plenty of Demand for Wireless Broadband").

Plenty of Demand for Wireless Broadband

Harris Interactive (Rochester, NY) recently released the results of a new survey of more than 69,000 Internet users that measured the perceptions of both current wireless broadband users and those planning (planners) to move to broadband DSL and cable modem Internet connections. The study estimated that approximately 38.9 million U.S. households connect to the Internet, and about 3.6 million U.S. households connect using a high-speed connection (cable modem, DSL, ISDN, or satellite data service). Most of the high-speed users use either cable modem (2.35 M) or DSL (0.85 M).

The study's results show that there is high interest in high-speed Internet connections among current Internet users. About one in eight of the households that connect to the Internet said that they planned to start using either DSL or cable modem service. The planners were about evenly split between DSL (2.4 M) and cable modem (2.6 M) services as their connection of choice.

The study revealed some similarities and some differences between DSL and cable modem users: According to the Harris Interactive Consumer TechPoll(SM) results, both DSL and cable modem users are happy with their connections. About 85 percent are satisfied with the reliability of their wireless broadband connection, and about 90 percent are satisfied with the speed of downloading pages and files. But the study also shows that all is not completely rosy with these services:

- Seventy-six percent of cable modem users were satisfied with the amount of time it took them to actually have service after they ordered it—much higher level of satisfaction than for DSL users (58 percent).

- Cable modem users seemed to find their service a bit easier to set up—81 percent of cable modem users were satisfied with the ease of set up versus 71 percent for DSL users.

These results show that while subscribers are happy with their wireless broadband connections once they get them, there is room for improvement in the provisioning of these services to shorten the wait time between order placement and functioning wireless broadband connections. There was little difference between perceptions among planners of DSL and cable modem services:

At the time of the survey, a projected 5 million Internet-using households planned to get either DSL or cable modem broadband services within the next 6 months—one-third more than were already using them. These intended subscribers saw little difference between DSL and cable modem services:

- An equal portion (30 percent) believed that connection speeds of both DSL and cable modem services were consistent.

- An about equal portion (31 percent) believed that both connections would be reliable.

- Very few (7 percent) thought that either service would be difficult to install and set up.

- Nearly half said they would choose the less expensive service.

- Fifty-seven percent said they would choose the service that had the higher top speed.

What's holding back revenues for wireless broadband service providers is not a lack of demand for wireless broadband services. The business is there to be had if service providers can get their provisioning acts together. What is interesting is how little difference wireless broadband planners see between the two dominant service types, DSL and cable modems. Thus, while the challenge now is provisioning, as service areas become more widespread, service providers will have to better differentiate their offerings unless they want to battle it out simply on price.

Harris Interactive Consumer TechPoll(SM) is a new multiclient study launched quarterly by Harris Interactive. It uses a sample taken from the Harris Interactive panel of more than 7 million online respondents. In addition to wireless broadband Internet connections, the study focuses on recent PC buyers and digital still camera and other technology hardware and services used by U.S. consumers.

Recently, StarBand[5] announced its two-way service, promising download speeds of up to 500 kbps, which is about 10 times faster than a 56K modem and slightly slower than DSL or cable modem service. Uploading, the company announced, would be at about 150 kbps. The service is expected to be widely available in the near future.

The StarBand service is being advertised with conspicuous swipes at other types of wireless broadband service. In one StarBand radio spot, a cheerful saleswoman from a cable modem provider tells a prospective customer: "Let's see, I can schedule an installation when hell freezes over or when pigs fly. Which would be better for you?"

Indeed, the demand for high bandwidth in the home has called attention to the fact that cable systems upgraded for two-way Internet traffic do not reach most rural areas. And DSL works only within 3 miles or so of a telephone central office. StarBand is a joint venture of Gilat, an Israeli satellite maker; EchoStar Communications, which operates the Dish Network television service; and Microsoft, which invested $50 million in the venture.

Hughes Network Systems, of Germantown, MD, is also preparing to begin a two-way service, which is essentially an upgrade to its DirecPC service, until now a one-way satellite link (see the sidebar, "Hughes Invests in Wireless Broadband Satellite System"). And Wildblue, a start-up in Denver, is building its own satellites to begin a consumer service in 2002.

Hughes Invests in Wireless Broadband Satellite System

Hughes Electronics Corporation's Spaceway has provided affordable high-bandwidth and high-speed communications for wireless broadband and multimedia applications. The first system is scheduled to begin operation in North America in 2003.

Hughes plans to work with global strategic partners to roll out additional systems with similar capabilities in other regions as the markets develop, including Europe, Middle East and Africa, Latin America, and Asia, thereby producing an integrated worldwide system. The FCC has already allocated Hughes orbital slots worldwide to operate the Ka-band frequency satellite system.

Once the geosynchronous orbit Spaceway system is operating, the next phase of Hughes' global wireless broadband plans is to introduce a complementary nongeosynchronous system. This system will have satellites operating in lower earth orbits and will expand the network capability to offer additional interactive wireless broadband multimedia communications services in high-traffic markets.

Spaceway has provided bandwidth-on-demand—the ability to transmit and receive data, video, voice, audio, and multimedia with customers using and paying for only the amount of bandwidth needed for the specific application, from e-mail to high-bandwidth, high-speed corporate networks. With Spaceway, large businesses, telecommuters, small office/home office (SOHO) users, and consumers will have access to two-way, high-data-rate applications such as desktop videoconferencing, interactive distance learning, and Internet services operating at speeds faster and at costs less expensive than those provided by such current land-based systems as Frame Relay. It will seamlessly integrate with existing land-based systems and will be fully compatible with a wide range of terrestrial transmission standards.

The Spaceway applications are marketed under variations of the *Direc* name already used by Hughes. The initial services offered by Spaceway include the next generation of DirecPC broadband Internet services and the DirecWay family of high-bandwidth very small aperture terminal (VSAT) services.

Hughes, through its Hughes Network Systems (HNS) unit, is already the market leader in VSAT corporate data networking and satellite wireless broadband Internet services. Existing HNS customers, many of which are Fortune 500 companies, have the opportunity to transition to Spaceway, which provides new applications for their businesses while keeping end-user costs low enough to provide competitive advantages over terrestrial offerings.

The satellite system employs innovative onboard digital processing, packet switching, and spot-beam technology to offer single-hop connectivity throughout the service area regardless of location. This connectivity, for example, allows customers to communicate directly via satellite with other customers without having to go through a retransmission service or hub. It also permits direct full-broadcast capability throughout the service area.

The North American network consists of two HS 702 geosynchronous orbit satellites built by Hughes Space and Communications Company, plus an in-orbit spare. HNS has led the development of the user terminals and overall ground infrastructure. Ground stations range from user terminals with antennas approximately 26 in in diameter to larger gateways for connectivity to terrestrial backbone networks.

PanAmSat operates the telemetry, tracking, and control center for the satellites in orbit and assists HNS in operating the network control center. PanAmSat also acts as a reseller of Spaceway capacity in certain market segments. DirecTV already markets to its subscribers several of the data services offered by Spaceway.

The demand for broadband data is expected to increase dramatically in the foreseeable future, with industry estimates projecting the U.S. market alone at $60 billion in 2006. Spaceway's technological advancements in frequency-reuse capability translate into an eight-fold increase in the satellite's revenue-generating potential at the wholesale level. With these advancements, the Spaceway platform allows Hughes to offer very competitive cost advantages and positions their offerings, such as DirecPC and DirecWay, to capture an increasing share of this rapidly growing broadband market.[6]

The service from StarBand and others requires the installation of a 24-in dish antenna, as well as a satellite modem, which together cost around $400, plus $199 for installation. The monthly fee starts at $60, slightly more expensive than cable modem and DSL service.

Everyone is improving their technology and decreasing their price points. StarBand customers can receive their Dish Network TV service on the same dish for about $100 per month.

The advantage of satellite service is that almost anyone almost anywhere can make use of it. All a satellite dish needs is a clear line of sight to an orbiting satellite. "If you can see the southern sky, you can get StarBand" is one of the company's marketing catch phrases.

To drive its point home, StarBand tested its service with a Havasupai tribe that lives on the floor of the Grand Canyon and receives no radio signals. StarBand provided the equipment, sending it down into the canyon by helicopter and mule train.

However, satellite-based data services have a reputation for being problematic. One annoyance with satellite systems is what is called *rain fade*. That is, heavy rainfall and wet snow can interfere with the signal. Also, high winds can knock the dishes out of alignment.

If it works, it is great, but if it does not work, it requires a technician's skills to repoint the dish. And since it is in remote locations, if you have a problem with your hardware, it can take days for a technician to get there.

Like cable modem service, satellite is a shared service. That is, downloading slows considerably, depending on how many people in one neighborhood are using the service at the same time.

Still another catch is choice limitation. A StarBand customer who signs up for the system through Radio Shack is required to buy a Compaq computer, which comes with the dish and the necessary cards for satellite reception already installed, for about $1200. But this option restricts the choice of Internet service providers to MSN. The service is also available through EchoStar distributors.

There is also a lingering psychological resistance to satellites. Not only can the move to a satellite-based Internet service seem intimidating, but a handful of satellite companies have suffered highly visible failures recently. In 1999, Iridium LLC, a global telephone venture backed by Motorola, Inc., declared bankruptcy, and others are struggling. People are scared!

Still, Internet users are increasingly obsessed with data speed, and the promise, any promise, of speed is delectable enough to make satellite service attractive. By the time enough people decide they simply cannot live without speedy Web connections, perhaps all the kinks will have been worked out.

Conclusion

Future satellite systems will offer an array of advanced information services. The trend is toward high-speed Internet access and wireless broadband multimedia and IP-based services over IP and/or IP/ATM networks. Services may range from e-mail and voice to wireless broadband multicasting and interactive video.

Finally, satellite architectures may employ OBP, OBS, and/or OBR to augment capacity or traditional bent-pipe transponders for simplicity and flexibility. Constellations may be LEO, MEO, GEO, or combinations thereof, depending on the coverage required and the services to be supported. The use of Ka-band and even higher frequencies will be increasingly common as available spectrum becomes more scarce. Higher frequencies also enable the use of smaller terminals and, potentially, greater mobility.

Perhaps most significant, the integration of emerging and future satellite systems with terrestrial networks can help bridge the last mile and expand the reach of Internet-based services to business and homes.

Endnotes

1. "ETNO Reflection Document on the Coexistence Between Fixed Service and High Density Fixed Satellite Systems, " ETNO Office Boulevard Bischoffsheim 33, 1000 Brussels, Belgium, 2000.

2. John Farserotu (CSEM) and Ramjee Prasad (Aalborg University), "A Survey of Future Broadband Multimedia Satellite Systems, Issues and Trends," *IEEE Communications Magazine,* IEEE Communications Society, 305 East 47th Street, New York, NY 10017, USA, 2000.

3. *Ibid.*

4. *Ibid.*

5. StarBand Corporate Headquarters, 1760 Old Meadow Road, McLean, VA 22102, 2000.

6. "Hughes to Invest $1.4 Billion in Broadband Satellite System," HNS Corporate Headquarters, 11717 Exploration Lane, Germantown, MD 20876 USA, 2000.

CHAPTER 21

Configuring Residential Wireless Broadband Access Technology

The teleworker (the employee who performs a portion of his or her work duties from a residence) may be the fastest growing part of the corporate work force. For some enterprises, connectivity needs for the majority of its teleworkers may be accommodated using the same technology and security measures used for roaming and remote access. For others, the emergence of residential wireless broadband services offers new opportunities for extending the corporate local-area network (LAN) to the residence-based employee. The high bandwidth, low latency, and *always-connected* characteristics of services based on digital subscriber line (DSL) or cable modem technologies allow teleworkers access to corporate LANs using network operating system (NOS) file, session, and printer services, including AppleTalk, Microsoft Network, and UNIX/NFS/X. These NOS services generally are impractical to use over traditional dialup services because of dialup's low bandwidth, high latency, and intermittent connectivity. Residential wireless broadband services thus allow a qualitative difference in teleworker activities compared with dialup services by enabling teleworkers to use the corporate network at home in the same way they do at the office.

The characteristics of residential wireless broadband services are similar to public switched data services such as Frame Relay and SMDS, with one noteworthy exception. Most Frame Relay and SMDS connections terminate at remote offices or corporate locations, where some site security policy is typically enforced: Employee identification is required, connectivity to the public Internet is restricted and protected by corporate firewalls, etc. Residential wireless broadband service, as the name implies, usually terminates in the home of a corporate teleworker. Because of this difference, the characteristics that make residential wireless broadband service attractive also may raise security concerns for some information technology (IT) managers.

Why is residential wireless broadband access to a corporate network so different from modem and ISDN dial access from a residence or hotel? Why are some IT managers cautious about bringing DSL or cable modem services into their enterprise? Are there ways to safely integrate residential wireless broadband into an enterprise network? Is one residential wireless broadband technology safer than the rest? Let's take a closer look.

NOTE   This chapter offers considerations for implementing security in enterprise networks where DSL-based services are applied. It does not profess to address every security issue for every enterprise IT manager. In the course of this chapter, security products are mentioned that may satisfy a security need for an IT manager and may direct the IT manager to a review of certain products. Any such mention does not represent an endorsement of any kind by this author.

Residential Broadband Services: Digital Subscriber Line and Cable Modem

Digital subscriber line (DSL) technology is used to provide layer 2 (data-link layer) access services. There are many different variants of DSL technologies. For example, Covad Communications Company's[1] TeleSpeed SM service is offered using IDSL, ADSL, and SDSL (see Figure 21-1).[2] The TeleSpeed SM service shares many characteristics with Frame Relay. Both are point to point, based on permanent virtual circuits (PVCs). A PVC is conceptually just a bidirectional pipe between two systems; data that are placed in one end of the PVC come out the other end unmodified. Customers can use any network protocol (AppleTalk, IP, IPX, etc.) over a PVC. PVCs transport data without examination; this means that the data can be encrypted, compressed, or otherwise transformed in ways agreeable to the systems using the PVC without affecting the PVC itself.

If your enterprise has already completed a risk assessment for Frame Relay, the security measures deemed appropriate for Frame Relay trans-

Figure 21-1
Covad's TeleSpeed SM service uses PVCs that originate at the tele-worker's residence as a DSL circuit operating over a copper twisted pair. This copper pair is connected to equipment in physically secured facilities in the tele-worker's serving central office. The PVC is relayed over a regional network and then onto a dedicated circuit to the customer's enterprise network.

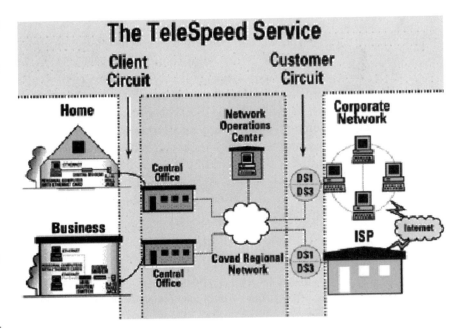

port probably can be applied to DSL-based services. For example, if your enterprise uses encryption over Frame Relay links, you can do so over TeleSpeed service links as well. This is true for many configuration and management issues as well. The same third-party trust model that companies understand and accept when dealing with other telephone and Frame Relay providers applies to alternative public data service providers as well. Basically, everything related to customer service is done at customer request. Alternative public data service providers set up new PVCs only when the customer submits an authorized service order. Furthermore, an alternative public data service provider setting up a new PVC is not enough to create a new connection into the customer's network; the customer also has to set up its own router or switch to handle the PVC. Like telephony providers, alternative public data service providers' facilities are physically secured, and only authorized personnel monitor and administer equipment.

Cable modem technology offers another method for providing residential wireless broadband services. Cable modems use two radiofrequency (rf) carrier signals *(channels)* from the CATV spectrum to provide high-bandwidth, low-latency, shared access service to residential customers. Cable modem operates a layer 2 service over a hybrid fiber-coax plant that passes residences in neighborhood to reach a cable company's central office for relay to a distribution hub (the *headend*), as shown in Figure 21-2.[3] Cable companies often collaborate with (or franchise services from) public Internet service providers (ISPs) for layer 3 (IP) service.

Whereas the DSL-based services offered by alternative public data service providers are point-to-point services, services based on cable modems are multipoint services. Cable modem service is similar to LAN service provided by shared-media (traditional, nonswitched) Ethernet. In security terms, shared-media Ethernet and cable modem systems (in the most common deployment configuration) are promiscuous media: All stations sharing the same media can read frames transmitted over the medium, and can write frames to the medium. When using cable modem services, data encryption is often warranted to ensure message privacy and integrity; this adds complexity and expense and can have an impact on performance.

NOTE   Unlike PVC-based services, shared-media services rely on stations to honestly identify themselves when transmitting data. Passive monitoring, forgery, and denial-of-service attacks are thus all greater risks with cable modem services than with DSL services.

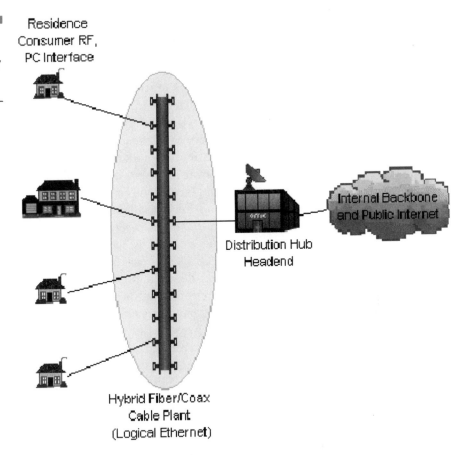

Residential Wireless Broadband Services and Security

Characteristics that residential wireless broadband services share that may be associated with security risk are

1. The residence is not a physically secured premises, at least not in the same way as other corporate facilities.

2. The residence has an always-connected link to the enterprise network.

3. The connection from residence to the enterprise network is a high-speed link.[4]

The first and second concerns are related and are problems common to all communications services used by teleworker and roaming employees who access corporate information resources remotely. Regardless of whether it is via analog modem, ISDN, or dialup bridge/router access, connectivity is typically automated. Because of this automated connectivity, the physical security of a teleworker's premises should be a concern for the IT manager regardless of whether access to the enterprise is achieved using on-demand or always-connected services.

For example, is DSL service a greater risk than remote LAN access using dialup ISDN service because DSL is always connected, given that ISDN router automatic dial-on-demand features are generally used by teleworkers? The answer, of course, depends on other factors, including the security measures in place at the corporate network and at the host computer(s) in the teleworker's residence; if all other factors are equal, the answer is usually *no, always-connected DSL service is no greater risk than automatic dial-on-demand ISDN service.* In many ways, in fact, always-connected DSL may be a lesser risk because it can only be used from a single premises. Dial-on-demand ISDN can be accessed from any ISDN-connected site anywhere in the world.

The third concern (that the connection from the residence to the enterprise network is a high-speed link) often proves to be the most troubling, especially in the case of remote or teleworker access to corporate servers. When corporate security is evaluated, the speed of a link is a weighting factor in determining risk. Simply put, if a low-speed link is compromised, information could be leaked from the enterprise network, but not nearly as fast as if a high-speed link is compromised. The rate at which a motivated intruder can access or collect sensitive information from a corporate server is more worrisome than whether the intruder is dialing in or is using facilities from a physically unsecured premises.

Let's examine several scenarios where these characteristics become issues for the IT manager and consider how they might be addressed. How an organization addresses security in these scenarios is greatly influenced by the perceived and real risks to corporate resources, the organization's financial and technological abilities to reduce or mitigate these risks, and the ability of the organization to implement and enforce the security measures chosen.

Scenario 1: The Teleworker Operates Systems that Do Not Fall under the Purview of Corporate Desktop Administration

By definition, teleworkers work outside the physically secured workplace. The IT manager may have little control over equipment at the teleworker's residence. The teleworker who runs unauthorized services (a Web, file, or mail server) and unapproved software may create vulnerabilities and compromise a secure perimeter established for an enterprise network. Network antivirus and intrusion-detection measures can be circumvented, and mail distribution, name resolution, or enterprise routing could be disrupted. Whether the result of accidental misconfiguration or malicious attack, activities initiated over the residential connection can interfere with or deny service to fellow corporate workers.

Recommended Policy and Best Practices for Desktop Security   It is easy to get caught up with concern over theft or modification of data transported over a network and overlook the more mundane issue of protecting stored information. Information is not any less sensitive because it is recorded on a removable medium (a Jazz drive) or hard disk of a laptop than if it is stored electronically. A security policy for both teleworker and mobile employee should consider the following:

- Desktop authentication
- Antivirus utilities
- Secure file storage and stored file encryption
- Desktop file security access controls
- Unauthorized services

DESKTOP AUTHENTICATION   This can be as simple as requiring that all personal computers (PCs), irrespective of location, use login and screen saver passwords with a small idle timeout. It also can be as sophisticated as requiring a security token, key, or card to access a PC or a removable medium. For example, Cylink Corporation offers products that require a physical token and password to access a PC. If you are interested in authentication based on biometrics, NEC and others offer affordable fingerprint recognition systems.

ANTIVIRUS UTILITIES   Teleworker PCs should run antivirus software to prevent the spread of email-borne viruses from the residential PC into enterprise networks. This is probably consistent with your corporate desktop security, but it is especially important if your network relies on network antivirus measures at your secure perimeter. MacAfee, Symantec, IBM Corporation, and several others offer fine antivirus products.

SECURE FILE STORAGE AND STORED FILE ENCRYPTION   There are a number of easy and effective applications for encrypting files stored on PCs and removable media. Often, the same application provides file deletion that prevents recovery *(electronic shredding)*. Pretty Good Privacy, Entrust Solo, and EMD Worldwide's Encryptor can be used for secure file storage and secure electronic mail. RSA SecurPC from Security Dynamics Technologies, EMD Worldwide, Software Shelf International, and Symantec offer products that are aimed at protecting enterprises from the loss or compromise of sensitive information resulting from the theft of laptops, and these alternatives are appropriate for teleworker PCs as well.

DESKTOP FILE SECURITY AND ACCESS CONTROLS File (folder) sharing on Windows 2000 is simple to use but too often ignored. Insist that teleworkers assign passwords to network users, and discourage them from allowing full access privileges to entire disks and partitions. Consider a centrally administered user-level access control list for network domains that include teleworker PCs. Use third-party products (EMD Armor) that offer advanced access control features for Windows 2000. For increased file security, consider Windows NT, which has a Windows 2000 look and feel, but its file system (NTFS) ACLs can be used to assign user permissions to files, directories, or other secured objects (devices, ports) and so offers more effective and granular access controls.

NOTE One way to motivate any worker to take file security seriously is to explain that personal or sensitive information stored on a PC in a residence or on a corporate LAN could be viewed easily by anyone in the corporation who sees that PC through Microsoft's Network Neighborhood.

UNAUTHORIZED SERVICES Consider a security policy that expressly prohibits services operating on desktop PCs that can expose the corporate network to attacks. It is not uncommon for IT managers to expressly prohibit FTP server applications or, nominally, prohibit anonymous FTP access from operating on all desktop PCs, including teleworker PCs. Web hosting applications present a number of security issues when operated on desktop PCs. Entire file systems can be browsed if file permissions on a Web server are not appropriately set, and the IT manager cannot exercise adequate control over the features, CGI scripts, and services operated, nor can he or she control the use applets and downloadable programs.

The IT manager may wish to prohibit the operation of mail, telnet, tftp, route, and domain name servers on teleworker LANs. Consider blocking or filtering of routing protocol updates, name server announcements, and SMTP messages used between mail transfer agents emanating from a teleworker connection.

NOTE This is only a partial list of servers that may be inappropriate for operation from an uncontrolled desktop.

Scenario 2: The Teleworker's Residence Has Multiple Physical Connections

Depending on how residential wireless broadband services are terminated at the corporate network, a second connection in the teleworker's residence can provide an unprotected access or backdoor into the corporation. There are several ways multiple physical connections can be introduced, as shown in Figures 21-3 and 21-4.[5]

Recommended Policy and Best Practices for Multiple Connections to the Residence The most commonly encountered second or alternative connection a teleworker may have is an analog modem or ISDN terminal adapter on the teleworker's PC. An IT manager can expressly prohibit modems and TAs, but a less stringent but more readily enforceable alternative is to prohibit incoming (data) calls.

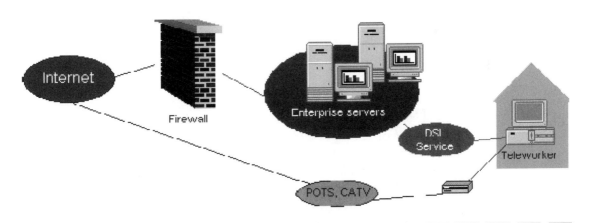

Figure 21-3 The teleworker has a PC with a modem, incoming calls are accepted by the modem, and software operating on the PC (PC Anywhere, Netopia Virtual Office, UNIX shell, Telnet) is compromised to allow an outsider to gain control of the PC. An extreme case of this configuration is one in which the teleworker has a second LAN NIC and uses this to connect to the public Internet via the DSL or cable modem.

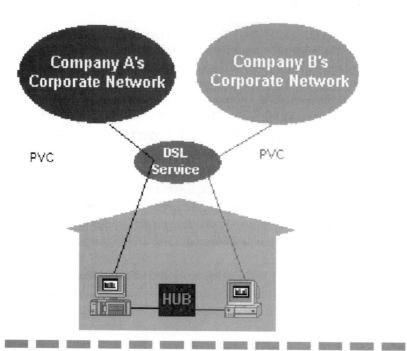

Figure 21-4 The teleworker of Company A operates a PC LAN at his or her residence, and a second system, e.g., a house partner's host or router, is connected to both the PC LAN and the public Internet. In this scenario, anyone who gains access to the house partner's PC also may gain unauthorized access to Company A. An extreme case of this scenario is where Company A's teleworker and a housemate share a PC LAN in the residence and where the housemate has a separate Internet connection or a connection to the housemate's corporate network (Company B).

Even with incoming call handling disabled and with a security policy that prohibits server operation from a desktop [including routing services (UNIX gated, NT R&RAS)], the IT manager must consider the security implications of client applications, especially Web browsers. Executable programs carried over an HTTP stream are especially dangerous in those situations where a teleworker has multiple connections, because the teleworker may unknowingly download active content using a Web browser. The downloaded executable might contain code designed to circumvent firewall or Web proxy defenses and provide an intruder with access from the outside. It may contain a virus or other undesirable software, and this could be propagated onto the corporate network. One security measure to consider is to require that teleworkers disable the download of active content (Java, ActiveX) to browsers or require that they utilize antivirus software to filter it out. Disabling active content should include disabling download of executables and archive files containing executables. Seemingly harmless applications can contain "easter eggs" or other suspicious code. A better long-term policy and practice is to implement strong public-key-based authentication between servers and clients (see the section "Universal Precautions" below).

LANs in the teleworker's residence can pose additional security problems. For example, Covad TeleSpeed service is commonly offered through a two-port router or bridge. One port is connected to the DSL service and another to the Ethernet segment to which the teleworker's PC(s) and perhaps printers are connected. Ethernet is commonly implemented in a residence using inexpensive hub technology. Unauthorized equipment attached to the hub can be used to gain access to the corporate LAN through the DSL router or bridge.

This chapter has mentioned how LANs shared between housemates are yet another form of multiple, unsecured connections in a residence (see "Residential Wireless Broadband Services and Security" earlier in the chapter). There are several ways to address this problem as a matter of policy or practice:

1. Do not permit the use of shared hubs; instead, use Ethernet crossover cabling between the DSL router and the teleworker's PC. This limits systems at the residence with DSL access to the router and the teleworker's PC.

2. Use managed hubs, port-switching hubs, or workgroup Ethernet switches at the teleworker's residence. Disable all but the authorized number of Ethernet ports on the hub using administrative controls only accessible to authorized IT staff. SNMP-manage the hubs and enable traps so that unauthorized attempts to modify the hub configuration are forwarded to IT management systems.

> **NOTE** Think of an always-connected medium as an asset rather than a liability. You do not have to enable and manage incoming calls at the teleworker's residence to manage hubs remotely over an always-connected DSL service.

3. Consider hubs or switches that offer advanced security features. Some equipment (3COM port-switch hubs and workgroup switches) has the ability to learn the MAC address of a station attached to one of its ports. Once learned, the hub or switch will disable the port and generate an alarm (to console or as an SNMP trap) should any address other than the learned address be seen on that port.

4. Use packet and MAC frame filtering. IT managers may wish to preconfigure network-level packet filters on routers or bridges to block access to well-known services ports of teleworkers' PCs, to block traffic from unauthorized addresses originating at the teleworker's LAN, and to block network protocols other than authorized protocols. Where bridging is used, IT managers may wish to configure filters that only permit forwarding of LAN frames originating from authorized MAC addresses.

5. Restrict routing and bridging protocols. For the majority of teleworker environments, static routing is sufficient and should be the only routing used between routers at a teleworker's residence and corporate routers. Similarly, a static forwarding database can be configured in many bridges, and learning can be disabled.[6]

Scenario 3: The Teleworker Requires Access to Application Servers and NOS Services that Would Otherwise Be Blocked by a Corporate Firewall

The kinds and locations of enterprise servers and NOS services that a teleworker may need to access depend on the nature of the work the teleworker is expected to perform from a residence and include (see Figure 21-5)[7]

- Intranet Web servers
- File and print servers accessed using network
- Operating system (NOS) protocols
- Client-server remote login
- Internal database and other networked application servers[8]

Figure 21-5
The teleworker requires access to application servers and NOS services that would otherwise be blocked by a corporate firewall.

In this scenario, the IT manager may have to terminate residential wireless broadband services behind the corporate firewall or make exceptions to an existing security perimeter to accommodate access to, for example, intranet file servers. Such actions introduce vulnerabilities. Existing methods for compartmentalizing LAN communications within the enterprise may not be accommodated from a common termination point within the corporate network.

Recommended Policy and Best Practices for Teleworker Access to Enterprise Servers   AppleTalk, Microsoft Network (SMB/CIFS), and UNIX/NFS/X cannot be used effectively over traditional dialup services, but residential broadband services easily satisfy bandwidth and delay characteristics for teleworkers, so they naturally will want access to the same LAN environment from home as they have in their office. There are several ways to accommodate LAN access. These should be implemented in conjunction with the best practices already described and include the following techniques:

- For teleworker access to intranets, consider products that allow you to build community-of-interest networks (COINs) based on strong user authentication.

- For NOS protocol support, use virtual private network (VPN) techniques to securely extend file, print, and other NOS services from enterprise networks to the teleworker (see "Encrypted Data Transport" and "Strong Authentication" later in the chapter).

- For client-server remote login, consider secure shell and secure Telnet applications.[9]

Universal Precautions

The measures described in the preceding can greatly reduce risks associated with common configuration scenarios associated with teleworker residences. They are largely based on security measures that generally are understood to be among the *best practices* in building secure networks. They are universal precautions and, where implemented, will be effective for mitigating and reducing certain risks, whether the user is a teleworker or mobile or office employee. Let's examine these more closely.

Strong Authentication

Strong authentication is perhaps the most important security measure you can implement. Access controls, accounting, message confidentiality, and message integrity are all based on the ability to require a user to prove that he or she is who he or she claims to be. If a user's or server's authenticity can be demonstrated with a high degree of confidence (assurance), IT managers can control access to specific hosts, information, and applications. They can exercise considerable control over the kinds of actions users can perform on secured objects, and they can dictate when message exchanges between users and objects should be conducted using encryption for privacy and integrity.

There are a number of strong authentication systems to choose from, and you may have already implemented these over corporate LANs and for remote access. These include Kerberos, one-time passwords such as Bellcore S/Key or RSA SecurPCTM (SoftID), and authentication token systems from Security Dynamics Technologies (SecurIDâ).

An increasing number of organizations that require strong authentication for Web-enabled applications make use of the Secure Sockets Layer (SSL) and Secure Hypertext Transfer (S-HTTP) protocols between Web servers and clients. SSL can be enabled on most commonly used browsers and servers to provide mutual, strong authentication between clients and servers. For applications that operate over TCP, strong end-to-end session encryption can be negotiated and employed as well. SSL uses public-key cryptography for strong authentication. For example, Aventail Corporation maintains a good reference site on SSL and SOCKS security resources. Secure HTTP (S-HTTP), an extension to HTTP, provides strong client-server authentication, *spontaneous encryption* and message integrity, and request/response nonrepudiation.

The use of a public-key-based authentication requires an infrastructure [a certificate authority (CA) for assigning personal and server certificates]. A CA not only issues certificates but also is used to assert the trustworthiness and validity of certificates as well. You can outsource CA to third parties such as GTE, Verisign, CyberTrust, and Thawte Consulting, or enterprises can use certificate servers from companies such as Xcert, Netscape, or Entrust to implement private CAs. Once implemented, teleworkers (indeed, all workers) acquire personal certificates for use and configure their browsers to only permit downloads of active content from servers that present trusted and valid certificates.

Encrypted Data Transport

Certain organizations may find it necessary to use encryption over any communications link that is not physically secured, and security policy may dictate that any intraenterprise communications exchanged over unsecured link must be encrypted. Consider VPN products based on Internet Protocol (IP) security (IPSEC) standards to fill this need. Layer 3 IPSEC tunnels provide IP-based virtual, secure connections. In this IPSEC mode, normal IP packets are routed between tunnel end points. Host systems or IPSEC routers can terminate tunnels. Tunnel end points can operate over any intervening network topology. Encapsulated within tunneled IP packets are IETF-specified security protocol headers that provide packet-level authentication (AH, authentication header) and data integrity and confidentiality (ESP, encapsulating security payload). These protocol extensions are IPv4- and IPv6-compatible. When used in conjunction with an Internet Key Management Protocol (IKMP), IPSEC protocols can be used with any authentication or encryption algorithm (MD5, SHA1, RC5, DES, 3DES, etc.). Products based on draft standards for tunnel or transport-mode IPSEC include the Cisco IOS routers, Compatible Systems IntraPort, RedCreek Ravlin, Timestep PERMIT, VPNet VSU-1010, and FTP Software Secure Client.

In situations where corporations wish only to encrypt certain data, application-specific or circuit-level encryption may be appropriate. For example, Aventail VPN servers encrypt application data transmitted over TCP connections. InfoExpress offers a VPN solution that proxies Windows Internet Naming Service (WINS) and Microsoft File Sharing for Windows environments. InfoExpress recently added AppleTalk proxy support to its virtual TCP secure remote VPN product. Electronic mail applications from Microsoft, Netscape, Network Associates, and others support either Secure MIME or Pretty Good Privacy. These products let you digitally sign and encrypt mail and attachments.

Intrusion Detection, Attack Recognition, and Response

Where you terminate residential wireless broadband services in the corporate network and the services you expect to provide to teleworkers may change the way you proactively monitor for intrusions and attacks. If you are already performing monitoring, logging, and auditing activities on all internal segments, subnets, and systems, consider extending the practice to include teleworker connections. If you only proactively monitor systems on DMZ subnets or systems on subnets that can be accessed by outsiders or partners, consider how these same practices can be extended to subnets where teleworker connections are terminated.

Proactive monitoring systems and software products represent one of the fastest growing segments in the security industry. FireWatch from Bellcore and UNIX tcpwrapper and tcpdump provide administrative assistance in collecting logs and creating reports for network auditing purposes. PingWare from Bellcore, Internet Scanner from ISS, or UNIX COPS proactively scan networks for known configuration flaws that are exploited by intruders. Products from Cisco Systems, Network Associates, and ISS take intrusion detection to the next level. These products scan networks searching for traffic patterns and content that match known attack signatures. NetSonarä from Cisco Systems, ISS SafeSuiteä, and Network Associates' (formerly TIS) Stalker products can intervene and reconfigure firewalls, screening routers, and servers when they detect an attack or misuse of a network.

Network Antivirus Protection and Content Filtering

Blocking and intercepting executable code from sources outside the enterprise is a persistent concern for IT managers. Again, where you terminate residential wireless broadband services in the corporate network and the services you expect to provide to teleworkers may change the segments and subnets you choose to restrict downloads and filter content (see "Intrusion Detection, Attack Recognition, and Response" earlier in this chapter).

Firewall-based VPN products from vendors such as Aventail Corporation, CheckPoint, Raptor, and Network Associates can monitor application data and can enforce security policies at a more granular level, for example, by blocking application protocol content like Java and ActiveX. Products that focus entirely on Web security and management to provide URL and content access controls also can be obtained from companies such as Netegrity (SiteMinder) and Caravelle (Webwatcher).

For example, Symantec's Norton AntiVirus for Firewalls and McAfee NetShield Security Suiteâ work with any firewall that supports the

Content Vectoring Protocol (CVP), a standard interface used by firewall clients to validate message content by passing requests to a scan server. The scan server checks HTTP, FTP, and SMTP requests for known virus signatures and repairs or deletes infected messages before they can be propagated inside the firewall. McAfee NetShield Security Suiteâ performs similar security services from a Windows NT server or workstation.

Conclusion

In this chapter, background information was provided for IT managers who must maintain tight security while also introducing new access technologies into the enterprise. It explained how residential wireless broadband services based on DSL and cable modem operate. The chapter also identified potential vulnerabilities that are sometimes associated with DSL-based services but are in many cases vulnerabilities exposed by many, if not all, services used by remote workers and mobile employees. It also discussed deployment scenarios you may wish to consider as you reevaluate corporate security policies regarding remote access and teleworker arrangements. Finally, through examples, this chapter also described how risks can be mitigated or reduced using commercially available security products. Hopefully, this chapter alleviated your concerns about DSL-based services and security and has helped you move one step closer to a successful teleworker deployment.

Endnotes

1. Covad Communications Company, 2330 Central Expressway, Santa Clara, CA 95050-2516, 2000.
2. David M. Piscitello, "Residential Broadband Access and the Teleworker: Security Considerations for the IT Manager," Core Competence, Inc., 3 Myrtle Bank Lane, Hilton Head, SC 29926, 2000.
3. *Ibid.*
4. *Ibid.*
5. *Ibid.*
6. *Ibid.*
7. *Ibid.*
8. *Ibid.*
9. *Ibid.*

PART 5

Managing Wireless Networks

Managing Wireless Broadband: Operations Management of LMDS Systems and Their Applications

Demand for high-speed Internet and data networks is growing exponentially, but only a few privileged large corporations have fiber access. Today's small and medium-sized businesses and upmarket households need more bandwidth. Around the world, telecom markets are liberalizing. New competitors and incumbents alike are positioning themselves to meet the demands of the new millennium.

Local multipoint distribution systems (LMDS) and other fixed wireless broadband technologies are emerging as a viable solution to this problem. LMDS offers wireless broadband speeds with a quick time to market, an attractive capital structure, and no need to dig up streets. In addition, LMDS supports multiple applications, delivering voice, video, and high-speed data—a major benefit given the trend toward convergence of data and voice networks.

In other words, LMDSs represent a new radio-based access technology with cellular architecture offering flexible high-capacity connections to private users and organizations. The systems employ a point-to-multipoint broadcast downlink with a total capacity of 34 to 38 Mbps per transport stream, giving high flexibility for inclusion of any type of data. The interactive channel, being a point-to-point connection, may employ different technologies depending on availability and user demand for capacity. This capacity basically may range from a few kilobits per second up to at least 25.6 Mbps. LMDS performance and management relative to other wireless broadband access technologies are discussed in this chapter. A major remaining development task is the establishment and verification of methods for coverage of normally shielded areas. The availability of cheap repeaters and possibly reflectors for increased coverage is a must, which will significantly improve coverage. The LMDS technology, now in its first stage of implementation, is expected to enhance development and management of wireless broadband services such as e-commerce and teleteaching.

With this in mind, the main focus area in communications today is the provision of efficient transport capacity at acceptable cost for the last-mile connection, the access network. The need for on-demand wireless broadband capacity for all types of users of communications has increased at a remarkable speed as a consequence of use of the Internet and the professional dependence on electronic document exchange and database technology.

The early growth phase of Internet-related applications coincides with the introduction of digital television by satellite, offering new and interesting possibilities such as interactive TV and supporting new wireless broadband services such as electronic commerce, tele-education, and telemedicine. Thus network operators are now facing the wireless broadband requirement challenge by improving existing technologies and developing new operation systems. The wireless broadband multimedia focus is the driving force in the ongoing development of technologies for both mobile and fixed networks and with strong requirements for efficient interoperation between the different network technologies.

Wireless broadband access network development is being forced from both the communications side and the broadcast side. Broadcast networks are developed into two-way networks through the addition of an interactive channel that very often is based on a different technology. The conversion of broadcast satellite networks and cable TV networks into interactive networks is a representative example. From the communications side, the existing copper network offers possibilities for transport capacities in the megabits per second range depending on the distance to the nearest node. Fiber to the home, the preferred solution, is expensive and time-consuming to install but is gradually becoming the main connection for demanding professional user groups.

New radio-based technologies such as stratospheric platforms and local multipoint distribution systems (LMDSs) are being developed and managed and put into operation. They have the advantage of a high-capacity downlink that can be shared by many users in a flexible manner.

LMDSs are now being introduced throughout the world. The U.S. frequency auction in March 1998 represented a start for mass introduction and production. In Europe, there were licenses in several countries in early 2000, and systems will be in operation within 2001. Broadcast in combination with the Internet will dominate the private market through the introductory phase, but there also will be a strong focus on home offices and smaller enterprises. The advantages of LMDSs are easy operation and deployment, flexibility in on-demand capacity allocation, and potential support for a broad spectrum of applications, allowing for future development and management. This chapter focuses on LMDSs and their operational management principles, their potential, and areas of application.

The Principle of Operations Management

LMDSs are combined high-capacity radio-based communications and broadcast systems with interactivity operated at millimeter frequencies. Early systems, however, were used mainly for analog TV distribution, and it all started with Cellular Vision and Bernard Bossard proposing a system for TV distribution in central New York City. Digital television opened for a combined transport of data representing TV programs, data, and communication. The possibility of implementing a full-service wireless broadband access network by rebuilding a broadcast network into an interactive network by functionally adding a communications channel for the return was a reality that coincided almost perfectly with growth of the Internet and data services.

Wireless broadband interactivity arrived with digitalization. Interactive LMDS has a point-to-multipoint downlink and a point-to-point uplink, as illustrated in Figure 22-1.[1]

The transmitter site should be on top of a tall building or on a high pole overlooking the service area. The transmitter covers a sector typically 60° to 90° wide. Full coverage thus requires four to six transmitters. The streams transmitted contain 34 to 38 Mbps of data addressed to everybody (typical TV) in the coverage zone, subgroups or individuals (typical communication, Internet). The capacity of the point-to-point return channels is determined by the needs of the individual user.

Operations management of an LMDS in an area normally will require a cluster of cells with separate base stations for colocated transmitter/receiver sites. One of the base station sites will serve as coordination center for the franchise area and connect the LMDS cells to external networks. Intercell networking may be implemented using fiber or short-hop radio relay connections. Colocation with mobile base stations allows for infrastructure sharing.

Operations management in the millimeter range imposes some restrictions. Precipitation effects lead to severe attenuation and limit the reliable range of operation to 3 to 5 km depending on the climatic zone and the frequency of operation. Line of sight is also required. Full coverage,

Figure 22-1

The operations management of LMDSs for broadcast and interactive services.

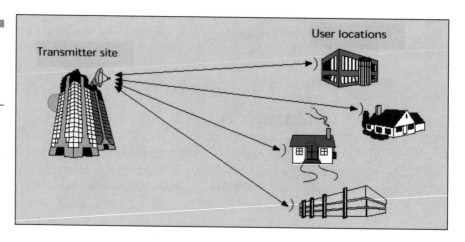

however will not be possible, and numbers quoted are normally in the 40 to 70 percent range, whereas something in excess of 95 percent is a minimum for a service offered to the public. Improved coverage is thus required and may be obtained in different ways. The numbers quoted refer to single cells. By introducing some overlapping between cells, it may be possible to obtain coverage in shielded areas in one cell from the neighboring cell transmission site. Repeaters and reflectors present other possibilities, but such a solution requires some additional equipment, which is compensated for by increasing the number of users. Thus different site-dependent methods of operation will solve the coverage problem. The most severe restriction may be the attenuation caused by transmission through vegetation. Buildings completely shielded by vegetation need an elevated rooftop antenna or some wireless broadband connection to an unshielded site. Propagation issues are by now well understood and are not considered a serious obstacle for reliable operation of millimeter-wave systems of cellular architecture. The problems are known, and proper precautions can be taken.

Trials performed in many countries have reported promising results. The ACTS project CRABS performed operational management and user trials in several European countries from Norway to Greece in the North-South direction and from the United Kingdom to central Russia in the West-East direction. The differences encountered did not severely affect operation, and the trials had convincing effects locally. Systems planning tools for availability and coverage based on digital maps are considered important for design of local systems architecture.

Frequencies of Operations Management

Even though the capacity in the millimeter part of the spectrum is considerable, there are many systems competing for frequency allocations, and it has been difficult to obtain a worldwide allocation for LMDSs. In the United States, 1.3 GHz in the 28- to 29-GHz band has been allocated, whereas European countries are allocating frequencies in different bands. The main high-capacity band is presently 40.5 to 42.5 GHz, with a possible extension to 43.5 GHz depending on decisions at the year 2002 World Radio Frequency Conference (WRC 2002).

Licensing and deployment in Europe now indicate that there will be systems in different frequency bands from 24 up to 43.5 GHz. The frequency band 24.5 to 26.6 GHz with subbands of 56 MHz has been opened for point-to-multipoint applications in many European countries. These bands may then be used for either LMDSs or related systems called *fixed wireless access* (FWA). The systems can then be typical multipoint business systems with some capacity for private users. Only systems addressing the business domain typically are based on Asynchronous Transfer Mode (ATM) technology.

The 40-GHz band normally will be shared among two or three licenses, limiting the available spectrum per operator to 500 to 2000 MHz with two polarizations. The licensing policy may vary from country to country, with stimulation to competition as the main guideline. The LMDSs have the potential of becoming the high-capacity access domain for private users.

Technologies Employed

Proven technologies required for service startup exist, and different companies have products available addressing the needs of small business customers and, to some extent, also demanding private users. In LMDSs, the high-capacity broadcast-based downlink is shared among several users in a flexible way. The front-end technology is still expensive at millimeter-wave frequencies, but existing high-electron-mobility transistor (HEMT) modules offer the required performance. The output power level needed per transport beam of 36 Mbps is about 25 dBm. A technology allowing for final stage amplification of several transport beams would reduce equipment complexity and cost. The hub transmitters, however, are shared by many users, and cost is not directly critical.

The front-end technology at 40 GHz is more expensive than at 28 to 29 GHz, and attenuation by precipitation increases with frequency, favoring the lower frequency ranges. The higher capacity offered at 40 GHz may compensate for these effects in the long run.

The number of transport streams is determined by demand and limitations set by available spectrum. This gives a scalable architecture, starting with relatively low capacity and adding transmitter modules as demand increases.

The transmission format for digital video broadcasting (DVB) satellite transmission based on quadrature phase-shift keying (QPSK) modulation has been adopted by both Digital Audio/Visual Council (DAVIC) and the DVB project and with the same IF interface, 950 to 2150 MHz, between the outdoor and indoor units. This allows for application of set-top boxes developed for reception of digital TV by satellite with data included in the transport multiplex. The IF is then fed into a set-top box interfacing a TV or a PC or both in parallel, depending on user orientation. Both options allow for interactivity, since set-top boxes are also equipped with a return channel connection to the public switched telephone network (PSTN)/ISDN. There are some differences, however. In DVB, IP or ATM data are included in the MPEG transport stream in combination with TV programs. DAVIC has separate high-capacity ATM-based data transmissions. Until now, the PC-oriented user has dominated the interactive world; the development of interactive TV, with possibilities for manipulation of content, inclusion of more advanced text TV, possibilities for e-commerce, different games, and active participation in competitions, will lead to an increased interest in interactive television with a low-capacity return channel.

The uplink is the individual connection, and different technologies may be used depending on demand. Two of the wireless broadband driving applications, interactive TV and the Internet, will require only low-capacity return links, and technologies such as general packet radio service (GPRS) and PSTN/ISDN will suffice. For more demanding customers, an in-band radio return link with on-demand capacity is required. The radio-based solutions for small and medium-sized enterprises do have a radio-link-type return link, allowing for symmetric connections or connections that may be asymmetric in either direction. However, it is felt that existing radio return solutions, with their requirement for isolation between transmit and receive implemented through the use of allocated bands isolated by filtering for transmit/receive, put limitations on flexible operations management and efficient resource management. A combined use of systems for broadcast and data for both private users and business organizations necessarily will result in strong variations in capacity for the two directions. Possible future time-division duplex (TDD) operation would solve this problem.

The main technological challenge is production of a real low-cost two-way user terminal for the private market; the mass market depends on it. The total capacity of a system is mainly determined by the available frequency resource. In a cellular system employing QPSK modulation, the capacity of a 2-GHz system is easily 1.5 Gbps per cell for downlink and uplink.

LMDS versus Other Access Technologies

LMDS provides a wireless alternative to fiber, coax, and asynchronous/very-high-rate digital subscriber line (ADSL/VDSL) and offers a high capacity locally compared with other radio solutions such as interactive satellite systems and stratospheric platforms. The different technologies contributing to wireless broadband access networking all have clear advantages and drawbacks. Figure 22-2 shows an access scenario for competition in the home market.[2]

There are basically two groups of technologies: wire-based, represented by optical fiber and copper pair; and wireless, represented by satellite, stratospheric platforms, and LMDS. In general, all wireless technologies have broadcast/multicast potential, making them well suited to TV distribution and multicast data distribution. The increasing storage capacity of PCs may lead to an increasing number of home servers, favoring the use of multicast and push technology.

Satellite systems, which have low individual capacity per user within the area of coverage, have the advantage of total coverage independent of local population density. They are thus well suited to broadcast, updating of servers in more local networks like LMDS, and wireless broadband to rural areas and in areas with poor infrastructure. LMDS is well suited to interoperation management with broadcast-based satellite systems for local distribution and the satellite system likewise for connecting remote LMDS cells. At IBC '98 in Amsterdam, a system for remote control of LMDS cells from a main cell in Norway was demonstrated by the ACTS project CRABS.

The stratospheric platform has yet to demonstrate its operability. From its elevated position, it will have good coverage. Attenuation effects will be approximately the same as for LMDS, and the capacity per square kilometer will be somewhat less. Operations management in Nordic areas will be difficult due to short days with reduced solar cell charging during the winter season.

Interactive cable networks will have 500 to 1000 households connected to each node. They have a limited capacity for the return channel and thus

Figure 22-2
Available access
technologies.

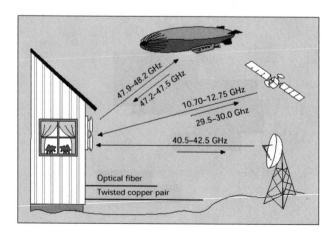

are not well suited when a high-capacity return channel is demanded simultaneously by many users. They have the advantage of combining delivery of TV, Internet, and telephony in an efficient manner.

The existing copper wire connections offer 2- to 5-Mbps downlink and 384- to 512-kbps uplink capacity through introduction of ADSL technology, sufficient for most private Internet users today but not for TV. The distance to the nearest node is somewhat critical and typically will be in the range of 2 to 5 km depending on the quality of the existing installations. If this distance is reduced below 1 km, the capacity may be increased to 25 Mbps for the downlink and 2 Mbps for the uplink. VDSL is also sufficient for TV provision in the form of separate TV programs but not for transport streams containing four to eight digital programs. xDSL technologies belong to existing operators; they have an upper capacity determined by the distance to the node and quality of the connection. They have reduced capacity for symmetric operation and represent a typical Internet and delivery technology.

Interactive systems are all in a way cellular systems if we consider the distance to the nearest node as the main parameter. In general, high interactive capacity of a system requires a short distance to the nearest node and either a high total node capacity, as in LMDS, or a high-capacity connecting cable, represented by the fiber solution. LMDS is favorable for operations management in urban and suburban areas and is definitely the preferred solution for operators without a copper network and as a supplement to the copper-based and interactive cable networks. Table 22-1 lists the capacities of different access technologies. [3]

Another important parameter is the total capacity per square kilometer. LMDS will, depending on cell diameter and licensed frequency range,

TABLE 22-1

Capacity Comparison of Some Available Access Technologies

Type	Uplink Data Rate	Downlink Data Rate	Max Range (km)
Analogue modem	14.4–33.6 kbps	14.4–33.6 kbps	N/A
ISDN	128 kbps	128 kbps	N/A
ADSL	384 kbps 640 kbps	2 Mbps 6–8 Mbps	6 2–3
VDSL	640 kbps 2 Mbps	13 Mbps 25 Mbps	1.4 0.6
Cable modems	0–384 kbps	30 Mbps (shared)	N/A
Satellite; DVB-RCS	2 Mbps	36 Mbps (shared)	Not limited
LMDS	0–8 Mbps typical 25.8 Mbps possible	36 Mbps (shared)	5

have a total capacity of 150 to 1500 Mbps/km^2, whereas other radio technologies such as low-earth-orbit (LEO) satellites and stratospheric platforms have 100 kbps and 1 Mbps, respectively, per square kilometer. The smaller cell size, however, reduces the strength of the broadcast/multicast function outside the local domain and makes it very efficient for distribution locally. Table 22-2 lists a few radio-based technologies illustrating the superiority of LMDS on local capacity. [4]

LMDS has the potential for playing a central role in the wireless broadband access network now under development, where different wireless broadband technologies such as xDSL, interactive cable systems, multimedia satellite systems, fiber to the home systems, and LMDS will exist in both cooperation and competition as important components of the network. In the third-generation mobile network with smaller cells than the LMDS network, the capacity of the LMDS system makes it well suited for connections to UMTS base stations.

Applications

LMDS is first of all a system of high flexibility, allowing for capacity on demand. Changing the cell size through reduction of either cell diameter or illumination angle increases total capacity. Its flexibility with regard to high on-demand capacity in both directions makes it well suited to home offices and teleteaching (see list of distant learning URLs at http://www.tnellen.com/school/distant.html) in the local domain. The first major applications are TV-, Internet-, and business-oriented, thus combining professional and entertainment use. In Europe, LMDS was considered a supplement/alternative to cable TV and actually was referred to as wireless broadband cable. With digital television, the possibility for convergence of TV, data, and communications opened up development of new wireless broadband applications. Hopefully, the availability of wireless

TABLE 22-2

Local Capacity of Some Radio-Based Access Technologies

Technology	Cell Area	Capacity per km^2
Terrestrial LMDS	2–20 km^2	150–1500 Mbps
GEO satellites	Up to semiglobal	Low
LEO satellites	3000 km^2	100 kbps
Stratospheric platforms	5–10 km^2	1 Mbps

broadband capacity will stimulate the growth of applications such as telemedicine and teleteaching, which have been recognized for some time without really taking off.

From Television to Interactive Television

The TV business has had strong growth, but the time spent by individuals watching TV has not changed very much. Digital TV represents new possibilities. The first step is the introduction and development of interactive TV, adding new and interesting functionality. More local TV programs will take advantage of LMDS. Interactive TV will stimulate growth in e-commerce, and the more local part of it, such as property trading, apartment renting, car buying and selling, and many other transactions, will take advantage of the possibilities offered by local wireless broadband networking. Telebanking and vacation planning are applications where interactive TV offers added functionality.

Teleteaching

Education, as well as updating/reeducation, is one of the major challenges in many countries today. Lack of educated and skilled teachers, particularly in technology, is a common concern. Young people of today may have to be reeducated and change their professional focus several times during their working lifetimes.

The local focus of LMDS makes it excellent for high-capacity connections to schools at different levels, connecting a group of local schools as well as providing connections to remote sites (distant learning). Locally, it would then also be possible to connect to homes and have lessons stored for the use of both pupils and parents.

> **NOTE** Distant learning is the ability to teach or communicate with large or small groups of people dispersed across a wide geographic area through the use of single or multiple telecommunications services. Distant learning networks help organizations develop communications networks and delivery systems that fulfill each organization's unique need to inform and each participant's need to know in a timely and cost-effective manner.

Finally, wireless broadband access will offer possibilities in education we have barely started to explore. The advantage of LMDS in this connection is the flexibility in capacity allocation and the multicast property of the downlink, allowing very efficient delivery for this type of application.

Conclusion

The wireless broadband access market is now emerging. In Europe, 2001 seems to represent a breakthrough for digital TV, ADSL, interactive cable networks, and LMDS. Wireless broadband access systems are gradually taking over connections to the home.

Licenses for LMDS are now being issued in many countries; deployment will take 3 to 5 years. During this first phase, LMDS seems to first become a technology chosen by the second and third operators. The business case looks attractive. Given a license for operation, the technology is rapidly deployed and brought into operation. The cost of establishing a backbone infrastructure connecting to the hubs of the individual cell sites by fiber, satellite, or radio link can be considerable, especially in countries with a poor telecommunications infrastructure. LMDS is a technology for a time of growing demand. It offers the flexibility for on-demand capacity required by the new TV-related interactive and high-speed data services combined with the increased demand for Internet access. It represents a complement to and competition for other wireless broadband technologies such as cable, satellite, and ADSL/VDSL. Most important, it is a contribution to wireless broadband access technology, stimulating growth and development of new applications in areas with a certain population density. It is not yet the technology for rural areas. Nevertheless, it is expected that availability of high-capacity access to every home will greatly stimulate the development of the information society and bring areas like teleteaching and e-commerce a major step forward.

Endnotes

1. Agne Nordbotten (Telenor R&D), "LMDS Systems and Their Application," *IEEE Communications Magazine*, IEEE Communications Society, 305 East 47th Street, New York, NY 10017, USA, 2000.
2. *Ibid.*
3. *Ibid.*
4. *Ibid.*

CHAPTER 23

Testing Wireless Broadband Satellite Networks for Onboard Processing of Multimedia Applications and Next-Generation RF Digital Devices

For future multimedia applications, satellites may play an important role. For broadcast applications, satellites are ideally suited to illuminate a large geographic area. However, multimedia applications are interactive and therefore are a combination of a broadcast mission and a multipoint-to-point mission. The natural question is, Can a satellite system compete with the capacity provided by terrestrial cable networks? If the answer is positive—and it will be shown in this chapter that it is—a second question arises: What new testing developments are required to migrate from the state-of-the art satellite technology to such advanced concepts? Taking the example of the European Space Agency's activities in this field, an overview of the required building blocks that make up a complete multimedia communication satellite is given. Based on this technological overview, a discussion of the testing systems developed by European space industries with support from the European Space Agency is given.

Testing Wireless Broadband Satellite Networks for Satellite Onboard Processing for Multimedia Applications

Until 60 years ago, each individual communicated with about 100 other persons, of whom 80 to 90 percent lived close by. Twenty years ago, this picture changed. Each individual communicated with about 500 other individuals, of whom 80 to 90 percent did not live close by. This was made possible by the emergence of advanced communications systems.

Until the mid-1980s, telecommunications, computing, TV, and consumer electronics developed in isolation. With the appearance of personal computers, computing and consumer electronics merged; with multimedia applications, personal computing and TV merged; and finally, with the Internet and the integrated services digital network (ISDN), personal computing and telecommunications are merging. With the rapid technological advances experienced until now, we can expect that very soon we will have information technology that includes telecommunications, computing, video, TV, videoconferencing, and consumer electronics in every building (home and/or business). The challenge of this is to provide multi-application networks [wideband (around 2 Mbps) services] accessible to everybody everywhere.

It is recognized that the terrestrial network, even with very large bandwidth, available as a result of optical fiber technology alone cannot meet the testing requirements. A large investment is required to bridge the last mile between the local exchange and the customer.

Satellites can play a complementary role by reducing the time to market. If a satellite is in orbit, the subscriber only has to install a satellite terminal and subscribe to the service.

Wide bandwidth is available already in over 40 million homes in Europe in the form of TVRO equipment. Existing installations in the home can be used to connect satellite interactive terminals (SITs). Such services can be provided by satellite onboard processing (OBP) systems.

More than two-thirds of the investment of a telephone network is required for the last mile (the connection between the subscriber and the local exchange). The transmission between the individual exchanges is equipped with a high-rate digital transmission system using coaxial cable but dominated already by optical fiber systems. Existing telephone networks are limited in providing high bit rates to subscribers. Investments on the order of several tens or even hundreds of billions of Euros are required by the individual telephone companies to provide high bandwidth to each subscriber via optical fibers.

Cable TV companies, on the contrary, have installed high-bandwidth transmission media (usually coaxial cable) for one-way distribution to subscribers. However, the density of cable TV subscribers is nowhere near as high as that of telephone subscribers. A merging of telephone technology and the cable TV distribution network is occurring.

However, to provide high bandwidth to everybody everywhere first requires an immense investment, and second, time to realize. The answer of network technicians is Asynchronous Transfer Mode (ATM). This concept is basically a multiplexer with a high-rate output (nominally 155 Mbps) and every possible lower rate at the input side. The answer of telecommunications managers to satisfy this demand is to provide temporary test solutions such as asynchronous digital subscriber line (ADSL) and high-rate DSL (HDSL).

Today in Europe, more than 40 million satellite TV receivers are installed. A small dish is located on the roof of a house, and in most cases the already existing TV cable can be reused to feed the received satellite signal toward a dedicated satellite receiver. Such a receiver converts signals received in the band from 950 to 2050 MHz to the existing standard TV set. If in the existing 40 million homes in Europe the TV receive-only set is augmented by transmit capability, a very cheap high-rate asymmetric user access can be realized.

In addition to the existing TV broadcast satellites, a switchboard must be installed on a satellite providing the transmission capacity of the transmit signal of individual subscribers with a VSAT terminal for interactive services. To allow reasonably small transmit power with small dish diameters, the satellite has to provide high-gain antennas, which consequently results in multibeam antennas to cover Europe or an equivalent geographic area. Multibeam antennas require switching capabilities between subscribers located in different beams. This means that the payload of a multimedia satellite must provide switching capabilities.

The very often quoted disadvantage of geostationary communications satellites, the large delay of about 250 ms for one uplink and downlink, is not very relevant for interactive data services and delivery of a large amount of data on request (typical multimedia applications). The delay is disturbing for voice. However, most voice traffic is carried by the terrestrial copper and optical fiber networks and the emerging cellular radio networks such as the Global System for Mobile Communications (GSM). In addition, so-called big LEO systems such as GlobalStar and ICO are competing with the terrestrial networks for voice applications. For wideband multimedia applications, geostationary satellites with several high-gain spot-beam antennas, onboard processing and testing, and switching are the logical step to migrate from pure TV broadcast to interactive multimedia services.

A satellite OBP test system designed and partially developed by the European Space Agency (ESA) provides for each user terminal (user traffic station, UTS) a high-data-rate reception capability, up to 32.784 Mbps and 384 kbps or even 2.048 Mbps (depending on the UTS type) transmit capability. The OBP test system is designed in such a way that a large number of UTSs (up to 150,000 for a 262-Mbps onboard switch capacity) could be served by the OBP network.

If a customer requires a wideband data connection (up to 384-kbps or 2.048-Mbps point-to-point or point-to-multipoint bearer service or up to 1-Mbps fast packet switching), he or she only has to install a UTS and perform the cabling within his or her premises. The functionality offered by the OBP test system is ideally suited to provide the services required by the information society of today. The elements making up the OBP test system are

- The UTS

- A switching payload onboard a geostationary satellite

- The master control test station[1]

The Capacity Limits of Satellite Channels

The capacity of fiberoptic cables is practically unlimited. The exact bandwidth limitation of an optical fiber is unknown but is in excess of several terabits per second. Considering that optical fibers are made from silicon, which is the second most common element of the planet earth (27.5 percent) after oxygen, and that most integrated electronic circuits are also made of silicon, an increase of transmission capacity by several terahertz requires only some grams of sand. Sand seems today to be the most important resource of the information society.

About 20 to 30 years ago, the only natural resource for the information society was the electromagnetic spectrum. Radio and TV are known to everybody as wireless broadband communications means that bring entertainment into each home. Satellite TV and mobile telephones are the latest evolution of wireless broadband technology.

For about a century, twisted-pair copper wires have been used to connect people all around the world by the largest machine on earth, the telephone network. Coaxial cables have found their way to the home as well, providing large amounts of entertainment as cable TV systems.

However, the unlimited communications capacity provided by optical fibers is rarely available today to the individual. The tremendous growth of satellite TV receiver installations has demonstrated that, in principle, every house is able to receive a large amount of information not offered by terrestrial networks. In 1995, a transponder capacity of about 120 GHz (using the C, Ku, and Ka bands) was installed in geostationary orbit by some 35 satellite operators.

A very natural question is, What are the limitations in terms of numbers of users (receivers and/or transmitters) and transmission capacity of satellite networks?[2] After some fundamental considerations, the relations for satellite capacity are as shown in Table 23-1.

TABLE 23-1

Uplink Capacity

R: Radius of the Satellite Orbit (km)	R_B Data Rate (bps)	S: Number of Satellites in Orbit	Total Number of Satellites
700	$121*10^{12}$	70	840
1000	$2.77*10^{12}$	11	66
1600	$1.25*10^{12}$	8	48
36,000	$22*10^{12}$	180	180

For the geostationary satellite case, a 2° spacing is assumed. For the other nongeostationary cases, the total number of satellites of the constellations is used. The possible total uplink capacity for a 2° spacing in a geostationary orbital arc is much more than is possible with nongeostationary satellite networks, except in the very low orbital case at 700 km altitude (the original Teledesic concept).

OBP Building Blocks

A key driver of the information superhighway is interactive multimedia or Internet services. Network connections are required by a large population; the target market is residential users. From the user toward the service provider, typically bursty traffic needs to be transported. From the service provider toward the user, compressed video ideally would be provided by a constant-bit-rate (CBR) channel. Packet transmission and video reception capabilities are needed for these applications. However, other applications, such as videoconferencing, would require point-to-multipoint or even multipoint-to-multipoint CBR connections.

Emerging and currently partly unknown applications that may make use of the capabilities offered by ISDN will grow in the future and require symmetric point-to-point circuits. Requirements for an OBP system are

- To provide services compatible with existing ISDN infrastructure
- To provide narrowcasting/multicasting services not offered by terrestrial ISDN
- To provide TCP/IP-compatible services for data applications
- To provide point-to-point or point-to-multipoint on-demand compressed video services[3]

A possible OBP system supports these services in the following way (see Figure 23-1).[4] First, the kernel of the system consists, for example, of a switch for digital signals located on a geostationary satellite. The basic service provided is a point-to-point ISDN circuit-switched connection. The user interface can be a basic rate, primary rate, or fractional primary rate access according to the International Telecommunication Union Telecommunication Standardization Sector (ITU-T) recommendations. Point-to-multipoint services are added and are named *extended network services* (ENS). In addition, the TCP/IP protocol suite is supported.

Figure 23-1
The onboard
processing system
architecture.

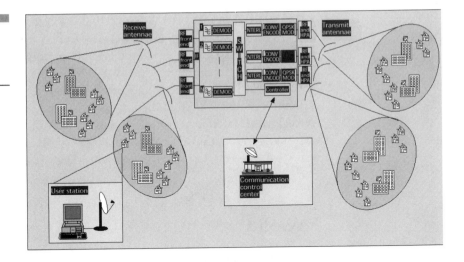

If a user wishes to communicate with another user in the ISDN scenario, he or she places his or her request via standard ISDN customer-premises equipment to the user traffic station. A special access scheme provides a connection via the satellite to a network control center located on the ground. The connection request is analyzed there, and the participating system elements (calling user station, satellite switch, and called user station) are configured from this control station via system-internal signaling messages. In case of ENS requests, another module in the network control station provides the necessary connection commands. For video services, according to the Digital Video Broadcast (DVB)/MPEG standard, the appropriate number of circuits is set up at the network control station. For TCP/IP service requests, the same physical onboard hardware is used as for the circuit-switched connections. However, the onboard circuit switch is augmented by a so-called onboard request handler, which analyzes packet switching capacity requests and provides, depending on actual circuit switch usage, the capacity for packet switching.

Another key technique, in addition to OBP, is efficient implementation of multiple access from users to the satellite switch. The OBP system uses a technique called *bit-synchronous multiple-frequency time-division multiple access* (MF-TDMA). This technique allows the TDMA system to be operated without any guard time, resulting in the highest spectrum utilization and highest traffic efficiency (low blocking probability).

The User Station

Each UTS consists of an outdoor unit and an indoor unit, and each can be equipped with an ISDN interface, an ENS interface, and a packet switch interface (TCP/IP compatible). Each UTS has a high-data-rate reception capability of up to 32.768 Mbps. A DVB-S signal can be received on a separate downlink (on a standard TV downlink), and a DVB-S module can be included as an option. The design driver for all user traffic stations is to achieve a low-cost design, enabling wide acceptance by users at an attractive price.

Payload

In addition to the equipment on a conventional communications satellite, the OBP payload contains onboard demodulators, a baseband switch, and modulators. The number of spot beams determines the mass and power consumption of the payload for a given geographic coverage area and information throughput. The major mass contribution is from the radiofrequency (rf) test equipment (which will be covered later in this chapter). Power consumption decreases when the number of spot beams increases, due to the reduced power to be transmitted per spot beam.

Developments to reduce the mass of the 30-GHz receive chain composed of low-noise amplifiers (LNAs), downconverters, microwave switching matrices, and so on are required. The downlink rf part contains mainly the TWTA and the output filters, multiplexers, and microwave switches. Advanced packaging techniques are key to minimizing mass and volume. Another major block is the demodulator and modulator. The number of these units depends on the number of uplink/downlink beams.

Figure 23-2

The multicarrier demodulator (MCD) block diagram.

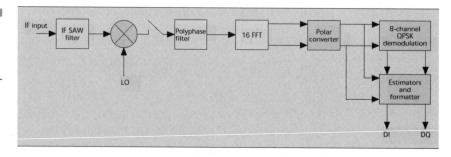

The demodulator is the most complex onboard device (see Figure 23-2).[5] Its task is to demodulate a group of uplink carriers, each modulated with TDMA signals.

The analog signal, after downconversion, is sampled at about 30 Msamples/s. The required filter bank is implemented by a dedicated DSP. The particular design uses a polyphase filter. The burst demodulator contains carrier and clock recovery circuits for each burst.

In addition to its function, the MCD (see Figure 23-3) measures the time of arrival and received power level of a steady state synchronization burst (SSSB) generated by each activated UTS. The measured results are transmitted via a reserved internal signaling channel that is inserted into the continuous downlink data stream. The UTS uses this information to adjust the uplink frame timing and rf power level.

The continuous data stream delivered by the MCD is the input signal for the onboard switch. A circuit switch and a fast packet switch are implemented to provide CBR and variable/available-bit-rate (VBR/ABR) services (see Figures 23-4 and 23-5).[6] The circuit switch consists of a time-slot interchange (TSI) switch realized by random access memory (RAM). The received data stream is written sequentially into the memory locations. Readout of the memory is controlled by another memory, the connection memory, which contains the switching table. This T-stage (see Figure 23-6) is surrounded by receive and transmit interface units.[7] A central control unit is needed to control updating of the connection memory via internal

Figure 23-3

The 32-channel 512 kbps MCD engineering model.

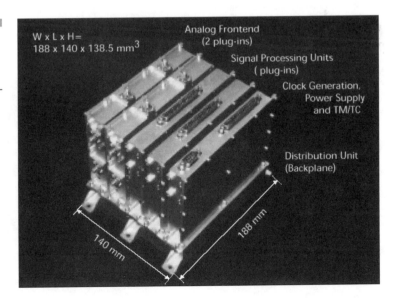

W x L x H = 188 x 140 x 138.5 mm³

Analog Frontend (2 plug-ins)

Signal Processing Units (plug-ins)

Clock Generation, Power Supply and TM/TC

Distribution Unit (Backplane)

188 mm

140 mm

Figure 23-4
Circuit switch
architecture.

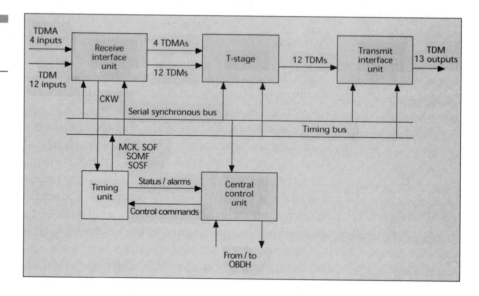

signaling messages and, for emergency situations, via the satellite TT&C links. In addition, the circuit switch contains the master clock module.

Fast packet switching requires large onboard memories for buffering. The most efficient use of the limited uplink capacity for circuit switching is achieved by the synchronous MF-TDMA uplink. For onboard packet switching, the achievable statistical multiplexing gain is limited because of the uplink access. The packet-switching principle is shown in Figure 23-7.[8]

Figure 23-5
The 262 Mbps circuit
switch engineering
model.

Figure 23-6
T-stage hybrid.

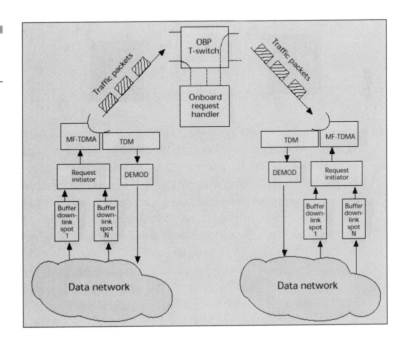

Figure 23-7
The packet switching principle in OBP.

Figure 23-8
Onboard request
handler architecture.

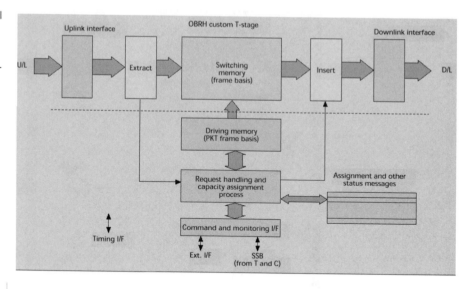

Another scheme was invented in which the packets to be transmitted are buffered inside the UTS. An arriving packet initiates a capacity request from the UTS to an onboard request handler (OBRH). The OBRH stores each request in a queue (see Figure 23-8).[9]

The OBRH observes the occupation of the connecting memory. If free capacity is detected, the OBRH reserves capacity and, via another internal signaling channel, commands the UTS to transmit the packet(s).

The Master Control Testing Center

Modern telecommunications networks are characterized by the penetration of computers into the traditional telephone network; more and more testing functions are performed by software. One key factor responsible for the tremendous economic growth of communication systems is interoperability of different computers, terminals, and transmission systems.

Any new network must be compatible with existing protocols and algorithms. This is achieved by a set of standards that allow information transfer between different systems.

The translation of protocols and algorithms of the subscriber terminals into commands to control the communication flow inside the wireless broadband satellite communications network is the task of the master control testing center (MCTC), as shown in Figure 23-9.[10]

Figure 23-9
Master control testing
center architecture.

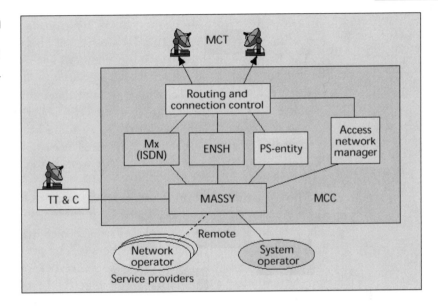

These communications control functions cover the entire range of services to be provided: circuit-switched, both ISDN and extended network services (ENS), and packet-switched services. The MCTC provides the processing functions for

- Overall communication control concept (internal protocols)
- Circuit/packet switch control
- Management of the whole network[11]

The development of network management and real-time call handling is a very costly undertaking. In order to limit effort and make optimal use of existing equipment and software, the following approach was adopted. The MCTC, located on the ground, is physically a terrestrial switching center. Only a few modifications in some software modules are needed to satisfy the OBP-specific requirements. A special interface unit, the routing processor, is to be developed for the task of translating the protocols used in the switching center into the satellite-specific protocols.

Systems

The pace at which the present generation of systems is evolving constitutes a revolution for the satellite communications industry. Global players are actively initiating new systems; maintaining an active R&D strategy will be an essential feature for survival of manufacturing companies.

The ESA has initiated three development activities. One is concerned with the development of the space and ground segments of the SkyBridge system; the other two are targeted to develop geostationary multimedia satellite systems, EuroSkyWay and WEB (WEST Early Bird).

The common feature of the three systems is that large capacity is achieved by using spot-beam techniques. The SkyBridge system will operate in the Ku band, and the other two systems will make use of the Ka band.

The SkyBridge system is an access network that provides the connection between users and the gateway via satellites in a 1400-km orbit. About 80 satellites form the constellation, projecting about 400 spot beams to the earth. About 160,000 subscribers can be served per spot. The gateways provide connectivity with the terrestrial network and, if needed, via another gateway with another SkyBridge subscriber. Different classes of user terminals are foreseen: residential and professional terminals, which provide different data rates for uplinks and downlinks.

The EuroSkyWay system is a satellite communications network using geostationary satellites. The basic characteristic is that a cell switch is located onboard the satellite. This switch provides unrestricted connectivity between any user located in the coverage of the satellite.

The WEB system provides connectivity between users located in a spot beam and a gateway dedicated to this spot beam. This concept is comparable with the SkyBridge access network. However, the difference is that WEB will use the migration path from existing broadcast satellites, compliant with the DVB-S standard, to interactive multimedia applications.

Testing Wireless Broadband Satellite Networks for Next-Generation RF Digital Devices

Cost (technology notwithstanding) continues to be the major challenge for next-generation wireless broadband communications products. These products, such as cell phones, are awaited eagerly by consumers who expect increased functionality without an increase in price. Currently, these products are in the development labs and nearing the next hurdle: economic volume production.

Major integrated-device manufacturers and foundries are moving from 200-mm fabs to 300-mm fabs to reduce manufacturing costs—until recently the single most expensive component of the end product. While automated test equipment (ATE) design continues to address the needs of ever-increasing device complexity with more complex and flexible systems, the cost of test has not been following the ever-falling average selling price curve. Obviously, this mismatch must be reconciled if these next-generation products are going to meet the demands of the consumer.

On the technology side of the equation, these next-generation rf devices are more complex, wideband, and linear than ever. Third-generation (3G) cell-phone ICs will be multimodal to satisfy consumer demand that phone appliances work anywhere at any time.

Not only will devices need to work in the cellular and personal communications service (PCS) bands, but they also must transmit and receive the standards of first-generation (1G) advanced mobile phone service (AMPS); second-generation (2G) service such as code division multiple access (CDMA), Global System for Mobile Communications (GSM), and North American digital cellular (NADC); and 3G service such as cdma2000 and wideband CDMA (W-CDMA) devices. First-generation service will remain in rural areas of the United States.

Market Demand for RF ATE

Cellular handset production continues to be the growth engine for rf devices. Production has grown 60 to 70 percent annually, and Dataquest projects 540 million handsets for 2001 and more than 2 billion annually by 2005.

To capitalize on this growth, component manufacturers are driving demand for rf ATE to new heights. This demand is expected to continue its rapid growth through 2006. Third-generation devices could make their debut in early 2002, with predictions that they will follow the trends of their predecessors by increasing both the demand for and requirements of rf ATE.

Technology Requirements for 3G-Ready ATE

Better connectivity, higher data rates, and wider information bandwidths are core consumer requirements of next-generation cell phones. In addition, service providers need greater system capacity, resulting in increased linearity and power-control specifications.

These requirements are prompting rf ATE vendors to rethink their solutions for 3G. Since the first commercialization of cellular technology in the early 1980s, the bandwidths associated with each generation of cellular phone have followed a logarithmic trend.

Earlier standards yielded channel bandwidths from 30 kHz (NADC) to >1.25 MHz (CDMA). Third-generation standards, such as cdma2000, have bandwidths more than three times larger than the widest current standards.

Today's ATE systems use a traditional narrowband measurement receiver design to test current 2G devices. This has resulted in traditional approaches in specifying and testing the parts.

The most obvious issue of applying a narrowband receiver to a wideband component is acquisition time. Despite the improved technology in data acquisition and digital signal processing (DSP), without the bandwidth to capture all the information at once, throughput and accuracy are compromised.

Reduction in throughput is easy to understand, but loss of accuracy is less intuitive. The time-varying nature of these modulated signals requires that the same snapshot of data be used when calculating parameters as simple as gain or the more complex adjacent channel power ratio (ACPR) to achieve the highest accuracy (Figure 23-10).[12]

However, with a narrowband receiver, the stimulus waveform must be replayed many times to capture the entire information bandwidth, which reduces accuracy and throughput. This approach also has resulted in new figures of merit to correlate the modulated behavior of 2G devices.

Figure 23-10
ACPR single-shot 15-MHz acquisition for accuracy and throughput.

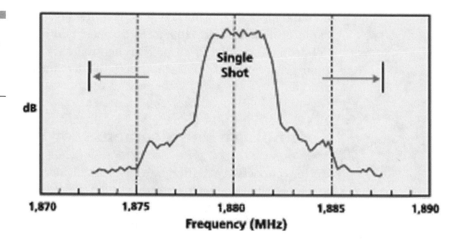

Faulty evaluation of the data has allowed good devices to be rejected, which drives up costs. It also has permitted defective devices to pass tests and then fail in the end application, which decreases quality. These traditional approaches are failing both the device supplier and the handset manufacturer.

The simple solution is to increase the measurement receiver's bandwidth and provide compatible modulation capability. As with most things in life, it is not this simple. Without improvements in other parts of the receiver's design, nonlinearity and noise also will increase with wider bandwidths, contrary to the demands of 3G devices.

ACPR, a key figure of merit for modulated power-amplifier linearity, is increasing from -55 to -80 dBc (decibels down from the occupied channel to the alternate channel). Modest device performance improvements in intermodulation distortion, -8 versus -10 dBm, and noise also are being implemented on the downconverter's data sheets.

An 80-dB spurious-free dynamic range now is a common request from customers evaluating next-generation rf ATE. Phase-noise requirements for 3G devices, due to more demanding bit error rate (BER) specs, also are forcing ATE vendors to design corresponding improvements in the measurement receiver.

Beyond the hard-core technical requirements of rf ATE is the issue of reducing the cost of test with the use of multisite ATE configurations that allow parallel testing. Tradeoffs in complexity and cost versus parallel test must be investigated and optimized. Many of today's rf ATE platforms claim multisite capability but actually operate serially to some degree due to the lack of parallelism in rf ATE design.

MVNA Technology

Modulated vector network analysis (MVNA) is a new technology for making classic rf measurements on wideband-modulated signals. It has the capability to make measurements in a user's environment, reducing the issue of correlating test to the end application.

At the core of this technology is modulated vector-corrected stimulus and measure. This capability allows you to make measurements with just one instrument that once required the use of network analyzers, spectrum analyzers, vector signal analyzers, and power meters.

In addition to the obvious cost savings, throughput and accuracy are enhanced. The same data captured in a single acquisition can be used to measure S-parameters, ACPR, error vector magnitude (EVM), and power (scalars).

Fourier proved why all this is possible. Every signal is a composite of an infinite sum of sinusoids. Consequently, the use of modulated signals necessary for testing 3G devices offers the ability to gather more information from the same data set. The amount of information gathered is a function of the stimulus applied and the information bandwidth of the measurement receiver.

S-parameters traditionally have been used by rf engineers to describe the device performance and offer the most direct way of correlating performance to the models used to design them. For device vendors, they also provide the best feedback to design, product, and modeling engineers on how the ongoing process variations are affecting performance and yield.

Unfortunately, traditional sinusoidal narrowband network analyzers do a poor job of predicting modulated behavior of S-parameters. Figure 23-11 illustrates the effect of applying a modulated signal versus a single sinusoid to an amplifier.[13] A single sinusoid allows measurements at a single power level and frequency. Depending on the power level, the amplifier may or may not be operating in its linear region.

Applying a modulated signal, like the CDMA signal in Figure 23-11, causes the amplifier to undergo linear and nonlinear operation continuously due to its inherent gain compression and the large peak-to-average power. Capturing and analyzing this kind of signal allow you not only to observe this real-world power response, as illustrated in Figure 23-11, but also to study all the embedded transient behavior as well. In contrast,

Figure 23-11
Linear-to-nonlinear response of an amplifier due to a modulated signal.

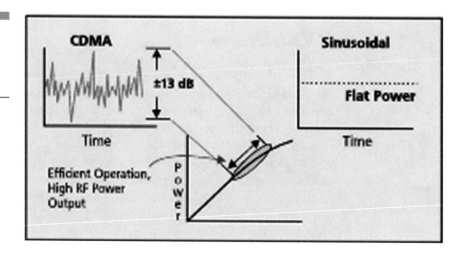

a constant-power sinusoid corresponds to only a single point on the transfer curve.

Following this line of thought, you would correctly suspect the S-parameter response would be quite different for a modulated signal. Indeed, measurements have shown decibels of difference in S21 (gain), even with an applied signal of small dynamic range.

Like a vector network analyzer (VNA), MVNA technology (see the sidebar, "A Next-Generation RF Test Solution") also can make swept S-parameter measurements of the modulated device, but with the actual power as opposed to an average power at a given frequency. Unlike a VNA, however, this swept response can be captured in a single acquisition, saving time and increasing accuracy.

A Next-Generation RF Test Solution

RFIQ, the next-generation subsystem for rf applications from Credence, meets the challenges of 3G cellular devices as well as the demands of current rf devices. The core of this system is MVNA technology, the capability to force and measure rf devices in their end-use modulated environment. Using Fourier concepts, MVNA technology decomposes these modulated time-domain waveforms into their multitone frequency components and then applies 12-term vector error correction.

Perhaps the simplest way to understand the application of MVNA technology is to compare S-parameter measurements on a classic VNA and a system using MVNA technology. S-parameters are a ratio of the incident and reflected or transmitted signals. However, to accurately measure them, imperfections in the test system and the device under test (DUT) interface must be eliminated.

Using two-port network theory, these imperfections, as seen by the DUT's input and output, are mathematically eliminated by the 12-term model. A VNA uses a single frequency stimulus, combines the raw measurements with the model, and extracts the actual S-parameter response.

In contrast, MVNA technology uses the multifrequency content of a modulated signal to perform these same measurements simultaneously. The number of measurements is limited only by the measurement receiver's information bandwidth (15 MHz for the RFIQ) and the frequency complexity of the stimulus signal.

When using a modulated signal, the actual power level at a given frequency is being applied and measured, so the real end-use response of the DUT is captured, not just the swept average power-frequency response. The measurements are a true reflection of actual device performance with increased throughput and accuracy.

Architecturally, starting from the right side of Figure 23-12, the RFIQ subsystem has eight 6-GHz rf ports.[14] Each port has the full modulated vector-corrected stimulus and measurement capability of MVNA technology. Backward fixture capability with the company's 1G rf solution, RFSS, was maintained to ease transition to RFIQ. The eight ports have been partitioned into two banks of four, each with a dedicated rf synthesizer.

Also, an auxiliary synthesizer provides a third stimulus to any of the eight ports. This gives you the ability to drive a third port, perform third-order intercept point (IP3) tests, or create an interfering signal to simulate real-world transmissions.

On the measurement side, each bank of four ports has two receiver channels. These channels function independently to make four simultaneous scalar measurements or in concert to produce differential, reflection (one-port), or S-parameter (two-port) measurements. This flexibility is suitable for true parallel multisite measurements.

In addition, each bank's pair of receiver channels has a dedicated measurement local oscillator (LO), allowing two different frequencies to be measured simultaneously for DUTs that have multiband functionality. All high-frequency hardware is fully integrated into the test head.

In the instrument rack are the rf synthesizers and the MVNA technology PCI card-based instruments, which provide the stimulus and measurement capability. The cards contain two integral 30-MS/s arbitrary waveform generators for I and Q signal generation along with four 60-MS/s measurement receivers. The software is backward-compatible, providing access to the company's DSP library used by Quartet and RFSS users.[15]

Since the effects of cable loss, mismatch, and other interface issues are removed, the actual performance of the DUT can be observed. Finding correlated figures of merit will become unnecessary and allow the next step in the rf device test (functional, as opposed to parametric, test) to become the norm in guaranteeing performance to the customer.

Figure 23-12
RFIQ block diagram.

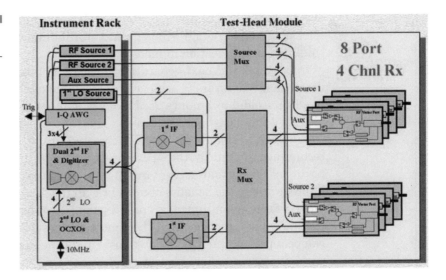

Conclusion

In broadcast mode, satellite systems provide a tremendous amount of capacity and in principle allow us to supply every human on earth with several gigabits per second of information. Broadcasting has been the major application for geostationary satellites for several decades. In Europe, more than 40 million satellite TV receivers are installed. In addition, satellites are also capable, in principle, of collecting a large amount of information from very many sources and delivering this information to a few sinks. To increase the capacity of satellites in orbit, new technologies are needed:

- Multiple-beam antennas to cover a large area and to allow low-cost user stations to transmit toward the satellite

- Onboard regeneration and decoding to improve the link budget

- On-demand onboard switching to provide unlimited connectivity and make the most efficient use of the capacity[16]

The key technologies required to implement these new satellite systems are already developed, and it is now possible to design and implement communications satellite systems for interactive multimedia applications. The tremendous increase of bandwidth for the information society in the twenty-first century is a good indication that the new generation of interactive multimedia communications satellite systems can complement the terrestrial network and will generate multibillion-dollar business for the satellite communication industry.

Finally, testing next-generation devices requires new techniques for device manufacturers to achieve their cost and quality goals. The narrow-band sinusoidal techniques used today will increase costs due to decreased yield and more customer returns.

Wideband, modulated, vector-corrected stimulus and measurement techniques offered by the MVNA technology will allow vendors to test parts in actual end-use environments. Throughput and accuracy will improve due to the benefits of collecting all the data in a single acquisition and performing multiple tests on this same set of data. It also will give the customer the assurance that the vendor understands the application and can be a partner in driving down costs and time to market.

Endnotes

1. Manfred Wittig (European Space Agency), "Satellite Onboard Processing for Multimedia Applications," *IEEE Communications Magazine*, IEEE Communications Society, 305 East 47th Street, New York, NY 10017, USA, 2000.
2. *Ibid.*
3. *Ibid.*
4. *Ibid.*
5. *Ibid.*
6. *Ibid.*
7. *Ibid.*
8. *Ibid.*
9. *Ibid.*
10. *Ibid.*
11. *Ibid.*
12. Terry Wilson (Credence Systems), "Test Challenges of Next-Generation RF Digital Devices," EE—Evaluation Engineering, Nelson Publishing, 2500 Tamiami Trail North, Nokomis, FL 34275, 2000.
13. *Ibid.*
14. *Ibid.*
15. *Ibid.*
16. *Ibid.*

CHAPTER 24

Troubleshooting Fixed Wireless Broadband Networks

This chapter describes an ongoing fixed two-way wireless broadband field experiment conducted by AT&T Laboratories (Research in Monmouth County, NJ) to help troubleshoot fixed wireless broadband networks. The AT&T Laboratories experiment, which is one of the first two-way broadband fixed wireless systems, offers end-to-end wireless broadband packet access service, with telecommuting as the primary application for their employee users. It operates in the 2.6-GHz MMDS spectrum and is based on cable modem technology. The company has developed a Web-based network monitoring/management tool that greatly enhances the ability to manage, diagnose, troubleshoot, and optimize the system. The lengthy period of operation has allowed AT&T to make observations about user behavior, weather-related channel impairments, and equipment performance. The company has identified several design issues related to the application of cable modem technology to the fixed wireless broadband environment. Also, AT&T Laboratories has measured a significant path loss effect arising from a combination of rain and foliage.

As explained previously, the experimental system offers a wireless broadband packet service to residential users. The experiment started in late 1997, and currently, there are 12 sites that are the homes of volunteer AT&T employees. This system is one of the first (if not the first) two-way fixed wireless broadband systems. It operates in the 2.6-GHz multichannel multipoint distribution service (MMDS) spectrum and is based on cable modem technology. The objectives of the experiment were to

- Install a field-grade wireless broadband two-way fixed wireless network

- Operate a wireless broadband packet access network offering high-speed access to corporate intranets

- Study various issues related to fixed wireless and broadband packet access networks[1]

The primary service that AT&T Laboratories *(http://www.research.att.com/)* was interested in providing was a seamless extension of the corporate TCP/IP intranet out to user homes. The approach taken in their experiment was to set up a network to provide a previously unavailable two-way, always-on, high-speed packet access service that users would use in their daily routine. The system was thus treated as a whole as the company investigated in depth the various components, such as radio receiver technology and Medium Access Control (MAC) protocol. The long-term nature of the project provided a unique opportunity to study user behavior patterns as well as radio performance issues related to weather.

The objective of this chapter is to provide a broad overview of the system. It briefly discusses fixed wireless broadband access, then describes AT&T's experimental system, and finally highlights the company's observations and lessons.

Fixed Wireless Broadband Packet Access Using MMDS

A fixed wireless broadband network is an attractive option for troubleshooting wireless broadband packet access networks. Such a network typically has base stations serving three to six (or more) sectors in a cell with 2- to 15-km radius. User sites have directional terminal antennas oriented toward a suitable base. Fixed wireless broadband networks are similar to hybrid fiber-coax (HFC) networks in that the access medium is a shared network carrying radiofrequency (rf)–modulated data signals. Fixed wireless broadband offers rapid and flexible deployment and a low initial cost; this makes it suitable for low-take-rate scenarios.

The AT&T Laboratories experiment uses the 2.6-GHz MMDS spectrum. Some of the first broadband fixed wireless data systems used this band. MMDS or *wireless broadband cable* systems were designed originally for broadcast video services covering a single cell with 10- to 40-km radius. The service and the technology were similar to cable television. The first MMDS data systems, as well as HFC cable systems, had a high-speed packet channel on the downlink, with the uplink provided by a telephone modem link. This constrained the uplink bit rate and also required a telephone line for the data service. Two-way wireless broadband overcomes these disadvantages, and this experiment is one of the first two-way MMDS systems. With the growing popularity of the Internet, MMDS systems have now evolved to two-way access networks.

In the initial single-cell systems, there was no cochannel interference, and the system could support the use of 64-quadrature amplitude modulation (QAM) on the downlink. In order to cover large metropolitan areas with sufficient capacity, the new MMDS systems have to use a cellular architecture that reuses radio spectrum. The preferred cellular designs involve moderate signal-to-interference ratios of 12 to 15 dB rather than the 25 dB required for a 64-QAM downlink. While (multicell) fixed wireless broadband deployments are expected to use modulation schemes such as quadrature phase shift keying (QPSK) and 16-QAM, AT&T Laboratories' single-cell experimental system uses 64-QAM modems, since these were the only modems available. Since 64-QAM modems are sensitive to channel impairments, this gave the company an opportunity to study channel effects closely.

The Experimental System Architecture

Figure 24-1 depicts the major components of the experimental system, which has been operating continuously since late 1997.[2] There are 12 user sites scattered across the Red Bank, New Jersey area within an 8-mile radius of the base station, which houses radio systems and Internet Protocol (IP) data networking equipment. The user sites are the homes of AT&T employee volunteers. An AT&T Labs research location is also one of the user sites. The base station is connected to the AT&T Labs IP intranet

Figure 24-1
The AT&T Laboratories' fixed wireless broadband packet access field experiment.

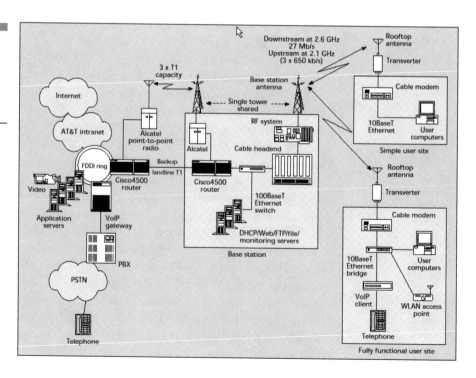

(5.3 miles away) by a point-to-point radio link with 3 x T-1 (4.5-Mbps) capacity and one backup landline T-1. The system is based on two-way cable modem technology and uses IP as the network layer protocol. This part of the chapter describes the radio network, the IP network, the services, and the network management.

Radio and MAC Subsystems

The experimental system is based on a commercial two-way HFC cable modem system. The base station houses a cable headend that operates at 44 MHz downstream (downlink) and 5 to 40 MHz upstream (uplink). Compatible cable modems are used at user sites. At both ends, the cable frequency signals are translated to the wireless broadband frequencies.

Base Station Equipment   For downlink signals (from the base station to user sites), the 44-MHz signal from the cable headend is upconverted to 2.6 GHz and transmitted at 48-dBm equivalent isotropic radiated power (EIRP) to user sites. The base antenna has a 15-dB gain, 180-s beamwidth (cardioid), and an effective height of 400 ft above grade level. Although the cable headend was developed before the current widely adopted Data Over Cable Service Interface Specifications (DOCSIS) standard, its specifications are similar to DOCSIS. The continuous 6-MHz-wide downlink uses MPEG-2 transport. It carries IP packets at 27 Mbps using 64-QAM at a 5-MHz symbol rate and forward error correction (FEC) overhead of 3 Mbps. The uplink signals are burst-mode QPSK signals within 600-kHz channels. The uplink signals received are downconverted to 5 to 40 MHz. The cable headend extracts user IP packets from the uplink signal at a post-FEC 650-kbps effective bit rate. The AT&T Laboratories system supports three uplink channels that are quasi-statically assigned to individual user modems. While the downlink is continuously on, the uplink is time-shared using polling-based multiple access.

User Site Equipment   Figure 24-2 shows the user site equipment, which is based on off-the-shelf products.[3] The user sites have 24-in roof-mounted antennas with 7.5-s beamwidth and 24-dBi gain and effective heights of 12 to 30 ft above ground. The antenna is connected directly to transverters that contain uplink/downlink amplifiers and mixers for up/downconversion. The downlink is converted to 285 MHz to match the cable modem specifications, whereas the upconversion matches the downconversion at the base station.

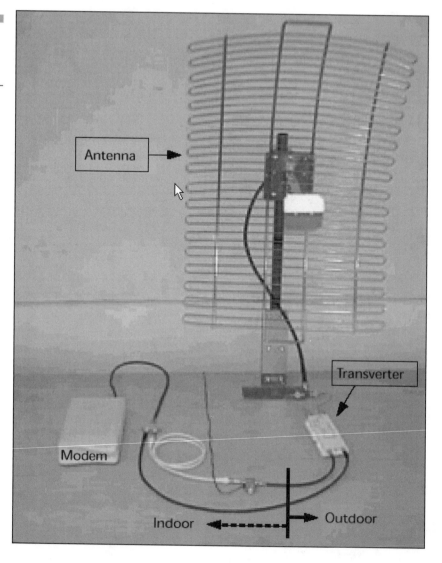

NOTE   There is a small amount of additional loss and distortion due to the concatenation of transverter and modem rf stages.

The transverters typically are mounted close to the antennas to minimize signal loss and connected via 75-ý coaxial cables to cable modems, which are placed indoors. If necessary, attenuators are used to match the signal power levels to the input dynamic range of the modems. The transverters are powered from indoors via the rf coaxial cable using a dc coupler. Cable modems communicate with users' IP device(s) using a 10-base-Ethernet interface.

IP Network and Applications

The IP network for the experiment essentially consists of three connected networks: the user subnet, the base station subnet, and the AT&T Labs intranet. All user IP devices are on the user subnet, and the headend routes IP traffic between this subnet and the base station subnet.

NOTE The traffic between any two user sites is treated as layer 2 traffic and does not involve IP layer routing.

The base station subnet uses switched 100baseT Ethernet and contains a Dynamic Host Configuration Protocol (DHCP) server and other application servers. A midrange IP router connects the base station subnet to the AT&T Labs intranet via the backhaul T-1 links. Another IP router terminates these T-1 links inside the AT&T Labs intranet and connects to the Internet as well as various internal application servers.

Applications The base station subnet has an FTP server and a Web server, which are used for testing and to provide network monitoring and management functions, as described in the next part of this chapter. This exploits the full capacity of the wireless broadband channel on the downlink, which exceeds the capacity of the backhaul T-1 links. The user applications supported by the system include

- Telecommuting
- Voice over IP (VoIP)
- Video-on-demand and video multicast
- Thin-client computing

TELECOMMUTING The principal use of the fixed wireless broadband packet data system is always-on telecommuting. Users at home can access file and print servers at their respective offices controlled by different Windows NT domains, as well as internal Web sites in the AT&T Labs intranet. Internet access is through the same firewalls that protect the AT&T Labs intranet. The families of the users also have access to the Internet, while AT&T intranet resources are protected by passwords. One user site is an AT&T Labs office building where some users use the experimental system routinely for their day-to-day office work. A modem at this location is connected to a wireless broadband LAN (WLAN) that supports several laptop computers. This system also offers seamless portability of laptops between work and home; users can use their laptops both at work and at home without any change in setup and get the same environment in both places.

VOICE OVER IP (VOIP)   The fixed wireless broadband system supports VoIP for a few user sites. The client devices at the user sites have two RJ-11 jacks to accommodate two analog telephones with separate numbers. Voice conversations are encoded using International Telecommunication Union (ITU) Recommendation G.711. The packetized voice is sent as IP packets to another client device or to a VoIP gateway in the intranet. The gateway interfaces with the corporate private branch exchange (PBX), and the client devices work like regular PBX extensions. Calls can be made using the PBX without additional dial tone. Weighted Fair Queuing (WFQ) is used to provide basic quality of service (QoS) for VoIP, and more sophisticated QoS approaches are being implemented and studied over the experimental system.

VIDEO-ON-DEMAND AND VIDEO MULTICAST   The users also access a video-on-demand service and live broadcasts of AT&T internal presentations. This service is enabled through IP multicasting from a server in the intranet over the fixed wireless broadband system and requires 50 to 500 kbps downlink bandwidth.

THIN-CLIENT COMPUTING   A thin-client computing service using Windows NT Terminal Server/Citrix MetaFrame is supported. Enabled by simple client software, users can run various Windows applications remotely on a high-performance server in the intranet, with local display and input devices. This includes several wireless broadband thin-client devices that are supported by the WLAN mentioned previously. These lightweight *wireless broadband pads* with pen-based input allow access to standard Windows applications on the remote server while roaming in the building.

Web-Based Network Management System

Configuring, monitoring, and debugging various network and computer devices initially required multiple separate interfaces (Telnet, tftp, Web), each with a separate login. Also, since the experimental system covers a substantial geographic area, frequent visits to user sites and the base station were required. This was very tedious, especially for a continuous long-term experiment. Therefore, a Web-based network management system was implemented by integrating several commercially or publicly available software systems around a commercial network management development platform. The system resides on a server inside the intranet and supports the following:

- Monitoring and configuration of any Simple Network Management Protocol (SNMP)–enabled device in the experimental system through a Web browser interface anywhere in the AT&T intranet

- SNMP management information base (MIB) manipulation for customized interface

- Real-time statistics collection, presentation, and manipulation on a Web browser using Java applets

- Alarms for device failure, signal quality degradation, and other customizable fault conditions via email, paging, fax, or Web browsers

- Remote control of various servers and user computers inside a browser window using Virtual Network Computing (VNC) Java servers developed by AT&T Labs (Using VNC, computers at user sites can be remotely configured to participate in experiments, performance measurements, and technical support.)

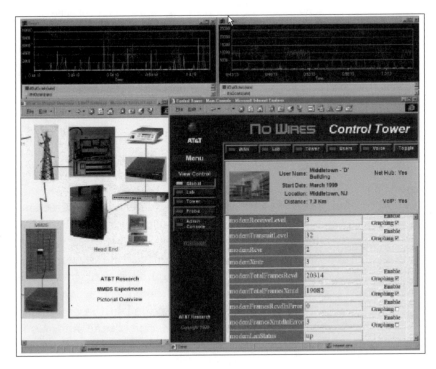

Figure 24-3
The Web-based network management system. (Top) Real-time statistics graphs; (bottom left) overview of major equipment with clickable image to access/configure details; (bottom right) top-level interface to the network management system.

■ Access to, and control of, packet capture probes deployed at various locations in the system (These remote-controlled software probes were placed in the base subnet, a user site, and the intranet, since current SNMP implementations do not provide enough detail about network traffic. The probes capture and analyze Ethernet packets to assist in debugging and measurement, including long-term measurements.[4])

The preceding capabilities significantly reduce the time and effort required for experiments, measurements, configuration, and maintenance on the system. This is significant because, compared with telephone networks, these functions are likely to be more complex in packet access networks. Figure 24-3 shows a screen shot of a typical view of the management system in several browser windows.[5] The windows show real-time statistics graphs, live information on individual sites, and a clickable image map for accessing/configuring most devices used in the experiment.

Observations and Lessons

This part of the chapter highlights some of AT&T Labs' observations about weather-related radio channel impairments, modem performance in wireless broadband systems, and user application performance.

Combined Rain/Foliage Effect On Propagation

Figure 24-4 shows the link-path loss for the various user site locations, along with the free-space loss and the predicted median loss based on the AT&T Labs path-loss model for fixed wireless broadband systems.[6] The link losses are 10 to 30 dB greater than the free-space loss due to scattering and diffraction from foliage, terrain, and buildings. The losses are consistent with the AT&T path-loss model. As part of normal operation, the network management system collects various statistics over time, including hourly downlink and uplink signal strengths for each site based on modem measurements. Although not as accurate as calibrated signal-strength measurements reported in the literature, these hourly records are collected over a longer period of time (approximately a year) than previously reported studies.

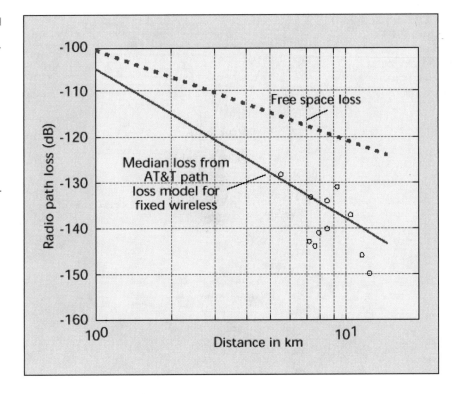

Figure 24-4

Radiolink path loss for user sites with 2.56 GHz of free space loss predicted by the AT&T path-loss model for fixed wireless broadband systems (tx height = 130 m, rx height = 10 m, light foliage).

One interesting finding from these records is the combined effect of rain and foliage on propagation path loss. Figure 24-5 shows the relative downlink power level variation observed at two sites along with the hourly rainfall record obtained from a nearby weather station.[7] The wireless broadband link between the base station and site 1 (approximately 5 miles long) has several large trees in the path near the house. With this relatively heavy foliage, the path attenuation increases by more than 12 dB under heavy rain. The limited dynamic range of the cable modem system is indicated by the clipping of the attenuation curve at the top. Thus the rain/foliage attenuation could be more than 12 dB in some cases. Site 2, which is approximately 3 miles from the base station, has a path partially obscured by a single tree branch. The relative path loss for this site compared with its nominal value is also highly correlated with rainfall, but the attenuation under heavy rain is observed to be less than 3 dB.

The comparison between the two sites suggests that the combination of heavy foliage and rain can cause a significant increase of path loss, whereas rain alone has a modest effect at 2.6 GHz. This is due to the increased scattering caused by wet leaves. As can be seen in the graph, the path loss of

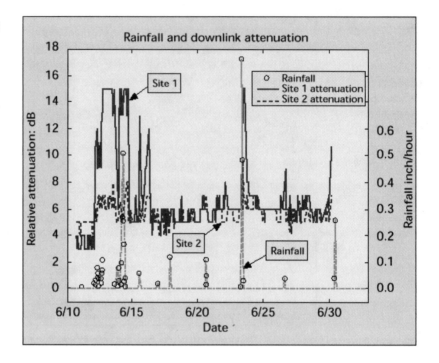

site 1 continues to stay high for several hours after a heavy rain, until most
of the water has dried/shed from the leaves. Records collected for other sites
also support the preceding conclusion. When planning for the coverage of a
fixed wireless broadband system, this rain/foliage-related attenuation must
be taken into account in addition to all the conventional margins for sea-
sonal, log-normal, and Rayleigh fading. This result is significant because
the 2.6-GHz frequency is often assumed to be unaffected by rain (as
opposed to 28- and 38-GHz systems), and AT&T Laboratories sees that this
is not so in some special foliage-related cases. Another important implication of this rain/foliage attenuation is that slow transmit power control,
receiver automatic gain control (AGC), and continuous equalizer adaptation are necessary for reliable service. Only a minor impact has been
observed due to snow accumulation on tree branches.

Applying Cable Modem Technology to Fixed Wireless

As described earlier, the experimental system is an adaptation of an early
two-way cable modem system to fixed wireless broadband applications.

Since cable modem technology continues to be a strong option, it is important to understand the issues involved in such adaptation. These issues are mainly due to differences in the HFC and wireless broadband physical media.

Symbol Timing and Downlink Equalization   According to simulations using channel models from and actual system tests, the downlink equalizer lengths of most cable modems (as short as eight feed-forward and eight feedback taps, and longer for more recent modems) are adequate for mitigating the delay spread of fixed wireless broadband channels, provided that the symbol timing error is kept small. However, most current implementations of cable modem equalizers (including the one used in this experiment) show inadequate symbol timing recovery performance. There are many effective methods to achieve low symbol timing errors, and longer equalizers or fractionally spaced equalizers improve this problem.

Equalizer Adaptation   The cable modem equalizers used in the AT&T Labs system do not continuously adapt after initial acquisition. Although this may be acceptable for the HFC environment, fixed wireless broadband channels are time-varying, albeit at slow speed. Over a period of several days, the downlink error rate increased at all user sites. To overcome this problem, the company forced equalizer tap updates by remotely resetting all modems twice a day when user activity was low. However, one of the user sites exhibited especially fast channel variation (on the order of tens of seconds). Since the channel time variation is not tracked by the equalizer, this site had the highest downlink error rate. These problems can easily be solved by slow equalizer channel tracking.

Carrier Recovery and Stability   In most cable modem designs, carrier recovery uses a second-order loop with a decision-directed (DD) phase discriminator and usually can correct carrier frequency errors up to 10 percent of the symbol rate under ideal conditions. The performance is worse with a low signal-to-noise ratio (SNR) and/or delay spread. This tolerance range is about 50 kHz for the AT&T Labs downlink and 5 kHz for the uplink. The carrier stability requirement is more demanding for the uplink, especially considering its bursty transmission. At 2.6-GHz carrier frequencies, an uplink transmit carrier stability of 2 ppm is required.

> **NOTE**   For an HFC system with uplink carrier frequencies under 100 MHz, the carrier stability requirement is about 100 ppm.

In the AT&T Labs system, uplink carrier stability has been the most common cause of service disruption, primarily due to the effect of temperature on outdoor-mounted transverters. User sites with high SNRs and little multipath delay spread operated reliably with up to 7-kHz carrier offsets, whereas user sites with low SNRs and/or larger multipath delay spread failed with only 3-kHz drifts. Achieving satisfactory performance at these sites required more stable (and more expensive) oscillators. Improving cable modem carrier recovery performance would be more reliable and cost-efficient than improving transverter oscillator stability. There are many simple synchronization methods to ease the carrier stability requirement in the literature.

RF Stage Control   The transverters used in the system are basic analog devices that cannot be controlled remotely. The preceding transverter-related problems can be eliminated if they are monitored and controlled by cable modems, e.g., by a control signal path between transverters and cable modems or integration of modem functions and rf functions.

Dynamic Range   The wireless broadband environment requires a much larger receiver dynamic range than does the HFC environment. The signal-level variation with weather/foliage needs to be addressed with suitable AGC and/or larger dynamic range. The static part of this variation can be compensated for by attenuators, and using programmable attenuators would avoid a complex installation procedure.

Modulation   As mentioned earlier, support for modulations such as QPSK or 16-QAM for downlink is preferable for robust operation in a wireless broadband environment with cochannel interference and/or to achieve better coverage.

Link-Layer Error Recovery   Cable modem systems usually have no mechanism for packet error recovery in the MAC layer and leave this function to higher-layer protocols such as TCP. This is a reasonable design in cable environments, where the packet error rate is low. However, for fixed wireless broadband systems, this is likely to be inadequate due to interference and fading, and link-level retransmission techniques are preferable.

Services and Application Performance

After initial equipment validation and improvement, most user sites have been continuously operational for about a couple of years, although a few of them have experienced short periods of outage while transverters were being replaced. These were due to the limited carrier recovery and equalization performance of the cable modem system combined with the carrier drift (up to 8 kHz) of transverters over time and temperature.

Best-Effort IP Data   The IP data performance of the system is determined by the cable modem system. Round-trip delays between user computers and the AT&T intranet measured by the ping program range from 10 ms when lightly loaded to 70 ms when many modems are active (especially on the uplink). The peak FTP throughputs are 7 Mbps for download (close to ideal over the 10baseT Ethernet interface to the modems) and 650 kbps for upload. Stress testing was conducted on the base station Web server and one user modem by simulating the workload of 200 Web users on one modem using the SURGE Web workload model. There were no impairments under load, and the performance was as if the computer were connected directly to the server over a regular 10baseT connection.

VoIP   In the AT&T Labs experiment, the company focused on the routers at the ends of the backhaul link between the user subnet and the AT&T intranet. WFQ was implemented on the routers to preferentially treat the VoIP traffic between the user subnet and the AT&T intranet. Consequently, even with heavy data traffic between the user subnet and the AT&T intranet, the voice quality of the VoIP calls had little degradation, and the packet round-trip delay between the VoIP gateway and client devices was kept under 20 ms.

Telecommuter Applications and Traffic   The measurement system records 1-minute averages of various IP traffic characteristics. Although this may not capture the true dynamics of IP packet data traffic, AT&T Labs found some interesting aspects of telecommuters' applications and traffic.

First of all, the main applications were Web browsing, email, network storage/printer access, database access, streaming and push applications (Real Audio, Pointcast, etc.), and IP multicasting. The use of streaming and push applications is increased due to the always-on nature of the service. Except for IP multicasting video service and Web browsing, most applications are symmetric (within a factor of 2) in terms of number of bytes as well as number of packets. Web browsing is symmetric in packets (due to acknowledgments) but fairly asymmetric in terms of bytes.

Second, AT&T Labs observed that many applications are very chatty. While most Web traffic is highly correlated with the input of users, other applications such as desktop productivity applications and server-based email applications generate traffic that is not well correlated with user activity. This is especially true for applications configured to use network storage. Such applications sometimes use network storage for temporary files, creating unnecessary traffic on the network.

Finally, many desktop applications do not react well to, or recover well from, packet losses due to short-term fading of wireless channels lasting several seconds or minutes. These include server-based email applications such as MS Exchange, domain login services, and many desktop productivity applications that use network storage. Most of them eventually time out and alert users with an unclear error message. However, the timeout periods of these wired-LAN-oriented applications are sometimes excessively long when waiting for server responses, and users often manually terminate them too early in the absence of status information. This is in contrast to Web browsers, where users may not even notice temporary channel degradations. This may be due to the fact that Web browsers running over TCP are designed to operate with various bandwidths ranging from dialup modem speeds to LAN speeds, whereas desktop productivity applications usually assume reliable high-bandwidth LAN connectivity.

User Experience   Several users report that there has been a fundamental change in their computing and work behavior since they joined the experiment. The always-on characteristic of the system encourages more efficient online time at home between other activities and enables quick lookup of email and information on the Internet for immediate use for professional and personal activities. Wireless broadband access enables them to participate in videoconferencing, provides access to multimedia streaming and multicast, allows access to/sharing of large files at work for collaboration, and lets them spend more time at home while maintaining higher productivity. Users also enjoy quick technical support via high-speed software download, remote configuration through SNMP and VNC, and early detection of potential problems by the management system. Also, they greatly appreciate the simplicity of having virtually identical computing environments at home and at work.

Conclusion

AT&T Labs has been operating a two-way fixed wireless broadband field experiment in the 2.6-GHz MMDS band for more than a year. It provides high-speed intranet and Internet access for telecommuting employees. The network has been operating continuously, except for short, isolated periods of outage related to failure of rf subsystems that were still early in their product cycle. The AT&T Labs experiment, which is one of the first two-way fixed wireless broadband field experiments, offers an end-to-end solution which the company's satisfied users use in their daily routine. AT&T Labs has developed a Web-based network monitoring/management tool that greatly enhances the ability to manage, diagnose, and optimize the system. The lengthy period of operation has allowed AT&T Labs to make observations about user behavior, weather-related channel impairments, and equipment performance. AT&T Labs has identified several issues in the design of cable modem–based systems that need to be tailored to the wireless broadband environment. Also, AT&T Labs has measured a significant path-loss effect arising from a combination of rain and foliage. Future directions for the experiment include

- Enhancements to IP network features such as QoS provisioning and network management
- Use of DOCSIS 1.1 modems that may address some of the performance issues raised in this chapter and provide voice/data integration features
- Provision of in-home wireless broadband LAN extensions at more user sites
- Continued measurements and analysis of user traffic and weather-related impairments
- Use of lower-order modulation schemes to improve robustness and coverage[8]

Endnotes

1. Byoung-Jo Kim, N. K. Shankaranarayanan, Paul S. Henry, Kevin Schlosser, and Thomas K. Fong, "The AT&T Labs Broadband Fixed Wireless Field Experiment," AT&T Labs-Research (T. K. Fong is now with @Home Corporation.), *IEEE Communications Magazine*, IEEE Communications Society, 305 East 47th Street, New York, NY 10017, USA, 2000.
2. *Ibid.*
3. *Ibid.*
4. *Ibid.*
5. *Ibid.*
6. *Ibid.*
7. *Ibid.*
8. *Ibid.*

PART 6

Advanced Wireless Broadband Networks and the Future Directions

Wireless Broadband Network Applications: Teleservice Model and Adaptive QoS Provisions

In today's telecommunications market, there is a strongly felt urgency for innovative wireless broadband services. There are many driving forces in this direction, including the following: High-capacity, high-reliability (mainly tethered) links are available for the transfer of large amounts of information, and technology is seen by the user as a means of augmenting senses in every field of experience. This means that enhanced services such as distance learning, teleworking, and telemedicine have now taken on the role of necessary means to improve the quality of life.

In such a scenario, the transition from monomedia narrowband services to multimedia wireless broadband applications is ineluctable. To complete the stimulating picture of the information age, we should not overlook the personalization of wireless broadband applications. This means proliferation of services fitting disparate user needs, arrangement of access techniques to the services, free user roaming, and finally overcoming the constraints of tethered systems. Accordingly, the wired backbone shall be made accessible through fixed (home and business) and wireless broadband (cellular handheld and satellite-based) terminals. The evolution scenario outlined gives rise to a problem, which is the main topic of this chapter: the quality-of-service (QoS) guarantee to wireless broadband multimedia services over heterogeneous wired-wireless broadband network platforms.

High-speed fixed networks, mostly based on Asynchronous Transfer Mode (ATM), mean nonfloating high-capacity links that can easily support wireless broadband multimedia services and guarantee the requested end-to-end QoS. However, still open issues are QoS guarantee to wireless broadband services over wired-wireless links connecting fixed-to-mobile or mobile-to-mobile users and the management of unreliable low-bandwidth mobile radio links.

In the future internetworked scenario, wireless broadband and narrowband network segments will coexist. As an example, in a wireless broadband ATM system, the information flows across both *hard-wire* links (optical fibers), over which the QoS requisites can easily be met, and *soft-wire* links (air), over which difficulties arise in guaranteeing target quality.

The scenario becomes much more complex when we consider user mobility, which means variable-capacity and reconfigurable end-to-end links. Roaming implies the risk of crossing areas that do not own sufficient resources to meet the requirements of a wireless broadband multimedia application. Furthermore, the interference level on the radio link changes rapidly, and services that occupy wider bandwidths undergo greater risks of experiencing great quality degradation.

The issue of effective handling and providing QoS to wireless broadband services in internetworked scenarios is well known in the research community. To provide a constant (hard) QoS during the call, resources are reserved according to the peak-rate requirements. This results in high costs and low resource utilization, which is inconvenient on the wireless broadband side due to scarcity and highly variable availability of bandwidth resources.

Recently, the idea of adaptive (soft) QoS control has begun to appear. According to this, the resources assigned to a connection adapt themselves to the dynamic variations of network and user exigencies during call progression. Consequently, the QoS of the connection changes dynamically as well. It is essential that the QoS be configurable throughout the system; therefore, the adaptive QoS approach is the only feasible solution for the handling of mobile multimedia applications.

This chapter presents a teleservice model for wireless broadband applications based on an adaptive QoS paradigm. According to this, a multimedia wireless broadband application is considered as a set of hierarchically ordered adaptable media streams that accept varying degrees of network-level guarantees depending on dynamic resource changes and user preferences. Some algorithms that match the proposed paradigm are designed for call and mobility management. Their performance is analyzed in a mobile multitier cellular system, including the satellite component.

In other words, this chapter describes a paradigm for wireless broadband multimedia applications matching the adaptive QoS approach and reports the test results of its flexibility in a high-bit-rate multitier mobile environment. The overriding concept is that the multimedia application is prone to accept a variable QoS within a given acceptability range to face a momentary lack of resources or overall degradation of a radio link. The teleservice model proposed in this chapter suggests how this adaptation can be performed simply and effectively.

Early studies on this model have been carried out within wireless broadband multimedia and wireless broadband ATM systems. In this chapter, the study is extended to multitier systems, trying to benefit from the adoption of the overlapping coverage, which is a consolidated means to increase the channel capacity in cellular environments.

Based on the paradigm of adaptive QoS guarantee, a class of algorithms for the integrated handling of originating and handoff calls from wireless broadband multimedia applications has been proposed. Results achieved are extremely interesting and testify as to how adaptive QoS helps in solving problems that cannot be faced successfully by means of mere (although powerful) multitier coverage.

Modeling the Wireless Broadband Application

From an adaptive QoS perspective, it is mandatory to decide which portion of the wireless broadband multimedia traffic must be presented at the user interface and which might be temporarily discarded/scaled to match radio-link fluctuations. The objective is, however, to preserve the information that has the highest significance to the call in order to maintain a minimum acceptable quality level.

The approach selected to make adaptive QoS actually effective consists of *entering* the wireless broadband multimedia flow and intervening on each single monomedia traffic component to adjust its rate or temporarily disable its transmission. This implies that the network looks at the multimedia call as a set of distinguishable components (a multicomponent teleservice model). The ability to act on a single media flow gives the network high flexibility and reliability.

Scaling/filtering the traffic flow is a common approach in the literature. This method adapts the transmitted traffic by changing its characteristic, e.g., by lowering the frame rate of a compressed video stream that adopts progressive or hierarchical coding (MPEG). A further level of adaptation can be conceived, consisting of dropping a single media component on a priority basis. This method temporarily deactivates some media streams during the multimedia call session due to network and/or user exigencies.

Network-driven dropping of components may occur following congestion due to impairments on the radio link or cell overloading. The advantage is guaranteed. Let us assume that the availability of resources at a given time cannot meet the requirements of the *scaled* multimedia flow, and its bit rate cannot be further reduced due to quality acceptability reasons. Then, if the call is handled as a unique traffic flow, without distinguishing its components, it must be terminated. Conversely, by exploiting the multicomponent model, the single media streams can be scaled, and in addition, the less significant components can be dropped. Thus the wireless broadband application can be maintained active at a negotiated lower QoS level.

The dropping of a component in the multimedia flow also can be user-driven. In the case of a mobile videophone connection, for example, the user can inhibit the video transmission for a while due to reasons of privacy. In any case, the filtered or dropped components can be reintegrated at the original rate when the user or network exigency is over.

From the multicomponent teleservice model, the necessity of separately conveying each media component on the air interface emerges. However, all the components logically belong to the same wireless broadband flow and thus need to be jointly handled. This is the basis of multibearer transport.

Multibearer transport best matches the dynamic multicomposite nature of a wireless broadband call. Indeed, each bearer fits the QoS requirement of a specific media stream. Furthermore, this solution harmonizes with the trend toward multilink usage for conveying multimedia information in high-speed networks.

The primary point in the multibearer approach is how to maintain a sufficient degree of user satisfaction even when the dropping of some components is conceived. Hence the next steps consist of

- Ordering the components of a multimedia call on a priority basis
- Defining the minimum acceptable quality for the application
- Trying to keep the components roughly synchronized on the air interface
- Conceiving ad hoc renegotiation mechanisms for QoS parameters
- Defining ad hoc quality indices[1]

Within the proposed multimedia teleservice model, let's exploit the notions of minimum set, static priority, and dynamic priority.

Minimum Set

At the start of a call, the user sets up a multimedia application session and declares the set of basic media components, the *minimum set*, which can guarantee an acceptable level of presentation quality. The minimum set is a way of specifying a minimum bound on the QoS of the whole flow.

A call is not blocked or terminated if enough resources are not found for the whole set of components, only if one of the minimum-set components has to be dropped. This implies that some media streams can be selected to be always present in the call. For example, in a teleconference session, the user can decide not to put through the call if both audio and video cannot be transmitted, and he or she can agree with suppression of the data component if this were necessary. In this case, audio and video will be tagged as components of the minimum set. If components not belonging to the minimum set are rejected, the multimedia connection is still maintained at a temporary lower QoS guarantee (adaptive QoS).

Static Priority

At call setup, the user interactively personalizes the multimedia application by assigning a *significance*, i.e., a level of static priority (SP), to each of its components. For example, a videophone call voice has reasonably higher SP than video, since dropping the voice would impair quality more severely than the lack of video. In other words, the user can accept some quality degradation during bad periods, and the videophone call could degenerate into a telephone call. Components with higher SP are those in the minimum set.

Minimum set and SP are included in the traffic contract. Other than the specifications on the negotiated characteristics of the whole connection, the contract consists of a traffic descriptor and QoS parameters for each component. Some (scalable) components can further declare a range of allowed values for their bit rate. The network is allowed to operate on two adaptation levels to adjust the quality of the multimedia connection: at call level (through the minimum bound specified by the minimum set) and at a component level (through the ranges of QoS parameters of each single component).

Dynamic Priority

The different time constraints of the component bearers and the delays suffered while crossing the air interface lead to the likelihood of losing the original interstream synchronization. A solution is addressed in and exploits the concept of dynamic priority. A sliding-window mechanism is used to couple the information of simultaneously generated components and to enable the system to monitor them in order to assess, on the receiving side, the degree of synchronization. Run-time processing can induce a system reaction by dynamically modifying the value of priority of each component.

Exploiting the Multicomponent Model in Multitier Environments

Let us focus on a multitier system, made up of microcellular, macrocellular, and satellite spot coverage, as illustrated in Figure 25-1.[2] Multitier coverage, including satellite, can be a very effective tool to increase system

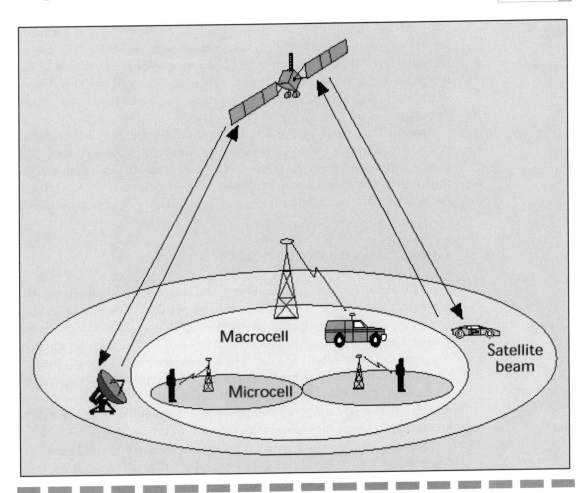

Figure 25-1 The reference multitier system.

capacity. But alone it may not be enough to guarantee the target QoS to multimedia traffic for the following reasons: The selected coverage layer risks being overloaded by the demanding need for bandwidth from broadband calls, and even if the selected layer has enough bandwidth, it might not fit the service constraints. For example, delay-sensitive components are prevented from using satellite links due to the long propagation delays.

To achieve flexible management of the radio spectrum and to match the QoS requirements of multimedia traffic, it is recommended that you couple multitier coverage with the multicomponent teleservice model and multi-bearer transport of information. The main advantage is the possibility of allocating each component on a different tier. For example, delay-sensitive components (video, voice) can be allocated on the microcell and macrocell layers, whereas delay-insensitive components (non-real-time data) can be moved to the satellite layer if insufficient resources are available in the terrestrial segment. Furthermore, in case of congestion and lack of resources in a given layer, some components can access a different layer to avoid call dropping.

An issue that needs further investigation is interstream synchronization when various components of the same wireless broadband flow are transported on different coverage layers. Let us now examine three multicomponent/multibearer algorithms: Progressive Layer Selection (PLS), Optimal Layer Selection (OLS), and Enhanced Optimal Layer Selection (EOLS).

Progressive Layer Selection

The PLS algorithm tries to allocate as many components as possible on the lowest microcell layer. If the whole call cannot find resources, PLS allocates the residual components on the macrocell layer. If bandwidth is not available on the lowest two layers, PLS tries to assign delay-insensitive components to the satellite layer. If some components still cannot be allocated, two alternatives are available: If some of them belong to the minimum set, the call is rejected, since the minimum QoS cannot be guaranteed, and otherwise, the nonallocated components are disabled, and the call is accepted at a temporary lower QoS.

The handover handling policy functions as well. Handover events are triggered on a component, not call, basis. Regardless of the current layer hosting a component, PLS tries to allocate it in a bottom-up way. The aim is to saturate the lowest layers before taking into consideration the resources on the higher layers, which are considered umbrella coverages with overflow resources.

Optimal Layer Selection

The OLS algorithm aims to scatter the components by allocating them on the most appropriate (optimal) layer. *Optimal* is defined here as a layer where

- The best statistical multiplexing with other calls' components can be achieved.
- The delay requirements of the component are fulfilled.

■ The likelihood of satisfying the component resource request is high.[3]

Obviously, it is not always possible to allocate each component on its optimal layer because of the unavailability of resources. In this case, OLS tries to move the component to suboptimal tiers; if it is not successful, it disables the nonallocated component (if not belonging to the minimum set) and accepts the call at a lower temporary QoS.

During handover events, the philosophy of OLS is always to bring each component to its relevant optimal layer as soon as possible. The choice examined in this chapter is to assign voice components to the microcell, video to the macrocell, and data to the satellite layer, according to the allocation sequences in Table 25-1.[4]

Enhanced Optimal Layer Selection

It would be interesting to allow wireless broadband data components not in the minimum set to make further allocation attempts on the lower lay-

TABLE 25-1

Features of the OLS Algorithm

Voice	Video	Non-Real-Time Wireless Broadband Data	Non-Real-Time Narrowband Data
First allocation attempt on the microcell layer	First allocation attempt on the macrocell layer	First allocation attempt on the satellite layer	First allocation attempt on the microcell layer
In case of resources lacking, second attempt on the macrocell layer	In case of resources lacking, second attempt on the microcell layer	In case of resources lacking, second attempt on the macrocell layer *only* if the component belongs to the minimum set; otherwise, it is rejected	In case of resources lacking, second attempt on the macrocell layer
In case of resources lacking, rejection of the component	In case of resources lacking, rejection of the component	In case of resources lacking, rejection of the component	In case of resources lacking, third attempt on the satellite layer
			In case of resources lacking, rejection of the component

ers when no resource is available on the satellite links. This approach is exploited in a modified version of OLS, EOLS. It allows temporary suboptimal allocation of wireless broadband data not in the minimum set that are waiting for resources to become available on the satellite layer.

Performance Results

To effectively compare the proposed algorithms it is essential to select (or redefine) suitable performance indices. An index useful for giving a measurement of the average QoS of a given call is the *QoS index* (QI). Other performance indices are the new call blocking and forced termination (due to handover failure) probabilities.

For comparison purposes, let's refer to a conventional algorithm, not based on the multicomponent model, called *Standard*. It supposes that the media streams are multiplexed in the mobile terminal, and an integrated multimedia flow is generated. Therefore, a multimedia call is handled as a unique connection and conveyed on a single wideband channel (single-bearer transport).

Standard tries to allocate a whole multimedia call on a given layer (the fixed QoS approach). The first attempt is made at the microcell, and the subsequent attempts at the macrocell layer and, only if no component has real-time constraints, at the satellite layer. A similar approach is adopted to handle a handover call. This algorithm is clearly not optimized for the mobile environment; the most penalizing feature is that a call is accepted successfully if and only if the whole multimedia flow is preserved.

The results reported refer to the case in which the system is loaded by mobile videophone applications, which generate traffic composed of voice, video, and data information. For those algorithms exploiting the multicomponent paradigm, voice and video are included in the minimum set.

Let's now refer to time-division multiple access (TDMA)–based air interfaces. Voice components request 1 slot per frame (each slot carries 13 kbps); video and wireless broadband data components request 4 and 8 slots, respectively.

The test configuration consists of a group of eight microcells, with two overlapping macrocells and one overlapping satellite spot. The average call duration is 120 s; the average permanence time in a microcell is 25 s and in a macrocell 100 s.

The number of channels in the micro, macro, and satellite layers is 20, 40, and 100, respectively. The system is planned to test the algorithm behaviors during congestion, which explains the high values of blocking

Figure 25-2
Blocking probability
versus multimedia call
arrival rate.

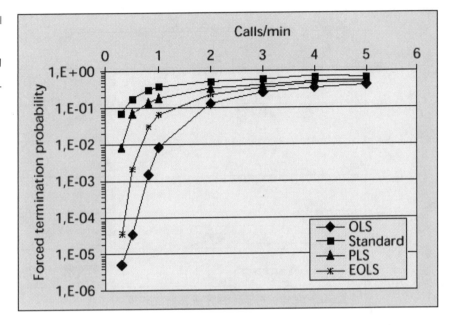

and forced termination probabilities; these, however, can be reduced by adequate cell channel planning. In Figures 25-2 through 25-4, the performance indices are shown versus the multimedia call arrival rate.[5]

As expected, the Standard algorithm is distinguished by high values of blocking and forced termination probabilities compared with the multi-

Figure 25-3
Forced termination
probability versus
multimedia call arrival
rate.

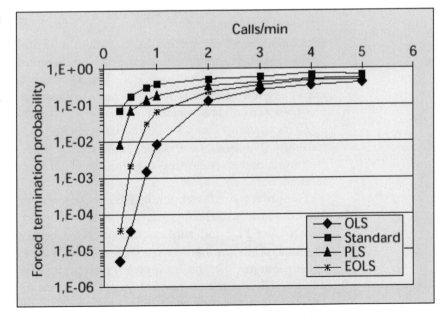

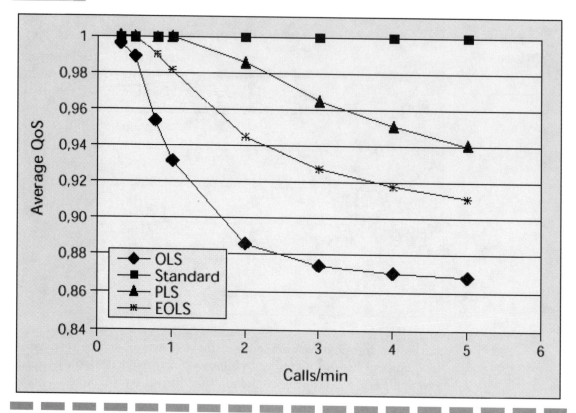

Figure 25-4   *Average quality (Q-1) of multimedia calls versus call arrival rate.*

component-based algorithms. On the other hand, its behavior is optimal in terms of average quality offered to established connections. The problem is that even at low offered load, excellent QoS can be guaranteed only to extremely few connections, due to the very low performance in terms of accepted and safely completed calls.

As for the multicomponent algorithms, both blocking and forced-termination probabilities for PLS are higher than those of OLS. The opposite trend is manifest regarding the QoS. The EOLS algorithm has an intermediate behavior.

The progressive attempts of PLS to allocate all the call components from the lowest to the highest layer is the main cause of its low performance. In fact, PLS underutilizes the spot resources and overloads microcells and macrocells compared with OLS. Thus blocking probability increases because channels in the low layers, which preferably should be allocated to delay-sensitive components, are occupied by data. Since preemption is not allowed, accepted data components subtract resources to voice and video components of new calls, which therefore undergo the risk of being rejected, being voice and video components of the minimum set.

This also explains why the forced-termination probability is quite high: Data components keep on trying to share the resources of the lowest layers with video and voice. Had a data component been allocated at the satellite layer: It would not have contended with the delay-sensitive components in the minimum set, and no handover request would have been made—the crossing of a satellite spot border being very rare during a call connection. This is the reason for the better behavior of the OLS algorithm, which tries to allocate data only on the spot layer and thus leaves more slots free at the lowest layers.

If you focus on the offered QoS in Figure 25-4, you will notice that OLS shows worse performance than PLS. This is due to the higher number of calls accepted and completed successfully. This turns into a slightly higher probability of the broadband data component not finding resources and being rejected. Due to the lack of this less important component, the calls accepted have a slightly lower average QoS.

The philosophy of the EOLS algorithm is to permit QoS performance to be increased just by sacrificing a little blocking and forced-termination probabilities, which still remain well below the values of PLS and Standard algorithms. The QoS of the call manifestly increases, without falling below 95 percent for a wide range of load variations. These are the effects of the slight increase in the resource occupation of the microcell and macrocell layers.

Conclusion

In this chapter, a teleservice model for wireless broadband applications is proposed in an adaptive QoS approach. The philosophy has been to match the composite nature of a multimedia application, being able to intervene on each separate component while always preserving the identity of the call as a whole. This implies the use of more bearer services for information transport on the air interface and the adaptation of the QoS guaranteed to each component stream to cope with the intrinsic variability of the mobile radio environment.

Some algorithms for call and traffic management, which exploit the proposed multicomponent paradigm, have been designed for a multitier cellular system, including a satellite coverage layer. Their performance is analyzed and compared with a conventional approach based on fixed QoS. Performance is evaluated in terms of a new QoS index, specifically conceived to capture the nature of multimedia traffic and the variability of capacity in wireless broadband networks. Valuable results confirm the validity of the proposed paradigm for managing wireless broadband multimedia applications in capacity-varying networks.

Endnotes

1. Antonio Iera (University of Reggio Calabria), Antonella Molinaro (University of Messina), and Salvatore Marano (University of Calabria), "Wireless Broadband Applications: The Teleservice Model and Adaptive QoS Provisioning," *IEEE Communications Magazine,* IEEE Communications Society, 305 East 47th Street, New York, NY 10017, USA, 2000.

2. *Ibid.*

3. *Ibid.*

4. *Ibid.*

5. *Ibid.*

CHAPTER 26

Residential High-Speed Internet: Wireless Broadband

The Internet revolution is here. Yet, for the average household user, it is becoming a painfully slow phenomenon. Analog dialup modems (by far the most common residential Internet access technology) are sufficient for email and occasional Web browsing. Streaming video, audio, and graphics files, however, can take minutes or hours to load.

At the end of 1999, three technologies had positioned themselves to compete for the residential high-speed market: cable modems, digital subscriber line (DSL), and wireless broadband. With almost 300 basic trading areas deployed, the market has been clearly established. Yet 2000's 2 million high-speed households represent fewer than 3 percent of U.S. households; the future of the market is far from certain.

With this in mind, there is some good news and some bad news. The bad news is that by the beginning of 2002, fewer than 2.7 million homes in North America will have access to multimedia applications and content using high-speed Internet, phone lines, cable modems, or wireless broadband services. The good news is that this number is expected to grow exponentially over the next few years.

Telephone companies, cable operators, wireless broadband/satellite providers, broadcast media corporations, and Internet service providers (ISPs) all want to have a hand in developing the high-speed Internet access technologies that wireless broadband applications require. These new wireless broadband networks will emerge as the platforms that open a whole new world of on-demand information and entertainment services to eagerly waiting end users all over the world. The goal of this chapter is to provide a rational and objective opinion of the wireless broadband Internet access market as it appears today and how it will evolve over the next few years.

Wireless broadband technology in this context means anything that sends multiple signals over a single line or transport carrier. This chapter will focus on those technologies which provide a bandwidth level of at least 1.5 Mbps, because this is considered a minimum for carrying simultaneous voice, video, and data. This chapter also will discuss the technologies that fall below this point if they provide multiple services over a single medium and will increase to higher bandwidth levels sometime in the near future.

Access in this context is the term commonly used to describe the transport connection between the service providers (Internet, telco, cable, satellite, wireless) and the customer premises. The Internet access connection is often referred to as *the last mile* and sometimes as *the first mile*. Another basic definition to be considered is that the *Internet* is the simple term generically used for the very complicated internetworking of networks and hosts connected by the Internet Protocol (IP).

This chapter also examines the implications of residential wireless broadband Internet access trends. It will focus on the commercial opportunities arising from the development of the new technologies. This chapter discusses all significant access technologies: DSLs, hybrid fiber-coax systems, fiber to the home, satellites, and terrestrial broadband wireless. In addition to analyzing the technological trends in today's Internet access market, this chapter also focuses on profiling the strategies, products, and services of all leading equipment manufacturers and service providers. This chapter also will provide detailed forecasts of all major high-speed Internet access products and services with an assessment of future strategies for both equipment vendors and service providers.

Residential High-Speed Internet Access Demand and Wireless Broadband Convergence

The single most important occurrence in the access world has been the massive entry by residential consumers and small business users onto the Internet. Most of this traffic has been centered on email and browsing the World Wide Web for specific information not found easily in other media formats. The other great solution provided by the data access mechanism has become the fulfillment of the long-standing need for inexpensive interconnections between business local-area networks (LANs). This shared access to remote files has become an immediate concern for the growing number of home-based teleworkers.

Residential Internet access to date has been agonizingly slow because the overwhelming method of connection is dialup. It is also common knowledge that the fastest growing Web sites are full of multimedia content, and the intense graphics, animation, sound, and video content benefits greatly from high-speed access. Until recently, almost all the propaganda has emphasized Internet access as opposed to voice and video services. This is all about to change.

Broadcast television continues to be the primary wireless broadband service that we see today. In the past decade, the tide began to turn. Personal computers (PCs) became the cornerstone for the new interactive information era, and the PC even passed the TV in sales in 1996. It is estimated more than 17 million homes in the United States now have two or more PCs, and analysts expect this number to double over the next few years. However, the PC also will evolve in the next few years. The powerful, general-purpose PCs that have dominated the industry for the past 20 years are now in the process of developing into Internet-access appliances.

The broadcast television industry recently has begun battling the Internet juggernaut with a new format called *digital television* (DTV) or *high-definition television* (HDTV). DTV will require many expensive changes to both provider and end-user equipment. The new digital TV sets will need massive amounts of processing power to reassemble the compressed MPEG-2 pictures and sound and will be quite expensive in the beginning, as are all innovative products in the early stages of their life cycle.

A prime example of the new types of devices resulting from the PC/TV convergence is *personal television* set-top devices and services. These can best be described as *on-demand TV,* and they are helping to change the traditional television landscape. These VCR-type boxes automatically record and store the favorite television programs chosen by the viewer in random-access mode (meaning it can record, pause, and play different sections of a show at the same time with the playback being slightly behind real time).

Broadcast television will continue to be a major medium for the delivery of video and audio content, but it also will become one of the major superhighways for the delivery of data to digital appliances and in-home media servers. Television also will finally be able to provide the interactive information marketers can use to target an appropriate advertising campaign to a person who actually cares about their product.

High-Speed Access Technology

For more than a hundred years, access to the customer has meant running copper wire from a central office or a cable headend to the customer's premises. Until recently, this had changed very little since the introduction of the telephone in 1876, especially for residential customers. The demand for high-speed Internet access has brought about a revolution in the way access is being approached by the various service providers.

Quality of service (QoS) technology will become the cornerstone of wireless broadband access. QoS refers to the ability to guarantee that a packet flow through the network is sustained at a maximum throughput and that some types of packets are able to get different levels of treatment based on header information. QoS has become a hot topic with the introduction of real-time data traffic on the IP (Internet) network.

▬▬ ▬▬ xDSL

DSL is the generic term for using the installed subscriber loops in place in and above the ground to deliver wireless broadband applications. This is accomplished by expanding the frequency utilization of the copper wires. An additional benefit is that unlike the current plain old telephone service (POTS) dialup analog modems or Integrated Services Digital Network (ISDN), which both continue to burden the telephone switching network, xDSL systems remove the data traffic from the voice switch at the central office. The data are routed to a data network that is more efficient at handling this type of information.

It is clear that DSL is seen as a way for telephone service providers to make a quick entry into providing higher-rate data services to their customers. Establishing standards for the consumer market will lead to lower equipment costs (by half approximately) and to more rapid acceptance in the consumer market. The standards also will reduce the cost and complexity of customer premises equipment (CPE) and will help eliminate truck rolls for installations. The International Telecommunications Union (ITU) G.Lite standard is the first to be ratified, and the standards for the other types of DSLs are expected to enhance deployments significantly.

High-Speed Usage, Awareness, and Demand: DSL or Cable

In the not so distant past, accessing the Internet from work was an activity reserved only for those employees who had a pressing business need to do so. In many cases, these lucky few even accessed the Web via individual modem lines. Of course, the Internet has since invaded every facet of the corporate world, and now companies are looking for economical ways to provide comprehensive Web access not only to all on-site employees but also to remote workers and home office networks.

Because simple dialup accounts are too expensive for large groups of disparate users, most companies use either DSL or cable modems for cheap wireless broadband access. Which solution is best for your company? This very question ignites a fiery and informative debate between industry analysts.

Underlying Technology　Cable modem technology, which leverages existing coaxial cable wiring in a home or business to transmit digital data, is largely based on Ethernet technology developed at Xerox Parc in the 1970s. Unlike xDSL, the connection between a cable modem and an ISP is not an individual line—it is a shared connection among all users assigned to the same network node. Each cable modem talks to a cable modem termination system (CMTS), which brokers all data requests. The best analogy for this setup is a large-scale client-server model with two-way communication between cable modems (clients) and a CMTS (server).

Because each node resembles nothing more than a large LAN, cable providers are able to use off-the-shelf hardware components and communicate with heterogeneous clients (such as Windows, Mac OS, and Linux) using standard TCP/IP protocols. Not only does this result in lower costs, which benefits consumers, but it also means that cable ISPs avoid having to write network drivers for every operating system. To realize just how crucial a benefit this is, try talking to an xDSL subscriber who is struggling to use his or her service after upgrading to Microsoft's new Windows Me operating system.

On the other hand, while cable works on a shared-network type of topology, xDSL is designed around other existing wide-area network (WAN) topologies. Basically, asymmetric DSL (ADSL) or symmetric DSL (SDSL) is designed to work like T-1- or T-3-type technologies. The DSL modem at the customer site connects the local Ethernet network (be it a router, a switch, or a direct connection to a PC) to the back-end Asyncronous Transfer Mode (ATM) network. This gives access to the ISP's network, which is providing the actual Internet access.

A DSL modem gives the user an Ethernet jack to plug in to, just like a cable modem does. There is no difference between the two technologies here at all, except for the cable industry's hype about how DSL is so difficult to set up.

Bandwidth Issues   As the cable industry claims in its commercials, cable sometimes offers more bandwidth than DSL for the same cost. But with cable you are sharing a limited amount of bandwidth with others on your segment. With DSL, each user has his or her own dedicated copper that goes directly to the phone company's central office. It is also true that if you want the higher bandwidth offerings of DSL, you must pay more. However, this is true of every other WAN option, and what's so weird about the idea of paying more for faster service?

Then, of course, there is upload speed. With DSL, there is a choice of both downstream and upstream bandwidth. Downstream is typically a guaranteed 384 kbps, with bandwidth up to 1544 kbps available depending on your line conditions and distance to the phone company's central office. Upstream speed is normally 128 kbps, just like cable. But DSL can be customized to the user's needs, whereas the upload speed of standard cable modem service is capped at 128 kbps. If you need both high downstream and high upstream bandwidth, SDSL allows 384 to 1544 kbps in both directions or even higher speeds if needed.

Nevertheless, because cable takes a shared-bandwidth approach, its performance can fluctuate with the number of users on a particular segment. The larger the number of users, the less bandwidth available for allocation to each individual workstation. Often this can result in performance fluctuations and degradation.

Many cable modem providers are working around this problem, however, by placing restrictions on the number of modems per CMTS and by blocking or filtering certain types of bandwidth-hogging IP traffic. Companies such as Lucent's Bell Labs are also amplifying the fiberoptics used in cable technology to make them operate at increasingly faster speeds, which also will decrease performance bottlenecks.

Industry averages for cable speeds usually check in around 750 kbps over a range of 500 kbps to 3 Mbps. Some vendors cap the upload speed at 128 kbps, but many vendors are also easing their cap rates up a few notches.

It appears that xDSL has an advantage here. Remember that the entire Internet is based on the notion of shared bandwidth. Thus, while the bandwidth of an individual DSL connection may not be shared, eventually all DSL connections will terminate at an Internet router, at which point these individual streams will merge together into one or more upstream connections, causing a potentially hazardous bottleneck.

Installation Hurts   Let's be honest here. Installing DSL can be more painful than undergoing gum surgery. Some say that DSL actually stands for "Damn, that service is lousy."

And what's up with having to use *microfilters* on all the telephones in your remote office anyway? DSL installations rely heavily on the quality of phone lines and the distance away from the phone company's central office. If you are more than 18,000 ft away from a central office, you can expect performance and installation problems, period.

In comparison, cable offers a painless installation process. In general terms, an existing coaxial cable plugs into the cable modem, and an Ethernet cable runs from the output of the modem to a network hub or network interface card. This simple process requires minimal software configuration on a user's workstation.

However, typical DSL installations can be pretty bad. As with any other very popular service, it can take weeks to get a DSL line installed. For early adopters, the demands on installation crews are not as intense as they are today. Fortunately, many DSL providers are now offering self-installation kits, and doing it yourself is no more difficult than connecting a few wires and installing a new phone jack.

Security Issues   When it comes to security, DSL wins hands down. There are two major issues here: overall network security and virtual private network (VPN) capabilities. As far as network security goes, DSL and cable offer similar features. With DSL, however, each end user has a dedicated connection to the central office. With cable, all users share the same cable with others in their neighborhood, which not only endangers privacy but also diminishes the overall bandwidth for each cable user.

As far as VPN capabilities go, DSL and cable should be identical. But some cable providers have clauses in their service agreements prohibiting the use of VPNs across their networks unless you pay a higher cost. This reminds one of the DSL cost structure that cable people complain about in their TV ads. In contrast, DSL providers have no such restriction, and a basic business DSL line, at least in some areas, is priced identically to a basic personal DSL line.

While it may be difficult for the cable company to detect if you are using a VPN across its network, the very thought of an institution restricting your IP-based services should be a big red flag to any responsible information technology (IT) department. And besides, do you really want to depend on your local cable company for your business Internet access? Most people would not.

On the other hand, DSL companies point to cable's shared bandwidth as a glaring, potential security hole, and they have some valid points. For example, if you open up the Network Neighborhood on your local PC, you will see everyone's PC that is attached to the cable network in My Neighborhood.

However, some companies such as Cox cable are taking very effective actions to address these security concerns. For example, some ISPs have turned off all the IP ports that support Windows file sharing, and others are allowing customers to call and request that file-sharing ports be blocked on an individual basis. In addition, the next generation of cable modems will support the Data Over Cable Service Interface Specification (DOCSIS), which provides numerous security hooks and safeguards for data transmission.

Some Parting Shots   Both cable and ADSL services have their merits. Because competition is a good thing for consumers, let's hope that both technologies flourish and provide us with two reliable and low-cost options. However, until xDSL can iron out its installation issues and do something about its distance limitations, cable is clearly the better choice.

Nevertheless, the last thing you would want is for your ISP to start blocking ports and filtering your Internet connection. Besides, Windows file-sharing ports are far from being the only vulnerabilities that need protection.

For the "soccer mom" users out there, or for those who cannot yet get DSL in their area, cable modems are a good choice. However, many users have had too many problems with their cable company in the past to ever trust their high-speed Internet access to it.

Hybrid Fiber-Coax Systems

Hybrid fiber-coax (HFC) is a tough architecture to beat. It is economical, has a significant level of coverage in North America, and has ample bandwidth for the present and future services in demand. The coaxial cable used in HFC architectures can carry many times the information the telephone company's twisted-pair copper plant can transport.

Some of the largest telephone companies are buying their way into the technology by acquiring both large and small cable companies. It is important when looking at this industry to remember that there are more than 12,000 cable systems in the United States and that fewer than 7 percent of these systems have yet deployed high-speed Internet access. There are very substantial opportunities for bringing wireless broadband access to the vast remainder of the cable systems not included in the merger hysteria.

Fiber to the Home

When someone thinks about the best method to get the most bandwidth to the customer's premises, the obvious thought is to run fiber all the way there. This approach has various names, such as *fiber to the home* (FTTH), *fiber to the curb* (FTTC), *fiber to the building* (FTTB), *fiber to the neighborhood* (FTTN), and *fiber in the loop* (FITL). All these approaches have in common the use of fiber technologies to bring the bandwidth as close to the customer as possible. Nothing has contributed more to the reemergence of FITL than the fact that telephone companies can now use their existing copper plant to carry everything but analog video at distances that allow them great leeway in the use of fiber.

Satellite Systems

With their almost ubiquitous coverage, satellite systems can receive and transmit broadcast and multicast content to millions of subscribers. The systems scale to any number of broadcast/multicast receivers with no incremental system cost. The growing use of IP multicast standards as a way of transporting a variety of content types has helped move providers away from proprietary protocols to standards-based systems and ensures that users have less expensive and more flexible access.

Satellite communications offer a natural medium for transporting IP multicast. With advances in other related areas, it is now possible to carry all content—data, video, and audio—in a consistent manner. Furthermore, products exist on the market to support the reliable delivery of data files, high-quality video, and even stereo audio in an IP multicast environment.

With this in mind, let's now look at a simplified and integrated analysis of the key design issues in the use of Ku-band satellite capacity and small earth stations for high-speed low-latency Internet access. These design issues involve a variety of interconnected technical and economic choices affected by the cost of the earth stations and that of the satellite capacity required to support a single user or small groups of users. This part of the chapter analyzes the performance of very small aperture terminals (VSATs) for high-speed Internet access under a variety of multiple access architectures: SCPC/DAMA, CDMA, ALOHA, MAMA, and SAMA.

High-Speed Internet Access Using VSATs

The use of Ku-band satellite capacity and small earth stations for high-speed low-latency Internet access presents a number of interconnected technical and economic issues that generally are not appreciated. In this part of the chapter, a simplified integrated analysis of these issues is presented. From the analysis, one can draw two primary conclusions.

It is sometimes said that satellite capacity is too costly for use as a thin-route high-speed access technology for the Internet. The first conclusion of this part of the chapter is that it is possible to find technologies and system architectures that make Internet access by satellite and small earth stations uneconomical. It is recommended that you do not use these technologies and system architectures. The second conclusion is that it is possible to find technologies and system architectures that can provide high-speed low-latency shared access to the Internet for large numbers of users at a low cost. The system architecture and economics of these technologies are the primary focus of this part of the chapter.

Definition of the Problem: High-Speed Internet Access General-purpose corporate very small aperture terminal (VSAT) networks transmitting and receiving data from a large number of locations have been in operation since the 1970s. In 1998, about 60,000 two-way Ku-band VSATs were installed, and by the beginning of 1999, about 300,000 two-way VSATs were in operation throughout the world. Almost all these VSATs are designed primarily to provide data for private corporate networks, and almost all two-way data networks with more than 20 earth stations are based on some variation of an aloha protocol for access.

In an aloha multiple-access channel, packets are buffered at each VSAT and transmitted over a common channel to a hub station (see Figure 26-1).[1] No control is imposed on the channel in order to synchronize transmission from the various VSATs, so packets from different users will be transmitted with a high probability of success if there is a moderate amount of traffic on the network. As traffic on the network increases, the probability of a collision between packets from different users increases.

The reasons for the general use of an aloha-based protocol in two-way VSAT networks with large numbers of terminals are not difficult to see. For transaction-based traffic, which is the primary application in many large corporate networks, the bursty nature of the network traffic provides a good match to the capabilities of aloha multiple access.

However, the peak data rate of aloha channels used for VSAT networks rarely exceeds 64 kbps. This data rate may be adequate for the return channel of a single user connected to a VSAT-based aloha channel, but 64 kbps is not adequate to support a large number of users accessing the Internet over a common shared channel. And conventional aloha channels cannot be scaled easily to provide the high data rates required by Internet applications of today. This limitation of conventional aloha will be addressed in more detail later.

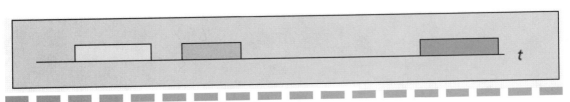

Figure 26-1 Packers in an ALOHA channel.

CLIENT-SERVER ARCHITECTURE   Almost all VSAT networks operate in a client-server configuration, with a group of VSAT terminals (the clients) transmitting on one or more multiple-access channels to the hub station (the server) and the hub station transmitting on a shared wideband broadcast channel to the VSAT terminals (see Figure 26-2). [2]

There are compelling link-budget reasons for this configuration. By requiring all traffic in the satellite-based part of the network to either originate or terminate in the large hub station, it is possible to decrease the size and cost of the VSATs in the network. A client-server configuration means that any intranetwork traffic from one terminal to another must traverse a two-hop path to the hub station and back again. Since most of the traffic in these networks is directed to or from the hub station, this limitation is not a problem, especially for the Internet applications of interest in this chapter.

Two-way interactive data networks involve much more than the combination of two one-way channels. The two directions of communication flow in the channels of a two-way VSAT network with a client-server configuration involve two fundamentally different forms of communication. In the direction from the hub to the terminals, the communication channel is one to many, or a broadcast channel. In the direction from the terminals to the hub, the communication channel is many to one, or a multiple-access channel.

Transmitting data from a single hub station to a large number of remote terminals (the broadcast channel) is a relatively simple problem. This channel architecture is almost always configured in a simple time-division multiplexed (TDM) mode. Furthermore, during 1998, the adoption of the European Telecommunications Standards Institute (ETSI) Direct Video Broadcast (DVB)/MPEG-2 standard encouraged the development of a variety of TDM-based transmitting and receiving equipment for the

Figure 26-2

Client-server configuration of a VSAT network.

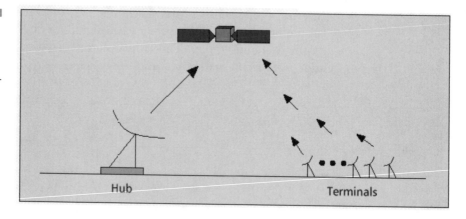

high-speed digital broadcast channel. The consequence of this development is discussed in more detail later.

Transmitting data from large numbers of remote terminals to a single hub (the multiple-access channel) is a much more challenging problem. The multiple-access problem for VSAT access to the Internet is the primary technology focus of this chapter.

SME MARKET (ILUS AND ALUS) High-speed low-latency access to the Internet for those users who can be aggregated within a single building in large enough numbers is usually not a problem. For these users, the connection to the Internet can be provided by a dedicated shared high-speed channel. The sharing of a high-speed channel among 100 or more users at a single location can bring the cost per month per user down to reasonable levels. And even in those parts of the world where an adequate terrestrial telecommunications infrastructure is not available, a dedicated high-speed data channel usually can be provided using a dedicated satellite channel. Of course, in some parts of the world, a high-speed (terrestrial or satellite) connection shared among large numbers of users is not easily available at a reasonable cost. A common symptom of this problem is a lower grade of service to these users as a result of inadequate sizing of the connection to the Internet.

At the other end of the spectrum, high-speed low-latency shared access to the Internet for a small number of users or even for a single user is available in an increasing portion of the metropolitan and suburban United States by means of both ADSL and cable modems. Where these options exist, no one expects VSAT access to the Internet to be competitive.

In both cases of users connected to the Internet by means of a dedicated shared high-speed channel and users connected by ADSL or cable modems, the primary limitations on system performance are those limitations provided by the Internet itself. The limitations of Internet trunk lines, Internet switches, and Internet servers will limit the grade of service to the user, and there is little to be gained by improving Internet access for such users. Let's refer to such users as *Internet-limited users* (ILUs), whereas all other users are referred to as *access-limited users* (ALUs).

The market of ALUs, composed of individuals and small groups (say, 2 to 30) with a requirement for high-speed low-latency Internet access, is both unserved and underserved today. The market of ALUs includes both the small-office, home-office (SOHO) and small- and medium-enterprise (SME) markets. This market is a natural market for two-way VSAT Internet access, and its technology and economics are the concern of the rest of this chapter.

Key Areas: Traffic Characterization   It is generally understood that traffic on the Internet differs greatly from conventional voice traffic and other forms of digital traffic in a number of ways. Furthermore, the properties of Internet traffic will depend on the population being measured, the applications available to users, and even the characteristics of the network over which the traffic flows. Because of these factors, it is difficult to characterize the statistics of Internet traffic with any precision in order to evaluate the performance of any given network architecture for Internet access. In particular, the fact that user traffic depends on the performance of the network means that there is an ongoing interaction between the statistics of user traffic, the network performance, and users' perception of network performance. Nevertheless, it is necessary to make some general assumptions about average user traffic in order to begin the process of network access design. In this part of this chapter, these assumptions are explained.

Since there is an interest in the industry in providing high-speed low-latency access by VSAT, one can assume traffic values typical of networks where the primary limitation on performance is determined by the Internet rather than by the access network. That is, let's assume traffic values typical of the ILUs. The goal of satellite Internet access design is to provide a service to ALUs that will transform each ALU into an ILU.

Since the amount of traffic in the broadcast channel typically is much greater than the amount of traffic in the multiple-access channel, it is convenient to first characterize the average amount of traffic per user per day in the broadcast channel. Without trying to be too precise on this number, let's take the value of 2 Mbytes per day per user as typical of the traffic to the user in the networks of interest. Certainly, there will be users who receive much more than 2 Mbytes per day, and there are days when almost any user of the Internet will receive more than this value. Nevertheless, let's take this number as a reasonable guide to the average amount of traffic delivered to a typical user over a long period of time.

In order to specify the average traffic in the multiple-access channel, let's assume a value for the asymmetry of the access network, i.e., a value for the ratio of the average amount of data sent in the broadcast channel to the average amount of data sent in the multiple-access channel. Again, this number is subject to a great deal of uncertainty and variation among different users as well as over time with a single user. However, with the same level of confidence and precision with which one assumes the average broadcast channel traffic in the preceding paragraph, one can assume the asymmetry of typical Web and email traffic to be about 6 to 1.

The characterization of the average traffic in the multiple-access channel and the asymmetry of the traffic in the two channels provides a necessary but incomplete description of the network traffic. The traffic in both channels, of course, is bursty, but the bursty nature of the traffic in the broadcast channel is not a critical factor in determining the performance of that channel. Since the broadcast channel provides a one-to-many communication link, the bursty nature of the traffic in the broadcast channel is smoothed by buffering in the hub transmitter. In the many-to-one multiple-access channel, however, the bursty nature of the traffic flow is smoothed to a much more limited degree.

CONNECTED ACCESS AND CONNECTION-FREE ACCESS The growth of the Internet as an efficient and effective tool for information retrieval is based on the shared utilization of high-capacity information resources. On the Internet, servers are shared, switches are shared, and the Internet backbone is shared among large numbers of users. In the case of ILUs, access to the Internet is also shared, and the sharing process makes possible high-speed access at a reasonable shared cost. By extending the sharing of resources from the Internet to the ALUs, it is possible to provide the same level of high-performance, yet affordable service to these users.

For ALUs, which are the focus of this part of the chapter, it is necessary to find a sharing mechanism for bursty Internet traffic that will permit the high-speed access required for the Internet applications of today. At the same time, such a sharing mechanism for access must use the satellite transponder resource in an efficient manner because it is expensive.

These considerations lead to the conclusion that high-quality access to the Internet for the ALUs of interest in this part of the chapter requires a connection-free wideband access architecture. A connection-free architecture for the multiple-access channel completely eliminates any connection-related overhead in the multiple-access channel. At the same time, a connection-free wideband architecture eliminates any latency caused by the connection process.

Eliminating the inefficiencies generated by a connection-oriented architecture in the presence of bursty traffic is an obvious advantage of connection-free operation. Another less obvious advantage of wideband connection-free operation of the multiple-access channel is the scalability and fungible nature of data flow in such a channel.

When a connection-oriented architecture is used, the question arises as to how large to make the connections or channels assigned in the network. If the connections established are at a low data rate, the transmission of data in the channels assigned may be too slow, whereas if the connections are established at a high data rate, utilization of the satellite resource may not be efficient. Some reasonable compromise must be made, but this *one-*

size-fits-all approach can lead to further inefficiencies when the channel traffic does not fit the choice made.

In a connection-free architecture, the data flowing within the channel are fungible. Thus, for a wideband connection-free channel with a throughput of 1 Mbps, the traffic can be provided by 10 users each with an average data rate of 100,000 bps, by 100 users each with an average data rate of 10,000 bps, by 100,000 users each with an average data rate of 10 bps, or by any combination of users as long as the aggregate average data rate does not exceed the maximum throughput of 1 Mbps. The value of this flexibility for the case of Internet traffic is important precisely because of the unknown nature of the traffic in this rapidly changing medium. It is difficult to specify the nature of the Internet traffic of today. The specification of the Internet traffic of tomorrow is much more speculative, so a scalable, fungible architecture insensitive to arbitrary traffic assumptions is highly desirable.

PROTOCOLS   When the communications channel resource is a limiting cost factor in system design, it is necessary to examine the suitability of how that resource is used. In the case of satellite channels used for Internet access, a major component of this use is the transmission of protocol information within the satellite channels. Of course, some protocol information is absolutely necessary for proper functioning of the communications path. In the case of Internet traffic, however, based in large part on the TCP/IP protocols designed in the 1970s, the time has come to reexamine the suitability of those protocols. This reexamination should consider the possibility of enhancing TCP to take into account the properties of the satellite channel and transparent methods of bypassing some of the most wasteful features of TCP.

Such a reexamination has been started by a working group of the Internet Engineering Task Force (IETF), and a working document describing ongoing TCP research related to satellites is available on the Web. Among the TCP modifications considered by the IETF working group, as well as other groups, are TCP header compression, data compression, modification of the TCP slow-start algorithm, and a variety of acknowledgment strategies bypassing existing TCP strategies.

TCP originally was designed with the goal of providing *robustness in the presence of communications unreliability and availability in the presence of congestion.* In the early days of the Internet, communications channels were almost always symmetric, so the addition of large amounts of TCP-generated overhead in the lightly loaded channel from the end user imposed little penalty on system performance. When the channels are not symmetric, however, and the capacity of the channel from the user is the critical resource, one must reexamine the effectiveness of transmitting this overhead.

In a multiple-access channel that includes a contention protocol, such as aloha or Spread aloha, the transmission of excessive overhead in the multiple-access channel will be self-defeating. In these channels, the overhead added will increase the contention traffic in the channel and decrease the probability that a given packet will be received correctly. In the case of aloha or Spread aloha, the addition of overhead not only will decrease the useful throughput of the channel but also will decrease the reliability of the channel because channel reliability decreases as the traffic on the channel is increased.

When transparent proxies are used to reduce the excess overhead generated by TCP for the multiple-access channel, the traffic asymmetry assumptions discussed earlier must be reexamined. Although such proxies will reduce the amount of data transmitted in both directions, the reduction will be proportionally greater in the multiple-access direction than in the broadcast direction. Simplified proxies of the sort available in 2001 can increase this asymmetry from 6 to 1 to 15 to 1. And examination of the basic form of the data transmitted in typical Internet applications indicates that a ratio of 150 to 1 can be achieved. When multiple-access-channel capacity is an expensive resource, as in VSAT Internet access applications, these efficiencies assume an importance in overall system design.

NOTE There are certain situations where satellite communications have important operational advantages over conventional terrestrial communications for Internet traffic.

Whenever a significant amount of traffic is broadcast or multicast from a central location, the broadcast physical medium of the satellite channel can introduce major efficiencies. In these situations, the satellite broadcast channel can deliver large amounts of data to an unlimited number of terminals with a single broadcast transmission. In addition to various forms of Internet radio and video transmissions, this capability is of value for the distribution of Internet caching information. And the enhanced caching capabilities made possible by satellite access can serve to decrease the user traffic requirements on the satellite access channel.

Economics of Satellite Access: The Broadcast Channel In 1998, the adoption of the ETSI DVB/MPEG-2 standard encouraged the development of TDM-based transmitting equipment and chips for the high-speed digital broadcast channel. The consequence of this development is that a variety of chips are now available that implement the receiver portion of the remote terminal. And since these chips are used in the large market for receive-only digital video transmission, the cost of the digital broadcast channel receiver (operating at data rates up to 90 Mbps) in two-way VSAT networks has been reduced to less than $40. Thus the cost of the equipment required to provide high-speed satellite access to a VSAT broadcast channel is now low enough that this equipment can be marketed to the single-user home market. And the existence of service offerings such as the Hughes DirecPC and equipment such as the receive-only satellite data boards sold by Broadlogic show that this market is now limited only by the lack of a multiple-access return channel.

Since the one-time equipment cost of the broadcast channel is now so low, the primary cost of providing VSAT Internet access to the user is the cost of the shared satellite channel itself. To calculate this cost, let's make the conservative assumption that the satellite broadcast channel is operated at a data rate of 30 Mbps. Then one can estimate the cost of satellite resources in the broadcast channel for a single user by using the traffic estimate of 2 Mbytes per user per day discussed earlier. Let's make the additional conservative assumption that all this traffic is transmitted within a 10-h business day interval, allowing only minimal use of the time zone shifting made possible by satellite footprints extending over multiple time zones. A fully loaded 30-Mbps DVB channel during this 10-h business day has room for

$$\frac{10 \times 60 \times 60 \times 30 \times 10^6}{2 \times 8 \times 10^6} = 67{,}500 \text{ users}$$

By taking advantage of packet buffering in the hub station made possible by the broadcast architecture, it is estimated that such a channel can be operated at a loading factor of 60 percent in the broadcast channel without significant impact on the QoS to individual users. This gives a capacity of about 40,000 users in a single satellite transponder.

The cost in today's market for a Ku-band satellite transponder capable of supporting the 30 Mbps that were assumed to be into a small (less than 1 m in diameter) earth station is about $200,000 per month. Thus the cost in transponder time for the broadcast channel is about $5 per month per user.

NOTE   This estimate is consistent with the pricing data available at the end of 1999 for the Hughes DirecPC service.

The price of this service ranges from about $20 to $35 per month per user for residential users and about $110 per month per user for business users. DirecPC uses the same architecture for the satellite broadcast channel to the user, although the satellite communications services (see the sidebar, "They're Back!—Iridium Signs Satellite Communications Services Contract with DOD") must rely on a dialup telephone line for the return channel from the user. Thus, DirecPC users can be characterized as ALUs, and one would expect the broadcast channel traffic of this service to be less than that of the ILUs of interest in this part of the chapter.

They're Back!—Iridium Signs Satellite Communications Services Contract with DOD

"Rumors of Iridium's death have been greatly exaggerated" (to paraphrase Mark Twain—alias Samuel Clemens). Update! Update! The Department of Defense (DOD), through its Defense Information Systems Agency, recently awarded Iridium Satellite LLC of Arnold, MD, a $72 million contract for 24 months of satellite communications services. This contract would provide unlimited airtime for 20,000 government users over the Iridium satellite network. The contract includes options which, if exercised, would bring the cumulative value of this contract to $252 million and extend the period of performance to December 2007.

The DOD has taken this action because the Iridium system offers state-of-the-art technology. It features on-satellite signal processing and intersatellite crosslinks allowing satellite-mode service to any open area on earth. It provides mobile, cryptographically secure telephone services to small handsets anywhere on the globe, pole-to-pole, 24 hours a day. The system and its DOD enhancements will provide handheld service currently not available.

Since the Navy has a requirement more than twice as large as the current capability, the DOD needs the capacity Iridium uniquely offers: small-unit operations in areas without satellite constellation coverage or during periods when various assets are being used in other contingencies. Special Forces operations, combat search and rescue activities, and polar communications also will be enhanced. Iridium will provide a unique resource to enhance DOD mobile satellite communications requirements.

Iridium not only will add to DOD's existing capability, but it also will provide a commercial alternative to its purely military systems. This may enable real civil/military dual use, keep DOD closer to the leading-edge technologically, and provide a real alternative for the future.

Iridium Satellite LLC is now purchasing the operating assets of Iridium LLC and its existing subsidiaries, pursuant to a November 22, 2000 order of the U.S. Bankruptcy Court for the Southern District of New York. Under the agreement, Iridium Satellite LLC will purchase all the existing assets of Iridium LLC, including its constellation of low-orbiting satellites and its satellite control network, and will have Boeing operate the system. The new bulk-rate service agreement offered and accepted by the DOD stands to provide the same critical augmentation capability at substantially cheaper rates.

Early in 2002, Iridium will offer a classified capability. Classified service not only will be provided for users already registered to the DOD gateway but also will be extended to new users from DOD, other federal agencies, and selected allied governments.

Since the cost of both the end-user equipment and the monthly cost per user of the shared satellite broadcast channel is so low, let's turn our attention to the cost per user of the satellite multiple-access channel.

THE MULTIPLE-ACCESS CHANNEL   In order to provide two-way satellite access to the Internet, it is necessary to complement the broadcast access described in the preceding with a multiple-access return capability. In this part of the chapter, the various architectures for VSAT-based Internet multiple-access capability are described.

SCPC (FIXED ASSIGNMENT)   Single-channel-per-carrier (SCPC) operation of a two-way satellite earth station is perhaps the most common mode of operation for VSATs. Indeed, approximately 150 such VSATs are used by high schools in Alaska for two-way Internet access today, although the cost per user of this configuration is extremely high.

In an SCPC architecture, a separate carrier is allocated to a given channel, and that channel is assigned on a fixed or on-demand basis to a given earth station. This part of the chapter will deal with fixed-assignment SCPC, and the next part will deal with demand assignment. The size of an SCPC channel is most often that of a 64-kbps voice channel, but this is not necessary for an SCPC-based architecture.

A single satellite transponder can be partitioned into about 400 64-kbps SCPC channels, so using the figure of $200,000 per month per transponder, the cost of an SCPC channel is about $500 per month per terminal for the multiple-access channel. Of course, each SCPC terminal can be shared among multiple users at the VSAT site in order to bring the cost per user down to a more reasonable level. There is a good deal of uncertainty in how many users can reasonably share a 64-kbps SCPC channel, but it appears that depending on the nature of the user community, a maximum of about 50 users is a generous estimate for ILUs. Above this number, the QoS for the user will deteriorate.

At 50 users per earth station, the cost of the multiple-access channel is about $10 per user per month. This figure is twice the $5 per user per month that is an estimate for the broadcast channel, but it is not prohibitive. The problem is that in order to achieve this figure in a network, it is necessary for each VSAT in the network to serve exactly 50 users. If fewer than 50 users are served by a given earth station, the cost per user will rise accordingly, whereas if more than 50 users try to share a given earth station, the quality of the Internet connection will deteriorate. Under the assumptions given in the preceding, C, the total cost of satellite resources per user per month, can be calculated as the sum of the cost of the broadcast channel and the multiple-access channel. This cost will be a function of n, the number of users sharing a single earth station in the multiple access direction.

$$C = 5 + \frac{500}{n} \text{ dollars per user per month}$$

Figure 26-3 sketches an estimate of the cost of satellite resources per user per month—indicating a soft limit on the number of users per VSAT.[3] From Figure 26-3 we see that if only 10 users share an SCPC channel, the cost of the satellite resources to support a single user increases to about $55 per month. In addition to the cost of the satellite resources, it is necessary to factor in the cost of the end-user equipment shared among all the users at a given earth station.

VSAT Internet access using an SCPC fixed-assignment architecture is a reasonable alternative for networks composed of clusters of users approaching 50 at a single location. However, the cost of this configuration is highly sensitive to variations in the number of users at the earth station location, so if the number of users sharing a single earth station is not close to 50, the cost per user rises rapidly (too few users) or the QoS degrades to an unacceptable level (too many users). The size of the user

Figure 26-3
The cost of SCPC
satellite resources
per user per month
(US$).

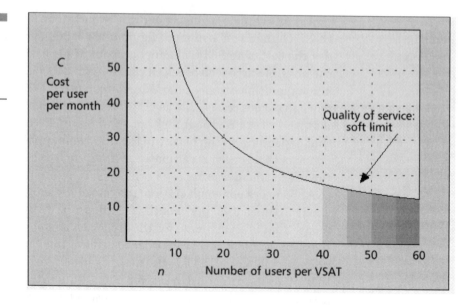

cluster required to make SCPC VSAT Internet access practical means that the antenna for these VSATs is usually 1.2 m or more in diameter. And the earth station configuration for these larger-diameter systems tends to be at the upper end of VSATs in both cost and performance.

SCPC/DAMA In the case of SCPC channels used for voice or file-transfer applications, the addition of a demand-assigned multiple-access (DAMA) capability can significantly decrease the cost of the satellite resource for an individual user. For these applications, the multiple access SCPC channel is used for significant periods of time (say 1 minute or more) by a single user. Under these conditions, the requirement of a setup time on the order of seconds is consistent with the scale of the data transmitted on the SCPC channel.

In the case of a cluster of users generating Internet traffic, however, the addition of a DAMA capability will not significantly decrease the cost of the satellite resources used for multiple access. With as many as 50 users sharing one multiple-access channel, there is little to be gained by assigning the channel on demand. The problem for this shared-multiple-access channel is similar to that of a single user employing a connection-oriented protocol, as discussed earlier. If the assignment of the channel is done on a burst-by-burst basis, the overhead and latency introduced by the assignment process are too large, whereas if the assignment is done on a session-by-session basis, the resources of the satellite channel are wasted for large intervals of time during the assignment. The situation here is even worse than that of a connection setup for a single user because sessions by different users will in general overlap at the VSAT.

aloha   In the case of both fixed-assignment and DAMA SCPC VSATs for Internet access, the basic problem is that the cost of a satellite channel dedicated to the traffic generated at a single earth station is too high. When this cost can be shared among enough users to bring the cost per user down (see Figure 26-3), SCPC-based access to the Internet can be practical. However, the requirement that the number of users at each earth station in the network be contained in some narrow band of acceptable values restricts the kind of networks that can employ SCPC for Internet access.

In order to justify the use of the high-cost resources of the satellite channel, it is necessary to find a flexible method of sharing a single channel among large numbers of users at several locations rather than at a single location. And it is necessary for this method of sharing to work well with a wide variation in the number of users sharing a single earth station. Conventional aloha channels provide the capability for this kind of sharing, but conventional (slotted or unslotted) aloha channels are limited to narrowband operation. Figure 26-4 illustrates three packets in a conventional narrowband aloha channel.[4]

There is no theoretical reason why the bandwidth of this channel cannot be increased in order to decrease the time to transmit a single packet and thus increase the total number of packets transmitted in the channel. However, if the time per bit is decreased, it is necessary to increase the instantaneous power of the transmitter to keep the energy per bit constant.

Safety and cost constraints on the instantaneous power output of a VSAT transmitter impose a practical limit (see Figure 26-4*b*) on the data

Figure 26-4

(a) Packets in a narrowband aloha channel; (b) packets in a wireless broadband aloha channel.

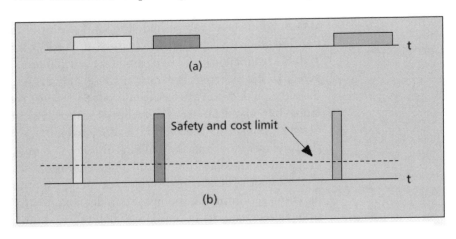

rate of an aloha channel that can be achieved from a VSAT. In practice, most aloha channels in Ku-band VSAT networks are limited to a peak data rate of about 64 kbps by these considerations.

A data rate of 64 kbps is not enough to support networks with the large numbers of users of interest in this part of the chapter. In the next part of the chapter, a discussion is presented on the use of multiple narrowband aloha channels within the same network in order to provide Internet access to large numbers of users.

NOTE   The use of an aloha protocol allows the sharing of a single channel by enough users that the cost of the satellite resources for multiple access can be decreased. Unlike the case of a shared SCPC channel, the cost per user of the satellite resources for multiple access in an aloha channel is independent of the number of users who share a common earth station. In an aloha channel, the cost per user depends on the total number of users at all earth stations sharing the same aloha channel.

If one uses the same numbers employed to evaluate the SCPC channel (a cost of about $500 per month per 64-kbps channel and about 50 users per channel), the cost of the multiple-access satellite resources necessary to support a single user is about $10 per user per month. Furthermore, as far as the cost of satellite resources is concerned, this figure is independent of the exact number of users at each earth station. Even the extreme case of a single user at each earth station imposes no additional cost on the network.

Of course, with only a single user, or a small number of users, at an earth station, the equipment cost of the earth station becomes a major system cost determinant. And this constraint leads to a requirement for small-dish-diameter low-cost earth stations in a network employing an aloha protocol for VSAT access to the Internet.

MAMA   aloha channels provide the kind of connection-free resource sharing that allows variable-size clusters of users at large numbers of earth stations to efficiently share a common multiple-access channel for low-cost access to the Internet. However, a single aloha channel ordinarily will not have the peak data rate or throughput to support the traffic generated by more than about 50 users distributed arbitrarily among some number of earth stations. It is therefore necessary to examine methods of increasing the total network capacity while retaining the connection-free architecture provided by the operation of the aloha channel.

Perhaps the most direct method of increasing the total network capacity while retaining the aloha system design advantages is to employ multiple aloha channels in an FDMA/aloha format for users within the same

Figure 26-5

A multiple-aloha multiple-access transponder.

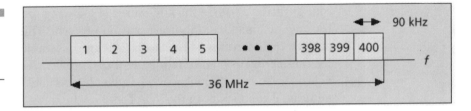

network (see Figure 26-5).[5] This option has been given the descriptive (if unduly maternal) acronym of MAMA (multiple-aloha multiple-access).

In a MAMA hub station, it is necessary to provide a separate receiver for each aloha channel. Using the number of 50 users per aloha channel for Internet traffic, one obtains the figure of 800 separate aloha receivers operating in the band covered by two separate 36-MHz transponders to service the 40,000 users supported by a single broadcast channel in a single transponder.

From a purely theoretical point of view, an architecture such as MAMA, which limits each user's power to a subband of frequencies, rather than the total available frequency band, will have lower capacity than if each user is allowed to use the total frequency band. This is true even if one ignores the guard bands used to separate multiple aloha channels at different frequencies. However, the primary disadvantage of a MAMA architecture is a practical, not theoretical, limitation.

As noted earlier in this chapter, the ability of an aloha-based architecture to provide efficient multiple-access capabilities for earth stations serving a small number of users, or even a single user, means that it is important to design low-cost earth stations with small (say, less than 1 m) dish diameters for use in such a network. Establishing adequate frequency stability in such a network composed of up to 400 narrowband FDMA/aloha channels in a single 36-MHz transponder is not an easy task for low-cost earth stations. Indeed, even in more costly VSATs in operation today, the 90-kHz carrier separation required is less than half the carrier separation commonly used. And any increase in required carrier separation will translate directly into higher cost per channel because fewer aloha channels will be accommodated in a single transponder.

An additional improvement over simply assigning individual users to a fixed aloha channel is to provide frequency agility at each individual earth station transmitter and select a transmission frequency at random on a packet-by-packet basis. This has the advantage of improved queuing efficiency to handle peak loads in a given channel at the cost of some hardware complexity: frequency agility at the VSAT. A frequency-agile MAMA configuration also has the advantage of allowing the transmission of long files by means of an aloha reservation protocol. This version of a MAMA architecture can provide a factor of 2 improvement in throughput over fixed-assignment MAMA (equivalent to increasing the number of Internet users served by a single narrowband aloha channel to about 100), but the additional complexity in the VSAT makes the target of low-cost earth stations even more difficult to achieve.

An even more serious limitation on the economical use of MAMA channels for VSAT Internet traffic is the size of the required antenna. The intersatellite interference at a 2-s satellite separation caused by the transmissions from multiple narrowband aloha channels is close to the allowable margin using a 1.2-m VSAT antenna. But the radiofrequency (rf) transmitter and antenna make up the major cost components of a VSAT using any kind of aloha multiple access. This means that the important cost savings available from the use of less than 1-m antennas may not be available if narrowband aloha, MAMA, or indeed any narrowband access technique is employed in the network. Because of these difficulties in implementing low-cost VSATs employing sub-1-m antennas in narrowband architectures, let's turn our attention to network architectures based on wideband access methods.

CDMA Code-division multiple access (CDMA) is a wideband multiple-access technique based on the separation of signals from different transmitters by the use of a different spreading code in each spread-spectrum transmitter. An immediate consequence of this coding separation is that a separate receiver tuned to each spreading code is required in the CDMA hub station for each possible transmitter in the network. Clearly, if the total number of potential data terminals in the network is much larger than the number of active terminals at any given time, this requirement can introduce considerable complexity into the design of a CDMA system.

Only two significant commercial CDMA networks had been put into operation by the end of 1999. The design of each of these two networks addressed the problem posed by the requirement of a separate receiver for each possible transmitter in a CDMA network in a different way. In the C-200 VSAT network implemented by Equatorial Communications, a separate receiver for every potential transmitter was in fact implemented. This connection-free architecture worked well for a small number of transmitters, but as the number of VSATs in the network increased, it became clear that the logistics of installing and maintaining a separate piece of hardware at the hub station for each user was not practical in a connection-free data network. The C-200 network is no longer in operation.

The second significant commercial CDMA network put into operation is the digital cellular voice standard designed by Qualcomm. In order to deal with the problem of multiple receivers, the CDMA digital cellular standard does not in fact implement a connection-free digital network but a form of on-demand connection-oriented network architecture where a fixed number (64) of code-agile receivers in the hub station are assigned on demand. The requests for channel access in the Qualcomm implementation system are transmitted on a separate low-data-rate aloha channel.

The spread-spectrum format of a CDMA signal provides considerable protection against the intersatellite interference problem that limits how small an antenna can be used in narrowband systems. However, the use of a connection-oriented digital cellular form of CDMA is a problem for VSAT Internet traffic. The connected architecture of this digital cellular standard is not a problem for the voice traffic of interest in cellular networks, where a 3- to 10-s setup time is not unreasonable for a 3-minute voice conversation. In the case of VSAT Internet traffic, however, the connection-oriented architecture of this form of CDMA leads to the operational difficulties and inefficiencies discussed earlier. Neither form of CDMA seems to provide a practical candidate for the operation of a wideband connection-free service suitable for a network composed of large numbers of low-cost VSATs providing access to the Internet.

SAMA Spread aloha multiple access (SAMA) is an advanced multiple-access technology that can provide the wideband connection-free multiple-access capabilities required for digital networks with very large numbers of remote terminals. SAMA combines the proven simplicity and operational flexibility of a connection-free aloha multiple-access channel with the high bandwidth of a spread-spectrum CDMA channel.

SAMA can be viewed as a version of CDMA that uses a common code for all remote transmitters in the multiple-access channel. In a SAMA channel, different users are separated by a random timing mechanism, as in a conventional aloha channel, rather than by different codes. Since only a single code is used in a SAMA channel, only a single receiver is required in the SAMA hub station rather than a separate receiver for each remote terminal, as required in CDMA. Furthermore, the use of a common code for all VSATs in the network removes the requirement for code agility in the user's terminal, further simplifying the implementation of SAMA VSATs.

The first spread aloha channel was built at the ALOHA Networks laboratory in San Francisco in early 1998. This channel operated with a spreading gain of 31 at an aggregate data rate of 2 Mbps over a 3-MHz channel. The maximum throughput of this channel is realized when the average traffic value (the average number of simultaneous transmitters) is equal to 15.5. As in the case of a conventional aloha channel, the spread aloha channel operates at a peak data rate of about 0.10 Mbps (corresponding to an average throughput of 200,000 bps). This corresponds to a value of G/r (channel traffic divided by spreading gain) of about 0.13, or about four simultaneous users in the channel with a spreading gain of 31 dB.

Spread aloha provides a wideband capability in the multiple-access channel that is essential for a network of low-cost terminals capable of serving large numbers of users at a reasonable cost. Because of the common code used in a SAMA architecture, both the SAMA hub and, more important, the large number of SAMA VSATs require none of the complexity introduced by code agility and code management. Frequency stability in one or a smaller number of wideband spread aloha channel(s) sharing a single transponder is much easier to achieve than the frequency stability required for up to 400 narrowband channels. And a spreading factor of 31 dB, such as used in the aloha Networks implementation of SAMA, provides an additional 14 dB of isolation for the intersatellite interference caused by the use of earth stations with diameters less than 1 m.

The 2-Mbps SAMA channel built by ALOHA Networks is equivalent in throughput to 31 separate narrowband aloha channels operating in the random frequency-agile MAMA mode described earlier. Each SAMA channel is capable of supporting the multiple-access Internet traffic of 31×100, or 3100, users without the use of the transparent proxies discussed earlier. Since the bandwidth of the SAMA channel is 3 MHz, one can support a total of 12 such channels in a single transponder, or about the same number of users (40,000) supported by a broadcast channel, also using a single transponder. Using these figures, one can estimate the cost of satellite resources to support a single Internet user as about $5 per month for the broadcast traffic, and $5 per month for the multiple-access traffic. If transparent proxies can be used to increase the asymmetry of the traffic flow to around 150 to 1, a single 2-Mbps SAMA channel could support about 40,000 users, and the cost of the satellite resources required for the multiple-access channel would decrease to about $.50 per user per month.

In addition to simplifying the design of VSAT terminals, the use of a common code provides an interesting operational advantage in combating the mutual interference of multiple transmitters in a SAMA network. In both CDMA networks discussed earlier, the use of code division presents a problem in the design of a family of spreading codes for spread-spectrum operation. In each system, the problem is solved by choosing the spreading codes at random. In a SAMA network, however, it is not necessary to find a family of spreading codes with a separate code for each transmitter. It is only necessary to find a single spreading code to be shared by all users. This problem is much easier to solve, and indeed, the performance of any specific code can be compared easily with the performance of the kind of random codes used by most CDMA architectures.

ALOHA Networks has developed tools to quickly evaluate the performance of any given spreading code. These tools were applied to large numbers of candidate spreading codes with spreading gain equal to $2k - 1$ for integer values of k from 2 to 11.

For these spreading codes, you should be able to evaluate the signal-to-interference ratio of a single user in the SAMA channel and compare this value with the equivalent signal-to-interference ratio in a CDMA network using random spreading codes (see Figure 26-6).[6] The signal-to-interference ratio of the SAMA codes is found to be that of CDMA, as shown in Figure 26-6. For the large values of spreading gain that have been investigated (up to a maximum of length 2047), the SAMA codes have been found to provide an improvement of 5.35 dB over CDMA. For the spreading codes implemented in the SAMA system built by ALOHA Networks, this improvement is 7.09 dB, or a factor of 5 over CDMA in the number of SAMA transmitters that can share a given wireless broadband multiple-access channel. This result means that in the important mutual interfer-

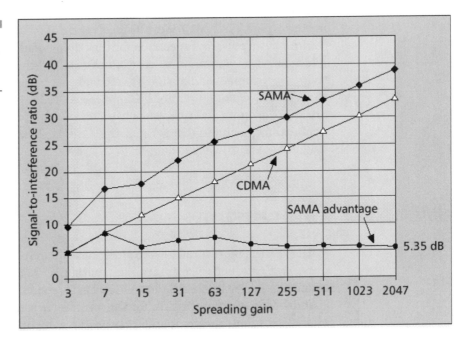

Figure 26-6

The signal-to-interference ratio of SAMA and CDMA.

ence-limited case, a SAMA channel can accommodate five times as many users as the equivalent CDMA channel.

Wireless Broadband

Finally, fixed broadband wireless technology seems ideal for solving the last-mile access bottleneck. The various wireless broadband spectrums being developed support almost any kind of access service a customer may need: voice, video, Internet, ATM, Frame Relay, or traditional T-1 services. Wireless broadband providers can provision service in days rather than the weeks or months it can take traditional wireline carriers to get a service up and running. And the cost comparison with wireline is not even close. In most cases, a point-to-multipoint wireless broadband connection costs less than one-tenth what it would cost to run wire to the same site.

Although line-of-sight (LOS) clearance is required for wireless broadband technologies to operate properly, new technology advances and substantial use of spectrum engineering systems are lessening the effects of this potential limitation. Another frequently cited problem is rain fade (or attenuation). The signal attenuation caused by rain and climate varies greatly by region, but equipment advances are enabling service providers to make it less of an issue.

Wireless broadband operators are just now realizing how powerful their medium is. AT&T, MCI/WorldCom, NextLink, WinStar, Teligent, and Sprint have all secured spectrum for the deployment of advanced point-to-multipoint systems as a low-cost, quick way to bring high-speed connectivity to consumers and businesses. To make things even more interesting, the Federal Communications Commission (FCC) also has begun the process of opening additional spectrum bands for fixed wireless broadband applications, including 25 MHz at the 4.6-GHz level and a huge block of 1.4 GHz at the 40-GHz level.

Conclusion

With even the most humble Web sites these days sporting drawings, banners, and interactive graphics, and with new Web development tools promising more multimedia in the future, there is expected to be a major rush by consumers to sign up for the wireless broadband access services offered by telephone companies and cable companies, according to the information presented in this chapter. This chapter claims that house-holds that have signed up for Internet access at speeds near or above 1.5 Mbps will grow from approximately 3.8 million at the present time to 53.9 million by 2005. Multimedia is expected to spur this growth because where, just a few years ago, the average file transfer from the Web was about 4 kB, today it is 17 times that amount, rendering traditional dialup service increasingly inadequate.

NOTE   The multimedia trend is likely to accelerate as multimedia on the Web becomes better in quality and Web-based entertainment increasingly competes with television entertainment. This chapter has envisioned such developments as online fashion shows with interactivity and e-commerce capabilities and online multimedia trade shows that would enable tele-workers to remain in their homes while learning about the latest develop-ments of their field.

Such developments clearly will require higher data rates to the home to make them effective. This chapter also examined the prospects for xDSL, cable modems, wireless broadband, and satellite—the main technologies that will be able to provide these higher data rates to the residential envi-ronment.

While some of the telcos continue to announce unrealistically optimistic plans for xDSL, this technology should at last start to come into its own in the year 2001. This is so because the new G.Lite standards (which are backed by such giants as Intel, Microsoft, Compaq, Cisco, Ericsson, Lucent, Nortel, and Siemens) provide an entry-level version of xDSL, while emerg-ing VDSL technology provides a migration strategy to the very high speeds that will be required by consumers in the not-too-distant future. The entire market for xDSL products and services will be worth approximately $32.6 billion by 2005, compared with $252 million in 1999.

This chapter also claims that the standardization of cable modems led by CableLabs should help make cable modems a familiar domestic appli-ance within a few years. As a result, the market for cable modem products and services will be worth approximately $10.8 billion by 2005, compared with $860 million in 1999, with most of the cable modems offering two-way service. For some years to come, cable modems and xDSL are expected to account for the bulk of wireless broadband residential access. However, there is some hope for wireless broadband access over satellite and wire-less broadband infrastructures.

This chapter says that two-way wireless broadband satellites still lie some way off in the future as residential access platforms, but the low infrastructure cost coupled with the ability to rapidly deploy this infrastructure could make wireless broadband technology the obvious choice for the many users who will not have cable modems or xDSL available to them for many years. MCI/WorldCom's acquisition of CAI Wireless and Sprint's acquisition of American Telecasting and Peoples Choice TV have vindicated MMDS as a residential access medium. And although most LMDS providers are currently targeting larger businesses, they ultimately may refocus on residential access.

Finally, the use of Ku-band satellite capacity and small earth stations for high-speed low-latency Internet access can be achieved using low-cost VSATs with dish diameters less than 1 m. In order to achieve these objectives in networks supporting large numbers of users, it is necessary to employ a wideband connection-free architecture in the multiple-access direction.

Endnotes

1. Norman Abramson (ALOHA Networks), "Internet Access Using VSATs," *IEEE Communications Magazine,* IEEE Communications Society, 305 East 47th Street, New York, NY 10017, USA, 2000.
2. *Ibid.*
3. *Ibid.*
4. *Ibid.*
5. *Ibid.*
6. *Ibid.*

CHAPTER 27

Wireless Broadband Hybrids: The Next Wave

Once disparate wireless broadband access strategies are beginning to coalesce around a tightly integrated hybrid wireline-wireless broadband platform that could pose significant new challenges to the dominant wireline players in cable and telephony. The idea of mixing fixed wireless broadband and wireline components into a single network (see Figure 27-1)[1] to accomplish wide and rapid penetration of the local marketplace started to take off in the spring of 1999 when NextLink Communications, Inc., suddenly bought out the local multipoint distribution service (LMDS) holdings of WNP Communications, the leading bidder in 1998's auctions with 40 licenses in major markets nationwide (see the sidebar, "Wireless Broadband Licenses Expected to Raise $15 Billion for the United States").

Wireless Broadband Licenses Expected to Raise $15 Billion for the United States

After months of legal tussling, the most precious natural resource of the information age (a large new batch of licenses to use the airwaves for wireless broadband communications) will finally go on sale soon in what experts say could become the largest auction ever held by the federal government. Based on auctions held by Europeans for licenses in early 2000 and the growing needs of American wireless broadband companies to fill out their national networks and aug-

Figure 27-1
Newbridge
multiservices
multiaccess platform.

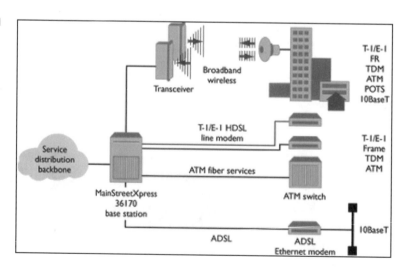

ment service in their existing digital wireless broadband telephone markets, some Wall Street analysts and industry executives estimate that the auction, which is scheduled to begin soon, could raise more than $15 billion.

Even though it appears as if many of the bidders for European licenses overpaid, telecommunications companies cannot afford to pass up the chance American regulators are now offering. The upcoming auction is for prime beachfront property.

The auction of 422 licenses in 195 markets, including some of the largest and most attractive, presents a chance for the biggest carriers, such as AT&T Wireless, Sprint PCS, and Verizon Wireless, to fill in holes, enter new cities, beef up capacity, and gain the true national footprint that has so far proved elusive (see Table 27-1 and Figure 27-2).[2] It provides an opportunity for second-tier players such as Nextel Communications, VoiceStream Wireless, and Cingular Wireless, a joint venture of SBC Communications and BellSouth, to expand.

And since many of the licenses are reserved for small businesses, minority enterprises, and rural companies, it also provides a chance for smaller niche players to develop particular cities or regions. Still, the action largely will center on the most populous regions.

If you look at the 15 largest markets, this is where the true battle will be. You will not reach the crazed prices that Europe reached, especially in the United Kingdom and Germany, but you will see much more aggressive bidding in those markets.

TABLE 27-1

Based on the Size of Their Good-Faith Deposits, These are Some of the Companies Expected to Bid for the Most Wireless Broadband Licenses in the Next Auction of a Key Portion of the Radio Spectrum

Company	Bid (millions)
Alaska Native	$238.8
Salmon PCS*	$238.8
AT&T	$150.8
Nextel	$150.8
VoiceStream	$150.8
Verizon	$131.1
Sprint	$ 69.8

*85 percent owned by Cingular, an SBC BellSouth joint venture.

Figure 27-2
The FCC is holding an auction to sell the rights to provide additional wireless broadband services in various areas across the United States.

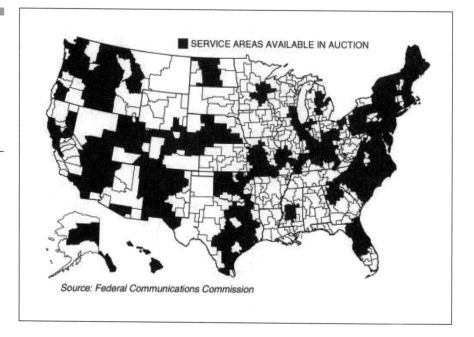

■ SERVICE AREAS AVAILABLE IN AUCTION

Source: Federal Communications Commission

The potential $15 billion or so that the government is expected to raise is staggering considering that the previous 30 auctions held by the Federal Communications Commission (FCC) throughout the last decade together produced total bids of no more than $25 billion. But it would still be considerably smaller than the total amounts paid by companies in Europe, where the auctions were for nationwide licenses as opposed to regional ones.

Germany recently concluded an auction of a portion of its electromagnetic spectrum in which six companies agreed to pay more than $46 billion for licenses. A few months before that, five companies won bids in Great Britain for licenses that yielded the government $35.4 billion.

Experts and analysts have concluded that many of the companies wildly overpaid for the spectrum in much of Europe. With recriminations flying, the planned wireless broadband auction in Switzerland collapsed in November 2000 after several participants pulled out, and Italy's auction attracted far less than expected because British Telecommunications withdrew from the bidding.

However, this is not stopping some of the same players who ran up the bidding to such heights from now turning their sights to the United States. Recently, Deutsche Telekom and NTT DoCoMo announced strategic alliances and major investments in American counterparts, pouring in billions of dollars that will enable the bidders to be more aggressive at the auction. The bidding will be very intense.

A recent analysis by Merrill Lynch estimated that the auction would raise about $18 billion if the companies made bids similar to those of the Europeans. Still, some analysts think that the European experience of paying so high a price for licenses may make some American companies more circumspect as they approach the auction for the so-called C and F blocks of the spectrum, bands that are concentrated primarily in the 1900-MHz range. Moreover, a spate of deal making and license swaps recently among large and small players in the United States may take the pressure off the companies to outbid one another at stratospheric levels.

However, others say that the opportunities presented by the auction may be unique, particularly since demand for mobile telephone service has been so high, and another long-awaited auction of even better licenses has been clouded by wrangling with broadcasters that now hold some of those licenses as part of the conversion to digital television and may be under no obligation to give them up for many years. The licenses being sold will allow companies to bolster their presence in some of the nation's most attractive and lucrative markets, including Boston, the Baltimore-Washington corridor, Chicago, Denver, Los Angeles, Minneapolis, New York, Philadelphia, Pittsburgh, San Diego, San Francisco, Seattle, and Portland, OR.

For all the raging popularity of mobile telephones, consumers agree that one of their biggest frustrations has been that they are less reliable than land lines. Cell phone users find that it is not uncommon to have calls dropped in midsentence, and sometimes it can appear impossible to make a connection after dialing a number, particularly in major cities and crowded airports. Experts say the coming auction can go a long way toward solving those problems by giving the carriers a far greater capability to handle more phone traffic.

While the licenses will be used primarily for voice and text messaging traffic in the first instance, some experts believe that they eventually may be part of the so-called third-generation digital phones that are able to browse the Internet. Sixty-three of the more valuable licenses in the auction have been bogged down in years of litigation and lobbying. They had been won in a 1996 auction by Nextwave, which had the high bid of $4.7 billion.

However, the company ultimately could not find the financing for its bid. After going into bankruptcy, the company and some of its investors waged a furious legal and lobbying campaign to hold onto the licenses. After a series of adverse court rulings and legislative setbacks, the company lost the licenses and now, barring any last-minute hitches, the FCC will begin the auction. Hoping to reduce the potential financial pressure and keep the auction from skidding out of control, some companies have begun swapping their current licenses to fill in gaps in a series of minideals first described by *Communications Daily,* a newsletter that follows industry and regulatory trends.

Cingular Wireless, for instance, and VoiceStream agreed to exchange licenses so that Cingular could operate in New York City and VoiceStream could increase volume in Los Angeles and San Francisco. In November 2000, Sprint PCS and AT&T Wireless also reached an agreement on spectrum swaps but did not disclose which markets were involved.

Many of the largest players also have struck alliances with start-ups and small businesses to succeed in an auction that reserves some of the licenses for the companies with assets of less than $500 million and gross revenues of less than $125 million in each of the last few years. In other words, the auction has been designed to be so large that smaller players can now participate. Bigger players need more for existing operations. Smaller players are likely to use this for innovative new technologies.[3]

This was a shot that was heard throughout the industry. Now, with MCI/WorldCom and Sprint acquiring multichannel multipoint distribution system (MMDS) spectrum in markets representing about 28 million households each and AT&T quietly moving forward on various other wireless broadband fronts, the message to the vendor community has been amplified many times over: Hybrid wireless broadband–wireline is the wave of the future.

It is not just a matter of the radio link on the air interface providing bandwidth on demand. It is a question of how can someone make sure that he or she can bill for such service and provide for the operations support system (OSS) over the interface the same way he or she does over the wireline connections.

NextLink is now the biggest player in LMDS, which operates at the spectrum tiers of 28 and 31 GHz. Along with acquiring A-block (1.15-GHz) licenses to 39 markets representing a population of 100 million people from WNP, NextLink has taken full control of 15 additional A-block and 29 B-block (150 MHz) LMDS licenses by buying out Nextel Communications, Inc.'s 50 percent interest in the two companies' joint wireless broadband venture, NextBand.

The ability to combine fiber and wireless broadband to reach small and medium-sized businesses gives NextLink an enormous advantage over companies that are either all wireline or all wireless broadband. In the wireline mode, the company can cost-justify extending fiber to buildings only about a quarter of a mile from the fiber rings it is installing throughout the metropolitan regions of the country, which would mean it would have to lease T-1 facilities from telcos for deeper reach into these markets if it did not have access via wireless broadband.

Wireless broadband gives NextLink buildings 2½ miles away from its rings and allows it to own the facilities. Eventually, the company will be able to extend the reach deeper, possibly moving fiber to the first points of wireless broadband connection as the revenue streams build and shifting the wireless broadband transmitters further out to encompass ever more territory.

Wireless Broadband–Wireline Integration

Wireless broadband–wireline integration is also key to the MMDS strategies of Sprint and MCI, although their agendas differ from each other and from NextLink's. NextLink intends to accomplish its local service goals using a patchwork of overlapping networks, including digital subscriber line (DSL), fiber, wireless, cable, or other means.

In MCI's case, use of the MMDS spectrum being acquired with the buyouts of Prime One and CAI Wireless and its affiliates will be focused on meeting the surging demand for high-speed data services in small business and institutional markets. Sprint, too, wants to be able to mix the use of DSL with MMDS to deliver integrated on-demand network (ION) services in the local market. In fact, the company wants to be able to integrate with its mobile Personal Communications Service (PCS) platform as well. In bridging services like unified messaging, you lose the distinction between wireline and wireless broadband.

In contrast to MCI, however, Sprint, with its acquisition of People's Choice TV and American Telecasting, also will design services, including TV entertainment, to accommodate the residential market. America Online (AOL) is making clear that it believes the ability of carriers to integrate across *multiple-access (multiaccess systems)* platforms is vital to its plans to deliver wireless broadband services ubiquitously across the country. As we look at wireless broadband, we are looking at a tapestry of network platforms. Even if AOL wins the battle for open access over cable, it will still need the other platforms.

With this in mind, let's now identify some of the key problems one encounters when thinking about multiaccess systems. Let's begin with a general discussion of nomadic computing and move on to issues of multiaccess in a distributed environment. Then let's specialize to the case of wireless broadband systems and identify some of the key considerations and algorithms that must be addressed in this environment. Lastly, let's identify some of the higher-level issues and principles one should properly keep in mind when investigating the design and behavior of these systems.

Integrating Across Multiple-Access Platforms

The issues involved with untethered communications are extensive. This part of the chapter discusses some of these from a high level with the purpose of addressing the considerations that extend across many of the detailed analyses and discussions. No single multiaccess scheme is considered in detail. Instead, the discussion centers around more general themes. Let's begin by discussing the larger field of nomadic computing and the issues of mobility, access, and service that arise as a result.

Nomadic Computing

The combination of portable computing with portable communications is changing the way companies think about information processing. It is important to recognize that access to computing, communications, and service now is necessary not only from one's home base, but also while one is in transit and when one reaches one's destination.

These ideas form the essence of a major shift to nomadicity (nomadic computing and communications). The focus of nomadicity is on the system support needed to provide a rich set of capabilities and services to the nomad as he or she moves from place to place in a transparent and convenient form.

Of concern are those capabilities which must be put in place to support nomadicity. The desirable characteristics for nomadicity include independence of location, of motion, of computing platform, of communication device, and of communication bandwidth, with widespread presence of access to remote files, systems, and services. The notion of *independence* here refers not only to the quality of service one sees but also to the perception of a computing environment that automatically adjusts to the processing, communications, and access available at the moment. For example, the bandwidth for moving data between a user and a remote server easily could vary from a few bits per second (in a noisy wireless environment) to hundreds of megabits per second (in a hard-wired ATM environment), or the computing platform available to the user could vary from a low-powered personal digital assistant while traveling to a powerful supercomputer in a science laboratory.

Today's systems treat radically changing connectivity or bandwidth/ latency values as exceptions or failures; in the nomadic environment, these must be treated as the usual case. Moreover, the ability to accept partial or incomplete results is an option that must be made available due to the uncertainties of the informatics infrastructure.

The concept of mobility in a nomadic environment takes on many meanings. One component of mobility is the desire to gain access to the informatics infrastructure when one arrives at different destinations. An example might be when one transports one's laptop from the corporate office to one's home or a hotel. In this case, issues of seamlessly managing the configuration settings of the nomad (TCP/IP address, netmask, Web proxy setting, domain name server, gateways, etc.) must be managed. Another component of mobility is the desire to gain access to the informatics infrastructure while in motion. In this case, issues of tracking, handoff, connectivity, and so on, as well as managing configuration settings, come to mind and must be addressed.

The need for nomadic computing support has been recognized recently, and an entire industry has begun to arise in response to this need. Now let's see the rollout of wireless broadband access (DSL, cable modems, wireless broadband access) from a number of suppliers (Copper Mountain, Paradyne, SBC, GTE, Lucent) and the rollout of subscriber management systems (Nomadix, Redback, Shasta). Most recently, it has become clear that one must shift from a *connection-centric* view (connectivity is now almost a commodity in terms of innovation and scarcity) to a *service-centric* view in which the focus is on providing services over those broadband pipes. No longer is it the "fat pipe" that matters but what goes through it. Local service is no longer simply printing and email; it is movie tickets, games, and pizza. Indeed, the Internet is becoming much more than connected networks and computers—it is becoming a service access and delivery system. Thus the ability to automatically adjust all aspects of the user's computing, communication, storage, and service functionality in a transparent and integrated fashion is the essence of a nomadic environment.

Shared Media and Multiaccess

In dynamic environments such as that of the nomad, it is necessary to find ways to share resources in an adaptive fashion. Indeed, one must deal with the problems of multiple users attempting to access common resources in a competitive fashion (multiaccess). Not only are companies faced with the queuing problems that arise from the stochastic nature of the demands, but they also are faced with the issue of allocating resources to a geographically distributed (and possibly mobile) set of demands. Were companies not in this distributed environment, queuing theory would provide them with the ultimate mean response time–throughput performance profile. However, most companies have additional loss of resources due to the cost of organizing the separated demands into some kind of cooperating queue that permits intelligent access to the available resources.

For the purposes of this part of the chapter (and at no loss of generality), let's assume that the shared resource is a communications channel and that the demands are message sources that require transmission of their messages over this shared channel. Here one is faced with controlling access to this channel from these distributed message sources in which the control information must pass over the same channel being controlled (or over a control subchannel derived from the data channel).

Let's characterize the classes of multiaccess schemes into three categories and observe that the previously mentioned cost of organizing these sources into a cooperative group also falls into three categories. The three classes of multiaccess control schemes are

- Fixed (static) control
- Random control

■ Dynamic control

The three sources of lost resources are

■ Wasted (idle) resources

■ Collision of resources

■ Control overhead[4]

In the first class of fixed control, all multiaccess schemes are included that rigidly assign a portion of the channel to each source. Examples include time-division multiple access (TDMA), frequency-division multiple access (FDMA), and so on. Fixed control is extremely easy to implement. However, the typical price paid for such a rigid assignment is that the channel assigned to a given source is wasted (lies idle) whenever the source has nothing to send in its assigned portion of the channel.

At the other extreme from the rigid approach taken with fixed control is that of no, or minimal, control, namely, the second class, random control. Examples include ALOHA, carrier-sense multiple access (CSMA), and so on. Random control is also relatively easy to implement. However, the typical price paid here (for poor or no control) is that of collisions that occur when two sources attempt to transmit in the same portion of the channel (the definition of *portion* could be time, frequency, code, space, or some combination).

With the third class, dynamic control, the channel resource is apportioned on a demand basis according to the needs of the sources. This control can take the form of polling (where a source waits to be asked if it needs channel access) or active requests from the source in the form of a request for access, such as asynchronous time-division multiplexing (TDM) or reservation ALOHA or others. In all such cases, the typical price paid is that of the overhead to send the control signals over the channel. Table 27-2 summarizes these tradeoffs.[5]

Of course, in the general case, one can combine some of these access control methods and then suffer a mix of their forms of channel cost. An example of mixed access control would be that of a dynamic control scheme in which reservations for data slots are made using a random access

TABLE 27-2		Idle Resource	Collisions	Control Overhead
The Price of Distributed Resources	Fixed control	Yes	No	No
	Random control	No	Yes	No
	Dynamic control	No	No	Yes

request control channel (say, ALOHA) and where the data slots themselves are allocated on a fixed TDMA basis as long as the source has data to send, after which the data slots are assignable to other sources as the demand arises.

The Issues of Wireless Broadband Access

It is clear that a great many issues regarding nomadicity arise whether or not one has access to wireless broadband communications. However, with such access, a number of interesting considerations arise that are discussed in this part of the chapter.

Access to wireless broadband communications provides two capabilities to the nomad. First, it allows the nomad to communicate from various (fixed) locations without being connected directly into the wireline network. Second, it allows the nomad to communicate while traveling. Although the bandwidth offered by wireless broadband communications media varies over an enormous range, as does the wireline network bandwidth, the nature of the error rate, fading behavior, interference level, mobility issues, and so on for wireless broadband is considerably different from wireline networks, so the algorithms and protocols to support wireless broadband access are far more complex than those for the wireline case. Whereas the location of a user or device is a concern for wireline nets as described in the preceding, the details of tracking a user while moving in a wireless broadband environment add to the complexity and require rules for handover, roaming, and so forth.

The cellular radio networks so prevalent today have an architecture that assumes the existence of a cell base station for each cell of the array. The base station controls the activity of its cell. The design considerations of such cellular networks are reasonably well understood and are being addressed by an entire industry. These will not be discussed further in this chapter.

There is, however, another wireless broadband networking architecture of interest that assumes no base stations. Such wireless broadband networks are useful for applications that require *instant* infrastructure, among others. For example, disaster relief, emergency operations, special military operations, and clandestine operations are all cases where no base-station infrastructure can be assumed. In the case of no base stations, maintaining communications is considerably more difficult. For example, it may be that the destination for a given reception is not within range of the transmitter, in which case some form of relaying is required. This is known as *multihop communications*. Moreover, since there are no fixed-location base stations, the connectivity of the network is subject to considerable change as devices move around and/or the medium changes its characteristics. A number of new considerations arise in these situations, and new kinds of network algorithms are needed to deal with them. At this point, it is convenient to articulate some of the issues and algorithms with which one must be concerned in the case of no base stations by decomposing the possible scenarios into the following three.

- Static topology with one-hop communications
- Static topology with multihop communications
- Dynamic topology with multihop communications

Static Topology with One-Hop Communications   In this case, there is no motion among the system elements, and all transmitters can reach their destinations without any relays. The issues of concern, along with the needed network algorithms (shown in italics), are as follows:

- Can you reach your destination?—*power control*
- What access method should you use?—*network access control*
- Which channel (or code) should you use?—*channel assignment control*
- Will you interfere with another transmission?—*power and medium access control*
- When do you allow a new *call* into the system?—*admission control*
- Is there sufficient bandwidth for your application?—*capacity assignment*
- For different multiplexed streams, can you achieve the required quality of service (bandwidth, loss, delay, delay jitter, higher order statistics, etc.)?—*multimedia control*
- What packet size should you use?—*system design*
- Is there a need for systemwide synchronization?—*global control*
- How are errors to be handled?—*error control*
- How do you handle congestion?—*congestion control*
- How do you adapt to failures?—*degradation control*[6]

Static Topology with Multihop Communications   Here the topology is static again, but transmitters may not be able to reach their destinations in one hop, so multihop relay communications are necessary in some cases.

The issues of concern, along with the needed network algorithms (shown in italics), are all the preceding plus

- Is there a path to your destination?—*path control*
- Does giant stepping help?—*power control*
- What routing procedure should you use?—*routing control*
- When should you reroute existing calls?—*reconfiguration control*
- How do you assign bandwidth and quality of service (QoS) along the path?—*admission control and channel assignment*[7]

Dynamic Topology with Multihop Communications   In this case, the devices (radios, users, etc.) are allowed to move, which causes the network connectivity to change dynamically. The issues of concern, along with the needed network algorithms (shown in italics), are all the preceding plus

- Do you track or search for your destination?—*location control*
- Which network reconfiguration strategy should you use?—*adaptive topology control*
- How should you use reconfigurable and adaptive base stations?—*adaptive base station control*[8]

These lists of considerations are not complete, only illustrative of the many interesting research problems that present themselves in this environment. Indeed, in this part of the chapter, only the network algorithm issues have been addressed, and the many other issues involved with radio design, hardware design, tools for computer-aided design (CAD), system drivers, and so on have not been presented.

Some General Considerations

In the foregoing, a number of issues and problems have been listed that arise in the case of nomadic and untethered communications. This part of the chapter focuses on some overriding principles and observations that are useful across this set of issues and problems. These principles and observations are simply a subset (albeit an interesting one) of guiding principles of value when discussing multiaccess in a distributed environment.

On the Latency Parameter a   In many distributed communication systems, there are three parameters that interact:

`C` is the capacity of the communication channel
   (say, in megabits per second).
`L` is the length of the channel (say, in kilometers).
`b` is the length of the data unit transmitted
   (say, in bits per packet).

These three can be combined into a single key system variable, *latency*, which is denoted by a and which is defined as the propagation delay (time for a bit to travel the length of the channel) divided by the time it takes to transmit a packet into the channel. It turns out that the system performance of many communications channels is closely tied to the latency. If we assume that it takes 5 μs for energy to travel through 1 km of the channel (this is approximately the value for a wireline channel), the latency is simply

$$a = 5LC/b$$

since $5L$ is the propagation delay (in microseconds) through the channel and b/C is the time (also in microseconds) to transmit a packet. It is interesting to observe the range of values taken on by a for some characteristic systems; these are shown in Table 27-3.[9]

   The thing to note from Table 27-3 is the enormous range over which the key parameter latency varies (six orders of magnitude). If the channel is a wireless broadband channel, and if the access method uses some version of CSMA, it is well known that the performance of the channel critically depends on the latency a. Since there is such a wide variation in a, it is very important to consider its effect on performance.

Power   In evaluating the performance of a system, the mean response time T is often compared with the throughput of a system. This profile typically looks like that shown in Figure 27-3.[10]

TABLE 27-3

Latency for Some
Common Systems

	Bandwidth (Mbps)	Packet Length (bits)	Propagation Delay (μs)	Latency (a)
LAN	10.00	1000	5	0.05
WAN	0.05	1000	20,000	1.00
Satellite	0.05	1000	250,000	12.50
Fiber link	1000.00	1000	20,000	20,000.00

Figure 27-3
Typical response
time–throughput
tradeoff.

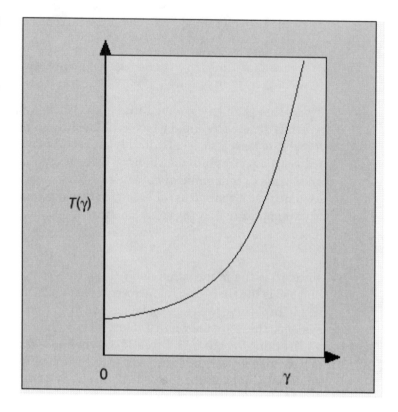

Figure 27-3
Typical response
time–throughput
tradeoff.

NOTE   At low throughput, you should get good response time, and at a high throughput, you should get poor response time.

It turns out that power is maximized at that point on the response time–throughput profile where a straight line from the origin first becomes tangent to the profile. Figure 27-4 denotes the optimal throughput operating.[11]

What is amazing about this result is that for all Matrix-Geometric (*M/G/*1) queuing systems, this point occurs where $E(N)$, the average number of messages in the system, is exactly one! What makes this interesting is that it is intuitively the correct operating point for deterministic systems.

NOTE   This chapter presents an algorithmic approach to find the stationary probability distribution of matrix-geometric (M/G/1) type messages which arise frequently in performance analysis of computer and communications networks.

Figure 27-4
The operating point
at maximum power.

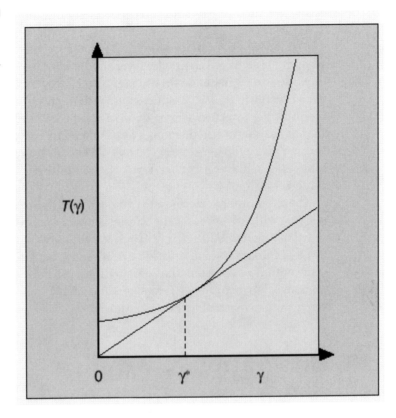

Giant Stepping   In the case of packet radio systems, a totally different consideration leads to exactly the same result that was just quoted earlier. Let us consider an ideal multihop packet radio system where the power in every radio is adjusted so that each hop covers exactly a radius R. Further, assume that the total distance a message must travel is $D \gg R$. Now, let $T(R)$ be the mean response time experienced by a message in traveling one hop, due to interfering traffic from other radios. It is clear that if you choose R to be large, $T(R)$ is large (more interference), but the number of hops is small, and vice versa for a small value of R. Thus you should desire to find that value of the step size R which uses an appropriate transmission power in a way that balances these two effects. This is called *giant stepping* and is a typical consideration in ad hoc network design. If you assume that there is a continuum of radios in the plane, the total mean delay along the path is clearly $T(R)$ (D/R). Differentiating this function with respect to R, you should find that the optimal value of R, which minimizes the total mean delay, is such that $dT(R)/dR = T(R)/R$. It is interesting to note that this solution is at exactly the same point as that shown in Figure 27-4.

A number of refinements can be made to this simplified model to account for some of the practical constraints of the problem (discrete locations for radios instead of a continuum). However, the beauty of this idealized result is that it provides a guideline for system design and enjoys the intuitive interpretations given in the preceding. For example, it says that at optimality, the load on a system feeding a pipeline should be such that, on average, there should be one packet per hop. It is this kind of intuition that leads to a higher level of thinking and understanding about these very complex systems.

Therefore, many pieces vital to such intuitions are coming together, starting with advances on the wireless broadband side that provide for the provisioning flexibility and QoS options that are common to wireline platforms. Moreover, some entities are already focusing on the integration issue with new products that employ Internet Protocol (IP) and other formats over Asynchronous Transfer Mode (ATM) as the primary means of tying transmission elements together at the local network edge points.

Integration of Wireline and Wireless Broadband Domains

Motorola Corporation and Cisco Systems, Inc., have agreed to pool resources in an effort to create an IP-based industrywide framework for integration of the wireline and wireless broadband domains. The two companies have pledged to spend $3 billion on the process, which they say could take as long as 4 years, although they are already beginning to deliver initial product lines built to suggested specifications of the framework. The reason Cisco is moving with Motorola on SpectraPoint is that it wants to get the best of breed radio frequency (rf) and fixed wireless broadband integrated into that architecture.

Facilitating Multiplatform Integration

SpectraPoint has a strong head start in the direction of facilitating multiplatform integration via IP and ATM, having been working with Cisco for

Developing Wireless Broadband Routers

Hybrid Networks, Inc., will integrate Conexant's InfoSurge single-chip broadband modem integrated circuit (IC) into the wireless broadband router (WBR) that is part of its two-way fixed wireless broadband system. The wireless broadband router converts data from personal computers to signals that are transmitted over radio frequencies, enabling two-way wireless Internet access. New modems using the InfoSurge wireless broadband modem IC will offer non-line-of-sight access. Products using the IC, which features a programmable MAC architecture, will be available in early 2002.[12]

most of 2000 to integrate router switches (see the sidebar, "Developing Wireless Broadband Routers") and other IP components into the LMDS access system. A lot of thought has gone into the integration of its system with Cisco's products.

The big performance gains in LMDS and other spectrum applications (see Figure 27-5)[13] of point-to-multipoint wireless broadband start with greater flexibility in the use of bandwidth than was possible heretofore. For example, SpectraPoint has introduced products that support dynamic changes in modulation from the more robust low-bits-per-hertz levels to the noise-sensitive high-capacity levels as weather conditions change or customers shift the tradeoffs they want to make between bandwidth efficiency and QoS.

Figure 27-5
Available spectrum:
LMDS band.

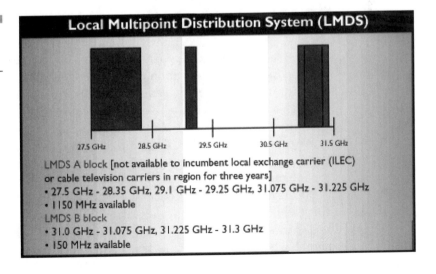

The radios SpectraPoint is shipping with their 2200 system support quadrature phase-shift key (QPSK) and 8, 16, and 32 quadrature amplitude modulation (QAM). By mid-2001, SpectraPoint probably will have software that supports dynamic shifts from one modulation level to the next.

One of the innovations vendors are applying to LMDS and other fixed wireless broadband products is the ability to transport everything in ATM while using time-division multiple-access multiplexing technology to dynamically alter the amount of bandwidth devoted to any one user's needs. In this way, all the users on a single rf LMDS channel, now at up to 45 Mbps and moving to 155 Mbps in 2002 on SpectraPoint's system, can pay for services on an as-needed basis, allowing service providers to more efficiently allocate bandwidth that is not in use from one moment to the next.

Another glimpse of what is to come can be seen in the plans of Ensemble Communications, Inc., a San Diego–based start-up that demonstrated the first iteration of its *adaptive IP* platform at Supercomm in June 1999. This company's system uses a number of innovations to greatly simplify the end-user connection process while allowing service providers to deliver a given channel of frequency on a shared-use basis to multiple buildings.

With current-generation systems, you have to engineer every link to the customer individually and allocate bandwidth on a fixed basis to every link. With Ensemble's system, customers will be able to take their customer premises equipment (CPE), hook it up, and turn it on, just like people do today with cellular and PCS systems.

Tight Integration of Multiple Delivery Platforms

Another leading LMDS supplier, Newbridge Networks, Inc. (see Figure 27-1), is promoting tight integration of multiple delivery platforms via TDMA/ATM interface cards, which employ compact design capabilities obtained through the firm's recent agreement to acquire Stanford Telecommunications, Inc. The Newbridge MainStreet Xpress ATM switch is designed to aggregate LMDS, MMDS, DSL, and eventually cable, each with its own interface card, at a local service node that also can serve as the wireless broadband base station.

Newbridge Networks' vision is to support a multiple-service network. Basically, the company has made the ATM switch a base station by designing an interface card that directly integrates ATM functionality into the rf signal, which turned out to be a very difficult thing to do.

At the same time, the company is developing a voice-over-DSL interface in conjunction with the DSL card that slides into the same ATM switching module that is used for the wireless broadband components, thereby providing for the complete integration of voice and data services over various wireline and wireless broadband platforms at the base station/switch. This new voice capability for DSL uses the GR-303 switch interface that allows the call provisioning and feature functionalities of central office switches to be supplied to the packet voice streams in the DSL connection, which is the approach to voice delivery being taken by most players in the DSL arena.

Where MMDS is concerned, operators are just now moving to the digital TV delivery capabilities that will allow them to go from about 30 channels of analog service to 100 or more digital channels. And they are also just introducing two-way, high-speed data capabilities, wide-scale deployment of which depends on what FCC officials say is the imminent issuance of orders in the reconsideration process attending 1998's grant of two-way authority to the MMDS sector.

At the cutting edge on both the video and data fronts is one of Sprint's targeted acquisitions, PCTV, which now has 160 channels of video along with a 60-Mbps downstream/10-Mbps upstream data service underway in Phoenix. The two-way data capacity can be repeated ad infinitum with various forms of spectrum multiplexing.

Expanding This Data-Carrying Capacity

Expanding this data-carrying capacity is a top priority for both MCI and Sprint, starting with use of multiple transmitters and sectorization of those transmitters, in contrast to today's deployments, where one transmitter, as in Phoenix, serves an entire metropolitan area. Sectorization means that each area served by a specific transmitter is divided into segments served by separate beams. In some vendor iterations, all the sector beams operate over the same 200 MHz of frequency through use of some means such as reverse polarization to prevent interference at the sector edges, while in other design approaches, adjacent beams use different frequencies in an alternating pattern that allows only 100 MHz to be used over any one beam. This latter approach, used, for example, by Spike Technologies, permits a much higher degree of sectorization, where, in Spike's case, a dozen sectors divide the territory into small slices of users contending for the 100 MHz of available bandwidth within each slice.

Ironically, MMDS, with a signal reach of 35 miles, could readily serve a metropolitan region with a minimum number of transmitters if it had the amount of bandwidth made available at the much higher frequencies set aside for LMDS, where licensees must cellularize to accommodate a signal reach of only 3 miles or so. The spectrum-allocation differences (see Figure 27-6) result from the fact that there are many competing applications in the low-frequency tiers where MMDS resides, whereas it was not until fairly recently that it became technically feasible to use the tiers occupied by LMDS for point-to-multipoint applications.[14]

There is considerable confusion about how these and other wireless broadband tiers can be scaled over multiple cells and what the effective comparative bandwidth-to-user ratios are from one tier to the other. Given the great disparities among them—which also include the 24-GHz category, where about 400 MHz is available; the 38-GHz tier, where several 100-MHz blocks might be amassed in any given marketplace; and the much more bandwidth-restricted categories in cellular at 800 MHz and PCS at 1.9 GHz—the players are always looking for ways to make their chosen tier look good against the others, which has produced some interesting claims.

For example, some experts are claiming the effective available band-width using MMDS technology at 200 MHz per territory is on a par with the bandwidth efficiency of LMDS at 1.15 GHz per license. However, such claims often demonstrate a lack of understanding of all the factors that

Figure 27-6
Available spectrum: MMDS band.

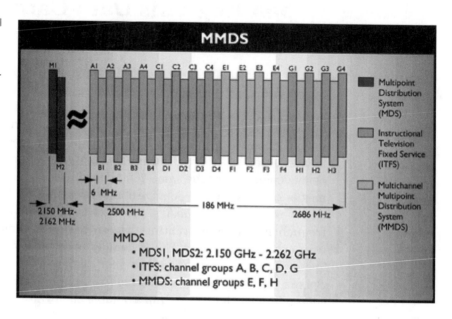

must be considered in weighing relative efficiencies among various wireless broadband spectrum tiers, where the propagation characteristics deteriorate as the frequency level goes up.

What you have to realize is that when you go to multiple cells, the limiting factor in terms of frequency reuse becomes the signal-to-interference ratio, and this is directly related to the modulation level you use, independent of the frequencies at which you are operating.

In other words, the sensitivity to interference at 64 QAM (quadrature amplitude modulation) is the same whether the propagation frequency is 2.5 or 28 GHz. This means that with its much greater signal reach, cell-to-cell interference for MMDS comes into play at far greater spacing of cells than is the case for LMDS, so any effort to chop a territory into a lot of MMDS cells in order to reuse the limited frequency to the point where it begins to even out the bandwidth advantage of LMDS is going to be hampered by the signal-to-interference problem.

With MMDS, you are not going to be able to get away with 64 QAM if you are counting on a reuse strategy to compensate for the limited bandwidth. Thus, with the loss of the higher bit rate per hertz of 64 versus 16 QAM, for example, which translates to about 5 bits per frequency cycle versus 2, the 200 MHz of frequency loses a lot of its aggregate throughput in exchange for a move to multiple cells.

Viewing Two Types of Platforms: LMDS and MMDS

The best way to look at the two types of platforms is to view LMDS as ideally suited for high-capacity service requirements in urban areas, whereas MMDS is better for lower-capacity requirements in less dense residential areas. The bottom line is that LMDS has the bandwidth advantage, but MMDS has the propagation advantage, and it is best to design systems accordingly.

With only 200 MHz to work with, cellularization is a likely step in Sprint's efforts to maximize bandwidth. It is doubtful that Sprint will put just one stick up in an area. The company is also looking at use of *intelligent waveguide technology* as a means of expanding bandwidth efficiency.

MCI is thinking along the same lines. It will break the serving areas up into smaller cell sizes. This would add substantial costs to the approximately $3 billion MCI is spending to acquire the wireless broadband cable properties.

Eventually, both companies intend to use the MMDS spectrum for delivering multiple-line packet voice services, although it remains to be seen how soon such services will be possible. Sprint will focus on delivering high-speed data in 2002, postponing to some undetermined time in the future the rollout of voice over MMDS.

PCTV already has tested the use of an IP voice phone over Sprint's two-way data channels and found the quality to be on par with circuit-switched service. It will take operators a long time, however, to achieve the back-office and operational integration essential to supporting voice services.

In fact, the technical challenges associated with use of wireless broadband have made the topic one of the most difficult questions for MCI's senior management to answer. However, with demand for high-speed data connections surging and the advantages MCI sees in owning wireless broadband facilities rather than leasing telco lines, as it must do with use of DSL technology, the company concluded that it had little choice but to make a move into fixed wireless broadband services once it became clear that two-way services were technically feasible.

Now MCI, which, like Sprint, will have coverage reaching some 48 million households and businesses through the announced acquisitions, is considering further moves in this direction. A good guess is that you have not heard the end of it yet.

Conclusion

The systems of interest discussed in this chapter were nomadic computing, multiaccess systems, and wireless broadband systems; these systems share a common need for control, access, and allocation. A key conclusion of this chapter is that in order to gain understanding of the behavior of complex systems such as these, it is often helpful to look for overriding principles of performance. For example, one way or another, one must pay a price for organizing distributed demands in their competition for use of a shared resource. It turns out that the price will be some mix of idle resources, collisions, and control overhead. Another factor discussed was that of latency. It often has a dominant effect, depending on a small set of basic system parameters. Two very different optimization problems were characterized using very simple and different models, and it was found that the same underlying principle applied: the notion of finding the knee of the appropriate curve as the optimal operating point.

The conclusion is that as a complement to detailed systems analysis, it is important to look for overriding principles of operation that transcend the specific systems and layers being studied. Indeed, one must span more than one layer of the communications stack when designing systems of the type described herein. For example, there must be awareness of the link-layer capabilities (bandwidth, delay, error rate) by the application and transport layers lest one try to send a full-motion color video to a monochromatic display on a handheld device over a limited-bandwidth wireless broadband link. The need for proxies at various points in the communications path and at various layers also can be of use in these situations. Think globally, and look for overriding principles.

Endnotes

1. Fred Dawson, "The Next Wave: Wireless/Wireline Hybrids?" *CED Magazine,* P.O. Box 266007, Highlands Ranch, CO 80163-6007, 2000.

2. Federal Communications Commission, 445 12th St. SW, Washington, DC 20554, 2000.

3. *Ibid.*

4. Leonard Kleinrock (Nomadix, Inc.), "On Some Principles of Nomadic Computing and Multi-Access Communications," *IEEE Communications Magazine,* IEEE Communications Society, 305 East 47th Street, New York, NY 10017, USA, 2000.

5. *Ibid.*

6. *Ibid.*

7. *Ibid.*

8. *Ibid.*

9. *Ibid.*

10. *Ibid.*

11. *Ibid.*

12. "Hybrid Networks to Develop Wireless Broadband Routers Using Conexant's IC," Communication Systems Design, 525 Market St., Suite 500, San Francisco, CA 94105, 2000.

13. Fred Dawson, "The Next Wave: Wireless/Wireline Hybrids?" *CED Magazine,* P.O. Box 266007, Highlands Ranch, CO 80163-6007, 2000.

14. *Ibid.*

CHAPTER 28

Next-Generation Wireless Broadband Networks

The number of cellular and PCS subscribers has grown dramatically, but cellular and Personal Communications Service (PCS) data access has not. However, the ability to access data and the extension of content to wireless broadband phones constitute the next big trend in the industry and a significant competitive shift.

Recently, this shift has been framed largely as part of the evolution to third-generation (3G) technologies. The realization of 3G technologies enabling high-speed Internet communications could dramatically transform wireless broadband phone applications and use. However, do not overlook the potential for intermediary fixed and mobile cellular and PCS data solutions (2.5G).

This chapter provides information beyond the typical overview of standards committees related to 3G systems. Based on detailed financial models and market research, this chapter analyzes the business case for mobile and fixed wireless broadband, looking at demand and financial viability.

First, let's look at 3G systems that will deliver higher bandwidth and offer a much fuller range of services including multimedia, high-quality real-time video, fast intranet and database access, and other data-intensive applications. This 3G technology will bring video to your wireless broadband phones, but Japan will lead the way in 3G deployments. In other words, video over wireless broadband is just around the corner in Japan, but if you want a video-capable wireless broadband device in the United States, you will have to wait.

3G Technology

A banker flies from New York to Tokyo, grabs a taxi, and heads to an important meeting. During the cab ride, the banker flips on a wireless broadband phone to get video feeds of the latest global financial news and to download pictures of the people he or she is scheduled to meet. An insurance adjuster drives to the scene of a natural disaster and uses a wireless broadband personal digital assistant (PDA) to send video images of damaged homes back to supervisors. And paramedics at a car crash send video of the victim's injuries to physicians at a trauma center over a wireless broadband connection.

The ability of a handheld device to send and receive voice, data, and video over a wireless broadband network offers some tantalizing possibilities for doctors, salespeople, and workers on the plant floor—virtually anyone whose job keeps him or her on the move. Obviously, today's handheld devices do not offer video, but the next generation of mobile networks will feature minicams and larger screens and will be able to deliver wireless broadband applications to untethered devices over the Internet. These end-user devices will include speech-only phones, multimedia phones that come equipped with keypads, PDAs, and laptops.

This 3G wireless broadband technology is also known as *IMT-2000*, the standard ratified by the International Telecommunication Union (ITU). 3G systems support data rates from 384 kbps to 2 Mbps, which is sufficient for video applications.

In 2002, NTT DoCoMo plans to roll out the world's first 3G service in Tokyo, Yokohama, and Kawasaki, Japan. Since launching its initial mobile Internet service called *iMode* in February 1999, NTT DoCoMo signed up more than 10 million subscribers. European wireless broadband operators are expected to introduce 3G systems in late 2002 or early 2003.

However, two factors (the lack of available spectrum and reluctance by wireless broadband operators to make additional infrastructure investments) will likely delay the arrival of pure 3G systems in North America until 2004. However, North American wireless broadband operators plan to introduce so-called 2.5G services as early as 2002. 2.5G technologies, including Ericsson's Enhanced Data Rates for Global Evolution (EDGE) and Qualcomm's High DataRate, let wireless broadband operators maximize their 2G infrastructure.

2.5G systems support packet-switched services, and while some 2.5G systems implementations may suffice for one-way video, 2.5G systems will not support two-way visual communication. 2.5G technology is similar to cable modem and asynchronous digital subscriber line (ADSL) technologies in that the download speed is faster than the upload rate, but specific data rates will vary depending on the service provider.

There is also some debate over which technologies are truly 3G. Ericsson calls EDGE a 3G upgrade and therefore insists that the United States will get 3G systems in 2002, but many analysts disagree and say that EDGE is a 2.5G technology.

Nevertheless, sooner or later we are clearly going to have 3G systems in the United States. However, in the United States, 3G systems will be evolutionary. Deployment will be slowed by the spectrum shortage and by North American wireless broadband operators waiting to invest in 3G technologies until there is a market demand.

Now let's look at some industries that are likely early adopters of video over wireless broadband.

Financial Services

Wall Street analysts, traders, and bankers depend on timely information. However, financial services professionals face heavy travel schedules. Most investment banking firms hold morning calls to review pending deals and strategy with analysts globally. The financial industry streams video of these calls and market-moving news clips to corporate desktops, but financial professionals on the go use their mobile phones more than computers.

We are just beginning to think about wireless broadband video applications. Streaming video of morning calls, research, and conferences must move beyond the limitations of the desktop. Being able to do these things without being tethered to the desktop is very attractive. Every investment bank is looking at doing this over wireless broadband.

Health Care

Because health professionals are often on the run and rarely sit behind desks, the health care industry is hungry for video over wireless broadband. Major medical centers and managed-care companies use so-called store-and-forward video and interactive videoconferencing for telemedicine.

Primary-care doctors consult with specialists by sending medical images desktop to desktop and interacting via real-time video connections over Integrated Services Digital Network (ISDN) or the Internet. Wireless broadband would let health professionals consult on cases as they move from place to place.

Currently, Mount Sinai Hospital in New York streams video from its operating room over the Internet for medical education. This will take telemedicine to a new level. You could stream a patient's tests including radiology, CT scans, or dynamic (moving) studies and transmit them instantly to anyone in the hospital. Wireless broadband is particularly useful for echocardiograms and ultrasound because the images are moving and therefore require more bandwidth.

The University of Arizona Medical Center has conducted more than 6000 clinical consultations via store-and-forward and interactive video in the past few years. The telemedicine program delivers services to prisons and rural areas.

There are communities in Arizona where people basically do not have land-line services. Wireless broadband could support those communities.

Insurance

With armies of adjusters moving from place to place, the insurance industry uses wireless broadband voice and data to reach its mobile workforce. Give this industry wireless broadband, and an array of tantalizing applications emerges.

In 1992, Hurricane Andrew caused nearly $25 billion in damages and wiped out entire city blocks in southern Florida. Adjusters had difficulty determining where streets and houses were located before the hurricane hit. Wireless broadband could have let them access images and video showing city blocks before and after Andrew. You could forward a video display of how an area looked before the hurricane hit. You could certainly compare that data with customer data, including the location of homes and the conditions of roofs.

Investigations are another application for video over wireless broadband. Insurance investigators frequently shoot video of people they are observing who are claiming bodily injury. The ability to transmit the video from the scene could boost efficiency. For example, Omega Insurance Services is an investigative services vendor to the insurance industry. On a big-dollar claim, the insurance companies want to know the information in real time. If you can send the video in real time, it gives you the opportunity to patch it through to somebody who can ID the person. They can say, "That's the right guy. Stay with him."

Automotive

One common fantasy that most people have about 3G wireless broadband is streaming multimedia to the backseat of a car so that you can watch Mickey Mouse while taking the kids to Disneyland. However, the auto industry also believes that video over wireless broadband could be useful in communicating with business partners, namely, dealerships and service technicians.

Telling the service technician how to replace a part might be a benefit of video. Since a lot of service centers and dealership service bays today are not wired with high-bandwidth capability, they potentially could benefit from 3G wireless broadband. However, universal wireless broadband capability is key to companies such as Ford Motor Company. Ford will be interested in 3G systems only if they are reasonably ubiquitous.

Besides key industries that will be early adopters of video over wireless broadband, there are several enterprise applications that cut across most industries, including sales, business to employee, business to business, advertising, etc.

Sales

Wireless broadband video likely will become a key tool for mobile sales professionals. For example, a sales representative for a factory construction company could show a prospective customer a video of a factory in action. In another example, real estate agents could show homebuyers video walk-throughs of houses.

Business to Employee

Business-to-employee applications include internal corporate communications and training. Corporate communications departments can leverage video over wireless broadband as a tool to reach employees during otherwise unproductive periods. Employees could receive video clips from the CEO's speech, from the new marketing campaign, or from a TV news story about a competitor on their wireless broadband devices and view them as they take the train to work or while waiting in an airport. Employee benefits could let managers send video clips to team members explaining the new health plan. Also, managers could join department meetings via mobile videoconferencing from virtually anywhere. Video over wireless broadband also has possibilities for employee education. If you could do training on demand in short bursts, 10 minutes here and 10 minutes there, you could finish a course.

Business to Business

Business-to-business applications for video over wireless broadband include viewing videos of parts and machinery used in manufacturing. A manager on the go can determine which goods and services to order. Wireless broadband video also will let companies communicate and collaborate with key suppliers in real time regardless of location. Engineers building an airport in the United Arab Emirates, for example, could review design plans with the project architect who is riding in a taxi in New York.

Advertising

A key driver for 2.5G and 3G wireless is *location-specific services.* This means that advertisers can track where people are and market services directly to them. For instance, operators will maintain detailed profiles of consumers. When those consumers drive to a shopping mall, their mobile devices will begin displaying visual advertisements for goods available inside the mall. 3G wireless broadband applications including video likely will change business models. Location-specific services will benefit brick-and-mortar businesses over pure dot-coms in that companies can target market to consumers based on which stores or locations they are physically near.

Sports

When Denver Broncos quarterback Gus Frerotte connected with wide receiver Ed McCaffrey in the end zone in November 2000 to seal a critical 38-37 victory over San Diego in the runup to the NFL playoffs, fervid Broncos fans wanted to know about it right away, wherever they may have been. Until the beginning of the 2000 season, however, if those fans were outside the stadium during the final moments, they had to be near a TV, radio, or PC to get the news.

Not anymore. The National Football League has kicked off an ambitious push into the world of wireless broadband. Beginning in the 2000 season, the NFL was offering users of one- or two-way pagers, wireless broadband-enabled cell phones and PDA access to headline news, final scores, and upcoming schedules—any time, anyplace. So far fans are responding. About 10,000 began using the wireless broadband system in the 2000 season.

There are a couple of strategies driving the NFL's wireless broadband play. In the short term, providing wireless broadband access to content is a good way to cement fan loyalty. This is particularly important to the NFL in these days of growing competition. Not only is the league facing a direct challenge from the soon-to-be-launched XFL (which began to play February 3, 2001), there are also more teams, a vast array of new sports, and an ever-growing field of TV and Web channels competing for fan attention.

Longer term, the NFL sees wireless broadband as a potentially significant additional revenue source. The NFL is going to wireless broadband to provide a service to its fans to allow them to be even more involved with the league, the teams, and the players and to express their passion for the game in an even deeper way. Down the road, the NFL certainly envisions wireless broadband becoming a revenue stream for it through the addition of advertising and e-commerce opportunities.

The league's move into wireless broadband is a milestone not only for sports leagues but for e-businesses generally, analysts conclude. This is so because the NFL is one of the first major consumer brands to attempt to take advantage of its clout by investing in the world of wireless broadband. The first wave of wireless broadband involved carriers and Web portals teaming up to provide content to wireless broadband consumers. However, they had no clear return on investment (ROI). Now we are seeing people with real skin in the game, like the NFL, betting that their brand will drive wireless broadband usage.

To be sure, the NFL has an enviable track record when it comes to keeping abreast of new technologies. The league launched its official Web site in 1995, becoming the first major sports league to go online. And NFL.com is one of the most frequently visited sports sites on the Web. In October 2000, the site ranked among the top 50 most-visited Web sites of all kinds, hitting number 46 with 6.5 million unique visitors.

Opening Play   The NFL's decision to jump into wireless broadband came almost as suddenly as a game-ending Hail Mary pass completion in the end zone. In the summer of 2000, only weeks before the scheduled start of the football season, NFL Enterprises looked at the rapid growth of wireless broadband technology users in the United States and Europe and decided to take the plunge. The league's biggest hurdle to getting wireless broadband off the ground was not finding content; everything it planned to put out on wireless broadband already existed on the Web site. The first challenge was locating the expertise to launch its wireless broadband initiative in time for the new season, which started September 3.

After a couple of weeks of research, the NFL decided to outsource development and hosting of its wireless broadband applications, signing on with Atlanta-based AnyDevice.com, Inc. Besides hosting wireless broadband applications, AnyDevice has software that translates Web-based content into formats that can be accessed from multiple wireless broadband device types. Within 2 weeks, AnyDevice and the internal NFL.com information technology (IT) group had evaluated which content they wanted to go on the wireless broadband system (scores, schedules, and news) and made the necessary protocol translations to provide that content to a variety of mobile devices, including short message service (SMS) pagers and cell phones, Handheld Device Markup Language–or Wireless Application Protocol–enabled phones (see a discussion of WAP later in this chapter), palm OS devices, and BlackBerry devices from Research in Motion, Ltd.

Just as the season began, the NFL.com site launched its wireless broadband service. Fans could sign up on the Web site and, by following some simple directions, learn how to access the NFL's wireless broadband services from their particular devices. They also could customize the service by choosing when they want to receive news alerts if, for example, they were using a one-way paging device. In addition, they could select which teams and schedules they wanted to track. The registration is free and allows NFL.com and AnyDevice to know which devices are proving most popular and what kinds of information are most valuable to users. So far the most popular devices have been SMS-enabled cell phones and pagers.

Moving the Ball   User feedback from email and focus groups is already prompting modifications to the service. The NFL has learned, for instance, that even brief headlines on the Web, such as "N.J. Jets Starting Running Back Out for Two Weeks with Injury," need to be cut back to something more brief, such as "Jets Running Back Out." It is easy to overestimate the amount of space on a cell phone screen.

Everything the NFL learns about the habits and preferences of mobile users moves it one step closer to its goal of turning its investment in wireless broadband into a profit center. Once the NFL reaches a critical mass of users (in the hundreds of thousands of users), it can offer advertisers intriguing opportunities, and they can explore the possibilities of offering e-commerce to mobile users. Down the road, the league may offer mobile users access to streaming video and audio of game highlights on a subscription basis, for instance.

No one knows yet how rapidly wireless broadband commerce will play out in the next few years. If you think e-commerce is still in its infancy, then m-commerce (mobile e-commerce) is still just a gleam in daddy's eye. While Gartner Group, Inc., of Stamford, CT, estimates that between $10 billion and $1 trillion worth of trade will pass through mobile devices each year by 2005, it remains unclear which wireless broadband standards or devices will be favored by users (wireless broadband standards will be discussed later in this chapter).

Fortunately for organizations such as the NFL that are taking the wireless broadband plunge early, the cost of entry is relatively modest, particularly via outsourcing. Pricing of products and services from companies such as AnyDevice vary, depending on whether customers choose to license the software platform and build the applications themselves or contract with AnyDevice to do the development and whether they choose to use AnyDevice as their application service provider. The NFL, which declined to say how much it is investing in its wireless broadband initiative, is using AnyDevice not only to develop and host its wireless service but also to provide user support. Setup fees for the software range from $10,000 to $100,000. Monthly hosting and support fees run $3000 to $15,000, in addition to usage fees that depend on traffic.

The NFL expects its wireless broadband investments to produce a big score eventually. The wireless broadband audience being built and the lessons the league is learning eventually will be used by individual teams and other units such as the NFL Films division. Already, some teams are launching their own wireless efforts. The San Francisco 49ers, for example, are testing wireless broadband systems that allow spectators at 3Com Park to access breaking news on other games.

Maybe it is not surprising that the league and some of its teams are aggressively pioneering the use of wireless broadband Web technologies. After all, in football (just like in e-business), when you see an opening, you have got to jump on it.

Management Concerns

For corporate IT managers, wireless broadband presents new management issues. Users will upload information into corporate databases from wireless broadband devices, and these databases may include rich media types such as video. This means that wireless broadband operators will invade a space that typically has been the exclusive province of corporate IT. The moment you add a wireless broadband net, the old schema of how you get that data and control access does not make sense anymore.

IT managers have got to realize that connectivity may not just be on their own local-area network (LAN). They have to architect today with the expectation that there may be other networks out there that will be secure. Besides mobility, 3G technology also will provide *fixed wireless broadband*, which means wireless broadband in fixed locations including homes and businesses.

3G systems will give you great flexibility, more bandwidth, and easier access than in a wired setting, which holds more than 800 wireless broadband patents. You could plop your laptop down anywhere and conduct a videoconference if you wish. Bluetooth, a specification for short-range radio links between mobile PCs, mobile phones, and other devices, will complement 3G systems for fixed wireless broadband. 3G and Bluetooth will let corporate users access *context-sensitive* information. This means that when we enter a conference room for a meeting, the agenda can pop up on our devices.

Japan versus North America

North American wireless broadband operators will wait until they prove the business case for 3G systems before investing in infrastructure upgrades. In the meantime, Japan is clearly leapfrogging the rest of the world in deploying 3G technologies.

NTT DoCoMo thinks users will embrace broadband applications, including video. So what is different in the United States? Internet penetration in the United States exceeds cell phone penetration, so the conventional wisdom is that demand for wireless broadband applications in the United States will trail that of Japan. Also, some analysts believe the American culture is less likely to crave wireless broadband multimedia applications.

Japan is a unique culture. The current generation of iMode has taken off because of unique cultural things in Japan. Downloading cartoon screen savers on cell phones in Japan is "big stuff." As 2.5G technologies have taken hold in the United States, wireless broadband operators may resist upgrading to full-blown 3G systems until 2004. However, many operators and technology providers will likely market 2.5G as 3G.

2.5G systems are expected to proliferate in a lot of places and potentially impede customer use of 3G systems. It will take such a long time to get 2.5G out. We had better get used to the idea that we are talking about a 100-kbps experience. It is better than what we have today, but it is not this unlimited euphoria.

Search for Spectrum

Besides the billions of dollars necessary for 3G infrastructure upgrades, the other factor delaying 3G systems in the United States is the lack of dedicated spectrum. In March 2001, the FCC auctioned spectrum in the 700-MHz band. However, some technology providers question whether this block is broad enough to support 3G services, namely, wideband code-division multiple access (W-CDMA). The problem with W-CDMA is that you need so much spectrum. Each channel is 500 MHz wide, and you need two channels to deploy it.

3G on Radar Screens

The bottom line is that wireless broadband operators will pay attention to the wireless broadband application demands of customers. However, operators will stop short of sinking billions of dollars into 3G upgrades until they are reasonably certain the investments will pay off. In the meantime, corporate IT managers should put 3G applications including video on their radar screens.

The advice to IT managers is to test some things out. Nevertheless, corporate strategists must think about how 3G wireless broadband will change network management models and plan for voice, video, and data over IP-oriented mobile networks.

Now let's look at the fundamental changes that have taken place in the development of international commercial wireless broadband telecommunications standards and trace the steps in this evolution. The development of the recommendations, technical specifications, and standards for the air interfaces for the next generation of commercial wireless broadband systems is used as an illustrative example of these changes. This next generation of wireless broadband, which is known as IMT-2000 in the International Telecommunications Union (ITU), is also referred to as third-generation (3G) wireless broadband. The process created by the ITU in developing recommendations for IMT-2000 sets a new framework for international cooperation in telecommunications standards development.

Harmonized 3G Wireless Broadband Standards Development

The ITU has long been a focal point for the development of international telecommunications standardization activities by developing documents known as *recommendations*. These recommendations are developed in each of the two sectors of the ITU—the Radiocommunication Sector (ITU-R) and the Telecommunication Standardization Sector (ITU-T). The efforts of the ITU have been supplemented for many years by a variety of national and regional telecommunications bodies. Within the last decade, however, the number of telecommunications standards development (both accredited and de facto) and technology proponent organizations has grown significantly. Many of these new organizations (the ATM Forum, SDR Forum) are international rather than national or regional in scope. Furthermore, many of these organizations were created for standardizing a very specialized technology, whereas others are more broadly based, although most are not as broadly based as the ITU.

In this changing environment, a critical need has developed for close coordination between these various standards development organizations and similar entities. This close coordination is needed

1. To ensure that there is no duplicative effort and that the *wheel is not reinvented*.

2. To ensure that the necessary standards are developed in an efficient manner such that the rapidly changing needs of the marketplace are met.

3. To address the fact that development of very complex systems with severe time-to-market challenges can no longer be completed by any single organization, entity, or company.[1]

In the commercial wireless broadband area, the focus of recent standardization activity has been on 3G systems, which are referred to in the ITU as *IMT-2000* (see the sidebar, "An Overview of IMT-2000"). Several international organizations were created in response to marketplace demands for the rapid development of technical specifications for 3G systems. Brief descriptions of these organizations known as *partnership projects* and *technology proponents* are provided in the sidebar, "Relevant External Organizations for Commercial Wireless Broadband Standards Development." Thus there are now a number of additional standards/specifications development organizations focusing on commercial wireless broadband that are international in scope rather than specifically national or regional. The ITU has responded positively to these new international wireless broadband specifications development organizations by creating a win-win atmosphere in which there is a role for all the national, regional, and international standards bodies.

An Overview of IMT-2000

International Mobile Telecommunications 2000 (IMT-2000) systems are 3G mobile systems that are scheduled to start service around the year 2000 subject to market considerations. They will provide access, by means of one or more radio links, to a wide range of telecommunications services supported by the fixed telecommunication networks (PSTN/ISDN/IP) and to other services which are specific to mobile users.

A range of mobile terminal types is encompassed, linking to terrestrial- and/or satellite-based networks, and the terminals may be designed for mobile or fixed use. Key features of IMT-2000 are

- High degree of commonality of design worldwide
- Compatibility of services within IMT-2000 and with the fixed networks
- High quality
- Small terminals for worldwide use
- Worldwide roaming capability

■ Capability for multimedia applications and a wide range of services and terminals

The air interfaces of IMT-2000 systems are defined by a set of interdependent ITU-R recommendations. Network aspects of IMT-2000 systems are being developed by the Telecommunication Standardization Sector of the ITU (ITU-T). While the current list of ITU-R recommendations on IMT-2000 is extensive, several, such as Recommendations M.1034 (requirements), M.1225 (radio interface definitions), M.1455 (key characteristics of the air interfaces), and M.1457 (detailed specifications of the air interfaces), are particularly significant to terrestrial commercial wireless systems.[2]

NOTE   Details on IMT-2000 and its related recommendations can be found at *http://www.itu.int/imt. Warning:* URLs are subject to change without notice.

Relevant External Organizations for Commercial Wireless Broadband Standards Development

There are numerous organizations that develop standards and technical specifications for commercial wireless broadband applications. The organizations most relevant to the ITU-R Working Party 8F process for developing recommendations on IMT-2000 and systems beyond IMT-2000 are described below. Other organizations may appear as progress is made on the "beyond" portion of IMT-2000 and beyond.

Third-Generation Partnership Project (3GPP)
This organization is an international organization based on the partnership between several regional and national organizations. The procedures of the Partnership Project are agreed on among the partners but, as far as possible, are founded on those of the bodies involved. The project's results will be published as technical specifications that may be adopted as formal standards by any of the partners. The 3GPP is responsible for

1. The technical specifications for the IMT-2000 CDMA direct spread air interface [also known as W-CDMA and as universal terrestrial radio access (UTRA) frequency-division duplex]
2. IMT-2000 CDMA TDD [also known as TD-SCDMA and as universal terrestrial radio access (UTRA) time-division duplex]
3. The evolution of Global System for Mobile (GSM)

There are two types of partners in the 3GPP: organizational partners and market representation partners. The organizational partners are the following regional/national standards development organizations (SDOs):

- Association of Radio Industries and Businesses (ARIB), Japan
- China Wireless Telecommunications Standard (CWTS) Group, China
- European Telecommunications Standards Institute (ETSI), Europe
- Standards Committee T1, Telecommunications, United States
- Telecommunications Technology Association (TTA), Korea
- Telecommunications Technology Committee (TTC), Japan

The market representation partners of 3GPP are the Universal Mobile Telecommunications System (UMTS) Forum, the Global Mobile Suppliers Association (GSA), and the GSM Association. An overview of 3GPP may be found at *http://www.3gpp.org/About_3GPP/3GPPdesc_copenhagen.ppt*.

Third-Generation Partnership Project 2 (3GPP2)

3GPP2 is an effort spearheaded by the International Committee of the American National Standards Institute's (ANSI) board of directors to establish a 3G partnership project (3GPP) for evolved ANSI/TIA/EIA-41, "Cellular Radiotelecommunication Intersystem Operations," networks and related radio transmission technology (RTTs). The 3GPP2 is responsible for IMT-2000 standards known as IMT-2000 CDMA multicarrier (this radio interface is also known as cdma2000). The regional/national standards development organizations that are members of 3GPP2 are

- Association of Radio Industries and Businesses (ARIB), Japan
- China Wireless Telecommunications Standard (CWTS) Group, China

- Telecommunications Industry Association (TIA), North America
- Telecommunications Technology Association (TTA), Korea
- Telecommunications Technology Committee (TTC), Japan

NOTE   Four of the organizations listed are also members of 3GPP. More information on 3GPP2 may be found at *http://www.3gpp2.org/*.

Universal Wireless Communications Consortium (UWCC)

The UWCC is known as a technology proponent and is responsible for the IMT-2000 TDMA single-carrier air interface (also known as UWC-136, which is specified by American National Standard TIA/EIA-136). The UWCC and the GSM Association have developed agreements for joint development of TDMA technologies such as EDGE. More information on UWCC may be found at *http://www.uwcc.org/*.

Market Organizations

The CDMA Development Group (CDG), the GSM Association, and the UMTS Forum are among the organizations that may be considered to be organizations that are primarily technology market organizations for 3G wireless broadband systems. The Universal Wireless Communications Consortium functions as a market organization as well as a technology proponent responsible for the development of technical specifications for UWC-136. Although these market organizations (with the exception of UWCC) do not develop specifications or standards per se, they have tight relationships with the partnership projects and technology proponents that do develop such materials.[3]

It is the purpose of this part of the chapter to describe this new paradigm of commercial wireless broadband standards development in the international arena and to show how this *new way of doing business* for commercial wireless broadband standards development will continue and can be a role model for other areas of telecommunications standards development.

Timeline of the Changing Wireless Broadband Landscape

Commercial wireless broadband systems generically are described by their *generation*. Although there is no precise definition of the generations, the following definitions can be loosely applied:

- *First generation (1G).* Analog mobile systems including analog cellular and its predecessors (AMPS, TACS, NMT)
- *Second generation (2G).* Digital mobile systems including cellular and personal communications systems (GSM, IS-136 TDMA, IS-95 CDMA, DECT)
- *Third generation (3G).* Digital mobile systems having greatly enhanced performance and service characteristics including high-speed data [up to 2 MBps (IMT-2000 technology family)].[4]

The evolution from 1G to 3G and beyond is usually depicted on a rough timeline. On the same time scale, the level of globalization of standardization activities associated with each generation is also depicted. The term *level of globalization* relates to whether the standards were developed (or at the very least had a predominate focus) at the national level, the regional level, or the international level. National-level organizations include organizations such as the Telecommunication Industry Association (TIA), American National Standards Institute (ANSI) Committee T-1, etc. These organizations are sometimes referred to as the *accredited standards development organizations* (SDOs).

NOTE   There are two generally accepted uses of the word *standards* in the context of this chapter. The first use is a generic reference to any of the documents produced by a variety of different *standards* organizations, such as recommendations from the ITU, technical specifications from organizations such as the partnership projects, and *standards* from recognized standards development organizations (SDOs) such as TIA, ANSI Committee T-1, etc. The second use of the word is that associated with the documents produced by the SDOs which are recognized by standards accrediting organizations such as ANSI. These documents are actually called *standards* as opposed to specifications or recommendations.

At the regional level, there are organizations such as the European Telecommunication Standards Institute (ETSI) that produce technical specifications. The first and second generations of commercial wireless broadband standards/specifications were developed by national and regional standards bodies with a marketplace focus at the national and regional levels.

As a result, the 1G systems tended to be national in scope and therefore incompatible with each other. The 2G commercial wireless broadband systems tended to be more regional in scope (e.g., the GSM system that was developed initially as a pan-Europe standard).

NOTE   As the marketplace evolved into a global market, these same technologies were refocused from a national/regional perspective to be *exported*, often with the addition of new local variants to the standards (e.g., PDC is an Asian market variant of IS-54 TDMA).

The development of 3G standards/specifications, guided by the global requirements developed by the ITU-R, was initiated by national and regional standards bodies such as ETSI, TIA, and ANSI Committee T-1 and other technology proponents in response to the ITU's call for submissions. Harmonized versions were later adopted (after *consensus building*) in ITU-R recommendations, thus giving these technical documents an international status and recognition. It was during this period (1997–2000) that the paradigm shift took place.

Going forward into systems beyond 3G, the standards community is starting with an international perspective in all aspects from marketplace requirements through the technology development cycle, including considerations of common global frequency bands and uniform international regulations. Having an international perspective at the start is important for end users, service providers, and manufacturers. The key is a global design adapted to local market specifics as opposed to a local design being extrapolated into an international marketplace.

Overview of the Paradigm Shift

Fundamental changes have taken place in the requirements for international wireless broadband telecommunications standards development and in the environment in which international standards are developed. In the past, the standards were driven by technology and engineering, were designed to meet the operating needs and requirements of the network operators and manufacturers, could be developed over the course of one or more ITU 2- or 4-year study periods, and tended to have a national or regional perspective. Today, standards are driven by the consumer and the marketplace, are developed with operators and manufacturers acting as surrogates for the end user, must be developed in very short periods of time to meet marketplace demands, and have a global perspective from the start.

The development of commercial wireless broadband standards is an example of the change in the international telecommunications standards development environment and processes. This changing landscape is summarized in Table 28-1 and will be described further in the following parts of this chapter.[5] Part of the change in commercial wireless broadband standards development was precipitated by the establishment of the partnership projects and other forums. However, the underlying driver was the need for standards development organizations to be more responsive to marketplace needs. The marketplace requirement for the timely development of standards that would accommodate the explosive changes in wire-

TABLE 28-1

International
Wireless
Broadband
Standards
Development
Landscape

	Historical Past	Recent Past	Current & Future
Drivers	Driven by technology and engineering	Driven by requirements of the consumer	Continues to be driven by the requirements of the consumer
Customer needs	Customer needs determined by the operators and manufacturers; designed to meet needs of the operators and manufacturers (system capacity and coverage)	Operators and manufacturers act as surrogates for the end-user requirements	Many entities now function and act as surrogates for end-user requirements, including content providers
Perspective	National or regional	Global perspective at the onset	Global perspective in design is now the baseline; design for global marketplace and customize locally
Technical developments	Major technical standards inputs were predominately by manufacturers (often just one or at most a few)	Major collaborative effort of manufacturers, operators, service providers, SDOs, and other proponents	Major partnership effort of manufacturers, operators, service providers, SDOs, and other proponents; more formalized and structured than previously
Services	Before Internet; predominately voice; data was a minor consideration	After Internet; data capability was a major thrust at the start	Beyond Internet; major realignment of access, networks, etc., the *IPing* of systems

less broadband technology was the reason that other international organizations came into being. However, this did not obviate the need for the
ITU because of its unique aspects, including the openness of the ITU's
processes, the need to accommodate the special needs of the developing
countries, and because of the stature of ITU recommendations in the international communications community. Furthermore, the ITU-R is the cen-
troid of international radio regulations related to the natural resource of
wireless broadband, i.e., spectrum.

The 1G and 2G Standards Landscape

The 1G and 2G of commercial wireless broadband standards were developed by national and regional standards organizations. The 2G standards could be considered to be largely regional in scope. For example, the GSM specifications developed by ETSI were developed for the European region. It was only after the standards were developed that the GSM standards were *exported* to other regions of the world, including Africa, North America, and Asia. Similar statements can be made about the 2G standards developed in North America, such as the standards for 2G CDMA and TDMA. These standards were developed from a North American perspective but were later *exported* to other regions of the world.

The 3G and IMT-2000 Standards Landscape   The marketplace requirement for the timely development of standards was the genesis of the partnership projects and technology proponents as well as the subsequent changes in the radio air interface specification (RSPC) recommendation development process. The development of RSPC was the start of the new paradigm in ITU-R recommendations development because of the wide-scale use of normative references in this part of the chapter. The unique use of references in RSPC as an integral part of this ITU-R recommendation is the result of the pioneering relationships developed between ITU-R and external organizations as part of the RSPC development process.

NOTE   RSPC was the initial informal name for ITU-R Recommendation M.1457, "Detailed Specifications of the Radio Interfaces of IMT-2000," which was approved by the Radiocommunication Assembly in May 2000.

NOTE   The term *external organizations* is used in this proposal to mean organizations external to the ITU such as the Third Generation Partnership Projects (3GPP and 3GPP2) and national and regional standards development organizations (SDOs) such as ANSIT-1, ARIB, CWTS, ETSI, TIA, TTC, TTA, etc., and technology proponent organizations such as UWCC.

The process developed and used by ITU-R in the creation of RSPC is a new process for international standards development. This process was designed specifically to provide a mechanism by which the ITU could be responsive to marketplace demands for 3G wireless broadband systems and services. The ITU Task Group 8/1 generated a request for the submittal of radio transmission technologies to the relevant external organizations, who also were requested to perform a self-evaluation as to how well their proposed systems met IMT-2000 requirements previously developed by the ITU. These evaluations and the technical specifications themselves were reviewed by Task Group 8/1 and assessed for compliance with the ITU requirements previously published as part of the M-series of documents on IMT-2000. Systems that implement this ITU-R recommendation and the technical specifications and standards developed by the relevant external organizations are expected to become operational in early 2002.

Of critical note is the phase entitled *consensus building*. One of the stated ITU-R design objectives of IMT-2000 was *that the number of radio interfaces should be minimal and, if more than one interface is required, that there should be a high degree of commonality between them*. The movement that this engendered in the industry was the nexus of the paradigm shift, in that it forced the collaborative partnering development environment now in place both among the external organizations and with the ITU-R. The factors included

1. Recognition of a global market.
2. Understanding that a particular technology was strengthened by incorporation of the best design elements from many sources.
3. Recognition that in the short timeframes allocated, a distributed and parallel development approach was desirable.
4. Recognition that the development effort must be a combination of work by manufacturers, network operators, service providers, and other stakeholders.
5. Finally, realization that to be commercially successful, the family of radio interfaces for IMT-2000 must be the minimal set required to satisfy the diverse marketplace factors.[6]

The ITU-R then compiled an extensive summary of all the air interfaces and an extensive list of references to the technical specifications published by the partnership projects and technology proponents (UWCC) and the standards published by the SDOs such as ARIB, CWTS, ETSI, T1, TIA, TTA, and TTC as delineated in the Recommendation M.1457 (see the sidebar, "Unique Attributes of the RSPC Standards Development Process").

Unique Attributes of the RSPC Standards Development Process

From this we can now ascertain that the unique attributes of the RSPC standards development process included

- Establishment of dynamic new relationships between the ITU and relevant external organizations
- Liberalization of the use of references in ITU recommendations
- A new fast-track process
- New roles for each of the major types of standards organizations:
  - The International Telecommunications Union
  - Radiocommunications Sector (the "R sector")
  - Telecommunication Standardization Sector (the "T Sector").
  - Standards development organizations (e.g., ANSI T1, ARIB, CWTS, ETSI, TIA, TTC, TTA, etc.)
- A place for collaborative entities and market-focused organizations to rally as developmental stakeholders:
  - The partnership projects (3GPP and 3GPP2)
  - Technology proponents (UWCC)
  - Market organizations (GSM Association, OHG, etc.)[7]

The Future Standards Landscape: We Are in a New Era

On the completion of ITU-R Recommendation M.1457, Task Group 8/1 was disbanded, and a new organization (Working Party 8F) was created by ITU-R Study Group 8. This new working party was created in recognition of the fact that the marketplace will be demanding extensions to IMT-2000 systems and probably systems beyond IMT-2000 to accommodate the need for even higher-speed data and wireless broadband access to the Internet. A key aspect of future wireless broadband standards development is that it will have an international aspect from the start and also will have in place a working cooperative, partnering, and synergistic relationship between the ITU and relevant external organizations at the onset. These future developments will build on the foundation established, will refine the concept of partnering, and will extend the vision of consensus building.

Let us now consider a view of the future standards landscape for extensions to the ITU-R recommendations on IMT-2000 and for systems beyond IMT-2000. The international standards development process for IMT-2000 and systems beyond IMT-2000 can be viewed as four sides of a pyramid.

Moving from the base to the tip on each of the four sides provides a national to regional to international perspective. The four sides of the pyramid are

- Marketplace
- Spectrum
- Regulation
- Technology[8]

The common meeting point for three of these four faces of the pyramid is the ITU. The three interrelated factors that come together globally only at the ITU are the spectrum (the natural resource of wireless), the regulation (the authorization to use the natural resource), and the technology (the mechanism to put the natural resource to work).

NOTE   The base is the *marketing organizations* that provide market drivers and requirements. The national and regional standards development organizations and the technology proponents and partnership projects are in the middle of the pyramid, and they develop the technical specifications and standards in coordination with both sectors of the ITU.

One of the key differences between the model used for *systems beyond IMT-2000* and the model used for the initial version of IMT-2000 is that the communication and coordination process between the ITU and the relevant external organizations is in place at the onset rather than being put in place at the end, which was the case for the first version of IMT-2000. This is important because it allows for the cohesive development of requirements between the ITU and the relevant external organizations.

NOTE   There is a large amount of interaction between the ITU and the relevant organizations from market requirements development; establishment of principles, frameworks, and technical requirements; through actual development of the technical specifications; and standards and recommendations. In other words, the interaction is throughout the process, not just at the end of the process, as was the case for the original version of the IMT-2000 standards.

3G CDMA Technologies

This part of this chapter will now cover the following 3G CDMA technologies:

- CDMA environments: DS/CDMA
- 3G mobile communications

- Common IP-based wireless broadband network
- "Smart" antenna systems
- MA-based intelligence for 3G mobile systems.

CDMA Environments: DS/CDMA

This section introduces the key concepts, organization, and operations of distributed sample-based acquisition systems, which have been introduced recently for fast and robust synchronization of the long-period scrambling codes in direct-sequence code-division multiple access (DS/CDMA) environments. In distributed sample-based acquisition (DSA) systems, the transmitter samples and sends the state of its main sequence generator, or main shift register generator, in a distributed manner over the short-period igniter sequence, and the receiver detects and applies the state samples to correct the state of its main shift-register generator SRG, thereby acquiring SRG synchronization after a round of state reception. Acquisition performance of DSA techniques is extremely fast and robust compared with typical correlation-based acquisition techniques of comparable complexity. This section discusses the operation and performance of DSA techniques in the DS/CDMA communications environment as well as their applications to intercell synchronous and asynchronous cellular systems.

In other words, with regards to DS/CDMA wireless broadband mobile systems, the first step of processing at the receiver in the mobile station is to synchronize the locally generated pseudonoise (PN) scrambling sequence to the tracking range of the received waveform. This process is generally known as *initial code acquisition* or *scrambling code acquisition*.

In scrambling code acquisition, fast acquisition is one of the most important goals, and a considerable amount of research has been done on this in the past few decades. The conventional serial search scheme is normally simple in hardware, but the acquisition time is very long for long-duration PN sequences because the mean acquisition time is directly proportional to the period of the PN sequence employed. Several fast acquisition schemes have been developed at the cost of increased complexity. For example, multiple-dwell approaches employed a fast decision-rate matched filter for initial searching and a conventional active correlator for verification. Various parallel acquisition schemes were employed for parallel acquisition processing, but the hardware complexity (the number of active correlators or matched filters) increased exceedingly as the sequence period increased. Several sequential test approaches that combined two threshold comparators with variable dwell time were introduced, and these were successful in reducing the acquisition time to an acceptable level. However, all these correlation-based acquisition schemes cannot provide fast acquisition performance without accompanying severe hardware or computation complexity when the PN sequence period becomes very long.

A novel approach that potentially can reduce the acquisition time tremendously at a small hardware increase can be found in directly estimating the state of the involved shift-register generator (SRG). In principle, it is possible to accomplish code acquisition in L time units if the current sequence of the transmitter SRG of length L is available. This indicates the possibility for tremendous acquisition time reduction because it would take $2^L - 1$ time units if conventional serial search schemes were used. In fact, some earlier schemes called *sequential estimation* attempted to implement this principle by making L consecutive hard decisions on the incoming code chips using the chip-matched filter and then loading them to the receiver SRG as the current SRG state. This attempt was indeed successful in demonstrating a speedy acquisition process but failed in practical application due to lack of reliable estimation of the chip values.

Recently, a new acquisition technique that realizes direct SRG acquisition through distributed SRG state sample transmission has been introduced under the name of *distributed sample-based acquisition* (DSA); a family of variations followed. DSA basically features two new mechanisms: distributed sampling correction for synchronization of the SRG and distributed conveyance of the state samples via a short-period sequence. Their combination turned out to be very effective in speeding up the acquisition process at low complexity and making performance reliable even in very poor channel environments.

DSA   In DSA, the state of the main SRG in the transmitter is sampled and conveyed to the receiver in a distributed manner, while the state samples are detected and applied to correct the state of the main SRG in a progressive manner. For conveyance of the distributed state samples, a short-period sequence, the *igniter sequence*, is employed.

ORGANIZATION AND OPERATION   Figure 28-1 shows a functional block diagram of the DSA system.[9] In the transmitter, the main SRG generates the main sequence $\{s_m\}$ of long period N_M, $2^L - 1$, which is used for data scrambling and whose fast acquisition is the ultimate goal. On the other hand, the igniter SRG generates the igniter sequence $\{c_m\}$ of short period N_I, $2S$. The time-advanced state sampling block takes the state sample z_n of the main SRG at time $(R + n - 1)N_I$ in advance, for a reference value R.

Figure 28-1

A functional block diagram of the DSA.

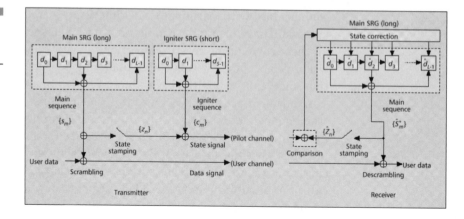

NOTE   The system description is given on a discrete time basis, with the unit time set to the chip duration T_c.

The state samples are scrambled by the igniter sequence and conveyed over the pilot channel. In the meantime, the user data are scrambled by the main sequence and transmitted over the user channel.

For safety against detection error, a verification process is appended to check whether or not the conveyed and receiver-generated state samples coincide V more times after the L comparison—*correction operations for a V chosen to meet the performance target.* If all the V state sample sets coincide, the receiver declares synchronization of the main sequence complete, and the tracking and estimation processes follow. Otherwise, the acquisition process is reinitiated.

A DSA-BASED DS/CDMA SYSTEM   Figure 28-2 depicts a functional block diagram of a DS/CDMA system employing the basic DSA scheme.[10] The DSA functional blocks in Figure 28-1 are embedded.

The transmitter part consists of a DSA spreader and a sample spreader, and the receiver part contains their despreading counterparts (DSA despreader and sample despreader). The DSA spreader-despreader pair takes the synchronization function, whereas the sample spreader-despreader pair take the sample conveyance function. These two functions are supported by the main SRG residing in the DSA spreader and the igniter SRG residing in the sample spreader.

In the transmitter (or base station, BS), the differential phase-shift keying (DPSK) modulator maps the state sample generated by the time-advanced sampling block to the corresponding PSK state symbol x_n and produces the DPSK pilot symbol f_n by adding the phase of x_n to the phase

Figure 28-2
A functional block diagram of the DS/CDMA system employing the DSA scheme: (a) transmitter; (b) receiver; (c) structure of the channel estimator.

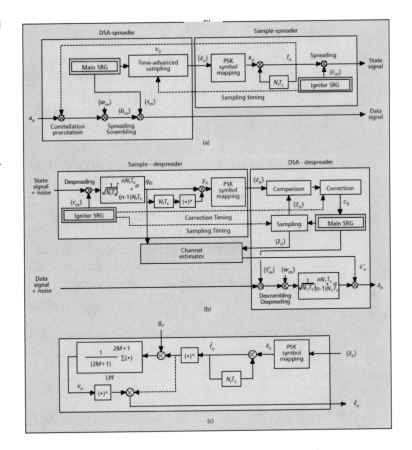

Figure 28-2
A functional block diagram of the DS/CDMA system employing the DSA scheme: (a) transmitter; (b) receiver; (c) structure of the channel estimator.

accumulated up to the previous time slot. The resulting pilot symbol is spread by a period of the igniter sequence and transmitted through the pilot channel in the interval $[(R + n - 1)N_I, (R + n)N_I]$. On the other hand, each user's data are multiplied by the pilot symbol f_n, spread by one of the orthogonal channelization sequences $\{w_m\}$, scrambled by the main sequence $\{s_m\}$, and then transmitted in the interval $[(R + n - 1)N_I, (R + n)N_I]$. The state signal (or pilot signal) and data signal are propagated over the same multipath fading channel to arrive at the mobile station.

The receiver (or mobile station, MS) first acquires the DPSK modulated igniter sequence employing the simple noncoherent threshold detector. It is assumed that the simple serial search method is applied to the igniter sequence acquisition, whereas any other search methods may be used to speed up the acquisition process. After the timing synchronization of the igniter sequence, the MS despreads the received state signal and differentially detects the conveyed sample z_n. Then the comparison-correction-based SRG synchronization process follows, as described in the preceding.

Figure 28-3 depicts the timing relations among various processes in the transmitter and receiver.[11] Once synchronization of the SRG is completed, the receiver despreads the data signal by multiplying the synchronized main sequence and the corresponding channelization code and then coherently demodulates the despread data by using the channel estimate obtained from the pilot channel sequence (or state signal). The relevant channel estimation process is discussed later in this chapter.

PERFORMANCE AND COMPLEXITY   In simple approximation, the overall mean acquisition time of the DSA scheme employing an active correlator is about $(N_I + L + V) \times N_I T_c$ (the sum of the igniter sequence serial search time and correction/verification time), whereas that of a conventional serial search scheme is about $(2^L - 1) \times N_I T_c$. Thus the relative acquisition time of DSA, normalized to the serial search case, is approximately $(N_I + L + V)/2^L$, which becomes extremely small as L increases. V is typically set to a value smaller than L. As a typical example, the relative acquisition time reduces to 0.004 when $N_I = 128$ and $L = 15$ and to 0.001 when $N_I = 256$ and $L = 18$.

For implementation, the DSA necessitates a main sequence generator, an igniter sequence generator, a state symbol generator, a (time-advanced)

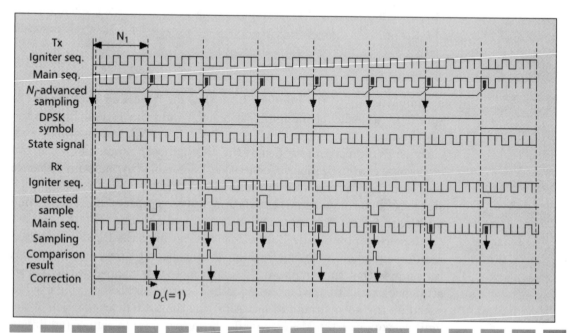

Figure 28-3   System timing diagram example $N_I = 8$, $D_c = 1$, DPSK modulation).

sampling circuit, a correction circuit, and a verification circuit. With all these functions, however, the required hardware and computation are very simple, so implementation complexity is very low.

CHANNEL ESTIMATION The typical DS/CDMA pilot channel signal takes the form of an unmodulated scrambling sequence itself, whose replica can be generated immediately once the timing synchronization is completed. However, in the case of DSA, the receiver cannot generate the perfect state signal even after timing synchronization because it has no information on the initial phase of the transmitter DPSK modulater.

NOTE This is called the *initial phase discrepancy problem.*

To overcome the phase discrepancy problem, arrange the transmitter pilot generation block to provide the phase information of the DPSK pilot symbols to the data generation block and rotate the data constellation before spreading. This process is called *constellation prerotation*. The receiver can now obtain the channel estimate by employing a simple channel estimator, as shown in Figure 28-2*a*.

THE DSA FAMILY The original DSA scheme was designed on the basis of binary orthogonal state symbol generation, in which the state signal was used directly as the channel estimation reference without employing data constellation prerotation. The DSA was then extended to batch DSA (BDSA) and parallel DSA (PDSA), which are capable of manipulating multiple samples concurrently, for application to general *M*-ary signaling or multicarrier DS/CDMA systems. The acquisition performance degradation that can happen when the number of concurrently manipulated state samples increases was resolved by introducing DPSK-signaling DSA (D2SA). For enhanced robustness of the DSA scheme in the worst-case channel environment, correlation-aided DSA (CDSA) incorporating the state symbol correlation process was introduced.

In CDSA, a state symbol correlation process is added as an extension to the original comparison-correction-based acquisition process. If the initial-stage acquisition, which is based on the comparison-correction process, fails to acquire synchronization within a certain time limit, the state symbol correlation process is activated based on the state symbol sequences that have been collected until that time. In this second-stage acquisition, synchronization is acquired by determining the shifted sequence that produces the maximum correlation energy as the truly transmitted sequence. The state symbol correlation process indeed provides a very high synchronization success probability even in poor channel environments, but the required additional memory or computation complexity is minimal.

DSA-Based Cell Search in DS/CDMA Cellular Systems   The DSA scheme, as it is, can be employed efficiently for cell search (the base station scrambling code acquisition of the cell where the mobile station is currently located) in commercial DS/CDMA systems such as IS-95, IS-95B, cdma2000-1X (cdmaOne Family), and wideband CDMA (W-CDMA). However, in commercial cellular applications, the robustness of the acquisition process against wireless broadband channel obstructions such as shadowing, fading, and frequency offset is as important as the acquisition time speedup. Fortunately, CDSA renders the added capability of robustness to such commercial applications.

SYNCHRONOUS DS/CDMA CELLULAR SYSTEMS: IS-95 OR CDMA2000 APPLICATIONS   An intercell synchronous DS/CDMA cellular system relies on an external timing reference source and uses different time-shifted versions of a single PN sequence as the forward link scrambling code of each cell site. This single-code scheme enables each MS to acquire the scrambling codes in a relatively short time with simple hardware.

Let's consider an intercell synchronous cellular system composed of 512 cells. Let's also assume the following on the overall system operation: A BS transmits multiple user data signals in parallel after orthogonal channelization. A complex extended m-sequence of period 215 is used for chip scrambling.

NOTE   In cellular applications, Figure 28-2 corresponds to BS-MS organizations, respectively. In this case, the transmitter generally transmits multiple data signals in parallel.

Each cell timing is aligned to the external timing reference such as global positioning system (GPS) timing. The scrambling sequence of each cell is a shifted version of the same scrambling sequence. The minimal sequence phase difference is 64. There is a one-to-one correspondence between the states of the I-phase main SRG and the Q-phase main SRG.

For CDSA realization, let's take multiple complex sequences of period 256 as the igniter sequence set elements. In the cellular applications, multiple igniter sequences are needed to prevent use of the same sequence in neighboring cells. The set size should be designed considering both the MS complexity and cocode cell interference. Let's set the size to 4 and adopt the orthogonal Gold sequences as the element sequences, while any other good sequences are equally applicable (the Golay-Hadamard sequences).

The four element sequences and their shifted versions, shifted by 64, 128, and 192 chips, constitute a set of 16 different igniter sequences that are also time-aligned to GPS timing. In relation to the state symbol correlation process, the number of candidate state symbol sequences (M_S) is 4, and the state symbol sequence period (N_S) is 128.

Because there is a one-to-one correspondence between the states of the I-phase and Q-phase SRGs, the BS takes the I-phase SRG state samples only and broadcasts the resulting state signal through the common pilot channel. The MS first identifies the igniter sequence used in the current cell and searches for its timing, which is usually accomplished by a parallel search of the four candidate sequences or other equivalent methods. When the igniter sequence search is completed, the comparison-correction process is conducted for synchronization of the I-phase main SRG. If the synchronization is not completed until B state symbols are detected, the state symbol correlation process is triggered. Let's take $B = 128$, which is the same as the state symbol sequence period. For state symbol correlation, let's take 4×128 correlations of 128-long sequences. Finally, the Q-phase main SRG state, frame boundaries, and channelization code boundaries are immediately searched on the basis of the system frame structure.

Figure 28-4 plots the resulting mean acquisition time performance of the synchronous cellular system employing the CDSA (or DSA) scheme compared with that employing the conventional parallel search acquisition (PSA) scheme operating four parallel correlators.[12] The operating chip rate is 1.2288 Mchips/s, and a 100-Hz Doppler Rayleigh fading channel is used. The chip signal-to-noise ratio (SNR) denotes the average ratio of the pilot chip energy to the one-side noise power spectral density. DSA and CDSA can complete the cell search about 30 times faster than PSA with comparable complexity in moderate SNR ranges. When the SNR becomes very low, the performance of DSA shifts to the level of PSA, but CDSA maintains the same level of acquisition time gain.

The cdma2000 specification contains multicarrier DS/CDMA transmission systems ($3 \times$ mode) as well as IS-95 single-carrier systems ($1 \times$ mode). The CDSA scheme also can be applied efficiently to the multicarrier mode once the multiple-state sample-based SRG synchronization problem is resolved. The multiple-state sample-based comparison-correction process is readily developed in; thus the application of CDSA to the multicarrier mode is straightforward.

ASYNCHRONOUS DS/CDMA CELLULAR SYSTEMS: IMT-2000 W-CDMA APPLICATIONS In contrast to an intercell synchronous cellular system, an intercell asynchronous cellular system assigns different PN sequences to different

Figure 28-4
Overall mean
acquisition time in
100-Hz Doppler
Rayleigh fading
channel with respect
to chip SNR. PSA
indicates the
conventional parallel
search algorithm.

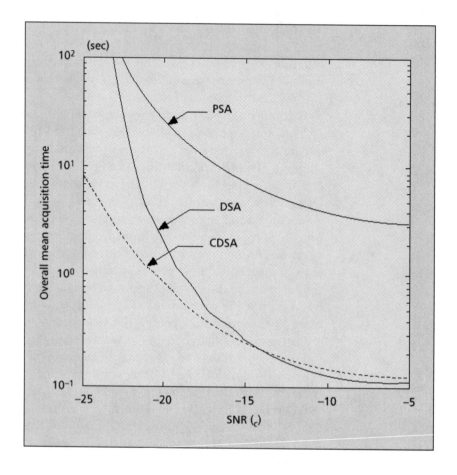

Figure 28-4
Overall mean acquisition time in 100-Hz Doppler Rayleigh fading channel with respect to chip SNR. PSA indicates the conventional parallel search algorithm.

cell sites, eliminating the dependence on external timing references. Consequently, very sophisticated and complex synchronization schemes are needed to acquire the scrambling codes within the allowed time limit, and the code identity and time shift have to be searched simultaneously.

Figure 28-5 depicts the functional block diagram of the BS and MS in a cell of an asynchronous cellular system that employs the DQPSK-based CDSA scheme.[13] The main SRG-1 and main SRG-2 generate the truncated complex Gold scrambling sequence of length $N_M = 38,400$, and the igniters SRG-1 and SRG-2 generate the complex igniter sequence of length $N_I = 256$. Since there is no external timing reference, the number of element sequences the igniter SRGs generate must coincide with the igniter sequence set size, for which 16 is taken. Each of 512 cells in the cellular system belongs to one of the 16 cell groups employing the same igniter sequence. Consequently, there are 32 cells in a cell group.

Figure 28-5

A functional block diagram of the acquisition-related part of the intercell asynchronous W-CDMA cellular system employing the DQPSK-based CDSA scheme: (a) base station (transmitter); (b) mobile station (receiver).

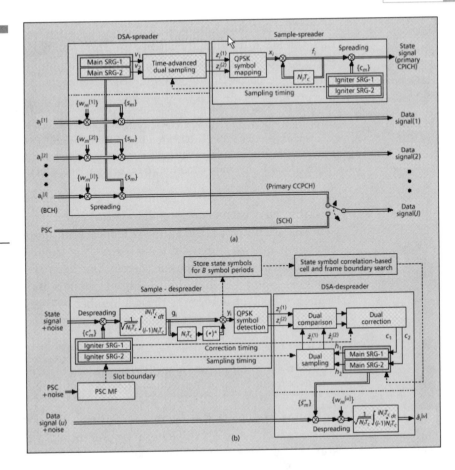

The BS takes a pair of state samples from the two main SRGs and maps them to the I-phase and Q-phase of the QPSK constellation to generate the state symbol x_i. The state symbol is differentially encoded, spread by the 256-long igniter sequence allocated to the BS, and then broadcast through the primary common pilot channel (CPICH). To speed up the frame timing acquisition, the primary synchronization code (PSC) is also broadcast once at the beginning of every slot, with the remaining interval of the slot used to transmit the primary common control channel (CCPCH) signal. In a CDSA-based W-CDMA system, secondary synchronization code (SSC) transmission is not needed.

The MS first searches the slot boundary by employing PSC-matched filtering and then identifies the igniter sequence of the current cell by comparing the correlation energy between the incoming state signal and each of the 16 candidate igniter sequences. Once the igniter sequence is identified, the MS differentially detects the state symbol, demaps it to a pair of state samples, and acquires the primary scrambling code through the comparison-correction-based main SRG synchronization process.

> **NOTE**   The key feature of the comparison-correction-based synchronization process applied to the W-CDMA system is that the state samples taken from each of the two main SRGs are always manipulated in pairs, which enables simultaneous search of the cell number as well as the frame boundary timing. Refer to the dual sampling, dual comparison, and dual correction blocks in Figure 28-5.

If the cell search is not completed until B (for which we take 150) state symbols are detected, the state symbol correlation process is activated in the following two steps. First, determine the frame timing by comparing the energies resulting from the correlations between the soft state symbol sequence $\{y_i\}$ and each of the 15 shifted versions of the Q-phase candidate sequence. Second, determine the cell number by comparing the correlation energies between the soft state symbol sequence $\{y_i\}$ and each of the 32 candidate I-phase sequences.

> **NOTE**   The initial state of the BS main SRG-1 is set on the basis of the cell number, while that of the main SRG-2 is set to a string of all 1s.

Figure 28-6 plots the mean acquisition time performances of CDSA compared with the Third Generation Partnership Project (3GPP) three-step cell search scheme.[14] The operating chip rate of 3.84 Mchips/s and a 200-Hz Doppler Rayleigh fading channel are assumed.

> **NOTE**   The SIR parameters I_{or}, I_{oc}, and N_o denote the total BS signal power spectral density (PSD), other cell interference PSD, and the background thermal noise PSD, respectively, measured in the MS.

The hardware or computation complexity is comparable for the two schemes or slightly less for CDSA. Let's observe why CDSA provides better acquisition time performance than the 3GPP scheme and the performance gap steeply increases as the channel environment becomes worse (in low signal-to-interference ratio or large frequency offset environments).

Now let's look at how transcoding proxies for mobile World Wide Web access have been developed. In the near future, wideband mobile communication systems such as IMT-2000 will emerge, and these proxies will have to cope with a variety of media such as video. This section identifies issues involved in viewing a video stream in a mobile computing environ-

Figure 28-6

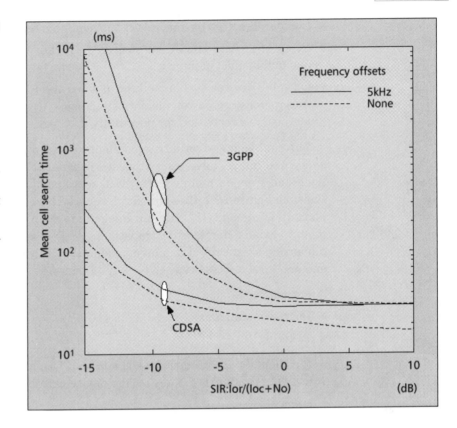

Figure 28-6
Overall mean cell search time performances in a Rayleigh fading channel with respect to SIR $[I_{or}/(I_{oc} + N_o)]$ for 5-kHz frequency offset and no offset. (It is assumed that the SCH/primary-CCPCH and primary-CPICH use 10 percent of the BS total signal power, respectively.)

ment. To handle these issues, a video transcoding system and its control method are proposed. These mechanisms provide stable transmission of video data and comfortable video viewing for user clients by estimating the communication conditions, client device capabilities, and user preferences.

3G Mobile Communications

Recent mobile communications systems (cellular systems, cordless phone systems) and client devices (notebook PCs, personal digital assistants, and cellular phones) enable us to access Web content on the Internet. Web content is becoming richer, including much multimedia data such as image and video. However, such multimedia content is not appropriate for mobile Internet access because of the following restrictions on the wireless broadband link and client devices:

- Compared with wireline access, the available bandwidth is narrow.
- Communications conditions such as error rate change dynamically due to the effect of fading.
- On small devices such as cellular phones and PDAs, device capabilities (processing power, memory size, display capability, and input method) are restricted for portability.[15]

In recent years, several transcoding proxies, which target markup language and image, have been proposed in order to mitigate these restrictions and provide mobile users with more comfortable Web access. As shown in Figure 28-7, these proxies receive Web content such as Hypertext Markup Language (HTML) and image data from Web servers and relay them to mobile clients after transcoding.[16] *Transcoding* is the process of converting a data object in one representation into another representation and has three process types:

- Format conversion
- Data size reduction
- Tailoring[17]

If a client device cannot support a type of format, a proxy needs to convert a data format into a format the device can support. The format con-

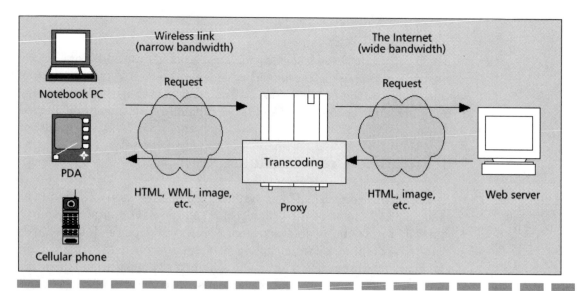

Figure 28-7   The basic architecture of transcending systems.

version can be carried out between media types (text to voice) and within media types (HTML to Wireless Markup Language, or WML). Also, data size reduction shortens response time. To obtain this effect, some proxies try to reduce the data size (in bytes) of an image by reducing its size (in pixels) and quality. In addition, to improve user viewing, some proxies tailor Web content. Since the display size of a portable device is very small, it is difficult to view Web content fully as designed for a desktop or notebook PC. Therefore, these proxies make a text summary by analyzing the context and reduce image size (in pixels) in order to fit the client display size.

In the near future, wideband mobile communications systems, such as International Mobile Telecommunications 2000 (IMT-2000), will emerge, and mobile users will enjoy high-quality video applications (video mail, videophone, visual news, games). However, when viewing a video stream in a mobile computing environment, there still will be some problems because transmission of video data is easily affected by communications conditions if the transmission continues for a long time, and the client device is not able to properly reproduce a heavy video stream, which is beyond its capabilities.

In this section, let's carry out a basic examination of a video transcoding proxy that provides stable transmission of video data and comfortable viewing for mobile users. The rest of this section is organized as follows: It will identify issues involved in viewing a video stream in a mobile computing environment. To handle these issues, it proposes a video transcoding system and its control method. The features of the transcoder that has been developed are shown.

Issues of Viewing a Video Stream in a Mobile Environment   In this section, issues involved in viewing a video stream in a mobile computing environment will be identified, and methods of handling these issues will be proposed. Video streams encoded by a high-bit-rate compression method (MPEG-1) require several megabits per second of bandwidth and are not suitable for a strictly band-limited environment. Therefore, video streams should be encoded by a low-bit-rate compression method (MPEG-4). MPEG-4 is appropriate for mobile access because it is robust to channel errors. From this point of view, some MPEG-4 codec large-scale integrations (LSIs) for mobile devices are under development, and MPEG-4 is apparently becoming the mainstream technique for mobile video use.

When communications conditions get worse and error rate increases in a wireless broadband link, transmission jitter increases because error packets are retransmitted based on Radio Link Control (RLC) protocol located at the data-link layer. If any packets are not recovered by retransmission using a reliable transport protocol such as the Transmission Control Protocol (TCP), error packets are retransmitted end to end. However, this causes more transmission jitter and throughput reduction. Also, if an unreliable transport protocol such as the User Datagram Protocol (UDP) is used, packets not recovered by retransmission and flooded by congestion on the communications link are discarded, so the rate of packets that arrive at the client decreases. As a result, in both cases the application layer throughput reduces, and video data cannot be transferred stably. Therefore, the data rate of a video stream needs to be adapted in accordance with communications conditions. In addition, jitter can be absorbed by preserving some video data on the client buffer.

As far as client device capabilities are concerned, display size, processing power, and memory size have to be taken into account. Since the display size of portable devices is small (on cellular phones both width and height are about 100 pixels at most), a video stream may be larger than the display size and is not easily viewed by mobile users. Hence both the width and height of a video frame have to be fitted to the display size. In another method, the size may be reduced by the user client. However, this places an extra load on the user client and is undesirable for mobile systems where the processing power of the client device is low.

If the client device does not have enough real-time video stream decoding power, a mobile user cannot fully view video streams. The amount of processing required for decoding is related to the number of video frames in 1 s (frame rate) and the total number of pixels in one frame (frame size). Therefore, the frame rate and frame size need to be adjusted to the processing power of the client device. As for memory size, the client device needs to have sufficient memory to preserve several decoded frames because, in encoding methods such as MPEG-4, the decoding process requires a few frames before and after the frame that is actually decoded.

Video Transcoding System Architecture   To resolve the issues described previously, let's take a video proxy approach. With this approach, if a content provider provides only one video stream, the video proxy performs transcoding properly for each user and provides converted video streams. Then it is possible to adjust the video stream to the variety of device capabilities and communication conditions at the time, and the extra work involved if content providers were to prepare and maintain content can be saved.

The architecture of the video transcoding system is illustrated in Figure 28-8.[18] The system consists of a client proxy that collects profiles required for transcoding and a video proxy that converts video streams sent from the Internet and delivers converted videos to mobile users.

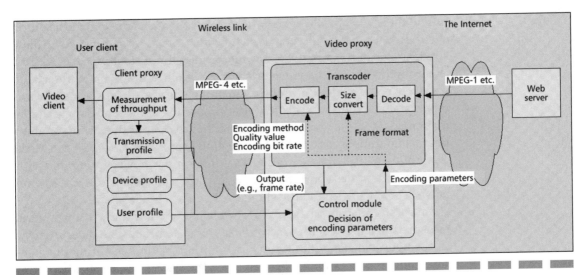

Figure 28-8 Video transcoding system architecture.

The video proxy has two components, a transcoder and a control module. The transcoder is an actual conversion engine of a video stream. It decodes an input video stream and then performs size conversion and reencoding. In decoding a video stream, for the decoder control timing at which video frames are read, the transcoding process can be synchronized with time, and it is possible to execute video transcoding in real time. In size conversion, it is necessary to specify the frame format (CIF and QCIF). The frame format indicates both width and height of the video stream. Furthermore, in encoding, the encoding method, quality value, and encoding bit rate must be specified. The encoding method is a compression method such as MPEG-4. The quality value is a value related to a table that is used for quantization of the video frame. In short, it indicates the quality of the video frame. Actually, applications are free to decide the relationship between the quality value and quantization table; that is, the quality value depends on applications. In this section it is assumed that a greater quality value indicates high quality, and the lesser the quality value, the lower is the quality. The encoding bit rate is the data rate at which the transcoder aims, and the frame rate is adjusted in the transcoder automatically so that the data rate may become the specified rate. As described in the preceding, these four encoding parameters must be specified in transcoding. Then the control module, based on profiles sent from the client proxy, decides on a set of encoding parameters appropriate for each user.

The client proxy relays the data between the video proxy and the video client. It keeps data size relayed to the video client; by adding up the data size in a specified interval, the download throughput can be measured. The client proxy notifies the video proxy of its result. Furthermore, the client proxy collects the device profile, which includes hardware and software information on the device (display size, processing power, and decoder information) and the user profile such as preference information, which enables the mobile user to control the transcoding process, and notifies the video proxy of them. In implementation, the client proxy may be integrated with the video client or separated from it; say, the video client is located on a notebook PC or PDA and the client proxy on a cellular phone.

One of the characteristics of the system is that download throughput is measured on a user client, which enables more accuracy than measurement on the network side (video proxy). In addition, by implementing the measurement process on an application layer, the system can implicitly control overall effects including lower-layer issues such as RLC and TCP/UDP.

The Control Method for Video Transcoding   This section describes a process wherein the control module decides four encoding parameters based on the profiles. In order to decide appropriate encoding parameters, decisions must be made by estimating the communications conditions, client device capabilities, and user preferences. Since each decision affects another, they must be made in the following order:

- Encoding method
- Encoding bit rate
- Frame format
- Quality value

ENCODING METHOD   From the device profile, the control module determines the encoding method (MPEG-4) by recognizing the available decoder on the client device. This decision enables the video proxy to adapt to a variety of decoders.

ENCODING BIT RATE   When throughput between the video proxy and client is less than the data rate of a video stream, some packets sent to the client will be delayed and lost. Therefore, the control module determines the encoding bit rate of a video stream based on the measured throughput so that the data rate may be adjusted to the available bandwidth of bottlenecked links. As a result of this decision, stable transmission of video data is possible.

TABLE 28-2

The Relationship
Between Frame
Format and Size

Frame Format	CIF	QCIF	SQCIF
Width (pixels)	352	176	128
Height (pixels)	288	144	96

FRAME FORMAT The control method determines frame format by estimating both the display size and processing power of the client device. This decision is made as follows: First, the control module derives the frame format for a video stream to be fit to the client display size. For instance, from a relationship of frame format and size such as in Table 28-2, the control module derives the largest frame format for which both width and height are within the client display size.[19] Next, the control module calculates the maximum frame rate (F_{max}) at which the client device can reproduce a video stream in real time on the frame format derived in the preceding (Figure 28-9).[20]

F is the frame rate of a video stream, while S is the frame size of a video stream and is derived by multiplying width by height. In calculating, since P_t differs with the capability of the CPU and video codec LSI present on the client device, P_t is determined based on the processing power information in the device profile.

Figure 28-9

F_{max} and restriction of
processing power.

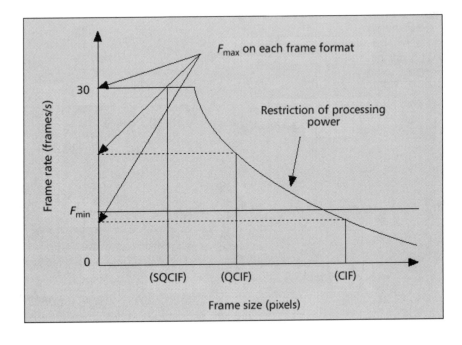

Finally, if either a content provider or a mobile user specifies the minimum frame rate (F_{min}) of a video stream, the control module estimates F_{max}. This situation may occur when the user wants the video proxy to guarantee the necessary video motion. As a result of this estimation, if $F_{max} < F_{min}$, the control module considers that the client device cannot reproduce a video stream with the necessary motion in the frame format derived in the preceding and selects a smaller frame format.

QUALITY VALUE   The quality value indicates the quality of the video frame. Under the conditions of a constant encoding bit rate and the same frame format, the more the quality value increases, the more the frame rate decreases; i.e., there is a tradeoff between quality and frame rate. Therefore, in the system, a quality value is determined based on user preference (frame-rate-weighted or quality-weighted).

Also, under the condition of the same frame format and constant quality value, the frame rate of a video stream after transcoding is proportional to the encoding bit rate up to 30 frames per second (Figure 28-10). Q_{max} and Q_{min} show the maximum and minimum quality value that can be set on the transcoder, respectively. However, this relationship depends on the features of the video stream and transcoder, and it is difficult to estimate

Figure 28-10
The relationship between frame rate and encoding bit rate for quality value.

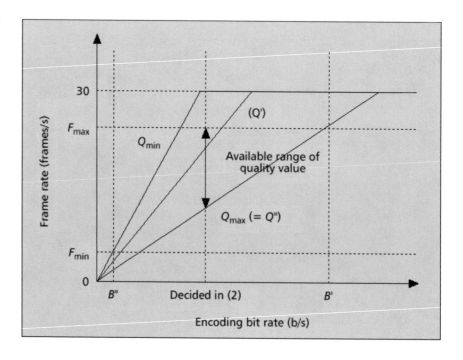

this dependence and reflect it in decisions in real time. Therefore, the relationship between encoding bit rate and frame rate for each quality value and each frame format in advance is acquired experimentally. And the control module, based on this relationship, determines a quality value so that the frame rate is between F_{min} and F_{max}, derived in the frame format decision above.

Actually, the control module executes a frame-rate-weighted control by utilizing the minimum quality value (Q') for which the frame rate is less than F_{max}. Furthermore, the control module executes quality-weighted control by utilizing the maximum quality value (Q'') for which the frame rate is greater than F_{min}. In addition, when a mobile user can select a preference from several steps (by a slide bar), it is possible to perform fine control. In this case, the control module determines a quality value by mapping the range of user preferences to the range of quality values between Q' and Q''. However, when a quality value for which the frame rate is less than F_{max} does not exist (say, where the encoding bit rate is greater than B' in Figure 28-10),[21] the following control must be performed to adapt to the device capability:

- Setting a lower encoding bit rate

- Increasing F_{max} by deriving a smaller frame format

- Eliminating video frames in the transcoder.[22]

Conversely, if a quality value for which the frame rate is greater than F_{min} does not exist (say, where the encoding bit rate is less than B'' in Figure 28-10), it is necessary to increase the frame rate by deriving a smaller frame format. Furthermore, the frame rate actually varies with the content of the video stream. Therefore, by referring to the frame rate after transcoding, the control module has to perform feedback control that varies the quality value temporally so that the frame rate is between F_{min} and F_{max}.

In the preceding decision processes, the control module decides four encoding parameters by estimating the communications conditions, client device capabilities, and user preferences. The preceding decisions must be performed periodically because communications conditions and profiles may change during transcoding.

Features of the Transcoder   In this section, using the transcoder, the relationship between encoding bit rate and frame rate that is needed for the quality value decision is derived experimentally. In the transcoder, an MPEG-1 video stream is converted into a Quality Motion (QM) 1 video stream in which the encoding bit rate can be set from 10 to 500 kbps and the quality value can be set from 1 (low quality) to 12 (high quality). CIF-to-CIF and CIF-to-QCIF size conversions are supported.

NOTE   Quality Motion, developed by KDD R&D Laboratories, is a low-bit-rate encoding method like MPEG-4.

In Figure 28-11*b* it is realized that the frame rate of CIF format is less than that of QCIF format. This is so because the number of CIF format bits in one frame is greater than that of QCIF format bits.

Now, let's look at one of the other 3G CDMA technologies.

Common IP-Based Wireless Broadband Network

Proponents of Internet Protocol, version 6 (IPv6), a controversial upgrade to the Internet's main communications protocol, have finally found their killer application: wireless broadband. Since early 2000, the focus of the IPv6 community has shifted from trying to convince traditional, hardwired ISPs to roll out IPv6. Instead, IPv6 researchers and product developers are responding to a groundswell of support from European and Japanese wireless broadband suppliers that need the unlimited supply of Internet addresses offered by IPv6.

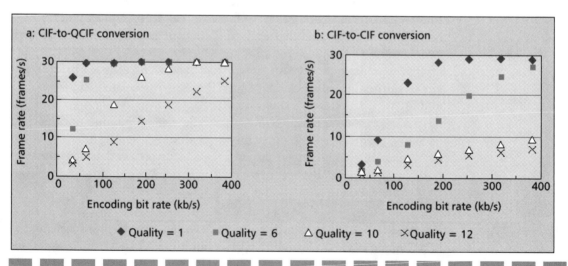

Figure 28-11   Experimental results of the relationship between frame rate and encoding bit rate.

The shift was evident as Sun, Microsoft, and IBM fully expected proliferation of Internet-enabled mobile phones and handheld computers to propel IPv6 into the core of the Internet. What caused the shift in momentum for IPv6 was the European wireless broadband community's decision in May 2000 to adopt the new protocol in its next-generation wireless broadband initiative, dubbed 3GPP for Third-Generation Partnership Project.

Adoption of IPv6 by 3GPP is the first real business case and the biggest business case for IPv6. IPv6 is practically what is needed for wireless broadbrand applications because it provides true end-to-end security and true end-to-end voice over IP.

3GPP has provided the ice-breaking leadership that will pull the fixed networks to IPv6. IPv6 is the Internet engineering community's answer to the problem of a rapidly depleting supply of Internet addresses.

The current version of IP (IPv4) uses 32-bit addresses to identify computers connected to the Internet. Theoretically, IPv4 can support 4 billion addresses. But due to a history of inefficient address assignments, half these addresses were already assigned. And only a fraction of the remaining addresses actually can be used because of shortcomings in the original IPv4 design.

IPv6 uses 128-bit addresses, which means the protocol can support a virtually unlimited number of computer systems and other devices connected to the Internet. In addition to enough addresses, IPv6 offers several advantages for wireless broadband applications, including built-in security and mobility and a simpler configuration.

Yet, despite its benefits, IPv6 has been slow to take off. Only a handful of companies offer IPv6 support in shipping products. Migrating to IPv6 will be time-consuming and expensive for ISPs and large corporations. And alternative technologies such as network address translation, which uses private rather than globally unique Internet addresses, are growing in popularity. However, with 3GPP looming as a real market for IPv6 products, network vendors are stepping up efforts to ship IPv6-compliant products.

Recently, Sun announced plans to ship an IPv6-compliant version of Java in early 2002, with beta software due next fall. Sun also will add support for mobile IPv6 and IP security to Solaris 8 in the fall of 2001.

Meanwhile, IBM executives are looking across IBM's product lines and service offerings to see where they can integrate IPv6 into upcoming releases. IBM was the first UNIX supplier to offer an IPv6 implementation back in 1997 and recently shipped IPv6 support for OS/390 systems. Now IBM is planning to add IPv6 to its OS/400, Linux, WebSphere, and Tivoli offerings.

IBM does not anticipate significant customer demand for IPv6 until 2002 or 2003, but it considers the technology a critical part of its e-business strategy. Pervasive devices and pervasive users are driving a whole new way of thinking about e-business. The Internet is not just about communicating with established customers and partners but with potentially hundreds and thousands of people all around the world. In order to do this, you have to make fundamental changes in the way you do business. IPv6 is one of these fundamental changes.

Hewlett Packard (HP) has offered an IPv6 developer's kit for 2 years and will add IPv6 support into its core UNIX operating system in 2002. HP also plans to offer IPv6 support in its handhelds, printers, and network management software.

Mobile networks will drive IPv6. When there is enough critical mass in the Internet infrastructure and services, the enterprises will come on board.

Microsoft also recently announced an upgrade to its IPv6 tool kit for Windows developers. Available as a free download since March 2000, Microsoft's IPv6 Technology Preview now includes a browser, basic utilities such as telnet and FTP, and support for tunneling IPv6 traffic over an IPv4 backbone.

However, Microsoft will not ship a commercial version of Windows 2000 with built-in IPv6 until 2002. Microsoft is focused on getting application developers to support IPv6 first so that the technology will be useful to consumers and businesses when it ships.

In other IPv6-related news, Ericsson announced its first IPv6-compliant wireless broadband router, the Realtime Router RXI 820, which was designed specifically for 3GPP. The 820 supports IPv4 and IPv6 and will be deployed in late 2001. Also, Compaq now offers full IPv6 support in its Tru64 UNIX version 5.1, which began shipping in September 2000. Compaq will add IPv6 support to its TCP/IP services for OpenVMS product later in 2001.

The only cloud on the IPv6 horizon is news that Cisco has slipped the ship date of the version of its IOS that will support IPv6. Originally anticipated for October 2000, IPv6 support instead will ship in the last quarter of 2001. Cisco officials say the change does not reflect a lack of support for IPv6 but rather results from the overall difficulty of getting new features added to software release schedules. IPv6 proponents downplayed the Cisco news.

Cisco is still keying delivery of its product to the 2001–2002 time frame for 3GPP. The fact that an early product release slips from October to March is not that big of an issue from a transition point of view. 3GPP rolls out in 2002, and Cisco thinks it will be there.

With 2002 quickly approaching, let's see why designers of wireless broadband systems are faced with meeting an FCC mandate for E-911 functionality. By combining "smart" antenna technology with direction-of-arrival (DOA) algorithms, engineers can develop systems that provide accurate location information.

"Smart" Antenna Systems

Enhanced 911 (E-911) technology is on the minds of most wireless broadband designers today. With 2002 just around the corner, the FCC-mandated rule to include E-911 functionality in all wireless broadband products is drawing near. Therefore, engineers need new technology solutions to bring E-911 capabilities to their system designs.

During 2000, "smart" antennas have emerged as a main technology for delivering E-911 functionality to next-generation wireless broadband networks. These antenna systems are powerful solutions because they can exploit the spatial and spectral characteristics of signals, providing very accurate location information. Smart antenna systems, which require complex digital signal processing (DSP), will apply DOA algorithms to this information. The challenge for the designer, however, is choosing the right DOA algorithm.

Across the board, there are a variety of DOA algorithms under development for use in smart antenna systems targeted at position-location applications. This section explores one of these algorithms—the multiple-signal-classification (MUSIC) algorithm. Additionally, the DSP requirements of smart antenna systems employing the MUSIC algorithm will be presented.

Antenna Array   A "smart" antenna array, for this discussion, consists of several omnidirectional antenna elements dispersed in a known physical pattern. The electromagnetic (EM) waves incident on the antenna array are represented as plane waves with various directions of arrival.

By using this type of antenna array, near-identical signals are received by each antenna element, a combination of the incident signals and any ambient noise. Each incident plane wave is received by the individual antenna elements at a different time. The plane waves are all somewhat out of phase, as determined by the DOA and the array geometry. A direct sum of all the received signals will result in some signals being canceled (those out of phase), with a very few contributing positively.

It is possible to apply a phase delay to the signals received at each antenna element, tuning the antenna array to optimally receive from a particular DOA. This concept is sometimes referred to as *beamforming* because this approach produces an antenna sensitivity lobe (or beam, in the case of transmission) in the DOA (see Figure 28-12).[23] The array's sen-

Figure 28-12
A "beam" formed by
a 12-element array
tuned to 30 degrees.

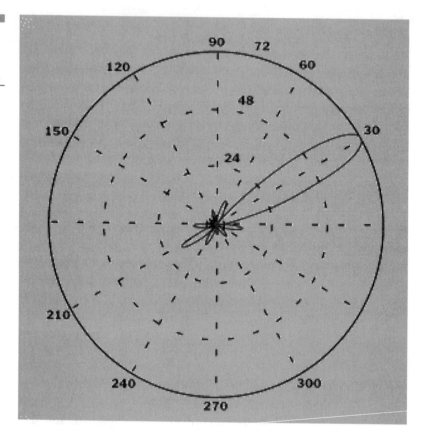

sitivity or overall power output would be increased by a factor equal to the number of antenna elements. The length M set of phase delays applied to a particular antenna array that causes it to point a beam in a particular direction is known as a *steering vector*.

The results obtained by using a DOA algorithm may be employed for E-911 position location or as input to a system interested in increasing the signal-to-noise ratio (SNR) in the direction of a particular user. The system simply can take the user's DOA and tune the array to improve reception.

MUSIC   The MUSIC algorithm is one of the most researched DOA algorithms due to its interesting breakdown of the principal components of input signals (see Figure 28-13).[24] The input signals provide information about the DOA of the received plane waves as well as the noise received at each element. Using the algorithm, engineers can obtain multiple delayed versions of the plane waves and the antenna array geometry. This makes

Figure 28-13
MUSIC algorithm
concept block
diagram.

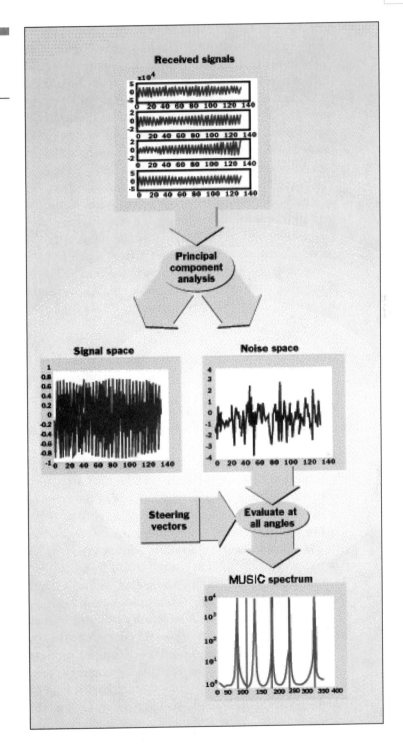

it possible to exploit the spatial and temporal correlation between the different received signals to determine the angles of arrival.

Performing principal-components analysis on the input signals breaks the data down into a basis, or set, of M-dimensional vectors capable of describing the statistical relationships between all the signals. The core concept of the MUSIC algorithm is that these vectors (called *eigenvectors*) can be divided into two subsets, one providing information about the correlated plane waves (signal space) and the other containing information derived from the uncorrelated noise (noise space).

The eigenvectors in the noise space are orthogonal to those in the signal space. Since the signal space contains information about the angles of arrival from each plane wave, the steering vectors from these angles are also orthogonal to the vectors in the noise space. The magnitude of the product between a steering vector from a plane wave's DOA and the noise-space matrix is zero. The inverse of the magnitude of the product between a steering vector from all possible angles and the noise-space matrix is known as the *MUSIC spectrum*.

Implementation   The purpose of the MUSIC algorithm is to derive the DOA from a number of sources incident on a "smart" antenna array. This frame-based process (performed on a number of samples at a time, known as a *frame*, instead of being computed continuously) begins by demodulating the signals received at each antenna element and producing a buffer of complex-valued samples. The samples are complex so that the phase information remains intact throughout the process. The frames are then transferred to the system that will run the MUSIC algorithm.

The first step in computation of the MUSIC algorithm is to compute the signal covariance matrix, which is one of the more computationally intensive sections (see Figure 28-14).[25] Each of the frame buffers is arranged into a vector containing K samples per frame, and there are M total frame buffers (one for each antenna element in the array). The covariance matrix is formed by multiplying each of the M frame buffer vectors by every offer frame buffer vector (taking the scalar product). Each vector multiplication takes K complex multiply-accumulates, and there are M^2 vector multiplications, for a total of M^2K necessary complex operations. Due to the symmetry of the problem, it is possible to reduce this by almost a factor of 2, but this is still a massive number of computations.

The second step in the MUSIC algorithm is to compute the eigen decomposition of the covariance matrix, and a typical method is the use of householder transformations followed by Givens rotations and backward accumulation. Although there are several possible approximations and alternate methods, most are still on the order of M^3 complex operations.

Figure 28-14
MUSIC algorithm
system block
diagram.

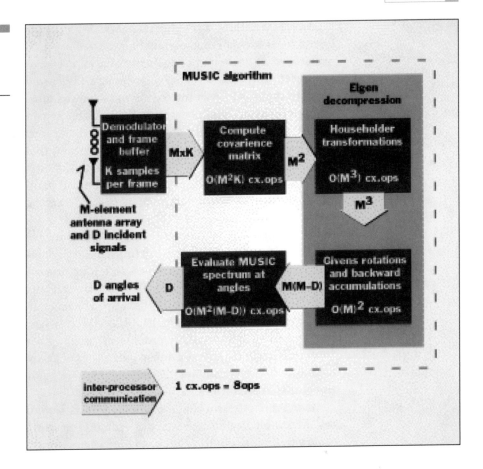

From the eigenvectors and eigenvalues of the covariance matrix, the MUSIC spectrum is formed and then evaluated at a particular angular resolution. For D incident signals and an angular resolution of $2p/L$, this results in $M^2(M - D)L$ more complex operations. For reasonable system estimates, such as $M = 12$ antenna elements, $K = 128$ samples per frame, $D = 6$ incident signals, $2p/L = 360$ angular resolution, and a frame rate of 1000 Hz, the total comes in at approximately 3000 millions of instructions per second (MIPS).

Spreading the Load   The number of operations involved in computing a typical DOA algorithm is massive, often so large that it prohibits implementation on even the fastest traditional DSP architectures. Algorithm designers have been forced to come up with new solutions or new applications of old solutions. One of these solutions that has come into favor recently is the concept of parallel computing.

Not a new technique by any means, today's DSP programmers are often forced to "throw horsepower at the problem" by adding multiple identical processors as a method of reducing overall cycle count. In a world where real-time processing is mandatory, cost and board space are usually less important—less important that is until passed along to the consumer.

Designers may ask how parallel computing helps the implementation of a DOA algorithm. Ideally, an engineer should be able to reduce the number of cycles required by a factor equal to the total number of processors used. Unfortunately, this is rarely the case due to the large amount of overhead inherent to parallel computing. The most prominent factors of this are the need for interprocessor communication and the transfer of intermediate results.

For example, in the computation of the covariance matrix for a 12-element, 128-sample-per-frame system, 78 (due to Hermitian symmetry) length-128 complex dot products are required. In a four-processor system, it is possible to reduce this number to $78 \div 4 = 19.5$ (rounds up to 20) of the same dot products. This is a considerable savings. However, this reduction requires that the entire input frame (a 12×128 matrix of complex samples) be distributed to each of the four processors, causing a significant amount of overhead. Additionally, the subsequent step of the MUSIC algorithm also demands that the complete covariance matrix be distributed throughout the multiple processors.

In order to perform the householder transformations, which is the initial step of modifying a covariance matrix into tri-diagonal form, it is necessary to derive length M householder vectors and transfer them to each processor for every one of the M^2 iterations. The result is the communication of M^3 intermediate results per frame. A parallel implementation of Givens rotations, the process of modifying a tri-diagonal matrix into a pure-diagonal matrix with eigenvalues along the main diagonal, and the backward computation of the eigenvectors is very efficient. It does not require any intermediate communications as long as the size M^2 tri-diagonal matrix is present on all processors. Finally, the computationally intensive process of evaluating the MUSIC spectrum also can be distributed among several processors efficiently, but only after the $(M - D)$ length M eigenvectors have been broadcasted to all processors.

Careful algorithm design can reduce data transfer, but not eliminate it. If it were possible to completely divide all operations and allow them to reside in their own separate processors without the need for any information from another, this would be the best-case situation. This interprocessor communication is exhausting, especially when one considers what is involved with each transfer.

Interprocessor Communication Traditionally, multiprocessor systems were limited to various interrupt-driven techniques in the methods of interprocessor communication (see Figure 28-15).[26] These methods were usually of the following sort:

- Processor A prepares a message for processor B, puts it in shared memory, configures DMA, and so on.
- Processor A signals an interrupt on processor B.
- Processor A continues its processing or waits for processor B.
- Processor B services the interrupt from processor A.
- Processor B processes the data from processor A.[27]

The disadvantage of a distributed communication scheme is that it is very difficult to predict the transfer times. Interrupt latency and processor bus timings are only a few of the factors that must be taken into account. Scheduling among the different processors becomes an extremely difficult problem, often eclipsing the original algorithm.

A new improvement in interprocessor communications is organization of the multiple-DSP system into clusters (see Figure 28-16).[28] A cluster provides complete connectivity between the attached processors, enabling data transfer between the processors in a deterministic fashion. Data are routed on cycle-by-cycle terms. There is no need to schedule or even worry about interrupts. The transfer cycle is simple. First, processor A executes a single-cycle instruction, sending processors B and C some data. When the next cycle arrives, processors B and C already hold the necessary data.

Figure 28-15
Distributed multi-processor system showing processor A to B transfer.

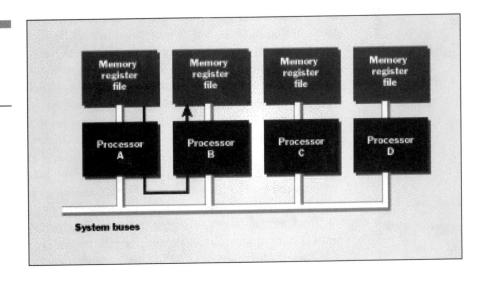

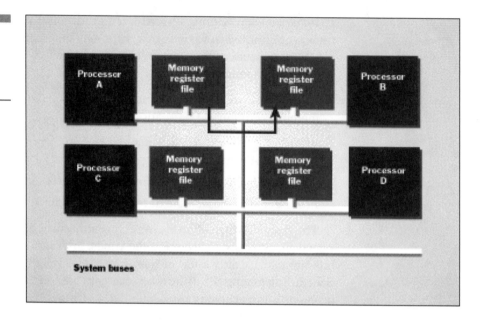

A clustered system enables the DSP algorithm programmer to design very tight parallel code. In an SIMD parallel implementation, intermediate results can be communicated in a single cycle, so there is no down time or latency. In the example of the MUSIC DOA algorithm, the communication of intermediate results would be a scheduling nightmare for a traditional multiprocessor system. In a clustered system, however, the intermediate results are sent and received in a known number of cycles, eliminating the need for any scheduling or interrupt handling. In fact, each transfer between tasks in Figure 28-14 can be performed in a single cycle, making the communication much less than the order of operations from the compute sections.

More Powerful Architectures   Obviously, the following generations of communication signal processing algorithms are going to require DSP manufacturers to come up with more powerful architectures. Multiprocessor systems are going to become mandatory, and scheduling of data-transfer operations may begin to eclipse the complexity of the original algorithms. In the case of the MUSIC algorithm, interprocessor communication can be virtually eliminated through the use of a well-designed data-exchange architecture such as a clustered system.

The DSP industry is striving to provide higher levels of performance to enable computationally intensive algorithms such as the MUSIC algorithm for "smart" antenna systems. All DSP architectures available in the marketplace will benefit from the faster clock speeds enabled by smaller process geometries. Many suppliers have introduced new products during the past few years that validate the need for parallelism in addition to faster clocks. Examples are the very long instruction word (VLIW) and superscalar architectures. While these incorporate instruction-level parallelism, the highest-performance architectures must incorporate all levels of parallelism instruction, packed data, and multiprocessing. Architectures that can deliver all these with simple-to-use programming tools will deliver the best levels of performance.

Now let's look at how high spectral efficiency and flexible data rate access are the main focus of future wireless broadband networks. Multiple channel allocation schemes have the potential of achieving this goal. By assigning multiple slots and/or multiple carriers to one user, it is possible to provide a flexible data rate with quite low complexity. In this section, a simple allocation scheme where each user is assigned a fixed group of carriers is proposed. These carriers are adaptively used depending on the interference situation within the system. The system performance in terms of average throughput is investigated for two different types of allocation schemes: a fully centralized scheme and a distributed one that uses frequency diversity as a means of improving the user link quality. The obtained results show that both schemes improve the system throughput over single-carrier allocation without affecting the capacity of the system in terms of number of users per cell.

MA-Based Intelligence for 3G Mobile Systems

High spectral efficiency and flexible data rate access are the main focus for future wireless broadband networks, as well as the development trend of existing networks toward the third generation (3G). To accomplish this goal, packet switching has been introduced to time-division multiple-access (TDMA)–based systems. For instance, the proposed general packet radio service (GPRS) for global system for mobile communications (GSM) and GPRS-136 for the North American standard IS-136 are forming the mainstream of evolution toward 3G systems. Triggered by this, the research work aimed at maximizing spectral efficiency by means of channel allocation schemes, partially involved in the frequency plan approach.

Different from the conventional channel allocation concept in that only one channel is assigned to uplink or downlink between a mobile station (MS) and its connected base station (BS), nowadays research work has been extended to three- or more-dimensional channel allocation to support high-data-rate services; i.e., more than one channel is assigned to an MS from its serving BS. These channels may be time slots and/or frequency bands. With multifrequency allocation, there is possible frequency diversity gain when the signal is transmitted over multipath radio channels. Conventional channel allocation can be catalogued into fixed channel allocation (FCA), dynamic channel allocation (DCA), hybrid channel allocation (HCA) of FCA and DCA, and random channel allocation (RCA). These channel allocation schemes try to maximize the total capacity of wireless broadband systems assuming a constant data rate per user. When variable data rates are needed, as for multimedia communications, a new dimension should be added to the allocation domain. A channel allocation scheme should maximize not only the capacity in terms of number of users per cell but also its throughput. Obviously, the design of the system becomes more complicated as more variables exist. A variable-rate system can be achieved through the allocation of multiple slots, multiple carriers, and/or link adaptation by using variable modulation and coding. Previous studies showed that multiple channel allocation combined with link adaptation can improve system throughput over single-channel allocation without affecting system coverage. In this section, a multicarrier allocation (MCA) scheme where a group of carriers is assigned to an MS from its connected BS is considered. To improve system capacity and promote fairness within the system, this MCA scheme is used in combination with frequency diversity. Thus a minimum required throughput can be guaranteed within the system even to users in bad fading positions.

The system model is introduced next, followed by a description of the MCA scheme. The simulation model used in this section, together with simulation results, is also given next.

The System Model   Let's consider a wireless broadband network with orthogonal frequencies. Each frequency provides a constant information data rate of R bits per second (bps). These frequencies could be the subcarriers of an orthogonal frequency-division multiplexing (OFDM) scheme or simply the carriers in an FDM scheme. These frequencies are used by the network to provide coverage over an area with N BSs.

In 1G and 2G cellular systems, the required user data rate is fixed, and the quality of service has to ensure a good connection during the duration of the call. The design in this case is based on minimizing the outage probability and at the same time trying to increase the capacity of the system in terms of users per cell. The outcome of this optimization results into a system reuse distance (cluster size) that defines the minimum distance between two BSs in which the same frequency can be reused. For instance, the analog cellular system AMPS has a reuse distance of 7, and the digital cellular system has reuse distances of 3 and 4.

For circuit-switched design, the outage probability should be kept small to ensure good connection (2 percent outage can be considered a good value). Even though it provides low outage probability, such a design procedure is not attractive for multimedia systems where the traffic is bursty and the user data rate changeable. In such a situation, it would take a long time to transfer files from one point to another and further require a large buffer at the transmitter. Therefore, some modifications are needed to increase the throughput.

Multicarrier Allocation Let's consider a system design based on the design procedure described in the preceding. Such a system is then characterized by its reuse distance and average outage probability.

One way to adapt this system to these new requirements is by transforming it into a system with universal reuse and assign a fixed group of *K* frequencies to any given user admitted into the system. Figure 28-17 illustrates this simple transformation.[29] Thus, depending on the interfer-

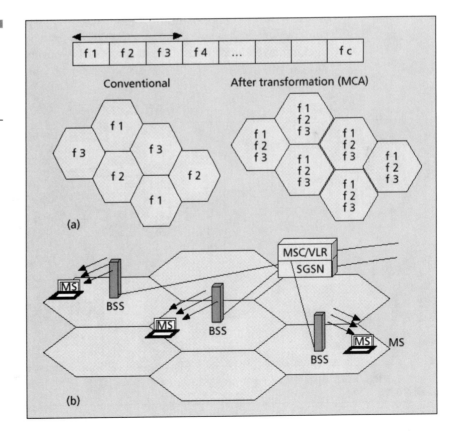

Figure 28-17
Multicarrier allocation: the transformation of conventional single-carrier allocation.

ence situation, every active user can use up to K carriers simultaneously. The average throughput of a user is then obtained as the sum of the effective data rate in K frequencies. Notice that the number of users per cell is not affected by this modification. In other words, by using this structure, the system will keep the same number of users, but each user can improve its peak throughput up to KR bps.

With such a scheme, all users close to their BSs will be able to use all the frequencies assigned to them, and users far away from their cells may be able to use only part of the K frequencies. A good degree of fairness also can be provided within the system by means of frequency diversity. Users who are unable to extract the full rate from each of their carriers can use transmitter (frequency) diversity and achieve their connections with a lower data rate.

This MCA scheme can be implemented centrally or distributively. These two schemes are described next.

FULLY CENTRALIZED SCHEME   In this scheme, the decision about what frequencies within each group should be used is taken in a centralized node, where measurements from all cells are available. Figure 28-18 gives the control flow of this scheme.[30] A group of frequencies is first assigned to a user, followed by computation of the SNIR experienced by each frequency within the system. The central node starts by shutting off frequencies

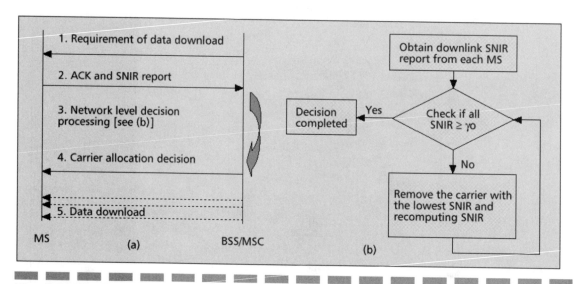

Figure 28-18   The fully centralized scheme.

having the lowest SNIR one by one until the point where all the remaining links have good connections.

Since all frequency groups are used in each cell, better system throughput is expected for the same capacity of users per cell. However, this scheme requires a lot of signaling where all link information needs to be reported to one node. Its computational complexity also increases with the number of users within the system. One way to reduce this complexity is to use a distributed scheme, where the selection of the appropriate frequencies for all mobile stations is done locally.

A DISTRIBUTED MULTICARRIER ALLOCATION SCHEME In this distributed scheme, each BS acts independent of all other BSs. Considering the downlink case (from the BS to the MS), each MS measures the link gain and total interference plus noise power appearing during demodulation of each frequency within its group. With this information, the MS computes the SNIR of each frequency. For instance, user n connected to BS i forms a vector of SNIRs of length K.

Based on this diversity combining, the distributed MCA scheme can take advantage of both the multipath fading channel and the interference situation within the system. The control flow of this scheme with diversity combining is shown in Figure 28-19.[31] Here, the transmission decisions

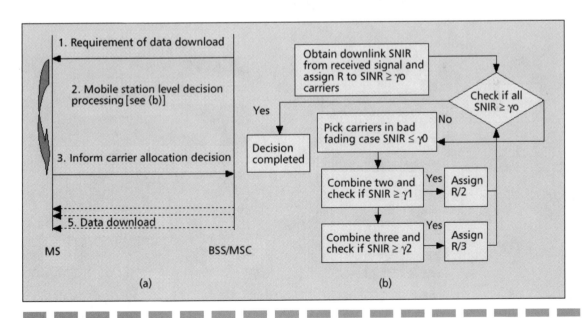

Figure 28-19 The distributed scheme with control flow operated by the MS (refer to conditions 1, 2, and 3).

and the way the BS should distribute the information intended for the MS over the different frequencies are made by the MS.

NOTE   Diversity combining also can be used in the centralized scheme described previously. Such a combination increases the complexity of the centralized scheme considerably, making it too difficult to use. The average throughput and the spectral efficiency of the distributed scheme are computed using the same procedure as for the centralized scheme where constant transmitted power is assumed.

Simulation Results: The Network Layout   Let's consider a finite network covered by N omni regular hexagon cells with a carrier set. The traffic is uniformly distributed with a heavy load. To analyze the performance of this system, take snapshots at different time instants. To simplify the problem, the mobile movement is neglected in this case.

RESULTS   To carry out the system simulation, a simulation package called RUNE was used (offered by Ericsson Radio AB). The parameters used in the simulation environment are listed in Table 28-3.[32] First, let's look at a conventional FCA scheme with different reuse patterns. For this, you should evaluate average throughput and spectral efficiency. Figure 28-20 shows the average throughput of the system with full load as a function of reuse distance.[33] Notice that higher reuse distance in single-carrier sys-

TABLE 28-3

Simulation
Parameters

Description	Parameters
Number of cells in the network	$N = 49$
Total traffic carriers	$K \in [1, 6]$
Cell radius (microcell)	$R = 800$ m
Shadow fading deviation	$\sigma_s = 4, 8, 12$ dB
SIR thresholds	$\gamma_0 = 10$ dB $\gamma_1 = 7$ dB $\gamma_2 = 6$ dB
Shadow fading correlation	$r_{ss}' = 0.5$
Propagation constant	$\alpha = 4$
Channel activity factor	100%
Results confidence	2000 times
Interval between snapshots	20 ms

Figure 28-20
The average throughput of the conventional single-carrier allocation scheme.

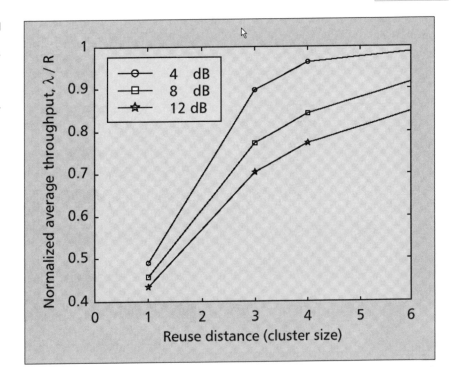

tems gives better throughput. By increasing the reuse distance, the outage probability is reduced, and as a result, the throughput is improved. However, increasing the reuse distance has a negative effect on system capacity. This is illustrated in Figure 28-21, where the normalized spectral efficiency gets poorer when increasing K.[34] Tighter reuse patterns give better normalized spectral efficiency but are limited by cochannel interference level as the time availability of a channel being used gets lower. In addition, higher shadow fading variance causes performance degradation. This can be explained by the trend of reuse pattern 7 for analog systems and 3 or 4 for digital systems.

Figure 28-22 illustrates the average throughput of the centralized and distributed MCA schemes as a function of the number of frequencies per group.[35] Notice that the average throughput per user increases with the number of frequencies per group K. It is also observed that the distributed scheme performs better than the centralized one, which is a good surprise. The reason for this is that the distributed scheme takes advantage of the diversity gain obtained through the combination of multiple frequencies instead of switching them off. Of course, adding this feature to

Figure 28-21
The spectral efficiency
of the conventional
single-carrier
allocation scheme.

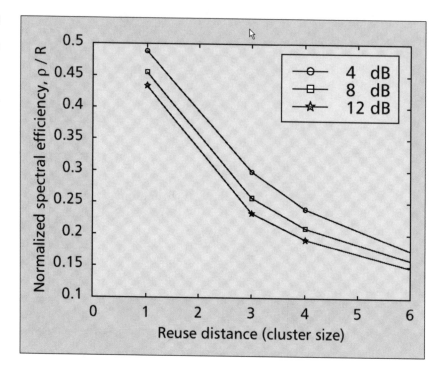

Figure 28-22
The average through-
put of the MCA
schemes.

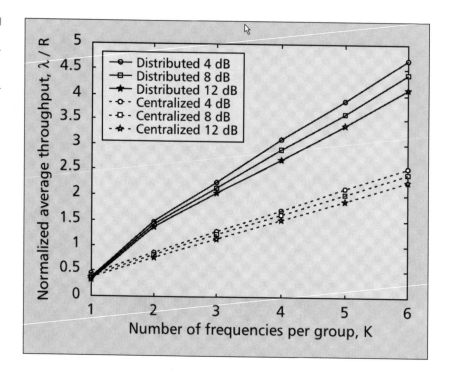

the centralized scheme will provide good gains in its throughput as well. However, as mentioned earlier, such a feature will increase the complexity of the centralized scheme considerably. Figure 28-23 illustrates the normalized spectral efficiency for the two schemes as a function of the number of frequencies per group K.[36] It is observed that the distributed scheme has worse normalized spectral efficiency for $K = 1$, but outperforms the centralized scheme for higher values of K. This is natural because transmitter (frequency) diversity can be applied when $K > 1$. Notice also that the normalized spectral efficiency of the centralized scheme is almost independent of K. Thus, for a cellular system with the parameters given in Table 28-3, the average throughput per user is a linear function of K with $\lambda_{cs} \approx 0.4K$.

The same tendency also can be observed for the distributed scheme, but with a much better throughput. Compared with the results of Figure 28-20, one can easily see that both schemes outperform the conventional scheme of single-carrier allocation. In fact, the distributed scheme provides a gain of about 70 percent in spectral efficiency. With its simplicity, this distributed scheme seems attractive and suitable for future multimedia applica-

Figure 28-23
The spectral efficiency
of the MCA schemes.

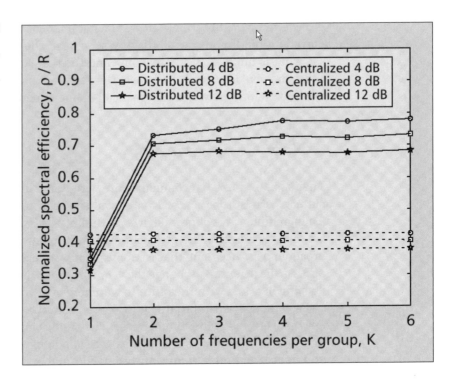

tions. One might think of using power control with this distributed scheme. With a proper adjustment of the transmitted power in the different links, better interference management can be achieved, and as a result, better throughput could be obtained. This point is left for further investigation.

Finally, let's look at "smart" phones and the 3G evolution. WAP technology will also be covered.

"Smart" Phones and the 3G Evolution

Finland is an unlikely technology country from a land better known for its reindeer and long Arctic nights than its cutting-edge gadgets. Today, Finland's telecommunications providers are helping people use their cell phones to do more—much more. And the impact of what they are doing is ricocheting around the world. Taking advantage of something called Wireless Application Protocol (WAP), a new system has been designed that allows mobile phones to tap into the Internet (see Chapter 29 for a detailed discussion on WAP technology).

For example, subscribers to WapIT not only can get sports results displayed on the liquid-crystal-display screens of their phones but also can see what is happening in museums and theaters, check the top 10 music chart, or even download the joke of the day. Demand for WAP phones is so hot that Nokia, the world's largest cell phone maker, cannot keep up.

A New Generation

Thanks in part to what companies are witnessing in Finland and throughout northern Europe, a post-PC age could be aborning in the United States. An incredible wave of new devices, including WAP phones, is beginning to hit the U.S. market. The products represent a new generation of wireless broadband services, one that combines mobile telephony with the Internet and has the potential to change the very way Americans communicate—from keeping in touch with the office to watching over the children to dating.

Few are suggesting that the PC—the product most threatened by the new gadgets—is going to disappear. The traditional desktop will survive for more complex functions such as digital photography, full-screen video and music, and manipulating words and numbers. But there is hardly a technology watcher around who does not believe that sales of easy-to-use "smart" devices and appliances will far outstrip PC sales in the not too distant future.

After two decades of experimentation, the PC is still considered too bulky, too expensive, and too complex for many people. Studies by various industry analysts show that a majority of users are frustrated. Among the reasons cited: poor technical support, confusing manuals, and overly complex software. By some accounts, as many as half the computers in people's homes are sitting in closets or in dusty corners largely unused. Millions of Americans, it seems, are resisting the future for one simple reason: It is too darn complicated.

Phoneland

PC ownership has stalled at around 52 percent of U.S. households, despite the advent of machines selling for less than $800. PC use is about 37 percent in Finland, but a full 69 percent of the population uses mobile phones versus only 30 percent in the United States. Such extraordinarily high penetration rates have turned the Nordic nation of 8 million into a virtual laboratory to experiment with the newest phones and services and the networks that allow them to function.

If Finland seems an unlikely harbinger of the future, consider that Silicon Valley used to be best known for growing fruits and nuts, not semiconductors. As for Seattle, well, it used to boast more longshoremen than software millionaires. Thanks in part to a national passion for staying connected across vast frozen distances, the Finns have created what they call a *mobile information society.*

Finnish teenagers are a major driving force behind the mobile phone craze. On buses and in the Helsinki train station, they can be seen yammering away on their Nokias or else punching out short text messages with their thumbs. They personalize their phones by downloading dozens of different ringing tones (from Finlandia to the Flintstones theme) from the Web site of Sonera, the largest of the country's more than 80 telecom service providers. For them, the phone is as important a personal statement as the latest pair of designer cargo pants is for American teens. Youngsters call their phones *kanny,* which means "extension of the hand."

In the realm of grown-ups, hundreds of thousands of Finns conduct personal banking from their handheld phones, order gifts of chocolate for friends, and even shop for apartments to rent. At least 400 different services are available. For American firms, the lesson is that they can expect an explosion in demand for their products and services if they can replicate the Finnish mobile experience. The Finns are showing the world the way to the future. Just about everything they have in Finland is on the agenda for global use. Internet phones on the U.S. market will offer full WAP services in late 2001.

Sprint PCS, AT&T Wireless, Bell Atlantic Mobile, and others are pushing a raft of telephone-based devices made not only by Nokia but also by Ericsson, Motorola, and Qualcomm. America Online (AOL) and Yahoo, meanwhile, are vying to become the portals that millions of mobile users will go through to get on the Web. AOL, pursuing a strategy called *AOL Anywhere*, is expected to begin offering an Internet-surfing device to new subscribers—free.

Bowing to the simplicity imperative, Internet appliances like i-opener and WebPAD are also hitting the market. They allow access to the Web without the seeming eternity it takes to boot up a PC. Offering more mobility, 3Com and allies such as OmniSky and Handspring want the cornerstone of the new era to be Palm-like personal organizers that communicate and surf the Net. In short, computer makers, phone manufacturers, telecom providers, and Internet companies are all rushing into the anytime, anywhere fray. Dataquest estimates that the sale of mobile Internet devices will increase from 807,000 in 2001 to 31.4 million in 2005. Prices, too, will drop sharply.

Less Is More

For every manufacturer, the new mantra is: "Give them just what they need when they need it." This is a lot different from the PC era, when everyone said, "Give me more memory. Give me more power. Give me more complex software."

Whether they admit it or not, the companies making the next generation of devices are responding at least in part to Nokia's skill in making easy-to-use machines. Unfortunately, many makers of computers, phones, and other gadgets know precious little about ergonomics and usability. For them, it is technology for technology's sake. How else to explain the mental gymnastics required just to program your VCR or to add new software to your Windows 2000 PC?

The Finns argue that users should not notice the complexity of computing and communicating. More raw power is coming, but it will be embedded in devices—in a box on your refrigerator that tells a Web grocer you need more milk, for instance. Rather than deciphering bewildering instruction manuals, users should be able to click on buttons to answer simple yes or no questions. Nokia, for example, has developed a *roller key* that allows users to scroll quickly through menus of options. Larger display screens and longer battery life also are improving the usefulness of handheld gadgets. Nokia wants to make the technology human and easy to use. The digital interaction should be natural.

What also makes the Nokia vision so compelling is that it is based on open standards controlled by no one company. By contrast, Microsoft's Windows CE and the Palm OS (operating system) are both proprietary systems.

Nokia Reboots

The WAP standard that Nokia has pushed addresses the problem of how Internet information is communicated to handheld phones that have smaller display screens than a PC. Nokia and Sweden's Ericsson, together with Phone.com and Motorola, started the WAP Forum in 1997 (see Chapter 29 for further details). Some 400 companies representing the vast majority of handset manufacturers have since signed on. WAP will do the same thing the browser did for the World Wide Web.

The key to WAP is a language called eXtensible Markup Language (XML), another open standard. This language tags all the data that are being distributed wirelessly and makes sure they are displayed in a way the user comprehends. It is like a *lingua franca*. Big Blue foresees 3 trillion "smart" devices connected to 3 billion users around the world in the not too distant future as part of what it calls *pervasive computing*.

How will those "smart" devices be designed? Again, Nokia is pushing a global standard, called *Symbian*, along with Ericsson, Motorola, Britain's Psion, and others. This defines the operating system of handheld devices. It is the equivalent of what Microsoft's Windows is for PCs and competes with Windows CE, the Seattle giant's attempt to extend its own proprietary software from the PC to the handheld segment. Symbian sets such things as the size and shape of screens.

To allow all these gadgets to talk to one another, Nokia has helped establish a third major standard called *Bluetooth*, named after a ninth-century Danish Viking chief who unified warring tribes. In this case, the Finns are working with Ericsson, Toshiba, IBM, Intel, and more than 3000 other companies to link devices with Bluetooth's radio signals. Right now, the most practical way to get different gadgets to communicate wirelessly is infrared, which is the way a remote control engages with a television.

Ordinary remotes have to be pointed directly at the infrared portal on the TV set from just a few yards away or they do not work. However, the

Bluetooth signals will be able to reach any device within a 10-yard radius, and the gadgets will not have to be pointed directly at each other. When Bluetooth products start hitting the market in greater numbers in 2001, users will be able to get their Palm organizers, for example, to synchronize address listings with their computers or cell phones simply by having them in the same room. The devices will communicate silently and invisibly, without wires. Existing gadgets can be retrofitted with Bluetooth, but it is expected that new devices made with this technology will work together more seamlessly.

These standards (WAP, Symbian, and Bluetooth) together mean that a sizable percentage of manufacturers now agree on how to make many wireless broadband devices and get them to function together. Microsoft and Intel are busy carving out roles in mobile Internet access, but they simply will not be able to dominate the new devices as they do the PC.

Simplicity

Will this emerging world actually be simpler? Not everyone is a believer. Some manufacturers will make the mistake of trying to cram too many functions into their gadgets. There is a temptation to transform a simple cell phone into a device that does everything. There is no way you can do this and also simplify it. The best new products include Nokia phones, the BlackBerry pager from Research In Motion and Bell South, and simplified Web browsers such as i-opener, iBrow, and WebPAD. Some early devices hitting the market are not well conceived. For example, the new Bell Atlantic Mobile pdQ made by Qualcomm is a fusion of a cell phone with a Palm, but it is awkward to both speak and use its Internet functions at the same time. It will be tough to maintain the agreement on various standards as manufacturers rush out products.

However, so many technology companies are pouring so much money into inventing the new era that progress seems certain. National Semiconductor, which retreated from PC chips, is now concentrating on selling its chips for devices such as the WebPAD. Several companies have launched *EasyPC* initiatives, and more are forming groups to make the next leap in ease of use.

Calling Dick Tracy

Networks, too, will get faster, greatly improving the performance of all these devices. Average users increasingly will be able to enter data onto the screen of a cell phone or wireless broadband device simply by talking at it. Faster networks also will one day permit video messaging so that you can see the person who just called.

Even though the champions of competing wireless broadband networks in the United States are not going to move quickly to a single technology, a relative handful of giants are emerging that will have national *footprints*—so it will not matter much.

Indeed, the big telecoms have spent an estimated $19 billion in 2000 alone to improve their systems. AT&T Wireless in 2001 will start testing a next-generation digital system called *EDGE*, which delivers 384 kbps of data versus 19.2 kbps today. Sprint PCS, which has the largest national all-digital network, is testing new technology that can deliver 2 Mbps of data, over 100 times faster than today. Vodafone AirTouch, meanwhile, is scheduled to launch a joint venture with Bell Atlantic Mobile in 2001 and will attempt to smash together multiple wireless broadband networks.

Nurturing these dreams of a wireless broadband world, Motorola, Lucent Technologies, Nortel Networks, and Cisco Systems, among others, are competing to devise new wireless broadband network equipment that big operators can use. Cisco is a major proponent of hooking up every device in the home to the Internet—from your sprinkler system to your thermostat.

The networked society that the Finns have created up near the Arctic Circle has convinced America's tech giants that their huge investments will pay off. Thus, if millions more Americans are soon connected, chalk it up, at least in part, to the Finns going "WAPpy" over their Nokias.

Conclusion

The standards process for commercial wireless has changed permanently. We have entered a new era in the development and evolution of complex systems that must meet the demanding requirements of a consumer-focused global market place. These systems must leverage a technology base offering common solutions customizable at the application level. To succeed in this environment it is necessary to recognize the following:

- There is no more *local-only* marketplace—global focus is the driver.
- The world of international standards has changed permanently.
- Continued rapid changes in the communications marketplace and in technology dictate the need for a *new way of doing business* in standards development, including a plethora of new specialized specifications development forums created by the communications industry.

- ITU-R has successfully developed and used a new model for standards development in this brave new world of dynamic changes in communications technologies, multiple international standards development organizations, and increased globalization.
- This model works for IMT development now and into the future.
- This model is applicable to other standards development outside the ITU-R.
- Efficient work management and coordination are the prime concerns, not organizational structure.

The fast and robust performance seen so far originates from the combination of several unique features of DSA techniques. First, the distributed processing adopted in state sampling, sample transmission, and state correction is essentially connected to reliable detection of samples in the practical wireless broadband channels without knowing the channel phase. This enables the time gap between successive state samples that results from distributed sample transmission being fully exploited for sample energy increase and differential encoding. Second, progressive comparison-correction processing for the synchronization of the receiver's main SRG well matches distributed sample processing. Comparison-correction-based synchronization, as well as implementation of the relevant circuitry, is firmly supported by distributed sample scrambling (DSS) theory. Third, the data constellation prerotation technique enables effective use of the DPSK state signal for channel estimation reference after completing timing acquisition. Fourth, the state symbol correlation process complementing comparison-correction-based synchronization substantially contributes to improving the worst-case acquisition performance at a minimal increase in memory space and complexity.

As we have observed so far, the CDSA scheme can be employed efficiently for fast and robust cell search in both intercell synchronous and asynchronous DS/CDMA cellular systems. The CDSA-based cell search scheme turned out to outperform the prevalent parallel search and 3GPP three-step search schemes of comparable system complexity. The nonorthogonality problem between the pilot and traffic channels can be resolved by introducing a simple pilot cancellation technique.

In this chapter, issues also have been identified that occur when viewing a video stream in a mobile computing environment and proposed methods of handling these issues. By taking the approach that a video proxy can perform the necessary operations, this chapter has described the video transcoding system architecture and control method that decides four encoding parameters based on the device profile, transmission profile, and user profile. In the system, download throughput is measured on an application layer at user clients so that accurate throughput can be measured, and the system can implicitly control overall effects including lower-layer issues such as RLC and TCP/UDP. The proposed control method also decides a set of encoding parameters by estimating the communications conditions, client device capabilities, and user preferences. These mechanisms provide stable transmission of video data and comfortable video viewing on user clients. Finally, based on the experimental results (see Figure 28-11), the features of the developed transcoder are shown.

Currently, a mobile multimedia data transcoding system (MMDTS) is being developed that contains three gateways: a mobile Web gateway (MWG), mobile push gateway (MPG), and mobile multicast gateway (MMG). The MWG targets normal HTTP Internet access. It performs the markup language conversion, image conversion (JPEG/GIF to JPEG/GIF/PNG), and video conversion described in this chapter. The MPG gets Web content at a specified time interval or a trigger obtained from a foreign function (location management node) and delivers transcoded contents based on the push procedure defined by the Wireless Application Protocol (WAP). The MMG receives layered video streams distributed by each multicast channel on the Internet, combines some layered video streams, and provides these to mobile users by unicast. At that time, a combined pattern of layered videos is decided in accordance with communications conditions and device capabilities. Using the MMDTS system, detailed system capabilities are evaluated, including the influence of time lag between change of communication conditions, its reflection on the transcoding process, and so on.

This chapter also presented a multicarrier allocation scheme that can provide radio links with different rates suitable for multimedia communications. This scheme is simple to implement because it does not require changing the modulation type or coding scheme to vary the information rate of a given connection.

Two different schemes have been presented: a centralized scheme, where all decisions are made at one node on the network level, and a distributed one, where each mobile makes the decision and informs the BS of how the information should be transmitted over the different frequencies of its group.

Finally, the results obtained show that the multicarrier allocation scheme achieves considerable gain in user throughput over single-carrier allocation schemes without affecting the total capacity of the system in terms of number of users per cell. A gain of about 70 percent in spectral efficiency was obtained. The distributed scheme provided better performance in average throughput than the centralized one. This is due to the fact that the distributed scheme uses frequency diversity to improve the link quality of more interfered frequencies.

Endnotes

1. Stephen M. Blust, "Wireless Standards Development—A New Paradigm," *IEEE Vehicular Technology Society News,* Strathclyde University, George Street, Glasgow G1 IXW Scotland, 2000.
2. *Ibid.*
3. *Ibid.*
4. *Ibid.*
5. *Ibid.*
6. *Ibid.*
7. *Ibid.*
8. *Ibid.*
9. Byoung-Hoon Kim (Global Communication Technology) and Byeong Gi Lee (Seoul National University), "DSA Techniques for Fast and Robust Acquisition of DS/CDMA Scrambling Codes," *IEEE Communications Magazine,* IEEE Communications Society, 305 East 47th Street, New York, NY 10017, USA, 2000.
10. *Ibid.*
11. *Ibid.*
12. *Ibid.*
13. *Ibid.*
14. *Ibid.*
15. Takayuki Warabino, Shinji Ota, Daisuke Morikawa, and Masayoshi Ohashi (KDD R&D Laboratories, Inc.), Hajime Nakamura, Hideaki Iwashita, and Fumio Watanabe (KDD Corporation), "Video Transcoding Proxy for 3G Wireless Mobile Internet Access," *IEEE Communications Magazine,* IEEE Communications Society, 305 East 47th Street, New York, NY 10017, USA, 2000.
16. *Ibid.*
17. *Ibid.*
18. *Ibid.*
19. *Ibid.*
20. *Ibid.*
21. *Ibid.*
22. *Ibid.*
23. Matthew Plonski, "Smart Antenna Schemes for E-911," *Communications Systems Design,* 525 Market Street, Suite 500, San Francisco, CA 94105, 2000.

24. *Ibid.*

25. *Ibid.*

26. *Ibid.*

27. *Ibid.*

28. *Ibid.*

29. Zhu Lei and Slimane Ben Slimane (Royal Institute of Technology, Sweden), "A Multicarrier Allocation (MCA) Scheme for Variable-Rate 3G Wireless Systems," *IEEE Communications Magazine*, IEEE Communications Society, 305 East 47th Street, New York, NY 10017, USA, 2000.

30. *Ibid.*

31. *Ibid.*

32. *Ibid.*

33. *Ibid.*

34. *Ibid.*

35. *Ibid.*

36. *Ibid.*

CHAPTER 29

Global Broadband Demand Methodology and Projections

The forthcoming mobile communication systems are expected to provide a wide variety of services from high-quality voice to high-definition videos through high-data-rate wireless broadband channels anywhere in the world. The high data rate requires broad frequency bands, and sufficient wireless broadband can be achieved in higher-frequency bands such as microwave, Ka band, and millimeter wave. Wireless broadband channels have to be connected to wireless broadband fixed networks such as the Internet and local-area networks (LANs). The future-generation systems will include not only cellular phones but also many new types of communication systems such as wireless broadband access systems, millimeter-wave LANs, intelligent transport systems, and high-altitude stratospheric platform station systems. The keys to the future generations of mobile communications are multimedia communications, wireless broadband access to wireless broadband fixed networks, and seamless roaming among different systems. This chapter discusses future-generation mobile communication systems and global wireless broadband demand methodology and projections.

Wireless Broadband Platform Demand Methodology Positioning

There has been an evolutionary change in mobile communications systems every decade. The first-generation (1G) cellular systems in the 1970s and the second-generation (2G) cellular systems in the 1980s were used mainly for voice applications and to support circuit-switched services. 1G systems were implemented based on analog technologies; however, 2G systems are digital systems such as the global system for mobile communications (GSM), IS-54 digital cellular, personal digital cellular system (PDC), and IS-95. These systems operate nationwide or internationally and are today's mainstream systems. The data rates for users in air links of these systems are limited to less than several tens of kilobits per second. International Mobile Telecommunications 2000 (IMT-2000), which will be introduced at the beginning of 2002 as the third-generation (3G) cellular system, can provide 2 Mbps and 144 kbps in indoor and vehicular environments, respectively. However, demands for higher access speeds for multimedia communications will be unlimited.

In this century, society and the economy will depend greatly on computer communications in digital format. Almost all information will become digital data instead of real-time voice. Another trend is that communications will make human activities free of spatial and time restrictions. Advanced personal communication devices will lead people to be nomadic. Mobile communications will become an essential part of our daily lives yet be transparent much like the air itself. They will be everywhere and commonplace, but people will not be aware of them. The key to the future generations of mobile communications are multimedia communications, wireless broadband access to wireless broadband fixed networks, and seamless roaming among different systems.

In this chapter, future generations include the fourth (4G) and fifth generations (5G), and 4G is used, in a broad sense, to include several systems, not only cellular phone systems but also many new types of communication systems such as wireless broadband access systems, millimeter-wave LANs, intelligent transport systems (ITSs), and high-altitude stratospheric platform station (HAPS) systems. When 4G systems are used in a narrow sense as cellular systems, they will be specified as *4G cellular*. Generations of mobile communications and their key words and typical systems are shown in Table 29-1.[1]

Figure 29-1 shows the future trend of mobile communications.[2] It is very clear that they have to satisfy the demands of high data rate, high mobility, and seamless coverage. However, it is very hard to give a clear vision of future-generation systems. In principle, it is difficult to realize a system that has both a high data rate and high mobility. In addition to this, system performance (cell size and transmission data rate) greatly depends on frequency bands. Taking these technical problems into account, future systems will include several different systems. Some will

TABLE 29-1

Generations of mobile communications and their keywords and typical systems.

B	1980s	1990s	2000s	2010s
Generation	First	Second	Third	Fourth
Keywords	Analog	Digital personal	Global world standards	High data rate High mobility IP-based
Systems	Analog cellular Analog cordless	Digital cellular GSM, IS-54, PDC Digital cordless DECT, PHS	IMT-2000 (3G cellular) Max. data rate 2 Mbps	4G cellular Broadband access ITS, HAPS Mini data rate 2–20 Mbps?
		Mobile satellite Iridium, Inmarsat-M		

Figure 29-1
Mobile communica-
tions systems.

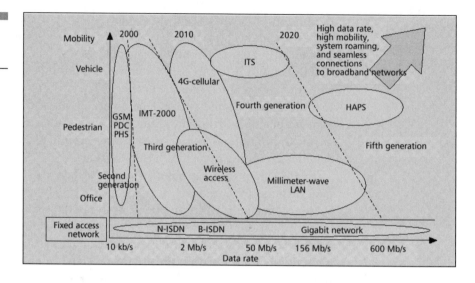

have high performance in providing high data rates, others in service coverage or high mobility.

If these systems are integrated with other systems, it will be possible to
enjoy both high data rates and high mobility. As candidates for future systems, 4G cellular, wireless broadband access systems, ITSs, and HAPS
systems have been attracting much interest in the mobile communications
field. In future systems, seamless roaming among these different systems
is a very important concept.

Seamless roaming among different systems will be added to high-data-
rate, high-mobility, and connection wireless broadband fixed networks.
This part of the chapter discusses not only so-called 4G cellular systems but
also other wireless broadband access systems as future generation systems.

Market Forecast

A forecast of the mobile communications market is shown in Figure 29-2
for Japan as an example.[3] The number of mobile communication subscribers is expected to reach 81 million by the year 2010. The dark line in
the figure represents the number of mobile telephone subscribers. As the
figure shows, from the current increasing ratio, this number will be saturated around 2006 with a penetration rate of approximately 70 percent.

Although the number of subscribers will be saturated, traffic will still
increase. The bars represent a forecast number of mobile Internet users as

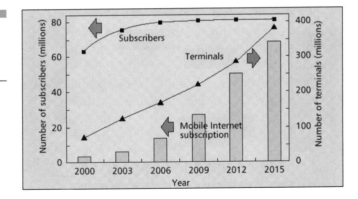

Figure 29-2

The mobile communications market forecast for Japan.

an example of new service subscribers. The number of mobile Internet users will continue to grow through the 2000s. In Japan, a new mobile Internet service called *i-mode* started in February 1999, and other operators followed to provide similar Internet Protocol (IP) access services called *EZweb* and *J-sky*. In these services, users can access Web sites and banking services and send email using mobile phones. As shown in Figure 29-3, the increase has been remarkable.[4] The number of total subscribers reached approximately 15 million at the end of July 2000. This shows that the *second wave* in mobile communications has arrived, and its main service will shift from real voice to Internet access communications. Mobile access to both the Internet and intranets will become increasingly popular and essential. Data size will continue to increase year by year, and higher-speed mobile communications systems will be required to satisfy user

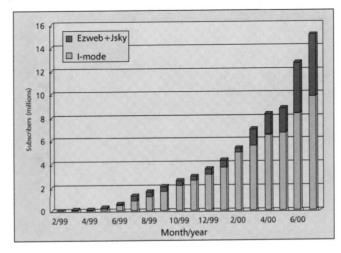

Figure 29-3

The growth of mobile Internet services.

demands. This trend will be accelerated by new types of applications such as electric tags on luggage, wallets, or even animals. The number of mobile terminals will continue to increase after 2010 to several times the number of subscribers.

Therefore, it is expected that mobile communications traffic will expand considerably. Future mobile communications systems should accommodate increased multimedia traffic in the 2010s. It should be not only high speed but also high capacity with low bit cost.

Traffic Forecast

When developing a new wireless broadband system, one of the most fundamental issues is to obtain the frequency spectrum necessary to accommodate the forecast traffic. In the spring of 2000, the International Telecommunication Union Radiocommunication Standardization Sector (ITU-R) task group TG 8/1 forecast future traffic and the necessary spectrum for IMT-2000. The calculation results for Region 3 are shown in Figure 29-4, where future traffic is compared in bits with traffic in 1999, which is considered one unit.[5]

From 1999 through 2010, voice-oriented services, which were the main services in the 1G and 2G systems, are expected to grow by 1.5 times in the

Figure 29-4

Forecast traffic for Region 3 in 2010 and after.

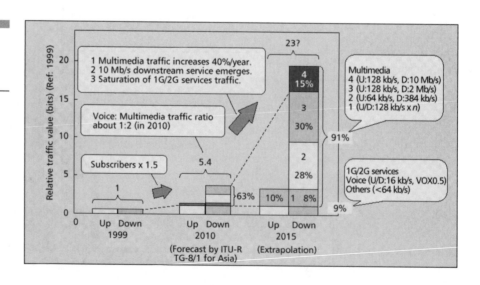

number of subscribers and double in amount of traffic. However, growth is not expected after that, and voice-oriented services will level off after 2010. After 2010, multimedia services, which will be widely introduced in the 3G system, are expected to expand considerably. The ratio between voice and multimedia traffic in 2010 will be approximately 1:2 for total up- and downlinks.

Assuming that multimedia traffic grows by 40 percent a year after 2010, it will be 23 times the current level, and the ratio between multimedia and voice traffic will be 10:1. This growth-rate assumption of 40 percent is based on the fact that the expansion rate of storage cell capacity, such as the memory and hard disks of personal computers that process information, as well as the number of pixels in Charge-Coupled Devices (CCDs) on which information is captured, is around 40 percent, and the number of Internet Web sites is growing at an annual rate of 40 percent in Japan and other countries.

The conclusion of the ITU-R TG 8/1 document was that additional frequency assignment will be necessary for 3G (IMT-2000) to accommodate the growing demand. The bandwidth to be added is assumed to be 160 MHz in 2010. However, the added bandwidth greatly depends on the growth ratio of traffic per subscriber, and traffic will continue to increase after 2010. Therefore, study of high-capacity 4G cellular systems with improved spectrum efficiency and a new frequency band is necessary to accommodate growing traffic in 2010 and thereafter.

System Requirements: High-Data-Rate Transmission

The 3G system covers up to 2 Mbps for indoor environments and 144 kbps for vehicular environments. The 5-GHz-band wireless broadband LAN and wireless broadband access systems being developed in Japan (MMAC), Europe (Hiperlan2), and United States (IEEE 802.11) have transmission speeds of approximately 20 to 30 Mbps. The user data rates of future generations will range from 2 to 600 Mbps depending on the systems. The minimum target speed of 4G cellular will be 10 to 20 Mbps, and at least 2 Mbps for moving vehicles.

High Mobility 4G cellular may be required to provide at least 2 Mbps for moving vehicles. Although realization of high mobility with high-data-rate systems is very difficult, it will be realized by intelligent transport systems, which will be operated in the 5.8-GHz band in the first phase. The ITS mentioned next is a dedicated system for transportation in the first phase; however, it will be expanded to cover pedestrians. The second phase of ITS will provide high-data-rate services with 50 to 200 Mbps in millimeter-wave bands.

A Wide Coverage Area and Seamless Roaming among Different Systems   Since the target data rate of future systems is more than two orders of magnitude higher than that of present systems, the cell radius will be decreased, resulting in a small coverage area. One option may be to use high-altitude platform station (HAPS) systems, which use large airships as communications platforms in a stratospheric layer 20 km above the ground. To extend penetration into buildings, wide-range variable-speed transmission is necessary. Smooth handover to other systems such as indoor wireless broadband LANs, outdoor wireless broadband access systems, and ITSs is a very important function for future systems. This concept can be called *roaming among different systems*. It may be the first step in realizing system roaming by constructing networks based on IP technology. Supporting the next-generation Internet, including IPv6 (see Chapter 28 for more information) and multicast, is important because every consumer electronic device can be connected to the network.

Higher Capacity and Lower Bit Cost   3G cellular system capacity will not be sufficient to handle the explosively growing multimedia traffic of the 2010s. Capacity per unit area for 4G cellular systems should be at least 10 times that of 3G cellular systems. The bit cost should be cut dramatically so that people can use it without worrying about communications charges.

Wireless Broadband QoS Resource Control   For Internet services, best-effort service is very attractive because it has the potential to lower service cost. However, wireless broadband systems use limited radio resources (frequency bandwidth and transmitting power) and suffer from congestion. Therefore, wireless broadband quality of service (QoS) resource control is necessary to maintain the service quality and to support various applications and service classes.

Candidates for Future-Generation Systems

In this part of the chapter, several candidates for future systems such as 4G cellular, wireless broadband access, LANs, ITSs, and HAPS systems are

Figure 29-5
The concept of
future-generation
mobile com-
munications.

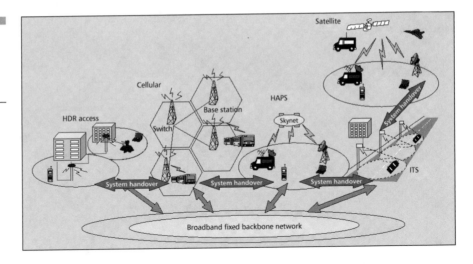

introduced. A concept of system roaming by system handover among different systems is shown in Figure 29-5.[6]

4G Cellular Systems   4G cellular systems should be not only high-speed but also high-capacity, with low bit cost and the ability to support the services of the 2010s. In order to achieve high capacity with reasonable frequency bandwidth, the cell radius of 4G cellular systems should be decreased from that of present cellular systems. However, current cellular radio access network (RAN) structures are not optimized for microcellular networks. Thus a new revolutionary RAN structure with reduced bit cost should be studied.

By constructing networks based on IP technology, seamless connection between 4G, 3G, wireless LANs (WLANs), and fixed networks will be possible. Not only the RAN structure but also the entire network structure should be considered to support various application services of the 2010s. The basic network structure concept for 4G cellular is shown in Figure 29-6.[7] The relationship between the network and applications in 4G can be divided into three layers. The physical network provides access and routing functions in an integrated format for both radio and core networks. The middleware environment acts as a bridge between the application and physical network. It provides functions such as QoS mapping, address conversion, plug and play, security management, and an active network. The interface between the physical network and the middleware environment will be an open IP interface. The interface between the middleware environment and applications also will be open interfaces, enabling third parties to develop and provide new applications and services easily.

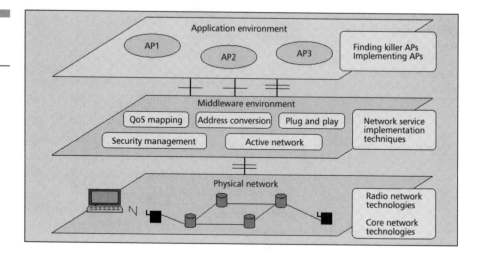

Figure 29-6
4G-cellular system
architecture.

Wireless Broadband Access and Local-Area Networks Wireless broadband access systems using 5-GHz and millimeter-wave bands have been developed. In 1996, Japan started a new research and development (R&D) program called *multimedia mobile access communications* (MMAC) systems. A MMAC is a high-performance wireless broadband system to be used after IMT-2000 that allows any person to communicate *anytime, anyplace*. The MMAC will provide two categories of high-speed wireless broadband access communications. The first will be serviced both outdoors and indoors. This is a wireless broadband mobile communications system that can transmit up to 30 Mbps using 5.2 GHz, which will operate starting in 2002. The second will provide ultra-high-speed WLANs indoors that can transmit high-speed signals (up to 600 Mbps) using the millimeter-wave radio band (60 GHz). These 5-GHz MMAC systems are similar to other systems in the world, and user data rates of these systems are very high, up to 30 Mbps. These systems cannot provide wide coverage areas, nor can they provide services in vehicle environments, and the main application is limited to a *hot spot* (covering indoors and premises). Prototype systems of millimeter-wave wireless broadband LANs have been developed to demonstrate the feasibility of 60-GHz WLAN systems with Asynchronous Transfer Mode (ATM) or 100-base Ethernet interfaces operating at data rates of up to 155 Mbps.

Intelligent Transport Systems The ITS is a new transport system that comprises an advanced information and telecommunications network for users, roads, and vehicles. The ITS is greatly expected to contribute much to solving problems such as traffic accidents and congestion. Not only solving such problems, ITS will provide multimedia services for drivers and passengers.

The ITS consists of nine development areas, including advances in navigation systems, an electronic toll-collection system (ETC), assistance for safe driving, and so forth. The first step of the ITS is an ETC, which is a nonstop toll-collection system using two pairs of 5.8-GHz bands. The ITS is appreciated as one of the most promising multimedia businesses, and the potential market is estimated at about 50 trillion yen. Telecommunications systems related to the ITS are divided into road-vehicle communications and intervehicle communications. The most important infrastructure is road-vehicle communications, in which many base stations are equipped along a trunk road to communicate with vehicles, and several control stations manage these base stations. Figure 29-7 shows the basic concept of ITS communications.[8] Along the roadside, optical fiber networks will be implemented to convey high-speed data to access points, which will connect fiber and wireless broadband links for moving vehicles. In ITSs, radio on fiber is one of the most important key technologies.

High-Altitude Stratospheric Platform Station Systems   A concept of a high-data-rate wireless broadband access network using HAPS is shown in Figure 29-8.[9] The HAPS system is very attractive for multimedia communications. It has the potential to become the third communications infrastructure after terrestrial and satellite communications. The platforms

Figure 29-7
The basic concept of ITS communications.

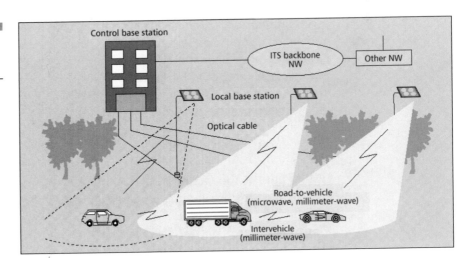

Figure 29-8

The concept of a HAPS wireless broadband access network.

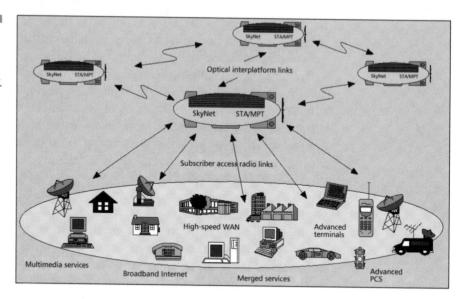

keep their positions at about 20 km high in the stratosphere. By optical intercommunication links, they make a meshlike network in the sky.

A wireless broadband access link is the link between the platform station and the user station. The frequency band of the access link is expected to use a millimeter-wave band. At the recent World Radio Congress (WRC) in Geneva, Switzerland, in November of 1997, a 600-MHz bandwidth in a 48/47 GHz band was allocated for the fixed services of high-altitude stations.

This system can support various types of user terminals, fixed terminals, portable terminals, and mobile terminals. The typical bit rate of the access link is 25 Mbps for most fixed and portable terminals, whereas a several hundred megabits per second link is available for limited fixed terminals with antennas larger than the typical ones. Because of the use of millimeter-wave bands, a small antenna with high gain is feasible. For example, a bit rate of 144 kbps can be provided for vehicles by only a 5-cm dish antenna with 20-dBi gain.

Key Technologies

In this part of the chapter, key technologies of future systems are discussed, and they are summarized in Figure 29-9.[10]

Modulation and Signal Transmission   High-speed mobile transmission in higher frequency bands suffers severely from frequency-selective fading. Robust modulation-demodulation schemes should be studied to find a way to withstand frequency-selective fading. Multiple carrier modulation schemes, including orthogonal frequency-division multiplex (OFDM) and single-carrier modulation with adaptive equalizers, are candidates. Another important demand for high-speed transmission is an extremely low required $E_b/N0$ value. Since the noise bandwidth at the receiver is wide in a high-speed system, low $E_b/N0$ values are required to achieve reasonable area coverage. High-speed transmitter power control (TPC) to mitigate Rayleigh fading and a pilot-added fast-tracking coherent demodulator are effective ways to achieve this goal. Frequency-domain antifading measures such as Range Acceleration Kill Evaluation (RAKE) combining spread-spectrum receivers or frequency-hopping techniques are also necessary. High-performance forward error correction (FEC) such as turbocoding, automatic repeat request (ARQ), and diversity are important factors in establishing high-speed large-capacity networks. All these measures to improve the required $E_b/N0$ value are also effective in increasing capacity.

Propagation   In radio propagation and link budget design, the mobile propagation characteristics of microwaves to consider for use in the future and wireless broadband signal transmission characteristics with the maximum of 20 Mbps are subjects for further study. Propagation studies at 60 GHz to analyze the characteristics of indoor multipath propagation found that the use of circular polarization and a directive antenna is effective in suppressing the effects of multipath and therefore significantly improve high-speed digital transmission characteristics. In addition to these indoor

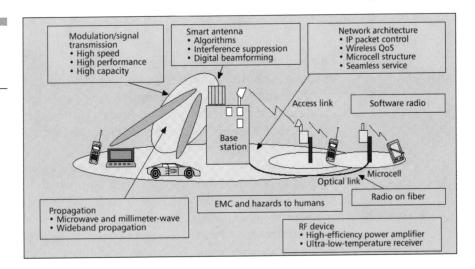

Figure 29-9
Key technologies in wireless broadband access networks.

multipath propagation experiments, measurements for characterizing various indoor construction materials also have been conducted to study their reflection and transmission characteristics, required for analyzing indoor multipath characteristics and modeling indoor propagation. Rain attenuation probability characteristics in the submillimeter-wave band are research subjects.

Software Radio   Software radio technology is one solution to realize the coexistence of several mobile telecommunications services. Software programs describe all telecommunications components in digital signal processing language, and adequate software programs are downloaded to digital signal processing hardware (DSPH) such as field programmable gate arrays (FPGAs) and digital signaling processors (DSPs) in accordance with the users' favorite wireless broadband telecommunications system. With software radio technologies, you should use only one terminal in different systems. However, in order to realize such a software radio technology, there remain several problems, including the following: The large volume of software depends on the required telecommunication systems, and in the implementation of the software in DSPH, many proprietary techniques exist. If a download-type software radio system is realized, all these confidential techniques will leak out.

In order to overcome these problems, a new configuration method for software radio systems has been proposed that is called a *parameter-controlled software radio system*. Moreover, an experimental prototype that realizes three-mode real-time radio communications systems [ETC, global positioning system (GPS), and personal handyphone system (PHS)] was developed using the proposed scheme, and its transmission and configuration performance was evaluated.

"Smart" Antennas   "Smart" antennas have intelligent functions such as suppression of interference signals, auto tracking of desired signals, and digital beam forming with adaptive space-time processing algorithms. Because of these characteristics, smart antennas have been considered key technologies for future mobile communications. One type of smart antenna, the adaptive-array antenna (AAA), is expected to reduce interference and lower transmission power. Interference canceling with an AAA and an interference-canceling equalizer (ICE) is promising to increase capacity. One problem in making these candidates feasible is implementing a fading-channel estimation circuit. Since channel estimation requires many calculations, the estimation algorithm and processor configuration are important issues to address.

Radio on Fiber   Radio-on-fiber (ROF) technologies have been considered very attractive and important subjects of R&D, especially in implementing the road-vehicle communications systems of the ITS. By using ROF, you can transmit a wireless broadband radio signal with low loss. Until now, a 60-GHz radio signal could be transmitted through the optical fiber. By using ROF technologies, you can transmit multiservice radio signals through optical fiber. In Japan, many wireless broadband services are available, such as digital cellular (PDC) on 800-MHz and 1.5-GHz bands, PHS on a 1.9-GHz band, VICS service on a 2.5-GHz band, FM commercial radio on a 76- to 90-MHz band, TV broadcasting a on 90- to 770-MHz band, and ETC on 5.8-GHz band. In order to decrease the number of air interfaces, a new transmitting technique based on ROF has been proposed.

Network Architecture and Protocol   The main subjects here include an air interface protocol suitable for IP packet transmission, location registration, and base station network configuration; wireless broadband QoS control; network configuration that facilitates the introduction of microcells; and integrated seamless service control with 3G cellular and wireless LANs.

In order to accommodate the enormous amount of traffic in dense urban areas, a spatial frequency reuse strategy is key. At this point, seamless geographic coverage with a microcellular structure is better than a hot-spot coverage strategy because the former can avoid geographic concentration of traffic.

Intelligent wireless broadband resource management is a key technique in handling multimedia traffic. For high-speed mobile communications, not only the spectrum resource but also the transmission power available in the base station and mobile station restrict the user's transmission speed. A wireless broadband resource manager should check the available resources, the quality of the forward and reverse links, and the application type and user class in QoS services and then assign the appropriate forward and reverse link speeds and transmitting power to the user.

The IP-technology-based network structure can handle IP packet traffic efficiently and at low cost. It also can easily provide the broadcast and multicast functions essential for push-type information services. The key issue is a routing/handover scheme and an authentication strategy that do not affect mobility or throughput.

Devices   Important components in high-frequency systems are radio-frequency (rf) circuits such as high-efficiency power amplifiers, ultra-low-temperature compact receiver amplifiers, and antennas. In particular, realization of millimeter-wave communications systems greatly depends on whether suitable devices are available for operation in high-frequency bands. Millimeter-wave components traditionally have been based on two-terminal devices and waveguide as active elements and transmission media, respectively. However, waveguide has disadvantages of bulkiness, heaviness, and rigidity. A remarkable technical advancement of high-speed three-terminal devices in millimeter-wave bands in the last two decades has changed components to integrated-circuit-based planar structures. Compared with a waveguide, they have advantages of compactness, light weight, and suitability for commercial production.

Indium phosphate (InP)–based high-electron-mobility transistors (HEMTs) have achieved a record high maximum oscillation frequency (f_{max}) of 600 GHz and superior low-noise performance from the microwave to millimeter-wave frequency ranges. Multistage millimeter-wave low-noise amplifiers (LNAs) have shown high performance (1.7 dB NF at 62 GHz).

Antennas operating in millimeter-wave bands are also key devices in future mobile communications. To avoid large attenuation in feed circuits in millimeter-wave bands, various types of antennas have been investigated and developed. Examples are a circularly polarized omnidirectional cylindrical slot-array antenna for base stations and a dielectric loaded gaussian beam antenna integrated with MMICs.

EMC and Hazards to Humans   Evaluations of electromagnetic compatibility (EMC) and hazards to humans are very important in frequency bands. This is especially true in higher frequency bands such as microwave and millimeter wave.

Before delving further into the global wireless broadband demand methodology and projections, the Wireless Application Protocol (WAP) must be discussed. After all, WAP is the de facto world standard for the presentation and delivery of wireless broadband information.

Broadband WAP Positioning

According to The Strategis Group, there will be more than 640 million wireless broadband subscribers by the year 2002. New estimates report that the number of wireless broadband subscribers will break the 2 billion mark by 2005, and *a substantial portion of the phones sold that year will have multimedia capabilities*. These multimedia capabilities include the ability to retrieve email and push and pull information from the Internet. In order to guide the development of these exciting new applications, the leaders of the wireless broadband telecommunications industry formed the Wireless Application Protocol Forum.

The Wireless Application Protocol (WAP) is the de facto world standard for the presentation and delivery of wireless broadband information and telephony services on mobile phones and other wireless broadband terminals. Handset manufacturers representing 91 percent of the world market across all technologies have committed to shipping WAP-enabled devices. Carriers representing more than 200 million subscribers worldwide have joined WAP Forum. This commitment will provide hundreds of millions of WAP browser–enabled products to consumers by the end of 2002. WAP allows carriers to strengthen their service offerings by providing subscribers with the information they want and need while on the move. Infrastructure vendors will deliver the supporting network equipment. Application developers and content providers delivering the value-added services are contributing to the WAP specification.

Enabling information access from handheld devices requires a deep understanding of both technical and market issues that are unique to the wireless broadband environment. The WAP specification was developed by the industry's best minds to address these issues. Wireless broadband devices represent the ultimate constrained computing device with limited CPU, memory, and battery life and a simple user interface. Wireless broadband networks are constrained by low bandwidth, high latency, and unpredictable availability and stability. However, most important of all, wireless broadband subscribers have a different set of essential desires and needs than desktop or even laptop Internet users.

WAP-enabled devices are companion products that will deliver timely information and accept transactions and inquiries when the user is moving around. WAP services provide pinpoint information access and delivery when the full-screen environment is either not available or not necessary.

The WAP specification addresses these issues by using the best of existing standards and developing new extensions where needed. It enables industry participants to develop solutions that are air interface independent, device independent, and fully interoperable. The WAP solution leverages the tremendous investment in Web servers, Web development tools, Web programmers, and Web applications while solving the unique problems associated with the wireless broadband domain. The specification further ensures that this solution is fast, reliable, and secure. It enables developers to use existing tools to produce sophisticated applications that have an intuitive user interface. Ultimately, wireless broadband subscribers benefit by gaining the power of information access in the palm of their hand.

The WAP Forum has published a global wireless broadband protocol specification based on existing Internet standards such as XML and IP for all wireless broadband networks. The WAP specification is developed and supported by the wireless broadband telecommunications community so that the entire industry and, most important, its subscribers can benefit from a single, open specification.

Wireless broadband service providers are able to offer a new dimension of service that complements the existing features of their networks while extending subscriber access to the unbounded creativity of the Web. Handset manufacturers can integrate microbrowser functionality at minimal cost because the WAP specification is open and public. Application developers gain access to a whole new market of information-hungry users while protecting and leveraging their current investments in Web technology. Subscribers gain real, anytime, anywhere information access with a simple and effective user interface available on a variety of networks and devices.

While the WAP specification solves the transport and content problems of the constrained wireless broadband environment today, the WAP Forum is constantly working to improve the state of wireless broadband access to information. By working to build liaisons with Association of Radio Industries and Businesses (ARIB), CDMA Development Group (CDG), European Computer Manufacturers Association (ECMA), European Telecommunications Standards Institute (ETSI), TIA and W3C, the WAP Forum will continue to ensure that a single, open standard will be available to meet the wireless broadband information needs of subscribers and industry participants worldwide. The WAP Forum is working with these standards bodies toward a goal of convergence with the Extensible Hypertext Markup Language (XHTML) and Hypertext Transfer Protocol (HTTP) standards in order to optimize them for the wireless broadband environment.

The WAP Forum

The Wireless Application Protocol Forum is an industry group dedicated to the goal of enabling sophisticated telephony and information services on handheld wireless broadband devices. These devices include mobile telephones, pagers, personal digital assistants (PDAs), and other wireless broadband terminals. Recognizing the value and utility of the World Wide Web architecture, the WAP Forum has chosen to align its technology closely with the Internet and the Web. The WAP specification extends and leverages existing technologies, such as digital data networking standards, and Internet technologies, such as Internet Protocol (IP), Hypertext Transfer Protocol (HTTP), Extensible Markup Language (XML), Secure

Sockets Layer (SSL), Uniform Resource Locator (URLs), scripting and other content formats.

Ericsson, Motorola, Nokia, and Phone.com (formerly Unwired Planet) founded the WAP Forum in June 1997. Since then, it has experienced impressive membership growth, with members joining from the ranks of the world's premiere wireless broadband service providers, handset manufacturers, infrastructure providers, and software developers. As of late 2000, the WAP Forum had more than 500 members.

The WAP Forum has drafted a global wireless broadband protocol specification for all wireless broadband networks and is contributing it to various industry groups and standards bodies. This WAP specification enables manufacturers, network operators, content providers, and application developers to offer compatible products and secure services on all devices and networks, resulting in greater economies of scale and universal access to information. WAP Forum membership is open to all industry participants.

The Goals of the WAP Forum

The WAP Forum has the following goals:

- To bring Internet content and advanced data services to wireless broadband phones and other wireless broadband terminals.
- To create a global wireless broadband protocol specification that works across all wireless broadband network technologies.
- To enable the creation of content and applications that scale across a wide range of wireless broadband bearer networks and device types.
- To embrace and extend existing standards and technology wherever possible and appropriate.[11]

The WAP Forum does not develop products but instead creates license-free standards for the entire industry to use to develop products. Each company's product line can then offer its own unique features while still conforming to the WAP specification. Since the WAP Forum is not a handset manufacturer, voice-mail vendor, or infrastructure provider, all companies in the telecommunications industry are assured that they are not competing with WAP because WAP does not promote any particular product or product line. Instead, the WAP Forum promotes and supports all companies that are developing products based on the WAP specification. In order to accomplish these goals, the WAP Forum has developed the WAP specification according to the design principles outlined next.

Build on Existing Standards   As much as possible, the WAP Forum seeks to use existing industry standards as the basis for its own architecture and design. For example, a WAP gateway is required to communicate with other Internet nodes using the standard HTTP 1.1 protocol. Furthermore, the specification calls for wireless broadband handsets to use the standard URL addressing scheme to request services.

It is also very important for the WAP Forum's standards to be developed in such a way that they complement existing standards. For example, the WAP specification does not specify how data should be transmitted over the air interface. Instead, the WAP specification is intended to sit on top of existing bearer channel standards so that any bearer standard can be used with the WAP protocols to implement complete product solutions.

When the WAP Forum identifies a new area of technology where a standard does not exist or exists but needs modification for wireless broadband, it works to submit its specifications to other industry standards groups. The WAP Forum currently has several different relationships with other standards bodies. For example:

- The WAP Forum is submitting its specifications to the European Telecommunications Standards Institute (ETSI). In addition to having a formal liaison between the two groups, the MExE (Mobile Execution Environment) subgroup within ETSI's Special Mobile Group 4 is cross-referencing the WAP specification to define a compliance profile. The Cellular Telecommunications Industry Association (CTIA) has an official liaison officer to the WAP Forum.

- The WAP Forum has established a formal liaison relationship with the World Wide Web Consortium (W3C) and the Telecommunications Industry Association (TIA). The WAP Forum is collaborating with these organizations in the area of WWW technologies in the wireless broadband sector. The W3C, TIA, and the WAP Forum intend to continue to work together in selected technical areas to jointly create and promote technical specifications of interest to all three organizations.

- The WAP Forum is in the process of forming a liaison relationship with the Internet Engineering Task Force (IETF).[12]

As new standards emerge, the WAP Forum will continue its active role in ensuring that these new standards remain compatible with the work of the WAP Forum. For example, the WAP Forum will be working with the W3C and IETF to ensure future convergence with HTML-NG (next generation) and HTTP-NG specifications and to provide input to these groups regarding the requirements of future wireless broadband network technologies. In addition, the WAP Forum is carefully watching the development of IMT-2000 (or often 3G) family of standards by the International Telecommunications Union (ITU).

Invite Full Industry Participation   The WAP Forum strongly believes that the best technology standards can only come about with full industry participation. With this principle in mind, the WAP Forum has been established as a forum open to any industry participant. By encouraging participation across the entire telecommunications industry, the WAP Forum is able to

- Produce open standards that result from many industry experts working together.
- Develop consensus in the industry for how all the components of a solution will interoperate.
- Produce standards through an open and collaborative process—no one vendor receives favorable treatment, and the entire industry benefits from the results.
- Benefit from the innovations of dozens of contributing companies rather than the efforts of only one or two vendors.[13]

To date, the WAP Forum has grown to a membership of more than 500 companies that all believe that an open standards process is the best way to develop solutions for wireless broadband Internet access.

Maintain Bearer Independence   To best address the needs of the widest possible population of end users, the Wireless Application Protocol is designed to work optimally with all air interfaces. This principle allows the largest number of service providers, software developers, and handset manufacturers to benefit from one unified specification. Service providers can implement a common solution across their own disparate networks so that every subscriber has the best possible user experience on each network. Applications can be developed using one standard that will work across a variety of networks. Handset manufacturers can use the same software in all their product lines, reducing development time and simplifying support issues.

By making minimal demands on the air interface itself, the WAP specification can operate on the widest number of air interfaces. It defines a protocol stack that can operate on high-latency, low-bandwidth networks such as the Short Message Service (SMS) or the GSM Unstructured Supplementary Service Data (USSD) channel.

Being air interface independent also makes the specification easy to extend to new networks and transports as they develop. As air interfaces become more sophisticated, the services they provide can be designed to comply with the WAP specification, further encouraging the use of one standard across all networks.

Maintain Device Independence   In addition to being air interface independent, the WAP specification is also independent of any particular device. Instead, it specifies the bare minimum functionality a device must have and has been designed to accommodate any functionality above that minimum.

Device independence offers similar benefits to bearer independence: Applications developed for one standard can operate on a wide variety of devices that implement the specification; network operators gain a consistent user interface for their services across multiple vendors' handsets; application developers do not have to write separate versions of their code for different devices; and service providers can choose any standard-compliant device that meets their own unique market requirements. Device manufacturers are assured that they will have many applications written for their device by implementing the specification yet are able to add their own brand features above and beyond the minimum standards to make their device unique in the marketplace.

Ensure Interoperability   Service providers must feel secure that their investments will yield benefits in the future. They will not be able to do so until equipment and software offered by different suppliers can be made to work together. The WAP specification has been designed to encourage easy, open interoperability between its key components. Any solution component built to be compliant with the WAP specification can interoperate with any other WAP-compliant component. Service providers can choose equipment and software from multiple WAP-compliant vendors, selecting each piece of the solution that is appropriate for the service provider's particular needs.

Bearer and device independence both help foster interoperability. But interoperability goes beyond these two principles to require that each WAP-compatible component will communicate with all other components in the solution network by using the standard methods and protocols defined in the specification.

Interoperability provides clear benefits for handset manufacturers and infrastructure providers. Handset manufacturers are assured that if their device complies with the WAP specification, it will be able to interface with any WAP-compliant server, regardless of the manufacturer. Likewise, the makers of a WAP-compliant server are assured that any WAP-compliant handset will interface correctly with their servers.

Encourage and Foster Market Development   The WAP specification is designed to bring Internet access to the wireless broadband mass market. By building open specifications and encouraging communication and technical exchanges among the industry players, the WAP Forum has already begun to open the wireless broadband data market in new ways. In 1998, the idea of a single wireless broadband data standard was unheard of, yet today the WAP specification is available to the public, and dozens of companies are promoting this vision of the future. The revolution is under way to bring information access to any handset at a reasonable price and in an easy-to-use form factor.

Why WAP Is Necessary

Providing Internet and Web-based services on a wireless broadband data network presents many challenges to wireless broadband service providers, application developers, and handset manufacturers. While the obvious limitations are rooted in the nature of wireless broadband devices and data networks, there are also more fundamental differences that are important to understand. The next part of this chapter outlines the challenges that must be overcome to make wireless broadband Internet access appealing to the average wireless broadband subscriber.

The Market Is Different   Bringing computing power to a wireless broadband handset opens an extensive new market for information access. This market is very different from the traditional desktop or even the laptop market because the subscriber has a different set of needs and expectations. Some of these differences include

- Ease of use
- Market size
- Price sensitivity
- Usage patterns
- Essential tasks

EASE OF USE   Despite the fact that using a desktop computer has become progressively easier over the last 5 years, a wireless broadband computing device must be dramatically easier to use than even the simplest desktop computer. These devices will be used by people who potentially have no desktop computing experience. Furthermore, they often will be used in a dynamic environment where the user is engaged in multiple activities. Subscribers will not be focused on their handset the way they are when they are sitting in front of a desktop computer. Therefore, the devices must be extremely simple and easy to use. Applications built for these devices therefore must present the best possible user interface for quick and simple use. There can be no installation scripts, complicated menu structures, application errors, general protection faults, or complicated key sequences such as Ctrl-Alt-Del or Alt-Shift-F5.

MARKET SIZE   The growth and size of the wireless broadband subscriber market have been phenomenal. There are more than 300 million wireless broadband subscribers in the world today. According to Nokia, there will be more than 2 billion wireless broadband subscribers by the year 2006. The wireless broadband market is enormous; it can afford and will demand optimized solutions.

PRICE SENSITIVITY   Even with today's sub-$900 computers, a price difference of $60 between two models is not considered significant. However, a difference of $60 between two handsets is very significant, especially after years of subsidized handset pricing by the service provider. Market studies have shown that a mass-market handset must be priced under $138 to be competitive. A solution must add significant value at a low cost to be effective in this market.

USAGE PATTERNS   Subscribers expect wireless broadband data access to perform like the rest of their handset. The service should be instantly available, easy to use, and designed to be used for a few minutes at a time. Hourglass icons telling subscribers to wait will not be acceptable.

ESSENTIAL TASKS   As soon as professionals step out of the office, information needs and desires change. Wireless broadband Internet subscribers will not want to use their handset to *surf the Internet*. They will have small, specific tasks that need to be accomplished quickly. Subscribers will want to scan email rather than read it all or see just the top stock quotes of interest. Receiving timely traffic alerts on the handset will be essential, whereas the same information may not be as valuable at the desktop. The best applications will give the user a comprehensive, personalized summary of important information and will allow them to easily drill down for more detailed information.

The Network Is Different   Wireless broadband data networks present a more constrained communications environment compared with wired networks. Because of fundamental limitations of power, available spectrum and mobility, wireless broadband data networks tend to have

- Less bandwidth
- More latency
- Less connection stability
- Less predictable availability[14]

Furthermore, as bandwidth increases, the handset's power consumption also increases, which further taxes the already limited battery life of a mobile device. Therefore, even as wireless broadband networks capitalize on higher bandwidth, the power of a handset always will be limited by battery capacity and size, thus challenging the amount of data throughput. Deployment of the WAP standard will accommodate more users per megahertz because it uses the available bandwidth at an extremely efficient level. The result of placing more users on a given amount of spectrum can yield lower costs for both the network provider and the customer. A wireless broadband data solution must be able to overcome these network limitations and still deliver a satisfactory user experience.

The Device Is Different   Similarly, mass-market handheld wireless broadband devices present a more constrained computing environment compared with desktop computers. Because of fundamental limitations of battery life and form factor, mass-market handheld devices tend to have

- Less powerful CPUs
- Less memory (ROM and RAM)
- Restricted power consumption
- Smaller displays
- Different input devices (a phone keypad, voice input, etc.)[15]

Because of these limitations, the user interface of a wireless broadband handset is fundamentally different from that of a desktop computer. The limited screen size and lack of a mouse require a different user interface metaphor than the traditional desktop graphic user interface (GUI).

These conditions are not likely to change dramatically in the near future. The most popular wireless broadband handsets have been designed to be lightweight and fit comfortably in the palm of a hand. Furthermore, consumers desire handsets with longer battery life, which will always limit available bandwidth and the power consumption of the CPU, memory, and display. Because there will always be a performance gap between the very best desktop computers and the very best handheld devices, the method used to deliver wireless broadband data to these devices will have to effectively address this gap. As this gap changes over time, standards will have to evolve continually to keep pace with available functionality and market needs.

WAP Specification

The WAP specification is a major achievement because it defines for the first time an open standard architecture and set of protocols intended to implement wireless broadband Internet access. It also provides solutions for problems not solved by other standardization bodies (W3C, ETSI, TIA, IETF, etc.) and is a catalyst for wireless broadband development and standardization. The key elements of the WAP specification include

- WAP programming model
- Markup language
- Specification for microbrowser
- Lightweight protocol
- Framework for wireless telephony applications (WTA)

WAP Programming Model   The definition of the WAP programming model as seen in Figure 29-10 is based heavily on the existing WWW programming model.[16] This provides several benefits to application developers, including a familiar programming model, a proven architecture, and the ability to leverage existing tools (Web servers, XML tools, etc.).

Optimizations and extensions have been made in order to match the characteristics of the wireless broadband environment. Wherever possible, existing standards have been adopted or have been used as the starting point for WAP technology.

Markup Language   A markup language adhering to XML standards has been designed to enable powerful applications within the constraints

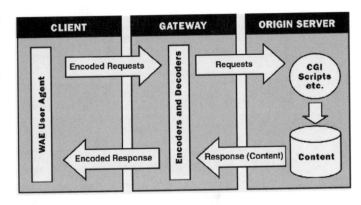

Figure 29-10
The WAP
Programming Model.

of handheld devices. The Wireless Markup Language (WML) and WMLScript do not assume that a QWERTY keyboard or a mouse are available for user input and are designed for small-screen displays. Unlike the flat structure of HTML documents, WML documents are divided into a set of well-defined units of user interactions. One unit of interaction is called a *card*, and services are created by letting the user navigate back and forth between cards from one or several WML documents. WML provides a smaller, telephony-aware set of markup tags that make it more appropriate than HTML to implement within handheld devices. From the WAP gateway, all WML content is accessed over the Internet using standard HTTP 1.1 requests, so traditional Web servers, tools, and techniques are used to serve this new market.

Specification for Microbrowser A specification has been defined for a microbrowser in the wireless broadband terminal that controls the user interface and is analogous to a standard Web browser. This specification indicates how WML and WMLScript should be interpreted in the handset and presented to the user. The microbrowser specification has been designed for wireless broadband handsets so that the resulting code will be compact and efficient yet provide a flexible and powerful user interface.

Lightweight Protocol A lightweight protocol stack to minimize bandwidth requirements, guaranteeing that a variety of wireless broadband networks can run WAP applications, has been implemented. The protocol stack is shown in Figure 29-11.[17]

Framework for Wireless Telephony Applications (WTAs) A framework for WTAs allows access, to telephony functionality such as call control, phone book access, and messaging from within WMLScript applets.

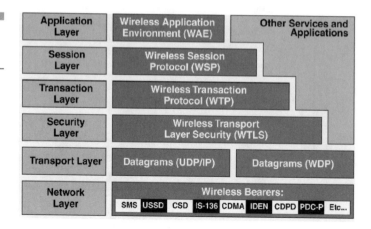

Figure 29-11
The WAP Protocol Stack.

This allows operators to develop secure telephony applications integrated into WML/WMLScript services. For example, services such as call forwarding may provide a user interface that prompts the user to make a choice between accepting a call, forwarding it to another person, or forwarding it to voice mail.

WAP Solution Benefits

The WAP specification was written to address the challenges of traditional wireless broadband data access within the context of the design objectives of the WAP Forum. This part of the chapter outlines how the WAP specification meets these goals.

Delivers an Appropriate User Experience Model The WAP specification defines a powerful and functional user interface model that is appropriate for handheld devices. Users navigate through cards with up and down scroll keys instead of a mouse. Soft keys allow the user to perform specific operations appropriate to the application context or select menu options. A traditional 12-key phone keypad is used to enter alphanumeric characters, including a full set of standard symbols. Navigation functions such as back, home, and bookmark are also provided, in keeping with the standard browser model. By using the existing Internet model as a starting point, this user interface provides familiar functionality for those accustomed with the Web. It also provides a user interface that is easy to learn and highly discoverable for the first-time user. The microbrowser allows devices with larger screens and more features to automatically display more content, just as a traditional browser does on a PC when the browser window is expanded on screen.

Leverages Proxy Technology   The WAP specification uses standard Web proxy technology to connect the wireless broadband domain with the Web. By using the computing resources in the WAP gateway, the WAP architecture permits the handset to be simple and inexpensive. For example, a WAP gateway typically will take over all Domain Name Service (DNS) services to resolve domain names used in URLs, thus offloading this computing task from the handset. The WAP gateway also can be used to provide services to subscribers and to provide the network operator with a control point to manage fraud and service utilization. A WAP gateway typically includes the following functionality: protocol gateway—the protocol gateway translates requests from the WAP protocol stack to the WWW protocol stack (HTTP and TCP/IP); and content encoders and decoders—the content encoders translate Web content into compact encoded formats to reduce the size and number of packets traveling over the wireless broadband data network.

This infrastructure ensures that mobile terminal users can browse a variety of WAP content and applications regardless of the wireless broadband network they use. Application authors are able to build content services and applications that are network and terminal independent, allowing their applications to reach the largest possible audience. Because of the WAP proxy design, content and applications are hosted on standard WWW servers and can be developed using proven Web technologies such as CGI scripting.

The WAP gateway decreases the response time to the handheld device by aggregating data from different servers on the Web and caching frequently used information. The WAP gateway also can interface with subscriber databases and use information from the wireless broadband network, such as location information, to dynamically customize WML pages for a certain group of users.

Addresses the Constraints of a Wireless Broadband Network   The protocol stack defined in WAP optimizes standard Web protocols, such as HTTP, for use under the low-bandwidth, high-latency conditions often found in wireless broadband networks. A number of enhancements to the session, transaction, security, and transport layers provide HTTP functionality better suited to the wireless broadband network environment. Here are just a few examples of these improvements:

■ The plain text headers of HTTP are translated into binary code that significantly reduces the amount of data that must be transmitted over the air interface.

■ A lightweight session reestablishment protocol has been defined that allows sessions to be suspended and resumed without the overhead of initial establishment. This allows a session to be suspended while idle to free up network resources or save battery power.

■ WAP provides a Wireless Transaction Protocol (WTP) that provides reliable transport for the WAP datagram service. WTP provides similar reliability as traditional TCP does but without behaviors that make TCP unsuitable in a wireless broadband network. For example, TCP transmits a large amount of information for each request-response transaction, including information needed to handle out-of-order packet delivery. Since there is only one possible route between the WAP proxy and the handset, there is no need to handle this situation. WTP eliminates this unnecessary information and reduces the amount of information needed for each request-response transaction. This is just one example of the optimizations WTP provides.

■ WAP's WTP solution also means that a TCP stack is not required in the phone, which allows for significant savings in processing and memory cost in the handset.

■ The improvements made in the WAP protocol stack lead to significant savings in wireless broadband bandwidth. Figure 29-12 compares the number of packets needed to process a stock quote query

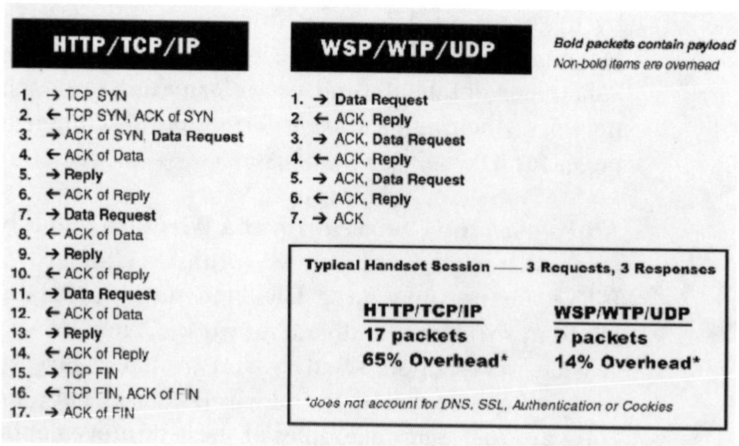

Figure 29-12
WAP protocols conserve wireless broadband bandwidth.

HTTP/TCP/IP	WSP/WTP/UDP	*Bold packets contain payload*
		Non-bold items are overhead
1. → TCP SYN	1. → **Data Request**	
2. ← TCP SYN, ACK of SYN	2. ← **ACK, Reply**	
3. → ACK of SYN, **Data Request**	3. → ACK, **Data Request**	
4. ← ACK of Data	4. ← **ACK, Reply**	
5. → **Reply**	5. → ACK, **Data Request**	
6. ← ACK of Reply	6. ← **ACK, Reply**	
7. → **Data Request**	7. → ACK	
8. ← ACK of Data		
9. → **Reply**		
10. ← ACK of Reply		
11. → **Data Request**		
12. ← ACK of Data		
13. → **Reply**		
14. ← ACK of Reply		
15. → TCP FIN		
16. ← TCP FIN, ACK of FIN		
17. → ACK of FIN		

Typical Handset Session —— **3 Requests, 3 Responses**	
HTTP/TCP/IP	**WSP/WTP/UDP**
17 packets	**7 packets**
65% Overhead*	**14% Overhead***

*does not account for DNS, SSL, Authentication or Cookies

from a desktop browser using HTTP 1.0 with the same query from a WAP browser.[18] The WAP protocol stack uses less than half the number of packets that the standard HTTP/TCP/IP stack uses to deliver the same content. This improvement is essential to best utilize the limited wireless broadband bandwidth available.[19]

Provides a Secure Wireless Broadband Connection   Many applications on the Web today require a secure connection between the client and the application server. The WAP specification ensures that a secure protocol is available for these transactions on a wireless broadband handset.

The Wireless Transport Layer Security (WTLS) Protocol is based on the industry-standard Transport Layer Security (TLS) Protocol, formerly known as Secure Sockets Layer (SSL). WTLS is intended for use with the WAP transport protocols and has been optimized for use over narrowband communication channels. WTLS ensures data integrity, privacy, authentication, and denial-of-service protection. For Web applications that employ standard Internet security techniques with TLS, the WAP gateway automatically and transparently manages wireless broadband security with minimal overhead.

Optimized for Handheld Wireless Broadband Devices   The WAP specification defines a microbrowser that is the ultimate thin client, able to fit in a limited amount of memory in the handheld device. The use of proxy technology and compression in the network interface reduces the processing load at the handheld device so that an inexpensive CPU can be used in the handset. This further helps reduce power consumption and extends battery life, meeting the needs of both handset manufacturers and wireless broadband subscribers.

Implements New Wireless Broadband Functionality   The WAP specification also defines new functionality that has not been defined by any other standard, such as a voice/data integration Application Program Interface (API) and the groundwork for wireless broadband push functionality.

The wireless telephony application (WTA) allows application developers to initiate phone calls from the browser and respond to network events as they occur. The WTA API accomplishes this by providing an interface to the local and network telephony infrastructure. The local interface allows WML and WMLScript to access a specific set of telephony functions, such as a function call to dial a phone number from the mobile handset. The network interface allows an application to monitor and initiate mobile network events so that the application can take action or update information based on these events. This functionality can be used to keep an updated list of the phone numbers dialed into an active conference call. These network and local APIs are powerful features that no other standard provides.

Standard HTTP has no support for *push* functionality. The WAP specification defines a push mechanism that will allow any Web server to send information to the client. This is an extremely important feature because it allows applications to alert the subscriber when time-sensitive information changes. There are a number of applications that make use of this functionality, such as traffic alerts and stock quote triggers or email and pager notifications.

Enables Application Development Using Existing Tools   Web developers will find it easy to develop WAP applications because the WAP programming model closely follows the existing WWW development model. WML is a tag-based document language specified as an XML document type. As such, existing XML authoring tools, as well as many HTML development environments, can be used to develop WML applications.

Since the WAP specification uses standard HTTP 1.1 protocol to communicate between the WAP gateway and Web servers, Web developers can deploy their applications on any off-the-shelf Web server. WML developers can use standard Web tools and mechanisms such as Cold Fusion, Common Gateway Interface (CGI), Perl, abstract service primitive (ASP) and others to generate dynamic WML applications. Developers can use either separate URLs for their HTML and WML entry points or a single URL to dynamically serve either HTML or WML content according to the requestor's browser type.

Although it is possible to translate HTML into WML using an automated system, in practice, the best applications use WML to tailor the interface to the specific needs of the wireless broadband user. This allows for the best possible use of the handset features, such as soft keys, and provides the best user experience. The most valuable parts of any Web application are typically the unique content it provides and the back-end database interaction, not the particular HTML that was written to interact with the user. Therefore, developing a corresponding WML front end leverages the previous engineering effort while providing significant user interface benefits.

Adapts New Standards for the Industry   Wherever possible, the WAP specification optimizes and extends existing Internet standards. The WAP Forum has taken technology elements from TCP/IP, HTTP, and XML, optimized them for the wireless broadband environment; and is now submitting these optimizations to the W3C standards process as input for the next generations of XHTML and HTTP (HTTP-NG).

The WAP Forum will continue to evolve the WAP specification to keep pace with new technologies. In the best tradition of Internet protocol standards, the WAP specification divides network functionality into several layers so that each layer can develop independently of the others. Low-level layers can be replaced to support new bearers without requiring changes to the high-level APIs or the intervening stack layers. This protects the initial investment in the protocol stack and makes the standard flexible as new and faster wireless broadband data protocols become available.

How Service Providers Benefit from Using WAP-Based Solutions

Service providers can add significant value to their existing voice offerings by adding a WAP-based solution to their wireless broadband networks. Enabling access to Web-based content is only the beginning. As service providers discover how they can use a visual interface to increase feature use and decrease operation costs, they will find that providing a WAP microbrowser-enabled handset to every subscriber will yield significant benefits. By choosing a WAP-based solution to deploy wireless broadband data, network operators will gain

- *A whole new dimension of relationship and communication with their subscribers.* Network operators can now use a visual interface to stay in touch with their subscribers and market new services to them. This creates new opportunities for improved customer service and increased use of network services.

- *Control of the data connection to their subscribers.* By using a WAP-based solution, network operators can ensure that they are part of the value proposition to their subscribers. Service providers can use the WAP gateway to track and bill for the service and provide general feature control, just as they do now for their voice services.

- *An easy method to deploy teleservices applications*, such as call feature control, prepaid wireless broadband recharge, and automated customer service. Since the applications are stored on a standard Web server inside the service provider's infrastructure, when new services are added or features are changed, these changes are instantly available to every subscriber in the network.

- *Immediate access to all WAP-enabled wireless broadband content.* Since WAP is a specification that many developers are using, service providers will benefit from an abundance of available content. This parallels the situation on the Web today, where any public Web page is available to anyone on the Internet with a Web browser.

- *Choice among open standards vendors.* Service providers can purchase their WAP gateway from one provider and use WAP-enabled handsets from several other vendors. Having the option to choose from several vendors helps keep pricing competitive for the service provider and ensures that competition will stimulate feature development.

- *Freedom to use and integrate new air interface technologies.* Since WAP is an open specification, service providers do not have to fear losing their wireless broadband data solution if they change or add a new air interface.[20]

How Handset Manufacturers Benefit from Using WAP-Based Solutions

Integrating a microbrowser into its product line allows a handset manufacturer to meet the demands of today's advanced service providers. By offering a WAP-based solution, handset manufacturers can

- Integrate a microbrowser into the handset at low cost, since the WAP specification calls for a low-profile browser that will not demand large memory or expensive CPU requirements.

- Offer one microbrowser that works on all WAP servers and therefore on all the networks that offer WAP-based services.

- Increase the perceived value of their handsets to subscribers.[21]

How Developers Benefit from Using WAP-Based Solutions

Application developers can reach the largest possible audience when they write their applications in WML because they are writing to an industry standard. Additional benefits for developers include

- Access to an entirely new, immense market of information-hungry wireless broadband subscribers while complementing their existing Internet services.

- Because WML is an XML-based language, it is an easy markup language for existing Web developers to learn.

- WML's basis in XML also positions it well as a future target markup language for automatic content transformation. The W3C is currently defining the eXstensible Style Language (XSL), which provides a powerful mechanism for the dynamic transformation of well-formed XML. Using an XSL style sheet, content written in XML-defined markup languages can be translated automatically into content suitable for either HTML or WML, as shown in Figure 29-13.[22] Likewise, content written in well-formed XML also can be translated to other XML-based markup languages using a different XSL style sheet.

- While the technology for universal content is still being developed, WML has been designed to be an integral part of this technology. Application developers can feel secure using WML today, knowing that there will be a migration path to the future.

- Since WML is part of an open standard and was developed by an independent organization, all developers can be assured that they are on equal footing with other developers. No single developer has unique access to APIs or special functionality.

- By writing in WML, a developer's work becomes available to any network and device that is WAP-compliant. WML and the WAP specification truly deliver on the *write once, use anywhere* promise.

- WML provides the application developer with the power to take full advantage of the user interface. Applications can map soft keys for easy user input and use special features to maximize the effect of displaying text on a limited screen.

- WML allows application developers to integrate their applications with device and network telephony functions. Applications that use these features can truly leverage the advantages of operating in an integrated voice and data device.

- WML allows the use of icons and bit-mapped graphics for devices that support them. One application will work equally well on a phone with or without graphics by offering alternate text to the phone that is not capable of displaying images.

- An application written in WML will look good on any device that is WAP-compliant. If one device is able to display more lines of text than another, the microbrowser will do so automatically, making the best use of the device's and application's capabilities.

Figure 29-13
The future of content
development.

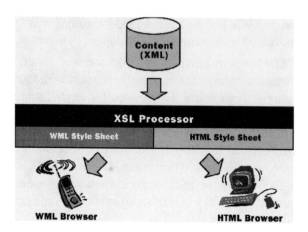

- An application can be customized to take advantage of a particular device's capabilities by using standard HTTP header mechanisms to learn about the device's capabilities.[23]

How Subscribers Benefit from Using WAP-Based Solutions

Ultimately, subscribers are the most important beneficiaries of the work of the WAP Forum. The WAP specification was developed and written by experienced telecommunications experts who understand not only the technologies involved but also the real needs of subscribers. Consequently, the WAP specification delivers significant value to subscribers. The WAP specification pulls together existing technologies and defines new standards to provide subscribers with

- Fast, efficient access to essential information from a wireless broadband handset.
- Peace of mind that all transactions are completely secure.
- An easy-to-use interface metaphor that meets the needs of users within the restrictions of a constrained network and device.[24]

The widespread adoption of the WAP specification is yielding these benefits:

- *A common user interface metaphor that is being used by all industry participants.* Just as the desktop metaphor is the de facto standard for applications on PCs, the WAP card metaphor provides a common interface to which all applications can conform.

- *Ubiquity of service.* Wherever subscribers go, they will have access to their own personal content using a WAP-enabled browser.

- *Wide selection of devices.* In addition to handsets with different features and form factors, subscribers will be able to use PDAs and pagers that are also WAP-enabled.

- *A large selection of applications.* Over the last few years, the Internet model has proven to be the least expensive and most effective way to deliver new applications and services to computing users. Now that this model has been extended to wireless broadband devices, subscribers will gain access to a wealth of applications.[25]

The WAP Forum Vision for the Future of Wireless Internet

Although the WAP specification has already been published, the work of the WAP Forum has just begun. As new handset technologies, network protocols, and Internet standards develop, the WAP Forum will take an active role in helping shape these new technologies and standards, making them relevant to the wireless broadband data market.

The WAP Forum is continually gaining membership and devoting resources to educate its membership on the best ways to make open, interoperable solutions from which the entire industry can benefit. The WAP Forum meets periodically to continue the evolution of its own standards and develop new standards to drive innovation in the industry in new and exciting directions. Recent submissions to the WAP Forum have covered topics such as

- Over-the-air provisioning (OTAP)
- Persistent storage
- SIM tool kit
- Location services
- Network management
- Broadcast services
- IMT-2000 (3G) multimedia capabilities
- Corporate data access[26]

Now, let's look at how communications satellites can be used to broadcast large volumes of data directly to extensive user groups. With the latest generation of high-powered direct broadcast satellites and the changing traffic and use patterns in the Internet, new ways of using satellites for delivering data directly to the end user have become viable alternatives to terrestrial point-to-point networks. In this part of the chapter, the software architecture of a distributed system, which has been implemented successfully and which supports online and offline interactive multimedia services, is presented. It is based on a method of carrying Internet datagrams over DVB/MPEG-2 transport systems intended for digital television. It relies on a configuration using a wireless broadband forward channel and a separate, usually narrowband return channel. The forward link is usually provided by a geostationary satellite, whereas the return channel uses a different network technology, such as dialup connection, a direct Ku-band return link, a low-earth-orbit (LEO) satellite network, or an Local Multipoint Distribution System (LMDS) local distribution system. A generic multicast system is presented that exploits the inherent capabilities of satellites to reach a large number of customers. The reliable multicast strategy chosen is shown to handle multiple applications, each with different reliability and timing requirements.

Estimating Satellite Internet Services and Equipment Using DVB/MPEG-2 and Multicast Web Caching

Communications satellites have been used in the Internet from its earliest days on; for example, the Atlantic SATNET connected the ARPANET with research networks in Europe. Geostationary communications satellites usually provide a backbone to interconnect regional computer networks or to support enterprise networks or local networks. The advantages and drawbacks of geostationary satellites are well known and include the long-fat-pipe property caused by the long signal propagation delay. On the other hand, communications satellites do offer advantages, particularly wide geographic coverage, reliability of transmissions, broadcast capabilities, and direct-to-home features.

The use of high-powered direct broadcast television satellites (DBSs) for data transmission offers an interesting alternative to terrestrial networks.

The use of DBSs (a one-way or unidirectional medium) requires certain changes in the network interface configuration because the traditional Internet interfaces are assumed to be symmetrical or at least bidirectional. Hence, for truly interactive services, an Internet station receiving data over a DBS interface will need a separate interface for the return link carrying traffic from the station into the Internet.

System Architecture

The Interactive Data Broadcast System (IDBS) represents an asymmetric network configuration making use of one or more channels on a DBS, the forward link, to transmit large amounts of data to the client station (end user) and using a separate network, such as a telephone dialup or similar low-speed network such as packet radio or another satellite return link, to access the Internet and connect to a server. This contrasts sharply with traditional configurations, where network access was mostly achieved in a *balanced* mode and under the assumption that the amount of data flowing into the network is of about the same order of magnitude as the amount of data flowing from the network to the end user. This model is changing rapidly with the introduction of new technologies such as asymmetric digital subscriber line (ADSL) and applications such as the World Wide Web. The information flow becomes rather *unbalanced* because users receive much more data than they transmit. This leads to the conclusion that an asymmetric, unbalanced network access, using separate networks for inbound traffic (forward link) and outbound traffic over the return link, is a viable alternative for end-user access.

Also, with the advent of DBS systems for the forward link, the most interesting technique is MPEG-2–based digital television, which can offer data rates up to 36 Mbps on Ku-band transponders and eventually 155 Mbps in the Ka band. Components developed for set-top boxes (STBs) are also being used to implement integrated receiver-decoder (IRD) cards that plug directly into the bus of a PC-class computer. This combination of high-speed forward and low-speed return links has been used for implementation of the IDBS system, which has been demonstrated since late 1996 over EUTELSAT satellites in Europe.

Figure 29-14 shows the IDBS configuration that requires some sort of packet forwarding at the uplink site to route the traffic across the respective network interfaces.[27] At the uplink site, a base station plays the central role for accessing the Internet. It is connected via a satellite gateway to the multiplexer, modem, and transmission equipment. At the client

Figure 29-14
The IDBS satellite net-
work configuration.

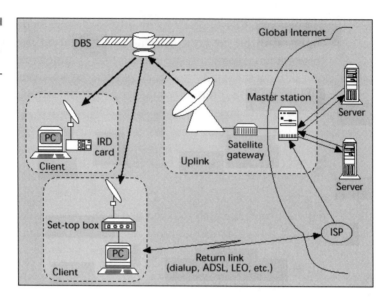

station, the signal is fed into an rf low-noise block and then into an integrated receiver-decoder. Finally, the data are delivered to the PC over the
internal bus and delivered to the appropriate protocol software. The return
path is routed over a separate network that connects the PC to the base
station; this connection can be temporary or permanent. Several communications systems have been used to implement a return channel,
including the standard public switched telephone network (PSTN)
telephone/modem or integrated services digital network (ISDN) links, Ku-
band and Ka-band satellite links via geostationary (GEO) satellites, and
packet radio networks. An interesting configuration for remote access
would be a combination of a GEO broadcast satellite for the forward channel and a LEO satellite system for the return channel.

The equipment needed at the user station consists, in addition to a typical PC, of a satellite interface unit (SIU) that performs all framing,
addressing, and forwarding functions for the data packets received from
the DBS interface. At the other end, a satellite gateway (SGW) must be
installed that interfaces on one side with the uplink channel to the satellite and on the other to the base station, which is an Internet server. Both
the SIU and SGW are combinations of hardware and software that take
care of all addressing, routing, and interfacing aspects so that no changes
or modifications to the Internet or TCP/IP protocol stack are required.

Digital Video Broadcast The digital video broadcast (DVB) system specified by the European Broadcast Union (EBU) is based on the cell-oriented packet transmission system defined by MPEG-2. MPEG-2 data streams carry video, audio, and data in digital form from a sender to a set of receivers. In addition, system internal signaling information is carried in the form of tables from the provider of a program to the receivers. The underlying communications channel is a broadcast medium such as a satellite transponder or a cable system with multiple access property; there is a certain similarity to a local-area network (LAN), the most popular infrastructure for computer networks today. The basic communications functionality is provided by protocol layers 1 (physical level) and 2 (data-link level). Since all stations connected to the broadcast channel can receive directly from any other station, no true level 3 protocol is required.

The physical level covers the modulation, synchronization, and encoding and is outside the scope of the MPEG-2 standards but defined by the EBU-DVB documents. The data link layer provides the point-to-point transport of what International Organization for Standardization/International Telecommunication Union (ISO/ITU) 13818-1 calls either the *payload* or *layer*. These layers, however, are not the protocol layers of the open systems interconnection (OSI) reference model (RM), but represent the service data units (SDUs) of the OSI architecture. A closer look at the transport stream (TS), table section, and packetized elementary stream (PES) of MPEG-2 reveals the layered structure shown in Figure 29-15.[28]

MPEG-2, DVB, and Protocol Layers Probably the best known architecture for layered network protocols is the OSI RM developed by ISO. It divides the functionality of interworking systems into seven layers, where

Figure 29-15
The protocol reference model for MPEG-2/DVB.

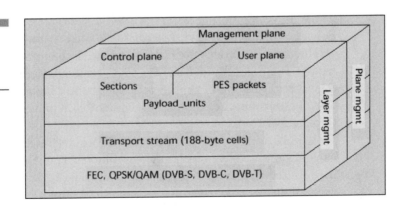

the lower three layers comprise the physical, data-link, and network layers. These layers handle the network access as well as the intranetwork functions such as medium access, error control, flow control, and routing. The upper layers are responsible for applications programs through middleware functions. All protocols are intimately integrated with the operating systems of the communicating host computers.

A related architecture model is the Protocol Reference Model (PRM) used for the definition of broadband ISDN (B-ISDN) by the ITU Telecommunication Standardization Sector (ITU-T). This model is also layered, but it distinguishes between a user and a control plane, and it also indicates the presence of additional system-related functions in a management plane that is itself further divided into layer management and plane management.

At first sight there is a striking similarity between the Asynchronous Transfer Mode (ATM) layers and the MPEG-2 architecture: Above the physical layer, the transport stream (TS) consists of fixed-length cells, and the next layer (the adaptation layer in ATM) transports payload_units that are segmented into and reassembled from sequences of cells. The cell header of the TS cell contains the packet identifier (PID), which defines a virtual broadcast channel. However, whereas ATM virtual circuits represent point-to-point links, the TS identified by one PID represents a logical broadcast channel with point-to-multipoint characteristics.

The lowest-level protocol that can be used for the transport of data payloads is the TS cell stream. A TS cell has a total length of 188 bytes, 184 of which are available for the payload. In case longer payloads have to be transported, the next-level protocol has to take care of the segmentation and reassembly of payload_units. In the case of the section and the PES, this function is performed automatically by the corresponding MPEG-2 entities.

Service Access Points   The MPEG-2 transport system offers two conceptual service access points (SAPs) where data units can be delivered: one for the PES packets and one for table sections. In addition, there is the SAP directly on top of the TS cell layer where individual cells are delivered. In case this variant is used, segmentation and reassembly have to be implemented by the user.

An integrated receiver-decoder (IRD) must be able to determine for each incoming cell to which payload it belongs and deliver it to the proper module (the next level of processing), which is either the PES handler, section handler, or a user-defined reassembly module. For MPEG-2, the information for this decision is the PID value, which is bound via the system information (SI) tables, in particular the program map table (PMT).

IP Over MPEG-2/DVB   IDBS uses standard IP for the network layer. IP packets are encapsulated according to the Multi Protocol Encapsulation (MPE) standard. The MPE specification of DVB uses private sections (using the section SAP in Figure 29-16) for the transport of IP datagrams and uses an encapsulation that is closely tailored after the IEEE LAN/MAN standards. Data packets are encapsulated in datagram_sections that are compliant with the DSMCC_section format for private data. This encapsulation makes use of a medium access control (MAC) level device address. The address format conforms to the ISO/IEEE standards for LAN/MAN.

The 48-bit MAC_address field contains the MAC address of the destination. It is distributed over six 8-bit fields, labeled MAC_address_1 to MAC_address_6 but rearranged in a different order. The MAC_address_1 field contains the most significant byte of the MAC address, whereas MAC_address_6 contains the least significant byte. How many of these bytes are significant is optional and defined by the value of the broadcast descriptor table. MPE is a solution that is neither elegant nor efficient, but it seems to be generally accepted, at least for the time being.

Another approach that was implemented earlier in the IDBS system is to use PES packets as containers for IP datagrams. This is a more straightforward solution that allows IP packets of up to 64 kB in length. The most elegant and efficient way to transport IP datagrams over the MPEG-2 cell stream is to use a private adaptation layer, similar to the solution chosen for ATM adaptation layer 5 (AAL5) in ATM networks, and also a private segmentation and reassembly layer. Although this can lead to a much more bandwidth-efficient solution, it is difficult to implement because the commercially available IRD components are tailored to the transport of PES and section structures only.

Figure 29-16

Schematic service access points for MPEG-2.

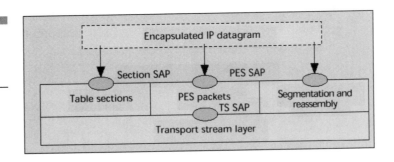

Routing Issues   IDBS is an efficient and potentially low-cost solution to deliver high-bandwidth services over wide geographic areas by using a unidirectional satellite link. The main problem with unidirectional links is that common routing protocols do not support this type of connection. To overcome this problem, it is possible to statically configure the IP routing at the master station. While this was done in the first IDBS network, static routing gets more and more complex as the number of stations grows, and radio transmission dependence can result in routing *holes*. This eventually can be cured by multihoming with a satellite plus a *normal* address, but better solutions are currently being discussed.

For larger networks, two different approaches have been defined by the Unidirectional Link Routing group: tunneling and routing protocol modifications.

TUNNELING   The lack of a back channel on the unidirectional satellite link is masked with the tunneling approach. In other words, in the tunneling approach, a link-layer tunnel to send routing information back to the master station is set up without requiring modifications to the routing protocol.

ROUTING PROTOCOL MODIFICATIONS   This allows the master station to send routing traffic on the unidirectional satellite link and receive routing traffic in the opposite direction on another interface. The lack of a back channel must be known to the routing protocol.

At this time, the tunneling approach is being deployed in the IDBS network. The second option is still a more research-oriented option.

Reliable Multicast Transport   Distribution of data via satellites using TCP at the transport level has to cope with the long-fat-network problem typical for reactive error-handling strategies: Automatic repeat request (ARQ) protocols are based on a feedback loop for error and flow control, and the long end-to-end propagation delay can lead to reduced performance. Especially for such a network, shorter transaction times, reduced bandwidth requirements, and faster service can be achieved if data are distributed in multicast mode, combined with an appropriate group management and error handling transport protocol.

NOTE   The end-to-end round-trip time (RTT) is the important element, not just the signal propagation delay. The critical factor is the product of the RTT and the data rate of the end-to-end link. Hence terrestrial networks with high queuing delays in routers are equally affected.

The transport layer of IDBS contains a lightweight reliable multicast protocol, called Restricted Reliable Multicast Protocol (RRMP), that

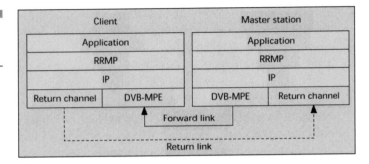

Figure 29-17
The IDBS protocol
stack.

provides end-to-end reliable data delivery service to higher-layer entities (Figure 29-17).[29] The traditional client-server model is not scalable to large communities of users due to duplicate data traffic and implosion problems. In order to avoid these problems, the proposed architecture is designed to work on connectionless transport/network protocols and the IP multicast model.

In RRMP, data are transferred without any prior connection establishment to avoid the handshake problem in client-server applications, since this problem introduces important latency to data transfer. This makes short data transfers particularly inefficient in case of long-delay network links (satellite links). Using IP multicast allows sending information only once to a large group of end users and consequently saving network bandwidth.

In most cases, information needs to be transferred reliably to multiple recipients. Since the underlying network protocol, typically UDP/IP, only offers best-effort data delivery service, it is very likely that data packets are lost due to congestion drops or link failures. To simplify the higher-layer design, RRMP implements error control mechanisms that focus on different return channel configurations, as well as on the problems specific to large-scale multicast. For example, the acknowledgment (ACK) implosion problem arises as the multicast group size increases because

- The transmitter complexity is proportional to the number of receivers.
- The latency grows, even for low error rates, because the number of retransmissions is proportional to the group size.
- The throughput is significantly reduced if the transmitter is kept busy sending retransmissions (sender implosion).[30]

Forward error correction (FEC) is an appealing approach to avoid this feedback implosion for satellite multicast transport. FEC techniques transmit additional redundant information to enable the receivers to correct a certain amount of lost data without requiring retransmission. Besides reducing the time needed to recover a missing packet, the FEC approach generally simplifies both the sender and receiver because no feedback channel is required. The technique is well suited to multicasting applications because different loss patterns can be recovered using the same set of transmitted data. Software-based burst erasure correction techniques at the transport level therefore are a good solution and can be used to enhance throughput efficiency by controlling the packet loss rate.

RRMP uses FEC error recovery in the limited reliable transport mode and FEC combined with negative ACKs (NAKs) (hybrid ARQ mechanism) for error control in the fully reliable transport mode. FEC error recovery in the fully reliable transport mode helps decrease the number of retransmissions necessary, and NAK suppression techniques help avoid necessary NAK(s).

Multicast Web Caching in the IDBS System

Communications satellites can be used to provide point-to-point services, but the real advantage lies in broadcasting large volumes of data directly to large user groups. In particular, for the dissemination of software releases or for Web-based multimedia applications, such a distribution system has an economic advantage over terrestrial store-and-forward solutions, even if they employ proxy techniques. It also could be in addition to a terrestrial low-speed delivery in a configuration where the satellite link provides a high-speed overlay.

With more and more image, audio, and video content on the Web, the demand for bandwidth at the end user increases. In many cases, accumulating individual requests and multiplexing the response, within a short time frame, by multicasting to all requesters constitute an efficient solution. If this multicast distribution service is combined with local caching and proxy techniques, novel services become possible that might be particularly attractive to content providers in the multimedia field.

A substantial fraction of all Internet traffic today is caused by Web applications. The caching of Web pages *near* the client is an important technique for reducing both network traffic and response time. Traditional caching strategies usually exploit hierarchical proxy cache structures developed for terrestrial lines without the capability to broadcast/multicast proxy cache information. Today's proxy caches use HTTP for data distribution. HTTP, which is based on TCP, has major drawbacks when used on high-delay links, notably high transaction times to deliver data to end users and lack of multicast features to lower-bandwidth usage.

Figure 29-18
TCP-based Web
caching.

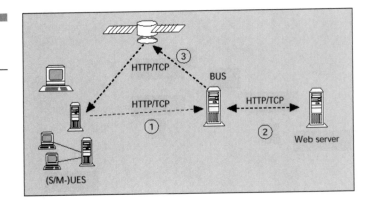

SiMPLE The Satellite Interactive Multimedia Platform for Low-Cost Earth Stations (SiMPLE) is a proxy/cache solution running at both the end user and broadcasting center using reliable multicast instead of TCP/IP to interactively and transparently request/return Web-based content. On request, it replicates Web content to many sites simultaneously, hence interactively keeping end-user caches up to date.

Figure 29-18 outlines a commonly used method to bypass the slow-speed last-mile telephone line by a direct-to-home satellite link.[31] In order not to modify the IP packet routing, the configuration uses a proxy at the wireless broadband uplink station (BUS). The browser on the user earth station (UES) directly communicates with the proxy at the BUS, which in return opens a second connection to the originating Internet server to obtain the content from the originating server. Given the constant yet noticeable satellite transmission delay (around 265 ms), a proper adjustment of TCP parameters (window size) is necessary to obtain reasonable transfer rates.

The preceding configuration imposes some major problems, however. First of all, the broadcast capability of the satellite link is not used at all, which makes use both inefficient (the data are being accepted by only one recipient, although they are received by everyone) and uneconomic (the recipient has to pay for point-to-point delivery). Second, the satellite link (even a full transponder) has limited bandwidth (typically up to 45 Mbps), and this bandwidth is shared by all simultaneous connections, which obviously does not scale well to thousands of simultaneous active users. Last but not least, each TCP transfer sets up a connection and uses slow start during connection setup and when packet loss occurs, which makes it not very responsive (especially for small objects) and slow (full throughput only after slow start).

Figure 29-19 outlines one potential solution that was adopted in the SiMPLE system.[32] Requests for Web objects are processed by a local proxy

Figure 29-19
Multicast Web
caching.

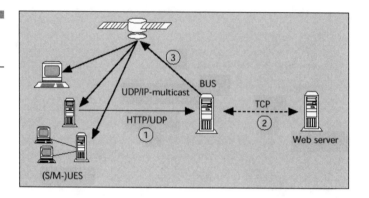

running on the client side (UES) and translated into UDP queries, which are forwarded to the proxy on the uplink side (BUS). The request is processed, and the reply is fetched from the Internet server by standard means (TCP) and then sent back via multicast to the requesting UES proxy. It is clear that the multicast transmission can now be joined by many UES proxies, which then update their respective local cache.

By monitoring and learning the pages that are frequently requested, the central proxy keeps a hot list of sites and pages that are of general interest. Automatically or on operator request, the latest versions of these pages are retrieved and then pushed to the client stations by means of a reliable multicast transmission. This prefetching dramatically decreases the latency and bandwidth requirements and improves the overall efficiency of the system, since pages can be distributed in advance without having been explicitly requested.

World Wireless Broadband Projections

Finally, let's examine world wireless broadband projections by first looking at network type, such as the HALO network. The High Altitude Long Operation Network is a wireless broadband metropolitan-area network (MAN), with a star topology whose solitary hub is located in the atmosphere above the service area at an altitude higher than commercial airline traffic. The HALO/Proteus airplane is the central node of this network. It will fly at altitudes higher than 51,000 ft. The signal footprint of the network, its *cone of commerce*, will have a diameter on the scale of 100 km. The initial capacity of the network will be on the scale of 10 Gbps, with growth beyond 100 Gbps. The network will serve the communications needs of each subscriber with bit rates in the multimegabit per second range. A variety of spectrum bands licensed by the Federal Communications Commission (FCC) for commercial wireless broadband services could provide the needed millimeter wavelength carrier bandwidth. An attractive choice for the subscriber links is the LMDS band. The airplane's fuselage can house switching circuitry and fast digital network functions. An MMW antenna array and its related components will be located in a pod suspended below the aircraft fuselage. The antenna array will produce many beams, typically more than 100. Adjacent beams will be separated in frequency. Electronic beam-forming techniques can be used to stabilize the beams on the ground as the airplane flies within its station-keeping volume. For the alternative of aircraft-fixed beams, the beams will traverse over a user location while the airplane maintains a station overhead, and the virtual path will be changed to accomplish the beam-to-beam handoff. For each isolated city to be served, a fleet of three aircraft will be operated in shifts to achieve around-the-clock service. In deployments where multiple cities will be served from a common primary flight base, the fleet will be sized for allocating, on average, two aircraft per city to be served. Flight operational tactics will be evolved and refined steadily to achieve continuous presence of the node above each city. Many services will be provided, including but not limited to T-1 access, ISDN access, Web browsing, high-resolution videoconferencing, large file transfers, and Ethernet LAN bridging.

Second, this final part of this chapter will discuss ramp-up to near-3G services to developing wireless broadband for fixed network access—2001 will see major moves in the deployment of wireless broadband services and technology introductions. This final part of the chapter also surveys the impending international changes and developments in the world of wireless broadband.

Trends by Network Type: The HALO Network

The markets of broadband, wireless, and multimedia network services are growing rapidly, as evidenced by the NASDAQ minting millionaires on a daily basis. These markets are demanding infrastructure that can be deployed quickly and economically. Services must be delivered to businesses and consumers, the end users of the network, at affordable prices. Quality of service (QoS) must be guaranteed. Also, the information bandwidth must respond dynamically to the needs of the end user with an imperceptible latency following a request for more bandwidth.

Innovative communications networks are being pioneered. The high-altitude long operation (HALO) network is a wireless broadband MAN consisting of HALO aircraft operating at high altitude and carrying an airborne communications network hub and network elements on the ground.

The HALO network combines the advantages of two well-established wireless broadband communications services: satellite networks and terrestrial wireless broadband networks like cellular and personal communication systems. Satellite networks to be deployed at low earth orbit (LEO), medium earth orbit (MEO), high elliptic orbit (HEO), and geosynchronous earth orbit (GEO) will offer quasi-free-space channels with, at worst, ricean fading due to clear line-of-sight signal paths offered by high look angles. However, their disadvantages include expensive high-power user terminals, long propagation delays, and stagnant performance growth. Also, system capacity will be practically fixed and can be increased incrementally only by adding satellites. In contrast, terrestrial wireless broadband networks have advantages such as low-cost, low-power user terminals, short propagation delays, and good scalability of system capacity. However, their disadvantages include low look angles, multipath channels with Rayleigh fading, and complex infrastructures. They require many base stations that must be interlinked over cables or microwave links in order to backhaul aggregated traffic. They often require significant reengineering to increase capacity when using cell-splitting techniques.

The HALO network will be located in the atmosphere at an altitude miles above terrestrial wireless broadband but hundreds to thousands of miles below satellite networks. It will provide wireless broadband services to businesses and small offices/home offices in an area containing a typical large city and its neighboring towns. To each end user, it will offer an unobstructed line of sight and a free-space-like channel with short propagation delay, and it will allow the use of low-power, low-cost user terminals.

The HALO network infrastructure is simple, having a star topology with a single central hub. Consequently, the deployment of service to the entire metropolitan area can occur on the first day the network is deployed, and the subsequent maintenance cost is expected to be low. The system capacity can be increased by decreasing the size of beam spots on the ground while increasing the number of beams within the signal footprint or by increasing the signal bandwidth per beam. The HALO network can interface to existing networks. It can operate as a backbone to connect physically separated LANs through Frame Relay adaptation or directly through LAN bridges and routers. It also can provide videoconference links through standard ISDN or T-1 interface hardware.

Figure 29-20
The system architecture of the HALO network.

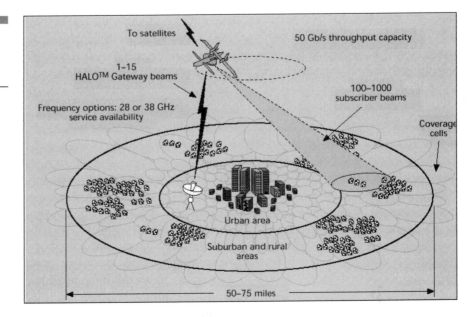

To satellites

50 Gb/s throughput capacity

1–15
HALO™ Gateway beams

100–1000
subscriber beams

Frequency options: 28 or 38 GHz
service availability

Coverage
cells

Urban area

Suburban and rural
areas

50–75 miles

The remainder of this part of the chapter is organized in four sections. A conceptual system architecture is presented. A corresponding reference model is proposed. The services provided by HALO networks is also discussed. The user terminals are described. The advantages of HALO networks are compared with terrestrial wireless broadband and satellite networks.

The System Architecture of the Halo Network   As shown in Figure 29-20, the HALO/Proteus aircraft serves as the hub of the wireless broadband communications network.[33] It carries the airborne network elements, including an ATM switch, spot-beam antennas, and multibeam antennas, as well as transmitting and receiving electronics. The antenna array provides cellular-like coverage of a large metropolitan area. ATM switches, now available, have capacities sufficient to satisfy the traffic volume requirements of the first network deployment and margins for growth.

The HALO/Proteus airplane shown in Figure 29-21 has been specially designed to carry the hub of the HALO network.[34] The airplane can carry a weight of approximately 2000 lb (900 kg) to its station-keeping volume. The airplane is essentially an equipment bus from which commercial wireless broadband services will be offered. A fleet of three aircraft will be cycled in shifts to achieve continuous service above an isolated city. In a multicity deployment, an average of two aircraft will be allocated to each city, and the fleet operations will be conducted from a common primary flight base as a

Figure 29-21
The HALO/Proteus
airplane.

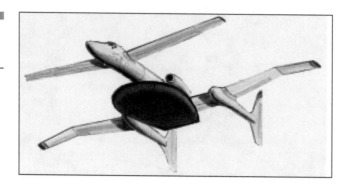

hub and spokes operation to achieve continuous service. Each shift on station will have an average duration of approximately 8 hours.

The HALO/Proteus airplane will maintain station at an altitude of 51,000 to 60,000 ft by flying in a toroidal volume of airspace with a diameter of about 5 to 8 nautical miles. The *look angle*, defined to be the angle subtended between the local horizon and the airplane with the user terminal at the vertex, will be greater than a minimum value of 20 degrees. The *minimum look angle* (MLA) for a given user terminal along the perimeter of the service footprint is defined to occur whenever the airplane achieves the longest slant range from that terminal while flying within its designated airspace. Under these assumptions, the signal footprint will cover an area of approximately 2000 to 3000 mi, large enough to encompass a typical city and its neighboring communities. Such a high value for the MLA was chosen to ensure a line-of-sight connection to nearly every rooftop in the signal footprint and high availability during heavy rainfall for most of the major cities in North America, especially for broadband wireless data rates propagated in the K/Ka bands (above 20 GHz).

By selecting millimeter-wavelength (MMW) frequencies, a wireless broadband network of high capacity can be realized, since carrier frequency bandwidths on the scale of 100 to 1000 MHz have been licensed and may be made available through partnerships. Small antenna apertures on the scale of 1 ft will provide beams with narrow beamwidths; thus user terminals can be compact but offer high gain. Also, a multiaperture antenna array can fit in an airborne pod with dimensions practical to an aerodynamicist.

A number of spectrum allocations could be used by a HALO network. The choice of which spectrum to use will be driven by pragmatic technical and business factors, including, but not limited to, practical link margins, licensed bandwidth, maturity and affordability of the user terminals, teaming agreements, spectrum access, and regulatory law. Prior publications have commented on the following two spectrum allocations as examples for creating a high-capacity HALO network offering wireless broadband services: local multimegabit data service (LMDS) at 28 GHz and the microwave point-to-point allocation at 38 GHz. The antenna array produces beams on the ground of two types. The shared beam provides services to 100 to 1000 subscribers, and the dedicated beam provides a connection to a gateway serving high-bandwidth users or to the network gateway through which a user from a non-HALO network can access the services of, and exchange information with, any end user of the HALO network.

The HALO network uses multiple beams on the ground arranged in a typical cellular pattern. Each beam spot in the pattern functions as a single cell. Each cell covers more than several square miles of area. Adjacent cells have different frequency subbands. The pattern has a periodic nature, and each subband in the set so chosen (each subband of the frequency-reuse plan) is used multiple times within the service area. Through frequency reuse, about 2800 mi of area can be covered. The total capacity achieved by only one platform can be in the range of 10 to 100 Gbps.

Figure 29-22 provides a map of the shared beam cells that, for the purpose of modeling, it is assumed would be produced by the antenna array carried by the HALO aircraft.[35] It is also assumed that there would be six rings of cells composed of 125 beams. The cells created by the antenna array would be fixed on the ground, and there would be no overlapping area

Figure 29-22
The footprint of shared beam cells.

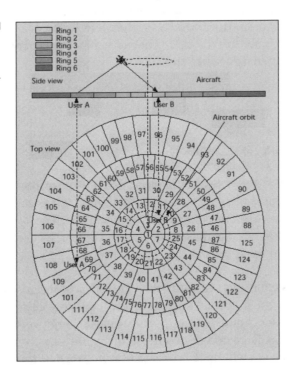

between adjacent cells. The cellular pattern would cover a metropolitan-scale area. The altitude of aircraft would be 16 km. It would have an orbit diameter of 14.8 km (ring 3 level). By assuming a constant ground speed, the orbit would have a period of approximately 6 min.

Each cell on the ground is covered by one spot beam. However, the spot beam that covers a particular cell changes due to the motion of the aircraft. A given beam covers a given cell on the ground for a duration of time called *dwell time*. Once the duration is exceeded, the beam must ratchet over by one or more beams to cover a new cell on the ground. The ratcheting action requires a burst modem in the user terminal and the use of electronically stabilized beams aboard the airplane. A beam-to-beam handover event may arise. Suppose that users A are connected by antennas 106 and 26 at time t. When ratcheting is completed at time $t + T$, they will both be connected by two new antennas: 108 and 27, respectively.

The System Reference Model of the HALO Network   As shown in Figure 29-23, the major elements of the conceptual HALO network are the airborne communications hub carried by the HALO/Proteus airplane, the premises equipment or user terminals, the network control station, the HALO gateway (HG), and the various interfaces.[36] The reference architecture shows the topology of the interconnected network elements.

The HALO network can be connected to non-HALO networks, such as ATM networks, the Internet, and Frame Relay, via an HG/interworking unit (IWU). Within the HALO network, four types of network elements can be connected directly to the onboard switch:

- Customer premises equipment (CPE, low-rate user terminals)
- Business premises equipment (BPE, high-rate user terminals)
- HG/IWU
- Network control station

CUSTOMER PREMISES EQUIPMENT   Since these terminals are equipped with the necessary interfaces to the HALO wireless broadband channels, they have direct access to HALO networks. The terminals can support either ATM or IP end users. If it is an IP user, IP over ATM will be implemented in the terminals.

BUSINESS PREMISES EQUIPMENT   This type of premises equipment is provided for a user group such as a company, university, factory, or another type of user group. Normally, there are local networks available within a user group. For example, a company may have a private ATM network, and its employees will have access to that network. If the private network has

Figure 29-23

The system reference
model of the HALO
network.

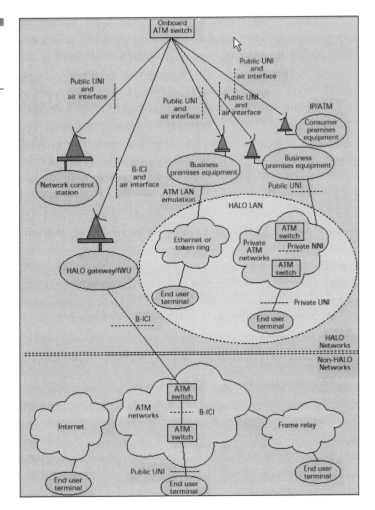

Figure 29-23

The system reference model of the HALO network.

HALO network–compatible BPE to serve as a bridge between the corporate network and the HALO network, all the users within the company will be able to gain access to the HALO network.

HG/IWU This equipment provides the portal and interfaces between HALO and non-HALO networks. As shown in Figure 29-23, only public ATM networks have direct connection to the HALO gateway/IWU because other networks are not compatible with the HG/IWU. Therefore, Internet and Frame Relay services have to be connected to the public ATM networks before they are connected to the HG/IWU.

NETWORK CONTROL STATION This is responsible for the maintenance, operation, and administration of HALO networks. Also, the connection admission control (CAC), processing of time-slot reservation or request generated by the medium access control (MAC) protocol, handover processing, and location management of mobile users are all managed in this control center.

According to Figure 29-23, there are four types of signaling interfaces between ATM networks and the HALO network. The public user–network interfaces (UNIs) are located between the onboard ATM switch and the CPE. The signaling interface between the HG/IWU and the onboard switch is B-ICI. If there exists a private ATM network within the local networks of the HALO network, both the private network node interface (NNI) and a private UNI will exist, as shown in Figure 29-23.

HALO Network Services   The HALO network accommodates the following design objectives:

- Seamless ubiquitous multimedia services
- Adaptation to end-user environments
- Rapidly deployable to sites of opportunity
- Bandwidth on demand for efficient use of available spectrum[37]

As shown in Figure 29-24, many types of organizations (schools, hospitals, doctors' offices, and small to medium-sized businesses) around the

Figure 29-24
HALO network services.

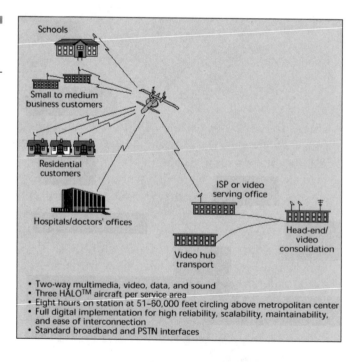

world will benefit from the low pricing of wireless broadband services provided by the HALO network.[38] Moreover, HALO can be used as a wireless broadband local loop (WLL) for mobile telephone services, two-way paging, one-way broadcasting, low-data-rate acquisition, and as a satellite concentrator. Standard broadband protocols such as ATM and synchronous optical network (SONET) will be adopted to interface the HALO network as seamlessly as possible. The gateway to the HALO network will provide access to the public switched telephone network (PSTN) and to the Internet backbone for such services as the Web and e-commerce. The gateway will provide to information content providers network-wide access for a large population of subscribers.

Various classes of service can be provided to subscribers sharing the bandwidth of a given beam, e.g., 1 to 10 Mbps peak data rates to small businesses and 10 to 25 Mbps peak data rates to business users with larger bandwidth appetites. Since each link can be serviced according to *bandwidth on demand*, the bandwidth available in a beam can be shared between sessions concurrently active within that beam. While the average data rate may be low for a given user, the instantaneous rate can be grown to a specified upper bound according to demand. A dedicated beam service also can be provided to those subscribers requiring 25 to 155 Mbps.

Subscriber Units (User Terminals) As shown in Figure 29-25, the user terminal entails three major subgroups of hardware: the rf unit (RU), which contains the MMW antenna and MMW transceiver; the network interface unit (NIU); and the application terminals, such as PCs, telephones, video servers, and video terminals.[39] The RU consists of a small dual-feed antenna and MMW transmitter and receiver mounted to the antenna. An antenna tracking unit uses a pilot tone transmitted from the HALO aircraft to point its antenna at the airplane. The antenna tracks the airplane with a mount possessing low-rate two-axis gimbals. Other schemes for performing the auto tracking function are feasible and appear to be competitive in cost. The high-gain antenna is protected beneath a radome from wind loading and the weather.

The MMW transmitter accepts an L-band IF input signal from the NIU, translates it to MMW frequencies, amplifies the signal using a power amplifier to a transmit power level of 100 to 500 mW, and feeds the antenna. The MMW receiver couples the received signal from the antenna to a low-noise amplifier (LNA), downconverts the signal to an L-band IF, and provides subsequent amplification and processing before outputting the signal to the NIU. The MMW transceiver will process a single channel at any one time, perhaps as narrow as 40 MHz. The particular channel and frequency are determined by the NIU.

Figure 29-25
User terminal
architectures.

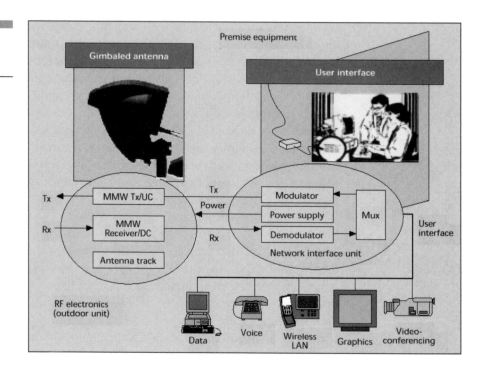

The NIU interfaces to the RU via a coax pair that transmit the L-band
TX and RX signals between the NIU and the RU. The NIU comprises an
L-band tuner and downconverter, a high-speed demodulator, a high-speed
modulator, multiplexers and demultiplexers, data, telephony, and video
interface electronics. Each user terminal can provide access to data at
rates up to 51.84 Mbps each way. In some applications, some of this bandwidth may be used to incorporate spread-spectrum coding to improve
performance against interference (if so, the user rate would be reduced).

The NIU equipment can be identical to that already developed for
LMDS and other wireless broadband services. This reduces the cost of
HALO network services to the consumer because there is minimal cost to
adapt LMDS equipment to this application, and you could take advantage
of the high volume expected in the other services. Also, the HALO RU can
be very close in functionality to the RU in other services (like LMDS), since
the primary difference is the need for a tracking function for the antenna.
The electronics for the rf data signal will be identical if the same frequency band is used.

Advantages Relative to Satellite and Terrestrial Networks   The
HALO network has several advantages over terrestrial wireless broadband

networks. The latter have complex geometries involving many base stations interlinked by cabling or microwaves. The communication paths have low look angles with multipath Rayleigh fading. Moreover, since each time-cell splitting is used to increase system capacity, the network can demand significant reengineering. On the other hand, satellite networks require more expensive terminals with high power to achieve the same data rates possible through the HALO network. Also, the longer propagation delays demand more complex algorithms to achieve interactivity. The capacity of a satellite network can be increased, but at higher expense than the HALO network, typically only by adding more satellites. And like terrestrial networks, reengineering of the entire satellite network may be required. The HALO network has striking advantages over proposed large LEO constellations, including ease of repair and rapidly evolving performance.

International Wireless Broadband Projections

The wireless broadband industry internationally has never been more exciting—or confusing. Collectively, the industry stands on the verge of introduction of near-wireless broadband services offering unprecedented data rates to users as so-called third-generation (3G) technologies are rolled out. Meanwhile, a slew of offerings in the fixed wireless broadband access arena promise major new opportunities internationally, as demonstrated by trials around the world of local multipoint distribution systems (LMDS). Behind the scenes, the industry has become a complex jigsaw of technology, spectrum availability, and pricing. In the face of high entry costs, business models must be extremely flexible. Above all, there has been a growing realization of the critical importance of radio spectrum and the possibility of competing technologies in different parts of the world.

Third-generation mobile cellular on the international stage has been referred to as the *universal mobile telecommunications system* (UMTS) or IMT-2000. Developing coordinated worldwide standards for 3G has been a complex task. Over the last 10 years, Japan, Europe, and the United States have all been at work on various formats approaching a 3G mobile technology for the 2-GHz band of operation in the radio spectrum. A global standard has been the objective to facilitate both roaming and economies of scale in the development and deployment of networks and terminals. From the user point of view, 3G has been specified to provide a high data rate service to support a wide range of services including multimedia applications.

Although the development of IMT-2000 and the overall international designation for 3G systems started with spectrum allocation in the early part of the last decade, several proposals competed on how to achieve the most appropriate 3G technology around the world. By the mid-1990s, several proposals were in contention. Following collaboration between Japan and Europe, the wideband code division multiple access (W-CDMA) technology, officially known as UTRA, emerged as a standards proposal. Harmonization has continued between the various proposals. As a result, IMT-2000 potentially could be implemented by up to five technology variants around the world. These include IMT-2000 CDMA direct spread, IMT-2000 cdma2000 multicarrier, IMT-2000 CDMA TDD, and two TDMA variants, one based on DECT in Europe and one based on UWC 136 in the United States as an IMT-2000 single-carrier solution. Internationally, it is expected that the IMT-2000 CDMA direct spread will be the primary candidate.

The W-CDMA format adopted in Japan and Europe remains distinct from the cdma2000 technology adopted for North America, where no spectrum was available for the international proposals for IMT-2000 and a narrowband CDMA system existed. Despite efforts to commonalize the technologies, significant differences exist between these two systems. The radio access part of the 3G standard regime has been separated from the core network part to permit operators to run different configurations. Three different modes of radio access, represented by the FDD direct spread, FDD multicarrier, and TDD technologies, are permissible.

These are for future, although near-term implementation. Exactly how telecom operators migrate to 3G systems from current 2G systems such as GSM, however, has been a subject of massive debate within the industry. It is possible to implement many wireless broadband data applications with the currently available GSM data rates of 9.6 kbps. The probable 3G standard internationally will be W-CDMA, to which the main digital cellular standards such as GSM and CDMA will migrate. While UMTS will offer data transmission speeds of 2 Mbps (for stationary users), compared with present capability of 9.6 kbps for most GSM handsets, technologies *on the way to UMTS*, such as general packet radio service (GPRS), will offer 144 kbps. Another option is high-speed circuit switched data (HSCSD). For multimedia and Internet applications, however, higher bandwidths should prove more attractive. Enhanced data rate for GSM evolution (EDGE), a new radio interface technology with enhanced modulation, increases HSCSD and GPRS data rates up to threefold.

The industry remains preoccupied with 3G and its implications, but for some observers, 3G is but a waystation toward a *true* mobile wireless broadband technology yet to be developed. One rationale for this is the continuing and prospective demand for mobile data services, unanticipated a decade ago when the first discussions took place at the World Radio Conference (WRC) for 3G spectrum allocation. While 3G can support 2-Mbps service, this would only be possible for stationary users near base stations. In other areas or for users on the move, it is likely to be considerably less, perhaps 384 kbps. The proposed 4G system (perhaps available in the 2010 timeframe) will support data rates much higher than the 2-Mbps limit of 3G and potentially deliver 10 Mbps on a downlink basis.

3G: The Big Challenge?

For much of the industry, the next big hurdle is undoubtedly the exciting prospect of 3G mobile cellular technology. It also presents enormous challenges that apply to all entrants, new or established 2G operators. Spectrum fees, new technology, new value chains and business models, network development costs, new skills, and staff are all issues that must be addressed. Perhaps most important, the prospective data market, generally assumed to be at the very heart of 3G revenue generation, is expected to boom in the next few years. Currently, however, there is no visibility of applications that will drive it, still less at what pace, what ultimate market size, and what overall profitability. Thus, for the time being, 3G may well have all the components of a highly risky business. In 2001, however, there is seen to be enormous operator interest around the world and numerous bidders in the major license contests. The key question is: Why does 3G remain attractive for operators even though they know that, in all likelihood, they will face a major challenge in their business?

A Last Opportunity? It is certainly arguable that 3G presents an opportunity to enter international markets (particularly European markets) and become a significant player. Of course, in many ways, the ultimate flavor of 3G in terms of business model and technology is quite different from existing 2G technologies such as GSM, the most prevalent international system. Even so, for players who have not achieved success in 2G markets, this may be the last chance to gain significant business in the mobile market of a given country. This rationale is most likely the primary driver for major European operators to bid for 3G.

If you look at the European telecom landscape after the fixed business deregulation phase and mobile license awards, it is evident that none of the major players has a full European footprint today. At least 5 to 10 players are seeking pan-European positions (Vodafone/Airtouch, Deutsche Telekom, and France Telecom/Orange are good examples). UMTS, therefore, is an additional opportunity for these players to enter markets where they do not currently have penetration. Alternatively, but arguably more difficult, is that they make acquisitions to access the remaining markets.

UMTS is also an opportunity for non-European players to step into Europe. TWI from Canada has been selected as the fifth player in the United Kingdom and is now reportedly seeking other European positions. It is also clear that NTT DoCoMo from Japan will want to be very active in European 3G to leverage its own home operations. DoCoMo, in fact, expects to be the first operator in the world to initiate 3G services (currently scheduled to begin in May 2001).

Pan-European operations (and, prospectively, global operations) are advantageous for several reasons. Operators can implement global services (such as unified voice mail and global mobile portals) and run major global branding exercises to differentiate themselves. Clearly, global positioning provides economics of scale in the sharing of service development costs, operational experience, tools and methodologies for network building, and market intelligence between different affiliates of a same group. Investors likewise perceive globalization and large operational footprints as necessary to be a happy survivor and reduce the risk of hostile takeovers during the inevitable consolidation phase in the marketplace.

The European telecoms are now in a phase of building this international presence. For example, France Telecom tried without success to enter Spain and the United Kingdom with UMTS and consequently acquired Orange to step into the the U.K. 3G business. France Telecom is thought to be targeting Sweden and Norway and may possibly acquire Sonera in Finland. France's Vivendi was more successful in Spain. Deutsche Telekom was unsuccessful in Spain but will try again in France.

The Big Squeeze   Another factor is the regulatory push to compress the licensing schedule. One estimate expects some 75 UMTS licenses to be active in Europe by the end of the schedule. These will be awarded by various means: by pure "beauty contest" (e.g., Spain and Sweden), by pure auctions (United Kingdom, Germany, Netherlands, and Belgium), or in some cases, by a mix of both (perhaps in France and Italy). Depending on the process, European governments stand to make a lot of money from spectrum (and make it quickly) in a 24-month period from the end of 1999 to the end of 2001. By comparison, it took about 5 years to award around 60 GSM licences for the same set of countries. This in turn means that operators may not have sufficiently thought through their exact business intentions. Bidding in some cases has taken place simply to prevent any competitive advantage.

Under the auction process, the system may seek to maximize the fees but cannot at the same time impose too many commitments in terms of launch dates, delivered services, or provided coverage. For instance, in the United Kingdom, 33 billion euros have been collected for five licences (equivalent to 6.5 billion euros per license) with no specific commitments regarding the network implementation or exact service launch date.

Alternatively, those who selected the "beauty contest" can put more emphasis on a 3G services launch date, percentage of covered population or territory, or network development pace—an aggresive launch date aims not only at stimulating the local market for 3G services but also at stimulating European industry to manage equipment delivery. More significant European, U.S., and Asian competition can be expected on the vendor side compared with the GSM cycle.

Launch dates vary. In Spain, a launch date of mid-2001 has been mooted by some candidates. In France (running a hybrid licence system), candidate operators selected through a "beauty contest" process will have to pay 5 billion euros each to access the spectrum. At the same time, they will have to commit to a launch date and network development pace. Commercial launch probably will take place around mid-2002.

UMTS: A New Age Business?   The economics of UMTS remain unclear, with high costs of entry and unproven and (at this point) potentially unattractive business cases. The business cases are, in fact, particularly difficult to analyze because eventual services are still indeterminate. No killer application has been identified. Pricing and subscriber forecasts are similarly hazy. Meanwhile, entry costs have shot up. The first 3G license auctions saw eventual spectrum fees reach more than US$33 billion—some 10 times more than initially expected. In the battle to enter 3G internationally, amounts may look large and perhaps even inconsistent to outsiders. France Telecom paid some 50 billion euros to acquire Orange and a 3G presence in the United Kingdom, whereas together with NTL, France Telecom had only a few weeks before giving up the U.K. 3G auction at 6 billion euros.

Of course, mobile Internet based on UMTS is one predictably popular application, but here there are concerns. Internet players of all types recently have experienced extremely high valuations if very poor cash flows. But the market also has changed as free Internet service providers (ISPs) have taken hold. Consequently, it will be extremely difficult for 3G operators to charge for Internet access—necessarily shifting value from access to content. The value chain is moving toward services and content for which subscribers are willing to pay. The merger between Time Warner and America Online and the latest partnership announcement between Vivendi and Vodafone indicate that the players are on the move to bring content through mobile Internet.

The next move probably will concern global access providers, together with portal/content providers, because there is a need for access providers to generate revenues formerly generated by access. UMTS is fundamentally a key in providing content to wireless broadband subscribers. One of two scenarios might be the eventual outcome: Either the content industry will try to move to its final customers through networks, or network operators will take over content providers to retain revenue streams. Either is possible, but one thing is certain: 3G operators will not look like 2G operators. In the meantime, there probably will be many partnerships between all players concerned, such as content providers, service providers, software platform providers, and of course, vendors, as well as classical operators who have a converged interest in making 3G happen as soon as possible. These alliances will help to raise the funds necessary to build networks. Afterwards, consolidation will be inevitable. In the meantime, 3G business, with its mix of content and services, will look like a new age business.

However, operators will need to address the costs of building access. Even with unprecedented spectral efficiency in the 2-GHz band, UMTS will require high base station density, probably comparable with that of GSM 1800 (i.e., a few hundred meters in urban areas). Equally, UMTS is an emerging, rather than a mature, technology, so startup costs inevitably will be more significant, especially where national coverage or high-quality indoor coverage is required. Capital expenditures on networks could range from 2 to 5 billion euros on a 15-year cumulative basis depending on the coverage areas and average bit-rate delivered. Payback optimistically may be on the order of 7 years but, according to some industry estimates, could be between 10 and 15 years if entry costs exceed 6 billion euros. High costs could spur a vicious circle: Higher service pricing would likely deter subscribers and lead to diminished revenue streams.

UMTS: Embracing Market Segments　From a business model standpoint, UMTS sits at the crossroads of mobility, bandwidth, advanced services, and a high value content that allows operators an unprecedented opportunity to develop innovative services. These features will allow operators to define focused strategies for different market segments. Ultimately, operators with nationwide UMTS coverage, excellent indoor reception, and an aggressive service policy will find that they will make a massive impact on the global telecom industry—and progressively the media industry as well.

In specific terms, consider residential fixed voice services. Internationally, GSM operators already have made major contributions to wireless broadband-wireline substitution. These contributions will be reinforced as the mass market is developed and new UMTS players enter the market with aggressive business development plans.

Wireless broadband, voice, and specific wireless broadband data services represent other opportunities. New UMTS players will reinforce competition in this already aggressive market. For example, the technical possibilities of UMTS on the Internet will enable or accelerate the substitution initiated in GPRS services. In 2001, an average residential Internet user experiences 128-kbps access, and early asymetric digital subscriber loop (ADSL) adopters experience a few hundred kilobits per second. By 2002, current ADSL capabilities will be enabled on air via UMTS. Thus a UMTS network deployed on a large scale by a new entrant offers potentially the prospect of a 2-Mbps wireless broadband local loop via UMTS to the final customer. UMTS will support lifestyle Internet use (such as e-commerce and audio CD/video download) with a mobility component.

Another promising segment will be corporate voice and data applications. Wireless broadband offers for corporate voice are currently on the way to the market. Again, 2.5G will educate the corporate market on wireless broadband data applications (such as access to database and Internet/intranet). 3G will further enhance this toward a takeoff point in a lucrative corporate market.

Finally, there is a real prospect of true multimedia, although it is still difficult to imagine how 3G will affect the TV, radio broadcasting, or CD communities. If technical capability, services, and prices are all right, on-demand and real-time video applications could open up entirely new revenue streams for operators.

What about Existing GSM? For those who currently operate GSM networks, the 3G story is quite different. In some cases, GSM networks have been established for nearly 10 years, and the market has matured into a vicious circle of subscriber increases, diminished network costs, and aggressive service pricing, leading to increased penetration. This has accelerated business payback; however, it is probable that after 6 or 7 years of loss, they will seek to improve their cash flow in the next few years.

While most operators believe that new revenues will come from data service, their interest is to minimize any extra investment needed to address this emerging wireless broadband data market and preserve cash flow. Consequently, HSCSD and GPRS investments are seen in the market. These are viewed as an evolution of GSM for data transmission. In turn, this may diminish the business incentive to go to true 3G networks. Equally, they also must plan for midterm scenarios, especially in countering new UMTS entrants that may implement aggressive services from scratch. Do these operators have to go to EDGE, do they have to turn to UMTS, and is there an optimal roadmap from 2G to 3G?

These are critical questions, since European regulators are both pushing the UMTS licensing process and offering quasi-guarantees to existing GSM operators to deliver a 3G license as soon as they can compete and pay for it. The issue for GSM operators is license acquisition to preserve their long-term business (and face high up-front costs) or be attacked by competitors, especially if that competition comes in the form of mass-market wireless broadband multimedia in which they probably lack spectrum.

However, some GSM operators may prefer a smooth evolution through GPRS to EDGE technologies, which in some cases may be more cost-effective for delivered services in quasi-competition with UMTS. In bit-rate terms, this evolution would be from a 384-kbps limit to a 2-Mbps EDGE service versus a 2-Mbps UMTS limit. In these circumstances, it would be difficult to say what UMTS would do for customers that EDGE cannot achieve. In turn, the main interest for existing operators would be preserved: Much existing technology is used, substantial capital expenditure is avoided, and spectrum competition is minimized.

The roadmap to 3G for an existing GSM operator is not entirely evident. It is probable that most operators choosing this route will go through GPRS from mid-2001 (for early adopters) to end-2002 (for late adopters). After this stage, it depends on market reaction to the proposed new data services. If the demand is widespread and requires additional bandwidth, an EDGE overlay to these networks may be practical.

Even so, observers expect that despite uncertainty in the ultimate business cases, most existing operators will compete for UMTS, but they will try to negotiate as far as possible minimized investment conditions for the license, especially when "beauty contests" are involved. This would involve a desire for lower spectrum fees, a progressive roll-out plan involving UMTS "islands," and a case-by-case basis for commercial launch dates (rather than imposition by the regulator). Equally, the community may push the vendors aggressively to supply dual-mode terminals as soon as possible so that 3G can be implemented gradually within existing GSM networks.

Despite high uncertainties and risks of the 3G business case, there are underlying strategic reasons for operators to compete for 3G and build networks. European regulators have understood this and are applying pressure to both initiate the schedule as soon as possible and generate as much fee income as possible. Meanwhile, the 3G business probably will move to a new era where equivalent voice services across all subscribers give way to some sort of specific content for each customer. It remains a high-stakes game but arguably a worthwhile one to produce a world based on wireless broadband multimedia.

TDMA, EDGE, and GSM/TDMA Convergence?

3G presents challenges for other cellular families, including TDMA technologies. While the current TDMA user base is significantly smaller than the existing GSM population, it is still substantial. According to the Universal Wireless Communications Consortium (UWCC), the main international TDMA industry body (which released figures at its recent international conference), there were 46.2 million TDMA subscribers worldwide at the end of 2000. This figure has grown from 9.2 million subscribers at yearend 1997 and 18.6 million subscribers at yearend 1998. Most TDMA subscribers are located in North America (20.3 million at yearend 2000) and Latin America (24.0 million at yearend 2000). There also were an estimated 30 million analog users within TDMA networks in 1999. Therefore, including these subscribers, TDMA networks served 65.1 million cellular subscribers at the end of 1999. Since the previous UWCC Global Summit, the organization developed a branding logo (TDMA-EDGE) and marketing line: "Taking wireless broadband beyond the call."

Another important development for the group was the ITU's acceptance of EDGE into the IMT-2000 specifications, which acknowledges the technology as a 3G solution. The two varieties of EDGE (compact and classic) are targeted for deployment in two phases in 2002 and 2003. In the United States, first-phase deployments likely will use EDGE compact in the 850-MHz band because it is a frequency-reuse technique for limited-spectrum situations. EDGE classic will be better suited for the 1900-MHz band in the United States because the operators have more capacity available there. The standard also will include a specification for voice over Internet Protocol (VoIP). Both versions of EDGE have data rates up to 384 kbps, but the deployment decision is based on spectrum availability.

Even with the ITU's acceptance and the UWCC's keenness to promote the standard as a 3G technology, is EDGE destined to be a poor man's 3G? Calling EDGE 3G is all positioning and nomenclature. It meets the ITU requirements. But EDGE follows the path that the TDMA operators are taking toward converging with the GSM world. But where the disconnect falls is that if the GSM world gets UMTS spectrum, then the manufacturing community is not going to put R&D effort and spending into EDGE in the way that the TDMA world will need it. There is only so much money to go around.

The TDMA operators have always been at a disadvantage in relation to GSM players in that they have not had the scale of manufacturers behind them. Manufacturers are currently under pressure to deliver general packet radio service (GPRS) handsets for commercial deployments this year. EDGE deployments are scheduled for 2002 and 2003, which is a timetable similar to early UMTS deployments. Vendors will be hard pressed to deliver not only the infrastructure for next-generation wireless broadband networks but also the handsets.

There is a window of opportunity for EDGE, but in Europe, the window is small. Given that most operators are deploying GPRS, they will not have time to fritter away with other technologies before moving to wideband CDMA. The EDGE deployments will be in the TDMA markets or where operators do not acquire UMTS spectrum. Ericsson's sees more opportunity for EDGE in Europe because it will be deployed in less densely populated areas, where UMTS would not be cost-effective to deploy. In Europe, the introduction of 3G will be a combination of EDGE and wideband CDMA. At the UWCC conference, speakers and attendees frequently said that this business is not about technology anymore—it is about what the technology can deliver. It is amazing to see how much column space and verbal energy are spent on minute differences in technology. This is about applications. Customers do not want EDGE; they want something that can do something for them. Telecoms have been trying to push data to people, but they should let people pull applications out of them. Telecoms have to educate the customer about what the applications can do. They must be careful not to overprice. Telecoms must avoid the comparison with surfing on the Internet at home. And it would be disastrous to say that 3G can do more than it can. Telecoms have to differentiate themselves and not just sell the Internet. Other panelists seemed less certain about what the future holds for 3G, expressing the challenge of dealing with reduced development cycles. It is what one does not know that one ought to be concerned about. About 50 to 60 percent of the roadmap was wrong over a 36-month period. Five years ago, this would make one break out into a cold sweat and worry about getting fired.

The message from the conference was the endorsement of EDGE as a 3G technology. While industry observers can debate the details on whether EDGE is 3G or not, the business issues for next-generation wireless broadband applications and services are universal regardless of the technology that delivers them.

Fixed Wireless Meets Broadband Although much attention has been given internationally to the development of 3G (mainly because of the spectrum auctions involved), it is clear that wireless broadband access using fixed wireless broadband technologies on a point-to-multipoint basis also has come of age. In particular, it seems that wireless broadband could be a critical technology to the development of competitive telecom operators at the network-access level. Such operators could roll out their networks to subscribers far more rapidly than infrastructure based on wireline broadband technologies, which require considerable public works infrastructure on relatively long timetables. While it is likely that some parts of 3G also will be used for such so-called wireless local loop (WLL) applications, emphasis is likely to be put on the various LMDS technologies now being tested internationally. LMDS systems typically work in multimegabit data rates in the 26- to 28-GHz band. One manufacturer, Alcatel, claims that LMDS can support high-speed Internet services to as many as 4000 customers within a 75-km^2 area. However, several frequency bands are contemplated for WLL services, and 3-GHz systems are in use. In some countries, the 40-GHz band is also contemplated.

Analysts predict that fixed wireless broadband services could generate as much as US$10 billion in 10 years. While North America will be the largest market, analysts expect more than a quarter of the global market to be in Europe and Asia-Pacific. Much of Europe has issued or is issuing licenses for wireless broadband services, including Germany, Switzerland, Spain, Portugal, and Ireland. France and the United Kingdom are in the middle of the licensing process. Many South American countries also have licensed or plan to license spectrum. This follows a burst of U.S. licensing activity in 1998.

Wireless broadband is set to follow UMTS into a license auction system in the United Kingdom. While it is not expected that fixed wireless broadband licenses will generate the same scale of fees that 3G did, it is still predicted that revenues could exceed US$1.5 billion. In the United Kingdom, 42 licenses are available to operate WLL services from 2001 on a 25-year basis. The licenses themselves cover 11 English regions, including Scotland, Wales, and Northern Ireland. There are also plans to develop the 40-GHz band in the future.

Meanwhile, there is an entirely separate but growing interest in providing fixed wireless broadband access in lower frequency bands, particularly in the 5-GHz region. Originally conceived of as being appropriate for wireless broadband LAN technology, experts note that there is a growing consensus to develop this platform for many different applications. In particular, momentum is growing to support the adoption of HiperLAN2 as a common worldwide wireless broadband LAN standard. HiperLAN2 offers up to a 54-Mbps wireless broadband connection in the globally allocated and free 5-GHz spectrum.

The standard is being promoted by a newly constituted industry association, the HiperLAN2 Global Forum (H2GF), which is backed by Bosch, Dell, Ericsson, Nokia, Telia, Texas Instruments, Alcatel, Adaptive Broadband, Axis Communications, Cambridge Silicon Radio, Canon, Grundig, Matsushita Communication, Motorola, NTT, Philips, Samsung, Siemens, and Silicon Wave. The forum says that wireless broadband LAN technology is the only one to support corporate, public, and home environments with high-speed access to multimedia applications and information, and similarly, the technology is also the only one that specifies complementing 3G cellular technology. This is an extremely significant issue because prospective demand for wireless broadband-based data services, particularly in "hot spot" areas such as central business districts and airports, may overwhelm the capability of 3G, which was conceived in a pre-Internet era when voice services still appeared to be predominant. It will bring seamless connectivity between communication devices and networks (including 3G cellular systems) and provide mobility, flexibility, and quality of service for future multimedia and real-time video applications. The forum says that increased interest in the HiperLAN2 standard ensures interoperability between different vendor equipment while offering best-in-class wireless broadband connectivity and access. The standard supports various fixed network protocols including Ethernet, ATM, and IP.

The Spectrum Dimension   Overshadowing all existing and prospective wireless broadband technologies is a critical piece of the jigsaw: spectrum availability. The high fee operators have been prepared to pay for access to 3G spectrum in Europe underscores once again that spectrum is a scarce resource. Allocating spectrum around the world is a complex job because of the many competing demands on the resource and the requirement that new applications do not interfere with existing ones. The focus of attention has been on the World Radio Conference (WRC), itself a marathon event, held about every 3 years. The WRC seeks to determine spectrum-allocation policies for the future. Most recently, WRC-2000 was held in Istanbul during May and early June 2000, a critical time for the international wireless broadband community.

To gain international recognition for new applications using the radio spectrum, the required frequency allocation has to be obtained at the WRC. If enough studies have been done and sharing is possible, the WRC usually will make such new allocations along with the technical conditions for the use of the newly allocated frequencies. If enough studies have not been carried out, then the conference may make provisional frequency allocations to be confirmed by the next WRC. Agreements are reached through consensus building, although some administrations occasionally take a reservation on certain decisions. Sometimes the divergence of opinion is too great, and no decision can be made. For example, in a certain frequency range, should preference be given to terrestrial systems or satellite networks? In these cases, a carefully worded resolution to further study the issue is agreed on, and the item is postponed to a future conference.

The WRC-2000 agenda contained more than 20 items. Some of the more controversial issues included replanning the ITU Region 1 (Europe and Africa) and 3 (Asia and Australia) for broadcast satellite services (BSS), confirming the equivalent power-flux density (EPFD) limits for frequency sharing between geosynchronous orbit (GSO) and non-GSO/fixed satellite service (FSS) satellites, the allocation of new frequencies for the radio-navigation satellite service (RNSS) to accommodate the proposed Galileo system, and issues related to IMT-2000/UMTS.

The replanning of the Region 1 and 3 BSS plan was the highest-priority item for Arab, African, and to a lesser extent, Asian countries. The WRC-2000 agenda item dealing with it called only for the results of studies on the feasibility of a Region 1 and 3 BSS replanning to be presented to WRC-2000, with the conference deciding the basis for replanning. The actual replanning was to be completed at the next WRC. However, during informal meetings with Europe, the Arab and African countries threatened to withhold support on items of great importance to Europe (EPFD limits and UMTS issues) unless Europe agreed to replanning of the Region 1 and 3 BSS plan at 2001's WRC. Europe agreed, and when the rest of the countries learned of it, they were upset that they had not been included in the negotiations. Eventually, all countries accepted the agreement, and the conference took the formal decision that the replanning of the Region 1 and 3 BSS plan would be done at WRC-2000. This, in turn, ensured the support of the Arab and African countries on the other items.

REGION 1 AND 3 BSS REPLANNING WRC-2000 adopted a new Region 1 and 3 BSS plan. This increased the number of channels assigned to each administration on average from 5 to 10 for countries in Region 1 and on average from 4 to 12 for countries in Region 3. Each channel has a nominal bandwidth of 27 MHz, although the channel spacing used in the plan allows for bandwidths as large as 33 MHz. In Region 1, there is a total of 800 MHz of spectrum allocated (40 channels in the 11.7- to 12.5-GHz range on the downlink), and in Region 3, a total of 500 MHz of spectrum is allocated (24 channels in the 11.7- to 12.2-GHz on the downlink).

The BSS plan is based on beams that cover only the national territory; therefore, in the majority of cases, such beams will never be implemented because it does not make economic sense to launch a satellite with only 10 (or 12) transponders. Planning often sterilizes the spectrum/orbit resource, since one administration cannot use the channels assigned to another. This was the reason that Europe had resisted replanning, preferring instead to access spare capacity in the plan through associated modification procedures that allow for supranational coverage and additional channels up to a total of 40 channels in Region 1 and 24 channels in Region 3. Modifications to the plan must be coordinated. Many such modifications had been submitted and had either been fully coordinated or were in the process of being coordinated. As a compromise, it was decided to include in the plan all systems that had been fully coordinated and for which due diligence information had been submitted.

FREQUENCY SHARING   The WRC-2000 agreed on EPFD limits on non-GSO FSS systems for both the Ku and Ka bands. This enables these systems to share frequencies and to protect GSO networks and networks in the terrestrial fixed service (FS). This agreement gives SkyBridge the necessary regulatory certainty needed to proceed with its Ku-band project to provide two-way wireless broadband services on a worldwide basis using its proposed constellation of 80 LEO satellites.

The previous WRC in 1997 granted access to these frequency bands to SkyBridge-type systems on condition that technical studies be conducted to develop appropriate technical parameters and rules in order to protect existing geostationary satellite and terrestrial communications networks from interference. WRC-2000 approved the results of those studies and adopted new provisions in the ITU Radio Regulations.

Conclusion

This chapter discussed, among other things, the future generation of mobile communications systems and key technologies. The forthcoming mobile communications systems are expected to provide a wide variety of services, from high-quality voice to high-definition video through high-data-rate wireless broadband channels anywhere in the world. High data rates require broad frequency bands, and sufficient wireless broadband can be achieved in higher-frequency bands such as microwave, Ka band, and millimeter wave. These wireless broadband channels have to be connected to wireless broadband fixed networks such as the Internet and LAN.

Future generations of systems will include not only cellular phones but also many new types of communications systems. The future systems under discussion are 4G cellular, microwave and millimeter-wave wireless broadband access, intelligent transport systems, and high-altitude platform station systems. The key terms in future generations of mobile communications are multimedia communications, wireless broadband access to wireless broadband fixed networks, and seamless roaming among different systems.

Furthermore, the WAP specification is a truly open standard that enables public content, corporate intranet, and operator-specific solutions to reach wireless broadband subscribers today. The WAP specification leverages and extends existing Internet standards, enabling application developers to tailor their content to the special needs of wireless broadband users. Handset manufacturers can enhance their product lines at minimal cost with new usability benefits. Wireless broadband service providers can establish a new and powerful way to interact with their subscribers through a vital point of control in their own network. The ultimate beneficiaries are wireless broadband subscribers, who can be more productive than ever before.

This chapter also showed you how the combination of broadcast satellite systems and multicast protocols can result in a powerful tool to distribute multimedia contents directly to end users. As described in the chapter, the unique advantage of the satellite is its broadcast capability; hence all sorts of multicast applications and distribution and dissemination services for multimedia can benefit from this type of network. Point-to-point (unicast) applications do not make efficient use of the capacity of GEO satellites and are better delegated to terrestrial networks or LEO networks. However, the rapidly growing field of Web-based multimedia services, which include audio and video clips and are frequently requested by large user communities almost simultaneously, represents a potential new service industry with enormous growth potential.

> **NOTE** For example, NASA experienced several million Web accesses shortly after the automatic laboratory landed on Mars and started reporting data from its experiments. Other examples are releases of new software versions by some major developers.

The next generation of direct broadcast satellites operating in the Ka band will provide bandwidth comparable with fiberoptics, thus increasing even more the potential of multicasting services. In the near future there will be a rapid development of these multimedia satellites that will become totally integrated into the global Internet and provide a second-level high-speed tier directly to the end user.

In addition, the HALO network will provide wireless broadband communication services. The feasibility of this network is ensured due to a convergence of technological advancements. The key enabling technologies at hand include GaAs rf modules operating at MMW frequencies, ATM/SONET technology, digital signal processing of wideband signals, video compression, ultradense memory modules, lightweight aircraft technology including composite airframes, and small fanjets capable of operating reliably at low mach and low Reynolds numbers. These technologies are available, to a great extent, from vendors targeting commercial markets. The HALO network is predicated on the successful integration of these technologies to offer communications services of high quality and utility to small and medium-sized businesses at reasonable prices. The regulatory climates of the Federal Aviation Administration (FAA) and FCC are favorable. While a variety of wireless broadband access modalities are promising for the U.S. markets, the HALO network may be a winner for "green field" deployment, especially in regions where the existing infrastructure is not amenable to an upgrade or retrofit.

Finally, the mobile satellite operators, especially Inmarsat, were seeking additional L-band spectrum allocations, but the recent WRC-2000 industry conference made no such allocations and decided instead that further studies were required to identify additional bands. The filing backlog at the ITU for satellite networks is now so large that if no new filings were received from today, it would still take 3 years to clear. The WRC-2000 conference adopted some measures intended to alleviate the situation. In addition, the identification of networks that new satellite networks must coordinate was simplified. The conference also drew up a tentative agenda for the next WRC, slated for 2002 or 2003. So many agenda items were proposed that it was difficult to decide which items to include, although, with much difficulty, a final list was compiled. This tentative agenda will receive further consideration by the ITU council, which meets yearly.

Endnotes

1. Shingo Ohmori (Communications Research Laboratory, MPT), Yasushi Yamao, and Nobuo Nakajima (NTT Mobile Communications Network, Inc.), "The Future Generations of Mobile Communications Based on Broadband Access Technologies," *IEEE Communications Magazine*, IEEE Communications Society, 305 East 47th Street, New York, NY 10017, USA, 2000.

2. *Ibid.*

3. *Ibid.*

4. *Ibid.*

5. *Ibid.*

6. *Ibid.*

7. *Ibid.*

8. *Ibid.*

9. *Ibid.*

10. *Ibid.*

11. "Wireless Application Protocol," WAP Forum, Ltd., 2570 West El Camino Real, Suite 304, Mountain View, CA 94040-1313, 2000.

12. *Ibid.*

13. *Ibid.*

14. *Ibid.*

15. *Ibid.*

16. *Ibid.*

17. *Ibid.*

18. *Ibid.*

19. *Ibid.*

20. *Ibid.*

21. *Ibid.*

22. *Ibid.*

23. *Ibid.*

24. *Ibid.*

25. *Ibid.*

26. *Ibid.*

27. Hilmar Linder, Horst D. Clausen, and Bernhard Collini-Nocker (University of Salzburg), "Satellite Internet Services Using DVB/MPEG-2 and Multicast Web Caching," *IEEE Communications Magazine*, IEEE Communications Society, 305 East 47th Street, New York, NY 10017, USA, 2000.

28. *Ibid.*

29. *Ibid.*

30. *Ibid.*

31. *Ibid.*

32. *Ibid.*

33. Nicholas J. Colella (Angel Technologies Corporation), James N. Martin (Raytheon Systems Company), and Ian F. Akyildiz (Georgia Institute of Technology), "The HALO Network," *IEEE Communications Magazine*, IEEE Communications Society, 305 East 47th Street, New York, NY 10017, USA, 2000.

34. *Ibid.*

35. *Ibid.*

36. *Ibid.*

37. *Ibid.*

38. *Ibid.*

39. *Ibid.*

CHAPTER 30

Summary, Conclusions, and Recommendations

Is the wireless broadband revolution unstoppable? Despite major issues regarding usability, reliability, and security swirling around wireless broadband communications, signs are pointing to a dramatic shift toward wireless broadband for conducting e-business. And if the predictions hold true, information technology (IT) departments will be at the center of an enterprise-wide business process reengineering effort.

On stage at the Fall Internet World 2000, in New York, IBM led the charge with a major mobile business presentation, at which the company predicted that as much as two-thirds of all e-commerce will be done via wireless broadband devices by 2003. IBM, in Armonk, New York, is basing its predictions on the work it is doing now with corporate clients and Web integrators.

This is the quiet before the storm. The top Fortune 2500 companies are preparing their wireless broadband strategy now and will start to see the results in the very near future. According to IBM, wireless broadband is so big that even "Big Blue" cannot handle all the business. Behind the scenes at Internet World, IBM was quietly recruiting Internet professional services companies, typically competitors, with its own services group. IBM asked the companies to sign up for its *wireless m-camps*, a series of 4-day seminars to be held in Austin, Texas, and Europe starting in 2001.

The m-camps (mobile camps) are meant to train and enlist the support of 200 to 300 professional services organizations to the WebSphere platform for wireless broadband deployments with the integrators, in turn, helping enterprise-level companies to implement an m-commerce (mobile commerce) business component.

Not everyone believes large enterprises will be the first to deploy m-commerce solutions, however. Right now, smaller businesses probably will deploy m-commerce first because it is easier to enable a few people wirelessly in your business than 140,000. However, once the economies of scale kick in, in terms of implementation and software, then we might see a shift more toward bigger businesses.

For example, BevAccess, an online business-to-business exchange for alcoholic beverages, is testing a wireless broadband system from Blueflame for its sell-side exchange participants. Wholesale trading partners can tap in to the BevAccess exchange via Palm VII devices to place orders and receive inventory updates and order confirmation. Despite frustrations with reliability and cost, the system does offer a competitive edge as well as an added value for partners.

BevAccess is offering sell-side trading partners a vehicle to use the exchange to their advantage. They are out on the road a lot, so with this tool they can generate orders wirelessly, which meets their needs. However, the system has had its problems: It is plagued by quality issues such as dead zones and slow speeds. For example, as when using your cell phone, if you run into an area without connectivity, you cannot make your trade or place your order. This is a source of frustration.

Wireless broadband may be disruptive at a much deeper level than dead zones and slow speeds, however. Nevertheless, wireless broadband will bring even bigger IT changes as it starts to push the technology envelope. Companies will see a whole new class of architectural componentry needed to manage the data coming in, and if you hit a home run on a wireless broadband opportunity, be prepared that it may scale.

Bandwidth is a major concern as wireless broadband commerce scales. Companies such as Focal Communications, Verizon, and Nextel are putting fiber infrastructure around the country that will connect wireless broadband receivers to the major switches to resolve any bandwidth issues. These companies sell wireless broadband virtual private networks (VPNs) with higher levels of security.

Wireless broadband is one of those so-called disruptive technologies, the effects of which ripple throughout a company. For example, companies such as Sony are already in the process of reengineering their business processes. In Sony's case, it is due to deployment in 2000 of a wireless broadband solution in its merchandising department.

By equipping its merchandising field force with Palms, Sony completely redesigned the way and the speed at which it gathers information about sales of its PlayStation line in retail stores. With wireless broadband, Sony was able to calibrate its marketing strategy on a real-time basis.

Kemper Insurance, in Chicago, uses a program called ActivePhoto from FlashPoint Technology, in San Jose, California, that helps it shorten the business process by giving appraisers the ability to send digital images wirelessly from the field to headquarters. However, if there is to be any drag on the speed at which wireless broadband is deployed, it will be because of usability and interoperability issues.

The Race for Wireless Broadband Space

Ready or not, here comes the wireless broadband revolution. As businesses in the United States untangle the technology behind wireless broadband data transmission, analysts are predicting a deluge of devices in the coming years that can deliver Web content to smaller form factors, wherever they may roam.

Despite all the hype over wireless broadband data access, only a handful of U.S. companies have taken the plunge to wireless broadband-enable their Web sites. The reasons why have more to do with what has gone wrong in the wide world of wireless broadband Web surfing than what has gone right.

No Single Standard

As opposed to Europe, which has sensibly backed the global system for mobile (GSM) communications standard, U.S. carriers use code division multiple access (CDMA), time division multiple access (TDMA), and GSM in their networks. Having different standards in use requires Web developers to duplicate their work to support each protocol and to support specific types of devices that use each protocol. Carriers and device manufacturers have, for the most part, agreed to support the Wireless Application Protocol (WAP), but WAP-compliant phones and pagers have yet to be seen in the market.

Slack User Demand

Unlike Europe or Asia, where land lines are difficult to get and Internet access is expensive, the United States enjoys a huge base of Web-connected PCs and numerous low-cost Internet service providers (ISPs). This spells lower demand for Web access via cell phones in the market and price sensitivity to per-minute cell phone charges. In places where telecom charges are really high, wireless broadband has taken off simply because it is more available and less expensive than wireline alternatives.

A Niche Market

Even as packaged Web applications tout their support of wireless broadband capabilities, boardroom executives in most companies have yet to come up with a compelling business case and return-on-investment (ROI) numbers for investing in a wireless broadband infrastructure. Wireless still has not really captured the imagination of the business community. A lot of companies are waiting for the "killer application."

Despite the murky waters, some companies, such as those in the financial services and travel industries, have found that the customer service benefits are worth wading in for. For example, banks and brokerage firms have deployed systems for serving up real-time stock quotes and enabling transactions on cell phones. Getting an early start will help those businesses prepare for increased demand for wireless broadband access in the years to come. The number of Web-enabled handsets is projected to surge in the next 5 years. The Yankee Group predicts that 60 percent of the U.S. population will be able to access data via their mobile phones by 2005. In certain vertical industries, wireless broadband data could become a big asset to the raw business structure.

Cutting Wires

Despite the wrangling over standards and development platforms, many companies have experimented with wireless broadband applications, believing that an early exposure to the technology will translate into a competitive edge in customer service down the road. For most, the Palm handheld personal digital assistant (PDA) has been the focus of early development because it has a large installed base of loyal users and uses a single standard, called Web Clipping.

Wells Fargo Bank and Bank of America are both in the process of deploying services for the Palm device and have ambitious plans to expand their projects over time. Wells Fargo's wireless broadband system will, by 2001, give U.S. customers the ability to check balances, transfer funds, and get alerts and stock quotes via Web-enabled phones or Palm VII devices. Bank of America, also ramping up its customer-facing efforts, later in 2001, will roll out a wireless broadband service in select U.S. markets that will allow customers to conduct transactions on a variety of wireless broadband devices. An earlier pilot program in California provided access to bank information via Palm VII devices and was popular with users.

Other industries forging ahead with wireless broadband include the shipping and airline industries, in which uninterrupted access to account information and schedules spells happier customers. In late September 2000, United Parcel Service (UPS) rolled out a program that allows customers to track packages, find dropoff locations, and learn the status of shipments via most Internet devices. These services are currently offered on Palm VII devices; the new services work with one- and two-way pagers, WAP-enabled phones, Research in Motion pagers, and PDAs. And UPS will extend the service internationally in late 2001. UPS wants this functionality available on any device. Where you really impact the marketplace is when you can hit all handheld devices.

To gain an edge in customer service, United Airlines is currently testing a system that will send alerts regarding flight delays, gate information, or upgrade status to a customer's preferred device. The system is currently available via PCs and Palm devices, and the pilot program will extend the service to Web phones and other devices. United intends to push more functionality to wireless broadband phones and devices, eventually allowing customers to change and book flights via a Web phone.

Getting Professional Help

For businesses new to wireless broadband applications and leery of messing with a working infrastructure, a new breed of integrators is prepared to help them out. Wireless application service providers (WASPs), as well as specialized software vendors and system integrators, have emerged that can create and deploy wireless broadband solutions on customer Web sites with minimal fuss. Some WASPs will even host a device-ready version of a company's Web site on their own systems for a monthly subscription fee. In addition, a trusted technology integrator can manage carrier relations and customer service issues pertaining to device support.

When adding support for wireless broadband devices, for example, both Bank of America and Wells Fargo leaned heavily on 724 Solutions, which translates the banks' content to device-friendly formats and serves it up in real time. Early adopter UPS agreed that a technology partner was essential, especially for nationwide deployments, and got its wireless broadband system up and running with help from systems integrator Air2Web.

There are over 300 carriers in the United States. Just working through that can be quite a maze. Working with an integrator, Air2Web, helped UPS to provide the content to its customers much sooner than what it could have done.

Now let's look at the latest designs being proposed/recommended in the network wireless broadband communications industry and how they are making use of digital intermediate frequency (IF)–based architectures. Modern test equipment, via the equipment vendor, also must migrate to this architecture to maintain correlation in simulation testing.

Wireless Broadband Test Equipment Vendor Perspective

As the designers, builders, and vendors of network wireless broadband communications systems look to cover the demand for enhanced performance of the base station, a myriad of innovative techniques is being implemented. One hybrid solution is through software-defined code formats that optimize bandwidth utilization in the allocated frequency that resides in the base station radio. This move toward the software-defined radio for third-generation (3G) wireless broadband products has taxed the capabilities of today's test methods.

New radio designs are implementing digital intermediate frequency (IF)– versus the traditional analog complex modulation (IQ)–based architectures. These changes force designers to test software-defined radio modules using both digital pattern generation and radiofrequency (rf) modulation analysis. The traditional model of injecting baseband analog IQ into the module and measuring the rf performance is not valid anymore. The software-defined radio modules require the multicarrier, multistandard signal to be injected into the radio as a digital IF rather than analog IQ.

The advent of highly linear analog-to-digital (A/D) and digital-to-analog (D/A) converters has enabled a new architecture for modern test equipment that matches the software radio evolution. The concept behind the test pattern is to provide a mirror-image signal scenario for the radio designer that provides for a *real-time* digital baseline to enhance the test process. This is possible due to the highly linear converters that enable the consolidation of numerous functions into one instrument. Using the software-defined radio or digital radio concept as the *baseline* or *standard* that must be met, the test equipment designer can now build modular virtual instruments with test equipment grade specifications. Using this concept, a full *transmit/receive* path for testing the latest wireless broadband standards can be implemented.

Test System Components

The latest designs being proposed in the network wireless broadband communications industry are making use of digital IF-based architectures. Modem test equipment also must migrate to this architecture to maintain correlation in simulation testing. The legacy test equipment available today typically is implemented using analog modulation techniques employing IQ modulators. This architecture was sufficient to test the older generation of communication devices.

To implement the software-defined radio as the solution for next generation deployments, all major components of the base station must be thoroughly characterized in the designer's test lab. To fully meet the designer's expectations at the platform level, these converters are coupled with gigabytes of solid-state memory and wireless broadband rf up- and downconversion. This provides for real-world conditions in the laboratory and ultimately at production test for both the digital-based radio and major subassemblies such as the amplifier, offering true base station simulation.

To further exploit the design options offered by the latest-generation converters, the test instrument incorporates a different architecture configured on the *digital radio* test concept. The digital radio concept emulates the process of quadrature modulation with the repeatability, accuracy, and control that only discrete systems can offer. After processing, the digital data stream consists of a real signal at a specified IF center frequency: digital IF. This digital data stream is converted to an analog IF signal by the D/A converter. The resulting signal is a real waveform at the specified IF frequency.

The analog IF signal can be translated to any required frequency through a highly linear, low-distortion upconverter. To implement the receive portion of the digital radio, a similar approach is used.

This process would consist of rf downconversion to a suitable IF frequency, A/D conversion to a digital IF, and signal processing to produce the IQ vectors. The immediate benefit of the digital IF signal-generation approach is that it allows for extremely low distortion and nearly immeasurable IQ impairments.

Why Software-Based Parameters Work

The advantage of a modular, digitally based test system that parallels the software-based radio is that it can be applied across the various subassemblies or components of the base station, providing complete design continuity. In testing power amplifier linearization, new digital linearization techniques can be tested to prove the latest algorithms.

The advantages and options that begin to emerge from the modular test platform are numerous and quite effective. Using the software-defined radio approach, the equipment can be configured to generate any number of multicarrier, multistandard signal scenarios using the vector-simulation software. The output of the vector signal generator is used to apply the stimulus to the amplifier. The vector signal analyzer portion of the instrument can acquire, analyze, and automate the performance measurements used to qualify the amplifier. Since all the stimulus-response and analysis occur within one instrument, there is immediate simplification for the user. Reconfiguring the functionality of this hardware allows receiver tests, interference tests, and additional system-level qualification tests to occur.

Typical testing for power amplifiers uses a signal generator based on an IQ modulator. While this was reasonably efficient for single-carrier generation, addressing the multicarrier requirements that exist today is much less effective than the modular test system with real-time digital and rf up- and downconversion capability. The nondigital, analog-based test sets feature dual D/A converters and analog IQ modulation circuits, waveform memory, and adequate capability for single standard test scenarios. These generators inherently have the same limitations that have forced base station designers to migrate toward the digital radio concept and, in turn, the digital-based test set.

Using the software-defined radio concept as the architectural basis of a vector signal generator, one can eliminate many shortcomings of today's IQ-based generators. This concept makes use of a single D/A converter and an IF- to-rf upconversion chain. This mimics the latest base station architectures. The addition of gigabytes of solid-state memory behind the D/A converters permits nearly unlimited flexibility in generating test scenarios. This provides for multicarrier, multistandard signal generation and the ability to record and play actual field spectral measurements.

This hardware, coupled with intuitive vector signal simulation software (VSS), gives the test engineer an endless array of multicarrier, multistandard spectrums for evaluation. The VSS software suite allows the designer to develop proprietary algorithms and custom modulation schemes independent of the equipment vendor.

The software-defined radio concept allows test equipment designers to use a modular architecture. The modular and software-defined test set gives the design team key design and test advantages. It offers the option to simulate both transmit and receive paths in a single test instrument and enables the designers of the radio, digital signal processor, and amplifier to work in parallel rather than in sequence. Finally, the modular test set offers the promise of reducing the capital equipment costs required for communication product design by replacing a number of stand-alone instruments.

Next, let's look at Internet Protocol (IP)–based services being implemented by service providers, such as wireless broadband data and voice over IP, that are showing continuous explosive growth. However, there are currently no technical standards in place for implementation of these new services. This final section outlines the new challenges this brings to service providers and addresses key properties that are critical to a robust wireless broadband provisioning system.

The Service Provider Perspective

Service providers face many challenges in implementing IP-based services. The network management, provisioning, mediation, and billing systems currently used by these service providers were not designed to accommodate these complex new IP-based services. To rapidly and reliably deploy these new services, providers must resolve a number of issues.

Market Challenges: Collecting Data from Innumerable Heterogeneous Elements

Providers must now contend with gathering data from a growing number of heterogeneous elements. Whether they are providing voice over IP, e-commerce, or video gaming, the data generated from each network element varies widely. Providers must be able to collect data from many diverse, proprietary sources and translate them into meaningful customer information.

Managing Enormous Volumes of Data   Many of the customer care systems used today require manual intervention. Operators enter customer information by hand into the various service elements required for provisioning. However, this mode of operation does not scale with the massive demand for service rollout. A backlog of requests builds up, and the risk of human error during the entry process results.

In addition, requesting new services over the phone will soon become a thing of the past. For example, inexpensive Web TV stations are now on the market. They will self-configure via telephone dialup when plugged in. It is estimated that millions of provisioning requests could be received over a holiday season. Providers who are unable to automate real-time provisioning and billing will risk an enormous loss of revenue.

Adapting Quickly to New Services and Requirements   Service providers will continuously offer new services, over new devices, all over an IP-based infrastructure. But the inflexibility of most customer care systems prevents operators from adding new service elements quickly and reliably. Providers need systems that can evolve to meet rapidly changing needs without straining the existing infrastructure.

System Architecture Requirements

Based on the market challenges addressed previously, the following criteria should be considered when selecting a broadband provisioning system:

- Automation
- Flexibility

- Distributed environment
- Consistent databases[1]

Automation   To compete in the high-growth IP-based service market, operators must provide for automated provisioning of IP services, cable modems, and other standards-compliant devices. Automated provisioning improves order accuracy and customer response times while significantly reducing labor costs.

Flexibility   Given the rate at which new services such as unified messaging are being deployed, the provisioning system must be nimble enough to add new service elements and workflow logic quickly and reliably. The provisioning system should be agnostic to the data record type.

Distributed Environment   If all service elements reside on a central server, it becomes difficult to distribute the various provisioning components where they are most needed. Implementing a distributed environment gives operators the flexibility to extend and deploy components based on the needs of those implementing the service.

Consistent Databases   Since many disparate systems need to be updated in order to complete the provisioning of a single customer, the potential for inaccurate reporting of partial operation failures increases. This causes additional work, confused customer service representatives, and dissatisfied customers. Developing consistency among all databases alleviates this problem.

Components of End-to-End Wireless Broadband Provisioning Systems

This part of the final chapter describes the network architecture and components that comprise an end-to-end wireless broadband provisioning system. The provisioning system integrates the existing operations and support systems (OSS) with the service delivery and provisioning elements.

Agents   *Agents* are the components that communicate directly with network services or network elements, bridges, and engines. In this case, the agent provides an adaptation function between the provisioning system and the various service elements in the network. Agents communicate with the bridge through a normalized usage application programming interface

(API). An agent registers itself with the bridge during agent initialization. There are two primary types of agents: provisioning agents and usage agents.

PROVISIONING AGENTS   These agents implement the normalized provisioning API and accept provisioning operations from the bridge, as shown in Figure 30-1.[2] Each provisioning agent controls a specific type of service element according to that service element's service provisioning API. The provisioning agent provides a translation function between the normalized provisioning API and the API of the service element, and vice versa in the case of data flowing from the service element toward the bridge (IP address changes, for example).

USAGE AGENTS   These agents implement the normalized usage API, pass usage information to the bridge, and ultimately deliver it to the OSS/billing system. An agent also performs a translation function between the usage-collection API and the normalized usage API. The agent translates for a variety of usage-collection technologies, including MIB II and flow-based systems.

Bridges   The bridge is a component of the provisioning system that provides necessary conversion, formatting, and communications capabilities to enable applications to transmit and receive data from any network element or service. The bridge is the entry point for provisioning information from the OSS system to the provisioning system and the exit point for usage information being delivered to the OSS/billing application.

Customer Premises Equipment   Customer premises equipment (CPE) terminates the service at the customer site. An example of a CPE is a PacketCable multiple terminal adapter (MTA). The MTA adapts the Packet-Cable voice-over-IP service to the residential twisted-pair infrastructure.

Network Element   A network element is any network-addressable device in the network. In this final chapter, a network address is assumed to be an IP address.

Normalized Usage API   This is a vendor-neutral API used to pass usage information between a usage agent and the bridge. The usage agent translates usage information to the format of the normalized usage API and then passes the information to the bridge for processing.

Normalized Provisioning API   This is a vendor-neutral API used to exchange provisioning information between the bridge and a provisioning

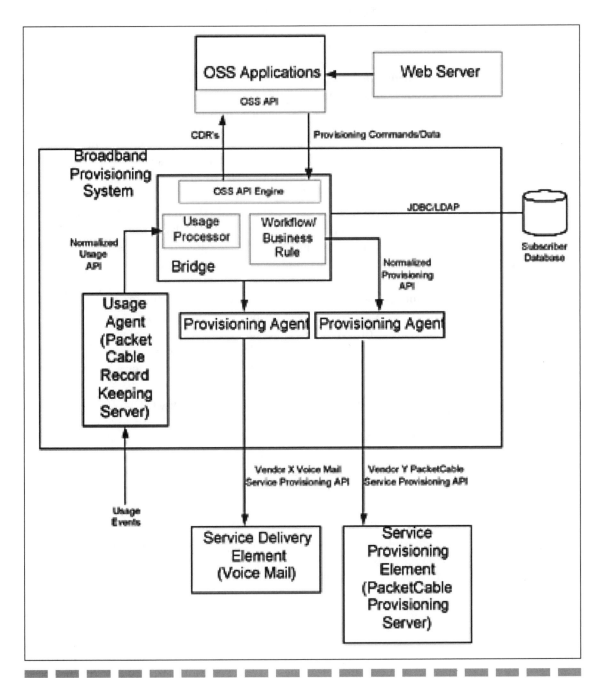

Figure 30-1 Heterogeneous service elements.

agent. The bridge translates provisioning information to the format of the normalized provisioning API and then passes the information to the provisioning agent.

Operations and Support Systems (OSS)   These systems automate the support and customer management functions of the carrier or service provider from a network and service point of view.

Service Delivery Elements   Service delivery elements are network infrastructure components that deliver an ongoing service to the subscriber for the duration of the subscription. Here are some examples of service delivery elements: First of all, you should have an email server providing POP3, Simple Mail Transfer Protocol (SMTP), and Network News Transfer Protocol (NNTP) service. This type of service delivery element would need to export a service provisioning API. The API would be used by the provisioning system to enable email service for a new data service subscriber, for example.

Second, you should have an IP router. This type of service delivery element may need to export a service provisioning API. In the event of a router implementing different levels of quality of service (QoS) with service level agreements (SLAs), the router would need to export a service provisioning API to allow QoS levels to be enabled (and enforced) for a particular customer according to the provisioned SLA.

A service delivery element is different from a service provisioning element in that the service delivery element is active in the delivery of service to the provisioned subscriber as long as the subscription lasts. A service provisioning element is only involved during the initial provisioning operation. For example, when a customer signs up for cable service, the service provisioning element activates the cable.

A service delivery element may or may not need to be provisioned. If updating the state of a service delivery element is required for successful provisioning of a subscriber, then that service delivery element must export a service provisioning API. This enables an agent to be developed for the service delivery element.

Service Element   *Service element* is a generic term that refers either to a service delivery element or a service provisioning element.

Service Provisioning API   A service provisioning API is an application programming interface exported by service provisioning elements or service delivery elements. The API is used by the provisioning system to direct the provisioning operations of the service provisioning element. Each service provisioning element or service delivery element whose state must be updated during a provisioning operation is required to export a service provisioning API. Service provisioning APIs may vary widely according to network element type and vendor.

Service Provisioning Element Service provisioning elements enable service on network elements with appropriate parameters. Service provisioning elements are specific to the types of customer premises equipment for which they provide service. An example would be a PacketCable provisioning server managing a neighborhood of PacketCable subscribers. This server provides Dynamic Host Configuration Protocol service for allocation of IP addresses and Trivial File Transfer Protocol (TFTP) service for download of operational parameter files into an MTA.

A service provisioning element is different from a service delivery element in that once the provisioning operation has taken place, there is no further involvement on the service provisioning element's part in the ongoing service for the subscriber. Service provisioning elements export a service provisioning API. Service provisioning elements may include service delivery element functionality.

Subscriber Database The subscriber database maintains the current state of the provisioning system. All updates to the database are performed under transaction control. At any given time, the subscriber database is consistent with all the service elements in the system. The subscriber database can be queried at any time to determine the state of customer data as they pertain to the services provisioned for them. A number of database technologies may be used for implementation of the subscriber database, such as the Lightweight Directory Access Protocol (LDAP) or relational database technology.

Provisioning System A provisioning system provides a provisioning mediation layer, enabling the end-to-end flow of provisioning and usage information between existing OSS applications and network and service elements provided by an ever expanding base of equipment and application vendors.

Web Server Subscriber self-provisioning is gaining acceptance in the marketplace in support of the retail model of CPE deployment. Placing a Web server near the OSS applications provides customers with online access to the OSS systems and provisioning processes.

There are at least two models for supplying information to the OSS from a Web server. The OSS system may export an API directly to a Web server by which the server can inject provisioning and subscriber update information to the OSS. Additionally, it is possible for a bridge component to be created to accept the provisioning data from the Web server. In this scenario, the bridge would then pass provisioning information upstream to the OSS as well as downstream to the provisioning agents.

Recommended Capabilities

In order to create a scalable and robust wireless broadband provisioning system, the underlying infrastructure must include a number of system-wide elements, which are described in this part of the final chapter.

Revenue Assurance   For more than 30 years, telephony carriers have developed mediation and billing system requirements that ensure the validity and reliability of their data. Customers will expect the same standards to the world of IP billing. To eliminate costly errors, it is important that provisioning systems have audit capabilities to guarantee the accuracy of each transaction. In addition, systems should be capable of performing duplicate and gap-checking functions.

Fault Tolerance   The provisioning system must always be available. There are various ways the system can provide for continuous availability, including

- Replicating system components, including network connections
- Electing primary and backup processors
- Replicating data stored on the system
- Detecting failure of the primary processor
- Enabling failover from the primary to the backup processor when failure of the primary system has been detected[3]

Several provisioning systems, including the AP Engines Provisioning Mediation System, can provide these capabilities on commercially available hardware and software solutions. For larger configurations where the number of transactions flowing through the system is greater, it may be necessary to apply a more significant hardware solution to the problem. Leading hardware vendors, such as Hewlett-Packard, Sun Microsystems, Stratus, and Compaq, among others, provide highly scalable and fault-tolerant solutions with Redundant Array of Independent Disks (RAID) disk technology. These high-end servers are appropriate for solutions that are required to scale to tens of millions of users.

Custom Business Logic   Each carrier's business model requires unique processing depending on how its business practices have evolved. It is recommended that the system allow for incorporation of custom business logic via a business rule. Once the business rule has been developed according to the API specification, it can be configured dynamically into the system.

Integration of Usage Collection with Provisioning   In the telecommunications world, reconciliation between carriers and service providers is critical to profitable business. This is a technical area that the IP world is just beginning to experience, but with the advent of open access between ISPs and carriers, it will become a major requirement in the future. Over time, an increasing number of billing events related to a subscriber will originate from IP usage events. Usage collection information will need to be integrated with the provisioning process to reduce manual intervention, ensure invoice accuracy, and increase ease of use of the system.

There are a number of IP usage collection technologies in use today. Companies such as AP Engines, Cisco, Nortel, and others are constructing systems for the collection of usage data for IP services. This information varies from raw byte and packet counters to detailed IP session information recording data on activity on the following application sessions: File Transfer Protocol (FTP), Hypertext Transfer Protocol (HTTP), and others.

If these usage events are to be used to generate billing events, issues may arise related to the nature of device addressing in an IP network. Many IP network providers assign IP addresses dynamically with protocols such as the Dynamic Host Configuration Protocol (DHCP). Once the IP address has been allocated, this address is then used for communications on the IP network.

It is possible that the IP address used by a device may change over the course of time for a number of reasons. One reason is that the DHCP maintains the concept of an IP address lease. When this lease expires, the IP device must obtain a new IP address. Since an IP end point may use a different IP address for communication at different points in time, there is the potential for serious billing errors. If the customer identification is correlated with the wrong IP address, customers will not be charged accurately for the services used. The requirement to generate billing activity from IP-based usage events means the architecture must meet the following criteria:

- The system must correlate a customer ID with the IP address currently in use for a particular IP end point.

- It may be necessary to notify the IP usage collection software that collection should be enabled for that particular IP address.

- Usage events identified based on an IP address must be correlated with the customer ID so that the charge will be placed on the appropriate customer's account.

■ Services may generate usage events to be delivered to different downstream applications depending on provisioning decisions.[4]

Distributed Component Model   Currently, there are very few programmatic APIs that the OSS and service network elements implement that can be taken advantage of for automating the subscriber management function. For the most part, each OSS and service network element implements a proprietary API for delivery of provisioning and usage data. The protocols and formats used in these APIs vary widely from SNMP to HTTP to an interface to an Oracle database to a TL1 provisioning interface. It is recommended that provisioning systems be designed to adapt these widely disparate OSS and network service elements so that they can be combined during configuration time without modification to any components.

Distributed Transaction Model   One of the problems operators are having with existing provisioning systems is the lack of transaction properties as applied to the provisioning operations. If the system does not have the properties associated with transactions (listed below), there is a high risk that the result of provisioning operations will be inconsistent.

For example, assume that a provisioning operation requires both that a device be provisioned and that a voice mail server be updated with an account. If the provisioning system fails in the middle of the provisioning operation, it is possible that the device was provisioned but that the voice mail server was not updated. The operator must be confident that when he or she receives a success code from the system, all the provisioning actions have indeed been completed and all the databases and service elements have been updated consistently. By the same token, a failure code should indicate that no service elements have been updated partially and that the system is in the state that existed before the failed provisioning operation. To accomplish this, provisioning transactions incorporate the following properties:

■ *Atomic.* Either all the actions of the overall provisioning operation happen, or none of them happen. The provisioning operation becomes all or nothing. There are no partial updates to the various network elements. If one of the provisioning actions fails, the operation is rolled back.

■ *Consistent.* All the network elements and databases remain consistent as a result of provisioning operations. When a service provisioning element is updated with customer information, the corresponding service delivery element will never neglect to be updated because of a partial failure. All the databases reflect the desired state with respect to a particular customer, even in the presence of failures.

■ *Isolated.* The operations on the various databases and network elements appear to happen at the same time. Partial updates are transparent to those observing the databases from the outside world.

■ *Durable.* All the preceding properties apply even in the face of system failures. Regardless of failures of the transaction software itself, sufficient information is saved during the provisioning operation to recover and complete any in-progress operations once the system has been restarted after a failure.[5]

A robust and scalable wireless broadband provisioning system is critical to the effective deployment of new IP-based services. To achieve this, several key properties should be inherent to the system, including

■ Automation of provisioning

■ Fault-tolerance

■ End-to-end audit capabilities

■ Correlation of usage collection and provisioning data

■ Incorporation of workflow and business rule APIs

■ Consistency of databases

■ Distributed environment

■ Distributed transaction model[6]

Finally, politicians profess a devotion to the cause of wireless broadband companies offering high-speed wireless broadband services, but this is unlikely to happen unless the U.S. military agrees to give up some precious airspace.

The Uncertain Future

Wireless broadband providers and their hardware partners view so-called third-generation (3G) services such as fast Internet connections and streaming video as a revenue windfall, as evidenced by DoCoMo's $9.8 billion investment in AT&T Wireless. These services will demand more airspace, or spectrum, and engineering surveys by the International Telecommunications Union (ITU) have identified only a few small bands that are compatible with 3G services.

The problem is that these bands all are occupied, some by commercial operations but the majority by more than a dozen government agencies, mostly military. There is a finite amount of airspace, or electromagnetic spectrum, that can be used for any wireless broadband operation, from a cell phone to a radio station. While most of this spectrum is already in use, government officials acknowledge that much of what is being used by federal agencies is not as efficiently allocated as it could be.

President Bush ordered government agencies to cooperate with the wireless broadband industry to find solutions to the spectrum drought, including the possible sharing or relocation of incumbents. However, at a meeting of government and industry representatives recently, the Department of Defense reiterated its inflexibility and emphasized its need for large swaths of airspace over major markets such as New York, Houston, and San Francisco, including all of Silicon Valley.

Sharing spectrum with commercial operators would be awfully challenging. Segmenting the spectrum band in question (1755–1850 MHz) into separate pieces is *more promising*. However, any dislocation of military operations would mean that the Defense Department would need access to some spectrum somewhere else and that the military would not hesitate to dislodge some other spectrum users. This could have a significant impact on companies and government agencies using other spectrum, particularly given that the wireless broadband needs of the military from everything to air-to-ground communications to tactical weapons systems could operate only in the lower frequencies of the radio spectrum.

Perhaps the biggest obstacle to achieving nationwide 3G services are the protected geographic areas the military has designated across the United States, which coincide with key military installations. To permit clear airspace for communications with aircraft and for satellite control, some of the largest metropolitan areas are all but completely blocked out by the military in the spectrum band in question. These include New York, Houston, Dallas, San Antonio, Denver, Miami, Philadelphia, Baltimore, Washington, Albuquerque, New Mexico, and the entire San Francisco Bay Area, including Oakland, Sacramento, San Jose, and the Silicon Valley. Other areas, such as Los Angeles, Seattle, San Diego, and Nashville, Tennessee, also would encounter some significant interference with military operations. Nevertheless, we cannot afford as a country not to move ahead on 3G wireless. We have no choice but to be very aggressive and active.

Other Spectrum Roadblocks

The military is not the only obstacle to spectrum availability. Along with the spectrum band the military operates in, President Bush instructed the Federal Communications Commission (FCC) to examine the 2500-2690-MHz band. A full 170 MHz of the 190 MHz in that band is already allocated to commercial fixed wireless broadband users, totaling about 4700 licensees across the country. Some of these licensees are educational institutions, but many are telecom providers such as WorldCom and Sprint that are rolling out two-way high-speed Internet access via a fixed dish and direct line-of-sight transmissions. The growth of these companies in 2000 means that this segment of spectrum is in a state of fairly rapid change.

The FCC is working on several scenarios that would consolidate fixed wireless broadband to 100 MHz and leave 90 MHz for 3G services. However, this could require some fairly substantive changes in the technology. Fixed wireless broadband officials oppose this because the industry already is on shaky ground financially, and a need to replace expensive equipment could cause investors to flee.

Fixed wireless broadband operators and others will have an opportunity to comment publicly on the FCC's ideas soon because the agency will begin a formal process for new rules by the end of 2001. President Bush in his executive order said that the FCC should issue new rules for 3G services by December 2001 so that auctions for the airwaves can be held by September 30, 2002. We will see if the new Bush administration will abide by the initial executive order.

Endnotes

1. "Selecting a Broadband Mediation System," AP Engines, Inc., One Clock Tower Place, Maynard, Massachusetts 01754 (Cable Datacom News, P.O. Box 59026, Phoenix, AZ 85076, USA), 2000.
2. *Ibid.*
3. *Ibid.*
4. *Ibid.*
5. *Ibid.*
6. *Ibid.*

Glossary

10base-T — Refers to a 10-Mbps Ethernet specification (also known as IEEE 802.3) that uses category 3 (CAT3) or category 5 (CAT5) twisted-pair wiring. As defined by the IEEE 802.3 Committee, it uses CSMA/CD technology to access the bus network or linear topology. The segment length is 100 m and is installed in star topology to the central hub.

2B+D — A basic rate ISDN line has two B-channels and one D-channel and 2-digit codes.

56K modem — The models of 56K modems made by Rockwell/Lucent and U.S. Robotics/3Com use different, incompatible standards for their speeds above 33.6 kbps. The Rockwell/Lucent standard is known as *K56flex*. The U.S. Robotics/3Com standard is known as *x2*.

AA — Accounting authority. This is an organization nominated on an activation registration form (SARF) to administer the billing and settlement of the communications charges incurred by a mobile earth station (MES).

AAIC — Accounting authority identification code. A unique code that is assigned by the International Telecommunications Union (ITU) to identify an accounting authority.

ABE — Alternative billing entity (or authority). The aircraft owner or other entity that is responsible for paying bills accrued by the AES. GES operators may, at their discretion, send bills direct to the ABE for payment.

Access approval — The document issued to the AES integrator setting out the terms and conditions under which a defined AES installation may be used in the satellite network.

ac (alternating current) — A continuously varying current that rises to a maximum value or flow (electron) in one direction, falls to zero, and then rises to a maximum value or flow in the opposite (reverse direction). When referred to, it follows a sinusoidal growth (increase) and decay (decrease) curve. In the United States, 110-volt ac power reverses direction 60 times per second (hertz).

ACK (acknowledgment) — A signal or message sent by a receiving device to a transmitting device indicating that it has successfully received one or more blocks of data.

Activation — Activation replaces the old term *commissioning*. Activation is the process of registering each new or modified mobile earth station (MES) or "smart" card in the electronic service activation system (ESAS). ESAS then notifies the satellite to globally activate the mobile identity and numbers in all satellite-related databases, including the land earth stations (LESs).

ADC (analog-to-digital converter) — A device that converts discrete level samples of an analog voltage waveform to a sequence of binary digits. Passing waveforms through an ADC introduces quantization noise.

ADN — Advanced digital network. Usually refers to a 56-kbps leased line.

ADSL — Asymmetric digital subscriber line. High-speed transmission technology using existing local loops to transmit POTS and data to and from a customer location.

AES identifier (AES ID) — A 24-bit binary number assigned to each AES, which is needed for signaling purposes within the satellite system. The number is unique to a particular AES installation on a particular airframe.

AES installation — A specific electrical and mechanical configuration of equipment installed on an aircraft that is designated by the AES integrator and which is intended to function as an AES.

AES installer — The person or entity responsible for carrying out the installation of an AES. The AES installer also may be the AES integrator.

AES integrator — The holder of the satellite access approval certificate for the particular type of AES installation.

AES licensee — The person or entity who holds a license to operate an AES.

AF (audio frequency) — Frequencies of air vibrations or electrical impulses that fall within the range of human hearing between 20 and 20,000 Hz.

Air time — The actual time spent communicating (transmitting or receiving voice, data, or fax) over the satellite system.

A-law — A standard algorithm for performing pulse code modulation (PCM). It is used in Europe and most other parts of the world.

Alpha version — Alpha version refers to the first working or upgraded version of a new product. In most cases, this version is tested within the company that designed it. The alpha version of a product is often used in the context of software.

AM (amplitude modulation) — A method of impressing or storing information on a carrier signal in which its waveform amplitude or magnitude is modified according to a plan agreed to by the transmitter and receiver.

Analog communications — The method of voice transmission used in today's telephone system. This method converts voice to electrical signals and amplifies them so the voice can be sent over long distances.

Analog signal — A continuously varying signal whose amplitude is proportional to another value, especially a voltage. Because of this correspondence, an analog signal may have virtually an infinite number of states. This is in contrast to a digital signal, which has a finite number of discrete states.

ANSI — American National Standards Institute. The primary standards organization for the United States, ANSI plays a significant role in defining ISDN standards.

Answerback — Telex equipment reply to "who are you" (WRU).

Antenna — A devise for transmitting (radiating) or receiving radiofrequency (rf) energy.

APC — Adaptive predictive coding (voice coding algorithm) or aeronautical passenger information.

Application — Software that provides a set of services such as electronic mail or file transfers of network management.

ASCII — American Standard Code for Information Interchange. The worldwide standard for the code numbers used by computers to represent all the upper- and lower-case Latin letters, numbers, punctuation, etc. There are 128 standard ASCII codes, each of which can be represented by a 7-digit binary number: 0000000 through 1111111. A standard governing the representation of various characters as a sequence of binary digits (bits). The ASCII character set includes all upper- and lower-case English letters, numbers, several special characters, and 32 control codes. A 7-bit binary number represents each character so that one ASCII-encoded character can be stored in 1 byte of memory. Various 8-bit extensions to the original 7-bit ASCII code set are not defined. ASCII is the main text file exchange format of a personal computer (PC) and email messages.

Asymmetrical — Data transfer where upstream and downstream data flow occurs at different speeds, usually a higher rate of speed downstream and a slower rate upstream. Reflective of typical end-user Internet usage patterns, where more data are received than sent, and no servers (such as Web server) are in operation.

Asynchronous — Data communication in which transmission is sent by individual bytes, not related to specific timing on the transmitting end.

Asynchronous communications — The form of data communications that transmits data one character at a time with start and stop bits. The method used for data communications over a plain old telephone system (POTS) using modems.

Asynchronous transmission — Refers to the transmission data, as groups of bits or characters, at irregular intervals. These characters, although transmitted at irregular intervals, contain bits that must be sent at regularly timed intervals within each group. Each character contains a start bit and one or two stop bits. When the receiving machine detects a start bit, it counts off the regularly timed bits that form a character and then returns to its "listening" state once all the stop bits are detected. The presence of these start and stop bits allows the time intervals between characters to be irregular or asynchronous.

ATM — Asynchronous Transfer Mode. High-bandwidth, low-delay, connection-oriented, packet-like switching and multiplexing technique requiring 53-byte fixed-sized cells.

ATU — ADSL transceiver unit. The ADSL Forum uses terminology for DSL equipment based on the ADSL model for which the forum was created originally. Thus the DSL end point is known as the ATU-R, and the CO unit is known as the ATU-C. These terms have since come to be used for other types of DSL services, such as RADSL and SDSL. ATU generally represents XDSL services.

ATU-C — ATU central office. ATU equipment placed in a carrier's central office in support of DSL-based services.

ATU-R — ATU remote. Equipment placed in a customer location in support of DSL-based services.

Authentication — A process used to verify the identity of an object (such as a "smart" card).

Authorization — Process of determining whether a certain level of access can be provided to an object (such as a mobile satellite terminal).

AWG (American wire gauge) — A standard for measuring nonferrous conductors (such as copper or aluminum) of wire. Gauge is a measure of the diameter or the thickness of a cable or wire with an inverse relationship. The higher the gauge number, the thinner is the wire or conductor, and the greater is the impedance and insertion loss per unit of length. Heavier gauge wires (those with lower AWG numbers) are more appropriate for electric power wiring where heat buildup from the resistance is frequently a problem. For example, heavy industrial or power line wiring may be no. 2 or no. 4, while indoor residential wiring is typically no. 12 or no. 14. In telephony, heavier gauges are required when used for long wiring runs. For example, wiring used for outside plant may be no. 19, no. 22, or no. 24, while wiring for inside a building is typically either no. 24 or no. 26.

Backbone — Equipment that provides connectivity for users of distributed networks and includes all the network infrastructure required to provide connectivity between the edge vehicles. In the context of the Internet, this term also refers to high-volume "primary" data carriers that make up the long-haul capabilities of the network.

Bandwidth — The capacity of a medium to transmit a signal. More informally, the "size" of a data pipe and its capacity to carry the files and messages.

Barring — There are two types of barring in a satellite system—technical, also referred to as "both directions barred," and financial, or "mobile-originated barred." (*a*) Technical barring of MES or "smart" card: This action suspends the use of the satellite mobile numbers (IMNs) for all services on the satellite network. When the IMNs are suspended, the customer loses the ability to use an MES or "smart" card to place or receive calls using the satellite system. (*Note:* If an unbarred "smart" card is inserted into a technically barred MES, the "smart" card user cannot place or receive any calls. Thus technical barring of an MES overrides the barring status of a "smart" card.) When an MES or "smart" card is technically barred, a message appears that says "not authorized" along with the code 15A1 for Inmarsat-B, -M, or Mini-M terminals, except for Thrane and Thrane terminals, which display the code 11A5. (*b*) Financial barring of MES or "smart" card. The following occurs when an MES is financially barred: (1) calls originating from fixed or Mini-M phones are successfully received by a mobile phone, (2) calls originating from a mobile phone are successfully connected to the called party, if a "smart" card is used to place the call, and (3) if a "smart" card is not used, the COMSAT operator intercepts the mobile-originated call, and the operator advises the user that the mobile ID is barred from use and that no calls can be placed. Thus the status of a "smart" card overrides the financial barring of an MES. When a "smart" card is financially barred, fixed-originated calls are received successfully by the "smart" card, and the COMSAT operator intercepts the mobile-originated calls. The COMSAT operator then advises the user that the mobile ID is barred from use and that no calls can be placed.

Baud — In common usage, the baud rate of a modem refers to how many bits it can send or receive per second. Technically, baud is the number of times per second that the carrier signal shifts value—for example, a 1200-bps modem actually runs at 300 baud, but it moves 4 bits per baud ($4 \times 300 = 1200$ bps). The signaling rate of a transmission channel (line), which is the number of transitions (voltage or frequency changes) that are made per second. The term is often used incorrectly to specify bits per second. One baud can be made to represent more than one bit, i.e. V.22 bis generates 1200 bps at 600 baud.

Baud rate — The actual symbol frequency being used to transmit data. Often used incorrectly as an equivalent to bits per second (bps). For example, both ITU-T V.22 bis (2400 bps) and V.22 (1200 bps) modems transmit data at 600 baud, but V.22 bis modems use 4 bits per symbol and V.22 modems use 2.

BBS — Bulletin board system. A computerized system that allows someone to upload and download files without an administrator being connected to the computer at the same time.

B-channel — A 64-kbps bearer channel used for delivering data or voice communications over ISDN. The satellite ISDN services include one B-channel. Also known as the "bearer" channel or the 64-kbps full-duplex (FDX) ISDN user-to-network interface channel. The basic rate interface (BRI) contains two B-channels, the North American primary rate interface (PRI) contains 23 B-channels, and the European primary rate interface (PRI) contains 30 B-channels. The B-channel carries circuit-oriented voice, data, or image traffic, not signaling information. Normally circuit switched by the network, the B-channel can be switched or dedicated access to an X.25 packet-switched network.

BE — Billing entity. This is an organization that may be nominated optionally on a satellite service activation registration form (SARF) in addition to an accounting authority to administer the billing and settlement of the communications charges incurred by an MES.

Bearer services — A communication connection's capability to carry voice, circuit, or packet data. The two B-channels in a BRI connection are bearer channels.

BER (bit error rate) — The amount of error that occurs during transmission. A BER of 1.0×10^{-7} means that 1 bit will be in error for every 10 million bits being transmitted.

Bit — A contraction of binary digit. The smallest unit of information in a binary number system. Eight bits are needed to create one byte or character.

Bit rate — A measure of the number of binary digits transferred over a given facility within a specific time interval. Usually measured in bits per second or in multiples thereof (example: kbps, Mbps, or Gbps).

Bits per second (bps) — The speed at which bits (electronic signals) are transmitted. A measure of the actual data transmission rate. The bps rate may be equal to or greater than the baud rate depending on the modulation technique used to encode bits into each baud interval. The correct term to use when describing modem data transfer speeds.

BONDING — Bandwidth-on-Demand Interoperability Group. The merging of two or more B-channels to form a single channel with a bandwidth greater than 64 kbps. For applications such as desktop video conferencing, BONDING combines the two B-channels for a total of 128 kbps to transmit video and audio. *Note:* BONDING is not possible with Inmarsat-M4 because only one B-channel is available for each terminal.

Bps — Bits per second. The unit of measurement for data transmission speed over a data communications line. A 28.8K modem can move 28,800 bits per second.

Branch office interconnect — A solution for providing data connectivity between branch offices, affiliates, and a corporate network.

BRI (basic rate interface) — A defined interface to ISDN that includes two B (bearer) channels and one D (delta) channel. Commonly referred to as 2B+D. A basic access ISDN line that uses an ordinary two-wire telephone line.

Bridge — A device that connects two networks as a seamless single network using the same networking protocol, such as TCP/IP. DSL modems are typically bridges.

Browser — A client program (software on a PC) that is used to look at various kinds of Internet resources. Netscape Navigator, Microsoft Internet Explorer, and Mosaic are three common Web browsers.

Byte — A group of bits, normally eight, which represents one data character.

CAA — Civil aviation authority: The national civil aviation authority of the state under whose authority the aircraft is operating. In the United States, the CAA is the Federal Aviation Authority (FAA).

CAG — A satellite's customer activation group.

Call appearances — A supplementary ISDN service that allows multiple incoming calls. Each directory number can have multiple call appearances depending on the switch type.

Caller ID — A telephone company service that delivers the calling party's telephone number to the called party, which can appear on an ISDN telephone, an LCD screen, a computer screen, or another device. *Note:* COMSAT's M4 service does not offer caller ID.

C band — Frequencies in the range 4 to 7 GHz.

CCITT — Comité Consultatif International de Telegraphie (International Telephone and Telegraph Consultative Committee). This organization is now called International Telecommunications Union (ITU). A United Nations organization that produces recommendations for standards for international ISDN.

CCS (common channel signaling or clear channel service) — When using CCS, all signaling goes over a common channel, which is separate from the data channel. Using SS7, ISDN keeps the signaling separate from the B-channels, thereby providing both faster dialing and the full 64 kbps. Those areas of the world which have not switched to SS7 can only offer 56 kbps.

CES — Coast earth station. A term formerly used in a maritime context for a land-based receiving and transmitting station that routes calls between Inmarsat MESs and shore-based subscribers.

Channel — A path along which a communications signal is transmitted.

Circuit-switched — The traditional method of providing dedicated bandwidth between sender and receiver in the form of a "time slot." End-to-end delay is predictable and constant for each connection. This type of network approach was designed for high-quality-of-service leased-line and voice connections.

Circuit-switched call — The entire transmission path, or circuit, remains "nailed up" end to end for the duration of the call. Network resources are set up at the beginning of a call and are dedicated to that call for the duration. Consequently, even if no one is talking or sending data, the "path" or "channel" between the two people remains up until someone hangs up (disconnects the call).

Circuit-switched data — Data sent over a circuit-switching network.

Circuit switching — A form of communication in which an information transmission path between two devices is routed through one or more switches. The path is assigned for the duration of a call.

Cisco — A major vendor of routers and switching products used on the Internet.

Class 1 — This standard provides minimal hardware support for sending a fax or data from a microcomputer.

Class 2 — This standard adds over 40 AT command set instructions and places more functionality into the modem while utilizing the onboard processor for fax operations.

Client — An intelligent workstation that makes requests to other computers known as servers. PC computers on a local-area network (LAN) can be clients.

Client modem — Modem that resides in your home that connects your computer to the analog telephone line.

Client-server computing — The foundation for networking, in which one computer acts as the host or server, and the other computer acts as a client. In the case of remote access, your PC acts as the client computer that connects to a server.

Cloud — A commonly used term that defines any large network such as ISDN wires (tip and ring) from your house that are terminated to the common carrier's switching equipment.

CO — Central office. A building used by telecommunications carriers to connect circuits to communications equipment. Also refers to the equipment located within the central office.

Codec (coder-decoder) — Transfers analog data into a digital data form and converts the digital data back to analog form. Since better accuracy is required for lower signal levels (because the quantization error is more significant compared with the signal), digitization values are assigned closer together for lower signal levels. This type of nonlinear analog-to-digital (A/D) converter is a codec (coder-decoder). There are two such nonlinearities standardized: μ-law (pronounced "mew law"), used in North America, Japan, and South Korea, and A-law, used in the rest of the world.

Common carrier — Telephone companies that provide long-distance telecommunications services, such as AT&T and MCI.

Compandor — Compressor-expander.

Compression — A process for reducing the number of bits required to transmit information.

CPE — Customer premises equipment. The DSL equipment located at the customer premises, which is either a DSL modem or a router for Internet access.

CSD — Circuit-switched data. An ISDN circuit-switched call for data in which a transmission path between two users is assigned for the duration of a call at a constant, fixed rate.

CSV — Circuit-switched voice. An ISDN circuit-switched call for voice in which the transmission path between two users is assigned for the duration of a call at a constant, fixed rate.

DAA (data access arrangement) — A circuit utilized by the modem to interface the analog telephone line to the codec.

DAC (digital-to-analog converter) — A device that reconstructs analog voltage waveforms from a sequence of binary digits.

DACS — Digital access and cross-connect system. A digital cross-connect device for routing lines among multiple ports. The connections are typically set up in advance of the call.

DARPA (Defense Advanced Research Projects Agency) — A U.S. government agency that in the early 1970s funded the initial research for the TCP/IP suite, as well as the Internet.

Data communications — The movement of bits of information (data) from one terminal device to another terminal device.

Data compression-decompression — The encoding (representation) of data to take less storage space using a mathematical algorithm and also the reverse.

Datagram — A packet.

Data protocols — Protocols or standards are formal descriptions of rules and conventions that govern how devices on a network exchange information. Simply put, they are the languages that computers and routers speak in order to share information across a local- or wide-area network. Common protocols on business LANs include NetWare, TCP/IP, and AppleTalk. The language of the Internet is TCP/IP; your computer must be running TCP/IP in order to communicate on the Internet.

dB (decibel) — Unit and scale used for measuring and comparing the amplitude of one signal to another signal, $dB = 10*\log(P_1/P_2)$.

DCE (data circuit termination equipment) — Converts information from a terminal device into electromagnetic signals so that it can be transmitted across a network or line. A modem is an example of a DCE. A DCE is a device that establishes, maintains, and terminates a session via a communications channel on a network. It also may convert or modulate signals for transmission.

D-channel — Delta channel. On a basic rate ISDN (BRI) line, a D-channel operates at 16 kbps carrying signaling information. For a primary rate ISDN (PRI) line, a D-channel operates at 64 kbps. The separate channel for out-of-band signaling between the user and the ISDN network.

DDS — Digital data service. Private-line digital service with data rates of 56/64 kbps.

Deactivate — Deactivation is the process of deregistering an MES or "smart" card in ESAS. ESAS then notifies the satellite to globally remove the mobile identity and associated IMNs in all satellite-related databases, including the LESs. A deactivated/not activated MES or "smart" card cannot use the satellite system for communication.

Demarc — The demarcation point. The point at the customer premises where the line from the telephone company meets the premises wiring. From the demarcation point, the end user is responsible for the wiring. The physical device that provides the means to connect the telephone company's wire to the premises wiring is called a *network interface box*.

Desktop videoconferencing — A PC-based videoconferencing system that allows people to conduct videoconferencing in real time from their desks. The basic desktop videoconferencing system includes a video camera, a video card, and an ISDN adapter card.

DHCP (Dynamic Host Configuration Protocol) — A service that lets clients on a LAN request configuration information, such as IP host addresses, from a server.

Dialup — Using the public switched telephone network (PSTN) to connect computers over modems with remote LAN access routers and/or terminal servers.

Digital pad — An attenuator that comes most commonly in 3- and 6-dB values, used in a network to reduce amplitudes.

DLCI (data link connection identifier) — The Frame Relay virtual circuit number used in internetworking to denote the port to which the destination LAN is attached.

DN (directory number) — Each BRI connection can have up to two directory numbers, one for each B-channel. Directory numbers are telephone numbers for ISDN.

DNS (Domain Name Services) — The collection of protocols and methods for mapping human-friendly domain names (rhythms.net) to machine-friendly IP addresses (127.192.11.34) for the purposes of accessing Internet services.

DNS registration — Domain Name Services (DNS) registration is the process of recording domain names in an Internet domain name registry (InterNIC) so that they are recognized by users of the Internet.

Domain — Part of an Internet naming hierarchy. An Internet domain name consists of a sequence of names (labels) separated by periods, e.g., netopia.com.

Domain name — The unique name that identifies an Internet site. Domain names always have two or more parts separated by dots. The part on the left is the most specific, and the part on the right is the most general. A given machine may have more than one domain name, but a given domain name points to only one machine.

Download — The process of transferring a file from a server to a client.

Downstream — Refers to transmission speed from the CO to the service user.

DP (dial pulse) — Pulses that a rotary telephone generates to signal a call.

DS-0 — A 64-kbps digital channel equal to one voice phone connection. In reality, it is limited to 56 kbps due to bit stealing used for signaling.

DS-1 — A standard service in the U.S. phone network, running at approximately 1.544 Mbps. A DS-1 is capable of handling 24 standard audio phone calls.

DS-2 — A T-2 (6.312 Mbps) digital channel format containing four multiplexed DS-1 channels. North American telephone companies needing more capacity than provided by a DS-1 have installed DS-3. Japan has deployed DS-2.

DS-3 — A T-3 (44.736 Mbps) digital channel format containing seven multiplexed DS-2 channels. Includes specifications for line rate, duty cycle, and framing structure and defines the signal format. DS-3 is typically associated with being the third step in the North American digital hierarchy. Also used on an unchannelized basis for access to network services such as ATM or SMDS and is a primary Internet backbone connection.

DS-4 — A T-4 (274.176 Mbps) digital channel format containing six multiplexed DS-3 carriers (4032 DS-0 channels). Includes specifications for line rate, duty cycle, and framing structure and also defines the signal format. Typically associated with being the fourth step in the North American digital hierarchy.

DSL — Digital subscriber line. DSL is a copper loop transmission technology enabling high-speed access in the local loop, often referred to as the last mile between the network service provider and service user.

DSLAM — Digital subscriber line access multiplexer. Provides high-speed Internet or intranet access over traditional twisted-pair telephone wiring through the use of xDSL technology. Provides simultaneous high-speed digital data access and POTS analog service over the same twisted-pair telephone line. Can be installed in the CO or at an Internet service provider (ISP) adjacent to the CO.

DSP (digital signal processor) — A microprocessor that is optimized and dedicated to performing the complex mathematical calculations inherent to processing digital and digitized waveforms.

DSSI — Digital Subscriber Signaling System No. 1. The network access signaling protocol for users connecting to ISDN. It includes the CCITT Q.931 and Q.932 standards.

DSU — Digital service unit. Digital loop device residing on customer premises providing interface to customer's DTE (data terminal equipment).

DTE (data terminal equipment) — Any device that converts information into digital signals for transmission or that reconverts digital information into another form. DTEs create and receive information to be sent and/or exchanged. A computer is an example of a DTE.

DTMF (dual tone multifrequency) — The technique using two simultaneous tones to represent digits used to signal a call (touch tone).

Duplex — Also known as full-duplex transmission, a communications service, telephony or telegraphy, that is capable of simultaneous two-way transmission.

E-1 — A standard in the European phone network, running at approximately 2.048 Mbps. An E-1 is capable of handling 31 standard audio phone calls.

Earth station — The points where signals traveling to and from satellites are terminated. Also, the point where connections are provided to either end-user equipment (e.g., mobile satellite terminal) or terrestrial networks (e.g., PSTN or ISDN networks) and which are in turn connected to end-user equipment (e.g., office phone, office PC).

EKTS — Electronic key telephone service. The National ISDN-1 standard for working with supplementary service on an ISDN telephone or analog telephone connected to an NT1 Plus device.

Electronic commerce (e-commerce) — An Internet service that supports an electronic transaction exchange between customers and vendors to privately and securely purchase goods and services.

Electronic mail (email) — A simple-to-use yet very powerful communications tool. Electronic messaging usually takes a matter of seconds to reach its destination, and consequently, communication is as easy with someone from another country as it is with someone in the office next door.

End terminal — A physical device (telephone, fax terminal, telex terminal or computer) connected to an MES.

Enterprise telework — A solution for providing remote access to corporate networks by teleworkers (telecommuters) from their homes or remote offices.

Ethernet — A baseband LAN specification invented by Xerox Corporation. Ethernet has become a series of standards referred to as IEEE 802.3.

ETSI ETS 300 102-1 — The name of EURO-ISDN standard.

FAQ — frequently asked question. FAQs are documents that list and answer the most commonly asked questions on a particular subject.

FCC — Federal Communications Commission. The U.S. federal regulatory agency responsible for regulating interstate, inter-LATA, and international communications.

FDDI — Fiber distributed data interface. A LAN Token Ring standard using fiberoptic cable.

FEC (forward error correction) — Corrects deficient data without requesting retransmission. FEC identifies where inside a message the error occurred and corrects the error by inverting the identified bit.

Fiber (fiberoptic cable) — Fiberoptic cable is made of pure glass. Digital signals, in the form of modulated light, can travel on strands of fiber for long distances. Signals travel at the speed of light, whether using fiber or copper wire. The primary advantage of using fiber is that, unlike copper wire, it can carry a greater amount of information. Fiber operates at a higher bandwidth.

Fiberoptics — A new generation of telecommunication wiring that uses light beams sent through thin strands of glass or other transparent materials. Fiberoptics can transmit large amounts of data from the physical transmission foundation for broadband ISDN.

File extensions — Extensions are letters or numbers (typically three) that appear at the end of a file name separated by a dot and indicate what type of file it is.

Firewall — A computer device and/or software that separates a local-area network from a wide-area network and prevents unauthorized access to the local-area network through the use of electronic security mechanisms such as IP filtering, address remapping, etc.

Firmware — System software stored in a device's memory that controls the device. The Netopia ISDN router's firmware can be updated.

FleetNET — Enhanced group call (EGC) service for broadcasting messages to groups of ships.

FORTEZZA — FORTEZZA is a registered trademark of the U.S. National Security Agency. In practice, it is a term used to describe a family of security products. This family includes PCMCIA-based cards, compatible serial port devices, combination cards (FORTEZZA/modem and FORTEZZA/Ethernet), server boards, and others. *FORTEZZA-enabled* and *FORTEZZA-certified* are terms applied to other hardware and software products that have had FORTEZZA security integrated. Examples include email, file encryptors, WWW browsers, databases, digital cellular telephones, and routers.

FRAD — Frame Relay access device. An interface between customer DTE (data terminal equipment) and a Frame Relay data circuit.

Frame Relay — A networking technology that uses a form of packet switching with variable-length frames over a shared data network and is protocol-independent.

Frequency — A measure of energy, as one or more waves per second, in an electrical or light-wave information signal. A signal's frequency is stated in either cycles per second or hertz (Hz).

Frequency reuse — The ability to use the same frequencies repeatedly within a single system, made possible by the basic design approach. Since each spot beam is designated to use radiofrequencies only within its boundaries, the same frequencies can be reused in other nonoverlapping spot beams with little potential for interference. The reuse of frequencies is what allows a satellite system to handle a large number of calls with a limited number of channels.

FRF (Frame Relay Forum) — An industry organization whose focus is Frame Relay technology.

FTP (File Transfer Protocol) — Internet tool for sending and/or receiving files from a server linked to the Internet.

Full duplex — The bidirectional communications capability in which transmissions travel in both directions simultaneously.

Functional devices — A classification of ISDN operational functions used to describe what tasks different components of an ISDN configuration perform. For example, the network termination 1 function defines the NT1 device that presents your premises as a node on the ISDN network. Another functional device is the terminal adapter, which defines the role of an adapter to convert some other form of communication to ISDN. For example, a TA allows an analog telephone to communicate over an ISDN device.

G3 — Represents a group of recommendations for facsimile (fax). A fax with the label G3 must support ITU Recommendations T.4 and T.30.

G4 — Represents a group of recommendations for facsimile (fax). A fax with the label G4 must support ITU Recommendations T.6 and T.30.

Gateway — A computer system that transfers data between applications or networks that use different protocols. A gateway reformats the data to make it acceptable for the new application or network before passing the data on. Gateways provide address translation services but do not translate data.

Ground segment — The satellite terrestrial communications network's group 3 (G3) fax. Currently, the most widely used facsimile protocol, which operates over analog telephone lines or with a terminal adapter over ISDN.

Group 4 (G4) fax — A facsimile protocol that allows high-speed digital fax machines to operate over ISDN.

GSM (global system for mobile communications) — The digital wireless standard for handheld cellular communications used in Europe and other parts of the world (GSM is not used in the United States). A time-division-based standard for digital wireless transmissions.

GUI (graphic user interface) — A computer environment, such as Microsoft Windows or MacOS, that graphically represents programs, activities, and services and is typically manipulated through both a keyboard and a mouse.

H.323 — A standard approved by the International Telecommunication Union (ITU) that defines how audiovisual conferencing data are transmitted across networks. In theory, H.323 should enable users to participate in the same conference even though they are using different videoconferencing applications. Most videoconferencing vendors have announced that their products will conform to H.323. However, it is uncertain at this time whether such adherence actually will result in interoperability.

Half-duplex — Data transmission that takes place in only one direction at a time. The channel or equipment is not capable of sending and receiving at the same time.

Harmonic distortions — Irregularities introduced into a signal (waveform) due to nonlinearities in the communications channel that produce harmonics (integer multiples) of the original signal.

HDSL (high-bit-rate digital subscriber line) — A technology to put two-way T-l/E-l service on normal unshielded twisted-pair wires without repeaters up to 20,000 ft.

Hertz (Hz) — The measure of frequency or the rate of repetitive recurrence of an electric signal, in cycles per second.

High-speed concentrators — A multiprotocol computer device that aggregates lower-speed connections into broadband circuits.

HLES (home land earth station) — Acts as a gateway to the public Internet. The SBS passes the user traffic (i.e., packets sent to and received from the MES) between the MES and its home LES. The home LES does not communicate directly with the satellite or the MESs.

Host — A single, addressable device on a network. Computers, networked printers, and routers are hosts.

HTML (HyperText Markup Language) — The coding language used to create hypertext documents for use on the World Wide Web. HTML files are viewed using a World Wide Web client program, such as Netscape or Internet Explorer.

HTTP (HyperText Transfer Protocol) — Protocol used by browser software such as Netscape to retrieve information from the World Wide Web (WWW). The protocol for moving hypertext files across the Internet. Requires an HTTP client program on one end and an HTTP server program on the other end. HTTP is the most important protocol used on the WWW.

HTTP (HyperText Transfer Protocol) server — Software running on one computer that allows a Web browser (running on another computer) to access and retrieve data from the computer.

HTU-C — HDSL transceiver unit—central office.

HTU-R — HDSL transceiver unit—remote.

Hub — A hub is a LAN device that serves as a central "meeting place" for cables from computers, servers, and peripherals. Hubs typically "repeat" signals from one computer to the others on the LAN.

Hybrid circuit — A circuit that makes the transformation from a two-wire transmission to a four-wire transmission and also the reverse.

ICAO 24- bit aircraft ID — A unique combination of 24 bits assigned to the aircraft by the address-relevant civil aviation authority of the state of registry.

IDSL — ISDN DSL using 2BlQ line code.

IEC — Interexchange carrier. The telephone company that provides telephone service outside the local telephone companies. For example, AT&T and MCI are interexchange carriers. Interexchange carriers are also referred to as *common carriers*.

IEEE 803.2 — The protocol that defines an Ethernet network at the physical layer of network signaling and cabling.

IETF — Internet Engineering Task Force. The primary working body developing new TCP/IP standards for the Internet.

ILEC — Incumbent local exchange carrier. Refers to the primary existing carrier, as distinguished from new competitive carriers with the advent of telecom deregulation.

IMAP4 (Interactive Mail Access Protocol version 4) — A protocol that provides support for multiple mail folders on the remote host. IMAP4 is a more powerful mail-retrieval protocol than POP3.

IMO (International Maritime Organization) — The organization responsible for making recommendations on maritime matters.

Implementation level — The level of implementation of an AES, which defines its level of compliance with the system specifications.

In-band signaling — Network signaling that is carried in the same channel as the bearer traffic. In analog telephone communications, the same circuits used to carry voice are used to transmit the signal for the telephone network. Touch tone signals are an example of in-band signaling.

Internet — The worldwide network of networks connected to each other using the IP protocol suite. The Internet provides file transfer, remote login, email, news, and other services. To be on the Internet, you must have IP connectivity (be able to telnet to or ping other systems).

Internet access — A solution for providing high-speed Internet services. (Also, generically, the provisioning of connectivity to the Internet.)

Interoperability — The ability of equipment from multiple vendors to communicate using standardized protocols.

Internet backbone — A high-speed, large (usually national) network run by a single corporate entity providing high-speed Internet connectivity to other companies and individuals. Examples of companies that operate Internet backbones are UUNet, Cable & Wireless, Teleglobe, PSINet, AT&T, and Sprint.

Interoperable — Two pieces of equipment are interoperable when they work together. Standards make devices from different vendors work with each other.

Intranet — A private network inside a company or organization that uses the same kinds of software that you would find on the public Internet but that is only for internal use.

Internet Protocol (IP) address — A 32-bit number assigned to any computing device that uses the Internet Protocol (IP). It is usually written in the form of four decimal fields separated by periods (208.204.46.4). Part of the address is the IP network number (IP network address), and part is the host address (IP host address). All machines on a given IP network use the same IP network number, and each machine has a unique IP host address. The system administrator sets a subnet mask to specify how much of the address is network number and how much is host address.

IP (Internet Protocol) — A standard describing software that keeps track of the internetwork addresses for different nodes, routes outgoing messages, and recognizes incoming messages.

IP number (address) — Internet Protocol number. Sometimes called a *dotted quad*. A unique number consisting of four parts separated by dots (185.123.113.5). Every machine that is on the Internet has a unique IP number.

IPSec (IP security) — Provides encryption of traffic and authentication of source.

IPX (Internetwork Packet Exchange) — LAN communications protocol used to move data between server and/or workstation programs running on different network nodes.

ISDN (integrated services digital network) — Provides circuit-switched access to the public network at speeds of 64 kbps or Nx64 for voice, data, and video transmission. Basic rate ISDN (BRI) and primary rate ISDN (PRI) are the two types of ISDN service.

ISDN address — The address of a specific ISDN device. It comprises an ISDN number plus additional digits that identify a specific terminal at a user's interface. An ISDN number is the network address associated with a user's ISDN connection.

ISDN telephone — A telephone designed for ISDN service. It typically includes programmable buttons for managing call features and an LCD display for viewing caller information.

ISL (interstation signaling link) — Automatically transmits service activation information from the network coordination station to all Inmarsat-C LESs.

ISO (International Standards Organization) — Within the communications industry, the ISO is best known for its Seven-Layer Open System Interconnection (OSI) Reference Model for communication protocols.

ISP (Internet service provider) — A vendor who provides access to the Internet and usually related services such as email and Web hosting.

ITU (International Telecommunications Union) — An organization under the United Nations that prepares telecommunications recommendations or standards, including many related to ISDN. The ITU was formally the CCITT. (Also see the *V. standards.*)

ITU accounting entity — Nominated by the AES licensee, it is responsible for acting as an intermediary for billing and settlement between an AES and the GES.

ITU-T V-class standards — The V-dot series of standards is designed and approved by the ITU-T, or International Telecommunications Union Telecommunications Standardization Sector (formerly called the CCITT) to deal with the transmission of digital data over the public switched telephone network (PSTN). These standards, among other things, specify transmission speed, data compression, and error control/correction techniques. The suffix *bis* is for revision two, and *ter* is revision three.

IXC — Interexchange carrier. All long-distance carriers; also known as *common carriers.*

Java — A highly flexible programming language for Internet and other applications.

JPEG — Joint Photographic Experts Group. A format for image files.

K56flex — The Lucent/Rockwell standard for 56K modems. A technology developed by Lucent Technologies and Rockwell International for delivering data rates up to 56 kbps over plain old telephone service (POTS). It was long believed that the maximum data transmission rate over copper telephone wires was 33.6 kbps, but K56flex achieves higher rates by taking advantage of the fact that most phone switching stations are connected by high-speed digital lines. K56flex bypasses the normal digital-to-analog conversion and sends the digital data directly to your modem over the telephone wires, where it is decoded. Lucent and Rockwell have announced that future K56flex modems will conform to the new V.90 standard approved by the ITU. Users with older K56flex modems will be able to upgrade their modems to support V.90. Although K56flex offers faster Internet access compared with standard modems, there are several caveats to using a K56flex modem: (1) the high speeds are available only with downstream traffic (data sent to your computer); upstream traffic is delivered using normal techniques at a maximum speed of 33.6 kbps, (2) to connect to the Internet at K56flex speeds, the Internet service provider (ISP) must have a modem at the other end that supports V.90, and (3) even if your ISP supports V.90, maximum transmission rates may not be achieved due to noisy lines.

Kbps — Kilobits per second; 1000 bits per second. It is a common way of specifying the speed of an Internet connection, i.e., the number of bits that can be transmitted over a wire in a single second. Most modem connections operate at speeds between 9.6 kbps (9600 bits per second) and 33.6 kbps (33,600 bits per second). The unit of measurement in thousands of bits per second for data transmission. ISDN has a data transmission capacity of 64 kbps for each B-channel.

Key systems — Telephone equipment with extra buttons that provides users with more functionality than regular telephones. ISDN phones and NT1 Plus devices that support analog telephone include key systems. A key system is a protocol invoked when you press a sequence of keys on the analog or ISDN telephone's dialing pad.

Kilobyte — A thousand bytes. Approximately 1024 (2^{10}) bytes.

L2TP — Layer Two Tunneling Protocol.

LAN — Local-area network. Privately owned and administered network for data communications. Usually a high bandwidth over a limited geographic area for communication between attached devices.

Land earth station (LES) — The land earth station (LES) acts as a gateway to the public switched telephone network (PSTN) and ISDN networks. The LES passes the user traffic and connects a call between the MES and public networks. LES provides the air interface between the MESs and the PSTN and ISDN network. The LES is the facility that receives and processes satellite signals to and from mobile terminals. The LES links calls to the requested destination either through landline carriers and/or through a satellite network. COMSAT Mobile Communications provides communication through several LESs that cover all four ocean regions. COMSAT-A: The stations that provide this COMSAT service are located in Southbury, Connecticut, for the AOR-E and AOR-W; Santa Paula, California, for the POR; and Kuantan, Malaysia LES. COMSAT-B, COMSAT-M, and COMSAT Mini-M (Planet 1): The stations that provide these COMSAT services are located in Southbury, Connecticut, for the AOR-E and AOR-W; Santa Paula, California, for the POR; and Kuantan, Malaysia, for the IOR. COMSAT-C: The stations that provide this COMSAT service are located in Southbury, Connecticut, for the AOR-E and AOR-W; Santa Paula, California, for the POR; and Aussaguel, France, and Raisting, Germany, for the IOR.

LAN switch — A network device that connects workstations or LAN segments.

Last mile — Refers to the local loop and is the difference between a local telephone company office and the service user; a distance of about 2 to 3 mi or 3 to 4 km.

Layer — One of the seven layers of the OSI Reference Model.

Layer 1 (physical layer) — Layer 1 is the part of the OSI Reference Model that defines the mechanical and electrical signaling standards for the transmission of data between systems in physical networks. All other layers rely on layer 1 to physically move their information (PDUs).

Layer 2 (data-link layer) — Layer 2 ensures accuracy of information transferred between two network points using a set of control or supervisory frames. Layer 2 is the part of the OSI Reference Model that is responsible for the transparent transport of layer 3 information between adjacent nodes in a network across an individual physical link. Layer 2 defines the format for data transmission (e.g., frames or cells).

Layer 3 (network layer) — Layer 3 allows access to transmission network. It takes large blocks of information received from layer 4 and breaks it into smaller packets that are addressed and routed through network. Layer 3 is the part of the OSI Reference Model dealing with network addressing, routing, and switching of data transmissions. Includes acknowledgments (ACK) that an entire message is correctly received and may include breaking a layer 4 message into packets of suitable transmission size.

Layer 4 (transport layer) — Layer 4 is the part of the OSI Reference Model responsible for reliable end-to-end connectivity between systems. The network itself is not aware of layer 4, since it operates only between end points. IP and X.25 are examples of layer 4 protocols. It should be noted that the TCP protocol has been effectively adopted as OSI TP4.

Layer 5 (session layer) — The part of the OSI Reference Model that allows presentation entities to organize and synchronize their dialog and manage their data exchange.

Layer 6 (presentation layer) — The part of the OSI Reference Model between the session layer (layer 5) and the application layer (layer 7) that specifies the format, coding, and possible encryption of communications between applications operating on different systems.

Layer 7 (application layer) — Layer 7 is the part of the OSI Reference Model that provides the means by which user programs access each other. Layer 7 sets up logical connections for passing ASE requests and responses between communicating entities.

L-band — Frequencies in the range 1.1 to 1.7 GHz.

Leased line — A dedicated circuit (private telephone line) between two locations, available full time for transmission of data or voice.

LEC — Local exchange carrier. LECs provide local transmission services.

Legacy network — A service that allows customers to continue to use their existing network along with network services based on more advanced technology.

Local loop — The pair of copper wires that connects the end user to the telephone company's central office, which is the gateway to the global telephone network. These wires, originally installed for analog communications, are the same wires used for ISDN service but require new equipment at the end user's premises and at the telephone company.

Logical channels — The three channels of a BRI connection, which are defined not as three physically separate wires but rather as three separate ISDN system channels.

LT (line termination) — Defines the local loop at the telephone company side of an ISDN connection to match the NT1 function at the customer end of the local loop.

Mbps — Megabit per second; 1 million bits per second. It is a common way of specifying the speed of a local- or wide-area network connection; the number of bits that can be transmitted over a wire in a single second. Ethernet LANs operate at speeds of 10 Mbps. A T-1 WAN connection operates at 1.544 Mbps.

MDF (main distribution frame) — Central point where all local loops terminate in the CO.

Megabyte — A million bytes. Technically, it is 1024 kilobytes.

MIB — Management information base.

Mobile earth station (MES) — The generic name used in both maritime and land-based contexts for the device used to communicate via a satellite. The MES sends customer traffic over a channel in a satellite beam to one of the LESs.

Mobility management (Mobman) — COMSAT mobility management: Facilitates the routing of fixed-to-mobile and mobile-to-mobile calls to a satellite, B and M terminals, and Planet 1 phones. It does this by directing the calls to the ocean region where the MES or "smart" card is logged (or where the terminal last made a call), without requiring the caller to know or to dial the correct ocean region. During the log-on process and after each successful call setup, the "smart" card and MES numbers and their associated ocean region code are registered in COMSAT's mobility management database (unless the ocean region registration is turned off). Example: A caller may dial the 872 ocean region code for the POR and reach an MES or "smart" card that is currently logged onto the AOR-E (871) as long as the call is being routed through a COMSAT LES.

MMSI (maritime mobile system identification) — Numbering system used by the ITU for the unique numbering of ships. The MMSI numbers are allocated by the national radio administration.

Modem — Data communications equipment that connects a computer to the telephone network. Technically, a modem converts a computer's digital signals to analog signals that can be transmitted over standard telephone lines. Digital or ISDN modems, also called *terminal adapters*, are used to connect computers to digital ISDN lines.

MSO (multiple system operator) — A cable industry term that describes a company that operates more than one cable TV system.

MTBF — Mean time between failure. A measure of hardware reliability.

Multimedia — Anything using more than one medium; graphics, sound, animation, text, and/or video generated by a computer into one "presentation" on screen.

Multimedia solutions — A combination of networking, computing devices, and software to improve business productivity by integrating voice, data, and video communication services.

Multiplexer — A device that enables several data streams to be sent over a single physical line or a device for combining several channels to be carried by one line or fiber.

Mux — Short for *time division multiplexer*. A mux combines multiple data streams into a single, higher-speed data stream for transmission to another location. A mux also receives the data on the high-speed aggregate and distributes or demultiplexes it to smaller data streams.

NAP (network access provider) — The NAP provides a transit network service permitting connection of service subscribers to NSPS. The NAP is typically the network provider that has access to the copper twisted pairs over which the DSL-based service operates.

NCS (network coordination station) — Satellite equipment that coordinates global communications between satellite MESs and LESs operating over the satellites.

NDIS (network design interface specification) — Used for all communication with network adapters. Works primarily with LAN manager and allows multiple protocol stacks to share a single NIC.

NEBS — Network equipment building standards. A set of requirements for the reliability and usability of equipment, established by Bellcore.

Netscape — The name of a WWW browser software. Also the name of the U.S. company that provides the Netscape browser.

Network — A collection of switches and interconnections providing one or more pathways from any access point to any other access point.

Network cloud — A cloudlike symbol in a diagram used to reduce an entire communications network into points of entry and exit. It infers that although there may be any number of switches, routers, trunks, and other network devices within the cloud, the point of interconnection to the cloud (network) is the only technical issue in the diagram.

Newsgroups — Also *usenet news*. Shared message conferences on the Internet, arranged hierarchically by subject matter.

NIC (network interface card) — The circuit board or other hardware that provides the interface between a communicating DTE and the network.

NID (network interface device) — An electronic device that connects the telephone line and the POTS splitter to the local loop.

N-ISDN — More commonly stands for *national ISDN*, less commonly for *narrowband ISDN*.

NMS (network management system) — The system that is responsible for managing a network and is typically run on a workstation that presents a GUI to the network manager. Provides access to a wide variety of information regarding network configuration, performance, and status. Exchanges information via a network management protocol, such as SNMP.

NOC (network operations center) — A centralized point of network management within a large-scale data network.

Node — A node on a network is usually formed by the presence of a router and user access equipment. Often, several leased lines are joined together at a network node.

Noise — Transmission noise in analog signals can cause errors to occur in information being sent.

NRO (national routing organization) — A company or organization responsible to a country's administration for authorizing the activation of an MES that is registered in that country.

NSN — Network service node.

NSP — Network service provider. Can include a local telephone company, ISP, or competitive local exchange carrier.

NT1 (network termination 1) — The device that connects to your ISDN hardware and works as a converter between an ISDN U-interface and an ISDN S/T-interface. Some ISDN adapters have an NT1 already built into them. Only required within the United States.

NT1 Plus device — A device that includes a built-in NT1 as well as ports to connect other devices (analog, ISDN, or X.25) to an ISDN line.

NT2 (network termination 2) — A device that handles network termination and switching functions, typically embodied in PBXs (private branch exchanges). An NT2 device performs intelligent operations such as switching and concentrating traffic across multiple B-channels in a PRI line.

NTU (network termination unit) — Equipment at the customer premises that terminates a network access interface.

Nx64 — Describes a contiguous bit stream at the 64-kbps rate to an application. Examples are LAN interconnect and point-to-point videoconferencing.

Ocean region — The coverage area of a satellite within which an MES may send and receive messages.

OC*n* — Optical carrier level *n* signal. The fundamental transmission rate for SONET. For example, OC3 operates at 155 Mbps.

Octet — A unit of measure, used in digital (data) communications, equal to 8 bits. It is the international version of the American byte. Using 8 bits allows an encoded representation of up to 256 discrete alphanumeric characters or different combinations.

Off-peak — The time of the day (traditionally after business hours or during weekends) when traffic volume over a satellite is reduced.

OSI (Open Systems Interconnection) Reference Model — Used in networking, OSI is a model of how data communications systems may be architected and interconnected. Communication is partitioned into seven functional layers. Each layer uses and builds on services provided by those layers below it.

Out-of-band signaling — Allows telephone network management signaling functions and other services to be sent over a separate channel rather than the bearer channel. ISDN uses out-of-band signaling via the D channel. Out-of-band signaling used in ISDN consists of messages rather than audio signals, as in the case with the touch-tone analog telephone system.

Packet — A formatted unit of data transmitted on a network.

Packet-switched — Primarily designed for data sent on a sporadic basis. This approach assigns packets, not time slots, to connections and allows for shared network resources. This results in variable delay and contention for network access.

Packet switching — In packet switching, all the data coming out of a machine is broken up into small segments, each segment has the address of where it came from and where it is going. This enables segments of data from many different sources to comingle on the same lines and be sorted and directed to different routes by special machines along the way. Packet switching is a data transmission method whereby data are transferred via packets. Packets are sent using a store-and-forward method across nodes in a network.

PAD (packet assembler-disassembler) — Divides original message into individual packets and later reconstructs the message.

Passive bus — Refers to the ability to connect multiple devices to a single BRI connection without repeaters to boost the signal. The configuration of the passive bus combines the terminating residence for all the devices connected to your ISDN line to add up to 100 ohms. The devices can share the same six-wire transmission facility and can transmit and/or receive at the same time.

PBX (private branch exchange) — A term generally used to refer to a corporate telephone system.

PCM (pulse-code modulation) — The method used to convert analog audio to digitized audio. At the customer's premise, the phone, fax, or modem generates an analog signal that is transmitted over a twisted-pair cable to the central office in the PSTN. At the central office, the switch digitizes the analog signal using a method called pulse-code modulation (PCM). PCM samples the analog signal at 8000 times per second and captures 8 bits per sample (or 1 byte per sample, since there are 8 bits in a byte). In other words, the height (or amplitude) of the analog waveform is measured 8000 times every second, and the amplitude is assigned a binary number between 0 and 255 (between 0000 0000 and 1111 1111).

Phantom power — The ability of NT1 to provide power to terminal equipment 1 or terminal adapters via two wires in an eight-wire cable.

Point-to-multipoint configuration — A physical connection in which a single network termination supports multiple terminal equipment devices. This configuration in supported by the S/T-interface.

Point-to-multipoint connection — A connection established between one device on one end and more than one device on the other end.

Point-to-point connection — A connection established between two devices through ISDN.

Point-to-configuration — A physical connection in which a single NT1 functional device supports only one device.

POP — Point of presence. A location where a network can be connected to, often with dialup phone lines. For example, if an Internet company says that it will soon have a POP in Belgrade, it means that it will soon have a local phone number in Belgrade and/or a place where leased lines can connect to its network. POP also refers to the point at which a line from a long-distance carrier (IXC) connects to the line of the local telephone company or to the user if the telephone company is not involved.

POP3 (Post Office Protocol version 3) — The method in which email software, such as Eudora, gets mail from a mail server. When a SLIP, PPP, or shell account is obtained, a POP account is usually established at the same time. By instructing your email software to use this POP account, you can get your mail. The POP3 provides message storage that holds incoming mail until users log on and download their mail. POP3 is a simple system with little selectivity. All pending messages and attachments are downloaded at the same time. It uses the SMTP messaging protocol.

POP server — A server that implements the Post Office Protocol (see POP3). A standard mail server commonly used on the Internet.

Port — A location for passing data in and out of a device and, in some cases, also for attaching other devices or cables.

POS (point of sale) — Any device used for handling transactions, such as card readers for credit card or debit card transactions.

POTS (plain old telephone service) line or phone — A plain analog telephone or phone line.

Powering — The powering of the ISDN line and CPE equipment. The ISDN line and any CPE connected to it must be powered locally. Usually, these powering capabilities are built into the NT1 or NT1 Plus device.

PPP (Point-to-Point Protocol) — A communications protocol that allows a computer using TCP/IP to connect directly to the Internet. New PPP/MP also allows different remote access devices to communicate with each other. PPP is an IETF standard for transmitting IP traffic. PPP has been accepted as the standard for IP over ISDN.

PPP/MP (Point-to-Point Protocol/Multilink Protocol) — The new Point-to-Point Protocol for ISDN connection that allows use of both B-channels for remote access to the Internet. PPP/MP also allows different remote access devices to communicate with each other.

Primary channel — For a single-channel MES, the only channel through which the MES can communicate. For a multichannel MES, the first numbered channel.

Primary rate interface (PRI) — In North America, a type of ISDN service that offers 23 B-channels at 64 kbps and one D-channel at 64 kbps (23B+D). In Europe, PRI provides for 30 B-channels and 2 D-channels (30B+2D).

Protocol — A formal description of message formats and the rules two or more systems must follow to exchange those messages. Protocol definitions range from how bits are placed on a wire to the format of an email message. Standard protocols allow different manufacturers' computers to communicate.

PS/2 — Powering for any ISDN devices connected to an NT1 or NT1 Plus device that does not have a local power source.

PSTN (public switched telephone network) — Refers to the country's telephone systems and networks collectively and in total.

Quality of service (QoS) — A premium class of data communications service in which the provider guarantees a level of service for mission-critical business data traffic.

Quantization — The process of assigning an absolute value or binary digital number to the amplitude or level of a discrete instantaneous sample of an analog voltage waveform. The larger the range between the highest and lowest possible numbers, the more exact the increments can be measured and the more accurately the digital sample represents the analog signal.

Quantization error (noise) — Refers to the error that occurs when the instantaneous sample of an analog voltage waveform (any value in an infinite range) is represented by a finite digital number system that, when converted back to a discrete level, is not equal to the amplitude of the original sample.

RADIUS (remote authentication dial-in user service) — Developed to allow separation of network and service provider roles in the Internet community. It is a client-server protocol used for access control (which involves authentication of a user or authorization to specific services) and accounting. RADIUS accounting starts when a call is initiated and may recur at any time during the call, as well as at the end of a call.

RADSL — Rate-adaptive digital subscriber line. Transmission technology that supports both asymmetric and symmetric applications on a single twisted-pair telephone line and allows adaptive data rates.

Rate adaptation — A system that allows two pieces of data equipment operating at different data transmission rates to interoperate. Non-ISDN equipment (such as a V.34 modem, G3 fax, or serial port) is often not capable of running at speeds of 64 kbps. For example, a serial port on a PC might be restricted to 19.2 kbps transmission. In such cases, a terminal adapter (TA) performs a function called *rate adaptation* to make the bit rate ISDN-compatible. Although the transport speed of the ISDN B-channel is 64 kbps, the effective data rate is constrained to the throughput of the non-ISDN device. Rate adaptation also comes into play when access to 64-kbps circuits is not available from one end of a connection to another. Since ISDN is currently not widespread, telephone providers must sometimes create an end-to-end digital connection using switched 56 kbps digital services, although the call originated on an ISDN link. In this case, the effective throughput of the link is limited to 56 kbps. This type of rate adaptation occurs commonly on international calls originating in North America or on calls that pass through multiple telephone carrier service areas. Most ISDN terminal equipment adjusts transparently to the lower rate.

Reference point — A specific point in the model of how ISDN works. Each component of this model is identified using a reference point. For example, the U reference point defines the local loop of an ISDN connection. These reference points are also called *interfaces*, such as the U-interface or S/T-interface.

Remote call center — A service concept where the traditional call center workstation is moved from a central office site to a teleworker's home or small office.

Ring — One of the two wires that make up the local loop; the wire that is connected to the ring on the jack that was used when operators would manually "patch" or connect switched calls. It is also a term for the energy on a POTS line that is required to activate the telephone's bell or ringer.

RIP (Routing Information Protocol) — A protocol used for the transmission of IP routing information.

RJ-11 — A telephone-industry standard connector type, usually containing four pins.

RJ-45 — A telephone-industry standard connector type, usually containing eight pins.

RJ-45 connector — A modular connector used for four- or six-wire analog devices. An eight-pin connector jack used with standard telephone lines and required by some ISDN hardware. A little larger than an RJ-11 jack.

RLES (regional land earth station) — An interface (or go-between) between the NCS and the SBS for the purpose of synchronizing mobile status information and for managing channel assignments. The RLESs, by themselves, are not capable of providing any of the commercial IPDS communication services. Thus, the RLES does not transmit or receive any user data packets to or from the MES. The RLES provides control of the signaling interfaces between the SBS and the NCS. The primary purpose of the RLES is to maintain an MES busy list and to authorize MESs for IPDS service.

Robbed bit signaling — An older technique used by the telephone companies that use T-1 digital transmission lines. The technique is to take the least significant bit and use it to control functions such a dial tone, ring, busy, answer, etc. This signaling method negatively effects V.90 by reducing the data rate.

Router — A device that interconnects LANs that can dynamically route data at layer 3, the network layer, based on destination and routes available.

Routing table — A list of networks maintained by each router on an internetwork. Information in the routing table helps the router determine the next router to forward packets to.

R reference point — The ISDN reference point that sits between the non-ISDN device and the terminal adapter (TA) functional device.

RS-232 — An industry standard for serial communication connections. The current version of this standards is RS-232C. Most PCs include one or more RS-232 ports for connecting devices, such as a modem and a mouse.

RSVP (Resource Reservation Setup Protocol) — A reservation setup protocol for the Internet.

RT — Remote terminal. Local loop terminates at remote terminal intermediate points closer to the service user to improve service reliability.

RTF — Rich text format. A word processing document format designed for compatibility with a wide range of computing platforms and software packages.

RTU — Remote termination unit. A device installed at the service user site that connects to the local loop to provide high-speed connectivity. Also referred to as the ATU-R.

SDSL — Symmetric digital subscriber line. Single-pair symmetric DSL.

SafetyNET — Broadcast system for maritime safety information using a satellite.

SBS (satellite base station) — Provides the air interface between the satellite MESs and the home LES (which is simply a gateway to the Internet). The SBS will contain channel units that will carry the IP packets to and from the MESs via the satellites.

Secondary channel — On a multichannel MES, all channels other than the primary channel.

Secure intranets — A network based on the Internet Protocol that supports intracompany communications between end users and employs security mechanisms such as firewalls, encryption, and authentication.

Secure extranets — A network based on the Internet Protocol that supports intercompany communications between end users and employs security mechanisms such as firewalls, encryption, and authentication.

Serial communication — The transmission of data one bit at a time over a single line. Serial communication can be synchronous or asynchronous.

Serial port — A connector on the back of a workstation through which data flow to and from a serial device.

Server — A device or system that has been specifically configured to provide a service, usually to a group of clients.

Server modem — A modem that resides at the remote server and is usually connected to digital lines.

Service activation — The process by which an MES is registered into a satellite system.

Shannon's law (theorem) — A theory that defines the maximum channel capacity or line speed in any given communications link between two points based on the impairments (including quantization noise) and the bandwidth of the channel.

Signaling — The exchange of information for call setup and control. It refers to the sending information on the phone network regarding phone numbers, busy status, call interruptions, hang-ups, etc. The tones that a touch-tone phone makes are part of signaling—the tones are interpreted by the local phone company as a phone number.

SIM (or SIM card) — Subscriber identity module: a "smart" card encoded with PID, IMN, and service-related information for the customer.

Simplex — A communications service, telephony or telegraphy, that is capable of transmission in one direction only.

SLIP (Serial Line Internet Protocol) — A standard for using a regular telephone line (a serial line) and a modem to connect a computer as a real Internet site. SLIP is gradually being replaced by PPP.

SMB/CIFS (server message block/common Internet filesystem) — Microsoft's file-sharing protocol that allows for remote LAN operation.

SMDS (switched multimegabit data service) — A high-speed switched data communications service offered by the local telephone company for interconnecting LANs in different locations. Connection to an SMDS service can be made from a variety of devices including bridges, routers, CSU/DSUs, as well as via Frame Relay and ATM networks.

SMTP (Simple Mail Transfer Protocol) — The main protocol used to send electronic mail on the Internet. SMTP consists of a set of rules for how a program sending mail and a program receiving mail should interact. Almost all Internet email is sent and received by clients and servers using SMTP; thus, if one wanted to set up an email server on the Internet, one would look for email server software that supports SMTP.

SNA (systems network architecture) — IBM's vendor-specific connection-oriented virtual circuit network architecture for terminal/host communication.

SNMP (Simple Network Management Protocol) — The network management protocol used with TCP/IP-based Internets.

SOHO — Small office/home office.

SONET — Synchronous optical network. A set of standards for transmitting digital information over optical networks. Uses fiberoptic ring technology.

S reference point — The ISDN reference point that represents where a CPE connects to a customer switching device, such as a PBX system. This type of device is called an *NT2 functional device.*

Subnet — A network address created by using a subnet mask to specify that a number of bits in an address will be used as a subnet number rather than a host address.

Subnet mask — A 32-bit number to specify which part of an address is the network number and which part is the host address. When written in binary notation, each bit written as 1 corresponds to 1 bit of network address information. One subnet mask applies to all IP devices on an individual IP network.

SWC — Service wire center.

Symmetrical — Data transfer where both upstream and downstream data flow occurs at the same speed. Beneficial in cases where servers (such as Web servers) will be operated and for which asymmetric data transfer would be undesirable.

Synchronous — Data communications in which transmissions are sent at a fixed rate, with the sending and receiving devices synchronized.

T-1 — A type of data circuit that provides 1.544 Mbps of bandwidth between two points. Can be provided through dedicated circuits or Frame Relay.

Terminal adapter (TA) — A terminal adapter is to an ISDN line what a modem is to a normal analog telephone line. It is an external device that connects a PC or Mac to an ISDN circuit, allowing non-ISDN equipment to use ISDN.

TCP/IP (Transmission Control Protocol/Internet Protocol) — A suite of communications protocols used by host computers to exchange information. TCP is layer 4, the transport layer, of the OSI Reference Model. IP is layer 3, the network layer, of the OSI Reference Model and provides connectionless datagram service.

TDM (time-division multiplexing) — Technique where data from multiple channels may be allocated bandwidth on a single wire pair based on time slot assignment.

Telework — A service concept that will allow customers to work productively and effectively using the same business tool environment from either work or home.

Telnet — A program that lets you connect to other computers on the Internet.

Universal asymmetric digital subscriber line (UADSL) — The newest member of the DSL family based on the G.Lite standard. UADSL is an asymmetric service that delivers data up to 1.5 Mbps upstream and up to 384 kbps upstream. This DSL service is targeted at the consumer market.

Upstream — Refers typically to the transmission speed from the user to the data network.

URL (uniform resource locator) — Used with the World Wide Web as an address (*http://www.icss.net*).

Usenet — A term used to describe the collection of newsgroups offered over the Internet.

UTP — Unshielded twisted-pair cabling.

VC — Virtual circuit. A logical connection or packet-switching mechanism established between two devices at the start of transmission.

VDSL — Very-high-bit-rate DSL. Generally refers to 25 to 50+ Mbps transmission over very short distances.

VLAN — Virtual LAN. Workstations connected to an intelligent device that provides capabilities to define LAN membership.

VPN — Virtual Private network, a networking service that is provided over a public network that allows the customer to utilize the service as if it was a private network.

Wall jack — A small hardware component used to tap into telephone wall cable. An RJ-11 wall jack usually has four pins; an RJ-45 wall jack usually has eight pins.

WAN — Wide-area network. A computer or communications network that covers a geographic area that is larger than a city.

xDSL — Another way of referring generically to any of the DSL variants: ADSL, HDSL, SDSL, RADSL, IDSL, or VDSL.

INDEX

E

F

N

ABOUT THE AUTHOR

John R. Vacca is an information technology consultant and an internationally known author. He has been a configuration management specialist, computer specialist, and was the computer security official for NASA's international space station program from 1988 to 1995. John has authored more than 28 books and written over 350 articles about wireless technologies and security since 1982. He was also one of the security consultants for the MGM movie *AntiTrust*.